FEMINIST INTERPRETATIONS OF NICCOLÒ MACHIAVELLI

NANCY TUANA, GENERAL EDITOR

This series consists of edited collections of essays, some original and some previously published, offering feminist re-interpretations of the writings of major figures in the Western philosophical tradition. Devoted to the work of a single philosopher, each volume contains essays covering the full range of the philosopher's thought and representing the diversity of approaches now being used by feminist critics.

Already published:

Nancy Tuana, ed., *Feminist Interpretations of Plato* (1994)

Margaret Simons, ed., *Feminist Interpretations of Simone de Beauvoir* (1995)

Bonnie Honig, ed., *Feminist Interpretations of Hannah Arendt* (1995)

Patricia Jagentowicz Mills, ed., *Feminist Interpretations of G. W. F. Hegel* (1996)

Maria J. Falco, ed., *Feminist Interpretations of Mary Wollstonecraft* (1996)

Susan J. Hekman, ed., *Feminist Interpretations of Michel Foucault* (1996)

Nancy J. Holland, ed., *Feminist Interpretations of Jacques Derrida* (1997)

Robin May Schott, ed., *Feminist Interpretations of Immanuel Kant* (1997)

Celeine Leon and Sylvia Walsh, eds., *Feminist Interpretations of Soren Kierkegaard* (1997)

Cynthia Freeland, ed., *Feminist Interpretations of Aristotle* (1998)

Kelly Oliver and Marilyn Pearsall, eds., *Feminist Interpretations of Friedrich Nietzsche* (1998)

Mimi Reisel Gladstein and Chris Matthew Sciabarra, eds., *Feminist Interpretations of Ayn Rand* (1999)

Susan Bordo, ed., *Feminist Interpretations of René Descartes* (1999)

Julien S. Murphy, ed., *Feminist Interpretations of Jean-Paul Sartre* (1999)

Anne Jaap Jacobson, ed., *Feminist Interpretations of David Hume* (2000)

Sarah Lucia Hoagland and Marilyn Frye, eds., *Feminist Interpretations of Mary Daly* (2000)

Tina Chanter, ed., *Feminist Interpretations of Emmanuel Levinas* (2001)

Nancy J. Holland and Patricia Huntington, eds., *Feminist Interpretations of Martin Heidegger* (2001)

Charlene Haddock Seigfried, ed., *Feminist Interpretations of John Dewey* (2001)

Naomi Scheman and Peg O'Connor, eds., *Feminist Interpretations of Ludwig Wittgenstein* (2002)

Lynda Lange, ed., *Feminist Interpretations of Jean-Jacques Rousseau* (2002)

Lorraine Code, ed., *Feminist Interpretations of Hans-Georg Gadamer* (2003)

Lynn Hankinson Nelson and Jack Nelson, eds., *Feminist Interpretations of W. V. Quine* (2003)

FEMINIST INTERPRETATIONS OF NICCOLÒ MACHIAVELLI

EDITED BY MARIA J. FALCO

THE PENNSYLVANIA STATE UNIVERSITY PRESS
UNIVERSITY PARK, PENNSYLVANIA

Library of Congress Cataloging-in-Publication Data

Feminist interpretations of Niccolò Machiavelli / edited by Maria J. Falco.
    p.   cm.—(Re-reading the canon)
Includes bibliographical references and index.
ISBN 0-271-02388-0 (cloth : alk. paper)
ISBN 0-271-02389-9 (pbk. : alk. paper)
1. Machiavelli, Niccolò, 1469–1527.
2. Feminist theory.
I. Falco, Maria J.   II. Series.

JC143.M4F46 2004
320.1'092—dc22   2004043860

The Pennsylvania State University Press is a member of the Association of
American University Presses.

It is the policy of The Pennsylvania State University Press to use acid-free paper.
Publications on uncoated stock satisfy the minimum requirements of American
National Standard for Information Sciences—Permanence of Paper for Printed Library
Material, ANSI Z39.48–1992.

Per due donne bellissime:
  Firenze, "La Città del Fiore" e
  New Orleans, "The City that Care Forgot"

Contents

Preface by Nancy Tuana   ix

Acknowledgments   xiii

Introduction   1

1   The Modernity of Machiavelli   39
    Donald McIntosh

2   Meditations on Machiavelli   49
    Hanna Fenichel Pitkin

3   Niccolò Machiavelli: Women as Men, Men as Women, and
    the Ambiguity of Sex   93
    Arlene W. Saxonhouse

4   Renaissance Italy: Machiavelli   117
    Wendy Brown

5   The Root of the Mandrake: Machiavelli and Manliness   173
    Mary O'Brien

6   Fortune Is a Woman—But So Is Prudence: Machiavelli's
    Clizia   197
    Catherine H. Zuckert

7   Machiavelli and the Citizenship of Civic Practices   213
    R. Claire Snyder

8   The Seriously Comedic, or Why Machiavelli's Lucrezia Is
    Not Livy's Virtuous Roman   247
    Melissa M. Matthes

9   Rhetoric, Violence, and Gender in Machiavelli   267
     Cary J. Nederman and Martin Morris

10   Beyond *Virtù*   287
     John Juncholl Shin

11   Machiavelli, Civic Virtue, and Gender   309
     Vesna Marcina

12   Rethinking Machiavelli: Feminism and Citizenship   337
     Jane S. Jaquette

13   Machiavelli and Feminist Ethics   367
     Andrea Nicki

     Appendix A   Summary of *La Mandragola*   387

     Appendix B   Summary of *Clizia*   397

     Selected Bibliography   407

     List of Contributors   409

     Index   411

Preface

Take into your hands any history of philosophy text. You will find compiled therein the "classics" of modern philosophy. Since these texts are often designed for use in undergraduate classes, the editor is likely to offer an introduction in which the reader is informed that these selections represent the perennial questions of philosophy. The student is to assume that she or he is about to explore the timeless wisdom of the greatest minds of Western philosophy. No one calls attention to the fact that the philosophers are all men.

Though women are omitted from the canons of philosophy, these texts inscribe the nature of woman. Sometimes the philosopher speaks directly about woman, delineating her proper role, her abilities and inabilities, her desires. Other times the message is indirect—a passing remark hinting at women's emotionality, irrationality, unreliability.

This process of definition occurs in far more subtle ways when the central concepts of philosophy—reason and justice, those characteristics that are taken to define us as human—are associated with traits historically identified with masculinity. If the "man" of reason must learn to control or overcome traits identified as feminine—the body, the emotions, the passions—then the realm of rationality will be one reserved primarily for men,[1] with grudging entrance to those few women who are capable of transcending their femininity.

Feminist philosophers have begun to look critically at the canonized texts of philosophy and have concluded that the discourses of philosophy are not gender-neutral. Philosophical narratives do not offer a universal perspective, but rather privilege some experiences and beliefs over others. These experiences and beliefs permeate all philosophical theories whether they be aesthetic or epistemological, moral or metaphysical. Yet this fact has often been neglected by those studying the traditions of philosophy. Given the history of canon formation in Western philosophy, the perspective most likely to be privileged is that of upper-class white males. Thus, to be fully aware of the impact of gender biases, it is imperative that we re-read the canon with attention to the ways in which philosophers' assumptions concerning gender are embedded within their theories.

This new series, *Re-Reading the Canon*, is designed to foster this process of reevaluation. Each volume will offer feminist analyses of the theories of a selected philosopher. Since feminist philosophy is not monolithic in method or content, the essays are also selected to illustrate the variety of perspectives within feminist criticism and highlight some of the controversies within feminist scholarship.

In this series, feminist lenses will be focused on the canonical texts of Western philosophy, both those authors who have been part of the traditional canon, and those philosophers whose writings have more recently gained attention within the philosophical community. A glance at the list of volumes in the series will reveal an immediate gender bias of the canon: Arendt, Aristotle, Beauvoir, Derrida, Descartes, Foucault, Hegel, Hume, Kant, Locke, Marx, Mill, Nietzsche, Plato, Rousseau, Wittgenstein, Wollstonecraft. There are all too few women included, and those few who do appear have been added only recently. In creating this series, it is not my intention to rectify the current canon of philosophical thought. What is and is not included within the canon during a particular historical period is a result of many factors. Although no canonization of texts will include all philosophers, no canonization of texts that excludes all but a few women can offer an accurate representation of the history of the discipline, as women have been philosophers since the ancient period.[2]

I share with many feminist philosophers and other philosophers writing from the margins of philosophy the concern that the current canonization of philosophy be transformed. Although I do not accept the position that the current canon has been formed exclusively by power relations, I do believe that this canon represents only a selective history of the tradition. I share the view of Michael Bérubé that "canons are at once the location, the index, and the record of the struggle for cultural representation; like any other hegemonic formation, they must be continually reproduced anew and are continually contested."[3]

The process of canon transformation will require the recovery of "lost" texts and a careful examination of the reasons such voices have been silenced. Along with the process of uncovering women's philosophical history, we must also begin to analyze the impact of gender ideologies upon the process of canonization. This process of recovery and examination must occur in conjunction with careful attention to the concept of a canon of authorized texts. Are we to dispense with the notion of a tradition of excellence embodied in a canon of authorized texts? Or, rather than abandon the whole idea of a canon, do we instead encourage a reconstruction of a canon of those texts that inform a common culture?

This series is designed to contribute to this process of canon transformation by offering a re-reading of the current philosophical canon. Such a re-reading shifts our attention to the ways in which woman and the role of the feminine are constructed within the texts of philosophy. A question we must keep in front of us during this process of re-reading is whether a philosopher's socially inherited prejudices concerning woman's nature and role are independent of her or his larger philosophical framework. In asking this question attention must be paid to the ways in which the definitions of central philosophical concepts implicitly include or exclude gendered traits.

This type of reading strategy is not limited to the canon, but can be applied to all texts. It is my desire that this series reveal the importance of this type of critical reading. Paying attention to the workings of gender within the texts of philosophy will make visible the complexities of the inscription of gender ideologies.

Nancy Tuana

Notes

1. More properly, it is a realm reserved for a group of privileged males, since the texts also inscribe race and class biases that thereby omit certain males from participation.

2. Mary Ellen Waithe's multivolume series, *A History of Women Philosophers* (Boston: M. Nijhoff, 1987), attests to this presence of women.

3. Michael Bérubé, *Marginal Forces/Cultural Centers: Tolson, Pynchon, and the Politics of the Canon* (Ithaca: Cornell University Press, 1992), 4–5.

Acknowledgments

The following individuals have been extraordinarily helpful in providing assistance with obtaining library research materials and interlibrary loans, and with technical advice on the finer points of the usage of search engines, the Internet, and e-mail generally: the reference staff of the Monroe Library of Loyola University of New Orleans, particularly Deborah L. Poole, Trish Del Nero, and Patricia Doran; the reference staff of Lower Township Branch of The Cape May County Library in the Villas, New Jersey, particularly Edward N. Carson and Virginia M. Sague; and the Information Technology staff of Loyola University of New Orleans, especially Steven Navarre.

For the use of previously published materials I should like to thank Hanna Fenichel Pitkin and The University of Chicago Press for permission to reprint Part 5, "Meditations on Machiavelli," chapters 11 and 12 from her book, *Fortune is a Woman: Gender and Politics in the Thought of Niccolò Machiavelli*, second edition (1999), 283–327 (copyright © 1984, 1999 by Hannah Fenichel Pitkin); Cath McNaughton for permission to reprint chapter 8, "The Root of the Mandrake: Machiavelli and Manliness" from Mary O'Brien's book *Reproducing the World: Essays on Feminist Theory* (1989), 103–32, and for the biographical material on O'Brien; Rowman and Littlefield for permission to reprint the following materials: chapters 5 and 6 from Wendy Brown's book *Manhood and Politics: A Feminist Reading in Political Theory* (1988), 71–123; Catherine Zuckert's article "Fortune Is a Woman—But So Is Prudence: Machiavelli's *Clizia*" from the volume *Finding a New Feminism: Rethinking the Woman Question for Liberal Democracy* (1996), edited by Pamela Grande Jensen, 23–37; and chapter 2 "Machiavelli and the Citizenship of Civic Practices" from R. Claire Snyder's book, *Citizen-Soldiers and Manly Warriors: Military Service and Gender in the Civic Republican Tradition* (1999), 15–43; Sage Publications, Inc., for permission to reprint parts of Donald McIntosh's article "The Modernity of Machiavelli" from *Political Theory* 12:2 (May 1984): 193–203 (copyright © by Sage Publications, Inc.); Arlene Saxonhouse for permission to reprint chapter 7, "Niccolò Machiavelli: Women as Men, Men as Women, and the Ambiguity of Sex" from her book *Women in the History of Political Thought: Ancient Greece to Machiavelli* (1985), 151–73, 196–98 (copyright © 1985 by Praeger Publishers, reproduced with permission of Greenwood Publishing Group, Inc., Westport, CT); The Pennsylvania State University Press for permission to reprint chapter 4, "The Seriously Comedic, or Why Machiavelli's Lucrezia Is Not Livy's Virtuous Roman," from Melissa M. Matthes's book *The Rape of Lucretia and the Founding of Republics: Readings in Livy, Machiavelli, and Rousseau* (2001), 77–97 (copyright © The Pennsylvania State University); Duke University Press for permission to summarize the Allan Gilbert translations of *La Mandragola* and *Clizia*, in *Machiavelli: The Chief Works and Others* (1989), vol. 2, 776–864.

I am also deeply indebted to Nancy Tuana, the editor of the series on Re-Reading the Canon of which this volume is a part, and to Sanford Thatcher, the director of The Pennsylvania State University Press, for their extraordinary patience and encouragement throughout the long seven-year period that it took to bring this volume to completion. My gratitude also to the contributors who stuck with this project despite the many delays.

Maria J. Falco
Metairie, Louisiana
February 2003

Introduction

Una questione che forse
Non si chiuderà mai:
La questione di Machiavelli.

One inquiry which perhaps will never be closed: the question of Machiavelli.
—Benedetto Croce, *Quaderni della "Critica"*

It is with this quotation from Croce that Isaiah Berlin ended his ground-breaking essay, "The Originality of Machiavelli,"[1] in which he attempted to distinguish, if not explain, the many different and often contradictory interpretations of Machiavelli's works in the more than 400 years since his death. As a Fulbright student at the University of Florence in 1954–55, I was myself exposed to a diversity of interpretations in a *corso singolo* titled *Machiavelli e gli Anti-Machiavellisti*. Since that time a profusion of works has added to that diversity, increasing almost in direct relationship to the lack of consensus that has prevailed. Virtually every line, every "jot and tittle" of every letter, play, poem, and essay, as well as every book, history, and "prayer" that he ever wrote, has suffered minuscule scrutiny. No other writer undergoing similar scrutiny today could hope to survive the range of accusations, denunciations, and praises—running the gamut from protofascist to protoliberal—to which Machiavelli has been subjected.[2]

It is not the purpose of this volume, however, to attempt to reduce this confusion or present any single harmonious explanation of Machiavelli's mindset or approach to politics, but rather to add another dimension to the discussion, namely that of feminism. In this volume we hope we have collected every major strand of feminist thought on *la questione di Machiavelli*, in order to enable the reader to see how feminists have generally been responding over the past few decades to the "modern" (or "proto-modern") approach to political thought that his work represents.[3] This collection is not exhaustive, however, since it does not present materials from outside the English-speaking community. It does demonstrate how at least these feminists have viewed, reacted to, and in some instances adapted for their own purposes those political and ethical aspects of Machiavelli's thought that they have found most critical to their understanding of their own time and place.

La Questione di Machiavelli

Let us begin with an introduction to the subject of this volume, Niccolò Machiavelli himself, and some of the reasons why, while there has been so little agreement over the interpretation of his works, there has indeed been universal consensus over the extraordinary impact that he and his thought, in all its interpretations, have had on modern political discourse. For it is no exaggeration to say that almost every day somewhere in the world someone is invoking his name, either as a cautionary plea against some specific political action or as a template for understanding particular events.[4]

Also, to attempt to understand the complex and somewhat inconsistent nature of his political thought as well as his views and attitudes toward women, it is necessary to consider the circumstances under which Machiavelli's intellectual and psychological formation occurred—whatever one concludes his resulting views to be. As Hanna Fenichel

Pitkin has pointed out, so little is known about Machiavelli's childhood or family life that one must broaden the scope of inquiry to include the cultural and political aspects of his times as well as his private letters and public writings if one wishes to "humanize" this sometimes "frightening" revolutionary thinker.[5]

Niccolò Machiavelli was born in 1469 of a minor branch of the Machiavelli family of Florence, Italy, during a time of transition in Florentine politics from that of a long-standing republic and communal city-state to one of the petty despotisms that were in the process of replacing many similar city-states throughout northern and central Italy. What set Florence apart was that it retained the semblance of republican institutions throughout this transition, except for the period from 1512 to 1527, almost until the final blow was delivered by invading armies during the devastating eight-month siege of the city in 1530.

Florence had served throughout the fourteenth and fifteenth centuries as the center of the ideological upheaval against feudalism, supporting the movement toward the civic life (*il vivere civile*), or republicanism. This movement was led by humanistic scholars serving as chancellors of the city during the period in which Florence was engaged in an almost life and death struggle against the despotic regime of the Visconti of Milan.[6] The belief in republican liberty was deeply engrained in the citizenry of Florence, even among the leading merchant families, but especially among the minor guilds (*arti*) whose members periodically revolted to obtain ever greater representation in the city government.

Machiavelli's father, Bernardo, was a middle-class jurisconsult and a respected student of the classics who obtained for his son an excellent education in Latin. Bernardo compiled an index of place names for an edition of Livy's history of the early Roman Republic and was given a copy by the publisher for his own library. The more prominent branch of the Machiavelli family provided to the city numerous elected members of the *Signoria* and *Priori* and at least four *Gonfalonieri* (Chief Executives).[7] Both father and son witnessed the gradual usurpation of power by the clever scions of the enormously wealthy Medici banking family, in particular by Cosimo and his grandson Lorenzo "the Magnificent." It was a usurpation more de facto than de jure, conducted through the use of influence, money, and the manipulation of the voting process rather than through the overt occupation of any particular office.

Machiavelli was a child of nine in 1478 when a conspiracy inspired by Pope Sixtus IV against Lorenzo and his brother Giuliano was perpetrated during High Mass in the Cathedral. Carried out by the Riarii and their Florentine allies, the Pazzi family, the incident was forever known as the "Pazzi Conspiracy" and resulted in the assassination of Giuliano and the narrow escape of Lorenzo. Machiavelli could not help seeing the terrible vengeance wreaked by the citizenry of Florence against the Riarii and the Pazzi families[8] and witnessed the conspiracy's political aftermath as well, in which the lists of candidates for all city elections were even more restricted than they had been under Cosimo.

Machiavelli was a young man of twenty-three when Lorenzo died in 1492, and he watched somewhat incredulously while Florence succumbed to the rhetorical powers of Fra Girolamo Savonarola,[9] the city's new leader, following the French invasion of Italy and the subsequent expulsion of the Medici in 1494 for having surrendered to Charles VIII virtually without a fight. The loss of the port city of Pisa in the mêlée further aggrieved the Florentines against the Medici, whom they had earlier so befriended.

The new constitution that Savonarola established for the Republic of Florence shortly thereafter made Florence the most democratic republic of northern Italy,[10] including Venice, after which it had been partially modeled. Upon Savonarola's execution for heresy in the Piazza della Signoria directly in front of the Palazzo Vecchio in 1498, the Florentines did something heretofore unheard of in such circumstances: they not only retained the democratic institutions Savonarola had established, but strengthened them as well. And in that same year, the twenty-nine-year-old Machiavelli, a member of the *popolani* (popular faction) but not of the *piagnoni* ("weepers") or followers of Savonarola, found himself elected both Second Secretary and Second Chancellor of the Republic. Some say he had the help of the new First Secretary, Marcello Virgilio Adriani, a lecturer at the *Studio,* or University of Florence.[11] For the next decade and a half Machiavelli continued to be reelected to that post until the government itself was overthrown and the Medici reinstated as de facto rulers of the city in 1512.

For most of that time he served under the administration of *Gonfaloniere* Piero Soderini, who had previously left the ranks of Savonarola's followers in disillusionment. Within a few years after his accession, Soderini was elected *Gonfaloniere à Vita* (for life) since the exceedingly short terms of the members of the *Signoria* made consistent and coherent foreign policy extremely difficult to maintain. Machiavelli became Soderini's chief advisor and preferred legate to foreign powers because of his brilliant analyses of difficult situations and his excellent reportage.

Machiavelli's first important mission as Secretary to the Ten, or Second Chancery, was to the remarkable Countess of Forlì, Madonna Caterina Sforza, in 1499. It was then that he received his first lesson in diplomacy: that a promise made one day could be broken the next before an agreement could be signed. This woman, for whom the term "virago" was said to have been coined,[12] thus taught Machiavelli what it meant to be a "fox" when one was too weak to be a "lion," and he rewarded her with citations of her tactics, successes, and losses in all four of his major political works.[13] Later, when Cesare Borgia failed to fulfill his hopes for a unified Italy, Machiavelli thought that Sforza's son, Giovanni delle Bande Nere, might succeed.[14] Instead it was that lady's grandson, Cosimo dei Medici, who became the first Duke of Tuscany under a system of near-permanent division of Italy. This division was rectified only by the upheaval in European politics that resulted from the French Revolution, the Napoleonic Wars, the Risorgimento, and the dissolution of the Papal States in 1870.[15]

During the period of his service to the Florentine Republic, Machiavelli was sent on many diplomatic missions to all the major courts of Europe and Italy. He helped conduct the war for the reconquest of Pisa and campaigned vigorously for the establishment of a citizen army (and succeeded briefly in recruiting a small contingent of ragtag peasants from the contado) after seeing the predatory and treasonous behavior of mercenary troops. These mercenaries were the mainstay of many Italian city-states in this age of large, highly disciplined, well-armed national armies elsewhere in Europe.

Machiavelli witnessed firsthand the brutal tactics of Cesare Borgia in conquering the renegade cities of the Romagna (including Forlì, the domain of Caterina Sforza) on behalf of his father, Pope Alexander VI. He pronounced the people of Cesena to be "gratified and awestruck" at the gruesome execution of Rimirro de Orco, Borgia's first in command, when he wanted to deflect their ire away from himself and toward his underling for some of the more rapacious activities of his regime. Machiavelli also recounted Borgia's carefully devised assassination of a group of conspirators in the town of Sinigallia after inviting them to join him for a "friendly" meeting—all of which turned out to be grist for Machiavelli's mill when he later wrote The Prince.[16]

This closely studied alliance between the papacy and a powerful, if unscrupulous, *Condottiere* (military leader) whose intentions for Italy mirrored what the rulers of Spain and France had recently done for their countries—i.e., the defeat of petty feudalities and the consolidation of large *stati* into what we today call nation-states—made a profound impression on Machiavelli. It should come as no surprise, therefore, that in 1513, a year after he witnessed the fall of the Florentine Republic, the reinstatement of the Medici, and the election of Giovanni dei Medici as Pope Leo X, he should call for just such a combination of papal and military might to lead Italy into what was rapidly becoming the "modern" world of absolute monarchies.

But before that could happen, Machiavelli was deposed as Second Secretary and investigated for possible participation in a conspiracy against the new Medici regime in Florence because of his close connection to Piero Soderini and some of the conspirators. He was imprisoned, tortured with the *strappado,* and released during the general amnesty that followed the election of Leo X.[17] He was fined and sentenced to remain in Florentine territory for a year, during which time he retreated to his tiny farm in Sant'Andrea in Percussina, near San Casciano just outside the city. He was recalled from time to time to give an account of the monies spent on "his" militia during his service in office. Machiavelli was now forty-three years of age.

It was during this desperate period in his life that Machiavelli turned to writing the works on which his reputation is based. That he was truly conflicted in his approach to politics is no secret. A dedicated republican at heart and a member of the middle class, he was literally impoverished by the loss of his position, and this former Second Secretary of the Republic was almost reduced to the status of a servant (tutor) except for the occasional assistance of his friends. Nevertheless, he considered himself to have been a servant of the state rather than of any particular regime, and proceeded to write a handbook for the new generation of absolute rulers of Florence in whom he placed his hope, not only for future employment, but for the unification of Italy.

Machiavelli first addressed *The Prince*[18] to Giuliano dei Medici, whom he partially credited with having assisted in obtaining his release from prison,[19] and later to Lorenzo, the Duke of Urbino, who became the de facto ruler of Florence. It is reported that the latter gentleman paid more attention to a gift of hunting dogs than he did to this slender volume.[20] Not so for the numerous political leaders who read it after the author's death and its publication in 1532. For this little book became the clarion call of the type of politics that ruptured the traditional bonds between ethics and politics cited throughout the history of political theory, from the time of Aristotle and Cicero through the Middle Ages and the pre-eminence of Christianity. According to what Giovanni Botero called "the reason of state,"[21] Machiavelli asserted the separation of the "is" from the "ought" in practical politics[22] and paved the way for the instrumentalism, impersonalism, and "rationalism"[23] that has so characterized "modernism" and its values.[24]

There is little doubt that Machiavelli's work also paved the way for the secular state divorced from any authority than that of the state itself. By redefining Roman *virtus* as *virtù* and excising the notion of honor and obligation from this practice of "manly" vigor and power, Machiavelli completely circumvented all appeal to the Christian virtues upon which the medieval handbooks for the guidance of princes had been written.[25] In adapting the Roman goddess Fortuna to the political term *Fortuna* in order to express not the goodness of nature but its fickleness, Machiavelli undermined the very notion of divine providence and asserted the ability of human will to overcome *Fortuna* at least "half of the time."[26]

This belief in free will was not unique to Machiavelli, of course,[27] but the context was. Thenceforth, the ability of a prince (or political leader, founder, reformer, or even a republic or state collectively) to overcome adversity would depend upon what actions he or she would be willing to take, good or evil, in the pursuit of his or her goals. What mattered was not the immediate evil consequent to specific actions but the ultimate purpose motivating those actions.[28] And, much to the confusion of his readers, that purpose was not evil for evil's sake, nor even self-interest or the attainment or maintenance of power exclusively, but the "common good."[29] Nor was this evil to be exercised indiscriminately, but through necessity only, and never in so extreme a fashion as to arouse the hatred of the people.[30] And always, the *appearance* of goodness (*bontà*), or virtue in its Christian sense, was to be maintained.[31] At least that was the strategy Machiavelli believed most successful princes pursued, no matter what their stated purposes.[32]

What upset his readers even more than this unfamiliar perspective, perhaps, was the implication that religion was also to be used as a tool of the state. While specifically condemning the activities of some individual popes on behalf of their own family interests, and the existence of the Papal States generally as the principal obstacle to the unification of Italy, Machiavelli also condemned the very ethic of Christianity as encouraging people to submit to their oppressors. And the *otium,* or leisure, that enabled everyone from the ancient Greeks to the medieval monastics to devote their time to contemplation of the "higher" or "better" aspects of spiritual or intellectual life, he saw as *ozio,* or laziness. It was the religion of the ancient Romans as established by Numa to bind those first unruly tribes to the new city-state that he most admired. Action, not contemplation, was the sign of a "virtuous" (having *virtù*) ruler.

And yet, Machiavelli also delivered an oration based on the *De Profundis* titled "An Exhortation to Penitence"[33] before one of the several religious charitable organizations of the city of which he was a member. The theme, again, was action, not just repentance, in order to take away the "opportunity for evil" through imitation of the works of St. Francis and St. Jerome, giving alms, and doing good toward one's neighbor. Was this, too, an exercise in "keeping up appearances" as some of his critics claim?[34]

Machiavelli's poignant appeal in the final chapter of *The Prince* to the Medici, who in 1513 controlled both the papacy and the city of Florence, to do what the Borgias had been unable to do—unite all of Italy under a single standard as had been done in France and Spain—invokes to this day a sadness and a regret for "what might have been." He likened such a leader to Moses and similar figures of biblical proportions, and believed that only extraordinary means could prevent the piecemeal dismemberment of the country by foreign powers and the disintegration of whatever integrity and dignity the people of Italy might still retain. The corruption of Italy's citizens due to weakness was far more obvious to him than whatever goodness may have been attributed to perceived meekness and humility. And this was the conundrum facing Machiavelli: while he condemned the Church, he needed it, but for the creation of the political entity necessary, in his view, to the survival of a people.[35]

Machiavelli also proclaimed the superiority of a republic to any form of monarchy, feudal or absolute. The entire *Discourses on the First Ten Books of Titus Livy* is a paean to the advantages of the liberty of republics over principalities, to the judgment of the populace over that of the prince, and to the need for diversity and what he called the occasional "tumult" (and what Jefferson echoed as "rebellion") for the health and stability of commonwealths.[36] In fact, after many years of unsuccessfully seeking employment from the new Medici rulers of Florence, Machiavelli was given a commission by Leo X (through Cardinal Giulio dei Medici, the future Pope Clement VII, his duly appointed Governor of Florence) in 1520 to advise them on ways in which the government of the city might be reformed. And it is in the document that ensued that all the ambiguities of Machiavelli's thoughts were manifest.[37] For not only did he advise the Pope on ways in which the rule of the Medici could be strengthened, he also suggested they use the republican institutions of Florence to do so! This was because, as he said, "in all cities where the citizens are accustomed to equality, a princedom cannot be set up."[38] Further, he stated (either with deliberate falsehood or extreme naiveté) that he knows that the Pope is "much inclined toward [a republic] and [would] defer to establishing [one]."[39] Was this the "triumph of hope over experience," or was it an attempt to "teach" (or manipulate) when he could no longer "do"?[40]

In that same year Machiavelli was given another commission by Leo X to write the history of Florence from its earliest beginnings.[41] He deliberately ended the book with the death of Lorenzo the Magnificent (1492) without criticizing in any way the methods by which the Medici came into power, because, as he told one of his many correspondents, he did not feel free to express his own opinions, and "what I am not willing to say as coming from myself, I shall have his [Cosimo's] opponents say."[42] It was turned over to the second Medici Pope, Clement VII, in its incomplete form in 1525.

In 1521 the only (quasi) theoretical book of Machiavelli's published during his lifetime, *The Art of War*, was issued. In it he stressed once again the importance of a citizen army as a means of rallying the people in defense of the state and of educating them in the discipline and values of citizenship.[43] Of all his works this was perhaps dearest to his heart, because in it he was able to sum up everything he had learned from his study of warfare as conducted by the Roman Republic while adapting it, even in his lifetime, to the battlefields of Renaissance Italy. That much of what he wrote was mistaken, ill-conceived, and insufficiently aware of the differences in war tactics brought about by the use of artillery goes without saying.[44] He nevertheless felt that such an army was absolutely essential to the revival of *virtù* in the people and necessary for the maintenance of the *stato*.[45]

During this same period, Machiavelli rejoined the community of discourse in the city and participated in many meetings of the *literati* in the *Orti Oricellarii* (Gardens) belonging to the Rucellai family. In addition to discussing his thoughts and works with these young men, initially in a somewhat guarded fashion,[46] he also turned to writing poetry, plays, short stories, and, for the entire time that he was unemployed, numerous letters to family, friends, and acquaintances throughout Italy,[47] some of them humorous, raucous, and bawdy, and some just eloquently sorrowful.[48]

Among the most important of these works are the two plays that are perhaps of most interest to feminists, *La Mandragola* and *Clizia*, the plots of which have been summarized in the appendices to this volume. The chief protagonists in both works are women who demonstrate without a doubt their ability to "rule a kingdom." *La Mandragola* is considered by many to be the most important comedy to have been written during the Italian Renaissance, despite its somewhat unsavory "moral" (if one may use this term in this context).[49] Other works from this period include *Belfagor, the Devil who Married; The (Golden) Ass,* a parody of the work of Apuleius; *The Life of Castruccio Castrocani*; several tercets, including one on *Fortuna*; several Carnival songs; three sonnets written to Giuliano dei Medici while he was imprisoned; and an *Epigram* for Piero Soderini, which perfectly sums up his attitude toward "good men" who do not know how to "play the game" of politics to win:

> That night when Piero Soderini died,
> His spirit went to the mouth of Hell.
> Pluto roared: "Why to Hell? Silly Spirit,
> Go up into Limbo with all the rest of the babies."[50]

Machiavelli's last years were indeed bittersweet. After years of asking friends like Francesco Vettori, the Florentine ambassador in Rome, and Francesco Guicciardini, the Papal Governor of the Romagna, to intervene on his behalf with Rome to allow him to obtain some means of employment beyond the occasional commission for manuscripts, Machiavelli finally decided to go to Rome, but only after the fall of Pavia in 1525,[51] in order to present his unfinished *Istorie* to the Pope and to plead the cause, not so much for his own employment,[52] but for the establishment of a national militia to help defend the country against the Imperial armies that were poised to invade Italy en masse, and for the immediate fortification of the walls of the city of Florence against such an attack.

Nothing came of his plea for a national citizen army in Rome, probably because Guicciardini argued against arming the people of the Romagna who might not be loyal to the Medici Pope.[53] But his constant efforts to warn Pope and Florentines alike of the need to strengthen the walls of the city, in anticipation of a siege by the combined German and Spanish armies of the Emperor Charles V, eventually led to the establishment of a body known as the "Five Curators of the Walls," with Machiavelli as its Chancellor. But neither he, nor the municipal government of Florence, nor the pleadings of Guicciardini could persuade Clement VII to spend the money necessary to complete the fortifications in time.[54] Instead, the Pope signed a series of truces with the Emperor and his rivals, the Colonna family of Rome, and, much to the dismay of Machiavelli and Guicciardini, disbanded his troops in an effort to save money [!]. Those truces were almost immediately broken and Clement VII was imprisoned until he was able to pay a large ransom.[55]

When, in 1527, those armies did indeed come south, Florence barely escaped their initial onslaught—but Rome did not. For eight days the starved, rapacious, undisciplined mob of German and Spanish troops sacked the city of Rome, killing, raping, and demanding ransom of thousands of the city's inhabitants—cardinals, clergy, nuns, merchants, children as well as adults, rich and poor alike—to the extent that the waters of the Tiber ran red with blood.[56] Clement VII himself was forced to seek shelter, first in the Castel Sant'Angelo (Hadrian's Tomb), and then in Orvieto, just south of Florence, where he fled into exile. The pike marks of the German troops can still be seen on the walls of the Raphael *Stanze* in the Vatican, where, it is reported, horses were stabled during the siege. The troops left Rome months later after destroying many of the works of art and libraries of the city, and retreated to Naples heavily laden with gold objects and religious artifacts from churches, homes, and monasteries alike.

The immediate effect was the overthrow of the Medici government in Florence and the return of the institutions of the Savonarolan republic. Machiavelli, now a worn out, sick man of fifty-eight, believed that since he was currently in the Chancery working to complete the necessary fortifications for the city, and also serving periodically as an emissary for the government and Guicciardini, he would be retained. Instead, the man who had served as Second Secretary under the just-exiled Medici was appointed to the position with no thought of Machiavelli or of all the work he had already put into the project.[57]

Having long been held suspect by the Medici for his republican connections, he now found himself distrusted not only for his Medicean connections, but also for his personal reputation as a *roué* and because many Florentines believed that his writings had served to teach the tyrants how to despoil them of their liberties.[58] Therefore, while others like

Vettori and Guicciardini eventually survived the overthrow, Machiavelli did not.[59] His social status was not sufficiently high enough for him to garner the kind of public support necessary for him to achieve a second political reincarnation under the restored republic, nor did he live long enough to join his friends Vettori and Guicciardini in the new Medici regime that was established in 1530.[60]

Machiavelli died on June 22, 1527, some say of a broken heart, but more likely of a ruptured stomach ulcer. The epitaph on his tomb in the Church of Santa Croce in Florence reads *"Tanto nomini nullum par elogium"* ("To such a name no eulogy is equal").[61] But perhaps a more apt epitaph should have read "I love my native city more than my own soul."[62]

The Feminist Inquiry

How have we as feminists reacted, almost five hundred years after Machiavelli's death, as we have struggled to come to grips both with the complexity of his thought and the depth of his influence on modern politics? In many ways we have been just as bewildered, intrigued, fascinated, and repulsed as anyone else who has ever grappled with his dark intelligence, his cynical humor, his raunchy escapades, or his despair. The chapters in this volume have all been written since the awakening of feminist consciousness following the civil rights movement of the 1960s. Some were written specifically for this volume. Several appear to be engaging in conversation with one another, as if to clarify and extend each other's thoughts. Sometimes there appears to be consensus on a point or two. But for the most part, there is disagreement; and perhaps that is as it should be. For after all, as Croce predicted, the inquiry on Machiavelli may never be closed.

However, one particularly interesting feature of this volume is the way in which feminist thought has tended to parallel mainstream critiques of Machiavelli over the past few decades. As analyses of his works other than *The Prince* have come to the fore, and, following Croce, as his quasi-liberal attitudes have been explored based upon *The Discourses*, his plays, and his extensive correspondence, both official and familial, a more rounded picture of this very complex and controversial personality has come into view. One might almost say that the mainstream and the feminist critiques have both swung from one pole to the opposite in just a few short years: from protofascist to protoliberal, and from extreme male chauvinist to "protofeminist," or at least, "female defender," depending upon which works or interpretations of which phrases and "stories" one chose to emphasize.

It took some time for feminists to begin to examine Machiavelli's works from a specifically feminine viewpoint, however. In 1978, for example, Mera J. Flaumenhaft turned the spotlight on *La Mandragola*, with the aim of comparing his purely political writings with his literary works to determine if the conclusions that could be drawn from each would be similar.[63] She concluded that they were indeed alike, though without addressing any specifically feminist issues or their importance to feminism in any way.

When Jean Bethke Elshtain wrote her book *Public Man, Private Woman* in 1981, she, too, claimed not to be speaking for feminism, but many in the feminist community agreed with her when she characterized Machiavelli's work as reinforcing the "war between the sexes" by confining each sex to a separate realm with different moral standards for each for distinguishing good from evil.[64] Women had no function in the public realm, she argued, primarily because of their lesser capacity for violence, while the civic actions of men in that realm were to be judged not by their intentions or motives but by the consequences of those actions.[65]

Three years later Donald McIntosh placed that same "battle of the sexes" in a Freudian context in the last section of his article "The Modernity of Machiavelli" (Chapter 1 of this volume).[66] Characterizing the struggle between *virtù* and *Fortuna* as "the outward manifestation of a battle . . . that raged within the soul of Machiavelli," specifically, "phallic narcissism" combined with "primary sadism," he asserted that "for him, politics was the continuation of sex by other means," and that the modern woman "must be passive, submissive, and expressive" in order to enable the man to be "active, dominating, and instrumental." Thus, "*Fortuna* is the creation of *virtù*, which cannot exist without her."

But he also issued a warning to mainstream as well as to feminist thinkers when he pointed out that the continuation of male dominance in a world that is no longer patrimonial persists today "purely on functional grounds," and that, because women "would have no group on which to displace their now unwanted passive and masochistic expressivity," the "full-scale entry [of women] into political and economic leadership would result in a dilution, a weakening, of the motivational syndrome that is the mainspring of modernity." Thus, he writes, "[t]he critics of feminism are entirely correct that this movement strikes at the basic values and institutions of modern civilization."

That same year Jack D'Amico challenged the "overly simplistic equation of fortune and woman, control and manly virtue," while arguing that for Machiavelli men have private as well as public roles, that one should not confuse those actions deriving from nature with those emanating from custom, and that only the latter are subject to free will.[67] In the play *La Mandragola*, Lucrezia may represent nature but she also shows a more astute sense of wisdom than Callimaco, and it is her *virtù*, exercised in her private world, that brings the comedy to a conclusion acceptable to the norms of society, or the public world. Both comedies, *Clizia* as well as *La Mandragola*, he argues, "show that we need to examine more carefully the assumptions about sex implicit in our reading of such key terms as *virtù* and *materia* [nature] in all of Machiavelli's works."[68]

It was not until Hanna Fenichel Pitkin published her monumental work *Fortune Is a Woman: Gender and Politics in the Thought of Niccolò Machiavelli* (1984) that the first inklings of a fundamentally feminist critique were perceived to be possible as well as necessary (excerpts from this book are Chapter 2 of this volume).[69] Utilizing a whole range of political, sociological, psychological, and philosophical theories, with a special emphasis on Freudian themes, in order to analyze Machiavelli's principal writings as they relate to her own efforts to understand autonomy and mutuality in politics, she created an "ideal type" called "Machiavelli at his best," and asserted that insofar as the real Machiavelli failed to achieve this synthesis of ideas it was because of his misogynistic fear of women and his projection of that fear upon *Fortuna*, resulting in his compulsive evocation of an exaggerated, protofascist notion of *virtù*—once again because of the classic battle of the sexes. Machiavelli's machismo,[70] she stated, was the principal cause of his being unable to break out of the cycle symbolized by the "Wheel of Fortune" and thus achieve a true liberation of the *vivere civile* from the paternalistic trappings of the past.[71] Suddenly, a window was opened for further exploration of exclusively feminist themes, even though Pitkin herself did not perceive that what she had done was necessarily "feminist" in tone. It was not long before other feminists joined in the fray.

One year later Arlene Saxonhouse, in chapter seven of her book *Women in the History of Political Thought*, took a major step away from the till-then radical dichotomization of Machiavelli's thought by concentrating on what she called the "Ambiguity of Sex" in his work, seeing his approach as positing the possibility of "Women as Men, [and] Men as Women" (Chapter 3 of this volume).[72] She claimed that Machiavelli was so intent on "breaking down the old hierarchies . . . that he makes the differences between what had been opposites so ambiguous that we can no longer tell good from bad or women from men." Thus, within four short years Machiavelli went from being the principal protagonist in the "battle of the sexes" to its major obfuscator—all the while engaging in a major "transformation of values" during the transition from the medieval to the modern.

Since effeminacy is as much the product of education as is masculinity, Saxonhouse explained, indolent, "effeminate" men can be remade by education in warfare into "masculine" men, while women (e.g., Madonna Caterina, Marcia, and the like), through revenge and necessity, can just as easily act as men in their ability to conspire and deceive.

To illustrate that, according to Machiavelli, women could be every bit as political as men and men every bit as weak and "effeminate" as women, Saxonhouse cited the comedies La Mandragola and Clizia, with Lucrezia "fit to rule a kingdom" in the former, and Sofronia "ruling the house" and determining the outcome in the latter. Therefore, she concluded, women are paradoxically "central" to Machiavelli's political thought yet "unimportant" to his concept of political life. He "leaves the status of women uncertain because all is uncertain," and in doing so "leaves open the movement to liberalism." And "[t]hrough its ambiguity, Machiavelli's work reveals the uncertainty at the foundation of modern political thought."

Three years later, in 1988, chapters five and six of Wendy Brown's book Manhood and Politics continued the feminist critique by exploring Machiavelli's interpretation of human nature as an attempt to reincorporate "into political thought that which . . . the Greeks [had tried] to eliminate—the body" (Chapter 4 of this volume).[73] Almost invoking a Darwinian interpretation in her study, she continued: "In contrast with the many political theorists who arrive at a definition of man by distinguishing him from other animals, Machiavelli suggests a very close and by no means unfortunate kinship between man and beast." It is man's "blind ambition" or "will to power" and domination, coupled with his weakness in the face of his natural environment, that prevents him from distinguishing between appearance and reality.

Thus, "[w]hile Machiavelli often portrays Fortuna as a goddess with mind, will, and intentions of her own, he also declares that *Fortuna* is nothing other than man's inadequate grasp of his circumstances." *Fortuna*, therefore, embodies the forces against which *virtù* must struggle.[74] "Conditions of political necessity, the conditions that demand and nourish *virtù*, are meant to be a human version of the conditions a wild animal faces." Faced with several options in this battle of "mind over matter/nature"—harmony with the feminine, conquest, or independence (homosexuality)[75]—without definitively choosing among them, "Machiavellian man creates a jungle of his own in civilization: Machiavellian politics."

In the final chapter of her book (not included in this volume), Brown joined Saxonhouse in attacking the dualistic interpretations of her feminist predecessors and called for a "post-masculinist politics" in which power is not eschewed or rejected by women, but is rather incorporated into a "distinctly feminist theory of political power" that "draws upon a Machiavellian insight" that "freedom, power, creativity, and struggle" are linked. She concluded that "the lessons [he] drew from the tumults of Rome need to be placed in the service of human life, genuine freedom, and equality rather than devotion to the state, imperialism, class, or gender domination."[76] Thus a full-blown and exclusively feminist critique was launched as a major theoretical enterprise, to take its place beside and be incorporated into the mainstream of political theory rather than simply being a minor if not digressing distraction from the principal work of the profession.

In 1989, chapter eight of Mary O'Brien's book *Reproducing the World*, a more narrowly feminist critique rather than an broader endeavor, approached the topic of Machiavelli's concept of "manliness" (*virtù*) through a theoretical treatment of *La Mandragola* (Chapter 5 of this volume).[77] In a variation on Elshtain's theme, O'Brien argued that "[h]is political work attempts to describe the theoretical and practical dimensions of an autonomous polity" (i.e., the separation of "the private realm of necessity" from "the public realm of freedom"), and that "Machiavelli believes that the major obstacle to this problematic glory . . . is Woman." She claimed that "from the standpoint of feminist politics, Machiavelli is correct: women do indeed reject the neurosis which sees nature as a cunning and powerful foe. Resistance to this pernicious doctrine, in which the endless defense of public and private violence as 'necessary evils' is posited as necessary to the common good, is an essential part of feminist struggle." "Feminists believe that the separation of the public and private realms does not merely institutionalize the dreams and realities of patriarchy; it ensures that politics *must* proceed from the violent exercise of power."

But O'Brien also held that "the material base of the persistent dualism in patriarchal thought lies in the dialectical structure of human reproduction. . . . Male participation in reproduction is . . . understood *politically* . . . in terms of a *right* to the child rather than in the value-creating reality of laboring to produce a child." Thus, "political man, having separated public and private, reason and passion, is left with little but undirected libido and a norm of aggression."

O'Brien then insisted, in a way that reflected but did not quite agree with Saxonhouse's argument, that *La Mandragola* demonstrates "exactly the opposite" of the separation of the political from the social realm. The dependence of the political upon the family in particular and the domination of the masculine over the feminine (*virtù* over *Fortuna*), the realm of control (polity) over the realm of necessity (family), shows that "manliness . . . is inseparable from the family which it must transcend, [and] is radically one-sided and contingent in terms of human life-process." Therefore, she concluded, Machiavelli "realized a peculiarly antihuman conception of politics in which manliness, divorced from humanity, finds its most apt expression in compulsive masculine militarism."

As this review of early feminist scholarship demonstrates, while most feminist authors during the 1980s viewed Machiavelli in a negative light, the overall assessment was not entirely so, and the years to follow would see a gradual shift in interpretation toward the positive, as the work of Saxonhouse, and to some extent Brown, began to have its effect. This was especially true in those writings that focused on the "civic virtue" and the republican aspects of his works, reflecting some similar evaluations by nonfeminist, "mainstream" critics.[78]

In 1992 Lenore Coltheart surveyed Machiavelli's treatment of women in her article "The Virago and Machiavelli"[79] as a way of examining, through the lens of feminist theory, how Machiavelli was able to "prepare the ground" for liberalism and modern politics. She stated that "Machiavelli's most profound achievement is his mediation of the politics of women's place," which substitutes realism for ethics as the modern political metaphor, and especially ignores Aristotle's emphasis upon ethics as male. Since this change in focus could have "disenfranchised" men, Coltheart argued, it was "for this reason that maleness is so heavily endorsed as the essential political virtue, and in this sense that Machiavelli provided the foundation for the work of Hobbes and Locke."[80]

Concluding that "Machiavelli averted his gaze from the virago, and political theory has not been able to look her in the eye since," Coltheart called for "[a] reappraisal of his writing that explores . . . [how] gendered power is accorded the force of scientific law, or common sense, [and how his] metaphors and contradictions . . . carry into the genre of political science and the discourse of Liberalism."[81]

In 1996 Catherine H. Zuckert explored Machiavelli's *Clizia* in her article "Fortune Is a Woman—But So Is Prudence: Machiavelli's *Clizia*" (Chapter 6 of this volume).[82] Taking her cues from both Pitkin and Saxonhouse, Zuckert asserted that in this play, Machiavelli "does not simply dismiss or demean women" but rather in the person of Sofronia he presents a woman who is "not merely . . . the rightful ruler of the household," but is "the embodiment of *virtù*," and suggests that "there is no essential difference between the sexes with regard to their potential for achieving human excellence." Thus he "appears to make way for—or even be the founder of—. . .'liberal feminism.'" The particular virtue Sofronia displays is prudence (practical wisdom), or the expression of her own self-interest, which, as it turns out, coincides with that of her husband and son as well. This is not the same as the ancient virtue of *sophrosynē*, because for Machiavelli, community is not based on love and trust but on "the one unchanging characteristic of all human beings: their attachment to their own lives, property, and standing in the eyes of others"— once again, the traditional liberal position. But more importantly, perhaps, in this article we see women already exercising not just the powers of *Fortuna*, but those of *virtù* as well.

In 1999, chapter two of R. Claire Snyder's book *Citizen-Soldiers and Manly Warriors: Military Service and Gender in the Civic Republican Tradition* explored what it meant to be a citizen of a republic post-Machiavelli, and how that has had an impact on women's lives in the modern and postmodern world (Chapter 7 of this volume).[83] It is a theme carried on through several of the papers that follow and is of primary interest to women, feminist or not, following the widespread recruitment of women into the armed forces in the current era.

Snyder held that for Machiavelli and the civic republican tradition, "the Citizen-Soldier constitutes a normative ideal that necessarily entails a commitment to a set of republican political principles, including liberty, equality, fraternity, the rule of law, the common good, civic virtue, and participatory citizenship," which she called a *citizenship of civic practices*. "According to this ideal, individuals actually *become* citizens as they participate together in civic practices, traditionally including those of the civic militia." Thus, "a 'citizen' is not a prepolitical identity"; it is neither ethnic heritage, class, nor living within certain borders but "engagement in civic practices [that] *produces* a common civic identity." But, to some extent agreeing with Elshtain, Snyder also asserted that these same martial practices can teach the opposite of civic virtues, including "selfless conformity" and "fraternity chauvinism"—a combative *armed masculinity* that is "both an enemy and the denigration of femininity." Therefore, "[w]hen service in the civic militia forms the primary civic practice constitutive of citizenship, the vices are more prominent."

Agreeing with Pitkin and Mark Hulliung that Machiavelli is both a republican and a protofascist when "martial practices are privileged over other possible forms of civic practices," Snyder nevertheless held, with J. G. A. Pocock, that the Citizen-Soldier embodies a commitment to civic republicanism, or secularism, which soon emerged in direct opposition to the Christian world-view and political order. Thus, "only a civic militia can be relied upon to defend a republic . . . [and] Citizen Soldiers fight to protect their secular political order and civic ideals . . . not . . . for God and His revealed Truth."

However, Snyder disagreed with Wendy Brown, in that men's "second nature" is more important than any "essential" masculine nature, and that "politics constructs manhood," not vice versa. Therefore, "if men's natures are subject to social construction through political practice, then so are women's . . . [and] perhaps female individuals could become republican citizens alongside 'men' if they began to engage in the same civic and martial practices." She concluded that "since both masculinity and citizenship are politically and socially constructed, the possibility remains of reconstructing the traditional configuration of gender and citizenship," but wondered (in part), "[w]hat would happen if women began to engage in civic practices that produce masculine citizen-soldiers?"

In chapter six of *Citizen-Soldiers and Manly Warriors* (not included in this volume) Snyder allowed herself to imagine a new form of masculinity, *civic masculinity*, as a way of destabilizing "traditional gender norms that have historically prevented 'women's' participation in republican citizenship," as well as a new form of femininity, *robust femininity*, that encompasses all of the traditional characteristics of the personal, domestic, and erotic spheres, which should be protected from "unwanted political incursion." Thus "all people, both male and female, would become both *civicly* [*sic*] *masculine* and *robustly feminine,* for all would participate as citizens in political rule and in the personal realm with those with whom they choose to make their lives."[84] This interpretation is interesting in that it suggests not entirely *eliminating* the division between the public and the private (so that the private *is* public), but rather reinforcing that division to protect the private from the public while allowing both genders to participate freely in both realms.

In 2000, Melissa M. Matthes approached *La Mandragola* from a somewhat different perspective in a chapter of *The Rape of Lucretia and the Founding of Republics* titled "Why Machiavelli's Lucrezia is not Livy's Virtuous Roman" (Chapter 8 of this volume).[85] Going somewhat further than O'Brien, she claimed that there is no distinction between the public and the private in this play; all there is for Lucrezia is "politics and the realm of appearances . . . the politicization of virtue." Thus "Machiavelli tries to demonstrate the necessity of making private morality answer to public necessity, rather than vice versa."

Unlike Livy, she stated, Machiavelli believed that the rape of the Roman Lucretia (an offense against the Senate) is not what led to the founding of the Roman Republic, but rather the people's consent to the revolt against the Tarquins because of their bad rule, and Lucrezia in his play represents the consent of the populace (all of the characters except her husband) against the rule of Nicia, her husband. Therefore, while Livy's Lucretia "forfeits her chastity in order to ensure her status as citizen," Machiavelli's Lucrezia "is willing to do this and thus personifies an ideal Machiavellian political actor." "[Her] conversion," Matthes concluded, "is not because she is corrupt . . . but because she is astute."

Matthes also argues that for Machiavelli, "*Fortuna,* like Lucrezia, must be seduced, not raped," "[f]or she, as the feminine principle of political action, cannot be completely dominated or annihilated." Seduction, for Machiavelli, is quintessentially political, and while conflict is a sign of vitality in politics, political action itself is about negotiation and accommodation and not about strict adherence to given principles. "The relationship which political actors have with *Fortuna,*" therefore, is one of "interminable seduction" despite Machiavelli's language of conquest. The "paradox of the feminine" for Machiavelli is that "[a]lthough his images of women are riddled with sexual violence, in his political narrative it is the feminine that ultimately makes politics possible."[86] "Lucrezia is a 'lesson' to men [because] she is Machiavelli's invitation to political actors to dissimulate." Thus, "antagonism with *Fortuna* as well as with femininity enriches men's *virtù* . . . and as a 'worthy enemy' Machiavelli grants women as personified by *Fortuna*, autonomous power." (No intermixing of *Fortuna* and *virtù* here!)

In Chapter 9 of this volume, Cary J. Nederman and Martin Morris examine the "economy of violence" in Machiavelli's rhetoric to determine if a "feminist corrective" may be applied. Agreeing with Pitkin that "the feminine is a source of fear that requires a forceful response," they argue that "Machiavelli's insistence upon rational discourse as the basis for fully civil life, in conjunction with his reduction of *Fortuna* to a feminized, naturalistic, and hence derationalized power, reinforces the antifeminist features of 'economy of violence.'"

Using Habermas's theory of valid communication and consensus, Nederman and Morris claim that Machiavelli illegitimately assimilates "natural contingency with social and political contingency" by treating both "in the same way." "Contingency and indeterminacy," they continue, "need not be dealt with by collective aggression embodied in the state if such factors are recognized among the very *conditions* of rational decision-making mediated by speech." Their conclusion is that "there is no good reason why women should be equated with irrational, unpredictable violence on the rhetorical republican model"; rather, such disturbances "ought to be treated at least the same way Machiavelli treats the 'tumults' of class conflict: as a healthy, appropriate aspect of republican rule."

Chapter 10, John Juncholl Shin's contribution to this volume, is written more from the perspective of a revisionist masculinist theorist than that of a feminist. He claims that Machiavelli's "discussion of Queen Giovanna [of Naples] isn't about women at all. Rather, it is about defining the contours of masculinity while claiming to criticize women." After contrasting Machiavelli's reflections on Giovanna in his *Florentine Histories* with what actually happened, Shin concludes that Machiavelli "should have commended her as a successful example of a prince who maintained her *stato* . . . with *virtù*, embodying all the qualities of masculine excellence necessary for success." Why then does he use her as a symbol of "ineffective leadership"?

In a claim reminiscent of McIntosh, Shin argues that Machiavelli's own misogyny prevented him from recognizing such excellence in a woman because it would have gone against his message to men that they must be more *virtuosi* than a "contemptible woman." Giovanna and others serve his "overall project of defining masculine citizenship" because

Machiavelli's masculinity entails not only *virtù* (activity, achievement, authenticity, and success) but "functionality" (passivity, dependence, and abstractness), that is, "that men must function in the name of and service of an abstraction outside themselves."

In characterizing what he calls "functionality" in a manner that others have labeled the "common good" and "civic virtue," and in an unexpected variation of the Saxonhouse theme (and to some extent echoing Snyder), Shin claims that "[w]omen . . . are, in the end, men in disguise, serving as examples of people who had *virtù* but did not use it functionally, and therefore are detestable and 'effeminate,' in Machiavelli's view."

Utilizing object-relations theory and the work of Descartes, Shin then sheds light on this concept of functionality by reviewing *The Prince* and *Balfagor* to show that these heroes "are not special in their possession of *virtù*. The difference between men and women is not that women lack *virtù* but their unwillingness to sacrifice themselves and their families' interests for some higher cause." By attributing women with *virtù*, and then emphasizing their lack of functionality, Machiavelli argues that men must be wary of attaining *virtù* alone, that men must balance their *virtù* with functionality to be considered truly great. Hence, a contradiction in the thought of Machiavelli is not really a contradiction if one considers the attribute of functionality as a component of *virtù* as well as of the "common good" (civic virtue).

"The ability and willingness to dispose oneself is a precondition for admittance into positions of masculine power," Shin writes, and "the difficulties of masculinity . . . are nothing more or less than a hazing process that, under the guise of 'making sure that they are masculine enough,' ensures that men, once admitted into the circle of power, would be loathe to leave." These acts of violence against men committed by men "are also arenas of patriarchy" and "serve the same purpose as violence against women and other groups constituting 'the other.' Only, while violence keeps 'the other' in positions of subordination, violence pressures men to stay within the fold of power." "The achievement of gender equality," he concludes, "requires the dissociation of male identity from masculine-functional identity," and to "reject the argument that being a man necessarily entails functionality and membership."

Vesna Marcina, attacking the same problem from a somewhat more positive perspective, also gives an analysis of earlier feminist interpretations of Machiavelli in Chapter 11 of this volume, basically siding with Saxonhouse in the belief that "women can be incorporated as citizens into [his] vision of the republic by showing that civic virtue is potentially an inclusive concept." She cites several of Machiavelli's works to show first that he depicts "women as men" as well as "women as women," and second that the concept of "civic virtue" requires both masculine and feminine behavior—that citizens must act like men *and* women. Acknowledging that some might object that "the submission and dependence of republican citizens are different from the traits of the same name traditionally ascribed to women," she nevertheless argues that those traits are "similar enough," and that "the phenomenon itself is the same." Thus, while not wanting to "erase" the differences between the family and the republic, she does want to "*privilege* the similarities"—a departure indeed from that of Shin's aversion to "functionality," but somewhat reflective of the view of Snyder.

Marcina maintains that, compared to Rousseau, Machiavelli appears like a liberal because he does not want to eliminate or transform a citizen's self-interest into a "general will." The interdependence of republican citizens is similar to that of the family, where men also depend on women (see O'Brien, this volume). And if women do not serve in armies there are other ways for them to learn civic virtue. Both men and women learn to submit their own interests to those of the family. So, Marcina asks, even if Machiavelli's republicanism is not inherently sexist, "why should feminists care whether or not we can salvage Machiavelli?" Her answer is that his works should be reread because he is useful in examining the genealogy of "submission and dependence, their gendered associations, and their value connotations." Also, he "points us toward an alternative conception of democratic citizenship" in that his "requirement of civic virtue from all citizens means requiring gender-bending of all citizens." One wonders, therefore, if the "functionality" that Shin wants to eradicate from the acculturation of men is not in fact essential in some form to both men and women in a republic.

Jane S. Jaquette takes the argument a bit further in Chapter 12 of this volume, "Rethinking Machiavelli: Feminism and Citizenship," and claims that "it is time to recover Machiavelli as an interlocutor rather than a foil for feminist theory." Disputing both Elshtain's claim that Machiavelli divides the public realm from the private and Pitkin's assertion that he condones the use of violence against women, Jaquette instead argues that "Machiavelli sees the two realms as virtually indistinguishable, with elements of realpolitik and compassion in both. He recognizes that women have the *virtù* to rule . . . and [d]espite his scorn for the 'feminine,' . . .

trains his prince in the art of deception, a quintessentially feminine form of power." But he does separate "the public from the private in one sense with which feminists and progressives can certainly identify: he distinguishes the public good from the pursuit of private interests."

Citing both *La Mandragola* and *Clizia*, Jaquette holds that in each the hero is a woman and that both roles are written to "make the audience familiar with the moral and practical issues [and] choices the 'new' prince must face," in particular, that "bad acts can bring about good ends." Further, she believes that Machiavelli's "attack on 'the feminine' is not an attack on women," since "[in] Galenist biology gender determined sex," and "[w]omen were not men's *opposites:* they were *lesser men.*"

Then, reviewing various readings of Machiavelli's pitting of *virtù* against *Fortuna*, including those that see this conflict as foreshadowing the conquest of nature by science, Jaquette holds that "Machiavelli would have been horrified at the world that Bacon imagined, where the scientific management of nature promised to bring a world of plenty . . . [since he] felt that the best states were formed where the land was less productive, because a life that was too easy would sap a nation's *virtù.*" And "men are first and last a part of nature. . . . Christian doctrine may suggest that nature can be transcended, but Machiavelli does not."

She concludes that "[t]his reading of Machiavelli does more than repel the charge of misogyny. It opens the way to a more balanced assessment." Citing Snyder, Jaquette too is optimistic that, since citizenship is constructed, "it should be possible to redefine both citizens and soldiers on grounds more congenial to feminism." Similarly, "[w]ith regard to citizenship, we owe important debts to Machiavelli, not the least his contribution to a secular, republican, and largely pluralist ideal of political community."

Perhaps the most critical question ever posed about Machiavelli's legacy involves his approach to ethics. In Chapter 13 of this volume, "Machiavelli and Feminist Ethics," Andrea Nicki cites a number of theorists of feminist ethics (Alison Jaggar, Sheila Mullet, Sandra Bartky, and Sarah Hoagland, among others) to build a case that "feminist ethics can benefit from Machiavelli's thought, and provide a sketch of a feminist Machiavellian account of morality."[87]

Using the work of Saxonhouse as her springboard, Nicki claims that a reassessment of Machiavelli's thought "proceeds from a rejection of classic utopian thought, which derives ethical principles from a vision of a perfect society. For Machiavelli, praiseworthy behavior is not based on knowledge of the Forms . . . but on unadorned truths of human social behavior." She continues, "What appears to be condemnable and vicious when examined in itself sometimes seems praiseworthy and beneficial when seen in a specific context."

After reviewing a series of situations and exhortations described in Machiavelli's works, Nicki states that "[t]he crux for Machiavelli is toward what aim 'evil' is being expressed," and contrasts his positions with those of Nietzsche and Sartre before returning to Saxonhouse's treatment of *La Mandragola* and *Clizia*. Nicki then uses Antonio Gramsci's distinction between the "diplomat" and the "politician," between preserving the status quo and changing it, to position Machiavelli as an agent for change, similar to the feminist who wishes to become "an instrument for social change."

With the caveat that "[t]he end of maintaining self-worth is not justified by any means *whatsoever*," Nicki concludes, in agreement with Jaggar, that "[f]eminist approaches to ethics 'must recognize the often unnoticed ways in which women and other members of the underclass have refused cooperation and opposed domination while acknowledging the inevitability of collusion and the impossibility of *totally clean hands*.'"

Conclusion

So where does that leave us in our attempts to come to grips with Machiavelli's politics, as feminists and as citizens of a twenty-first century republic that is undoubtedly as much unlike sixteenth-century Florence as Machiavelli could ever have imagined? Many questions ensue: Are we striving too much to see the similarities and the relevance of his message where perhaps there are few or none? Or is Machiavelli truly a force to be reckoned with, even today, as women adjust to their new-found status as presumed "equals" in what is obviously a challenging political environment?

More specifically, do women have to "play the game" as Machiavelli depicted it, in order to be taken seriously in this political arena? Are we as women undergoing the same kind of political transformation today as we make the same transition from the status of nonparticipants to full citizenship that men underwent when they, too, emerged from the status of subjects to that of citizens? Did men have to "put down" women in order to achieve their sense of liberation and independence (autonomy), just as teenagers have a tendency to turn against their parents when they approach adulthood? Were women just the obvious foils for men to use in their grasp for freedom because of their status as mothers and primary authority figures for children, as some feminists and Freudians believe? If so, are women obliged to react against men as slave-holders and oppressors in order for them to achieve their own sense of independence and freedom (autonomy)? Is this psychopolitical journey the same for both sexes, although women have enlisted in the undertaking more recently than men? Is it also the same or similar for all conflicts, political as well as social, economic as well as martial? Or is this drive for autonomy simply a cultural phenomenon confined to the modernist period of Western civilization from which we may just now be emerging?

Is it possible, now that both genders have arrived at the consciousness of what citizenship and freedom entail, that we can finally join ranks to achieve a mutual understanding of the *vivere civile* for all individuals and generations, as well as all races, religions, classes, and whatever other ideologies may have divided us in the past? If that most primal division—sex, or gender—can be overcome as a political obstacle, may we then hope to see other barriers falling as well, as we enter upon a new political horizon in which not differences but similarities bind us together in the civic enterprise? Are we at the point in our history when our humanity overrides our cultural, as well as our biological, differences and provides the glue that will eventually hold the world community together?

Fortunately, there are some signs that this may indeed be beginning to happen—at least in this country, if not yet worldwide. After the events of September 11, 2001, we must all look at the world somewhat differently. As one television commentator said, according to my recollection, immediately after that tragedy, "It was a case of the eighteenth century being confronted by the twelfth." The Enlightenment and its aftermath was too much of a threat to certain traditional societies to be allowed to go unchallenged. World globalization, the spread of secularism and women's liberation, and all the changes they implied for traditional values were too much for fundamentalists of whatever stripe to countenance.[88] Certainly, the ways in which Americans came together as one people in the face of that challenge were remarkable to say the least. One could see the outlines of a new ideology for the third millennium beginning to take shape as we rephrased and adapted our Enlightenment (and even postmodern) ideals to meet the new situation.

What is relevant about Machiavelli in this *novus ordo seculorum* is that, of all proto-Enlightenment political theorists, he was the most instrumental in articulating the vision that would eventually lead to the almost total break with the past, politically and culturally, that the Renaissance itself represented. His challenge to traditional values appears harsh even to our minds, but, like sherbet to the palate, it may have been just what was needed to force a reconsideration, and perhaps a cleansing, of our preconceptions regarding the world and humanity's place in it.

From this vantage point, Machiavelli's dualism seems not so much public versus private, male versus female, *virtù* versus *Fortuna*, as human versus bestial. Since, according to Pico della Mirandola, Machiavelli's contemporary, humans were created to occupy a position midway between the beasts and the angels and could determine for themselves the level to which they would rise or fall,[89] perhaps we should admit, with Machiavelli, that certain conditions will bring out the beast in any human sufficiently provoked. But Machiavelli went even further in that he advocated the deliberate, if controlled, use of the nature of the "brute," especially in his references to the centaur, the lion, and the fox, and that necessity instead of ethics should determine the limits of that use.

Ethically, Machiavelli's prescriptions for political behavior cause so much distress today because they seem more suited to the enemies of his goals than to his would-be "liberal," civic humanist, and republican followers. The question, therefore, upon which this volume closes remains as critical and as unanswered as when we began: Should feminists, too, become Machiavellian, with all that term implies? Some of this book's contributors have replied in the affirmative, while others have joined the opposition. Perhaps the problem is with the question itself. Perhaps, after all, the problem lies not with Machiavelli, but with the dichotomization of his thought, although not completely without justification, imposed by his critics. For it was Machiavelli after all who wrote: "For there is such a difference between how men live and how they ought to live that he who abandons what is done for what ought to be done learns his destruction rather than his preservation."[90]

The problem is that it was just such an admonition that caused his critics to cry "Foul!" Machiavelli never claimed to be either a philosopher or an idealist. To criticize him, therefore, for not being either is beside the point. To depict him as being a misogynist, considering his time and place, is plausible in light of certain of his works, but not all. To expect him to have been ideologically consistent in that dangerous and politically ambiguous time in which he lived may be imposing a criterion upon him that we would not want to have imposed upon ourselves in similar circumstances—where one's life and well-being hung in the balance. He stood at the headwaters of vast political as well as religious change. Alternatively, to see him as a protoliberal and a protofeminist, therefore, is not only to make allowances for such circumstances, it is also an attempt to adapt his ideas to the current condition. And this is what interpretations and interpretative essays are all about. We look for insights and relevancies applicable to the present wherever we can find them. We try to advance our understanding of ourselves by looking to the past—especially to those "moments" that have heralded radical changes in our perceptions of ourselves and of our societies.

Without a doubt we have entered another period of radical change, perhaps for the entire world. The sight of the wife of a President of the United States calling out for the liberation of women entrapped in twelfth-century *burqas* in a country so far removed from us in cultural time and space may have a surrealistic character to it, but can anyone doubt that recent events and the ensuing shock to our sensibilities, from our vantage point, made just such a pronouncement not only welcome but also inevitable?

Machiavelli presented us with a similar shock in his unapologetic and unvarnished portrait of ourselves as we were in the sixteenth century. It should come as no surprise that we now look to him to see if some of *his* pronouncements are still relevant today. And I am certain that at other "moments" of radical change in the future, other scholars from totally different vantage points will continue to take up the task of reexamining *la questione di Machiavelli,* because there is something both visceral and compelling in his thoughts and the language he used to communicate them—thoughts that are not only chilling and depressing in their pessimism about human nature, but also optimistic and inspiring in their ultimate unwillingness to yield totally to the consequences of this condition. And indeed no matter what the pronouncement or observation, Machiavelli always expressed himself conditionally and not absolutely, always pointing out alternatives that might prevail under different circumstances. Perhaps it was just this tendency that gave rise to the many perceived contradictions and inconsistencies in his works. And perhaps someday someone will graph all those alternatives on some gargantuan "decision-tree" in one more attempt to clarify the mysterious mind of

Machiavelli. But one wonders how such an empirical exposition might be any more revealing than all the other multitude of attempts to resolve the enigma that is Machiavelli.

Notes

1. Isaiah Berlin, *Against the Current: Essays in the History of Ideas* (New York: Penguin Books, 1979), 25–79.

2. A recent interpretation and application of Machiavelli's doctrines as a democratic thinker may be found in an article by John P. McCormick, "Machiavellian Democracy: Controlling Elites with Ferocious Populism," *American Political Science Review* 95 (June 2001): 297–313.

3. See Donald McIntosh, Chapter 1 of this volume.

4. The information covered in the following pages owes much to the following biographies of Machiavelli. See Pasquale Villari, *The Life and Times of Niccolò Machiavelli*, 2 vols., trans. Linda Villari (1892; reprint, New York: Haskell House, 1969); Roberto Ridolfi, *The Life of Niccolò Machiavelli*, trans. Cecil Grayson (1954; reprint, London: Routledge & Kegan Paul, 1963); Maurizio Viroli, *Machiavelli* (New York: Oxford University Press, 1998); Viroli, *Niccolò's Smile: A Biography of Machiavelli*, trans. Anthony Shugaar (New York: Farrar, Straus and Giroux, 2000); Federico Chabod, *Machiavelli and the Renaissance*, trans. David Moore, with an introduction by A. P. D'Entreves (New York: Harper & Row, 1958); John Hale, *Machiavelli and Renaissance Italy* (London: English Universities Press, 1961); Quentin Skinner, *Machiavelli* (New York: Hill and Wang, 1981); and Sebastian de Grazia, *Machiavelli in Hell* (Princeton: Princeton University Press, 1989). To see examples of how his name is invoked, one need only examine the multitude of references in the editorials and commentaries of newspaper and magazine columnists over the appointment of Henry Kissinger by President George W. Bush to the commission to investigate the September 11, 2001, bombings in November 2002. See also Michael A. Ledeen, *Machiavelli on Modern Leadership: Why Machiavelli's Iron Rules are as Timely and Important Today as Five Centuries Ago* (New York: St. Martin's Press, 1999).

5. Hanna Fenichel Pitkin, "Afterthoughts," in *Fortune Is a Woman: Gender and Politics in the Thought of Niccolò Machiavelli* (Chicago: University of Chicago Press, 1999), 332.

6. See especially Hans Baron, *The Crisis of the Early Italian Renaissance* (Princeton: Princeton University Press, 1966). The Florentines saw themselves as heirs to the Roman Republic carrying on the classic tradition of self-government. However, Peter Godman claims that " 'Civic' humanism, during the late Quattro- and early Cinquecento, did not exist. Its origins lie in the political and intellectual history of the Weimar Republic." *From Poliziano to Machiavelli: Florentine Humanism in the High Renaissance* (Princeton: Princeton University Press, 1998), 293.

7. Ridolfi puts the number at twelve *Gonfalonieri* and fifty-four *Priori* (*Life of Niccolò Machiavelli*, 2). In fact, another Niccolò served in the Signoria during our Niccolò's lifetime, which caused considerable confusion for early historians.

8. See the sketch by Leonardo da Vinci of the hanging of one of the conspirators in de Grazia, *Machiavelli in Hell*, 12. For a recent account of the conspiracy, see Lauro Martines, *April Blood: Florence and the Plot against the Medici* (Oxford: Oxford University Press, 2003). Martines writes that one of the conspirators was a Girolamo Machiavelli from the more prominent branch of the family (44–45).

9. Ridolfi writes that Machiavelli implied that Savonarola was a "fraud" and a "liar" when he wrote in a letter to Ricciardo Becchi two months before the friar's execution that "he acts in accordance with the times and colors his lies accordingly" (*Life of Niccolò Machiavelli*, 9). See Letter 3, March 9, 1498, in James B. Atkinson and David Sices, ed. and trans., *Machiavelli and His Friends:*

Their Personal Correspondence (DeKalb: Northern Illinois University Press, 1996), 8–10. However, Marcia L. Colish argues that Machiavelli's objections to Savonarola had more to do with his use of politics to promote religious objectives than with any criticism of the republican structures of government Savonarola imposed on Florence, in "Republicanism, Religion, and Machiavelli's Savonarolan Moment," *Journal of the History of Ideas* 60 (October 1999): 597–617.

10. For extensive analyses of the reforms initiated by Savonarola as well as for detailed biographies of this Dominican monk, see Pasquale Villari, *The Life and Times of Girolamo Savonarola*, 2 vols., trans Linda Villari (1888; reprint, New York: Haskell House, 1969). See also J. C. L. de Sismondi, *A History of the Italian Republics*, with an introduction by Wallace K. Ferguson (1966; reprint, Gloucester, Mass.: Peter Smith, 1970) for a one-volume summary of the history of the major Republics of Italy from the eleventh to the eighteen centuries.

11. Godman disputes this, saying that there is no evidence that Machiavelli was ever a student of Adriani at the *Studio* (*From Poliziano to Machiavelli*, 149).

12. For a biography of Caterina Sforza, see Ernst Breisach, *Caterina Sforza: A Renaissance Virago* (Chicago: University of Chicago Press, 1967). For an analysis of the accuracy of Machiavelli's portrayal of Madonna Caterina, see Julia L. Hairston, "Skirting the Issue: Machiavelli's Caterina Sforza," *Renaissance Quarterly* 53 (Autumn 2000): 687–712. For Lorenzo di Credi's portrait of Sforza, see J. H. Plumb, *The Italian Renaissance* (1961; reprint, Boston: Houghton Mifflin, 1989), 140.

13. For the original report Machiavelli wrote of his encounter with Caterina Sforza, see Christian E. Detmold, ed. and trans., *The Historical, Political, and Diplomatic Writings of Niccolò Machiavelli*, 4 vols (1882; reprint, New York: Houghton, Mifflin & Co., 1891), 3:6–26. Machiavelli cites her activities in *The Prince*, chap. 20; *The Discourses*, Book 3, chap. 6; *The Art of War*, Book 7; and *The Florentine Histories*, Book 8, chap. 34. See Niccolò Machiavelli, *Chief Works and Others*, ed. and trans. Allan Gilbert, 3 vols. (1958; reprint, Durham: Duke University Press, 1989). Hereafter, all works by Machiavelli unless specified otherwise are from Gilbert's *Chief Works*.

14. Letter 305, to Francesco Guicciardini (March 15, 1526), in Atkinson and Sices, *Machiavelli and His Friends*, 382–83.

15. For a history of these events, see Spencer M. Di Scala, *Italy from Revolution to Republic: 1700 to the Present* (Boulder, Colo.: Westview Press, 1995); and Rene Albrecht-Carrié, *Italy from Napoleon to Mussolini* (New York: Columbia University Press, 1950).

16. For Rimirro de Orco, see *The Prince*, chap. 7; for the assassinations at Sinigallia, see *The Prince*, chap. 8. For the more detailed account written for the *Florentine Histories* but never included in that volume, see Machiavelli, *Chief Works and Others*, 1:163–69.

17. See Letter 206 to Francesco Vettori (March 18, 1513) on his "pride" in having survived six pulls of the rope and 22 days in manacles in the *Stinche:* "I consider myself more of a man than I believed I was" (Atkinson and Sices, *Machiavelli and His Friends*, 222). For a description and sketch of this particular form of torture, see de Grazia, *Machiavelli in Hell*, 36–37.

18. *Princeps* in Latin, meaning "First Citizen," previously the title of the leader of the Roman Senate, a republican title preferred by Augustus to that of Dictator assumed by Julius Caesar. For more on this distinction and its implications, see Leo Paul S. de Alvarez, *The Machiavellian Enterprise* (DeKalb: Northern Illinois University Press, 1999), chap. 1.

19. Letter 206, Atkinson and Sices, *Machiavelli and His Friends*, 222.

20. Godman writes that it is more likely that Lorenzo never received the manuscript because "[t]he gloved hand of the lay censor had reached out to Rome" (*From Poliziano to Machiavelli*, 236). For an in-depth analysis of the *eminence gris* overshadowing all of Machiavelli's efforts to gain employment from the Medici and his latter-day limited success only after the temporary fall from grace of the First Secretary, Marcello Virgilio Adriani, see Godman, *From Poliziano to Machiavelli*, especially chap. 6.

21. See Maurizio Viroli, *From Politics to Reason of State: The Acquisition and Transformation of the Language of Politics, 1250–1600* (New York: Cambridge University Press, 1992); and Friedrich Meinecke, *Machiavellism: The Doctrine of Raison d'État and its Place in Modern History*, trans. Douglas

Scott, with an introduction by W. Stark (1957; reprint, New York: Praeger, 1965). For an extensive evaluation of Botero's work, see Victoria Kahn, *Machiavellian Rhetoric: From the Counter-Reformation to Milton* (Princeton: Princeton University Press, 1994), 60–84. For an excerpt of Botero's work, see Eric Cochrane and Julius Kirshner, ed. *Readings in Western Civilization*, 5 vols. (Chicago: University of Chicago Press, 1986), 5:230–51.

22. On this point see Chabod, *Machiavelli and the Renaissance*, 140–42.

23. See Cary Nederman and Martin Morris, Chapter 9 of this volume.

24. That Machiavelli himself was the dispassionate rationalist he is so often depicted is a matter of some dispute. See Anthony J. Parel, "Machiavelli Minore," in *The Political Calculus: Essays on Machiavelli's Philosophy* (Toronto: University of Toronto Press, 1972), 179–208.

25. See Ptolemy of Lucca, in de Grazia, *Machiavelli in Hell*, 265.

26. On this point, see de Alvarez, *Machiavellian Enterprise*, 124–26. See also Thomas Flanagan, "The Concept of *Fortuna* in Machiavelli," in Parel, *Political Calculus*, 127–56.

27. See Pico della Mirandola's *Oration on the Dignity of Man* (1486); and Erasmus's *A Disquisition Upon Free Will* (1524). For a humanist's conflicted view of the matter, see also Lorenzo Valla, "Dialogue on Free Will," in *The Renaissance Philosophy of Man*, ed. Ernst Cassirer, Paul Oscar Kristeller, and John Herman Randall Jr. (Chicago: University of Chicago Press, 1948), 155–82.

28. This concept has frequently been translated as "the end justifies the means," based upon the statement made in chapter 18 of *The Prince*, "*si guarda al fine*." For the original Italian and a much more accurate translation of this phrase, see Mark Musa, ed. and trans., *Machiavelli's "The Prince": A Bilingual Edition* (New York: St. Martin's Press, 1964). For other interpretations of this phrase, see also de Alvarez, *Machiavellian Enterprise*, 90; and John M. Najemy, *Between Friends: Discourses of Power and Desire in the Machiavelli-Vettori Letters of 1513–1515* (Princeton: Princeton University Press, 1993), 187–88. In my opinion, this last is the most accurate in assessing the sense implied by the phrase.

29. For different interpretations of the concept of "prudence," see Catherine Zuckert, Chapter 6 of this volume. See also de Alvarez, *Machiavellian Enterprise*, 103; Eugene Garver, *Machiavelli and the History of Prudence* (Madison: University of Wisconsin Press, 1987); and Parel, "Machiavelli's Method and his Interpreters," in *Political Calculus*, 3–32.

30. For an interesting analysis of Machiavelli's revolutionary "moral philosophy" and his "Un-Golden Rule," see de Grazia, *Machiavelli in Hell*, chap. 12.

31. *The Prince*, chap. 18.

32. On the difference between *imaginazione* and *la verità effettuale* in Machiavelli, see Najemy, *Between Friends*, 190. See also *The Prince*, chap. 8.

33. Machiavelli, *Chief Works*, 1:170–74.

34. For the more prominent negative criticisms of Machiavelli's intentions, see Leo Strauss, *Thoughts on Machiavelli* (Glencoe, Ill.: Free Press, 1958); Harvey C. Mansfield Jr., *Machiavelli's Virtue* (Chicago: University of Chicago Press, 1996); Mark Hulliung, *Citizen Machiavelli* (Princeton: Princeton University Press, 1983); and, to some extent, Vicki B. Sullivan, *Machiavelli's Three Romes: Religion, Human Liberty, and Politics Reformed* (DeKalb: Northern Illinois University Press 1996). Even Viroli thinks it merely a "commissioned" piece (*Niccolò's Smile*, 258), and Godman calls it "an exercise in an official genre, a sign of Machiavelli's gradual return and partial acceptance" (*From Poliziano to Machiavelli*, 282). However, in "Machiavelli Minore," in *Political Calculus*, Parel argues otherwise. Regarding the possibility that Machiavelli may have been a "closet" atheist, and for a discussion of how that term was used in the sixteenth century and why "[n]ot until the end of the eighteenth century would a few Europeans find it possible to deny the existence of God," see Karen Armstrong, *A History of God: The 4000-Year Quest of Judaism, Christianity, and Islam* (New York: Alfred A. Knopf, 1993), 287. For a refutation of these criticisms of Machiavelli's religious beliefs, see Cary J. Nederman, "Amazing Grace: Fortune, God, and Free Will in Machiavelli's Thought," *Journal of the History of Ideas* 60 (October 1999): 617–39.

35. For a fascinating account of how the Medici used Machiavelli and made it impossible for

him to complain when Agostino Nifo literally gutted the manuscript and published his own version as a whitewashed handbook for princes, see Godman, *From Poliziano to Machiavelli*, 255ff.

36. See Machiavelli, *Chief Works*, 1:175–529.

37. "A Discourse on Remodeling the Government of Florence," in Machiavelli, *Chief Works*, 1:101–15. For an analysis of this document as well as one written earlier, see Viroli, *Niccolò's Smile*, 200–201 and 219–20.

38. Machiavelli, *Chief Works*, 1:106. Of course he suggested some tinkering with the elections process (à la Cosimo), but he also advised that the Great Council, one of Savonarola's most successful inventions, be retained.

39. Ibid., 1:107.

40. Godman thinks Machiavelli and others were actually duped by Giulio dei Medici (later Clement VII): "Machiavelli was made to seem the cardinal's man" (*From Poliziano to Machiavelli*, 300).

41. Although Machiavelli titled this work *Istorie*, or "Histories," Gilbert and others prefer to use the singular "History."

42. Quoted in Machiavelli, *Chief Works*, 3:1028.

43. Ibid., 2:561–726.

44. At one point he attempted to drill some soldiers in a manner he thought appropriate and failed miserably. His hero at that time, Giovanni delle Bande Nere, smiled at his efforts and then showed him how it should be done. Ridolfi, *Life of Niccolò Machiavelli*, 229; Viroli, *Niccolò's Smile*, 241.

45. For the various ways in which Machiavelli used this word, see Mansfield, *Machiavelli's Virtue*; and Viroli, *From Politics to Reasons of State*.

46. They were originally supporters of the Medici but later several became involved in a conspiracy against them. Was this through Machiavelli's influence on his listeners as he read sections of the *Discourses* to them? See Ridolfi, *Life of Niccolò Machiavelli*, 202; and Viroli, *Niccolò's Smile*, 220.

47. For some of the more recent collections and analyses of his letters, see Najemy, *Between Friends*; and Atkinson and Sices, *Machiavelli and His Friends*.

48. See especially Ridolfi, *Life of Niccolò Machiavelli*, 172: "*Io rido e il rider mio non passa drento; Io ardo e l'orison mia non par di fore.*" (Freely translated: "I laugh and my laugh enters not within; I rage and my cry exits not without.") See also de Grazia, *Machiavelli in Hell*, 240.

49. Ridolfi suggests it is the "best Italian play of all time" (*Life of Niccolò Machiavelli*, 175).

50. Machiavelli, *Chief Works*, 3:1463. For the original Italian, see Allan Gilbert, ed. and trans., *The Letters of Machiavelli* (New York: Capricorn Books, 1961), 28.

51. The defeat of the French army, Florence's traditional ally, opened up the entire country to invasion by the Imperial armies on their way from Milan to reclaim Naples as well.

52. He had earlier been offered a high-paying job as advisor to Prospero Colonna in Rome but turned it down because he preferred to stay in Florence. Viroli, *Niccolò's Smile*, 203. It may also have been because the Colonna were viewed as enemies of the Pope and acceptance might have endangered his life and family in Florence. It was Soderini who informed him of the position during his own exile and before his death.

53. Ridolfi, *Life of Niccolò Machiavelli*, 213.

54. Hale, *Machiavelli and Renaissance Italy*, 167–69.

55. Viroli, *Niccolò's Smile*, 243; Hale, *Machiavelli and Renaissance Italy*, 169.

56. For a detailed description of these events, see André Chastel, *The Sack of Rome, 1527*, trans. Beth Archer (1977; reprint, Princeton: Princeton University Press, 1983).

57. Interestingly enough, it was the plan devised for those fortifications by Michelangelo that was eventually accepted and acted upon by the city and that withstood an eight-month siege by the imperial forces in 1530.

58. Ridolfi, *Life of Niccolò Machiavelli*, 248.

59. Both Vettori and Guicciardini fell out of favor after the fall of the Medici in 1527, but returned to become part of the new Medici regime under Duke Cosimo I. See James Cleugh, *The Medici: A Tale of Fifteen Generations* (New York: Doubleday, 1975), 275; and Felix Gilbert, *Machiavelli and Guicciardini: Politics and History in Sixteenth-Century Florence* (Princeton: Princeton University Press, 1965), 274.

60. Hale, *Machiavelli and Renaissance Italy*, 175.

61. Quoted in Villari, *Life and Times of Savonarola*, 2:508.

62. Letter to Francesco Vettori (April 16, 1527), in *The Letters of Machiavelli*, 249. See also Atkinson and Sices, *Machiavelli and His Friends*, 416; and Chabod, *Machiavelli and the Renaissance*, 141, who instructs us that the term Machiavelli actually used was *patria*. For the epitaph that Machiavelli jokingly said his friends had composed for him, see de Grazia, *Machiavelli in Hell*, 385. De Grazia also holds that Machiavelli's true "love" expressed in his letter to Vettori was for Italy rather than for Florence per se (156, 351ff.).

63. Mera J. Flaumenhaft, "The Comedic Remedy: Machiavelli's 'Mandragola,'" *Interpretation: A Journal of Political Philosophy* 7 (May 1978): 33–74.

64. Jean Bethke Elshtain, "Machiavelli Makes His Move," in *Public Man, Private Woman* (Princeton: Princeton University Press, 1981), chap. 2, 92–99. This article was to have been included in this volume but had to be omitted because of lack of space. It nevertheless served as a catalyst for the inclusion of Machiavelli in the discourse of feminism.

65. Ibid., 98–99.

66. Donald McIntosh, "The Modernity of Machiavelli," *Political Theory* 12 (May 1984): 184–203. The excerpt included in volume is on pp. 193–203 of the original.

67. Jack D'Amico, "The *Virtù* of Women: Machiavelli's *Mandragola* and *Clizia*," *Interpretation: A Journal of Philosophy* 12 (May 1984): 261–73. Quote is from p. 262.

68. Ibid., 273.

69. See the "Afterthoughts" in Pitkin's *Fortune Is a Woman*, 2d ed., for an especially revealing analysis of the motivations and processes that went into the writing of this book.

70. A term also used by McIntosh to translate the word *virtù*.

71. This brief summary hardly does justice to the broad scope and the complexity of the argument of Pitkin's book. It is unfortunate that a summary of the entire book was impossible to accomplish (although it was attempted three times by this editor), and that only the last two chapters could be reprinted in this volume because of limitations of space. Although some readers may prefer some other chapter selections over these, it was the judgment of this editor that the overall evaluation of Machiavelli's thought by Pitkin could only be effectively assessed from the vantage point of her own political philosophy.

72. Arlene Saxonhouse, "Niccolò Machiavelli: Women as Men, Men as Women, and the Ambiguity of Sex," in *Women in the History of Political Thought: Ancient Greece to Machiavelli* (New York: Praeger, 1985), chap. 7, 151–98.

73. Wendy Brown, "Machiavelli: From Man to Manhood," in *Manhood and Politics: A Feminist Reading in Political Theory* (Totowa, N.J.: Rowman & Littlefield, 1988), chap. 5, p. 71.

74. Brown distinguishes *virtù* from the Greek *aretē* in that the latter signifies a "struggle toward perfection" or a "consummation of man's nature," while *virtù* is "a secular quest for reification of man's limitations vis-à-vis his goals" (ibid., 83).

75. Brown calls the "self-sufficient/independent political actor" androgynous, or "manhood in drag . . . attempting to use both male and female powers in the struggle with other men" (ibid., 118).

76. See also Cary Nederman and Martin Morris, Chapter 9 of this volume, on this same point.

77. Mary O'Brien, "The Root of the Mandrake: Machiavelli and Manliness," in *Reproducing the World: Essays in Feminist Theory* (Boulder, Colo.: Westview Press, 1989), chap. 8, 103–32.

78. The debate between those who saw Machiavelli as secular, "evil," and "anti-Christian"

versus those who emphasized his "liberal" and republican attributes heated up as well in this period. For support of the former position, see Hulliung, *Citizen Machiavelli*; Kahn, *Machiavellian Rhetoric*; Mansfield, *Machiavelli's Virtue*; and Mansfield, *Machiavelli's New Modes and Orders: A Study of the Discourses on Livy* (Chicago: University of Chicago Press, 1979). For support of the latter, see Benedetto Croce, *Politics and Morals*, trans. Salvatore J. Castiglione (New York: Philosophical Library, 1945), and Croce, *My Philosophy and Other Essays*, trans. E. F. Carritt (London: Allen & Unwin, 1949); Baron, *Crisis of the Early Italian Renaissance*; Pocock, *The Machiavellian Moment: Florentine Political Thought and the Atlantic Republican Tradition* (Princeton: Princeton University Press, 1975); Parel, *Political Calculus*; and de Grazia, *Machiavelli in Hell*.

79. *Stereotypes of Women in Power*, ed. Barbara Garlick et al. (Westport, Conn.: Greenwood Press), chap. 8, 141–55. This article was also omitted from this volume because of space limitations.

80. Ibid., 145.

81. Ibid., 153.

82. Catherine A. Zuckert, in *Finding a New Feminism: Re-Thinking the Woman Question for Liberal Democracy*, ed. Pamela Grande Jensen (Lanham, Md.: Rowman & Littlefield, 1992), chap. 1, 23–37.

83. R. Claire Snyder, "Machiavelli and the Citizenship of Civic Practices," in *Citizen-Soldiers and Manly Warriors: Military Service and Gender in the Civic Republican Tradition* (London: Rowman & Littlefield, 1999), 15–43.

84. Ibid., 15, emphases in the original.

85. Ibid., 161.

86. Melissa M. Matthes, *The Rape of Lucretia and the Founding of Republics* (University Park: Pennsylvania State University Press, 2000), chap. 4, 77–97.

87. See especially Nicki's citation of Hoagland's references to *Sophie's Choice* and to Lucy Andrews, who petitioned a South Carolina court to allow her to become a slave during the antebellum period, in Chapter 13 of this volume.

88. On this point, see Karen Armstrong, *The Battle For God* (New York: Ballantine Books, 2000).

89. Pico della Mirandola, *Oration on the Dignity of Man*.

90. *The Prince*, chap. 15, 57–58.

References

Albrecht-Carriè, Rene. *Italy from Napoleon to Mussolini*. New York: Columbia University Press, 1950.

Alvarez, Leo Paul S. de. *The Machiavellian Enterprise*. DeKalb: Northern Illinois University Press, 1999.

Armstrong, Karen. *A History of God: The 4000-Year Quest of Judaism, Christianity, and Islam*. New York: Alfred A. Knopf, 1993.

———. *The Battle for God*. New York: Ballantine Books, 2000.

Atkinson, James B., and David Sices, ed. and trans. *Machiavelli and His Friends: Their Personal Correspondence*. DeKalb: Northern Illinois University Press, 1996.

———. *The Sweetness of Power: Machiavelli's "Discourses" and Guicciardini's "Considerations."* DeKalb: Northern Illinois University Press, 2002.

Baron, Hans. *The Crisis of the Early Italian Renaissance*. Princeton: Princeton University Press, 1966.

Berlin, Isaiah. *Against the Current: Essays in the History of Ideas*. New York: Penguin Books, 1979.

Breisach, Ernst. *Caterina Sforza: A Renaissance Virago*. Chicago: University of Chicago Press, 1967.

Brown, Wendy. *Manhood and Politics: A Feminist Reading in Political Theory*. Totowa, NJ: Rowman & Littlefield, 1988.

Chabod, Federico. *Machiavelli and the Renaissance*. Trans. David Moore. New York: Harper & Row, 1958.

Chastel, André. *The Sack of Rome, 1527*. Trans. Beth Archer. Princeton: Princeton University Press, 1983.

Cleugh, James. *The Medici: A Tale of Fifteen Generations*. New York: Doubleday, 1975.

Cochrane, Eric, and Julius Kirshner, ed. *Readings in Western Civilization*. 5 vols. Chicago: University of Chicago Press, 1986.

Colish, Marcia L. "Republicanism, Religion, and Machiavelli's Savonarolan Moment." *Journal of the History of Ideas* 60 (October 1999): 597–617.

Croce, Benedetto. *Politics and Morals*. Trans. Salvatore J. Castiglione. New York: Philosophical Library, 1945.

———. *My Philosophy and Other Essays*. Trans. E. F. Carritt. London: Allen & Unwin, 1949.

D'Amico, Jack. "The *Virtù* of Women: Machiavelli's *Mandragola* and *Clizia*." *Interpretation: A Journal of Philosophy* 12 (May 1984): 261–73.

Detmold, Christian E., ed. and trans. *The Historical, Political, and Diplomatic Writings of Niccolò Machiavelli*. 4 vols. New York: Houghton, Mifflin & Co., 1891.

Elshtain, Jean Bethke. *Public Man, Private Woman: Women in Social and Political Thought*. Princeton: Princeton University Press, 1981.

Flanagan, Thomas. "The Concept of *Fortuna* in Machiavelli." In *The Political Calculus: Essays on Machiavelli's Philosophy*, ed. Anthony J. Parel. Toronto: University of Toronto Press, 1972.

Flaumenhaft, Mera J. "The Comedic Remedy: Machiavelli's 'Mandragola.'" *Interpretation: A Journal of Political Philosophy* 7 (May 1978): 33–74.

Garlick, Barbara, et al. *Stereotypes of Women in Power*. Westport, Conn.: Greenwood Press, 1992.

Garver, Eugene. *Machiavelli and the History of Prudence*. Madison: University of Wisconsin Press, 1987.

Gilbert, Felix. *Machiavelli and Guicciardini: Politics and History in Sixteenth-Century Florence*. Princeton: Princeton University Press, 1965.

Godman, Peter. *From Poliziano to Machiavelli: Florentine Humanism in the High Renaissance*. Princeton: Princeton University Press, 1998.

Grazia, Sebastian de. *Machiavelli in Hell*. Princeton: Princeton University Press, 1989.

Hairston, Julia L. "Skirting the Issue: Machiavelli's Caterina Sforza." *Renaissance Quarterly* 53 (Autumn 2000): 687–712.

Hale, John. *Machiavelli and Renaissance Italy*. London: English Universities Press, 1961.

Hulliung, Mark. *Citizen Machiavelli*. Princeton: Princeton University Press, 1983.

Jensen, Pamela Grande, ed. *Finding a New Feminism: Re-Thinking the Woman Question for Liberal Democracy*. Lanham, Md.: Rowman & Littlefield, 1992.

Kahn, Victoria. *Machiavellian Rhetoric: From the Counter-Reformation to Milton*. Princeton: Princeton University Press, 1994.

Ledeen, Michael A. *Machiavelli on Modern Leadership: Why Machiavelli's Iron Rules are as*

Timely and Important Today as Five Centuries Ago. New York: St. Martin's Press, 1999.

Machiavelli, Niccolò. *The Letters of Machiavelli.* Ed. and trans. Allan Gilbert. New York: Capricorn Books, 1961.

―――. *Chief Works and Others.* Ed. and trans. Allan Gilbert. 3 vols. Durham: Duke University Press, 1989.

Mansfield, Harvey C., Jr. *Machiavelli's New Modes and Orders: A Study of the Discourses on Livy.* Chicago: University of Chicago Press, 1979.

―――. *Machiavelli's Virtue.* Chicago: University of Chicago Press, 1996.

Matthes, Melissa M. *The Rape of Lucretia and the Founding of Republics.* University Park: Pennsylvania State University Press, 2000.

McCormick, John P. "Machiavellian Democracy: Controlling Elites with Ferocious Populism." *American Political Science Review* 95 (June 2001): 297–313.

McIntosh, Donald. "The Modernity of Machiavelli." *Political Theory* 12 (May 1984): 184–203.

Meinecke, Friedrich. *Machiavellism: The Doctrine of Raison d'Etat and its Place in Modern History.* Trans. Douglas Scott. New York: Praeger, 1965.

Musa, Mark, ed. and trans. *Machiavelli's "The Prince": A Bilingual Edition.* New York: St. Martin's Press, 1964.

Najemy, John M. *Between Friends: Discourses of Power and Desire in the Machiavelli-Vettori Letters of 1513–1515.* Princeton: Princeton University Press, 1993.

Nederman, Cary J. "Amazing Grace: Fortune, God, and Free Will in Machiavelli's Thought." *Journal of the History of Ideas* 60 (October 1999): 617–39.

O'Brien, Mary. *Reproducing the World: Essays in Feminist Theory.* Boulder, Colo.: Westview Press, 1989.

Parel, Anthony J., ed. *The Political Calculus: Essays on Machiavelli's Philosophy.* Toronto: University of Toronto Press, 1972.

Pitkin, Hanna Fenichel. *Fortune Is a Woman: Gender and Politics in the Thought of Niccolò Machiavelli.* Chicago: University of Chicago Press, 1999.

Plumb, J. H. *The Italian Renaissance.* Boston: Houghton Mifflin, 1989.

Pocock, J. G. A. *The Machiavellian Moment: Florentine Political Thought and the Atlantic Republican Tradition.* Princeton: Princeton University Press, 1975.

Ridolfi, Roberto. *The Life of Niccolò Machiavelli.* Trans. Cecil Grayson. London: Routledge & Kegan Paul, 1963.

Saxonhouse, Arlene. *Women in the History of Political Thought: Ancient Greece to Machiavelli.* New York: Praeger, 1985.

Scala, Spencer M. di. *Italy from Revolution to Republic: 1700 to the Present.* Boulder, Colo.: Westview Press, 1995.

Sismondi, J. C. L. de. *A History of the Italian Republics.* Gloucester, Mass.: Peter Smith, 1970.

Skinner, Quentin. *Machiavelli.* New York: Hill and Wang, 1981.

Snyder, R. Claire. *Citizen-Soldiers and Manly Warriors: Military Service and Gender in the Civic Republican Tradition.* London: Rowman & Littlefield, 1999.

Strauss, Leo. *Thoughts on Machiavelli.* Glencoe, Ill.: Free Press, 1958.

Sullivan, Vicki B. *Machiavelli's Three Romes: Religion, Human Liberty, and Politics Reformed.* DeKalb: Northern Illinois University Press, 1996.

Valla, Lorenzo. "Dialogue on Free Will." In *The Renaissance Philosophy of Man,* ed. Ernst

Cassirer, Paul Oscar Kristeller, and John Herman Randall Jr. Chicago: University of Chicago Press, 1948.

Villari, Pasquale. *The Life and Times of Girolamo Savonarola.* Trans. Linda Villari. 2 vols. New York: Haskell House, 1969.

———. *The Life and Times of Niccolò Machiavelli.* Trans. Linda Villari. 2 vols. New York: Haskell House, 1969.

Viroli, Maurizio. *From Politics to Reasons of State: The Acquisition and Transformation of the Language of Politics, 1250–1600.* New York: Cambridge University Press, 1992.

———. *Machiavelli.* New York: Oxford University Press, 1998.

———. *Republicanism.* Trans. Anthony Shugaar. New York: Hill and Wang, 1999.

———. *Niccolò's Smile: A Biography of Machiavelli.* Trans. Anthony Shugaar. New York: Farrar, Straus, and Giroux, 2000.

1

The Modernity of Machiavelli

Donald McIntosh

Elsewhere I have argued the following points: First, in premodern times the prevailing ethical approaches mainly occupied positions on the continuum between a purely ritualistic and purely expressive ethic, with the instrumental dimension playing a secondary role because of the invariable fatalism or providentialism. In the modern era the instrumental approach has become predominant. Second, Machiavelli is the first important thinker to adopt an uncompromisingly instrumental stance. He thought highly of the pagan virtues, but insisted that even these must be abandoned when necessary to achieve a worthwhile result. Third, instrumentalism stands or falls on the ability of *virtù* to master *Fortuna*. Fourth, in the realm of political and military action instrumentalism fails this test. The conclusion follows that Machiavelli's ethical stance was unrealistic and, since he was in a position to know better, irrational. Why then did he adopt this stance? In an attempt to answer this question, I shall introduce some rather speculative ideas about the psychological origins of Machiavelli's views, with the hope of throwing some light not only on his own thought but also on modern instrumentalism in general.

It is quite striking the extent to which Machiavelli's treatment of the relation of *virtù* to *Fortuna* is sexualized. *Fortuna* invariably is portrayed as a woman, and not in flattering terms. She is powerful, malevolent, and treacherous, lying in wait to attack and envelop her male opponent at the slightest sign of weakness. This is a far cry from the usual picture of a charming but fickle creation, now smiling, now frowning at those who woo her.

Virtù, on the other hand, is a male principle, as befits its etymological origin in the Latin *vir*: male. It exhibits boldness, courage, initiative, perserverence, foresight, adaptability, ruthlessness, and "greatness of spirit," along with a kind of exhibitionist élan or "virtu-osity."[1]

The two principles are locked in a fierce and implacable battle of the sexes. This theme, which runs throughout Machiavelli's writings, finds its most dramatic and well-known expression in chapter 25 of *The Prince*:

> Fortune is a woman and it is necessary, in order to keep her under, to cuff and maul her. She more often lets herself be overcome by men using such methods than by those who proceed coldly; therefore always, like a woman, she is the friend of young men, because they are less cautious, more spirited, and with more boldness master her.[2]

Those who have studied the political thought of the Italian Renaissance often complain that there is no good English equivalent for the key concept of *virtù*. There is, however, an excellent translation available for the special way in which Machiavelli uses the word, which though colloquial and of foreign origin exactly captures his meaning. It is "machismo."

In Freudian terms, activity that displays machismo is on the phallic level, and has a narcissistic meaning. *Fortuna* is the object in relation to

which one demonstrates one's prowess as a sexual athlete, one's "greatness of flesh." But the relation of *virtù* to *Fortuna* is not wholly narcissistic. There is an addition a strong (anaclitic) object relation, which takes
the form of sadism. Freud distinguished two stages of sadism. In the first,
one simply takes delight in mastery, control of the other. The narcissism
is tempered by hatred, by a desire to subdue, inflict pain, or destroy. The
second stage, which might be called "sadism proper," is far more com-
pelx. It is crucial to sadism on the second level that the victim recognize
the mastery of the aggressor and take pleasure in being dominated. We
have here a genuinely adult (genital) relation in that the sadist *cares*
about how the victim feels. The point is conveyed by the jest that a sadist
is a person who is *nice* to a masochist.[3]

Our sexual impulses, says Freud, have a two-fold duality: libidinal and
aggressive,[4] active and passive. The sadist fulfills the active and aggressive
impulses via direct action, the passive and libidinal impulses vicariously
via projective identification with the victim.

From my reading of the texts, I judge that the predominant emotional
tone of Machiavelli's attitude toward *Fortuna* combines phallic narcissism
with primary sadism. The libidinal satisfaction is derived from admiration
of one's own prowess, and the aggressive satisfaction from the subjection
of the hated and feared opponent.

The prototypical act of primary sadism is rape, and indeed some feminist critics have charged the basic relation of the modern instrumental
male to women to be that of a rapist. In a similar vein, modern science
and technology have been accused of the "rape" of mother nature. While
such charges are too sweeping if they intend to have more than a metaphorical force, the case of Machiavelli suggests that they may contain a
kernel of psychological truth.

Despite what seems to be a preponderance of primary sadism in the
Machiavellian relation between *virtù* and *Fortuna,* there is also a distinct
element of sadism proper, as illustrated by the above quotation, in which
Fortuna is portrayed as yielding willingly to bold and manly force. Here
we begin to see the underlying projectivity of Machiavelli's attitude
towards *Fortuna.* This projectivity emerges strikingly in a letter he wrote
describing his visit to a prostitute. All would have gone well, he said, if
he had not lit a lamp, revealing the following:

> Ugh! I nearly fell dead on the spot, she was so ugly. The first thing
> I saw was a tuft of hair, half white, half black, piebald, that is,

with age, and although the crown of her head was bald—which baldness enabled one to see a louse or two taking a stroll—still a few sparse hairs mingled with the whiskers sprouting round her face; and on top of her meagre and wrinkled head was a fiery scar which made her look as if she had been branded in the market. There were colonies of nits in each eyebrow; one eye looked up, the other down, and was larger than the other; the tear ducts were full of rheum, the rims hairless. Her nose was screwed into her face at an angle, the nostrils full of snot, and one of them was half missing; her mouth was like Lorenzo de Medici's, but twisted up on one side, and it drooled a little: as she had no teeth she could not keep her saliva in. Her upper lip had a scant but fairly lengthy moustache. Her chin was long and sharp, pointing up a little, whence a scanty dewlap dangled to her Adam's apple.[5]

Both John Pocock and Quentin Skinner have remarked on Machiavelli's tendency to exaggerate for effect,[6] but we have here something more than that. What is notable about this passage is not the obvious fabrication but the *overvividness* of the detail, which is so precise and striking that it establishes a sense of insidious distortion. This is not realism: it is *sur*realism.

The belief that Machiavelli was a supreme realist is nonsense. Despite the sharpness of his observation and the penetration of his comments, the overall picture he draws has the same relation to political and military reality as Dali's watches have to actual timepieces. As with all surrealism, what is revealed is not the objectivity of the world but the subjectivity of the observer.

The syndrome is the one typically associated with the exaggerated maleness of machismo, and its psychodynamics are quite familiar. We are all, Freud pointed out, bisexual, with both a male and a female identification and identity. In this case there is an intense fear and loathing by the male of his female identity, its repression, and its projective outward displacement. The struggle between *virtù* and *Fortuna* is thus the outward manifestation of a battle of the sexes that raged within the soul of Machiavelli. That is why the enmity is so implacable and total victory so imperative.

It is this unconscious struggle that, I surmise, also accounts for the obsessiveness and ambivalence of Machiavelli's attitude toward femininity. The female is loathsome yet irresistably attractive, dangerous yet desirable, weak yet strong, modest yet wanton, moral yet ruthless, striving to dominate yet ready to surrender. Machiavelli's most withering term of opprobrium is "effeminate," yet the conquest of *Fortuna* is the highest goal.

Sex and politics were the only two things that truly interested Machiavelli; indeed, as I have tried to show elsewhere, in his mind the one flows into the other. For him politics was the continuation of sex by other means.[7]

The interpretation that I have advanced explains, I think, the strange blend of realism and unrealism in Machiavelli's work, as well as the points of contrast between his formulation of the relation of *virtù* and *Fortuna* and those more typical of his time. It does not explain why instrumentalism became the dominant orientation to action in the modern era—indeed, according to Weber, its very defining characteristic.[8] That question is beyond the scope of this article. The case of Machiavelli exemplifies but does not explain the thoroughgoing instrumentalism of modernity. Nevertheless, the way in which ethical instrumentalism is sexualized in Machiavelli's thought throws light on some important features of modern social action.

The instrumental and expressive aspects of action are not necessarily mutually exclusive. A given act can combine the two in an undifferentiated way. It is the *rationalization* of action in one or both modes that drives the wedge between the two principles. A frequent result of such rationalization is the differentiation of action into separate instrumental and expressive components.

For example, medicine formerly combined healing (instrumental) and caring (expressive) aspects. The integration is exemplified by the prototypical "laying on of the hands": the touch is both a healing and a caring act. But the instrumental rationalization of medical practice (maximum results via specialization, efficient use of the doctor's valuable time, and so forth) drains it of its expressive meaning. So the two aspects become differentiated: The doctor does the healing and the nurse does the caring. (Eventually nursing itself becomes rationalized instrumentally and loses its expressive meaning, as in many nursing homes.)

As has been pointed out, for Machiavelli instrumentally rationalized political action has a strongly masculine character. Here we find modernity following his lead, for in the modern era instrumental action and instrumental rationality uniformly have been the prerogative of the male. Concomitantly, the female has been assigned the expressive role.

In their book on the family, Parsons, Bales, Olds, Zedlich, and Slater identify such a role differentiation as universal across cultures and time.[9] But in doing so they unjustifiably read the modern distinction into premodern society. For example, they label child care expressive and hunting instrumental. Since it is almost universal for women to do most of the child rearing and men most of the hunting, the division of labor seems to support their thesis. But the former is expressive and the latter instrumental to the modern mind only. It is much less so for premodern society, and the farther back one goes in social evolution, the less the instrumental-expressive distinction applies. In primitive societies both childrearing and hunting combine the two modes in an undifferentiated way.

The fact that the contrasts I have been drawing between modern and premodern are not absolute, and the fact that modernity itself has been far from monolithic in these matters should not be allowed to obscure the main point: In contrast to premodern civilization, modernity has been characterized by the differentiation and sex stereotyping of instrumental and expressive action. By modernity I mean here not a period of time but a historical trend made up of a constellation of interconnected traits. In these terms, the generalization is the most valid for the most typically modern segments, that is, the commercial, industrial, and administrative classes of mature capitalism: The nuclear family where the husband goes to work and the wife stays home and takes care of the house and children. (We by now are well past the crest of this phase.)

The fact that the role assigned the modern woman includes both emotional and ethical expressivity explains an apparent contradiction. The female is a child of nature, giving direct and spontaneous expression to her emotional impulses, while the male is controlled and restrained, keeping his emotions under rigid check. However, the woman observes and fosters a strict moral rectitude, especially the Christian virtues: She is "God's own police,"[10] while the male is willing to cut corners in his drive toward his objective (i.e., he is a Machiavellian).

These two aspects of the feminine role are simply two kinds of expressivity. They are kept from conflicting with each other by a de-emphasis or sidetracking of the instrumental meaning of the act. Sexual activity is an excellent case in point. In its nature sex inextricably combines instrumental and expressive elements. In instrumental terms the goal is to have sexual intercourse with someone; but sexual intercourse is also normally an expression of one's sensual and emotional nature.

Modernity has split this unity apart. For the male, sex is an instrumental activity. He pursues the female in exactly the same way that he pursues economic gain or political power. ("Candy is dandy," says Ogden Nash, "But liquor is quicker.") What matters is not the expression of one's sexuality, but the conquest, which is even and absurdly measured in quantitative terms (as befits advanced instrumental rationality): the number of ejaculations per night, or the number of women conquered. Or it may be the cleverness with which the conquest is achieved, as in Machiavelli's La Mandragola. Indeed Machiavelli's attitude toward the feminine so precisely captures this syndrome that I am inclined to suspect that to lay bare its psychological origins in him is to say something about modernity itself.

The modern woman deinstrumentalizes sex through a passive and masochistic orientation: a strategy that has the advantage of enabling the ethical purification, or at least the sterilization of sex. It is the reverse of the pattern we have seen in Machiavelli. The male identity is externalized and projectively identified with the male conquerer. The woman partakes vicariously in her own conquest. As the victim she is not to blame, and so remains morally pure.

It is important to recognize that the passivity of this orientation concerns only the overt relation to the object. "Every insinct," says Freud, "is a piece of activity,"[11] a vigorous and assertive search for pleasure; and masochism is no exception. With this proviso, Freud identified masculinity with an active and femininity with a passive orientation toward sex. But he also asserted that this was not based primarily on biological difference.[12] Furthermore, he held that the libidinal drive is basically the same in both sexes.[13] The passive, masochistic, narcissistic woman pictured in his writings thus emerges not as woman herself, but as modern woman, a necessary counterpart to the modern machismo male exemplified by Machiavelli.

The huge success of modernity has depended on a ruling stratum that adopts an uncompromising, single-minded, and unconflicted (hence highly motivated) instrumentalism: that is, modern man. But you cannot have modern man without modern woman. The expressive and passive-masochistic strivings that all humans have must be nullified somehow in the male. They cannot be repressed more than partially, for repression reduces motivation and would blunt the insatiable drive for conquest. The solution is to displace these unwanted elements outward via projective identification. The conflict is externalized and serves to strengthen rather than to weaken the intensity of the drive.

But the victim must act according to the script. She must be passive, submissive, and expressive, because this is precisely what enables the man to be active, dominating, and instrumental. Just as there can be no master without a slave, no victor without a vanquished, so there cannot be modern man without modern woman. As in Machiavelli's mind, so in the modern era: *Fortuna* is the creation of *virtù*, which cannot exist without her.

So far my argument has been that the motivational impetus that has produced and sustained modernity functionally requires a role differentiation between the dominant instrumental male and the subordinate expressive female. Functional explanation, however, has its limits. It can explain how a given system works, but not how it came into being or even why it continues to endure. Such questions require a more historical approach.

While instrumental-expressive role differentiation is, as I have argued, distinctively modern, the subordination of women is not. In the many and varied patrimonial (large-scale agricultural) systems that preceded modernity, women as a group uniformly were regarded as inferior, and denied any significant political or economic power outside and even often within the household. But when we go back to hunter-gatherer or small self-sufficient agricultural societies, or to systems that show only a partial evolution toward patrimonialism, we find many cases where the sexual role assignment is not invidious, and where there is a partial or even complete sharing and/or equality of political and economic power among men and women.[14]

It is clear, therefore, that it will not do to account for male dominance solely on the basis of universal psychological or biological traits such as a genetically endowed greater male aggressiveness or the ubiquity of a psychological syndrome such as Machiavelli exhibited.[15] Instead any explanation of the historical origins of male supremacy must be found in features special to patrimonial systems, or to some but not all prepatrimonial societies. Such explanations could drawn on biological or psychological differences, but only in the context of such special features. Two often cited arguments may be mentioned here:

1. That in patrimonial society the crucial importance of military power in attaining and keeping the basic economic resource, arable land, coupled with the special nature of warfare, in the face of the lesser physical strength of women and the time limitations imposed

on their activities by childbirth and child rearing, made it inevitable that military and hence political and economic power be a male
prerogative.[16]

2. That the evolution of a market economy featuring commodity exchange outside the household, in the face of the degree to which
the functions of motherhood bound the female to the home, led
to male supremacy and indeed to the woman herself becoming a
commodity.[17]

Modern civilization emerged out of patrimonial society, but has developed into something quite different. While it is plausible to assume that
initially male domination was simply a holdover from the past, it is open
to question that its continuance has rested on the same foundations as it
did in antiquity. Certainly the two explanatory accounts alluded to above
seem highly doubtful when applied to twentieth-century industrial civilization.

The possibility suggests itself that by now male supremacy rests *purely*
on functional grounds: that is, that the modern sexual role assignment
continues to exist only of its own momentum via the cultural transmission of the internalized roles. In recent decades, perhaps in response to
changes in the structure of social action is late capitalism, the attitudes
of women toward work, family, and sex appear to be undergoing major
changes, and they have begun to show an increasing unwillingness to
accept the role in which they have been cast. The feminist movement
both reflects and promotes such changed attitudes.

Although change is under way, we must not expect women as a group
to adopt the dominant male ethos. Such a one-sided instrumentalism is
surely unattainable to them because, in contrast to the male, they would
have no group on which to displace their now unwanted passive and
masochistic expressivity.[19] Thus their full-scale entry into political and
economic leadership would result in a dilution, a weakening, of the motivational syndrome that is the mainspring of modernity. Furthermore, as
I have pointed out, the intensity of the male's instrumental drive depends
on its lack of inner conflict, and this is achieved via the externalization
of discordant elements. Refusal by women to play their part in this cha-
rade would break the externalization, and reintroduce the conflict within
the male. As a result the sharp impetus of instrumentalism would be
blunted. The critics of feminism are entirely correct that this movement
strikes at the basic values and institutions of modern civilization.[19]

Notes

1. Here is where Machiavelli's concept of *virtù* contains a distinct element of emotional-artistic expressivity despite the prevailing instrumentalism. My thanks to George Kateb for this point. It is not until we get to puritanism that every trace of expressivity—ethical, emotional, or aesthetic—is systematically eliminated.

2. Niccolò Machiavelli, *The Prince*, 92, in *The Chief Works and Others*, trans. Allan Gilbert (Durham: Duke University Press, 1965). Except where indicated, all quotations and citations of Machiavelli are from this edition.

3. The locus classicus of Freud's treatment of sadomasochism is *Instincts and Their Vicissitudes* (1915), in *The Standard Edition of the Complete Psychological Works of Sigmund Freud*, 24 vols. (London: Hogarth Press, 1966–1974), vol. 14.

4. The libidinal-aggressive polarity emerges fully only later in Freud, *Beyond the Pleasure Principle* (1920), in *Standard Edition*, vol. 18.

5. Machiavelli to Luigi Guicciardini, Verona, December 8, 1509, in Niccolò Machiavelli, *Literary Works*, ed. and trans. J. R. Hale (London: Oxford University Press, 1961), 124–25.

6. J. G. A. Pocock, *The Machiavellian Moment* (Princeton: Princeton University Press, 1975). Quentin Skinner, *The Foundations of Modern Political Thought* (Cambridge: Cambridge University Press, 1978), vol. 1. I am much indebted to these two works in the preparation of this essay. Berlin points out that "[Machiavelli's] habit of putting things *troppo absolutamente* had already been noted by Guicciardini." Isaiah Berlin, "The Originality of Machiavelli," in *Against the Current* (New York: Penguin, 1982), 28 n. 1.

7. The close connection between sex and politics in Machiavelli's thought is pointed out by John R. Hale, *Machiavelli and Renaissance Italy* (New York: Collier Books, 1963), 24–25. His discussion of *La Mandragola* is especially penetrating (159–161). The play depicts the rape-seduction of an apparently inaccessible woman by means of a combination of audacity and cunning. Here in the private world of sexual intrigue we have an exact replica of the relation of *virtù* to *Fortuna* in the public realm of politics.

8. The case is argued in Donald McIntosh, "Max Weber as Critical Theorist," *Theory and Society* 12 (1983): 69–109.

9. Talcott Parsons, Robert F. Bales, James Olds, Morris Zedlich, and Philip E. Slate, *Family, Socialization, and Interaction Process* (Glencoe, Ill.: Free Press, 1955).

10. The phrase is from Mary P. Ryan, "Femininity and Capitalism in Antebellum America," in *Capitalist Patriarchy and the Case for Socialist Feminism*, ed. Zillah R. Eisenstein (New York: Monthly Review Press, 1979), 155. My thanks to Kathy Ferguson for the citation.

11. Freud, *Instincts and Their Vicissitudes*, 122.

12. Freud, *Three Essays on Sexuality* (1905), in *Standard Edition*, vol. 7, 219 n. 1 (added in 1915).

13. Freud, *New Introductory Lectures of Psychoanalysis* (1933), in *Standard Edition*, vol. 22, 131.

14. Peggy Reeves Sanday, *Female Power and Male Dominance* (Cambridge: Cambridge University Press, 1981).

15. For example, Beatrice Whiting, "Sex Identity Conflict and Physical Violence: A Comparative Study," *American Anthropologist* 67: 6, pt. 2 (1965): 123–140.

16. Marvin Harris, *Cannibals and Kings* (New York: Vintage Books/Random House, 1975).

17. Eleanor Leacock, "Woman's Status in Egalitarian Society: Implications for Social Evolution," *Current Anthropology* 19 (1973): 247–55. (The basic argument goes back to Engel's *Origin of the Family, Private Property, and the State*.)

18. That is why the plaint of Henry Higgins and Simone de Beauvoir, "Why can't a woman be like a man?" must be in vain. For a discussion of Beauvoir, see Jean Bethke Elshtain, *Public Man, Private Woman* (Princeton: Princeton University Press, 1981), 306–10.

19. My thanks to Jean Bethke Elshtain, Kathy Ferguson, Eric Plaut, and the editors of *Political Theory* for helpful comments on a previous draft.

2

Meditations on Machiavelli

Hanna Fenichel Pitkin

As a political theorist, Machiavelli is difficult, contradictory, and in many respects unattractive: a misogynist, frequently militaristic and authoritarian, uncomplimentary about human nature. What nevertheless makes him worth taking seriously is that his works contain an understanding of politics, autonomy, and the human condition, which is profoundly right in ways that really matter. That understanding consists of a set of syntheses holding in tension seemingly incompatible truths along several dimensions. It is therefore difficult to articulate and to sustain, and Machiavelli does not always sustain it. But the understanding is there, and even when he loses the syntheses he is a better teacher than many a more consistent theorist, because he refuses to abandon for very long any of the aspects of the truth he sees. Thus he manages to be both political and realistic even while articulating a theoretical vision of human achievement.

This chapter, therefore, frequently refers to the ideas of a thinker called "Machiavelli at his best" and offers an account of how and why the historical Machiavelli diverged from those ideas. In the process, it also makes some suggestions about the relevance of those ideas for our time. For all these reasons, this chapter is speculative and personal, less grounded in evidence.

At his best, Machiavelli formulates an understanding of human autonomy that is activist without megalomania, insisting on our capacity and responsibility for choice and action, while nevertheless recognizing the real limits imposed by our historical situation. He understands the open-ended, risky quality of human interaction, which denies to politics the sort of control available in dealing with inanimate objects. Yet he insists that the risks are worth taking, are indeed the only way of securing what we most value. He also formulates an understanding of autonomy that is highly political. He assumes neither the solidarity postulated by organic theorists nor the atomistic, unrelated individuals postulated by social contract theorists. Instead, he focuses on the way in which citizens in political interaction continually recreate community out of multiplicity. He formulates an understanding of autonomy, finally, that is neither cynical nor hortatory, but realistic: tough-minded about political necessities and human weaknesses without being reductionist about our goals and potentialities. Justice, civility, and virtue are as real, in that understanding, as greed and envy, or as bread and air (though of course people often say "justice" when they are in fact speaking of mere interest or expediency).

Although he rarely cites Aristotle and probably had only contempt for the Thomistic Aristotelianism he is likely to have encountered, Machiavelli's best understanding of politics is importantly reminiscent of Aristotle's teaching that man is a political animal, meaning not that people are always found in a *polis*, but rather that, first, politics is an activity in which no other species engages and, second, engaging in it is necessary to the full realization of our potential as humans.[1] For Machiavelli as for Aristotle, this means that we are neither beasts nor gods, neither mere products of natural forces nor beings with unlimited power. We are capable of free agency, but always within the bounds of necessity. We are the products but also the makers of culture, law, and history. We develop our humanness only in the company of others, yet our sociability is never automatic but rather requires effort and care. Finally, for Machiavelli as for Aristotle, our political nature is a function of our unique capacity for judgment. The human being is the *polis* animal because it is the *logos* animal, capable of speaking, reasoning, distinguishing right from wrong, and thus of freely chosen action.

In terms of Machiavelli's conflicting images of manhood, the right understanding of human autonomy he offers is closest to the image of the fraternal Citizen. Yet it transcends the misogynist vision and manages to combine the commitment to republican, participatory politics with the fox's deflation of hypocritical and empty ideals, as well as the appreciation of authority, tradition, and generativity associated with the Founder image.

This best, synthetic Machiavelli holds in tension apparently incompatible truths along at least three interrelated dimensions of what it means to be human, political, and autonomous; dimensions so fundamental to these topics that any political theory must address them, if not expressly, then by implication. Autonomy is problematic for creatures such as ourselves in relation to the past, in relation to our contemporaries, and in relation to nature, both around and within us. It is problematic in relation to the past because we are the creatures of history. Our present situation and our very selves are shaped by the past. What can freedom mean for such a creature? Call that the dimension of action. Our autonomy is problematic in relation to our contemporaries because harmony among us is not automatic, as among the insects. We are distinct individuals with often conflicting needs and desires, yet we are also products and shapers of shared societies. Call that the dimension of membership. Our autonomy is problematic in relation to nature because we are both rooted in the natural and capable of transcending it, because we have bodies that need food and shelter and are mortal, and psyches, minds, or spirits that render us capable of distinguishing and choosing right from wrong, good from evil, just from unjust. But what is the relationship between natural need or drive and standards of judgment, and what is the basis of those standards—convention, nature, or some transcendent source? Call this the dimension of judgment. A right understanding of autonomy requires synthesis along all of these dimensions, and that is what Machiavelli at his best has to offer.

Yet Machiavelli often loses the synthetic tension along one or another dimension and falls into that endless circling among incompatible alternatives which Hegel associated with "bad infinity."[2] And the psychological and familial themes he employs, though they partly support, ultimately tend to undermine, those syntheses. To be sure, those syntheses are problematic and unstable also because each of the dimensions involves fundamental philosophical problems built into the very structure of our conceptual system, perhaps of our human nature. The dimension of action involves the problem philosophers sometimes call the "freedom of the will"; the dimension of membership, that of "universals and particulars"; the dimension of judgment, the problem of "value relativism" or " 'is' and 'ought.' " These are surely among the most formidable, difficult problems ever taken up by philosophers. And Machiavelli was no philosopher; he was not interested in resolving such problems nor particularly self-conscious about them. This is both a strength and a weakness. Precisely because he is not a philosopher, Machiavelli never leaves political reality for very long; but by the same token, he is also not fully aware of the conceptual or philosophical difficulties that complicate his theorizing.

The syntheses are problematic not only philosophically, however, but also politically. Machiavelli demanded of himself that his theorizing be relevant to the political realities of his time. Politically, the dimension of action requires that theory guide us about "what is to be done," help us to delineate here and now those things that we must accept as "given" from those that are open to change by our intervention. The dimension of membership requires, politically, that theory speak to power and plurality, that it not merely articulate abstract truths but make them relevant to an audience that has—or could generate—the power actually to do what the theory suggests must be done. And the dimension of judgment requires, politically, that justice and right be tied, if not to expedience, then at least to possibility; what is truly impossible cannot be politically right. The political realities of Machiavelli's situation, as was remarked at the outset, were extraordinarily troubled and intractable. The real difficulties facing Florence, and particularly Florentine republicanism, were just about overwhelming, seeming to defy even the best understanding that political theory might devise. In demanding of himself that his theory address those realities, Machiavelli was sometimes forced into utopian fantasies and enraged distortions—the very kinds of theorizing he rightly condemned in others.

But even when allowance has been made for the philosophical difficulties of the subject matter and the political difficulties of his situation,
it nevertheless remains true that Machiavelli's best synthetic understanding is frequently further undermined by the personal and familial themes
he himself invokes. The very metaphors and images he employs to convey
his insights repeatedly distort or destroy those insights. Whether this is
because of his own psychic needs and conflicts, or because of his efforts
to address the psychic vulnerabilities of his audience, must remain ultimately undecided. What matters is to understand the connections between political and psychological considerations in the texts.

Mankind is the species that makes itself, not just biologically as every
species perpetuates its kind, but culturally, through history. Human beings are born less completely developed toward adulthood than any other
creature. Thus their development is shaped more by the particular circumstances into which they are born; and those circumstances are less
purely natural, more cultural and social than those of any other species.
Using our capacity for language and abstract thought, and our opposed
thumbs and ability to make tools, we produce a material and nonmaterial
culture that forms the environment in which the next generations of
humans grow up. Thus to be human is to be the product of a particular
society and culture, which is the product of past history. Yet to be human
is also to have a share in making history, transmitting, preserving, and
altering culture, shaping society. It is we who enact the forces that shape
us. As Hobbes said, man is both the "matter" and the "artificer" of "commonwealth," of community and civilization.[3]

Those facts pose a mystery, or rather, whole clusters of mysteries: philosophical, political, psychological. How can a product of causal forces
also be a free agent capable of action, creativity, responsibility—to be
praised and blamed for its choices and deeds? What does it mean to say
that this person *did that,* is responsible for it, could have done otherwise?
On what basis do we make such judgments? Every action has antecedents
and every person a past, so is an action really different from an event, a
person from an object? What will count as initiating something new
rather than just continuing preexisting processes? Do these distinctions
mark something objectively real in the world, or are they merely conceptual conventions that we impose arbitrarily and, in the end, inconsis-
tently? These are among the questions with which social and ethical
philosophers must deal.

But the political theorist is not merely, or not exactly, a philosopher. Philosophy investigates those aspects of the human condition that could not be otherwise and that are so basic we are ordinarily not even aware of them. But politics concerns matters that might well be other than they are; it concerns the question "what shall we do?" Insofar as it directs itself toward matters that cannot be changed, it is misguided and will fail. Politics is the art of the possible. To theorize about politics, then, is not exactly like philosophizing about the human condition or the nature of being. Political theory does teach us about fundamental necessities, not merely those that are given to all humans in all ages but also those that are merely inescapable for *us*, here and now; but it does so with reference to, and in order to distinguish them from, those other matters that are subject to our choice and power, with regard to which we might success-fully act. Thus the political theorist is concerned not merely with the philosophical problem of whether humans can ever break the causal chain of history to make a new beginning, but even more with the politi-cal problem of how and where and with whom we might take action, given our present circumstances. He delineates, one might say, "what has to be accepted as given" from "what is to be done."

But this delineation is not really as simple as the drawing of a line between unchanging regions. For the political world is composed of human activities and relationships and habits, all of which are anchored in human thought. Change people's understandings of themselves and their political world, and they will change their conduct, and thereby that world. The political theorist is thus always a teacher as much as an observer or contemplator, and to the extent that his teaching succeeds, his subject matter will alter. So the distinguishing of necessities from possibilities is less like the drawing of a line than like a *Gestalt* switch: a reconceptualization of familiar details so that realities we feel we have always known suddenly become visible for the first time, familiar things suddenly take on a new aspect.

We live our ordinary lives in the particular and the concrete, largely unaware of our remote connections to people we never see, the long-range and large-scale consequences for others of what we do, for us of what they do. On the whole, we know how to use the resources at hand for the immediate tasks we face, how to do what we must daily do. But the factual particulars among which we live can be organized and inter-preted by many different theoretical schemas. That is why, as Machiavelli says, "the people" may be deceived "in judging things in general," but they "are not so deceived" about "particular," "specific things," "things individually known."⁴ It is not so much that we do not see the forest for the trees, as that more than one theoretical forest is compatible with the many trees among which we live. The political theorist, one might say, invites us to a new organizing schema for making sense of our concrete reality. If we accept the invitation, our familiar world will seem changed, and as a result we shall live differently in it. Yet whether we accept the new schema will depend on whether it makes sense of what we already know, makes meaningful what was before confused, chaotic, or intractable.

Obviously this will depend both on the truth of a theorist's vision and on his power as a teacher. Nothing is harder than to get people really to *see* what has always been before their eyes, particularly since such a changed vision will have implications for action (which may make uncomfortable demands on them) and interest (which may make it offensive to those who now hold privilege and power). Thus the political theorist faces a special problem of communication: in order to be understood, he must speak in terms familiar to his audience, from within a conceptual framework and an understanding of the world that they share. Yet he wants not to convey new information to them, but rather to change the terms, the conceptual framework through which they presently organize their information. It may seem an impossible task; and political theorizing accordingly has its dangers, from ridicule to martyrdom. Yet sometimes it does happen that people are ready for a new understanding, when the old explanations no longer make sense, the old rules no longer guide, the old procedures no longer produce satisfactory results, the old ceremonies no longer sanctify. Then a new vision—the right new theoretical vision—may "take" among a large audience and even produce basic political change.

Every political theory must expressly or by implication take its stand on these matters, since every theorist has both something to say and some reason for saying it. He wants to convey to an audience some truths, some matters he hopes people will recognize as "given," so that about other matters they will subsequently act differently than they now do. Even the most radical or relativistic theorist thus teaches respect toward something, and even the most conservative or pessimistic hopes by his teaching to produce some change.

The idea of fortune in the largest sense—not just the personification of Fortune as woman, but that figure together with her various (partial) equivalents, such as nature and opportunity, and their male counter-players, such as *virtù*, the Founder, and the *vivere civile*—this whole configuration of ideas is Machiavelli's particular response to these perennial problems of political theory. Fortune in this largest sense is his way of relating man the "maker" to man the "matter" of "commonwealth," of relating action to necessity and initiative to tradition. It is his way of addressing an audience in terms they will understand about a changed understanding of their political world that would—if they accepted it— bring them to change their conduct, and thereby their world. What are the consequences of this particular way, Machiavelli's way, of doing it?

Machiavelli presents a political universe that is neither a fixed, sacred order nor a meaningless accident. We face neither eternally valid abstract standards of right that it is our duty to try to approximate, nor inevitable forces moving to predestined goals, nor yet a randomness that defies understanding and effort. Coping with necessity is neither a worshipful seeking nor a scientific predicting. Nor is it a throw of the dice. Instead, it is like dealing with a person—a difficult, unpredictable, even sometimes malevolent person, to be sure, and one larger and more powerful than ourselves, but nevertheless a being with personality like ours, intention like ours, moods and foibles like ours, open to influence to some extent and in some ways, just as we are, yet never wholly within our control. That being can be known as any person can, which is to say, imperfectly, but sufficiently to make the effort worthwhile. The kind of knowledge that will be relevant here will be the kind we have of people, knowledge that leads us to expect the unexpected. It will involve not primarily causation and technical control, but relationship, intention, communication, meaning.

But Machiavelli's fortune is neither merely a person nor just any person; and the personification of our relationship to the universe was hardly an invention of Machiavelli's. The medieval Christian conception of the world, for example, was also personalized, a relationship to the Father, the Virgin, Christ, and the many saints. Yet it was a very different conception from Machiavelli's. For God was not merely a father, but also the creator of the world, ultimately beyond human comprehension. He presided over an order beyond human influence in which fortune was a relatively minor figure.

Machiavelli's Fortune, by contrast, is part of no righteous eternal system, subordinated to no male divinity. She enacts not some predestined justice, but her own whims. But by the same token she is open to human influence, not through prayer or supplication, but rather through court-ship, manipulation, and bold challenge. Above all, she is female and thus simultaneously inferior and dangerous.

The conception of fortune as responsive to human effort, the revival of *virtù* as symbolizing that effort, and the specific interpretation of that symbol in terms of virility were widespread in the Renaissance. But it is Machiavelli who presents man's relationship to the outcomes of human action in terms of sexual conquest—less violent than rape but more forceful than seduction. Thereby he not only anthropomorphizes and sexualizes the givens and the outcomes of human action in history but invests them with those specific desires, fears, and attitudes his male read-ers already bear toward woman—as unreliable nurturer, as sexual object, as "other." The consequence is both empowering and constraining; it promotes the striving for autonomy yet renders that goal inaccessible.

Personifying Fortune in this way means that the boundaries between necessity and possibility in Machiavelli's world are above all changeable, subject to the whims of fortune on the one side and human effort on the other. What has to be accepted as given varies, for him, with the particu-lar situation and with our own capacities and efforts. We are never all-powerful, but always subject to countless necessities. Yet the limits are always partly up to us to determine, expanding and contracting as we vary in skill, energy, and imagination.

Most of all, Machiavelli is an activist, urging us to hopefulness and effort. In drawing the line between what had to be accepted as given and what might be changed, Machiavelli had to address a mixed audience: many of them discouraged about the possibilities for action, others active enough but only in private concerns, particularly the pursuit of wealth, a few driven by ambition to activity in the public sphere, but in a hubristic and selfish manner that only increased the chaos and corruption of public life. His task thus was to rouse men to action, but to action that recog-nized some limits to human capacities, that did not assume perfect cer-tainty or unlimited human power. So Machiavelli's activism is of a peculiar kind. It is founded in no promise of guaranteed success or mas-tery, no alliance with providence or historical necessity. If anything, it is founded in challenge rather than promise. Against Christian otherworld-liness, Church hypocrisy, Stoic withdrawal, bourgeois acquisitiveness, factionalism, and envy, Machiavelli summons his contemporaries to *virtù* and to glory. In the cause of community welfare and political liberty, he tries to enlist their concern for manliness, their fear of dependence, their craving for sexual gratification. Machiavelli's ultimate challenge to his contemporaries is to shame them: stand up, and act like a man!

The image of fortune as woman, then, challenges men in terms of their masculine identity: she is there for the taking—if you're man enough. The political universe is meaningful and manageable, yet the image cautions that not just any action will succeed and prepares men for possible failure. It thus challenges what Machiavelli called "ambition," without promoting the excessive ambition entailed in imagining humans as having godlike power.

And yet, the image also has more indirect implications with almost the opposite effect. Machiavelli's was a time when sexual and familial relationships were in flux and were the focus of considerable conflict. We know, in addition, that certain features of Florentine family life at the time were likely to intensify infantile conflicts. Appealing to the pride in masculinity of men who grow up in such circumstances is likely to be rhetorically effective; but it is also likely, first, to reinvigorate and import into political life the anxieties that trouble their relations with women: their fear of the feminine, their need to prove manliness, and as a consequence, violence, hero worship, relations of command and obedience. Second, insofar as relations between the sexes are troubled by unresolved infantile conflicts, invoking woman means invoking mother and tends to return men to childhood fears and fantasies, trapping them in their own past. That is likely to stir up and import into political life fears of trust and nurturance, yearnings for omnipotence and merging, misleading fantasies of what adulthood means. Machiavelli undermines the very teaching he wants to convey by appealing to his audience's desire for manliness and thereby also summoning up childishness: fantasies of huge engulfing mothers and rescuing fathers, relationships of domination and submission, an unstable combination of cynicism and exhortation, and misleading conceptions of action, membership, judgment, and autonomy. The appeal to machismo can move men all right, particularly men troubled about their manliness, but it cannot make them free.

The problem of action concerns human creativity and our relationship to the past, issues Machiavelli confronts in the image of the Founder, in the authority of ancient Rome, and in the doctrines of imitation and the "return to beginnings." Yet each of these topics remains itself problematic, and specifically so in relation to familial and sexual themes. The Founder image, meant to solve the mysteries of creativity in history, merely reexpresses them. The Founder is the very essence of generative authority, yet must murder his sons. He is supposed to make men out of babies or beasts, yet must assure that they do not themselves aspire to Founder status. He, the solitary patriarch, is supposed to serve as inspiration for fraternal mutuality. Possibly the transition from patriarchal domination to the *vivere civile* is to be made by a liberating Brutus. Yet Brutus is himself a problematic Founder figure, his conspiracy effective only if the citizenry are already free in all but a formal sense.

The Founder is a myth, as Machiavelli the fox well knows, and thus cannot be a genuine solution to any problem in the real world. Yet the problem he is meant to solve—how to "get there from here"—*has been solved* from time to time in the real world. People have been formed into communities, barbarians civilized, republics founded, corrupt institutions renewed. There must be ways to do it. Though there are no Founders, capital F, there are sometimes founders, people who act so that the world is creatively altered after their passing. The image of the Founder, however, blocks rather than facilitates understanding of what human founding is really like. Conjured up as a counterweight to the mythical feminine power, it remains an escapist fantasy, for the mythical proportions of both threat and rescuer dwarf any merely human achievement. Meant to comfort the self, the Founder is actually a fantasy of self-denigration. Instead of empowering, it leaves people helpless, "blaming the princes" for their fate.

The doctrine of imitation and the "return to beginnings" are similarly ambiguous and may be read in terms of either paternal rescue or one's own generative capacities. Thus, imitating the Romans can mean copying their forms and formulas, or it can mean, like them, copying no one. Returning to beginnings can mean recovering terror to renew reluctant obedience, or it can mean dereification, recovering the self—both its capacities and its real commitments. The one reading offers escape from the engulfing matriarch, but only at the price of self-annihilation, whether through merger or murder. The other is genuinely empowering but liberates only at the price of risk. Read in the latter way, founding can be understood as a universal human potential, so that every moment is an opportunity for initiative (though the options are always limited), and every citizen is a potential (co-)founder. Then the Founder image reappears as a symbol of the human capacity for action, but a misleading symbol. For if founding is a shared human capacity, it is neither solipsistic nor a creation *ex nihilo*.

Even the wisest and most charismatic founding fathers are leaders of persons, not molders of material; their authority is the capacity to induce the free actions of other persons. This is not a denial of ancestral authority but the extension to ancestors of that manner of leadership Machiavelli called "the way of freedom." From this perspective, it is precisely the "irreverent" questioning of inherited tradition, the insistence on one's own equal freedom to choose and change, that constitutes true reverence, recognition of one's origins, and renewed contact with the founders. It is true reverence, first, because creating something valuable and lasting is a much more magnificent achievement for fallible human beings than it would be for divinities. It is true reverence, second, because unquestioning dutiful obedience means an implicit denigration of the self by comparison with the sacred ancestors. Therefore it masks a hidden resentment and rebellion; inside the Founder image lurks the fox. And, third, the implicit self-denigration is a partial denial of one's own capacities—to judge and change, but therefore also to defend and augment the tradition. Adults with full awareness of their powers and responsibilities are more effective guardians of what is to be preserved than dutiful children.

To repeat, such an understanding of ancestors and action is offered by Machiavelli but also blocked by his invocation of mythical engulfing mothers and rescuing fathers. For the personal and psychological counterpart of the political theory problem of action is our relationship to our parents: the human problem of growing up. For the small child, adults are indeed larger than life, authors of timeless, sacred, and unchangeable rules. The child feels by turns helpless in their power and omnipotent by assimilation to them. It regards the rules as sacred, although it has not mastered them, but is in fact ready to accept any innovation presented to it as authoritative.[5]

Growing up means acquiring a more realistic view of authority, both the authority of parental figures and that of the principles and practices by which one's community lives. At the same time it also means becoming oneself competent at those practices and capable of parenting others. It means becoming a master of the rules, a responsible custodian and interpreter of the inherited culture. To the extent that our growing up is troubled or incomplete, traces of the earlier understanding remain in us all and are likely to be evoked by certain images and situations, particularly in times of stress.

The transition from total subservience under a godlike authority to autonomous liberty, so problematic in Machiavelli's political argument, thus does take place in normal psychic development, but as shift in perception, not in reality. The small child normally perceives in ways that in an adult might be called myth and reification. Parents are not really gods; indeed, the psychological theory examined in this chapter suggests that such infantile images are more likely to linger into adulthood in proportion as actual parenting was inadequate, the parents absent or unreliable. In any case, the sense in which the transition is a psychic reality does not make it politically feasible. Citizens, or even privatized adults who might become citizens, are not children. And while no doubt we all need authority, adults do not need the kind of authority parents exemplify, and particularly not the kind exemplified by the small child's images of parents. The projection of those images into politics can only distort political reality.

But recognizing that parents are merely human, like oneself, and that our conventions are humanly made must not be confused with the hubristic suppositions that one had no parents, that our conventions have no authority, or that *every* option is open to us, here and now. Growing up is not the transition from regarding parents as demigods to regarding oneself as a demigod, but the acceptance simultaneously of the human powers and limitations of self and parents. Reification and hubris are equally childish. Growing up means coming to terms with this ambiguous authority of the past: that it is not sacred beyond our challenge, yet that it is *in* us, and without it, we would not be who we are.

To say it another way, growing up means coming to terms with the arbitrariness of the past. Though history is humanly made, it is inescapable. The past is given; the future is open to our action. We are "thrown" into the world, as Heidegger puts it, suggesting a random cast of dice, into some particular time, place, and circumstances not of our choosing. Yet only the unique configuration of circumstances and events that are my life could have made me. We begin helpless and unindividuated; only by being initiated into some particular culture do we become human individuals, capable of autonomy. So my origins, arbitrary as they are, must be accepted, for they are the preconditions of my capacity for choice and action.

That is what Nietzsche called *amor fati*, learning to love the accidents that have befallen us, to redeem them as sacred, by our will. It is an extraordinarily difficult doctrine to articulate. It does not forbid tampering with authoritative tradition but says that we *cannot* change what is past. The will cannot act on the past, Nietzsche says, and martyrs itself in trying. We act always in the present, but all too often the real motivation of our action is the wish to undo some past event, rather than to alter its results in the present. Nietzsche called such backward-looking action "reaction," because it was not free; and he said it was the product of weakness and *ressentiment*. Freud called it neurotic and said that neurotics expend vast inner energy continually trying to obliterate something in the past that cannot be obliterated because it is graven in the self. This cripples them and makes their actions ineffectual. Only if one can—in one sense—wholly ratify as if sacred everything in the past and thus everything about the world and oneself is one free to act effectively to change what—in another sense—needs changing about them.

But ratifying the past as if sacred does not mean imagining it as sacred. On the contrary, it requires recognizing the historical past as a product of human controversy and choice, at every step actually or potentially political. In Machiavelli's terms, we must not worship the ancestors and ape them but connect their achievements to our own potential. The past that to us looks so inevitable—partly because it is past and therefore for us inescapable—was for past actors a series of opportunities and choices, often fought out in political controversy, in which some won and others lost. And all that welter of conflicting views, policies, efforts is our heritage. In recovering the past and seeking out ancestors, we thus have some choice about whom to seek and how to see them—whether, for example, our origins are Roman or Tuscan, and what the choice implies for us now.

Both Nietzsche and Freud thought, paradoxically, that enslavement to the past could be cured only by the right sort of recovery of the past. For Freud, neurosis is cured by remembering the past that was repressed into the unconscious. Nietzsche's metaphor is digestion: to be free for action one must deal with the past in a way that incorporates it, once and for all, and be done with it. Machiavelli speaks not in such psychological and personal terms, but characteristically in political ones, yet his teaching is much the same.

The political counterpart of what Nietzsche called *ressentiment* Machiavelli called corruption. Corrupt people are obsessed with past injustice, desiring vengeance more than any direct gratification. "The reward they desire from victory is not . . . glory" but rather "the satisfaction of having conquered the others."[6] Thus when they come to power they kill or exile their enemies, making laws "not for the common profit but altogether in favor of the conqueror."[7] Their real desire being to undo the past, which is impossible, they cannot let the past go or look rationally toward the future. They would rather "go back over past things" endlessly than "provide for future ones" in ways designed to "reunite, not to divide the city."[8] So they launch escalating feuds or even ally themselves with their own state's enemies abroad. No law is "more dangerous for a republic," says Machiavelli, "than one that looks back for a long time."[9]

But a different sort of "looking back for a long time," one that renews contact with origins and founders and recovers the self, is also Machiavelli's cure for such factional resentment. Only, as already argued, this curative looking back can be understood in either of two ways: the one misogynistic and ultimately crippling, the other genuinely liberating. Developing the former understanding, Machiavelli, like Nietzsche, links resentful factionalism with femininity. Resentment is the passion of the effeminate; factional vengeance is the weapon of fortune within men. So the cure seems to lie in renewed contact with the saving masculinity of forefathers, who will impose murderous discipline. But that cure fails in its liberating intent, for it leaves people still trapped in the past, reliving instead of resolving childhood conflicts.

Alternatively, the curative recovery of origins and ancestors can mean recognizing one's kinship with their great, but human, achievement. It can mean recovering simultaneously one's own capacity to judge and change or augment what they created, and one's commitment to that creation which constituted both self and community. This would leave autonomy linked still with adulthood, but no longer with gender; the past would liberate not from feminine but from mythologized parental power. Here, however, the problem of action merges with those of membership and judgment, for an individual is not really free to change the traditions of his community by himself, and not just any action we take will be a right action. Even though free to create, we are nevertheless bound to be reverent toward something already given, and respectful of others with whom we must act if our action is to have political meaning.

Concerning the problem of membership, Machiavelli is neither a contractarian nor an organicist. He takes it for granted that we are somehow both distinct individuals, each unique and capable of action, and yet objectively interconnected, achieving individuality only in interaction with others. What really interests him, as always, is politics: the possibility of an active, intentional membership enabling us jointly to take responsibility for our objective interconnections, the large-scale consequences for each other of what we are actually doing. Particularly in the Citizen image of manhood, he sees politics as the activity by which free individuals, already objectively interdependent in a society but (therefore) also at odds in terms of interest, need, outlook, desire, repeatedly make themselves into a community, restore and redirect their community, defining it and themselves in the process. Politics thus both partly presupposes and creates both individuality and communal ties.

In deliberation and political conflict citizens are forced to bring their individual or class interests and "humors" into relationship with the interests and "humors" of others, producing a renewed recognition of their interdependence and shared membership. In the process, old connections are discovered and new ones made, and all are reminded of their stake in the community, in its policies and the ways those policies are made, in its ways of life and ethos, and in each other. This is neither a transformation of self-interest into dutiful self-sacrifice to something external called "the public," nor a mere refinement of self-interest to the longer-range and more rational, but something like a redefinition of the self, an enlarged awareness of how individuality and community are connected in the self.

This political struggle involves both power and principle, each side mustering what power it can, yet also appealing to the other in terms of law, right, justice, and the common good. Indeed, in the *vivere civile* might and right are interrelated, for law and justice are themselves partly resources of power; and, conversely, a purely abstract "right" that serves no community needs and can muster no community support is politically ineffectual and wrong. Because we are simultaneously both distinct and connected, politics always simultaneously concerns both the distribution of costs and benefits among competitors and the nature and direction of their shared community, both "who gets what, when, why" and "who we are." Every law or policy allocates, advantaging some and disadvantaging others; but every law or policy also affects their shared common life and the principles for which they stand. Neglecting either aspect is naive and potentially disastrous. Neglect the former aspect, and you are likely to be exploited under cover of attractive slogans about the public good or to formulate unrealistic policies that do not work. Neglect the latter, and you court "corruption"; your political community is likely to dissolve into factions, each poaching on a public good and on principles for whose maintenance it takes no responsibility.

For Machiavelli at his best, the real point is not some unified harmony at which politics theoretically aims, but the activity of struggling toward agreement with and against each other, in which citizens take active charge of the historical processes that would otherwise direct their lives in hidden ways. And that activity is no mere courtly dialogue, but a genuine conflict, in which needs and important interests are at stake. Without passion and struggle there can be no liberty, but only reification, habit, and drift. Yet political conflict must also always be kept within limits; politics is not civil war. The struggle must be kept open and public, rather than clandestine and private. It must involve a genuine appeal to principle, to what is reasonable and what is just; the public and principled aspect of politics must be kept lively in it. And citizens must be kept aware of their interdependence, their shared stake in fair rules and right principles, the civil limits (i termini civili) that forbid wiping out their opponents. These requirements are both prerequisites for and products of a healthy politics (which is one reason why the initial founding of a vivere civile is such a puzzle).

The essential element in membership so understood is mutuality; politics is not the domination of some by others, but a relationship among peers; the vivere civile means neither to dominate superbamente nor to serve umilmente. It resembles that outlook Kant later discerned as fundamental to morality: the recognition of other human beings as persons capable of action, like oneself, as members of the "kingdom of ends," not to be exploited for one's own purposes like objects but to be encountered in dialogue as peers with purposes of their own. Yet politics is not morality, and the reciprocity required of citizens lacks the intimacy of moral relationship; political deliberation is not dialogical but multivocal and impersonal. Although citizens must certainly share some degree of commonality to be and remain one community, there is room for much difference and conflict among them; and the mutuality politics requires is a recognition of similarity within difference, a peerhood that does not presuppose total equality, a capacity to continue to live and act with others who are substantially, even offensively, different from oneself.

Instilling this capacity for mutuality within difference is a crucial part of Machiavelli's effort at the political education of his factional fellow Florentines. But the sexual and familial imagery he invokes again partly undermines this effort by calling up images of domination and fears of dependence. The counterpart in personal and psychological life of the political theory problems of membership is our relationship to the "other": to someone we recognize as simultaneously like ourselves and yet dangerously different. It begins with the task already discussed, of learning to see our parents as human, as persons like ourselves; but it continues into relationships with our contemporaries. To relate actively, without masochistic resentment and yet within civil limits, with a recognition of mutuality, to persons defined as significantly different, in conflict with oneself, requires a certain self-confidence and tolerance for ambiguity. The "other" threatens the psychic integrity of the self. Whoever is excessively anxious about internal unity, purity, and consistency, who finds it difficult to acknowledge the "other" inside the self—parts of the self that seem alien, dangerous, in conflict with the rest—is likely to project that otherness onto external groups and persons defined as different, and therefore to deny mutuality with them. Ascribing to such external "others" forbidden parts of the self, we then relate to those others as we feel about those parts of the self. This happens in ethnocentrism and in many cultures' treatment of aliens and outgroups. It happens also between social classes and races, particularly as privileged and dominant groups project forbidden wishes onto subordinated groups, denying their humanity or at any rate their equality, perceiving them as simultaneously contemptible and dangerous: childish, passionate, physical, irrational, uncanny, mysterious. So white Americans tend to see people of color, so gentiles tend to see Jews, so the rich tend to see the poor, so men tend to see women.

Relations with the opposite sex are perhaps the most common and certainly the most intimate example of this encounter with the "other," of the difficulties in achieving mutuality within differences.[10] The difficulty exists for both sexes, but, on the whole, men are in the role of the dominant and privileged group here. Women tend to signify infantile relationships for us all, because the care of children is assigned mainly to women in our culture. But it is only for men that the infantile comes to be associated with "the opposite sex," that group and those individuals encountered as fundamentally different. In Dorothy Dinnerstein's terms, insofar as a boy's infantile relationship with his mother remains unresolved and unworked through, he is likely to project it onto his perceptions of all—or all significant, or all motherly, or all authoritative—women; and that relationship is more difficult for a boy to work through than for a girl precisely because he is socially constrained to keep mother at arm's length as "other," as fundamentally different from the self.[11] To the extent that our infantile experience remains unmodified, Dinnerstein says, we all perceive "the threat to autonomy which can come from a woman . . . as more primitively dangerous, than any such threat from a man"; thus we may even welcome male domination as "a reasonable refuge" from the female. "We come eventually, of course, to resent male authority, too," but not wholeheartedly.[12] Thus Dinnerstein says that when we abandon the risks of free self-government for the security of some "male tyranny, the big, immediate thing we are feeling the need to escape is not freedom," but our recollections and fantasies of that "earlier, and more total tyranny" of the mother's power, as experienced by the infant.[13]

Consequently, men's definition of the female as radically "other" both stimulates and undermines their struggle for freedom.

> Even in the efforts [misogynist] man makes to *overthrow* male tyranny—male tyranny over males, that is—he rests on the vassalage of woman. Reassured that he has the original despot under control, he can play with the notion of emerging from under the wing of the new one.[14]

But he can only play with that notion rather than effectively pursue the goal, because his feeling of strength is unstable.

> He is drawing strength from the subservience of woman for a struggle against the tyranny of man; but he can keep woman subservient only with the strength he draws from the sponsorship of the male tyrant. . . . He is balancing terrors, dependencies, against each other; the balance keeps tipping and he keeps slipping back into the patriarchal trap.[15]

Accordingly, relations between the sexes can be taken as one measure of the capacity for mutuality, and thus for the type of citizenship Machiavelli envisages. That is, I think, what Marx meant in claiming that the "species being" of humanity is "sensuously manifested, reduced to an observable fact" in the relationship between the sexes. From this relationship, he thought, one can judge the "whole level of development" of a people:

> the extent to which man's natural behaviour has become human, or the extent to which . . . his human nature has come to be natur[al] to him. In this relationship is revealed, too, the extent to which man's need has become a human need; the extent to which, therefore, the other person as a person has become for him a need—the extent to which he in his individual existence is at the same time a social being.[16]

The relationship between the sexes is suffused with natural animal drives and primitive psychic impulses; to the extent that it is nevertheless a civilized, moral relationship of mutuality, each recognizing and indeed needing the other as a person, an end rather than a mere means, our animality has been humanized. This humanizing transformation has occurred only to the extent that the civilized and moral type of relating has become a fulfilling expression of physical and psychic impulse, rather than a duty reluctantly performed.

Similarly, Hannah Arendt has suggested a correlation between the attitude men take toward women and their understanding of human action and politics. She sees that correlation exemplified in Christian thought by the choice between the two biblical versions of the creation story. Thus she says that Paul, for whom "faith was primarily related to salvation . . . insists that woman was created 'of the man' and hence 'for the man'" (1 Cor. 11:8–12), while Jesus, "for whom faith was closely related to action," cites Genesis 1:27: "he which made *them* at the beginning made them male and female" (Matt. 19:4).[17] Arendt does not elaborate, but the point is clearly related to her observation that action, the human capacity to create relationships and make history, always presupposes a context of plurality, "because we are all the same, that is, human, in such a way that nobody is ever the same as anyone else who ever lived, lives, or will live." This plurality within likeness "is specifically *the* condition—not only the *conditio sine qua non,* but the *conditio per quam*—of all political life."[18]

Certainly in Machiavelli's texts, misogyny works to undermine the vision of political liberty. Yet if one seeks to generalize about actual politics, no simple equation between free politics and mutuality between the sexes will do. Given the frequency with which actual participatory republics in history—examples of what Machiavelli would have called the *vivere civile,* from ancient Athens to modern Switzerland—have excluded or even severely oppressed women, one can hardly argue that democracy presupposes sexual equality, let alone that mutuality between the sexes would promptly produce a just and democratic polity. Even in the psychological and sociological theories examined in this chapter, the relevant variable is not actual relations between men and women, but how the citizen-men and the child-rearing women feel about those relations. In the second place, a free and participatory political life depends on a lot more than the psychic state of the citizens; that can surely be at most one factor among many economic, social, and cultural considerations. And, in the third place, as Machiavelli's writings indicate, the appeal to machismo really can move men toward intense bonds with their fellow males, and toward energetic, heroic action. However, the action so motivated is not likely to be coordinated with any public good, and the bonds so motivated are likely to require a rigid, authoritarian discipline.

Misogyny, overtly directed only against women, is also and necessarily directed against parts of the male self, since virtually every man was once mothered by a woman and began the formation of his self in relation to her. Needing therefore to expunge or deny those parts of the self they experience as feminine or childish, men who are anxious about their masculinity will be severely limited in their capacity for genuine mutuality—for the combination of trust with conflict—even in relation to other men. Unable to trust beyond their immediate circle of family and friends, unwilling to acknowledge their interdependencies, they would likely lead privatized lives—not, of course, confined to the household like their women, but concerned with business, for instance, or family status.

If such men do move into public life, they do so in order to escape and deny their private selves, the vulnerabilities of the body and their troubling relations with women and children in the household. Fleeing their bodily and domestic selves, they march out to ravage "the sheepfolds of others." To the extent that they feel threatened by "inner" conflict, psychic or political, they will lack that capacity for limited struggle among peers that differentiates citizenship from civil war, political dispute from the factional disintegration of a community. And so their community is likely to be an army, women safely excluded, the apple tree dutifully left untouched, and their mortality and private particularity left behind as they turn their rage outward against a (psychically) safely external "other." Theirs, in short, will be a zero-sum world in which the only possible conception of public life is of domination; they will be either fragmented and thus vulnerable to the domination of others or unified and dominated by a single commander for the purpose of dominating others.

Machiavelli's writings never transcended the conventional misogyny of his time. Like the other men of Renaissance Florence, he had virtually no experience of women as citizens or peers, though he had at least some significant experience of the exceptional woman *virago,* notably in his disastrous early diplomatic encounter with Caterina Sforza. This chapter has tried to show that his failure to deal with the "otherness" of women as a worldly, realistic difference rather than an uncanny and threatening mystery is not merely unfortunate for women—whose cause he might otherwise have given some early, though doubtless futile, assistance—but also has profound consequences for his teachings about men, about humanness, politics, and autonomy. Because he could not think (or at any rate, did not write) about women as fellow citizens but instead rested even his republican politics on a misogynyist ideal of manliness, his own metaphors and images constantly cast doubt on what he most wants to teach. Two great failures of mutuality, one might say, flaw his best vision of political relationship, the one a sin of omission and the other of commission. The one is his exploitation of—his failure to challenge—the misogyny of his time; the other is his militarist imperialism, his failure to extend into international relations the vision he fashioned of political life within a community. This chapter has argued that the two are intimately interrelated.

As with the problem of action, so with that of membership, Machiavelli's sexual and familial imagery, meant to challenge men out of their concern with private, household matters of wealth and family into the more "manly" realm of political life, also has the opposite effect, arousing images of domination and submission and undermining that capacity for mutuality which citizenship requires. There is, moreover, this difference between the two cases: while Machiavelli's best understanding of action does represent adulthood, an overcoming of childishness, and an acceptance of mature powers and responsibilities, the same cannot be said of his association of political membership with masculinity. Adults are more fit for citizenship than children. Men are not inherently more fit for citizenship than women and will appear so only in a society where women are confined to household and private affairs and denied access to public life. Thus while the equation of humanness with adulthood can lead to distortion if interpreted in terms of an anxious and defensive understanding of adulthood, the equation of humanness with masculinity is distorting not just in terms of an anxious and defensive understanding of masculinity, but in terms of any understanding of masculinity at all. Men who deny the humanity of women are bound to misunderstand their own.

The problem of judgment grows out of the relationship of what is distinctively human to what is natural: our own bodies and animal instincts as well as the natural world around us, out of which we construct civilization, technology, morality, politics. The latter, in turn, imply standards for action and judgment, right and wrong ways to do things, good and evil conduct. The status of those standards is a mystery, a cluster of mysteries. The problem of action earlier raised the question of what constitutes the "beginning" of a community or an individual, how causation and the animal turn into the capacity for action and the human. Now come these closely related questions: How does the causally determined natural turn into the moral and political, capable of choosing right from wrong, of judging and being judged? What is the origin of concepts such as justice, virtue, civility, honor, and the practices connected with them? How does any human individual make the transition? And what, accordingly, is the status of our norms of right conduct and judgment, the basis of their validty? Are they merely conventional? Or are they anchored in nature or in some transcendent authority guaranteeing their validity?

Such philosophical questions become politically acute in times like Machiavelli's, when there is a great disparity between the inherited ideals and standards, on the one hand, and people's actual activities, needs, and feelings, on the other. Traditional forms and ceremonies are experienced as empty, and they no longer sanctify. Traditional rules virtually guarantee failure, for their is "such a difference between how men live and how they ought to live that he who abandons what is done for what ought to be done learns his destruction rather than his preservation."[19] Inherited theories no longer make sense of the world, and actual practice remains chaotic, inconsistent, untheorized. It may be time for new theory, for the (re)creation of value and meaning. But where are they to come from?

The political theorist is not merely an observer but also a teacher, a bridge builder offering a new vision of the familiar world and trying to make it accessible to people through and despite their old ways of seeing. But how does one teach in such times of dislocation in judgment and action? Confronted by such conditions, a theorist may feel that the most urgent task is to destroy the remaining pretensions of existing ideals and unmask those who exploit them. Moved by a yearning for truthfulness, a rage at the prevailing hypocrisy, he may speak in the cynical mode, teaching that ideals are fraudulent devices, not merely conventional but foisted by the powerful on the credulous. He may, that is, equate truth telling with the systematic description of current, exploitive, and hypocritical practice.

Or he may, instead, choose the other side of the gap between ideals and practice, cleaving to the standards to which others only pay lip service—or to some different, perhaps historically earlier, set of ideals—and exhort his audience to live up to those standards. But if the corruption of the time has gone very far, neither of these modes of teaching is likely to be effective. The cynical mode may win popularity but can offer no cure, for it tells only a partial truth and can neither restore nor replace the old commitments. Yet exhortation is likely to fall on deaf ears, for everyone has learned to ignore the familiar cant of preachers and teachers, since taking it seriously so frequently means disaster "among so many who are not good."

Machiavelli is sometimes drawn to each of these modes: cynical in the image of the fox, horatory in relation to the Founder. Yet at his best he transcends and synthesizes both into what one may justly call a political and humanist realism: a truth-telling theory that perceives in the objective world not only the corrupt and exploitive practices currently pursued, but also their disastrous results, and therefore also the potential practical reality that ideals have. He seeks to theorize the *verità effettuale della cosa,* but that includes human achievement and potential along with human failure and corruption.[20]

The cynical theorist, one might say, wants to define human nature by what is most basic in us, to find a secure foundation on which to build: "*Erst kommt das Fressen, dann kommt die Moral.*"[21] The horatory theorist, by contrast, defines human nature by what is highest in us, our capacities for transcendence. Machiavelli ultimately rejects both alternatives and the choice between them. At his best, he retains the cynical fox's animus against utopian, empty, and hypocritical ideals, but not the conviction that all ideals are of necessity like that. He retains the foxy premise that standards of right are human artifacts, and thus cannot be legitimated by their origins, but not the conclusion that they must therefore be illegitimate. His deepest commitment here, as on so many topics, is to action, but responsible, creative action: glory. We are the creatures capable of transforming what is basic into what is glorious. That capacity makes possible real but limited—limited but real—human greatness, and so it defines our responsibilities. Precisely because ideals are humanly made, leaving their care and maintenance to some transcendent power amounts to a failure of responsibility. Yet precisely because some ideals promote an objectively better life for human beings than do others, the cynical refusal to judge and act is equally a failure of responsibility.

But here again the sexual and familial imagery Machiavelli invokes tends partly to undermine his teaching. Challenging his audience to a manly acceptance of the burdens of human self-fashioning, his imagery often makes that task seem more than human, suggesting a flight into either cynicism, excusing us from the effort, or submission to some rescuing father who will make the effort for us.

Machiavelli teaches that ideals like virtue and honor, justice and civility—both how we conceive them and how we practice them—are humanly determined. The goals people pursue, the standards by which they judge and act, are shaped by their upbringing, training, and experience, what Machiavelli in the largest sense calls *educazione*. This includes parental example and admonition, schooling, the discipline of law and public authority, military discipline, religion, and the whole way of life (*modo del vivere*) into which members of a community are initiated.[22] Yet each of these shaping elements is itself subject to human choice and sustained only by effort. All of them were arranged better in ancient times than in corrupt modern Florence.

Some conclude that consequently Machiavelli must also teach that there is no absolute, objective right and wrong, such standards being merely conventions and the only absolute being our origin in nature, which makes no moral distinctions. Indeed, there are passages in Machiavelli supporting such a reading, for the vision of the fox is a cynical vision. But this is not his final or his best position. Rather, he wants to maintain that although man-made and sustained only by effort, ideals enacted are as real as any natural phenomenon. The tyrant is "deceived by a false good and a false glory," which is to say that the difference between false and real glory is as objective as any other fact about which some may be deceived.[23] No mere convention can change such deception into truth. The ideals and practices we create are anchored on the one side in natural need and capacity, on the other side in their practical consequences for human life.

These questions can be fruitfully explored in Machiavelli's treatment of the great Ciompi Rebellion, the revolt of Florence's wool workers, "the poorest of the people." At the height of his account of the rebellion, Machiavelli presents an invented speech he ascribes to a man identified only as "one of the most fiery and of greatest experience among" the rebels.[24] It is a cynical speech, in effect claiming that all property is theft, all power domination, every relationship exploitative and concluding that the workers should take by force whatever they can, in order to dominate and exploit their former masters.

By "nature," the speaker argues, all men are equal; some claim to be of ancient and noble lineage, but that is mere convention, "for all men, since they had one and the same beginning, are equally ancient." The fundamental reality is nature; all else is mere convention and as superficial as clothing on the body.

> Strip us all naked; you will see us all alike; dress us then in their clothes and the[m] in ours; without doubt we shall seem noble and they ignoble, for only poverty and riches make us unequal.

Poverty and riches, moreover, are both equally unnatural, for "God and Nature have put all men's fortunes in their midst," so that wealth goes to those who take it. In the resulting struggle, theft is more effective than work, "the bad arts" more effective than "the good."

Indeed, great wealth, power, and status are always illegitimate at their origin, "attained . . . by means of either fraud or force." Only the "rapacious and fraudulent" ever emerge from poverty, only the "unfaithful and bold" from "servitude." Small crimes may be punished, but "great and serious ones are rewarded"; and the successful conqueror, whatever his means, is never "disgraced" by what he has done. After seizing what they want "with trickery or with violence," the conquerors "conceal the ugliness of their acquisition" by imposing a legitimizing terminology of ideals. Under such "false title," their ill-gotten gains come in retrospect to look "honorable" to the credulous exploited. Thus the wool workers should not be either "frightened" or "shamed" by the invocation of terms like "noble" and "ignoble," by appeals to conscience or to "ill fame," the judgment of others. All of these are mere conventions deployed by the winners to fool the losers. One must look behind ideals and conventions, including religion, to the natural realities of physical life: "When people fear hunger and prison, as we do, they cannot and should not have any fear of hell." Those who heed the call of "conscience" are naive, disappointingly inadequate as "men," since their credulity prevents them from acting. "Spirited men" act boldly to seize "the opportunity that Occasion brings," that is "offered . . . by Fortune."

On this basis, the agitator teaches the wool workers not merely that they should act, but specifically that they ought "to use force" whenever they "get the chance." Since all power is illegitimate in origin, relations of domination and exploitation are the only possible ones. The only issue is who will be on top, and the speaker urges the wool workers to take their turn, so that the former masters "will have to complain of and fear you," as the wool workers now complain of and fear their masters.

Here is an eloquent formulation of the view that "beginnings" are illegitimate, a return to nature and the body and to force. Anything beyond force, fraud, and the physical is mere convention externally imposed for exploitative purposes. But does Machiavelli mean it? The speech is written with verve and relish; one imagines Machiavelli enjoyed its writing. It is peppered with familiar Machiavellian maxims, suggesting a continuity with the main body of his works. And it is, of course, an invention, inserted in the *Florentine Histories* without any logical necessity.

But Machiavelli frames the speech in disparaging commentary. He says that it was made "in order to arouse" the workers and succeeded in "greatly inflam[ing] their spirits, which were of themselves already hot for evil."[25] The person in the Ciompi Rebellion for whom Machiavelli expresses admiration is not this anonymous (though "experienced") speaker, but Michele di Lando, a real historical figure who became the leader of the rebellion in its later stages but resisted the extreme claims of the poor, "determined to quiet the city," and who "publicly proclaimed that nobody should burn or rob anything."[26] Machiavelli says that Michele di Lando surpassed all others in his time "in courage, in prudence, and in goodness," and that he deserved "to be numbered among the glorious few who have greatly benefitted their native city."[27]

It is not obvious what to make of Machiavelli's praise for Michele di Lando and of the moderate framework in which the cynical speech is set. His letters indicate that Machiavelli felt constrained in writing the *Histories* by the fear of offending the powerful, particularly the pope who had commissioned the work. So it is in principle possible that the moderating framework is deception, the speech expressing his real views and teachings.

That interpretation becomes impossible, however, if one recalls the overall theme of the *Florentine Histories*, Machiavelli's investigation of why the Florentine Republic, unlike the Roman, was always unstable. His explicit answer to that question, it will be recalled, concerns factions, "unreasonable and unjust" demands, and a failure to observe limits in dealing with the opposition. Indeed, the preface to the book of the *Histories* that deals with the Ciompi Rebellion attributes Florentine weakness to the fact that whenever any group or faction gained power in the city, it tried to destroy its opponents utterly, making laws "not for the common profit but altogether in favor of the conqueror."[28]

Although the speech does invoke something like courage ("spirited men") and "honor" and does mention the hope of having "more liberty . . . than in the past," and although it mentions the wool workers' complaints about the masters' "avarice" and "injustice," it does not really, consistently address the ideals implied in such words.[29] It addresses only conquest and revenge, a simple inversion of past oppression, not liberty but what Machiavelli in the preface to the next book of the *Histories* identifies as "license." Florence, he says there, has never been well organized, having had at most a "semblance of republican government," fluctuating as its ruler and constitutions varied,

> not between liberty and slavery, as many believe, but between slavery and license. The promoters of license, who are the people, and the promoters of slavery, who are the nobles, praise the mere name of liberty, for neither of these classes is willing to be subject either to the laws or to men.[30]

In a city that can rightly "be called free," by contrast, there is reciprocity between opposing classes and groups, and an awareness of common membership in an association valuable to all.

By these criteria, the speech to the wool workers is licentious, advocating a politics without limits or mutuality, and counseling the workers to exploit the public life for their private advantage by threatening "damage" to "the city."[31] The speaker acknowledges that the consequence of the kind of politics he advocates is "that men devour one another," but he can envisage no alternative. On the contrary, precisely from the observation that men devour each other he concludes they should therefore use force whenever they can.[32] The speech thus displays a fundamental inconsistency characteristic of the fox's cynical stance. It employs terms like "fraud" and the conventional contrast between "bad" and "good" ways of getting ahead, "bad" and "good" men. Yet it also insists that

standards of good and bad are based on fraud and force, all equally exploitive. If the world is as the speaker claims, the conventional terms and
distinctions are meaningless, and he is not entitled to their use. Thus
it does not fully make sense to claim that moral standards originate in
exploitation and fraud, for the latter terms already imply the existence of
standards; if there is no such thing as virtue in mere nature, there is no
such thing as fraud, either.

Not only is the speech incoherent in this sense, but there is also a
problem, given the speaker's premises, about the nature of collectivity in
his audience or in the city. "You see the preparations of our adversaries,"
he says, "let us get ahead of their plans."[33] Thus he presents two opposed
collectivities: "we" and "they." Hitherto "they" ruled "us"; soon "we"
shall dominate "them." It is taken for granted that "I" gain if "we" win.
But what will be the relations among "us" if all human power is based on
force or fraud? If what the speaker says is true, then surely the audience
ought to be as suspicious of his motives as of the masters', and indeed of
each other's as well. The only "natural" unit, it seems, is the isolated
individual. There is no reason for anyone among the oppressed to suppose
that he will gain even private liberty if "our side" wins, for all that unites
"us" is our common oppression, which will disappear when "we" win.
Having won, or perhaps already in the process of winning, we shall do
what men have always done: "devour one another." Yet if we do not trust
each other, we cannot win; as the speaker points out, it is precisely because the masters are "disunited" that "we" have hopes of seizing power
now: "Their disunion will give us the victory."[34]

Despite its eloquence, despite its use of Machiavellan idiom, then, the
speech to the wool workers is not an articulation of Machiavelli's views,
both because he does distinguish between truth and fraud, benefit and
exploitation, and because he believes in and teaches about the value of
collectivity based on a well-founded mutual trust that is not naive. The
fact that standards are human artifacts does not make them fraudulent or
illegitimate, for such notions are themselves the products of standards.
Still, how any conventional creation can be (or become) more than arbitrary does pose a mystery, like the mysteries of how matter can be (or
become) animate, how animal can be (or become) human, how individuals can be (or become) collectivity.

Another approach to that mystery, the apparent opposite of cynicism, is
the edifying exhortation to duty. It, too, attracts Machiavelli, yet is ulti-

mately rejected by him. And though opposed to cynicism in a way, it is actually cynicism's flip side: inside the Founder image lurks the fox. Consider the famous charge leveled by Edmund Burke against the *philosophes*, that their irreverent questioning of authority would soon destroy "all the pleasing illusions which made power gentle and obedience liberal," leaving mankind exposed in all its "naked, shivering nature." What sort of illusions? Burke illustrates: to the *philosophes* "a queen is but a woman, a woman is but an animal—and an animal not of the highest order."[35]

Calling such beliefs "illusions," Burke ratifies through his choice of word the cynical view he means to oppose, that a queen is nothing more or other than an animal. To believe otherwise is to hold an illusion, he says, but one with vitally important practical consequences. Where such illusions are believed, power will actually be gentle and obedience liberal. Indeed, the urgency of Burke's larger argument makes clear that he thinks even more—the survival of civilization itself—is at stake in such illusions. Why, then, does he insist that people must believe *illusions* to preserve the very tangible and *unillusory* benefits civility and culture bring to all? Why cannot those benefits directly motivate a knowing, disillusioned civility?

Several answers are possible here, all part of Burke's argument at some point. First, there is the problem of human passion. People—or at least most people, or people of certain social classes—lack sufficient self-control to do what is prudentially in their best interest, unless it is reinforced by certain illusions that engage stronger passions than prudence ever can. Second, even in merely rational and prudential terms, while everyone clearly benefits from civilization, an individual might perhaps benefit even more if *everyone else* were moral and civilized, while he alone was consummately selfish. Third, the prudential outlook itself, which calculates consequences in terms of costs and benefits, may require a character structure tending to undermine morality and the public good.

To some extent, Machiavelli shares each of these views. He says that most men will "be good" only out of fear; that most people want only security and gain rather than glory; that anyone introducing important innovations must manipulate popular illusions, because "many good things are known to a prudent man that are not in themselves so plainly rational that others can be persuaded of them."[36] And yet Machiavelli also at times envisions a secular reverence achieved without reification, a human autonomy that is neither dependent on illusion nor furthered by hortatory preaching. Maurice Merleau-Ponty calls it a political "principle of communion" and says that "by putting conflict and struggle at the origins of social power," Machiavelli "did not mean to say that agreement was impossible," but only "meant to underline the condition for *a power which does not mystify*, that is, participation in a common situation."[37]

At his best, Machiavelli envisions a free politics of citizens holding themselves and each other to the civil limits defined by their particular tradition, a tradition they recognize to be conventional yet honor or alter as conscious "co-founders." They not only live by their principles but choose those principles consciously, and collectively take responsibility for them. Thus Machiavelli anticipates Kant's claim that moral autonomy requires not just acting in accord with principles, but positing those principles for oneself. Kant even calls this positing "lawmaking," but he is speaking metaphorically.[38] Machiavelli, as always most political, thinks that full autonomy requires not just metaphorical legislation in the mind to govern one's own conduct, but literal and public political engagement by which the members of a community together continually (re)define their shared way of life.

Such a citizenry cherish their shared *nomos* despite its conventionality and the arbitrariness of its origins, both because it defines who they now are, and because of the way of life it now secures. Thus they look to prudential consequences, yet not in narrowly self-interested ways; they look to glory and the public good, but these ideals have tangible content in their lives; tangible content includes not just profit but principle. Thus they think in terms of a glory that transcends, yet remains connected with, interest and need; and in terms of a self that is distinct from others, yet remains connected with them and with principle. The glory is made meaningful by its content of practical gratification; the needs it gratifies are enlarged and humanized by being tied to glory.

As with respect to action and membership, so too with respect to judgment, what is needed is synthesis: a transcendence that is also a continuity. To be human, our standards must transcend the animal, the natural, the necessary, mere force. Yet to be meaningful for us they must also retain—and so we must frequently renew—contact with their "origins" in natural need, the body, infancy, and its earliest relationships. A right understanding of the problem of judgment, a reverence without reification, thus rests as the *vivere civile* does on the mature human capacities for mutuality and limitation, for judicious trust and trustworthiness. And since these in turn are anchored in the "basic trust" of infancy, once again Machiavelli's best teaching is threatened wherever his imagery evokes misogynist fears and unresolved infantile conflicts.

The psychological counterpart of the problem of judgment in political theory is, in Freudian terms, the difference between repression and sublimation, the former corresponding to superego domination, the hortatory false piety toward authority associated with the Founder image; the latter corresponding to ego strength and an authority that is not reified. Freud himself never systematically explicated the difference between repression and sublimation.[39] Both are possible outcomes of the encounter of infantile libidinal drives with parents, significant other people, and the world of physical objects and processes. Repression occurs when a forbidden libidinal wish, blocked by the child's fear of punishment, is forced into the unconscious, where it continues to press for gratification. Energy is continually expended in keeping it unconscious, and neurotic symptoms may result from the inner conflict. Alternatively, however, the libidinal drive may be redirected to a substitute goal that is not forbidden, as when sexual energy is rechanneled into artistic, scientific, or cultural endeavor. Here the substitute activity is a genuine gratification that satisfies the libidinal drive, so no continuing expenditure of inner energy is required. Repression concerns the perpetual struggle between id and superego, which the ego attempts to mediate; sublimation concerns how the ego itself is constituted. A certain amount of repression, a certain amount of instinctual renunciation, is inevitable for anyone in any society; indeed, in his later, pessimistic writings Freud argues that neurosis might well be the necessary price for civilization.[22] But without sublimation, without the rechanneling of libidinal energy into acculturation, we could not become human persons at all.

We all begin in infancy, with our instinctual drives. And in a certain mood it may seem that the infant we once were was our only true self, all of its subsequent development a mere overlay of social pressures and external demands. But that does not really make sense, for it would leave the self an impoverished thing indeed. The infant is not yet a developed person, is incapable of action or meaningful choice; its needs and pleasures are infantile. Furthermore, that would mean that the whole development of human culture and history, the self-creation of the human species, was a series of accidents, a process devoid of any agency. If the adult person who acts is only an alien overlay over the core of true self, then not only the true "me" is incapable of action or responsibility, but so were my parents, grandparents, and their ancestors. "Society" shaped us all, but society itself is merely a collection of such nonagents, and no one is responsible for anything.

No matter how radically conceived, the liberation of the true self from alien social impositions cannot mean a return to infancy, for then there would be no self to liberate, no one *there* to take advantage of the liberty, but only total dependence. The *id* is not a self. The initial instinctual drives are essentially the same for all of us at the start of life; what makes us into unique individuals is the living of a human life, or at least the living through of a human childhood. In that sense, the self is a history much more truly than it is an infant, a body, or an id. Only through our initiation into the cultural world of our parents, ancestors, and peers do we each become capable of particularity as a human self.

To be sure, *some* of the habits and attitudes we acquire in growing up really are and remain alien impositions, and at some point in adolescence or later we may reject them, more or less successfully, as demands that others imposed on us but that we do not ratify. But the self that rejects this or that aspect of its upbringing, of itself, is also a product of that upbringing. It makes no sense to suppose that I might reject as alien every aspect of myself, or even every aspect except those rudiments of self with which I was born. For the very capacity to make such rejections, and the standards by which I make them, are the products of my development. By the time I am capable of choice, undertaking deliberately to change myself or the world, I already am some particular individual person with concepts, commitments, standards, expectations, ideals, some of which may be alien impositions I have been indoctrinated to accept, but not all of which can be.

In that sense, the individuated self, the person capable of responsible action, is the product of convention, not nature; or rather, of the interaction between nature and convention, infant and world. For there is, of course, historical continuity between the infant I once was and the person I become. And my individual psyche, although it is equivalent neither to my body nor to its natural drives and needs, nevertheless can exist only—how should one put it?—in the most intimate, necessary, one-to-one relationship with this particular body. Psychic life remains embedded in physical life. Furthermore, at least some of the social convention internalized as we grow up becomes so fundamental a part of our selves that it is as if natural, a kind of "second nature" that behaves and must be regarded *for us* just like the truly or originally natural. And this second nature includes not merely powers and impulses, but also standards of conduct and judgment, goals, ideals.

Of course we can be and indeed often are wrong about ourselves, about what in us is alien and what must be accepted as given, or even revered as authoritative. We do not always live up to our own standards (that is part of what is meant by standards of conduct); but we violate them only at a price to ourselves.

Although a community is not a person, still, much of this is true of human communities as well. They, too, are formed not just at a moment of "birth" or founding but, on the one hand, have an underlying "nature" that would-be founders must accept as given, and a continuing "natural" life of productive and reproductive needs and activities, and, on the other hand, develop through their history, which they both make and suffer. They, too, might be said to acquire out of that history something like a "second nature"—cultural features so fundamental to the members' character and relationships that they must be regarded as if natural *for this community*. And this second nature also includes some of the community's standards and commitments. So Machiavelli, for example, speaks of the hereditary ruler as a "natural" sovereign or prince, allegiance and deference to whom has become an unquestioned part of his subjects' very selves.[41] Yet communities, like individuals, frequently have illusions about themselves and their nature; in particular, they frequently have ideological illusions maintained because they serve the interests of some, to the detriment of others and of the whole.

For both individual and community, then, one can say: the self is a product of its history, and thus conventional, yet remains rooted in nature, defining the very self. Nevertheless, that core may be mistaken and violated by the self in action and judgment. Then there can be moments of insight, in which we recover aspects of the self that have been lost, distorted, or violated. Such moments may be quotidian, or sufficiently dramatic to be experienced as a "rebirth." That means: a starting over afresh because no longer "hung up on" the past; a recovery, therefore, of the self as free actor, of capacities that had been hidden by reification; a recovery, also, of the self as the product of its history and of those parts of that history that had been distorted or disguised.

That way of thinking about Machiavelli's "return to beginnings" appeared already in discussing the problem of action; now a different aspect emerges in the context of judgment. The return to beginnings is a new and right insight into what ideals, standards, and commitments are sacred to us and simultaneously a recognition of our capacity to make—and concomitant responsibility for making, revising, sustaining—them. For the individual, these are moments when "ego comes to be where id was," to paraphrase Freud; moments when repression is replaced by sublimation. For a community, they are moments when the citizens recover awareness of their stake in the public and at the same time redefine the public in terms of justice, thereby becoming free to act effectively as a community instead of being deadlocked in factional strife or resentfully bound to the past in the form of political vengeance. Though a community is not a person, still there are political counterparts to repression and sublimation: the former, a polity of domination, where some make the rules by which others are forced to live; the latter, a polity of mutuality, where the citizens share jointly in self-government.

Machiavelli does not talk in psychological terms, yet he does address the problem of human drives and natural needs and discuss how they must be transformed in order to make men fit for the *vivere civile*, to make animals human. What he says about them differs to some extent, depending on which sort of need he is considering and which image of manhood is most salient at the time. But in general, Machiavelli at his best teaches, first, that human drives and appetites are natural and have to be accepted; ideals that ignore them are vain. Second, however, too much of any of these drives, or the wrong way of handling them, destroys civilization and *virtù*; thus they are the weapons of mystical feminine power implanted in men. But, third, their open and direct expression and reasonable gratification is the right way of handling them, the way to prevent their excesses. His successful synthesis is a vision of sublimation; its failure takes the form of a vision of repression, the punitive discipline of the Founder.

Machiavelli discusses three groups of such drives: hunger or greed, ambition with its concomitant aggression, and sensuality or lust. Politically, each of them threatens to corrupt public life through privatization. Ambition, however, is also the source of civilization and a healthy public life; avarice is more difficult to transform into public terms, and sexuality Machiavelli mostly leaves to repression (and the occasional evasion of repressive authority). In each case, the key to transforming need into value, and private into public, is the capacity to acknowledge limits. Each natural need must be given its due but must be distinguished from its unhealthy extension into limitless craving, when the natural need is mediated by anxiety and becomes obsessive and insatiable. The truly human life requires acknowledgment of and provision for our real needs but is undermined by the distorted extensions of drives beyond need. Proper provision for needs also helps to prevent such unhealthy extension. So the greatest danger is the denial of human drives, the setting of ideals for man that are unrelated to his real needs, the sort of "humility, abjectness, and contempt for human beings" that is taught by the Church.[42]

Ambition, and the closely correlated problem of aggression, are most instructive here. Ambition in itself is not a vice but a normal part of human nature that must be accepted; yet it is also a fury that does evil among men. Were it not for ambition, the desire for mastery, men would never grow up, would never leave the matriarchal household or create civilization and the city. Yet excessive ambition, ambition handled in the wrong way, is also what undermines civilization and politics. The distinctions to be drawn here are between two forms ambition may take, and two ways it may be handled. Direct and relatively self-confident ambition, the desire to grow, to develop one's capacities and be admired for one's achievements—these are all healthy features without which we could not reach human maturity; they are also capable of (intermittent) satisfaction, like any natural hunger. And they are ready, under appropriate conditions, to be channeled toward public ends and thereby to make men genuinely public spirited; they are capable of producing a right understanding and pursuit of glory. They are to be contrasted to the resentful, envious, self-denigrating, masochistic ambition that knows no limit because it wants to undo the past. Similarly, the open and direct expression of ambition must be distinguished from its indirect and hidden pursuit; the institutions that politicize ambition and make it public, from those that privatize it and drive it underground.

The resentful and insatiable sort of ambition is by its very nature depoliticizing and makes people unfit for citizenship. It leads them to prefer vengeance to success at any other undertaking; thus they court disaster, for instance by inviting foreign forces into the city to support their side in a factional dispute. Where this condition becomes widespread, even men of *virtù* find it almost impossible to pursue the public good, for the resentfully ambitious are filled with envy of other men's glory, "grudging," "ungrateful," ever ready to "censure" and bring others down, even if all suffer as a result.[43]

The wrong sort of ambition can be minimized, and its dangerous effects for political life controlled to some extent, by acknowledging the right sort of ambition as natural, acknowledging the right sort of conflict as healthy, and providing institutional channels for their expression. "The malignant humors that spring up in men" must somehow "find vent," and where they are not permitted "lawful" and open expression, the will find "unlawful" methods of private revenge that produce factions and civil war.[44] Institutions for the public, open expression of ambition and anger, like the Roman institution of "accusations," will minimize both the formation of resentful, private ambition and its danger to public life by forcing all into public channels and exposing false, merely envious charges for what they are. Ambition and aggression then must be acknowledged, even encouraged, and brought out into the open.

The case of hunger and avarice or greed is less clear-cut. Obviously, human beings have bodies that need food; and hunger and the desire "to acquire" are therefore natural and inevitable. Only a fool would locate a city where it might look "glorious" but its inhabitants have no way to make a living. Natural hunger, however, is also capable of (intermittent) satiation through human effort. Its extension into avarice, greed, the insatiable craving for further acquisition for its own sake, is a different matter. It may, in a way, grow out of the natural need, yet it can outweigh even that need itself: the miser will starve himself in order to add to his riches. Avarice is, one might say, natural hunger transformed by anxiety, a vain attempt to provide against all future hunger; it reflects a fundamental distrust of the adult capacity to feed oneself (and others).

Like the resentful sort of ambition, avarice privatizes and sets people in rivalry with each other in destructive ways. Being insatiable, it instigates action without the recognition of limits, of commonality, promoting factionalism in the city and displacing the craving for glory by petty and private goals. Machiavelli's charge against the Florentine bourgeoisie is that there is no "limit or measure to their greed." They "plunder" each other of their goods; they avoid paying their taxes; they "sell justice"; and they "thirst not for true glory but for despicable honors depending on hates, enmities, disputes, factions."[45] Like Churchmen, "men in trade" are incapable of soldiering, the direct expression of aggression; thus they are incapable of autonomy, forced to follow "the Fortune of others."[46] All Florence's "evils," Machiavelli wrote a friend, "proceed from our being in the hands of priests and merchants; neither the one nor the other knows how to manage arms."[47] What is worse, neither understands the meaning of glory, so they pursue the wrong sort of goal.

Ideally, Machiavelli would like to treat this problem in terms of the opposing interests and "humors" of different classes, reintegrated through political struggle. Bourgeois avarice must be tempered by the nobility's military spirit and ambition for glory. But in the absence of a Florentine nobility, he must try to teach men of avarice about the value of glory, an extraordinarily difficult task of theoretical bridge building. For the only appeal the merchants can understand is to self-interest, yet their orientation to avarice and self-interest is precisely what must be overcome. Speak to them of glory, and they cannot hear; but speak to them of interest, and you cannot express your message. So Machiavelli insists, on the one hand, that *virtù* and the *vivere civile* are the only effective ways to secure wealth, that "riches multiply in a free country," and on the other hand, that the concern for wealth privatizes people and tends to destroy *virtù*: "Well-ordered republics" keep "their treasuries rich and their citizens poor."[48] In addition, the topic of avarice is also psychologically more troubling than that of ambition, for ambition draws men away from infantile dependence and is not itself an impulse of sensuality or nurturance. For men troubled about dependence, ambition is thus a "safer" drive with which to deal than either avarice or lust. Sensuality, sex, and lust are, in a way, most difficult of all for Machiavelli. Here there seems to be no way to transmute private into public welfare, and the best that can be hoped for is the imposition of a severe, public discipline in support of monogamy and patriarchy, combined with clandestine private freedom for men to pursue sexual pleasure. The reproduction of the species is of course beneficial to the community as well as instrumentally pleasurable, but Machiavelli is not prepared to argue, in accord with Church teaching, that good men will find their sexual pleasure only in the begetting of legitimate children. Nor is he prepared to challenge the mores of his time by suggesting that species reproduction might be reorganized in ways more consonant with human needs and pleasure. Thus "women" remain, in his theory, the most mysterious and in a way the most dangerous threat. Again, there is not much point in blaming Machiavelli for having failed to challenge the misogyny of his time—a topic that surely would have seemed to him remote from his explicit concerns—yet misogyny repeatedly works counter to his best political teachings.

Concerning judgment, once again Machiavelli summons us to an acknowledgment of our adult human powers and responsibilities; but he does so by summoning males to their manhood. And once again that turns out to defeat as much as to serve his purpose. For insofar as adulthood and full humanity are pursued out of anxiety about dependence, their pursuit will be distorted by childish fantasies and fears, the need to prove what cannot be proved because it is forever in anxious doubt. Men anxious about dependence will fear to trust anyone or anything and thus will be inclined toward cynicism. They will fear the feminine "other" inside themselves and will thus be powerfully drawn to hortatory hero worship and to repressive ideals. Fearing nurturance or other sensual gratification except under stringent safeguards of discipline, they will seethe with impotent anger, prefer vengeance to direct gratification, and identify with their—real or fantasied—oppressor, all of which tends to generate a conception of autonomy that blocks access to its real achievement.

Machiavelli urged people to assume deliberate, active, collective control over the conditions of their lives. Yet he urged action framed by the recognition of limits: limits on what is historically possible, here and now, and humanly possible anywhere; limits on what is politically acceptable, capable of enlisting the support of fellow citizens; limits on what is right and deserving of true glory. In teaching this delicately balanced multiple synthesis, Machiavelli also articulated a right understanding of that topic so central to Renaissance experience: autonomy.

A wrong understanding of human autonomy, by which Machiavelli himself was frequently tempted but from which he tried to wean us, is as a kind of sovereignty, a self-contained isolation, a solipsistic fantasy of omnipotence. Here, to be autonomous would mean either to be utterly alone, needing no one and nothing outside oneself, or else to be singular in privilege and power—the only person among objects, the only human among animals, the only god among humans—capable of dominating and free to exploit whatever is outside the self.

Machiavelli at his best, by contrast, teaches an autonomy that acknowledges our necessary interdependencies: that human freedom lies not in eradicating or escaping our necessary connections with others like ourselves, but in acknowledging them and using them to liberate us from other, unnecessary dependencies. "If men wish to be free," as Hannah Arendt has said, "it is precisely sovereignty they must renounce."[49] That is the point of Machiavelli's distinctions between liberty and license, between true glory and that false glory by which tyrants are deceived, between genuine autonomy and "doing whatever you want." Both princes and republics, he says, need "to be regulated by the laws; because a prince who can do what[ever] he wants to is crazy; [and] a people that can do what[ever] it wants to is not wise."[50]

True autonomy is a matter of accurate self-knowledge and responsible self-government. For both individual and community, it is a matter of getting right the synthesis between our determinant past and our freedom to act, between our objective interconnectedness and our individual agency, between our natural beginnings and our capacity for transcendence. Only through recognizing our particular past and the present world and self it has created do we become free to act effectively. Only in shared political interaction can we come to know accurately, and to take responsibility for, what we are doing. That limits our personal freedom because each of us is only one among many citizens but also expands it because together we can take charge of the social conditions that we collectively create, that would otherwise constrain our individual lives as alien powers. Only by transforming instinct into authority, recognizing the demands of both nature and our human commitments, do we become free simultaneously of and in our necessities.

That is the essence of Machiavelli's understanding of action within a context of necessity, of individual *virtù* within a context of interdependence, of transcendent value as anchored in particular, secular, historical life. The breakdown of synthesis along any one of these dimensions is "corruption": the corruption of passivity, of privatization, of cynicism, but also the corruption of mindless action for its own sake, or of hypocritical exhortation to "public" or "higher" duties that are empty. Along each of these dimensions synthesis has always to be actively made. Yet its making is not arbitrary but requires a certain reverence toward self, world, and ideals. The experience of political action among fellow citizens was for Machiavelli the best way to achieve this sort of self-knowledge. Where that process broke down into corruption, as it always tended to do, the next best hope for its restoration lay in leadership, of the sort employing "the way of freedom." Where even the necessary leadership seemed lacking, or people were so corrupt that available leadership could not help them, there was perhaps an outside chance that political theory might serve. In each case the point was returning people to themselves: to their connection with past and future, to their connection with each other, to their connection with nature and human values, to their capacity for action and a right understanding of the context in which that action must take place.

That is the heart of what Machiavelli has to teach us. Yet he himself was not able to sustain this vision. On certain subjects, such as relations between men and women, he never achieved it; on others, such as international relations, he at most defined a set of problems and questions pointing toward it. Even in discussing the *vivere civile* he was unable to sustain the vision consistently. Where he lost it, the loss was correlated with images and metaphors about sex roles and familial relations; particularly with the fear of dependence and of malevolent feminine power, and consequently with an anxious and defensive stress on autonomy, solipsistically conceived, and machismo, whether expressed in the cult of violence, in cynicism, or in submission to a supermasculine leader.

Machiavelli summons us from apathy, private acquisitions, and reactive violence to heroism and to glory. How shall we assess that summons? Heroism, like so many familiar and apparently simple concepts, turns out on closer inspection to be a profoundly ambiguous notion. Consider two contrasting views of what it might mean; call them the traditionally "masculine" and the traditionally "feminine" view. In the traditionally masculine view, the summons to heroism is a call to leave behind lower for higher things; to give one's life meaning and purpose by the willingness to sacrifice physical comfort and even life itself for some noble ideal; to leave the household for the public realm, there to express one's unique individuality in connection with something larger and more valuable than self. Without such opportunity to pursue heroism, human life would be impoverished. And so the men march out to war in pursuit of glory.

But now comes the subversive, the traditionally "feminine" view. The women watch the men depart, look at each other, and shake their heads: there they go again, the fools, making themselves feel important with all that fine rhetoric and shiny equipment, pretending to be fierce to hide their vulnerability. They are marching off to kill other people like themselves—and like us!—just so that they can get away from us and the kids for a while. And we are left, as usual, to cope with the true realities: to tend to the children, the harvest, the cooking and weaving that keep bodies alive.

What shall we say of this ancient confrontation of views? Surely there is something right in each. Surely the summons to heroism and glory is often a mask for privilege and exploitation, or for anxious flight from reality. But surely also a life confined merely to the household and care of the body is impoverished. Exclusion from community self-government and a share in making history is a deprivation. To lose or to flee contact with either the public or the private is to lose a part of our humanity. That is as true for the housewife whose life is empty as for her executive husband who imagines that clean shirts appear in his drawer by magic; as true for the alienated worker or apathetic peasant as for the privileged "movers and shakers" who live off of, and are utterly dependent on, the productive labor of others.

Machiavelli at his best summons us to heroism rightly understood: to public action for higher goals that nevertheless serve our natural and private needs, action that recognizes both our vulnerability and our capacity as creators and judges. He strives for, and sometimes achieves, a synthesis of the traditionally "masculine" and "feminine" views of heroism. But insofar as he excludes or encourages his readers to exclude the women and things feminine from the vision, the synthesis is bound to be lost. Heroism becomes machismo and embodies the wrong conception of autonomy, as sovereignty and domination. The participatory, republican politics of freedom does coexist in Machiavelli's political theory with protofascism; the key to their complex relationship lies in the metaphor that "Fortune is a woman."

Notes

1. I do not mean to suggest that Machiavelli's and Aristotle's political thought run parallel in all important respects; obviously they do not.

2. Georg Wilhelm Friedrich Hegel, *Wissenschaft der Logik*, 2 vols. (Nuremberg: J. L. Schrag, 1812–16; reprint, Frankfurt: Suhrkamp, 1969), 1: 152–56, esp. 155.

3. Thomas Hobbes, *Leviathan*, ed. Michael Oakshott (New York: Collier, 1962), 19.

4. Niccolò Machiavelli, *The Discourses*, in *Chief Works and Others*, ed. and trans. Allan Gilbert (Durham: Duke University Press, 1989), 1:291–93. Hereafter, all works referred to by Machiavelli appear in *Chief Works and Others*.

5. On the child's understanding of rules, see Jean Piaget, *The Moral Judgment of the Child*, trans. Marjorie Gabain (New York: Collier Books, 1962), esp. 13–109.

6. Machiavelli, *Florentine Histories* 3: 1146.

7. Ibid.

8. Ibid., 4: 1202.

9. Ibid., 3: 1143.

10. For the first formulation of the idea in these terms see Simone de Beauvoir, *The Second Sex*, trans. H. M. Parshley (New York: A. A. Knopf, 1961), esp. 57, 129. See also Philip Mason, *Prospero's Magic: Some Thoughts on Class and Race* (London: Oxford University Press, 1962).

11. Dorothy Dinnerstein, *The Mermaid and the Minotaur* (New York: Harper and Row, 1976), 107.

12. Ibid., 112, 175. See also 161, 178.

13. Ibid., 187.

14. Ibid., 196.

15. Ibid., 196–97.

16. Robert C. Tucker, ed. *The Marx-Engels Reader*, 2d ed. (New York: W. W. Norton, 1978), 83–84.

17. Hannah Arendt, *The Human Condition* (Chicago: University of Chicago Press, 1974), 8n.

18. Ibid., 8, 7.

19. *The Prince*, chap. 15, 57–58.

20. At least in this respect, Martin Luther faced the same problem in the north of Europe as Machiavelli faced in the south. Striving to become a monk, he was obsessively scrupulous and plagued by doubt, unwilling to make the hypocritical compromises customary in his time. His superiors prescribed the traditional exercises: fast, pray, perform rituals. If you behave like a monk, in time faith will come. But Luther could not accept that solution, feeling that the performance of ritual acts without faith was itself sinful—in effect, hypocrisy toward God—and could produce only more sin, never salvation. Confronting the gap between ideals and practice, he insisted on cleaving to the former; and his personal solution turned out to be meaningful for much of Europe. Machiavelli would have scoffed at the proposition that the problems he was addressing were theological in nature, yet he too refused to settle for hypocrisy, to live with the gap between ideals and practice. And he, too, associated the recovery of meaning, value, and virtue with a renewed and more direct access to true paternal authority.

21. "First comes food, then the moral." But the impact of Brecht's *Fressen*—the German verb for the way animals eat—is lost in translation. Bertolt Brecht, *The Three-Penny Opera*, sc. 6, "Second Three-penny Finale: What Keeps Mankind Alive?" in *Collected Plays*, vol. 2, trans. Ralph Mannheim and John Willett (New York: Random House, 1979).

22. *Discourses* 2: 331; 3: 490; 3: 500; 3: 521; 3: 525; Machiavelli, *Opere* 1: 496, 501.

23. *Discourses* 1: 220; 1: 302.

24. *Florentine Histories* 3: 1159–60 for this and the following quotations.

25. Ibid., 1161.

26. Ibid., 3: 1166.

27. Ibid., 3: 1168.

28. Ibid., 3: 1140.

29. Ibid., 3: 1161, cf. 1160; 3: 1158.

30. Ibid., 4: 1187.

31. Ibid., 3: 1161.

32. Ibid., 1160.

33. Ibid., 1161.

34. Ibid., 1160; cf. 1161; and Mansfield, "Party," in *Machiavelli and the Nature of Political Thought*, ed. Martin Fleischer (New York: Atheneum, 1972), 262.

35. Peter J. Stanlis, ed., *Edmund Burke: Selected Writings and Speeches* (Garden City, N.Y.: Doubleday, 1963), 458.

36. *Discourses* 1: 225.

37. Maurice Merleau-Ponty, *Signs*, trans. Richard C. McCleary (Evanston, Ill.: Northwestern University Press, 1964), 215, my italics.

38. Immanuel Kant, "Metaphysical Foundation of Morals," in *The Philosophy of Kant*, trans. and ed. Carl J. Friedrich (New York: Modern Library, 1949), 186.

39. Sigmund Freud, *Standard Edition of the Complete Psychological Works of Sigmund Freud*, ed. James Strachez, 24 vols. (London: Hogarth Press, 1953–74), esp. 11: 53–54, 14: 94–95; but also 9: 161, 171, 175, 187–89, 197; 11: 78, 132–36, 178–90; 14: 245–48; 19: 207.

40. Ibid., esp. 21: 96–97, 103–5, 108, 139, 143–45; and 9: 193; 11: 190.

41. *The Prince*, chap. 3, 16.

42. *Discourses* 2: 331.

43. "[Golden] Ass," ch. 1, lines 97–99, 752; *La Mandragola*, prologue, 778.

44. *Discourses* 1: 112–16.

45. *Florentine Histories* 3: 1146.

46. Ibid., 1: 1079.

47. Quoted in Ferrara, *Private Correspondence*, 46.
48. *Discourses* 2: 332; 1: 272.
49. Hannah Arendt, "What Is Freedom?" in *Between Past and Future* (New York: World Publishing, 1963), 165.
50. *Discourses* 1: 317.

3

Niccolò Machiavelli

Women as Men, Men as Women, and the Ambiguity of Sex

Arlene W. Saxonhouse

The Female and the Transformations of Values in *The Prince* and *The Discourses*

Readers of Machiavelli's writings always face both the ambiguities and the outrageousness of his words. Machiavelli intends to startle, to shock his readers into questioning their values, their beliefs, and especially the certainties on which they have based their lives. What had been accepted as true is now to be questioned. Natural hierarchies, clear lines of author-ity are undermined as Machiavelli confronts his readers with a chaotic world subject only to an order imposed by the extraordinary efforts of individuals capable of employing extraordinary means to achieve their ends. He had been a Florentine civil servant until his exile during the reign of the Medici at the end of the fifteenth and the beginning of the sixteenth centuries.

During his exile Machiavelli turned to writing what were to become his most famous (or notorious) works, *The Prince* and *The Discourses on the First Ten Books of Titus Livius*. In these works he attempts in a variety of ways to overthrow and transform the certainties on which political thought of the previous two millennia had been based. In the process of breaking down the old hierarchies, he reassesses the sources of political order and turns good into bad, bad into good, virtue into vice, men into women, and women into men—or, more precisely, he makes the differences between what had been opposites so ambiguous that we can no longer tell good from bad or women from men.

To effect this series of transformations of certainties into uncertainties, Machiavelli employs a variety of shocking techniques. One is to use old forms to suggest radically new perspectives. The "mirror of princes" pamphlets, common in Renaissance Italy, which Machiavelli's *The Prince* imitates, had exhorted princes to act according to Christian principles. Machiavelli uses his pamphlet to exhort princes to deceive, to kill their enemies, and to eschew reliance on God. While previous authors had urged the prince to be Christlike, to imitate the man-God, as he ruled the city, Machiavelli says that the prince must imitate the man-beast, the centaur, if he is to be successful in his rule.[1]

Key to his task of teaching men to lower their aims, in effect to learn to be "bad," is the rejection of classical utopian thought. Thus he encourages us, in his oft-quoted phrase, to look at how men act rather than how they ought to act.[2] We must yield our vision of the perfect society, whether it be Plato's city in the *Republic*, Augustine's City of God, or Cicero's Rome, and instead attend to what it is men can do. With powerful rhetoric he calls for a focus on the "effectual truth," that which matters in this life. That "truth" tells us that men act out of self-interest and it underlies the claim, intended to shock all good Christians of his time, that "a man who wishes to make a profession of goodness must come to grief among so many who are not good."

Beginning with chaos, with men as they are, Machiavelli gives his readers the opportunity to create, to found new political regimes, new orders and modes of relationships. There are no preexisting models into which everyone and every regime must fit: there are no ideals, no perfection of form, no ends. Along with the terror with which he confronts his readers as he condones the fratricide, the cruelty, the deceit that must accompany the creation of political order, there is also the opening up of possibilities, of new ways of defining old terms, of changing roles for men and for women, for princes and for subjects released from the world of precise hierarchies characteristic of the medieval period.

Among the certainties that Machiavelli is willing to question creatively is the perspective on the female, which had been captured and crystallized during the Middle Ages by the opposition between Mary and Eve, between good and evil, and, with particular significance for Machiavelli, between submission and action. This dichotomous view of women needs, in Machiavelli's vision, to be reassessed because of its stark opposition between good and evil and because of its failure to recognize the limits of submission and the advantages of domination.

Mary and Eve in Medieval Thought: A Preface to the Transformation of Values in Machiavelli

The medieval mind had thrived on analogy and symbolism to explain the relationship between the human being and the divine, between the individual and the universe. Throughout the Middle Ages, Eve and Mary participated in symbolic representations as opposing female forces. Eve, the temptress, was, in Tertullian's famous phrase, "the gateway to hell." She was sexually provocative, arousing the male's carnal passions and thus preventing his total devotion to the divine spiritual world. The sexuality of Eve and the female in general gave her a power that threatened the male, that caused the original Fall, and that continued to make men act as they should not. Popular among the medieval legends, for example, was that of Aristotle and Phyllis, the mistress of Alexander. So taken with Phyllis's charms was Aristotle that he agreed to get down on all fours and allow her, whip in hand, to ride upon his back. This story, often depicted in the art of the period through the sixteenth century, illustrated how even The Philosopher, as Aquinas called him, could be controlled by female sexuality.[3] The response to this threat was subjection and denigration of women in the art and the literature of the time.[4] The female was to be restrained lest she drag men to their downfall, as Eve and Phyllis had.

Yet Eve also plays a different role, for she reappears for some as a new Eve in the person of the Virgin Mary,[5] just as Christ in some interpretations had become the new Adam. Mary replaces the woman who originally led to the Fall: now, as the mother of Christ, precisely through her passivity and submission, she becomes the source of redemption, she *through* whom God acts, *through* whom the Son of God is born. Though in the early Christian era the focus on Mary was more common in the East, after the twelfth century there was in the West an intensification of the adoration of Mary as the gentle reminder of the potential for salvation.[6] As the bride of God, Mary was analogically associated in Christian theology and iconography with the Church, the bride of Christ. As Mary offered redemption to man through her marriage with God, so the Church offered redemption through its marriage with Christ. The bride analogy, as it is related to the Church, carried with it meekness and submission. In the writings of Paul, the Church and its subservience to Christ parallels the wife in her submission to her husband:

> Wives submit yourself unto your own husbands as unto the Lord. For the husband is the head of the family, as Christ is the head of the church: and he is the saviour of the body. Therefore as the church is subject unto Christ, so let the wives be to their own husbands in everything. Husbands love your wives, even as Christ also loved the church and gave himself for it.[7]

Mary's grace, purity, and redemptive power conform to her submissive role, a role expected of the wife in the family and of the Church before Christ.[8] Her virginity and grace set her up as an ideal of human perfection to counter the image of Eve.

Although these characterizations of Eve and Mary hardly capture the multiplicity of themes surrounding the two female forces in the Christian West at the end of the Middle Ages and into the Renaissance, they do suggest the contrast between action and domination (the evil Eve) and passive submission (the holy Mary). Machiavelli was to take these two portraits of women, transfer them to the men about and for whom he wrote, and transform them by turning the model of the active Eve, exploiting all of her capacity to control others through their passions, sexual or otherwise, into a positive portrait while the passive Mary, subordinate to others, is the symbolic cause of the enslavement of Italy. Throughout Machiavelli's writings, domination, submission, and liberty emerge as central themes. Liberty depends on the capacity to act—indeed, to dominate others, a trait embodied by the seductive Eve, who manipulates others not by her physical power but by sexual means. Slavery is the result of inactive, manipulable men, trained only in the art of submission, of men who in their submission to the Church and to God have become similar to Mary, the Bride of God.

Machiavelli's transformation of the two models of womanhood inherited from medieval thought and iconography underscores the fundamental transvaluation going on in his political philosophy in general. He is an author who can turn pity into cruelty, stinginess into magnanimity, deceit into a virtue, and submission—whether to a husband, Church, God, or the enemy—into a vice.[9] His writings revolutionized political thought by calling into question the traditional virtues, and the virtues and vices of women needed to be as thoroughly transformed as those of the men. Previous certainties for both sexes are made ambiguous. The certainty of the good Mary no longer plays against the evil Eve. The submissive female may not be better than the active, seductive Phyllis who can control the Philosopher who talks of ends and perfection. Indeed, as will be suggested below, men must, in Machiavelli's vision of the world, imitate Eve's capacity to dominate (as captured by his portrayal of *Fortuna*), and they must avoid Mary's submissiveness (as captured by his portrayal of effeminate Christians).

The images of women loom large in Machiavelli's explicitly political works, but women themselves play a relatively minor role. In the following sections we shall consider women's primary role as metaphor or image and their occasional brief appearance in the myriad historical examples that sprinkle Machiavelli's political writings. Here we shall see as well the ambiguity of sex and Machiavelli's own assimilation to the manipulative style of the female. In the second half of this chapter we shall look at Machiavelli's comedies, in which women and men enact roles not prescribed for them by standard social morality, but that show that along with the questioning of good and bad goes the questioning of what it means to be male or female. The disappearance of the old distinctions between virtue and vice parallels the disappearance of the old distinctions between male and female.[10]

Fortuna: The Female as Dominant

In the title of chapter 25 of *The Prince*, Machiavelli asks: "How much is Fortuna able to do in human affairs and in what ways may it be opposed?" He begins to answer his own question noting that some hold that worldly affairs are governed by *Fortuna* and by God. Already there is a tinge of blasphemy, since Machiavelli thus separates God and *Fortuna*. In medieval theology, *Fortuna* is an expression of divine will. She appears capricious because mortals are unable to comprehend the plan behind the apparent chaos of everyday events,[11] but that does not mean the plan is not there. Machiavelli, instead of collapsing God and *Fortuna* into one force, removes God from the equation: "So that our free will not be eliminated, I judge that it may be true that Fortuna controls half our actions, but that she leaves the other half, or so, to us." Thus man and *Fortuna* (not God) face each other and determine the movement of history.

After offering advice on how men must be able to adapt to changing circumstances in order to control, rather than be controlled by, *Fortuna*, Machiavelli explicitly introduces the metaphor of *Fortuna* as a woman. The metaphor is not unusual: from Roman times *Fortuna* had appeared as the fickle female. Machiavelli, though, is to see in this feminine *Fortuna* the exhortation to action, rather than submission to whatever she may bring. Earlier in this chapter, Machiavelli had compared *Fortuna* to violent rivers "that when aroused, inundate the plains, tear down trees and buildings . . . everyone flees before them and everyone yields to their force, without being able in any fashion to stand against them." This *Fortuna*, like Tertullian's woman, is the gateway to hell. She destroys those who have not built dikes against her. Princes (or men), according to Machiavelli, must be prepared to meet this threat: they must build floodgates and embankments so that when the river rages (when the female threatens with her sexuality), her power is confined within prebuilt channels. But when Machiavelli clarifies how we are to contain *Fortuna*, he urges us to become like her. Key to limiting the effects of *Fortuna* is the capacity to change—just as *Fortuna* herself does. The vision of virility that has the soldier standing firm, the warrior never yielding, is in Machiavelli's world a recipe for disaster. Men must instead become women in their capacity to be fickle. They must learn from the female *Fortuna*.

However, after suggesting that most men find it difficult to imitate

women, to "deviate from that to which nature inclines them," he proposes a more traditional masculine confrontation with the feminine force
of mutability when he uses the language of forcible rape. "For Fortuna is
a woman, and it is necessary for one wishing to hold her down to beat
her (batterla) and knock against her." The alternative to learning from
her is violence. Machiavelli adds that Fortuna yields more readily to those
who act boldly than to those who are "cold," those who can match her
passion with their own passion, her actions with their own actions. Indeed, this feminine Fortuna defines how men must act to assert their
masculinity. The male depends on the female and must assimilate himself
to her, whether it be by learning to be fickle or to be bold.

In answer to the question he had asked in his chapter heading, Machiavelli insists that Fortuna the woman can control us completely, if we do
not learn from her how to act. Human affairs can be ruined for those who
meekly submit, and neither adapt nor protect themselves through action.
Man conquers Fortuna only by acknowledging her power and foreseeing
that the stream may turn into a raging torrent. We must, Machiavelli tells
us, deal directly with that passion rather than deny it: indeed, we must
appropriate that passion to ourselves, if we are to survive the torrent.

As Machiavelli engages in his transformation of value terms, he takes
the most fundamental moral term, "virtue," and gives it a new meaning,
playing on the ambiguity in its etymological origins. The word derives
from the Latin virtus, which has as its root the Latin vir, "male." Virtus
is manly excellence, demonstrated by service to the state, whether in war
or in political leadership. In the Christian appropriation of the term,
virtue became the moral goodness of the Christian individual, the one
who loves (submits to) God and practices the moral precepts of humility
and universal love preached by Christ, the one active in the city of God,
not of men. Machiavelli takes this value-laden term and focuses on its
masculine origins: virtue is the attribute of those who act in a virile
manner, who practice not humility but self-assertion. The female imagery
in the latter part of chapter 25 of The Prince, where Machiavelli establishes the opposition between virtue and Fortuna, draws out the masculine roots of virtue in opposition to what he sees as the feminization of
virtue by Christian dogma extolling submissiveness.[12]

The sexual image in the confrontation of chapter 25 is violent. The
man must "beat" and hold down the female. It is the young, Machiavelli
tells us, who have the physical, and particularly the psychic, strength to
attack Fortuna in this way. He continues: "Therefore, as a woman, she is

the friend of the young, for they are less cautious, more fierce, and command her with more boldness." There is a peculiar shift: from conquest we find the emergence of friendship. Being "held down" does not mean submission here. Eve does not become Mary as the result of this encounter. The acceptance and acknowledgment of her power, yet the willingness to resist and to subdue her, leads to a partnership not possible for those who either deny her or passively submit to her. Interaction between male and female creates an order otherwise unattainable. Her force here is tamed, but it must also be employed. For this to happen, she must be made friendly. The sexual confrontation as an analogue of the political confrontation suggests that the task of the prince is not only to dominate but also to create, to give life to a new being. In contrast with other Christian authors, Machiavelli sees in sexuality an act of positive creation, not the sign of man's frailty.

In an earlier chapter of *The Prince*, Machiavelli discusses princes who have conquered without relying on *Fortuna*. These are men who acquired new principalities "with their own arms and by *virtù*." *Fortuna* gave them nothing but "occasions." She was not their friend: there was no sexual encounter. "And in examining their actions and life we see that they got nothing else from Fortuna than the occasion which gave them the material which they were able to put into whatever form pleased them; and without such occasion the virtue of their spirit would have been spent and without such virtue the occasion would have come in vain."[13] Such princes include Moses, Cyrus, Romulus, and Theseus, heroes from the realm of myth. These men function without the friendship of *Fortuna*, without her as a sexual counterpart to their manliness. They can give birth to the new principality parthenogenetically, ignoring the role of the female.[14] In contrast with these mythical heroes are the humans who must rely, as Machiavelli tells us in chapter 25, on *Fortuna* for half their affairs, who must make her their friend through adaptation, audacity, and action. They must respond to sexuality and transform that power into a source of order. For the young, bold men of chapter 25, Machiavelli has eliminated God, but he has not taken away the female. Humans must acknowledge and accommodate the feminine forces—indeed, utilize those forces—as the almost divine heroes of the earlier chapter did not have to.

Christianity and the Effeminate Male

In contrast with the vibrant female force *Fortuna*, it is the male who has become the complacent female, meekly submitting to those who dominate, who threatens the meaningful survival of the Italians of Machiavelli's day. In the final chapter of *The Prince*, immediately following the one in which *Fortuna* is compared to a woman, Machiavelli offers his "exhortation to liberate Italy from the barbarians [the French]."[15] The image of the female again appears vividly. This time, in marked contrast with the previous chapter, it is the passive female, awaiting her savior. She has been beaten (*battuta*) and ravaged. Her weakness called forth violence. Machiavelli's response is to encourage the Italians and their potential leaders to act, to transform their passivity into action (to change from Mary to Eve). He urges the princes to see "how she [Italy] prays to God that He command someone to redeem her from this barbarian cruelty and insolence." Having in the previous chapter replaced God with *Fortuna*, Machiavelli now tells the Italian princes that God is with them, sending the manna, opening the seas.

The final chapter is filled with references to God, precisely because the Italians, unable to meet the challenge Machiavelli sees facing them, have become dependent on another (God) to save them. Religion and God, both systematically eliminated from political life in the earlier chapters, are brought back into this exhortation to the Italians because, in their submissiveness, they must rely on others, as *Fortuna* the female and the men who are willing to confront her do not. Having become slaves to others, even or especially to God, these Italians are now unable to free Italy. She waits in vain for her knight, who will not come; the men and princes of Italy, as submissive females, accept divine providence. *The Prince* is filled with admonitions to defend oneself and not rely on others; the "female," be she the meek wife, the submissive Mary, or the effeminate Christian princes and armies of Italy, cannot do so. The weak depend on others for protection. The men who confront *Fortuna* and acknowledge her power act on their own.

The question of the dependence on others is often captured in Machiavelli's writings with the example of fortresses. Chapter 20 of *The Prince* has the heading "Whether fortresses and many other things which are frequently done by princes may be useful or not useful." The answer he provides with regard to fortresses is ambiguous; the answer depends on the particular circumstances of a prince—whether he can expect the support of his people. There is, however, one example of a fortress being especially useful: "Nor in our time do we see any profit to any prince which comes from fortresses, except in the case of the Countess of Forlì when the count Girolamo her consort died." A woman ruler needs a fortress because she relies on others. Similarly, if the men of Machiavelli's

world are women—if, losing the capacity to fight, they have become feminine—then fortresses are necessary.

In *The Discourses*, the book dealing with republics, Machiavelli answers in the title of another chapter the question he had raised in chapter
20 of *The Prince*: "Fortresses are generally more harmful than useful."[16]
In this chapter he reports the quip of a Spartan, whose city looked to
"the virtue of her men and no other defense to protect her." When asked
by an Athenian whether he did not think the walls of Athens beautiful,
he responded, "Yes, if the city were inhabited by women." As with the
example of the Countess of Forlì, it is women—be they male or female—
who need fortresses.

Throughout Machiavelli's work there are not only the physical walls
that release men from relying on their own valor; there are also the religious walls on which humans depend to avoid direct confrontation with
the disorder of the world in which they live. Effeminate men, like the
princes of Italy appealed to in chapter 26 of *The Prince*, rely on the fortress of religion. They turn to God, and thus do not act for themselves.
Religion, fortresses, and effeminancy are all intermingled in Machiavelli's
attack on the failure of his contemporaries to pursue freedom. When men
exhibit true virtue, they rely on themselves, needing neither fortresses
nor religion. Then they become men. In a world in which order must be
imposed by human endeavor, actions and self-reliance are the virtues that
receive praise and encouragement. Such men's virtue does not always
conform to the virtue of Christianity as it has come to be practiced.
Instead, throughout *The Discourses* Christianity is associated with indolence rather than action.

The Discourses is a complex compendium of maxims, history from both
ancient and modern times, and reflections on the possibilities of reintro-
ducing ancient virtue such as found in the Roman Republic to the modern world, a world that changed radically with the introduction of
Christianity. Machiavelli introduces the first of the three books of *The
Discourses* with an attack on the indolence (*ozio*) that "prevails in most
Christian states."[17] In Book 2 he reflects on "why it happened in ancient
times that the peoples were more enamored of liberty than in this time."
He concludes: "I believe it comes from the same cause that men were
stronger, namely the difference between our education and that of the
ancients, which is based on the difference between our religion and that
of the ancients." He continues: "Our religion has glorified men who are
humble and contemplative rather than active." But, he complains, "This

mode of living has made men weak, easily controlled by evil ones who act, allowing themselves to be beaten down (*battituta*) rather than seeking vengeance."[18] Machiavelli describes this situation as the worlds having become "effeminate and Heaven unarmed," and blames this not on Christianity but on those who have interpreted it as a religion that encourages *ozio* rather than virtue as he understands it. The problem is with those who have turned from a world of affairs to a world we can neither see nor know.

In Book 3 Machiavelli discusses the failure of contemporary princes and republics to take charge of their armies, "so as to avoid themselves the cares and dangers of attending it," and castigates those "indolent princes or effeminate republics, who send generals to battle with orders to avoid action."[19] Weakness and the avoidance of any engagement in the affairs of the world are associated throughout Machiavelli's political writings with effeminacy—and that in turn with Christianity.[20]

With effeminacy perceived as the inability and/or unwillingness to engage in battle or to assert physical and social domination, the escape from effeminacy depends on making men soldiers who defend their states, making them participate in the world of action. In Book 1 of *The Discourses*, Machiavelli turns to an example from fourth-century Greece. After Pelopidas and Epaminondas liberated Thebes from Spartan rule, "they found a city accustomed to servitude, and themselves in the midst of an effeminate population. . . . Such however was their virtue" that they put the Thebans under arms, took them out to battle, and demonstrated that "not only in Lacedaemonia were men of war born, but they were born in any other place where one might find someone to teach them military techniques."[21] The effeminate, indolent inhabitants were remade into men through an education in war.

Two chapters earlier, Machiavelli felicitates Rome for her fortune in having kings who complemented each other; while Numa was peace-loving, his successor was eager to train the Romans in "the *virtù* of Romulus . . . else this city would have become effeminate and a prey to her neighbors."[22] Near the end of *The Discourses*, Machiavelli reflects on what makes men more harsh or more effeminate, differences that, he notes, characterize families as well as cities. These differences cannot be genetically passed on, "by blood," because marriage brings so much diversity into a family.[23] The reason is the difference of education in each family. Thus, effeminacy is the product of education, as is manliness. The task for leaders of cities is to understand how impressionable the very young are and to avoid anything that might educate toward effeminacy. For Machiavelli this can be done. His writings are his attempt to make the effeminate Italians masculine. The power of his language and of his images, and his shocking examples, are to move the Italians out of the feminine passivity so that they can act to shake off the barbarians, rather than wait whimpering for God to send manna, to open the seas, to send his messenger.

The importance of discipline and training in overcoming effeminacy is emphasized when Machiavelli titles a chapter "The reason why the French have been and still are judged at the beginning of a fight more than men, but following a fight less than women."[24] He accepts the notion that the early fury of the French could be part of their "nature," but then insists that proper discipline could preserve their fury to the end of the fight. Again, he believes that those who have become women because they have been improperly educated in the art of war can be trained to exchange their effeminacy for masculinity. Thus, they *could* end the battle as men. On the other hand, he castigates the Italians, who lack the nature and the discipline. These armies are completely useless. They begin as women and end as women. Machiavelli seems to leave us a question: Is there any hope? Yet the fact that he writes—and does so in Italian—suggests an affirmative response. His is a battle of Eve against Mary that he, overturning Christianity, suspects he can win. Man is caught between the two models of womanhood. Machiavelli works to reinstate Eve over Mary.

Women and History in *The Discourses:* Models for Machiavelli?

Machiavelli's writings are filled with historical examples. One learns not from the Bible nor from moral philosophers of old, but from past deeds; not from thoughts, but from actions. Machiavelli relies in part on the ancient historians Livy and, to some degree, Tacitus. We find Lucretia, Verginia, Tullia, and Dido. However, apart from Dido, who appears in *The Prince* as a model of a new prince in a new state, Machiavelli has very little to say about the women to whom he briefly refers.

For example, Lucretia, fabled in Livy's story of the downfall of the Roman kings, is virtually ignored in Machiavelli's version. Tarquinius lost his kingdom "not because his son Sextus had raped Lucretia, but because he [Tarquinius] had broken the laws of the kingdom and governed as a tyrant." Machiavelli adds that even "if the incident of Lucretia had not taken place, there would have been some other incident to produce the same effect."[25] Similarly, while Livy devoted several pages to the role of the Verginia incident as the impetus to the uprising against the Decemviri, Machiavelli barely touches on the incident in his description of the faults of the Decemviri and the cause of their downfall.[26]

Although Machiavelli largely ignores women in the history he records, he urges the princes and potential leaders of republics to whom he addresses his works to recognize the importance of women. Their importance, however, derives not from their erotic qualities, but from their being part of a man's definition of himself. Therefore Machiavelli encourages rulers to be particularly careful about interfering with the women in a man's life, for should the ruler so threaten a man, the offended husband or father will pose a potential danger to the ruler. In *The Prince*, in a chapter entitled "On fleeing contempt and hatred," he advises his prince that hatred and contempt will follow if he is rapacious and usurps the "belongings and the women of his subjects."[27] On the other hand, chastity is a "virtue" of the prince, not because it is good in itself, but because others care about it.[28]

In the longest chapter of *The Discourses*, Machiavelli warns that of the actions that incite revenge, and thus conspiracy, the most serious are attacks on men's honor, particularly those directed against their wives.[29] The two stories that he uses to support this general maxim, though, hardly support it. The first story alludes to an incident described in an earlier chapter, the homosexual rape of Pausanias by a minister of Philip of Macedon.[30] Philip did not avenge the rape, as he promised, and eventually Pausanias assassinated him. The second story at least has a woman in it: the tyrant of Siena gave his daughter as wife to a certain Giovanni Bonromei, then took her back. For this insult Bonromei conspired against the Sienese tyrant, and almost killed him. Clearly, sexual passion does not motivate these conspiratorial men. The females are almost incidental—if they are even present. Rather, the argument is that the ruler must understand the human psyche and his subjects' desire for self-respect; if that self-respect is violated, the ruler must be prepared for the revenge that will follow. Instead of revolution to defend the chastity of Lucretia, it is the violation of the male that calls forth conspirators.

Chapter 26 of the last book of *The Discourses* has women in its title:

"How because of women a state is ruined." It is clear, though, in reading the primary example of this maxim, that women do not ruin the state; internal divisions do. A young woman of wealth in the city of Ardea is sought in marriage by a plebeian and an aristocrat. Since her deceased father had not chosen a husband for her, a conflict arises between the mother, who favors the aristocrat, and the girl's guardians, who favor the plebeian. This becomes a class conflict in which each side seeks outside aid; the conflict is resolved only when the state becomes subject to outsiders and thus loses its independence.

Machiavelli concludes: "There are in this text several things to note: First, one sees how women are the cause of much ruin to states and that they cause great damage to whomever it is who governs the city."[31] He then goes back to the cases of Lucretia and Verginia, whom he had previously dismissed as not being the causes of "much ruin and great damage" to their respective regimes. Why does he here blatantly contradict himself, within the same chapter? Forgetfulness might be one answer, but another is to be suspicious of his blaming women here after exonerating them earlier. In the cases of both Lucretia and Verginia the regimes fell because of their inadequacies: tyrannical rule and a blatant rejection of ancestral customs. The women who have been cited by others as the causes of downfalls of states were merely indications of a more general misrule by the political leaders. The causes of ruin were more profound. Similarly in the case of Ardea, that city's subjection to its neighbors is caused not by the "woman" but by the divisions between the plebeians and the nobles.

Women are the cause of the ruin of states, not because of any peculiar characteristic but because they indicate the divisions that exist among the human beings who make up the state. On one level there are male and female. They must be joined to continue the city. The city of Ardea is divided, like the human species, in two. It must be joined in order to preserve itself. The unmitigated opposition of the two factions means the death of the city, just as unresolved conflict between male and female would mean the death of the species. As Machiavelli concludes his long work about foundations and the preservation of republics built up out of diverse elements, he acknowledges the instability of any regime that must reconcile opposites, be those opposites male and female or nobles and plebeians, as was the case in Rome. Thus, women do not "ruin" cities, but they do underscore diversity within the state, a diversity that will always be a source of danger for any community.

A few specific women do stand out in Machiavelli's historical examples, particularly in the chapter on conspiracies in *The Discourses* (3.6). In each case, though, the women act more like men than women, thus succeeding because of the male's failure to foresee that women under the yoke of necessity or revenge can act like men. Most dramatic is the story of Madonna Caterina. She appears when Machiavelli comments that there only remains to speak of the dangers that follow the execution of conspiracies: One must kill all who might seek vengeance. There may be sons or brothers, but the particular story that he tells is of a wife whose husband, the king, was killed by conspirators. When the people of the city held out against the conspirators, Caterina, a prisoner along with her children, offered to go into the city to win the people over to the conspirators, leaving her children behind as hostages. Once in the city she mockingly spoke from its walls to the conspirators; uncovering her genitals, she rebuked her enemies for not realizing that she still had the means to have more children. Thus, she kept the conspirators from the city. Machiavelli does not use this story to show the "unnatural" female who could so crassly yield her children for the sake of revenge; rather, he uses it to comment on the conspirators, who showed little wisdom and much negligence in ignoring the powerful passion of revenge. Even a woman can become a man in such circumstances.

Two other cases stand out in the same chapter. Epicarus, the mistress of Nero, was accused of participating in a plot to overthrow the emperor. Though guilty, she steadfastly denied her involvement and thus assuaged Nero's suspicions. Then there was Marcia, concubine to Emperor Commodus. He foolishly left a list of those to be executed where she might find it. When she discovered her name on the list, "necessity forced her to be brave." Showing herself to be feminine in the manner of *Fortuna*, she became manly (changed with changing circumstances) and successfully conspired to kill him. There are no longer divisions between male and female. For Machiavelli a world in flux allows men to become women and women to become men.

In the last chapter of Machiavelli's long work on Livy, women reappear, this time in a conspiracy to kill their husbands. Though the title of the chapter focuses on the "providence" necessary to take daily precautions to prevent republics from losing their liberties, it recalls the plot by Roman wives to poison their husbands. Many succeeded before the plan was discovered. Machiavelli uses this incident and other large-scale crimes to discourse on the difficulties of punishing large numbers of male-

factors and to praise the Romans for introducing the practice of decimation, whereby every tenth individual (or military unit) suffers death. All
cannot be punished. Thus, decimation has the benefit of inducing fear
without destroying all. To punish all the women of Rome for the crime
of poisoning or planning to poison their husbands would mean the end
of Rome.

However, the incident of the mass poisonings at the end of Machiavelli's book may not tell us only about the Roman style of punishment;
indeed, it seems to tell us little about the "daily precautions" in the title
of the chapter. Rather, these women poisoners at the end of *The Discourses* give us a portrait of women to whom Machiavelli must assimilate
himself, just as those men who are to conquer *Fortuna* must be like the
fickle female. When he wrote both *The Prince* and *The Discourses*, Machiavelli was in exile, a state of enforced leisure (*ozio*) that he says throughout his works turns men into women. He was also old, no longer enjoying
the youthful audacity of those men who conquer *Fortuna* by violence.
Thus he was cast, in a sense, into the role of the woman. He was not
active politically, nor did he have the passion of youth. But, learning a
lesson from these female poisoners of Rome, eager to change the regime
that exalts the passive Mary, eager to undermine the world view of sixteenth-century Italy and the Christianity on which it was founded,
Machiavelli must apply his own poison in secret and corrupt from within
rather than from without.

Machiavelli's writings are similar to the poison of the Roman matrons
because, in his particular condition and at his particular age, he cannot
do otherwise. His chapter on conspiracies had told us that within a state
there will always be those who are prepared to conspire and to resist. His
chapter on women as the cause of much ruin to states had suggested the
internal divisions that plague all communities, divisions waiting to be
exacerbated by skillful manipulators. The Romans least expected their
wives to conspire to poison them; they did not see in them the source of
internal corruption of the regime, and thus did not take daily precautions
against them. Machiavelli, living in political exile, a weak man lacking
an army and youth, hardly seems a political threat to the princes of Italy
and especially the Medici of Florence; but precisely because men least
expect the apparently submissive female to be a subversive force, they
are least prepared when she is. The women of Rome rely on secretly
administered poison. Thus, the weak can cause the downfall of those who
are presumed to be strong. And thus Machiavelli, presumed to be weak,

can become surprisingly strong, adapting to the *Fortuna* who may mock his age and his political position, and who may have chosen to discard the old man.

The last paragraph of the last chapter of *The Discourses* praises Fabius Maximus, who restructured the citizen rolls of ancient Rome to limit the effects of the indiscriminate introduction of new citizens into the city. The leaders of Rome must carefully monitor those who can participate in the political regime. Fabius' great success, the reason he was called "the greatest [*maximus*]," was that he prevented subversive forces from participating in the city. Machiavelli's work (and the women of this last chapter) illustrate how even those excluded from direct participation within the regime can control it. Machiavelli, who in *The Prince* had praised the young able to beat and hold down the feminized *Fortuna*, now seems to learn his lessons from the weak women who can subvert because their strength is unexpected. He himself transcends the model of both Eve and Mary to find a mode of participation more compatible with his aims and his particular status.

Machiavelli's Comedies

Though the feminine forces of Eve and Mary permeate Machiavelli's explicitly political works, women as individuals appear infrequently. However, Machiavelli also wrote plays treating domestic relations in which women are active participants in the struggles for authority and security. Analogically, the family appears as a little principality, supposedly exhibiting the rule of the father over the other participants in the household. However, as in the principality, the lines of authority are not so simply drawn, conspiracies develop, rulers deteriorate and must be replaced, external and internal threats develop, orderly households are undermined and (since this is comedy) refounded. We will look at two of Machiavelli's comedies to see how his analysis of familial relations and women's roles therein illuminate his political thought, for by studying relationships on the personal level, Machiavelli crystallizes some of his political teachings.[32]

In both of the comedies discussed below, the motivating force is lust. In both a beautiful young woman is desired by one who should not have access to her. The enamored male tries to manipulate a variety of others so as to have the chance to sleep with her. In *Clizia* the girl so desired is never seen on stage. However, her foster mother controls the situation; she is the true prince—or, rather (as Machiavelli perhaps envisions himself), the one who begins as adviser but then takes over the rule.[33] In *La Mandragola* the beautiful young woman and her mother appear actively on stage, but this time the daughter ultimately controls the situation. She accomplishes this by exemplifying Machiavelli's insistence on the transformation of the meaning of virtue. By choosing adultery over fidelity, she ensures the stability and continuation of her little principality. Had she remained chaste according to the dictates of traditional virtue, destruction would have descended on all. A character in the play describes her as "fit to rule a kingdom."[34] Her willingness to assert a new understanding of virtue demonstrates this capacity.

La Mandragola

In *La Mandragola* a young Florentine named Callimaco falls in love with Lucrezia, the wife of a profoundly stupid old man named Nicia, who "allows himself to be governed by her."[35] Lucrezia's name is intentional. The entire story recalls Rome's original Lucretia, the chaste maiden discussed so proudly in Livy's history and dismissed so hastily in *The Discourses* (for a summary, see Appendix A).

Livy's Lucretia, once violated, commits suicide as she calls upon her husband and father to seek revenge for her rape. In Livy's Rome, violation of a female could lead to the downfall of a regime. Machiavelli's vision is of the greater happiness that will ensue when the violation is accepted and, indeed, embraced. According to Machiavelli's presentation in *La Mandragola*, one need only accept what has previously been considered sin, and an intolerable state of affairs can become perfectly tolerable. Lucrezia learns that she cannot be good and preserve her chastity in a world in which most others are not good. The rule of *The Prince*, chapter 15, changes her from an ancient Lucretia to a modern Lucrezia. The mandragola is a medication that supposedly gives life by killing. Though in the play its potency is a sham, Lucrezia's transformation mimics this death and birth. The old chastity dies for the sake of the new life of happiness. The cure does not come from the bottle, but from a transformation of the values of the main female character.

As Machiavelli develops the theme of rebirth in this play in a rather new context, he also works with the notion of age and youth. The old man, the fool, must give way to the young, inventive conspirators. In chapter 25 of *The Prince*, Machiavelli had indicated that the young have more success conquering *Fortuna* than those who are old and less daring. In *La Mandragola*, Callimaco is the young man, the modern man who gains control over the woman, outmaneuvering the impotent Nicia. Lucrezia enjoys his strong embraces and chooses to support him in his corruption of the family. But Callimaco takes *Fortuna* as his friend not by violence, not by rape, but by trickery. Nicia is tricked by a story about the mandragola's powers. Callimaco, despite his amorous ardor, is something of a fop, avoiding the battles of his country and staying far from military adventures. He shows none of the virtue of the true prince or the citizen of the Roman Republic. Ancient virtue does not conquer *Fortuna* in today's world of lesser men. The method must be trickery, deceit, camouflage rather than simple boldness—and in the end must depend on the will of a woman.

As the play develops, we are always aware of the strength of Lucrezia, one "fit to rule a kingdom," for she sees through the foolishness of those around her and resists, at least at first, the attempts to corrupt her. She is the one who must decide whether to reveal the ruse to her husband or to assist in the subversion of his authority. Like the powerful *Fortuna*, she supports the young and thus allows the play to end on a happy note. She is the one who makes the final choice: Nicia, who thinks he controls her completely, is controlled by her. She decides what is to happen in this Florentine family. In the kingdom of the home, she is not only fit to rule, she does rule. But she does so in the end only because she accepts a change in the meaning of virtue and agrees to become an accomplice to the tricks being played on her husband. In *Clizia* we meet another type of woman, one who rules through her simple good sense when all others around her lose theirs.

Clizia

La Mandragola is an original play: *Clizia* is Machiavelli's adaptation of a comedy, *Casina*, by the Roman playwright Plautus. Machiavelli has altered the plot in several significant ways, giving a more sympathetic role to the wife and mother. The general plot is the same as in Plautus' play (for a summary, see Appendix B).

Behind the whole story stands Sofronia, the mother and wife, who is distressed not at the infidelity of her husband but at his transformation from an upstanding citizen and father into a slobbering old fool. She devises a trick to foil his plans and cause him the shame that will bring him back to his old ways. Nicomaco is thoroughly shamed after this incident, accepts that he must mend his ways, and leaves all things to the stewardship of Sofronia. She does not allow Cleandro to marry Clizia either, until—as happens in plays of this sort—Clizia's father appears and, revealing his noble ancestry, opens the way for the wedding of Cleandro and Clizia. The fortunate arrival of Clizia's father contributes to the happy ending, but the joyous conclusion depends far more on the wisdom and self-assurance of Sofronia, her insight into human nature, and her concern with the welfare of the family as a harmonious community.[36] She was able to overcome the *Fortuna* that went against her when the lots were drawn, while her son had to wait for *Fortuna* to bring Clizia's father to Florence.

Machiavelli writes in the Prologue that this play is to be "instructive to the young," those eager to have *Fortuna* as their friend. But the young learn at least two things from this play: youth is not all they need to enjoy *Fortuna*'s smiles, nor is masculine authority enough. Sofronia demonstrates the wiles and craftiness necessary to manipulate others in order to make things turn out as one wishes. The young may think that success is defined by the assertion of power in war or love, and thus conflate the two in their songs, but Sofronia shows that the female, no longer young, can bring order within the principality of the family, can acquire rule for herself and build a strong, viable community while all the males, both old and young, produce only chaos.

Sofronia, according to her name, is the one who suffers or endures; at the beginning of the play she endures an aged and incompetent[37] ruler. As in *La Mandragola*, the aged ruler is a fool, but in this play he becomes the fool because he allows the love of a girl to interfere with his duties as a citizen of Florence. In a speech absent from the *Casina* of Plautus, Sofronia describes the former Nicomaco (see Appendix B).

As Machiavelli presents the interaction between Nicomaco and Sofronia, it is not at all "reasonable" that Sofronia submit to the rule of Nicomaco. Nicomaco's decline supports the overthrow of what traditionally was reasonable: there is no natural order that determines the rule of male over the female. Since there is no natural order, humans must impose the order whereby they live. Nicomaco, rather than imposing that order, now contributes to the disorder; thus it must be left to the female to structure the world around her and bring it back to its original principles. Sofronia is the adviser to the prince who takes the kingdom away from the prince.

At the end of the play, Nicomaco is completely overwhelmed by Sofronia's trick and transfers all his power to her: "My Sofronia, do what you will . . . govern as you wish."[38] When her son arrives, she recalls Nicomaco's words: "He wishes that I govern him according to my own wisdom." Nicomaco falls as a ruler; his authority is usurped by a woman who knows how to rule the family and how to use tricks to become the ruler. She says to Nicomaco, "I confess to have managed all sorts of tricks that have been played on you to make you change and reform. There was no other way than to make you ashamed."[39] Tricks indeed work against *Fortuna*. *Fortuna* did not favor Sofronia: the lot drawing went against her by giving Clizia to the one who would share the maid with her husband, but her skill and commitment to the family overcame her bad fortune.

Once again we must relate Machiavelli to the female; like Sofronia he suffers, endures the rule of foolish men, but lacks the stature and strength to overturn their authority. He must find other means to assert his control: trickery. As the successful female who does not meekly submit to a foolish ruler, to one who no longer properly educates his young, to one who pursues a shadow we never see, Sofronia is a potent model for a weak Machiavelli. She offers a model of action the males in the play do not provide. Among the others, Cleandro in particular relies on *Fortuna*. After the lots are drawn, the youth laments: "O Fortuna: being a woman you are a friend of the young, but this time you have been the friend of the old" (see Appendix B).[40] He builds no dikes: he is tossed about on the waves of fortune and does not conquer it. He fails to act as Sofronia does.[41]

Clizia portrays the victory of the woman who gains power. It thus represents an inversion: those who traditionally rule do not; those who traditionally are submissive are not. Because of the disruptive impact of the passions, the old guidelines for human action do not lead to order. Sofronia understands and manipulates those passions. She knows how to shame her husband and make him a proper Florentine gentleman again. The weakness of the female sex does not mean that she lacks efficacy. While in *La Mandragola* the inversion is one of vice becoming virtue, fornication replacing chastity, in *Clizia* it is of a woman "governing all things." In both cases the inversion indicates the inadequacy of the traditional expectations. It may be good that the father not know whether the child is his, as will happen when Lucrezia's child is born, and it may be good that the female rules within the family, as is the case in Nicomaco's household. Machiavelli's world sets up no precise guides. Thus, in his comedies adultery and the rule of a woman can become the new virtues.

Conclusion

Machiavelli is never completely open about his intentions. Some have seen him as an advocate of tyranny; others, as the spokesman for republican virtues; others, as the prince of evils; others, as simply trying to manipulate his way back into power in Florence. Through its ambiguity Machiavelli's work reveals the uncertainty at the foundation of modern political thought. The forms of Plato, the hierarchy of Aristotle, the political service of the Stoics, the God of Christianity all offered certainty. Machiavelli retreats from such precision, a retreat captured by the ambiguity of his political teachings. Within that ambiguity women play various roles. None of them, though, is definitive. *Fortuna* is a woman, but so is the weak man trained in the art of submission by Christian dogma. Men can become women and become fickle, changing with the changing times, as Machiavelli does; or men can become women and become submissive, yielding to whatever happens as they allow others—be they males or females—to dominate. While the images of women are central to Machiavelli's presentation of his political thought, women are unimportant in political life; they are easily dismissed by Machiavelli from the traditional tales that had emphasized their influence. Women in historical situations may have been the source of conflict among men, but here they are little different from property or the male's sense of self-respect.

Fluidity dominates Machiavelli's vision of world affairs. The task of the prince or of the rulers of a republic is to impose an order on that fluidity; in the process such leaders will specify the role of women in society. In *Clizia*, in particular, we see a woman capable of ruling; in the case of Madonna Caterina we see another woman capable of the greatest deceit. The flux of nature does not determine who or what women will be. Machiavelli leaves the status of women uncertain because all is uncertain, subject to manipulation. Thus, Machiavelli leaves open the movement to liberalism. The earlier models of women in society, as varied as they may have been, limited their role. These are cast down by Machiavelli as he destroys all hierarchical relationships. Men can become—indeed often must become—beasts, private citizens can become rulers, men can become women, and women, as he has a character in *La Mandragola* say, can be "fit to govern a nation."

Notes

1. Niccolò Machiavelli, *The Prince,* in *Chief Works and Others,* ed. and trans. Allan Gilbert, 3 vols. (Durham: Duke University Press, 1989), chap. 18.

2. Ibid., chap. 15.

3. For a discussion of the Phyllis story, see Horowitz, "Aristotle and Woman," *Journal of the History of Biology* 9 (1976): 183–213, esp. 189–91, and the further references in her notes 20 and 21. See also Natalie Zemon Davis, *Society and Culture in Early Modern France* (Stanford: Stanford University Press, 1965), 135–36.

4. Henry Krauss, *The Living Theater of Medieval Art* (Philadelphia: University of Pennsylvania Press, 1967), chap. 3, esp. 42.

5. Angela M. Lucas, *Women in the Middle Ages: Religion, Marriage, and Letters* (New York: St. Martin's Press, 1983), 15; Joan Ferrante, *Woman as Image in Medieval Literature* (New York: Columbia University Press, 1975), 30–35.

6. Eleanor Commo McLaughlin, "Equality of Souls, Inequality of Sexes: Woman in Medieval Theology," in *Religion and Sexism: Images of Women in the Jewish and Christian Traditions,* ed. Rosemary Radford Ruether (New York: Simon and Schuster, 1974), 246.

7. Ephesians 5:22–25.

8. In some authors the Church becomes the bride of God through analogy with the bride of the Song of Songs in the Old Testament. Some of those writing on the Song of Songs even asked men "to identify with a woman as the bride represents all of mankind" (Lucas, *Women in the Middle Ages,* 17). Ferrante, *Woman as Image,* 29, writes about St. Bernard, whose "devotion to the Virgin is such that he can identify himself, through her, with a woman's role, and speak of himself as a mother to his monks." See also Carolyn Walker Bynum, *Jesus as Mother: Studies in the Spirituality of the High Middle Ages* (Berkeley and Los Angeles: University of California Press, 1982), 15–18, and chap. 4, for a detailed discussion of the attraction of the female image for religious men, especially monks.

9. For a further discussion of Machiavelli's transformation of the meaning of traditional terms, see Clifford Orwin, "Machiavelli's Unchristian Charity," *American Political Science Review* 72 (December 1978): 1217–28.

10. Since this chapter was written, an extremely interesting discussion of Machiavelli and women has appeared: Hanna Fenichel Pitkin, *Fortune Is a Woman: Gender and Politics in the Thought of Niccolò Machiavelli* (Berkeley and Los Angeles: University of California Press, 1984). Though the orientation and concerns are quite different from those expressed in this chapter, it illustrates the centrality of women and the feminine for Machiavelli's work.

11. Ferrante, *Woman as Image,* 46–49, has a helpful discussion of this issue in her treatment of Boethius. His discourse with the feminine Philosophy "makes him see that Fortune is part of the

workings of fate and not a separate hostile entity, that it was his perspective that was wrong and not her actions" (47).

12. Quentin Skinner, *The Foundations of Modern Political Thought: The Renaissance* (Cambridge: Cambridge University Press, 1978), l. 176–79, comments on the public-private dimensions of *virtù*. The *virtù* in Machiavelli, he argues, relates to a public excellence, to the virtual exclusion of the private. Attaching the male and female connotations to the public-private dimensions, we can see how Machiavelli's virtue is here masculinized.

13. For the Italians of Machiavelli's time, Moses certainly does not come from the realm of myth: it is part of Machiavelli's heresy to include him in the same category as such characters as Romulus and Theseus.

14. Compare here the highly sexual language of chapter 26 of *The Prince*, to be discussed below.

15. Chapter 26. The subsequent quotes in this paragraph come from this chapter.

16. *The Discourses*, 2.4.

17. Ibid., 1. Introduction.

18. Ibid., 2.2.

19. Ibid., 3.10.

20. Harvey C. Mansfield Jr., *Machiavelli's New Modes and Orders: A Study of the "Discourses on Livy"* (Ithaca and London: Cornell University Press, 1979), 195 n. 12, suggests that *ozio* can also mean the leisure for contemplation. Thus, "the affinity of Christianity and philosophy is again suggested." Elsewhere in his study of *The Discourses*, Mansfield associates philosophy with that which is womanly (390ff).

21. *The Discourses*, 1.21.

22. Ibid., 1.19.

23. Ibid., 3.46.

24. Ibid., 3.36.

25. Ibid., 3.5.

26. Ibid., 1.40.

27. *The Prince*, chap. 19.

28. See the discussion of Scipio in *The Discourses*, 3.20.

29. Ibid., 3.6.

30. Ibid., 2.28.

31. Ibid., 3.26.

32. These analyses will have to be limited to how the comedies highlight the place of women in Machiavelli's political thought: thus, much of the complexity of the plays' themes and plots will have to be ignored. For discussions of Machiavelli's plays, with a focus on their political implications, see particularly Mera J. Flaumenhaft, "The Comic Remedy: Machiavelli's "Mandragola," *Interpretation* 7 (May 1978): 33–74; and Martin Fleisher, "Trust and Deceit in Machiavelli's Comedies," *Journal of the History of Ideas* (July 1966): 365–80.

33. *The Prince*, chap. 23. Here Machiavelli notes that a prince who is not wise in his own right may, by chance, have a counselor who is a very prudent man. This situation, though, does not last long, "since such a governor would in a short time take the state from him."

34. *La Mandragola*, 1.3.

35. Ibid., 1.1.

36. Fleisher, "Trust and Deceit," notes that in the *Casina* there is no emphasis on the welfare of the family.

37. Nicomaco's impotence is an issue of no small comic interest during the preparations for the wedding night. *Clizia*, 4.2.

38. Ibid., 5.3. See Davis, *Society and Culture*, 124–51, for the social role of "Women on Top" in transitional societies.

39. *Clizia*, 5.3.

40. Ibid., 4.1.

41. Ibid., 5.5.

4

Renaissance Italy: Machiavelli

Wendy Brown

Machiavelli's understanding of politics stands in sharp contrast to that of Aristotle. Machiavelli makes no grand claims for the exalted nature of man, he does not cast political life as the whole of life, he is infamous for having divorced politics from ethics and for distinguishing the virtues of the political man from virtue itself. In the tradition of political theory, Machiavelli is unique by dint of his passionate devotion to political *action*. He loved the subject matter of political theory—politics itself—to a degree unparalleled by any other theorist of equal repute. Ironically, the consequence is that through five hundred years of interpretation, Machiavelli has probably been more maligned and disparaged than any of his fellows in the tradition of political theory. In fierce and uncompromising fashion, Machiavelli pierced to the quick of Western politics and the men who comprise it; weaker hearts have rebelled.

Above all, Machiavelli reincorporated into political thought that which we watched the Greeks try to eliminate—the body. For Machiavelli, politics is a visceral, earthly, flesh and blood affair. His is a politics seething with irrepressible drives and urges, a politics that transpires on earth and through the body. There are no unchanging "forms" or spiritual ideals in Machiavelli's political world, no ultimate *telos* that man fulfills, no gods to whom he pays homage with his political activity. Politics is not an aesthetic ideal, but life itself.

However, the particular constructions of body, desire, and need in Machiavelli's politics are profoundly gendered. The life in which this politics is situated is the life of men bent upon control and domination, the life of communities ruled by those who care for ruling and the expansion of their power above all else. Similarly, while "necessity" figures largely in Machiavelli's musings on politics, this necessity too is narrow and one-sided, signifying for Machiavelli the limitations and dangers to one's quest for power and, conversely, the spur to greatness—it has little to do with daily, concrete human needs.

Machiavelli's sharply gendered view of human beings and politics lead him to subvert some of his own understandings about the political world. Despite his attunement to the intricacy and complexity of political life, he often urges the political actor to use the bluntest of instruments and force in this realm, advice that secures fleeting victories at best and more often increases the actor's vulnerability to threatening and incomprehensible forces (*Fortuna*). Similarly, Machiavelli's commitment to demystifying the political world is thwarted by his own reification of power's consequences in the character of *Fortuna*. This chapter explores the ways in which these tensions in Machiavelli's work grow out of his devotion to and development of an ethos of manhood.

For Machiavelli, politics emerges from what he takes to be the nature of man, *and* develops men into creatures of true manliness. In contrast to the Greeks, this development does not involve bringing man's nature to "perfection" through political life, but transforming, overcoming, or harnessing to specifically political purposes a number of the unwieldy qualities he perceives as indigenous to man. For Machiavelli, men are the raw material of politics and require a form superior to that which naturally inheres in them if political life is to flourish and if they are to achieve individual and collective glory. This superior form embodies the Machiavellian politics. Moreover, for Machiavelli, politics always bears the limitations of the transformative possibilities for man's nature. Machiavelli harbors no illusions about the usefulness of a political theory based upon "men as they might be" rather than men as they are or can be.

We begin, then, with a close inspection of the nature of "unmodified" Machiavellian man. Here it will be evident that while Machiavelli has much to say about "human nature" and identifies human beings as creatures of the natural world, his exploration of human nature is based upon a very particular kind of man. From the beginning, Machiavelli assumes men to be alienated from themselves and their surroundings, driven by a kind of random desire for power and conquest, inherently short-sighted and frustrated in their aims and ambitions.

Machiavelli's writings are replete with remarks about man's nature. Most of his political "advice" begins from or culminates in statements about one or more immutable characteristics of man. Thus, for example, when discussing Scipio's failure to quell rebellion in his troops, Machiavelli concludes, "this came from nothing else than not fearing him, because men are so restless that if the slightest door is opened to their ambition, they at once forget . . . all love for a prince."[1] Enumerating the difficulties of political innovation, Machiavelli cautions, "men don't really believe in anything new until they have had solid experience of it."[2] His teachings to the would-be leader of an insurrection are capsulated in the doctrine, "men are driven by two things: love and fear."[3] Nowhere, however, does Machiavelli offer a comprehensive portrait of man's nature. Rather, his ruminations on this subject are scattered throughout his writings and are synopsized only in the repeated declaration, "the nature of man is everywhere and always the same."[4] Thus, we must elicit a composite drawing of Machiavellian man from the diverse and partial testimony Machiavelli offers throughout his literary and political works.

We begin with Machiavelli's appreciation of man's animality. In contrast with the many political theorists who arrive at a definition of man by distinguishing him from other animals, Machiavelli suggests a very close and by no means unfortunate kinship between man and beast. Most familiar in this regard is chapter 18 of The Prince, in which he praises ancient allegory for its frequent depiction of the apprenticeship of would-be princes to Chiron, the centaur.[5] The mythical creature who is half-man, half-beast, is the symbolic figure of perfection in *The Prince*, a book of teachings and models for political success. On a first reading, it would seem that the most effective political actor is he who draws closest to his animal nature. On the other hand, the discussion of Chiron and the "lion and fox" allegory that follows might be read as an attempt to distinguish the nature of animals from the nature of man. Identifying man as a "creature of law" in this discussion, Machiavelli appears to make this distinction explicitly:

> You need to know, then, that there are two ways of fighting: one according to the laws, the other with force. The first is suited to man, the second to animals; but because the first is often not sufficient, a prince must resort to the second. Therefore, he needs to know well how to put to use the traits of animal and man.[6]

However, several matters contradict the seemingly clear opposition between man and beast put forth in this passage. First, Machiavelli never treats politics as something that has a nature independent of the men who generate it. Thus, insofar as successful political action requires the qualities of beasts, it is because bestial creatures have constructed the political conditions facing political actors. Seen in this light, the reference to man as one who fights according to law appears ironic, as a statement of what most people *think* men are, while the nature of politics suggests, indeed proves, quite otherwise.

We need not rely upon subtle methods of interpretation for this point. For once Machiavelli proceeds to expound the details of a prince's political education at the hands of Chiron, the human "half" of man's character drops from sight. The human qualities upon which political success depends are *worked into* the animals Machiavelli chooses as worthy models for political actors. The fox is selected for his clever scheming and sharp wits, the lion for his brute strength. The fox represents what is traditionally considered the distinctly human element of the man-beast amalgam. The fox's talents are also insufficient for precisely the reason man's are: while he harbors the cunning needed to avoid entrapment, he lacks the raw force necessary to frighten and fight an enemy.

There are many other passages in *The Prince* and *The Discourses* in which Machiavelli likens men of a certain character or condition to beasts. The following remarks on liberty are only one example:

What great difficulty a people accustomed to living under a prince has later in preserving its liberty, if by any accident it gains it. . . . And such difficulty is reasonable because that people is none other than a brute beast which, though of a fierce and savage nature, has always been cared for in prison and slavery. Then if by chance it is left free in a field, since it is not used to feeding itself and does not know the places where it can take refuge, it becomes the prey of the first one who tries to chain it.[7]

Even these instances of Machiavelli's use of analogy to establish man's proximity to the rest of the animal world do not yet plumb the depths of Machiavelli's radical assessment of man qua animal. For a full sense of this assessment, Machiavelli's literary endeavors are more revealing than his explicitly political writings. Particularly interesting in this regard is his allegorical poem, *The Golden Ass*.[8]

In one of the several vignettes contained in *The Golden Ass*, the narrator has stumbled into a strange forest where he is greeted by a beautiful woman leading a large flock of wild and domestic animals.[9] The shepherdess explains to Machiavelli that he has come to a netherworld from which he cannot escape and is doomed by order of her queen (Circe) to become a member of her flock. "In the world," she explains, "these animals you see were men like yourself."[10] She then shows him that the "men" of this habitat were not arbitrarily transformed into particular animals; instead, each was given the body of the creature his nature most resembled in his human life.[11] Moreover, the "transformation" is not complete; the animals retain some generic human characteristics as well as some of the specific idiosyncrasies each had in his particular life as a man.

Before the hapless protagonist of the story is transformed into animal shape, the shepherdess brings him to her abode for several days where he shares her food, her bed, and gains acquaintance with the strange world into which he has fallen. The story concludes with a tour of the grounds where the tame animals reside permanently and the wild ones rest at night. In this setting, Machiavelli muses on man's place in the animal world. His survey of the barnyard scene begins with a description of the animals who have lost or abused their respective virtues. Instead of graceful or magnificent, these creatures appear pathetic and helpless:

I saw a lion that had cut his own claws and pulled his teeth through his own counsels, not good and not sagacious. A little

> further on some injured animals—one having no tail, another no
> ears—I saw standing blockish in utter quiet. Then I saw an ass in
> such poor condition that he could not carry his packsaddle much
> less anything more . . . I saw a hound that kept sniffing at this
> one's muzzle and that one's shoulder as though he were trying to
> find his master . . . A stag I saw that was in such great terror,
> turning his course now here now there, such a fear of death he
> had.[12]

In short, the human individuals who so closely resembled these beasts
had, in their humanness, done a kind of civilizing violence to their natures. By breaking the bounds and balance of their natural animal virtues,
they incapacitated or mutilated their most useful instincts and rendered
worthless or self-destructive their natural abilities. The *genuine* ass is revealed as more noble, able, and useful, as well as happier, than the man
in ass's clothing.

The rest of the poem is a deeper exploration of this theme. The narrator wishes to speak with one of the animals and for this purpose, the
shepherdess chooses a huge, filthy hog bathing in a mud wallow. She also
grants Machiavelli the power to remove the hog from this setting and
return him to his human shape if the hog so desires. When Machiavelli
greets the hog with this offer, it is vehemently refused and the hog offers
a lengthy sermon about the superiority of his life as a beast to the life of
man. It is in this speech that Machiavelli offers his most thorough account of man's bungled relationship with his own animal nature.

"We," proclaims the hog, "seek the climate friendly to our way of life,
as Nature who teaches us commands." On the other hand, man goes
"exploring one country and another, not to find a climate either cool or
sunny but because your shameful greed for gain does not confirm your
spirit in a life sparing, law-abiding and humble."[13] Similarly, the hog
explains contemptuously, animals are generally stronger than men, purer
of spirit (having received a "richer gift of hearts invincible, noble and
strong") and purer of motive:

> Among us are done bold deeds and exploits without hope of a
> triumph or other fame, as once among those Romans who were
> famous. In the lion you see a great pride in a noble deed, and at a
> shameful act a wish to blot out its memory.[14]

Furthermore, the hog continues, "there are animals among us who would die before enduring the life of slaves, or be robbed in any way of their liberty."

The most poignant aspect of this harangue is reserved for the final verses. "How hapless you are above all other earthly creatures!" this section begins. Animals are in every way "closer friends to Nature." While every animal is born "fully clad," man alone is born "devoid of all protection."[15] Animals always have one or more very keen senses, while man's are relatively dull. And where nature does provide men with some things potentially advantageous such as hands and speech, she sends a curse along with them—"ambition and avarice, with which her bounty is cancelled."[16] The poem concludes,

> To how many ills Nature subjects you at starting! Yours are ambition, licentiousness, lamentation and avarice . . . No animal can be found that has a frailer life, and has for living a stronger desire, more disordered fear or greater madness. One hog to another causes no pain, one stag to another; man by another man is slain, crucified, plundered. . . . If any among men seems to you a god, happy and rejoicing, do not believe him such, because in this mud I live more happily; here without anxiety I bathe and roll myself.[17]

Machiavelli presents man as a creature who lives by desire rather than need, a creature with few innate tools for living other than his wits, and even these are a mixed blessing, often turning on him because they are placed in the service of his appetites and ambition. Man lives in a state of extreme vulnerability—without hide or scales—and he begins his life in tears and utter helplessness. He rarely seeks a habitat compatible with his needs but "often into an atmosphere rotten and sickly, leaving a healthful climate [he] shifts [him]self."[18] He does not find his way about the world easily nor in self-beneficial ways, and knows not by instinct even "what any plant is, whether harmless or injurious."[19] He has little capacity for dissimulation and flexibility in the interest of "pursuing his own well-being and avoiding distress."[20]

In short, hardly a single feature of man is "natural" or makes him fit to live in the natural world. Yet Machiavelli, unlike so many other political thinkers, does not therefore conclude that man lives above nature in a higher, better world. The conundrum of man is precisely that he, like all other animals, must cope with nature and his own needs but is severely ill-equipped and ill-tempered for doing so. Prior to the modern age, most political theorists conceived of politics as the activity that sets man apart from beast and issues from the former's intelligence, will, and capacity for conscious action. For such theorists, politics is the highest expression of man's superiority over animals. Machiavelli turns this formulation on its head: man is a poor sort of being and constructs a political world out of his poverty—his vulnerability, passion, and precarious bearing in the natural world. Whatever its prospects for individual or collective glory, Machiavelli insists that politics emerges from and in accord with man's weakness rather than from his superiority.

In *The Golden Ass*, Machiavelli depicts man as a creature who is highly alienated both from himself and from nature. Because of this alienation, *within* nature, man has no dignity and little chance of survival. Ironically, man seeks to resolve the ill effects of this alienation by means that drive it further, that make him even less "at home" in his world, and that make his existence anything but commodious, self-subsistent, or peaceful.

If Machiavelli were pressed to capture in a word that feature of man least shared by other animals and most salient as a political quality, inarguably the word would be "ambition." "What province or what city escapes it? What village, what hovel? Everywhere Ambition and Avarice pene-trate."[21] These "two furies sent to dwell on earth"[22] are the source of nearly all that man does or creates, especially that which is destructive or self-destructive. "If they had no existence, happy enough would be our condition . . . [but they] deprive us of peace . . . set us at war . . . and take away from us all quiet and all good."[23] Ambition and avarice never arrive anywhere alone but bring their necessary companions, Envy, Sloth, and Hatred, who in turn are always accompanied by Cruelty, Pride, and De-ceit.[24] Machiavelli considers ambition an utterly ineradicable feature of individuals and of the human condition as a whole: "when man was born into the world, [ambition] was born too."[25] And in *The Discourses* he says, "whenever men cease fighting through necessity, they go to fighting through ambition, which is so powerful in human breasts that whatever high rank men climb to, never does ambition abandon them."[26]

Machiavelli does not have moral objections to the drive he has labelled ambition; indeed, he considers it the spark and fire of political life. But he does identify a number of problems created by ambiton, problems that together make up the framework upon which his entire political theory is built. Machiavelli begins his political theorizing from the assumption that man's craving for power is boundless, his interest in domination unquestionable, his need to control a given. However, while Machiavellian man is insatiably appetitive and restless, this energy and ambition is polymorphous in character—it has no particular object and by itself is not political. "Nature has made men able to crave everything but unable to attain everything."[27] Even Hobbes did not cast men as so voraciously and indefatiguably desirous; the boundless quest for power in Hobbesian man has its root in self-preservation whereas for Machiavelli ambition is its own engine. Joseph Mazzeo captures the unbounded and unfocused nature of Machiavellian man's ambition in a comparison with Dante:

> Machiavelli, like Dante, sees man as driven by infinite desire, but the infinite goal and the ladder to it have disappeared. The enormous energies which Dante had seen as focused on the infinite, Machiavelli sees as unleashed in the world. . . . In Machiavelli, man appears in fundamental conflict with his universe for he is hopelessly incontinent . . . desirous . . . ambitious, yet his survival depends upon some degree of renunciation and restraint.[28]

In Machiavelli's view, the ubiquitous, polymorphous character of ambition is useless in its raw form for man's survival as well as for political projects. Indeed, much of his political thinking is concerned with the means of harnessing man's random quests for power to the project of Italy's redemption.

A second and related problem with the kind of ambition Machiavelli considers indigenous to man pertains to the competitive, individualistic elements it insinuates into human community. One cannot pursue one's own desires without making others fear for the status of their aims. "Every man hopes to climb higher by crushing now one, now another . . . To each of us another's success is always vexatious, and therefore always . . . for another's ill we are watchful and alert."[29] Such a mentality is more than a mere consequence of ambitious activity. Rather, the fearful or defeated condition of another is instrumentally essential to one's own success. Machiavelli makes this explicit in a discussion of the battles for power between plebeians and patricians in ancient Rome:

> Desire for defending its liberty made each party try to become strong enough to tyrannize over the other. For the law of these matters is that *when men try to escape fear, they make others fear*

and the injury they push away from themselves they lay on others, as if it were necessary to either harm or be harmed.[30]

Yet a third problem with ambition is that while "it is very natural and normal to wish to conquer,"[31] ambition interferes with the achievement of its own end. Even when ambition is "joined with a valiant heart"[32] or is rewarded "only in those who seek support by public [as opposed to private] means,"[33] its individualistic root remains a problem for politics and for man. The constructive possibilities of politics, a strong, rightly ordered and regenerative state, are at odds with the life energies of politics—individual striving, appetitiveness, and quests for glory. Furthermore, the nature of ambition undermines other qualities required for the achievement and maintenance of power, qualities such as analytical keenness, effective political judgment, and a right measure of subtlety and patience. Machiavelli even suggests that political ambition and political judgment have an inverse relation: "as men lessen in vigor as they grow older, [they] improve in judgement and prudence."[34] Ambition blinds men, thereby subverting the promise of their aspirations.[35]

Finally, if ambition is the eye through which men view their world, they will inevitably see it differently from one another and differently according to their constantly shifting ambitions. "As men's appetites change, even though their circumstances remain the same, it is impossible that things should look the same to them, seeing that they have other appetites, other interests, other standpoints."[36] The problem ambition creates for accurate perception and judgment is more active, more practical, than the familiar debilitation of truth by subjectivity. If men unselfconsciously view the world through the prism of their desires, they conceptually locate themselves and these desires at the center of a universe that actually has quite a different axis or no axis at all. They fail to see the "poison lurking underneath a pleasing policy" and they deceive themselves generally about the difference between appearance and reality.[37] The result is men vigorously acting in a world they understand insufficiently to be effective. They act according to a zealous passion for power rather than out of concern with realistic possibility, need, public or even private good.

However aware Machiavelli is of the problems and perils of ambition, he establishes it as the central dynamic of political life. Ambition, whether of a political or nonpolitical sort, is Machiavelli's way of talking about man's unbounded "will to power," his drive not simply to experi-

ence himself as a being of power but to have power over others. Even
when ambition is collectivized, it is rooted not in the good for a community but in a community's drive for power and domination. It is this
impulse toward mastery and conquest that Machiavelli locates as the essence of man's uniquely human nature, and that gives all shape and bearing to political life.

What we are seeing in this creature driven and plagued by ambition is
the development of a particular kind of man first uncovered in ancient
Greek political life. As I have argued elsewhere, once man alienates his
head from his body, once he conceives of the body as something to be
mastered, once he institutionalizes that conception in the organization
of social life, he is set upon a course in which he strives to conquer,
master, dominate, or control all that threatens his precarious freedom
from the body. The head that is separate from the body and subjugates
the body is threatened and spooked by what it has suppressed, and it must
be eternally vigilant in sustaining its "achievement." The mastery is
never complete, never final, and the amorphous drive for power at the
center of Machiavelli's conception of man is at least in part a consequence of this dynamic.

One of the most striking features of the distorting effects ambition has
upon perception and judgment is formulated by Machiavelli as a tendency to reify gaps or failures in one's own understanding of the world.
An excessive emphasis upon appearances—a confusion of appearances
with reality—is one manifestation of this reification. A man "blinded by
ambition" is too caught up in his own desires to perceive what lies underneath superficial appearances. But by far the most extreme expression of
this reification is that which Machiavelli joins with his predecessors in
denoting as *Fortuna*. I want only to suggest the extent to which *Fortuna*
is constituted by the limitations of man's understanding of the world and
his place within it—limitations spurred by his excessive ambition.[38]

While Machiavelli often portrays *Fortuna* as a goddess with mind, will,
and intentions of her own, he also declares that *Fortuna* is nothing other
than man's inadequate grasp of his circumstances. The former is how
Machiavelli knows most men regard *Fortuna* while the latter is his own
view of her existence. Machiavelli's most explicit discussion of the relationship between subjectivity and *Fortuna* occurs in a letter to Piero Soderini.

I believe that as Nature has given each man an individual face, so she has given him an individual disposition and an individual imagination. From this it results that each man conducts himself according to his disposition and his imagination. On the other hand, because times and affairs are of varied types, one man's desires come out as he had prayed they would; he is fortunate who harmonizes his procedures with his time, but on the contrary he is not fortunate who in his actions is out of harmony with his time and with the types of its affairs. Hence it can happen that two men working differently (in different circumstances) come to the same end, because each man adapts himself to what he encounters. . . . Thus because times and affairs in general and individually change often, and men do not change their imaginings and procedures, it happens that a man at one time has good fortune and at another time bad.[39]

Here Machiavelli portrays *Fortuna* as a function of the relative *fit* between a given man's temper and actions, on the one hand, and the conditions under which he is acting, on the other. Machiavelli thereby solves the enigma that inspired this meditation, i.e., how both Hannibal and Scipio, with their very different temperaments and methods, each achieved political and military success. Their different methods were suited to their respective circumstances. "One of them with cruelty, treachery and lack of religion . . . the other with mercy, loyalty, and religion . . . got the same effect . . . [and] won countless victories."[40] Machiavelli concludes the letter to Soderini:

And certainly anyone wise enough to understand the times and the types of affairs and to adapt himself to them would always have good fortune, or he would protect himself always from bad, and it would come to be true that the wise man would rule the stars and the fates.[41]

Machiavelli has thus punctured the mysticism and superstition of his age through a brazen confession: men call *Fortuna*, "fate," or "providence" that which they fail to comprehend or control and these things are therefore actually problems or figments of mind, not some external agency. He issues the same theme in *The Discourses:*

> Many times I have observed that the cause of the bad and of the good fortune of men is the way in which their method of working fits the times, since in their actions some men proceed with haste, some with heed and caution. Because in both of these methods men cross the proper boundaries . . . in both of them they make errors.[42]

And in *The Prince*, Machiavelli links the problem of flexibility and fortune more closely to the problem of ambition considered earlier:

> No man, however prudent, can adjust to . . . radical changes [in circumstances] not only because we cannot go against the inclination of nature, but also because when one has always prospered by following a particular course, he cannot be persuaded to leave it. . . . If only he could change his nature with time and circumstances, his fortune would never change.[43]

Machiavelli does not limit this understanding of *Fortuna* to individual experiences of her. Because ambition penetrates "every province . . . every hovel" and because ambition results in rigidity of method and shortsightedness about circumstances and consequences, to this impulse Machiavelli ascribes the rise and fall of whole cities and empires. While gains and losses of power are perceived by the ignorant as due to the mysterious vicissitudes of *Fortuna*, the true cause is ambition—its blinding effects on judgment, on the selection of appropriate political methods, and the formation of political goals. In one of his soliloquies in *The Golden Ass*, Machiavelli muses:

> That which more than anything else throws kingdoms down from the highest hills is this: that the powerful with their power are never sated. From this it results that they are discontented who have lost and hatred is stirred up to ruin the conquerors; whence it comes that one rises and the other dies; and the one who has risen is ever tortured with new ambition and fear.[44]

Similarly, in the "Tercets on Ambition," Machiavelli establishes unleashed ambition as the cause of every shift in the winds of *Fortuna*. "From [ambition] it results that one goes down and another goes up; on this depends, without law or agreement, the shifting of every mortal condition."⁴⁵ Law and agreement, we recall from Machiavelli's "lion and fox" discussion in *The Prince,* are the forms of struggle conventionally viewed as "appropriate to man." But Machiavelli has made clear that the most prominent feature of man—the raw drive for power—makes a farce of this account of human conduct and politics. Man has his own peculiar animalistic nature, whose drive and raison d'être is ambition. Ambition renders him a creature *in* but not *of* the jungle, a creature who has both more and fewer tools for his own survival than any other animal, a creature who eternally complicates the means of his own existence, and stands in awe and bewilderment at the problem he makes for himself.

For Machiavelli, the cultivation and exercise of *virtù* is the one hope men have of redressing the vulnerability resulting from their infinite passions, scarce natural endowments, and incompatibility with their environment. *Virtù,* like *aretē,* connotes active excellence yet it differs in significant ways from the Greek notion. In Machiavelli's account, man's excellence is measured against his natural inadequacies. Where the problem is poor judgment, *virtù* is keen insight; where laziness or idleness would prevail, *virtù* is energetic activity; where men would incline toward cowardice or effeminacy, *virtù* is courage and willingness to risk life. *Virtù* is an expression of freedom where any kind of enslavement threatens, strength where weakness is commonplace, action where inertia or passivity reigns. In short, the common quality in the diverse applications and meanings of *virtù* in Machiavelli's writings is *overcoming* and this is what distinguishes *virtù* from *aretē.* While *aretē* entails strain and striving, this effort was viewed by the Greeks as a movement toward the perfection or consummation of man's nature. *Virtù,* on the other hand, entails a struggle against man's natural self-indulgence, unfocused passions, laziness, or passivity. Strain and exertion are common to both, but one is a struggle toward perfection while the other is a secular quest for rectification of man's limitations vis à vis his goals.

Virtù is required to channel amorphous passions—especially ambition—into worthwhile, often public, aims. *Virtù* turns greed for gain into calculating, albeit spirited, plans for enlarging one's power. As Machiavelli repeats tirelessly, it is not enough to want something very badly, one must have the correct combination of discipline, patience, foresight, cunning, and strength to achieve one's ends, and this composite is *virtù.*⁴⁶ *Virtù* is also required to temper the excesses of powerful, passionate men; the best example of this dimension of *virtù* is drawn from Machiavelli's favorite pair of antagonists, Hannibal and Scipio. There was a danger, Machiavelli says in *The Discourses*, that each of these characters would bring about their own ruin by virtue of the very qualities that yielded their successes: Hannibal through making himself too much feared and Scipio by being too well loved. "From either one of the two courses can come difficulties great enough to overthrow a prince: he who is too eager to be loved gets despised; he who too much endeavors to be feared . . . gets hated."[47] *Virtù* saved each from these extremes:

> [One] cannot keep exactly the middle way, because our nature does not allow it, but . . . must with extraordinary *virtù* atone for any excesses, as did Hannibal and Scipio. . . . It does not much matter which method a general practices, if only he is able to impart a good flavor to either way of behaving . . . in either one there is defeat and peril if extraordinary *virtù does not correct it.*[48]

From this passage it is evident that contrary to the claims of many of Machiavelli's interpreters, *virtù* and ambition are by no means synonymous in his writings.[49] In fact, only when ambition is converted into desire for public glory does ambition cease to rival *virtù* and instead join forces with it. In all of his remarks about ambition, Machiavelli never links it with *virtù* yet the quest for fame and glory are expressly cast in terms of *virtù*. In his pastoral for Lorenzo de' Medici, Machiavelli concludes his litany of praise, "and by no means as something less excellent [virtuous] appears your natural desire for gaining fame that will make your glory evident."[50]

The road from individualistic ambition to public pursuit of glory is no easy one. In this task, *virtù* is called upon for two quite distinct and ultimately conflicting purposes. First *virtù* must supply the keenness of insight into conditions and farsight about consequences ordinarily hindered by man's ambitious nature. Second, *virtù* fosters a bold and determined approach to gaining one's ends. The first matter is an often neglected aspect of Machiavelli's conception of *virtù*. While *virtù* is most commonly associated with action (and finds its supreme expression there), effective action is predicated upon a thorough understanding of what Machiavelli calls "the times" and, as we have seen, this understanding is most elusive to the mind of men driven by ambition. In addition to developing the capacity for perceiving "opportunity,"[51] *virtù* of insight and foresight entails the exercise of patience and the inglorious work of establishing and maintaining solid foundations and fortifications.[52] The *virtù* of overcoming man's natural short-sightedness involves obtaining a long and accurate view of things and planning or ruling accordingly. It involves remedying diseases of state in their early stages, waging a war one does not have to wage in order to prevent one later where there would be less advantage, and seeing opportunity in what appears to others as chaos or seething social corruption.[53] In this regard, *virtù* is the reclamation of all the powers of vision and subtle uses of strength that ambition diminishes.

The problem is that such reclamation is nearly impossible and never absolute. Repeatedly Machiavelli laments that "men are more attracted by immediate than by remote events,"[54] and that even men of great *virtù* are incapable of understanding their circumstances and suiting their actions to the times. In this mood, Machiavelli's advice and formulation of *virtù* turns one hundred eighty degrees: be blunt, be bold, seize your world and impose yourself upon it. When *Fortuna* (bewildering or antagonistic circumstances) is upon you, be impetuous and audacious. The famous lines bear repeating: "It is better to be impetuous than cautious . . . [*Fortuna*] is the friend of young men because they are less cautious, more spirited, and with more boldness master her."[55]

As far as possible, then, one must know and work with the times and in this regard, *virtù* is historical knowledge, appreciation of patterns and cycles in human affairs, construction of political and military foundations, and intense, penetrating vision. But then the *virtù* of will, strength, and boldness takes over; force and firmness of purpose gain an importance rivaled only by the flexibility and caution Machiavelli counsels as virtues when there is space, time, and capacity for them. "Many times one achieves with impetuousness and audacity things that could never be achieved by ordinary means."[56]

Thus *virtù* not only involves both physical and mental strength, there are two sorts of each of these and they are ultimately in conflict with one another. In action, the importance of building foundations, carefully constructing conditions, and altering one's methods when the shifting winds call for it is overwhelmed by the call for unequivocal, bold, brute attack. In intellection, the *virtù* of insight and foresight is at odds with the *virtù* of a single-minded and opportunistic perspective. Utterly antagonistic to the open, searching mind needed to apprehend one's world is the mentality required for *virtù* in action where the bold exercise of will requires a relatively narrow, calculating, instrumental rationality. In the latter, contemplation has no place at all, and deliberation is relevant only in the most superficial—militaristic or strategic—sense of the term; what is wanted is a mind attuned solely to the relation between its aims and the opportunity to achieve them. Not only must such a mind avoid external distractions, it must hush all the inner sentiments, doubts, and conflicts that would subvert the fixity of its purpose and means of achieving it. As Jerrold Siegel remarks, "it [is] indecisiveness to which audacity is most strongly opposed, and this links it most closely to the necessity which creates *virtù* in Machiavelli's mind: both are opposites of choice and *virtù* dissolves in the realm of choice."[57]

Indecisiveness is only the extreme expression of what Machiavelli perceives as subversive of *virtù*. Any mental moves that deflect focus from a chosen goal will amount to assaults on the *virtù* of the mind intent upon this goal. Reason itself, unless tethered firmly to the task at hand, weakens a man's control over his world.[58] Undisciplined reason is no more trustworthy in Machiavelli's account than in Hobbes's. Harnessed to a purpose, however, reason becomes as powerful a force as physical might in shaping the world according to one's desires. "Force and fraud," Machiavelli's two pistols of politics, are simply different elements of the same medium. Neither is a mode of working *with* one's circumstances; both make up the activity of imposing form on matter, or combatting another form (generally mysterious and in the guise of *Fortuna*) with one's own. To this end, the mind must be cleared of all that makes it "soft" or "effeminate"; not only moral considerations but deep, reflective thought itself must be suppressed. Only as the mental equivalent of an invading army can the mind be marshalled as a force adequate to the task of conquering the unknown.

One can see this *virtù* of mind modeled in the very character of Machiavelli's own writing. Machiavelli's literary style is famous for its starkness and definitiveness—a situation is either "this" or it is "that," one must do either "a" or "b." This either/or, black and white motif Federico Chabod calls "a perfect formal expression of a mode of thought which is always based upon the precept that *virtù* in a politician consists entirely in making prompt and firm decisions."[59] No one is more aware than Machiavelli of the subtleties and nuances in the conditions of political action and relationships. Yet Machiavelli insists that descending into the depths of these subtleties and nuances portends disaster for political men. What one cannot be sure of, one must never pause before but, rather, bludgeon or overwhelm. Mental *virtù* entails suppression of the distinctly human reaches and byways of thought and brings man closer to being an animal driven by fear or voraciousness. As Felix Gilbert puts the matter, "man's control over his world depends on his attaining a level of instinctiveness where he becomes part of the forces surrounding him."[60]

Instinctiveness is indeed the characteristic Machiavelli looks to *virtù* to supply but he neither expects this to yield absolute control over one's world nor believes that such instinctiveness results in blending into surrounding forces. For Machiavelli makes clear that even in actions of the greatest *virtù*, man remains at odds with his world and controls only what he strongarms, what he imprints with his own form. *Virtù*, in the sense of boldness and courage, impetuousness and audacity, does not bring the actor in line with the times but rather, signifies his determination to shape the times rather than pander to them or mix with them. *Virtù* of this sort involves courage, risk, and acting in an occupied space. It is, as Machiavelli says repeatedly, the opposite of relying upon time or *Fortuna*.[61] It is also the opposite of relying upon others or upon institutions not of one's own making.[62] In this regard, *virtù* embodies a quest for control, for mastery of one's surroundings, but such control and mastery are achieved only to the degree that all manifestations of power other than one's own are subdued. This kind of *virtù* has nothing to do with bringing one's actions and intentions into accord with one's surroundings, with what Machiavelli has designated as *Fortuna*, and it therefore intensifies the battle with *Fortuna*. *Fortuna* and *virtù* remain locked in permanent combat; the war between the sexes is, for Machiavelli, *the* paradigm of politics.

What is becoming clear is that Machiavelli's comprehension of the complex nature of the political realm—complexity rooted in boundless human potentialities as well as limitations—is failed by the kind of actor he inaugurates into this world. Machiavelli urges control and mastery where he knows that they are ultimately impossible, he counsels blunt domination of circumstances that he has revealed as nuanced and shifting. The *virtù* of bold action is at odds with Machiavelli's understanding of the fluid, nuanced, and strongly contextual nature of political life. This kind of *virtù* is realized through shows of determination, firmness, and lack of equivocation. One must adhere to the path one carves and makes events or *Fortuna* flow around it—if that were possible.

Hence, while *virtù* is posed as a remedy to the alienation and relative powerlessness to which man's amorphous drive for power had given birth, it intensifies this alienation as well as the distance between everyday life and the realm called politics. Not only does the cultivation of *virtù* increase the intensity of struggle between political actors, it increases the extent to which the political realm is an arena of battle among the few for power over the existence of the many. Moreover, the domination of certain elements and forces, which is entailed in the exercise of *virtù*, increases the mysteriousness and dangerousness of that which is dominated or suppressed. To this matter we now turn.

As we approach Machiavelli's thinking on the subject of that which mysteriously undermines or threatens man's intentions in the political realm, we are once again confronted with his brilliance of insight subverted by his ultimate attachment to manliness. For Machiavelli is one of the few theorists of politics to have recognized the power borne by that which is oppressed, power generated by the very act of oppression, power that must be perceived and addressed by any successful political actor. Machiavelli saw in stark political terms what Freud would many centuries later put forth in refined psychological language: what is dominated, suppressed, or repressed does not disappear or die but takes on a life of its own in an underworld, eternally threatening and dangerous to that which has sought to lock it away. Yet even as Machiavelli so perceptively explores this phenomenon in political life, he turns his back on its implications and ultimately seeks to overcome it, despite the futility of this attempt. The language of "form" and "matter" permeating Machiavelli's political discourse is a perfect example of this self-subverting twist in his thought.

Before we explore Machiavelli's form-matter paradigm, a brief etymological digression is in order. "Matter" and "material" stem from the Latin *mater*, which, in turn derives from the Greek *ule*. The Greek and Latin terms both signify "mother" as well as "matter" and the Greek term also signifies "wood," "forest," "timber," "stuff of which a thing is made," and "trunk of a tree." From this array of meanings two possible explanations for the mother-matter connection suggest themselves: (1) Man perceives wood or forests as matter for his enterprises in a similar way as he regards mothers, i.e., as "the stuff of which a thing (an artifact or a child) is made." This corresponds especially to Aristotle's account of the reproductive process in which woman supplies/is the material for conception and man supplies/is the principle or seed; (2) If mothers and women are ideologically synonymous in patriarchal culture, then matter signifies women generally, not just mothers. In this case, *mater*'s multiple meanings reveal a more general facet of man's relationship to women and his genderization of the world: women are perceived as material for his use, service, or imposition of form and conversely, wherever man sees the possibility of imposing his form in the world, he sees himself (man) against "the other" (woman). In other words, woman-matter-mother is set up in opposition to man-form-father and the former not only exists for the use of the latter but is seen as given shape and purpose by it.

The significance of this for Machiavelli's work emerges clearly when we recall that the Italian *virtù* comes from the Latin *virtus* and the root of both words, *vir*, means "man." *Virtù* connotes manly activity, as "virtuoso" signifies a great and accomplished man and "virility" a potent and powerful man. For Machiavelli, the two definitive expressions of *virtù* are the act of giving form (*forma*) to matter (*materia*), especially in founding a city-state, and the act of defeating or outwitting *Fortuna*. Both are supremely gendered constructions, of course, and both involve a construction of manliness that entails not mere opposition to but conquest of woman.

On close inspection, Machiavelli's "form-matter" model of political action and political foundations is both revealing and deceptive with regard to his understanding of the nature of political life. It reveals that all Machiavelli's talk of the importance of flexibility in a political actor does not attenuate his conviction that one can only overpower events and circumstances one does not understand by forcefully assailing them, imposing one's form upon them.[62] However one translates the famous passage in chapter 25 of *The Prince*, Machiavelli's stance here is clear: *Fortuna* is to be cuffed and mauled, beaten or raped, anything but handled respectfully, gingerly, or flexibly.[63] *Virtù* opposes itself to what *Fortuna* represents in this case—the fluidity of setting and circumstance a man faces. Machiavelli calls this battle the imposition of form upon matter and portrays it as the sexual conquering of woman by man.

The deception lies in the fact that what Machiavelli calls *Fortuna* or "matter" does not have the passive qualities either term evokes but instead embodies a different kind of power than the one available to man or used by him when he is exercising *virtù*. *Fortuna* and "feminine power" *appear* mysterious, capricious, intangible, and utterly subversive to man if he does not effectively guard and prevail against them. Machiavelli repeats this theme tirelessly in his political, dramatic, and literary works. In "How a State Falls Because of a Woman," he concurs with Livy: "Women have caused much destruction, have done great harm to those who govern cities, and have occasioned many divisions in them."[64] The hero of *La Mandragola* is a man who has lost all interest in his worldly pursuits for love of an unavailable woman.[65] One of Machiavelli's lesser known plays, *Clizia*, is also a study of the corrupting effects of love on a man and of the indefatiguable power of a woman intent upon preventing a man from his desire. In this play, Nicomaco, the old man smitten by his adopted daughter, is described by his wife as a man who was "serious, steadfast, cautious . . . spending his days in dignified and honorable pursuits."[66] But "since this infatuation for that girl has got into his head, his farms are going to ruin, his business ventures fail, everyone has given up respecting him and makes a game of him."[67] Even though Nicomaco is master of his home and has all the social and economic power his wife lacks, it is she who wins the battle to get him away from the girl after whom he lusts (for a summary, see Appendix B).

Still another example of Machiavelli's identification of women's enormous capacity for subversiveness arises in "Balfagor: The Devil Who Married." This work has as its central theme the question of whether wives are the cause of their husbands going to hell.[68] Predictably, the tale ends with an answer in the affirmative and along the way Machiavelli also muses upon the difference between male and female power and the ability of the latter to undermine the former.

In none of these depictions of women's power is the power at issue a political or institutional sort. Women did not have such power and Machiavelli never assumes that they did.[69] But it is female power—mysterious, seductive, vengeful, cunning, associated with the impenetrable and unpredictable ways of Nature—that Machiavelli calls "matter" or *Fortuna* elsewhere in his writings. While many interpreters of Machiavelli regard *Fortuna* and "matter" as passive entities, obstacles rather than direct threats to men's interests, this misreads what Machiavelli is saying about women and about all the elements of man's universe he does not understand and control.[70] *Fortuna* and female power not only conspire to undo men but are also the very things man is acting against, in an effort to master, control, or escape.[71] He must avoid being bewitched by them as well as being thrashed by them; again, we glimpse the extent to which the enemy man perennially fights is within himself. When Machiavelli expounds on the perils of love, it is not the power of women qua women that is so deeply threatening but the passions a man feels toward them, his experience of being in thrall to his needs, that make ruins of the rest of his life and undermines his institutional power over women. It is self-mastery that is preeminently endangered. Since he has fallen in love with

Lucrezia, Callimaco complains in *La Mandragola*, he cannot sleep, eat, or return to his work in Paris.[72] Not Lucrezia but his own lust has undermined his self-mastery.

The other way Machiavelli speaks of female power—as vengeful, surreptitious and elusive—is also a mirrored image of man's inadequacies. It represents the unknown and incomprehensible against which man is powerless to prevail. To women and to *Fortuna* are ascribed whatever powers and abilities men experience themselves as lacking.[73] Machiavelli makes this clear each time he chastises a prince or a people for blaming upon *Fortuna* what is actually caused by their own paucity of ability, by their own lack of *virtù*.[74] But to know this intellectually, while partially demystifying "female power," does not vitiate that power, and Machiavelli's concern is with the strategies of battle between male and female, *virtù* and *Fortuna*, not with the origins or deep structure of the contest.

The stakes in this battle are both freedom and manhood. The man who succumbs to or attempts to rely upon *Fortuna* sacrifices both.[75] Conversely, men and states whom Machiavelli calls "effeminate"—without fortifications, discipline, energy, *virtù*—are the first to fall to the blows of *Fortuna* and womankind.[76] "Female power" must be confronted directly and with no moves toward reconciliation; avoiding dependence upon *Fortuna* is a theme Machiavelli repeats as often as he argues the need to fortify against her unpredictable blows.[77] *Fortuna* must be deciphered and paralleled in some instances, bludgeoned in others, and the real man must be able to do both. Says Robert Orr,

> Boldness . . . is the one advantage of character that men hold permanently over *Fortuna*. Up to a point, we have to fight her with her own female weapons—variety, flexibility, effectiveness. But we hold an additional weapon, which, if we did but know it, can be made an ace. She is a woman and we are men, able to move with speed, which carries with it a certain quality of determination, and even some negligence of consequences.[78]

Virtù is the paradigmatic symbol of manhood; exercised to its fullest, it rids a man of all softness in himself and all dangers of being enveloped, overcome, or seduced by the goddess who would undo or enslave him. The acquisition of *virtù* is also the acquisition of freedom. But what an expensive and precarious freedom it is! Instrumental in its essence, *virtù* storms everything in its path and quells even other dimensions of the actor, dimensions that come to haunt him in the guise of *Fortuna* and female power. All but the aim become tools or obstacles in the pursuit and expression of *virtù*.[80] Everything in the field and vision of the virtuoso is rendered either as an opposing force to be squelched or as matter upon which form must be imposed.[81]

Recall from whence the man of *virtù* has come. Naturally, polymorphously, desirous and ambitious, *virtù* shapes these drives into public, political ones and focuses man's cravings upon glory and public power. Ill-suited for and uncomfortable within his habitat, Machiavellian man seeks to resolve his vulnerability by commandeering his surroundings, reshaping them under his own auspices, stamping his world with his own projects and purposes. Limited in rationality and foresight by his boundless desires, *virtù* focuses his mind more intently upon the means and opportunities for achieving them and inspires him to boldly seize these opportunities. Intellectually and physically, man must become fierce, resolute, and in a sense, one-dimensional, if he is not to be overwhelmed by his weakness in the world. Freedom in the sense of *virtù* has peace as its antagonist or enemy, the sacrifice of collective sociability and security as its cost.[82]

We have come full circle: From Machiavelli's depiction of man as a poor specimen of animal, through the perils of harnessing man's ambitious nature, to the development of the man of *virtù* who rekindles the animal in himself and acts as one who is either hunted or hunting—swiftly, deliberately, without regard for convention, ethics, or the general order of things, except insofar as they are instrumentally useful for his purposes. Yet there is something very curious about Machiavelli's cultivation of this "magnificent animal." Humankind, after all, does not live in a jungle, nor, if one reads its annals, does it strive to make civilization in the image of the wilderness. Yet the man of Machiavelli's making, poised for political action, is meant to view his world in just these terms. Put the other way around, conditions of political necessity, the conditions that demand and nourish *virtù*, are meant to be a human version of the conditions a wild animal faces and, as will become clear in the next segment, the human version is a profoundly disturbing one.

The drive toward domination constitutive of Machiavellian man issues partly from an alienation from the body first articulated in Greek political philosophy. In the previous segment, we saw how this drive shapes and complicates man's posture on earth, especially his endeavors in collective life. These perspectives may now be drawn into an exploration of the purpose, characteristics and ethos of Machiavellian politics.

In the course of this exploration, some earlier themes will recurr: the need for perceptual clarity thwarted by unbridled desire; the reification of gaps or failures in perception as *Fortuna* or female agency; the ultimate call to conquer what cannot be fathomed. But we will also witness the way in which politics itself removes man further and further from concrete "reality," the way politics comes to transpire in a realm of appearances, as a game, as theater. While Machiavelli seeks to root politics in the body and in "life," the male bodies and lives in which he roots it produce a politics distant from and threatening to life and the body. As with the Greeks, Machiavellian politics issues from aspects of alienated man that create and sustain a struggle "above" the cultivation and concerns of life. Politics becomes its own cause, its own glory, its own pernicious and bloody battle for manhood and freedom. This frenzy in which political men are ensnared also casts its curse upon all that is outside the official purview of politics, whether men, women, children, or external nature.

Machiavelli opens the *Discourses on the First Decade of Titus Livius* with a problem seemingly quite peripheral to issues of politics and power: in what kind of climate and terrain should a city ideally be established?[83] This discussion at first appears either anachronistic or trivial—perhaps Niccolò's own particular manner of warming up his pen for a lengthy treatise on infinitely more complex and demanding subjects. But the paradox Machiavelli sets forth in the discussion of geographical considerations turns out to be a major theme in the 500-page symphony that follows.

> Because men act either through necessity or through choice, and because *virtù* appears greater where choice has less power, it must be considered whether for the building of cities it would be better to choose barren places, in order that men, forced to keep at work and less possessed by laziness, may live more united, having because of the poverty of the site slighter cause for dissensions . . . Such a choice would without doubt be wise and most useful if men were content to live on their own resources and were not inclined to govern others. . . . Since men cannot make themselves safe except with power, it is necessary for them to avoid such

barrenness of country and to establish themselves in very fertile places, where, since the richness of the site permits the city to expand, she can both defend herself from those who assail her and crush whoever opposes himself to her greatness.[84]

Men perform best and are least self-destructive when their activities are dictated by genuine and pressing need, but they have other inclinations making governance by external nature impractical. They require collective power, both for satisfaction of their own desires and for defense against omnipresent predators with similar desires. Machiavelli establishes the need for this kind of power as the prime mover in the formation of political communities.

> Cities built by men native to the place [arise] . . . when the inhabitants, dispersed in many little places, perceive that they cannot live in safety. . . . Hence . . . they unite to dwell together in a place chosen by them, more convenient for living in and easier to defend.[85]

The problem is that men are not naturally inclined toward building the collective power they require. Man's ambitious nature leads him to grasp for wealth and dominion via methods that do not necessarily engender or sustain virtue, strength, or community. Thus, in Machiavelli's view, ambition and slothfulness are frequent companions; men will take whatever appears to be the easiest road to their gainful ends. This also means that prosperous societies are frequently ridden with corruption; instead of enjoying or safeguarding their luxury and tranquility, men will incessantly and invidiously seek to augment it in their own personal or partisan favor.

Because men are "not content to live on their own resources" and are always "inclined to try to govern others," natural necessity is an inappropriate remedy for individual and collective laziness, decadence, and corruption. The power derivable from abundant resources rightly employed is essential for defense and attack, for success in domestic as well as international affairs. Thus, in order to reduce the evils arising from the prosperity prerequisite to power, Machiavelli calls for an arrangement of laws that will "force upon [a city] those necessities which the site does not."[86] Such a city, Machiavelli says, should imitate wise cities placed in countries very pleasant and fertile and likely to produce men lazy and unfit for all vigorous activity. They, to forestall the losses which the pleasantness of the country would have caused . . . have laid such necessity for exercise on those who are to be soldiers that through such an arrangement better soldiers have been produced there than in those countries that are naturally rough and barren.[87]

In formulating law as mitigating the corrupting effects of prosperity, it is clear that law has quite a different place in Machiavelli's political metaphysic than it does in the liberal tradition. While we are accustomed to regarding law as that which liberates us from nature (from the "state of nature" in Hobbes's and Locke's accounts) and yields civilized society, Machiavelli looks to law for the replication within society of the demands of a life lived in constant struggle with nature. Law supplies necessity and thus compensates for, rather than gives birth to, civilized existence:

Men never do anything good except by necessity . . . Where there is plenty of choice and excessive freedom is possible, everything is at once filled with confusion and disorder. Hence it is said that hunger and poverty make men industrious and laws make them good.[88]

Again, it is from the wilderness that Machiavelli has drawn what he considers an essential ingredient of man's individual and collective well-being. Necessity is the food that keeps animals sinewy and strong, active and alert; ease renders them fat and sleepy, destined to dependence or death and no little contempt. But for humans, the manufacture of neces-sity in society entails a good deal more than constructing constraints against ease or imposing conditions in which body and brain are routinely exercised. Yet even rigorous laws and military discipline are insufficient stays against the fragile character of individual and civic *virtù*. Deliberate and at times contrived construction of conditions of necessity is the only sure guarantee against the decay or corruption of a polity.

Prosperous, libertine polities are utterly unimpressive to Machiavelli. Equally unappealing are tyrannies, whether they are achieved on the foundations of a rich or poor economy, a rebellious people or a resigned one. It is individual heroic *virtù* and collective civic spirit that breeds a polity worth having and a political world worth exhausting oneself within the ceaseless turmoil indigenous to it. Such spirit and involvement are utterly dependent upon the existence of conditions—real or apparent—that *demand* them. "As long as necessity forced the Veientians to fight, they fought most savagely, but when they saw the way open, they thought more about fleeing than fighting."[89] Necessity makes a city strong where its absence "would make her effeminate or divided."[90] Indeed, Machiavelli posits necessity as the impetus for all great human accomplishment:

> The hands and tongue of man, two most noble instruments for making him noble, would not have worked perfectly or brought human actions to the height they have reached if they had not been urged on by necessity.[91]

"Necessity makes *virtù*," Machiavelli declares forthrightly[92] and when it does not do so directly, as in a situation where one either battles gloriously or is destroyed, it does so in more roundabout fashion, by giving rise to an entire culture of competitiveness, covetousness, and very rapid pace.[93]

There are resonances here of the relationship between the cultivation of *aretē* and the agonistic nature of Greek public life. Intense competition for glory and success is certainly one aspect of Machiavelli's appreciation of the dependence of *virtù* upon necessity. But *virtù* is more than accomplishment, more than excellence in deed—it is also vitality, largeness of purpose, and fierce determination in the face of adverse conditions. Necessity's nurturance of *virtù* is a central concern for Machiavelli because of its role in the development of political *strength* and *power*. This is most apparent in his praise of the "tumults of Rome" chronicled by Livy. In the chapter title of this discussion, Machiavelli declares that "the discord between the people and the Roman Senate made that republic free and powerful"—free because the people had to exercise their freedom in order to maintain it and powerful because the ceaseless discords and quests for power within the city made the people into citizen-warriors of the strongest sort imaginable.[94] Forced daily to fight for their civic status in order to maintain or enhance it, plebeians and patricians alike contributed to the enormous strength and vitality of the Roman state. Necessity unifies and focuses ambition and it cultivates vigor where its opposite threatens. "That kingdom which is pushed on to action by energy or necessity will always go upward."[95]

Ambition generates striving, striving breeds competition, competition nourishes *virtù*, the existence of *virtù* intensifies man's experience of scarcity, narrowed options, or necessity. Yet, as has already been intimated, Machiavelli does not find the need for conditions of necessity in politics satisfied through this chain of social-psychological reaction. Particularly in building civic *virtù*, political and military leaders must often construct the *appearance* of necessity in order to muster forces conducive to political success. *Perceptions* of circumstances as well as political time and political space all must be manipulated by political actors in the effort to bring necessity into play where it is useful and to disguise it where recognition of necessity by an enemy would be damaging.

In an essay on Machiavelli's concept of *fantasia* ("imagination" or "subjectivity"), K. R. Minogue notes that even necessity, seemingly the most concrete of political imperatives, is a function of imagination, of seeing no options in a situation.[96] It is in this vein that Machiavelli counsels a prudent general to "open to the enemy a road you could close and to your own soldiers close a road you could have left open."[97] He who wishes that a city be stubbornly defended "ought above everything to impose such necessity upon the hearts of those who are going to fight."[98] Concluding this discussion, Machiavelli approvingly cites a Volscian leader's speech to his soldiers: "Come with me, not wall or ditch but armed men oppose armed men; you are equal in courage; in the last and chief weapons, necessity, you are superior."[99]

To create the appearance of necessity where it is not actually present, both time and space must be manipulated or distorted. The prince of true *virtù* no more allows himself to be ruled by time than by that of which it is a subset, *Fortuna*. Rather, he uses time as a weapon by shortening or lengthening it as needed. The trick in politics is to obtain as much time as possible for oneself, to shorten time for those one wants to force into acting and to lengthen it for those one wants to defeat through their own confusion and delay.[100] Similarly, the successful political actor wrestles with the dimension of political space to create or dismember the apparent nature of political conditions. Because men respond to what is close at hand and to the superficial appearance of things, a wise prince uses this knowledge in his presentation of circumstances to his constituency and to his enemies.[101] Similarly, he capitalizes upon the distortions that spatial dimensions entail, heeding Machiavelli's belief that "so much more at a distance than nearby the things that make a show are feared."[102]

By now, it should be evident that the kind of "necessity" relevant to

Machiavellian politics bears little relation to what might be called the "real necessities" of human existence. Even when Machiavelli speaks of necessity as being imposed externally rather than as a condition fabricated by a political leader or imposed through institutions, it is not actual human or social needs but the imperatives of a particular political milieu and particular political goals to which he is referring. Political necessity arises from a conception and practice of politics rooted in the achievement, maintenance, or defense of individual and collective *power*. Political necessity is of an entirely different order from and moves on a different plane than human needs for material well-being, security, or freedom. Under the auspices of political necessity come such things as allying with another state to strengthen one's international position, or expanding one's state in order to fortify its existing power.[103] Thus, imperialism, domestic repression, acts of cruelty by a prince, and elaborate exercises in popular deception all constitute examples of political necessity.[104] True enough that Machiavelli's concern with political necessity stems from his belief that natural necessity, the struggle with nature, makes men strong. But human culture, while at times taking cues from the natural world, does not simply duplicate it; power it was that initially wrested men out of the jungle and into cities and power it is that dictates what political man "needs." Machiavelli calls for contrived conditions of necessity in civilization in order to push man past a tendency to recline into satisfaction of material wants or into other private desires. Necessity makes men of *virtù* out of mere men.

The political world Machiavelli analyzes is therefore one in which artificial necessity starts the dynamic of political events and the imperatives of success in the established political system perpetuate this dynamic. The basis of politics is the slight satisfaction men get from what they have and the concommitant need to defend themselves against other men who would prey upon them. From this arises the "necessity" of developing individual and collective power as well as the need to foster apparent "necessity," which will nourish and sustain that power. But once this world is operating at full pitch, it generates demands or necessary actions of its own accord: ominipresent striving, competitiveness, and power struggles issue a set of imperatives to any individual or state that would survive let alone gain in such a world. Not that the individual or state actually "need" the offerings or rewards of this struggle but that if one partakes of the rewards of that world at all, these imperatives become that by which one operates.

The manufacture of necessity intensifies the problems of accurately perceiving or assessing political conditions or "the times." The manipulation of time, space, and general conditions in order to make "necessity" appear or disappear according to one's strategy results in a perpetual distortion of the setting in which political judgment and political action occur. The construction of the appearance of necessity is a process of substituting appearances for reality and then acting upon those appearances such that they gain a kind of reality of their own. Myths, deceptions, and fabrications become a second-order environment for political action and further complicate the actor's struggle with knowing where he is, what time it is, and where he stands in relation to enemies, allies, and objectives. Hence, political life is not only several paces removed from human or social "needs" but also from any autonomous political "reality." In Machiavelli's account, politics transpires in the frenzied realm of appearances—a realm in which the political actor is half blinded by his own ambitions but is also threatened by camouflaged mine fields and false images of insurmountable passes constructed by his adversaries. We move now to a closer inspection of this milieu.

One modern interpretation of Machiavelli stands out amidst the massive literature on his thought. This is a reading that casts him neither as political scientist nor philosopher, but as political playwright. According to Norman Jacobson,

> Someone once inquired of Demosthenes, "What is the chief part of an orator?" "Acting," replied Demosthenes. "What next?" "Acting." "What next again?" "Acting!" . . . Were we to inquire of Machiavelli the chief part of his *Prince*, we would undoubtedly receive the identical reply: acting.[105]

For Machiavelli, so this interpretation goes, the political realm is a stage, there is no essential reality more important than appearance, there is real political power in symbolic action and events, in myth, faith, exuberance, good scenes or bad. Moreover, there is no authentic man but only the masks that he wears—predictable and transprent if he is a poor actor-politician and many, varied, and fluid if he is a clever and successful one.

> Machiavelli's . . . new political art . . . is utterly devoid of content, its teaching precisely the opposite of "Be yourself." Its precept is

instead "Be your roles." The object is to create a man of a thousand faces, a master performer who eventually does become his
roles.[106]

"After all," says Merleau-Ponty in his kindred reading of Machiavelli,
"a face is only shadows, lights and colors."[107] And Jacobson corroborates,
"in *The Prince*, political art is the capacity of the unique man to transmute words and events into appearance."[108] From Machiavelli's oft-
quoted precept, "in general men judge more with their eyes than with
their hands . . . everyone sees what you appear to be, few perceive what
you are."[109] K. R. Minogue surmises, "politics is then, in a deep sense, an
exercise in theatricality."[110] Hannah Arendt develops the theatrical aspect of politics discerned by Machiavelli into a metaphysical principle.
Genuine politics, she argues, can only occur in a bounded public realm
where "appearance—something that is being seen and heard by others as
well as ourselves—*constitutes* reality."[111] From Arendt's remark, N. O.
Brown concludes that political organization is theatrical organization.
"To see through this show, to see the invisible reality; is to put an end to
politics."[112]

Arendt's and Brown's characterization of the theatrical dimension of
politics is not quite true to Machiavelli, whose political world includes
but is not wholly constituted by the realm of appearances. Machiavelli
does not give us inauthentic man, pure role-player, and from him reach
inauthentic politics, a politics of nothing but roles and "seemings." To
the contrary, Machiavelli begins with men who distinctly crave power
but must reorder reality, dissimulate, and fabricate appearances to reach
their desires. Machiavellian man is a creature of intense subjectivity and
identity—he does not blend easily into the roles and forces that political
success demands. He climbs into the realm of appearances for purposes
instrumental to his real ends or is caught up in the order of appearances
because he does not know better. But he cannot possibly hope to succeed
in his endeavors if he takes events, conditions, or individuals at face
value. Political man must constantly strive to pierce the appearances
thrown up by others while creating appearances useful to his own ends.[113]
Thus, while Machiavellian politics has a theatrical element, it contains
elements the theater does not (unmasking the rest of the world while
masking one's own character and plans), elements distinctly at odds with
dramatic success (absence of a script), and elements opposed to theater
(plays whose own underlying desires and intentions dictate their roles).

If the identity between politics and drama is not so complete as some interpreters of Machiavelli have implied, the *role* of drama and especially of appearances does figure largely in his understanding of politics. Machiavellian politics is never quite real, it is never quite about real things. The spur of politics—ambition or the amorphous quest for power—is itself of an ultimately intangible quality and spins a world of unreality. In the Western tradition of "masculine" politics, political life is always at some level a game played by juvenile delinquents, and this is precisely what Machiavelli confesses as he portrays politics in dramaturgical terms. Still, Machiavelli's concern with the problem of appearances in politics is also about that most concrete of political goods—the construction and wielding of political power. That something so ephemeral as contrived appearances could be partly constitutive of something so tangible and determinate as power is not only an intriguing enigma but one that opens up another dimension of Machiavelli's distinctly masculine construction of politics.

The most overt sense in which Machiavelli treats appearances as constitutive of power arises in his discussions of a prince's efforts to frighten an enemy and to win the loyalty or commitment of his own people. In both cases, it is an emotional calculus with which the prince is working, an appreciation and use of the psychology of civic and political behavior. (Calculated manipulation of basic human drives, dreads, and responses is the way we would speak of this matter today.) The primary emotions to which a prince appeals in his constituency have already been touched upon in the discussion of ambition. He works on his subjects' desire for gain and on their insecurity or fear of loss.[114] But he also seeks to inspire them and command their loyalty through appeals to their sense of vengeance and hatred on the one hand,[115] pride and dignity on the other.[116] Above all, he works on the precept that "the masses are always impressed by the superficial appearance of things, and by the outcome of an enterprise."[117] He capitalizes on spatial and temporal distortions related to their short memories and short vision; he gives them the appearance of what they want or need, or the appearance of being forced by necessity, in order to obtain what *he* needs from them—whether it be timid obeisance or blood-thirsty citizen warriors. The clever prince arranges and rearranges appearances—his own and that of his surroundings or adversaries—for the purpose of securing or mobilizing power. Religious rituals as well as purely secular proclamations are useful to this end, and Machiavelli bears no scruples about mixing one with the other.[118]

A prince also builds power within his state through careful attention to his reputation. Not what he is but what he seems to be determines the extent to which he is in control of his dominion, and in turn, the extent to which his state is a powerful one.

> What makes the prince contemptible is being considered change-able, trifling, effeminate, cowardly, or indecisive; he should avoid this as a pilot does a reef and make sure that his actions bespeak greatness, courage, seriousness of purpose and strength . . . Any prince who gives such an impression is bound to be highly esteemed, and a man with such a reputation is hard to conspire against, hard to assail, as long as everyone knows he is a man of character and respected by his own people.[119]

Note how quickly Machiavelli moves from the seemingly superficial elements making up a prince's public image to his actual power in the world. In his account, dissimulation is not an alternative to power but a component of it. The lion is powerless without the fox; force may be useless where fraud is indispensable.[120]

Up to this point, I have intimated that however powerful and prominent the realm of appearances in Machiavelli's politics, this realm remains distinct from an order of "objective reality." Yet Jacobson insists that the drama—the superficial appearance of things—is the only relevant matter in Machiavelli's political world. And K. R. Minogue identifies Machiavelli's ontological view of "reality" as "an unstable part of a flux in which everything is dissolved into appearance by being continually construed as the product of imagination."[121] For these thinkers, Machiavelli did not so much discover the role of appearances in politics as that politics *is* the appearances generative of and generated by that realm. "If Machiavelli has a 'philosophic significance,' it is the rejection of any reality behind the one that appears to us."[122] Or again, in N. O. Brown's words, "to see . . . is to see through, to put an end to politics."[123]

What is eclipsed by these interpretations is Machiavelli's repeated insistence that the successful politician must be able to distinguish what *seems* to be the case from what is in fact the situation; he must be able to pierce the order of appearances if he is to work that realm in his own advantage. No one is more ill-fated than a prince who responds to the reputation rather than to the concrete power of another prince,[124] or who makes the error of trying to *be* what he must appear to be.[125] Whether external conditions or his own image are at issue, a prince who is duped by either is bound to fail. Machiavelli advises the political actor to play the game of appearances from outside of its clutches for political phenomena have an "underlying reality" even if few can grasp it and even though false appearances can transmute into power.

Yet this advice, like Machiavelli's advice to fit one's actions or methods to "the times," is ultimately futile, thwarted by the very problem that has made it necessary. The Machiavellian political actor cannot pierce appearances to grasp what lies beneath them because he is not capable of such judgment, because the underlying reality of men questing voraciously and blindly after power is what has given rise to the "game" that is politics. If the political world is full of illusions, political man is also a creature of delusions. Important as it is for him to see through the fabrications thrown up by others, his judgment is cloaked by its own particular burden, its inseparability from the distorting effects of the intentions and passions that focus it. Add to this the tremendous pace of political events making thoughtful inspection of motives, actions, and circumstances so difficult, and we have a picture of Machiavelli's political men incapable of the necessary, doomed by the impossible. Ruled by time and conditions distorted and manipulated by all, politics is a race through a riot by half-blind men who must plow through this chaos in order to face and create still more chaos at the next turn. The only means to averting utter victimization in such a world lies in developing and consolidating institutionalized power—power rooted in something more solid than appearances and reputation.

The ancient Greek philosophers were interested in power but disdained the quest for power for its own sake. For them, politics was about the good life and power-mongering was a symptom of corruption.[126] The Athenians forfeited their status as the "school of all Hellas" when they declared to the Melians that "the strong do what they can and the weak suffer what they must."[127] After this turning point in Thucydides' history of the Peloponnesian War, the book becomes a self-conscious chronicle of shattered Athenian principles and future prospects. In the Greek view, it is not power that corrupts, but power as the dominant principle of political purpose, organization, and action that is anathema to an understanding and practice of politics as the "good life." Justice, not power, must be the centerpiece of rightly constituted public life.

Machiavelli's view is quite different. Concern with a public or common good is by no means absent from his cares and writings, but politics is rooted in and revolves around quests for power. The common good is dependent upon power, constitutive of power, and lasts only so long as a polity exercises or increases its power. Moreover, for Machiavelli, power is a relevant and exciting issue even when it is detached from a concern with the public good.

The elements constituting political power in Machiavelli's account range from the obvious and uncontroversial to the surprising. Predictably, quantities of resources are significant—money, soldiers, arsenals, and so forth. However, even these goods do not translate into power unless they are effectively ordered and used within an effective order.[128] "Order" is the term Machiavelli most frequently utters in the same breath with power and is his term of praise for a well-regulated collective entity—a city, army, or government.[129] Order signifies a fortress against nature and against a world that will control man if he does not control them. What a man or his state does not control, he does not really have, even if he owns them in a technical sense. This seemingly banal point Machiavelli considers unheeded by most political actors and he returns to it tirelessly. It is the basis of his doctrines that one must occupy rather than merely annex territories one has taken in battle;[130] muster, discipline, and lead one's own armies;[131] avoid alliances with superior powers;[132] and purge or depower disaffected classes or individuals within one's polity.[133] Machiavelli insists that the most common and grievous political error is to rely upon someone or something not entirely under one's own sway.[134] Similarly, one cannot rely upon anything not stamped with one's own identity, even if it seems superficially suitable to one's purposes. Power, then, is linked centrally to self-sufficiency, autarky, or independence, as well as to stamping one's surroundings with one's own form.

"The man who makes another powerful ruins himself."[135] Power, while it can be distributed in various ways, cannot be shared. What a man does not control is not merely useless to him, it opposes or endangers him. Machiavellian man cannot know what he has not made or does not control, and in their illusiveness, such phenomena become threatening. Thus, albeit via a very different road than the one Aristotle traveled, Machiavelli returns to the ancient conception of autarky as the most valuable political and human good. Machiavelli, however, forthrightly admits something that had to be teased out from under Aristotle's utterances: power always relies on something, is always generated or produced by someone or something other than itself, and it threatens its own foundations whenever it tries to eschew or sever this relation. Aristotle sought to circumvent this dilemma with his "parts/wholes" construction of the *polis-oikos* relation. Machiavelli confronts more directly the problem of how one establishes the foundations that are the source of power while simultaneously seeking to acquire an autonomous experience and use of the power derived from these foundations. Independence is the goal and articulation of power, yet power is generated through interdependent relations. Power is always obtained from somewhere or something—it is not autoinseminating—yet when power's purpose is more power, it necessarily repudiates or attempts to depower its sources. This is the contradiction at the heart of a masculinist politics in which power becomes its own end and thereby subverts itself.

A prince may seize power without what Machiavelli calls "foundations," but he does not actually have and hold power unless he has such foundations, unless his rule is rooted in the people. This rootedness has its concrete expression in good armies, good laws, and the people's faith, loyalty, and willingness to sacrifice. It is, in fact, a misnomer to call power any manifestation of rule that lacks these foundations; such rule is not power but mere command. And "the first unfavorable weather destroys [such princes]."[136]

While power is drawn from sources outside of those who hold it, it cannot be shared with these sources and they must be denied their status *as* sources. The ruled must be convinced of the need for the ruler while the obverse must be obfuscated.[137] Yet even if this is accomplished, the problem of power's origins in relation to its projects is not resolved. For real power, the power that makes possible political action and success, entails much more than a prince's acquisition of ideological, emotional, and military support from his people. The power of a great state like that of ancient Rome has its basis in empowering and energizing the people themselves.[138] For Machiavelli, the sign of a truly powerful state is not a bold or even notorious prince but a tempestuous people, ever ready to do battle with each other or against an external enemy. But what is the relationship between the power of a vigorous and energetic people and the power of the head of state? The latter becomes partially determined and directed by the former. An empowered body politic exacts this price from the head because it is an assemblage of many bodies who have at least partly recovered their own heads. Control and order are thus both essential and impossible in building power from below.

Consider again Machiavelli's form-matter metaphor of political action. Machiavelli's treatment of political founding, rule, and action as the process of giving form to matter is rooted in the dictum that if you do not strive to make the world in your own image, it will make you. Form-giving is the highest expression of *virtù* where *virtù* is understood as pitting oneself against givens, nature, *Fortuna*, or self-doubt. Yet while Machiavelli speaks of form as something that is imposed upon circumstances, entities, or people without form, the fact is that such "matter" always has a form prior to the one imposed upon it by a political actor. (There is no such thing as formless matter.) Thus, form-giving of this sort is an intensely violent act, involving the usurpation of other forms, including the indigenous form of any given "matter," for the imposition of one's own. Even in the "dispersed matter" Machiavelli describes as the material for the rise of Moses, Cyrus, Romulus, and Theseus, a prior form, however impoverished or corrupt, had to be destroyed from the works of these men to be brought into being.[139] "Matter" may be forced to understand itself as formless but when such matter is a people, that understanding is always an ideological act, a conversion in the people's self-understanding at the hands of the aspiring form-giver, much as we saw Aristotle arguing that slaves and women are without purpose or function unless they have masters to rule them and to provide the higher end to which they contribute. Ideologically too, then, there is violence (destruction of old understandings) in the act of form-giving. A people or city must be made to conceive of itself as "matter" in need of form.[140]

If there is violence in this mode of founding, there is also domination inherent in maintaining such a relationship. Machiavelli's "new prince" is not Rousseau's Legislator, meant to remain powerless and exit from the community as soon as his blueprints are operational. To the contrary, a new prince acquires a principality in the interest of gaining, keeping, or using its power for his own ends. The form he imposes upon his "matter" is not absorbed by and perpetuated by the people because it is imposed for his sake, not theirs. It is the prince's power (or, in a republic, the power of the state) that is at stake, and he forms his world accordingly. The matter to which he gives form constitutes his foundations for power; thus, his relationship to this matter or these foundations never loses its instrumental character.[141]

The form/matter problematic can also be approached through close attention to Machiavelli's use of metaphor and gender pronouns in political discourse. Consider the following passage:

> A republic, being able to adapt herself by means of the diversity among her body of citizens, to a diversity of temporal conditions

> better than a prince can, is of greater duration than a princedom
> and has good fortune longer. Because a man accustomed to acting
> in one way never changes . . . when the times as they change get
> out of harmony with that way of his, he falls.[142]

Machiavelli, of course, is neither the first nor the last political thinker to
refer to a "body politic" as female. But this passage both reveals something about that "innocent tradition" and moves beyond its usual pale.
The body of a state is a woman, its head or heads are male. Male (head)
gives form to female (body, material, citizenry). The head does not move
in accord with the body but has intentions and actions of its own and
relates to the body as the executor of its will or as foundations for its
strength. The body of a republic, although still stamped with form meant
to produce power for external use, tends to have a closer, more organic
relationship with its head. A republic has greater longevity than a princedom because it has a relatively less alien relationship to its head. Yes, a
republic also suffers from being slower on the uptake and more indecisive
than a princedom[142]—bodies are sluggish things in comparison with the
pace of heads—but these are disadvantages only in an environment of
fierce predators, i.e., where there are other heads seeking to mutilate or
subjugate new bodies.

The whole notion of a "body politic" contains a mystification that
Machiavelli lays bare even while he perpetuates it. The "body" is not
headless without its official head, the "body" is not "matter," the "matter" is not formless. The matter is not inert but substance and sustenance,
the source of all power. The matter is mother with her procreative powers
ideologically usurped, institutionally denigrated, and structurally confined to a menial, prepolitical status.[144] The politics of form-giving seeks
to convert the power of the "body politic" into the sustenance of the
"head" by means of forced relations of dependence. The prince claims
the "body's" power for his own and the presence of many princes makes
her incapable of surviving without him. "[A new principality] being the
prince's actual *creation*, knows it cannot stand without his friendship and
power; therefore it will do anything to maintain him in authority."[145]
The body is dependent upon her prince for survival only because there
are others like him. She needs him for protection against other princes,
but she needs nothing for protection in a world without princes. The
omnipresent rapist keeps woman's security in the hands of the individual

man bound to protect her. There is no guarantee, of course, that she will not be raped by her protector:

> When the Duke took over the Romagna, he found it controlled by weak lords who instead of ruling their subjects had plundered them. . . . He judged that if he intended to make it peaceful and obedient to the ruler's arm, he must of necessity give it good government. Hence he put in charge Messer Remirro, a man cruel and ready, to whom he gave the most complete authority. This man in a short time rendered the province peaceful and united, gaining enormous prestige.[146]

Because the weak rulers had only bruised and aggrieved the body, the Duke, when he took her over, brought in a true savage to beat her into submission. But, however much terror such cruelty may instill in a people, it does not inspire genuine loyalty from them and does not therefore empower the prince.[147] So, the story of the Duke's dealings with Romagna continues:

> Then the Duke decided there was no further need for such boundless power, because he feared it would be a cause for hatred. . . . And because he knew that past severites had made some men hate him, he determined to purge such men's minds and win them over entirely by showing that any cruelty which had gone on did not originate with him but with the harsh nature of his agent. So . . . one morning . . . he had Messer Remirro laid in two pieces in the public square with a block of wood and a bloody sword near him. The ferocity of this spectacle left those people at the same time gratified and awestruck.[148]

At this point the people have been rendered submissive, grateful, and loyal, conditioned to view themselves as a body requiring the protection and guidance of a strong head. What plunder by weak masters could not accomplish, thorough brutality by a strong prince achieved. This Machiavelli condones despite his insistence that the primary desire of the people is "not to be oppressed."[149] Or perhaps it is because of this characteristic: merely wanting "not to be oppressed" cannot stand up to the pursuit of power by men of real *virtù*. Just as the corrupt priest in La Mandragola declares that "good women can be bamboozled because they are good,"[150] a self-sufficient people can be transformed into the *material* of an ambitious prince's design.

In addition to the violence and domination inherent in the form/matter relation, the prince must constantly suppress certain features of his own creation. A people empowered by good laws, *virtù*, energy, or purpose will burst the bounds of the form externally and instrumentally imposed upon it. Thus a prince must strive for a kind of order and static quality in his dominion that is unnatural or inimical to the nourishment of power, and at odds with the perpetuity of a regime.

Machiavelli's Polybian view of historical cyclicality offers further insight into this problem. For what Machiavelli casts as providential or naturalistic cycles of political renewal and decay turn out to be rooted in the tensions between political power and political order, between the form given to a polity and the tendencies of its "matter" to burst the bounds of this form. Two of Machiavelli's many references to the cyclical history of political regimes are of interest here. The first occurs in the *History of Florence*:

> In their normal variations, countries generally go from order to disorder and then from disorder back to order . . . from good they go down to bad, and from bad rise up to good. Because ability brings forth quiet; quiet, laziness; laziness, disorder; disorder, ruin; and likewise from ruin comes order; from order, ability, from the last, glory and good fortune.[151]

In *The Discourses*, Machiavelli offers a more political account of these historical cycles. He explains, according to abuses of power, the shifts from a princedom to tyranny, to aristocracy, to plutocracy, to popular government, and then back to monarchy.[152] Naturalistic as Machiavelli's descriptive terms of these cycles may be, there is nothing organic about them. What he makes clear in this discussion is that as a form of government nourishes the power from within that a prince requires, either the prince or the people begin to abuse, resist, chafe against, or outgrow that form. A man or state requires foundations for power but these foundations are in a real people who potentially have as much ambition, skill, and power as that which would appropriate their power. The more of this potential that can be tapped, the more powerful becomes the state and the more endangered its structure *as* a state. Machiavelli cites Rome as an example of a state that played this tension to the extreme: only through

continuous expansion could Rome avoid tearing itself apart over the conflict between an enormously energetic and powerful people and the external form this power was designed to fulfill.

The form-matter paradigm of political order thus entrenches the problem of political rigidity raised in the previous sections. On one hand,
order is a sine qua non of political foundations: a prince gains foundations
and power through instilling order in a people, an army, or state institutions. On the other, this kind of order is at odds with the inherent fluidity
or flux of human affairs. Machiavelli posits order as that which will fortify
a state against the sweep of time and the flow of events. Yet order cannot
move a polity toward synchronization with the backdrop, context, and
real nature of political events; rather, it is a bulwark against losing control
to or over these things. Order is a strategy for defeating political alienation with political power. Yet it drives man further away from himself
and from any possible reconciliation with the conditions he created that
require this overlay of power onto confusion, mystery, and chaos. Order
is Machiavelli's masculine response to fluidity and change, a response
that intensifies man's myopia, inflexibility, and need for self-sufficiency,
all of which were what originally produced a threateningly incomprehensible world.

Paradoxically, Machiavelli's formulation of order both provides the
state with the power it needs and undermines its capacity for functioning
within, rather than against, its context and sphere of activity. Order, like
other forms of renitence, is what brings a state to power and what dashes
it against the rocks when circumstances change. Order, like other means
of control through force, fights *Fortuna* successfully only through resisting
her with force, but it can be undermined by the myriad other kinds of
power she had. Order is a bulwark against a chaotic world, but when the
chaos is manmade, order turns out to be the source of the cycles of political rise and fall that Machiavelli sometimes casts as exogenous. When an
order has exhausted its own interiors, it becomes a wall that is as impris-
oning to those within as it is a fortress against external adversity.[153] Order,
in Machiavelli's sense of the term, can be the cause of political decay as
well as political success; order is an external form imposed upon matter
that responds to it but does not absorb it. Order answers to a need for
control but does not address or resolve from whence the need for this
kind of absolute control came.

As noted earlier, Machiavelli invokes *Fortuna* in a variety of ways for a variety of purposes, but these may be divided into two general sorts.[154] One has already been mentioned and will be elaborated further: *Fortuna* represents the limitations of man's perceptual and predictive wisdom— she is the reified consequences of the short-sightedness resulting from this ambition. The other is the more familiar version of *Fortuna*, the one most frequently developed in modern interpretations of Machiavelli, which locates him firmly in an age of superstition. In this portrayal, *Fortuna* is a vengeful goddess who supplies luck to the undeserving, sudden calamity to the strong, and jealously undermines man's reach for glory. Brief consideration of this depiction of *Fortuna* will reveal it to be nothing more than the popular face of the first version.

While references to *Fortuna* as a capricious goddess are scattered through Machiavelli's works, they are presented synoptically in his "Tercets on *Fortuna*."

> She turns states and kingdoms upside down as she pleases; she deprives the just of the good that she freely gives to the unjust. This unstable goddess and fickle deity often sets the undeserving on a throne to which the deserving never attains. She times events as suits her; she raises up, she puts us down without pity, without law or right . . . And this aged witch has two faces, one of them fierce, the other mild; and as she turns, now she does not see you, now she beseeches you, now she menaces you.[155]

Fortuna made Castruccio Castracani mortally ill just when he was ready to consolidate his victories and secure great power for himself.[156] *Fortuna*, "never satiated," caused ceaseless and pointless discords in sixth-century Italy.[157] *Fortuna* punished Benedetto Alberti for trying to do good among the many who were wicked.[158] Although *Fortuna* treated Machiavelli himself cruelly,[159] he also spoke of her as his only possible redeemer.[160] In these and countless other instances, *Fortuna* seems to stand in a simple and uninteresting way for the element of luck in human affairs and to date Machiavelli as a superstitious believer in supernatural deities. *Fortuna*, he says, in the famous chapter of *The Prince* devoted to her, "is the mistress of one half of our actions," leaving only half, or perhaps less, to our own responsibility.[161]

The first blow to this reading of *Fortuna* comes in the "Tercets on *Fortuna*" where Machiavelli carefully distinguishes "Luck" and "Chance" from *Fortuna*. Luck and chance are not synonyms for *Fortuna* but part of her palace decorations; they sit "above the gates of her palace . . . and are . . . without eyes and ears."[162] Now eyes and ears are the very things with which *Fortuna* is richly endowed—if man's senses rivalled hers in acuity, he would never run afoul of her, he would see as carefully and as far as she does, and her power would be dismantled. Moreover, *Fortuna*'s palace contains not merely one wheel dictating who is to be cast down and who raised to glorious heights, but "as many wheels are turning as there are varied ways of climbing to those things which every living man strives to attain."[163] The problem then becomes the familiar one: a man chooses a path and succeeds on it for a while when *Fortuna* suddenly "reverses its coure in mid-cycle."

> And because you cannot change your character nor give up the disposition that Heaven endows you with, in the midst of your journey *fortuna* abandons you. Therefore, if this he understood and fixed in his mind, a man who could leap from wheel to wheel would always be happy and fortunate.[164]

The refrain is the same as that in Machiavelli's letter to Soderini: the man who could change his ways in accordance with the changing times would be master of his actions and his fate, completely unfettered by *Fortuna*. She is thus the amalgamated consequences, a reified expression of the effects of man's rigidity and subjectivity in a world that moves more quickly and divergently than his own understanding and capacity to adapt to it.

Still, one might argue that even these "many wheels" indicate a kind of determining structure, prior to and autonomous from man's own actions and creations. But in the "Tercets," Machiavelli declares that it is "Laziness and Necessity which whirl [these wheels] around;" the former "lays the world waste" while the latter "puts the world in order again."[165] This is no small confession on Machiavelli's part. He has devoted an entire poem to the fantastic and arbitrary ways of a deity only to proclaim in the midst of it that her substance is wholly human, that she is moved entirely by ourselves. Machiavelli has made clear that laziness can be averted through the construction of necessity and that cyclicality in politics results from a very specific practice of political organization wherein form is imposed upon matter for purposes of producing power for a ruler. *Fortuna* is thus the shadow side of man's single-minded devotion to perpetuating his power, with all the inflexibility and tendency to undercut power's sources that this devotion entails. *Fortuna* is the consequence of man's pursuit of a political aim or construction of a political order that strives to convert context into dominion by means of domination.

Fortuna embodies the Machiavellian actor's alienation from his context or political environment. She is a figment of culture ideologically conceived as anthropomorphicized nature. *Fortuna* is the seemingly naturalistic aspect of the political realm—the "new jungle" that man must fight in the "civilized" political world he has made. She is the setting within which he acts, and she is also the enemy with whom he eternally wrestles. Yet she differs profoundly from the jungle with which savage man struggles because her power derives from man's thought and activity, not from his essential needs, let alone from some autonomous existence of her own.

Just as Machiavelli casts cycles of political decay in natural or supernatural terms when their root is wholly conventional, so *Fortuna* is portrayed as a natural or supernatural element of politics when she is a product of the peculiar effects of Machiavellian man in action. Man's struggle for survival in the political world is shaped by the institutionalized forms of competition, power, and action originating from his ambitious and overwrought nature. But as these institutions come to appear "natural," his alienated condition comes to appear as his "nature," and his battle with *Fortuna* comes to hide the truth that it is a struggle with his own individual and collective shadow.

Neal Wood has suggested that "Machiavelli's politico is cast in the mold of the warrior" and that war is the paradigmatic scenario for expression of *virtù*.[166] Wood's insight is accurate enough, but he fails to stretch its implications toward an even more fundamental feature of Machiavellian politics: politics is utterly dependent upon the presence of an enemy, it is at all times a fight, and dissolves when opposition is not present or is too weak to inspire consolidated struggle.[167] This is why Machiavelli insists that peace always gives rise to laziness, decadence, or a state of effeminacy.[168] Politics manifests itself only when necessity is present and politics is experienced only as against something or someone. Thus, the frequent observation that Machiavellian political thought is relevant only to kill-or-be-killed circumstances is actually the wrong way of putting the matter.[169] For Machiavelli, the apparent or actual existence of a kill-or-be-killed environment is the precondition for politics as well as the raison d'être of politics. This is not merely to say that "politics is struggle" for, in Machiavelli's account, struggle without an end is as corrupting of *virtù* and political life as is idleness or passivity. "The vigor that in other countries is usually destroyed by long peace was in Italy destroyed by the cowardice of those ceaseless wars . . . from 1434 to 1494."[170] Rather, it is to say that politics only appears when there is something to conquer, overcome, ambush, or resist. Wars, Machiavelli writes in the *History of Florence*, are not for purposes of peace but for the enlargement of power and thus necessarily entail resolution through total conquest rather than truces or compromises.[171] Peace, besides being an intangible good, is the death of politics.[172] War, by contrast, presents what Wood calls "the archetypal battle between *virtù* and *Fortuna*," a battle, of course, which is itself the archetype of Machiavellian politics and political action.[173] Wood elaborates:

> [War is the contest] between all that is manly, and all that is changeable, unpredictable, and capricious, a struggle between masculine rational control and feminine irrationality. War is the supreme test of man, of his physique, of his intellect, and particularly of his character . . . As the tide of battle changes adversely, as the peril mounts, and as the sands of time run out, at such unnerving moments, the *virtù* of the captain is on trial. His character, his self-confidence, strength of will, fortitude and courage, become of greater importance than his brains and bodily strength. Cunning and prowess of arms will be of no avail where there is a failure of nerve. Against overwhelming odds, the leader must often discard his carefully prepared battle plan and rally his forces by a determined and audacious improvisation.[174]

If war is the archetype of the political, Wood adds, then nonmilitary political situations always contain characteristics of war, and success in these situations requires the abilities and sensibilities of the warrior. "The model of civic life is always military life, the model of civic leadership is always military leadership."[175] Certainly most of the terrain we have traveled thus far corroborates this interpretation. Machiavelli's concern with necessity, with order, with constructing and piercing appearances, and with mustering *virtù* to battle with the unknown all have their ultimate expression in combat and derive from the requisites of military battle.

How can we have come to this pass? Politics, whose very etymology is rooted in the Greek association for the "distinctly human," has become one with the activity least distinguishing us from the rest of the animal kingdom. According to Arendt, war is "prepolitical"; according to the classical liberals, it is the "state of nature," prior to or outside the bounds of civil society. And by almost all accounts, war is the phenomenon against which politics' meaning and purpose is juxtaposed. Even Clausewitz's infamous declaration that "war is the continuation of politics by other means" is trumped by Machiavelli's literal collapse of the distinction between war and politics.

Our initial encounter with Machiavellian man revealed a creature neither glorious nor powerful; he lived uncomfortably in his habitat and experienced himself as uncontrolled and without control over his world. He craved everything and comprehended too little of himself and his surroundings to pursue his desires with much dignity or success. Politics developed this man but it also reflected and entrenched this nature. Political life intensified the struggle against his nature and gave it a new arena; it also raised the stakes for a good many of his shortcomings. In politics, man must project himself everywhere—he must strive for control or be ruined by his vulnerability; he must attack or be overrun by all the forces within and without that he inadequately understands. Cowardice, effeminacy, pandering to the demands of the body, peace, otherworldly cares, apathy, idleness, and irresoluteness are all anathema to this effort. Political man must re-form himself by reducing all tenderness, vulnerability, and inclinations toward peace, and by overcoming bodily cares such that the body is reduced to an instrument, a foundation for his power. The body's mortal and easily injured character as well as its incessant demands for food, rest, sex, and absence of pain must be supplanted with a single-minded treatment of the body as potential strength. The head, with its boundless yearnings, has larger and higher purposes for the body than its mere satisfaction. As the body becomes martyr and servant to the head, body and head also become alien to one another. Politics demands this alienation of body and head, but it also demands the power of both. Politics is not for bodies, but it does not dispense with them, Plato notwithstanding.

As political man tries to make himself hard and determinate, he wars against softness, flexibility, vulnerability, and equivocation everywhere— within, without, in mind, body, citizen, polity, and nature. Yet he gives a new power to these things as he tries to purge them from his being, his surroundings, and his creations. They constantly conspire to steal his manhood or *virtù* from him through *deception*, through *seduction*, or through *satisfaction*.[176] These correspond respectively to the intangibility of the political world and the problem of appearances; to *Fortuna* and women; and to peace or idleness. Political man struggles against all of these things through manufacturing necessity, establishing order, pursuing ideals of glory, and seeking larger scopes of control. He fights by attacking or constructing barriers against the seductive, the satisfying, the intangible and elusive and so also renders these forces more powerful as he grows more distant and alien from them. ("So much more at a distance than nearby the things that make a show are feared."[177]) These forces tempt and torment him, they foil and threaten him—just as women do.

Recall all that woman has come to symbolize. She is the "matter" that is man's own vulnerable and overwrought as well as potentially cowardly nature; the "matter" that is political situation or context; the "matter" that is a maleable people or polity. She is *Fortuna*—times or situations man cannot fathom, always threatening to thwart or depower him. To all of these kinds of "matter," Machiavellian man must strive to give form. Consider again the kinds of powers Machiavelli ascribes to women themselves. At times he suggests that women have power over men because men want something from them that is infrequently given. In this case, the power of women stems from their chastity in the face of insatiable male desire.[178] In other instances, Machiavelli portrays women as vengeful, calculating, shrewdly subversive of men's plans and activities.[179] This second kind of female power has an important relation to the first.[180] Women's intervention in the male world arises not from desire of him but for purposes of her own interests and power.[181] Thus, what man views as woman's power over him actually issues from his unrequited cravings. Man is controlled by her indifference to him or by her preoccupation with concerns that are mysterious to him because he does not share them. She appears to have power because both the motivations and the mode of her conduct are incomprehensible to him; when she rises against him, he neither understands where she came from nor what she is hitting him with.

In this battle, Machiavelli presents man with several options. He can struggle to fathom woman's nature and intentions and try to make his actions and desires intersect with hers. This is the *virtù* of insight, timing, perception, caution, and flexibility. Still, he must not pander to her, or he will have no *virtù* at all, he will be controlled by woman and thus be considered effeminate. Even if man manages to cooperate without pandering and maintains his focus upon his own desires, this mode of involvement with her has its costs: he must temper his own aims as they are submitted to or harmonized with hers. It also has its danger: she is unreliable. However much he tries to harmonize his actions with hers, she may make a sudden turn, leaving him perplexed and powerless precisely because he heeded her so much, only to discover it was not enough.

He can also try to conquer her, to so fill the world with his power that she is forced to submit to him. This is the *virtù* of audaciousness and forcefulness in which his desire has largely been supplanted by angry enmity against the degrading experience of being in thrall to female power. Rapture becomes rape,[182] the weakness of desire gives way to the brutality of conquest, but man is not yet free. His forcefulness blinds him, he becomes more vulnerable as he strikes more sharply at a single target. Her many faces and dimensions appear to multiply as his focus and weapons have narrowed.

Finally, man may seek to acquire utter independence of woman, to become "self-sufficient" or, as it were, homosexual. This in no way means that he ceases to have any dealings with her nor that he ceases to fight other enemies, including himself. The *virtù* of independence, self-reliance, or self-sufficiency vitiates only one aspect of female power over man, and that is his *desire* for her offerings. He reduces her power by reducing his need for her. He seeks to form and control his world independently of her and to deal only with other hard, tangible enemies rather than with fluid or elusive ones. At the same time, he seeks to appropriate some of her techniques for himself—the use of illusion, deception, coyness, cunning, and masked intentions. Thus, the self-sufficient/independent political actor is, in a sense, androgynous. He is manhood in drag, that is, clothed in his *perception* of female garb, attempting to use both male and female powers in the struggle with other men.

Machiavelli's ideal—a lively, tempestuous polity spurred by the necessity of preserving itself against others and against time, making a few men glorious and all men free, striving for individual and collective immortality—has its darker side. Born of a "need" for power, it is nourished only by power, yet this power is without location in a purpose other than glory and political necessity. The polity keeps itself going through contrivance and war, for it will collapse without spurs to greatness and explode without outlets for its surplus power. Thus, it must create enemies when it does not actually face them. The polity's value and *virtù* is indicated by its capacity to project itself beyond its boundaries, its strength is measured by its armaments, ardor, and order. It is threatened by tranquility and by time as well as by surprise attacks from others like itself. The flexibility essential to its survival is rendered almost impossible to achieve by the kind of order that is key to its existence at all and by the requisite obdurateness of the men who lead it.

The form or head of the polity is forever in tension with its matter or body, with its foundations or source of power, with what it has repressed, rejected, or reshaped to make itself strong. The head of the polity needs everything for its strength; yet very little that the head dominates actually needs the head—the matter is not actually formless, not actually in need of a ruling principle, not actually without function. The head is also perpetually threatened by its surroundings as well as by its body for these things move in directions, have needs or intentions quite different from those of the head.

The power of mental and physical force are man's greatest weapons in this kind of politics. The shortage of these powers, by comparison with other animals, was precisely what weakened and disadvantaged Machiavellian man in the wilderness. But in politics, his vulnerability is turned to aggression, his blindness is compensated by brutality, his precarious bearing in the world is cloaked by his *virtù*. Unfit to live in the jungle of the natural world, Machiavellian man creates a jungle of his own in civilization: Machiavellian politics.

Notes

1. All Machiavelli citations are from *Machiavelli: The Chief Works and Others*, trans. A. Gilbert (Durham: Duke University Press, 1965) and are cited by work and page number. *Discourses* 3.21, 478.

2. *Prince* 6, 26.

3. *Discourses* 3.21, 477.

4. Ibid., 1.58, 315; 1.11, 226; 3.43, 521.

5. *Prince* 18, 64.

6. Ibid.

7. *Discourses* 1.16, 235.

8. While this poem derives its title and even some of its fanciful structure from Lucius Apulieus' classic tale of the same name, Machiavelli clearly wrote the piece for his own pedagogical and comical purposes; the *content* of his poem bears almost no resemblance to the tale told by Apulieus.

9. Following the structure of Apulieus's allegory, the narrator of the story is the author himself but transformed into an ass. Since Machiavelli's poem is the story of how this transformation comes about, the narrator is actually an ass recounting the experiences that befell him while he was still of human form.

10. *Golden Ass*, 754.

11. Thus, as Machiavelli is first introduced to the various sorts of fierce animals in her brood, the shepherdess says: "at the first entrance are the lions . . . with sharp teeth and hooked claws. Whoever has a heart magnanimous and noble is changed . . . into that beast, but few of them are from your city . . . If anyone is excessive in fury and rage, leading a rude and violent life, he is among the bears in the second house . . . He who delights in good cheer and sleeps when he watches by the fire is among the goats in the fifth troop." Ibid., 765.

12. Ibid., 767–69.

13. Ibid., 771.

14. Ibid., 771.

15. Ibid., 772.

16. Ibid., 772.

17. Ibid., 772.

18. Ibid., 771.

19. Ibid., 770.

20. Ibid., 770.

21. "Tercets on Ambition," 735.

22. Ibid., 736.

23. ibid., 735–36.

24. Ibid., 736.

25. Ibid., 735.

26. *Discourses* 1.37, 272.

27. Ibid., 272.

28. Joseph Mazzeo, "The Poetry of Power," *Review of National Literatures: Italy, Machiavelli 500*, vol. 1, no. 1, 40.

29. "Tercets on Ambition," 737.

30. *Discourses* 1.46, 290, emphasis added.

31. *Prince* 3, 18.

32. "Tercets on Ambition," 737.

33. *Discourses* 3.28, 493.

34. Ibid., 2. Preface, 323.

35. "The ambition of men is so great that when they can satisfy a present desire they do not imagine the ill that will in a short time result from it." Ibid., 2.20, 383.

36. Martin Fleischer, "A Passion for Politics: The Vital Core of the World of Machiavelli," in *Machiavelli and the Nature of Political Thought*, ed. Martin Fleischer (New York: Atheneum, 1972), 132.

37. *Prince* 3, 54.

38. This is not the only source of *Fortuna*'s existence, but it is an extremely important one and explains especially her centrality in political life.

39. *Letters*, 896–97, emphasis added.

40. Ibid., 896.

41. Ibid., 897.

42. *Discourses* 3.9, 452.

43. *Prince* 25, 91.

44. *Golden Ass*, 762.

45. "Tercets on Ambition," 736.

46. Thus, the French armies, for all their passionate zeal, lacked *virtù*, and ended up, in Machiavelli's words, "less than women." Without discipline, plan, and method, passion is worse than useless. *Discourses* 3.36, 510.

47. *Discourses* 3.21, 478.

48. Ibid., 478–79.

49. See, for example, Friedrich Meinecke, *Machiavellism: The Doctrine of Raison d'État and its Place in Modern History*, trans. D. Scott (London: Routledge, 1957). Plamenatz denies ambition a place in the elements which make up *virtù* but even Plamenatz does not go far enough in probing the relationship between the two qualities. See "In Search of Machiavellian *Virtù*," in *The Political Calculus: Essays on Machiavelli's Philosophy*, ed. A. Parel (Toronto: Toronto University Press, 1972).

50. "A Pastoral: The Ideal Ruler," 98. Fame and glory do not occupy the same kind of place in Machiavelli's thought and Renaissance culture that they did in ancient Greece, but a place they certainly had. And as for the Greeks, fame was linked by men of the Renaissance to possibilities for immortality with one another: "No man is so much exalted by any act of his as are those men who have with laws and institutions remodeled republics and kingdoms . . . No greater gift, then, does Heaven give to a man [than] . . . that of giving you power and material for making yourself immortal, and for surpassing in this way your grandfather and father's glory," 114.

51. "I remember having heard the Cardinal de Soderini say that among the reasons for praise permitting anyone to call the Pope and the Duke great was this: they are men who recognize the right time and know how to use it very well." From "On the Method of Dealing with the Rebellious Peoples of the Valdichiana," 162.

52. Thus Machiavelli calls for standing armies (never mercenaries) and insists "a prince should never turn his mind from the study of war; in times of peace he should think about it even more than in war times . . . this is the only art for a man who commands and it is of enormous *virtù*." *Prince* 14, 55, and see *Discourses* 1.40, 284.

53. "Truly, if a prince is seeking glory in the world, he should wish to possess a corrupt city, not to ruin it wholly like Caesar, but to reform it like Romulus. Truly the Heavens cannot give a greater opportunity for glory, nor can men desire a greater." *Discourses* 1.10, 223. See also 1.11, 225.

54. *Prince* 24, 88.

55. *Prince* 25, 92.

56. *Discourses* 6, 26.

57. Jerrold Siegal, "Virtù In and Since the Renaissance," *Dictionary of the History of Ideas*, ed. Philip Wiener (New York: Scribners, 1973–1974), 4:482.

58. Recall Machiavelli's assault on reason in *The Golden Ass*. Felix Gilbert also remarks, "to Machiavelli, animals possess the pristine genuineness which in man is weakened by reason." *Machiavelli and Guicciardini* (Princeton: Princeton University Press, 1965), 197.

59. Federico Chabod, *Machiavelli and the Renaissance*, trans. David Moore (New York: Harper and Row, 1965), 128.

60. Gilbert, *Machiavelli and Guicciardini*, 197.

61. *Prince* 3, 17.

62. *Prince* 18, 66.

63. *Prince* 25, 92.

64. *Discourses* 3.26, 488–89.

65. *Mandragola*, 778–80.

66. *Clizia*, 835–36.

67. Ibid., 836.

68. "Balfagor: The Devil Who Married," 869–77.

69. Machiavelli is more honest in this regard than some of the later historians of the Renaissance. Burckhardt asserts that "perfect equality" prevailed between men and women of the period. He has contributed heavily to the myth of the Renaissance as a "feminist epoch." Women were so

far advanced in the Renaissance, says Burckhardt, that there was no need for feminism—they were "beyond feminism." Jacob Burckhardt, *The Civilization of the Renaissance in Italy*, trans. S. G. C. Middlemore (Vienna: Phaidon Press, 1890), 203–6. Joan Kelly-Gadol challenges this position in "Did Women Have a Renaissance?" in *Becoming Visible: Women in European History*, ed. R. Bridenthal and C. Koonz (Boston: Houghton Mifflin, 1977).

70. See, for example, Leonardo Olschki: "*Fortuna* is the passive and *virtù* the active forces of political action," in *Machiavelli the Scientist* (Berkeley: University of California Press, 1945), 38; and Anthony Parel, who agrees with Olschki, in "Machiavelli's Method and His Interpreters," in *The Political Calculus*, 10.

71. Lest it seem that I have made too much of the female symbolism in *Fortuna* and of Machiavelli's other references to gender, let Machiavelli speak for himself (for a summary, see Appendix B). "Certainly the man who said that the lover and the soldier are alike told the truth."

72. *Mandragola*, 780, 784.

73. There are two levels on which this projection of power occurs. First, as I have already argued, man tends to reify in the guise of *Fortuna* the consequences of action which misfires; and second, femininity embodies a number of human powers that are eschewed by "manly" men—sensitivity, perceptiveness, receptivity, nurturance. Both of these dimensions of Machiavelli's account of female power are further elaborated below.

74. *Prince* 24, 89; *Discourses* 2.30, 412.

75. Similarly, any man who loses to or is ruled by a woman is portrayed by Machiavelli as a slave and a wimp. Such are the characters of Nicia in *La Mandragola*, Nicomaco in *Clizia*, and Balfagor in "The Devil Who Married."

76. *Discourses* 1.7, 210–11; and *Prince* 19: "What makes the prince contemptible is being considered changeable, trifling, effeminate, cowardly or indecisive; he should avoid this as a pilot does a reef and make sure that his actions bespeak greatness, courage, seriousness of purpose and strength . . . he lays down decisions not to be changed." 68.

77. *Prince* 6, 25, 26; and 10, 42. *Discourses* 3.31, 498.

78 Robert Orr, "The Time Motif in Machiavelli," in *A Passion for Politics*, 204.

79. In Neal Wood's view, "*virtù* represents the principle of freedom" in Machiavelli's writings. "Machiavelli's Humanism of Action," in *The Political Calculus*, 46.

80. Plamenatz, "In Search of Machiavellian *Virtù*," 176.

81. *Prince* 20, 79.

82. This is not too high a price, however, for one's "humanity" and "manhood" according to Neal Wood: "Whoever behaves, ceases to act . . . not only is he reduced to being the creature of his own uncontrolled impulse but also he may be readily enslaved by the manipulation of tyrannical power seekers. Those who place themselves in thralldom to *fortuna*, by ceasing to act lose their freedom, and in a very significant way endanger their manhood and their humanity." "Machiavelli's Humanism of Action," 46–47.

83. *Discourses* 1.1, 193–95.

84. Ibid., 193–94.

85. Ibid., 192.

86. Ibid., 194.

87. Ibid., 194.

88. *Discourses* 1.3, 202.

89. *Discourses* 3.12, 462.

90. *Discourses* 1.7, 210–11.

91. Ibid., 459.

92. *Discourses* 2.12, 355.

93. Jerrold Siegel, "*Virtù* In and Since the Renaissance," 482.

94. *Discourses* 1.4, 202.

95. *Golden Ass*, 763.

96. K. R. Minogue, "Theatricality and Politics: Machiavelli's Concept of Fantasia," *The Morality of Politics*, 153.

97. *Discourses* 2.12, 460.

98. Ibid., 462.

99. Ibid., 462.

100. *Discourses* 3.44, 523.

101. *Discourses* 1.53, 303.

102. *History of Florence* 2.19, 1057.

103. *Prince* 21, 84; *Discourses* 1.6, 210.

104. Today these things go under the name of "national security" or "national interest."

105. Norman Jacobson, *Pride and Solace* (Berkeley and Los Angeles: University of California Press, 1977), 35–36.

106. Ibid., 27–28.

107. Maurice Merleau-Ponty, "A Note on Machiavelli," *Signs*, trans. R. C. McCleary (Evanston, Ill.: Northwestern University Press, 1963), 212.

108. Jacobson, *Pride and Solace*, 35.

109. *Prince* 18, 66–67.

110. Minogue, "Theatricality and Politics," 156.

111. Arendt, *The Human Condition*, 50.

112. Brown, *Love's Body*, 235.

113. See "Advice to Raffaelo Girolami," 116–119. For four pages, Machiavelli details the acquisition of these two skills.

114. *Discourses* 1.53, 303; *History of Florence* 4.27, 1219, 1220; and 4.31, 1227.

115. *History of Florence* 4.26, 1218 and 1.31, 1227.

116. "Remodeling Florentine Government," 110, 112; *Discourses* 1.25, 253.

117. *Prince* 18, 82.

118. *Discourses* 1.15, 233–34 and 1.14, 231–33.

119. *Prince* 19, 68.

120. In the *History of Florence*, Machiavelli gives accounts of entire wars carried out under auspices other than their actual ones, unbeknownst to everyone, on both sides, before, during and after the fighting. See 5.17, 1255–56, and 5.18, 1257.

121. Minogue, *The Morality of Politics*, 152.

122. Robert Johnson, "Machiavelli and Gramsci," unpublished manuscript, 23.

123. Brown, *Love's Body*, 235.

124. *Discourses* 2.11, 352.

125. *Prince* 18, 66.

126. Plato, *Gorgias* 482–527 (dialogue with Callicles) and *Republic* 336–51 (dialogue with Thrasymachus).

127. Thucydides, *Peloponnesian War*, 331.

128. *History of Florence* 3.13, 1160–61.

129. *History of Florence* 5.1, 1232; *Art of War* 2.614, 619–20.

130. *Prince* 3, 14, 16; *Discourses* 2.19, 378.

131. *Art of War* I, 585; *Legations* 2.53, 136–137; *Discourses* 1.21, 246; *Prince* 6, 24–25 and 12–13, 46–55.

132. *Prince* 21, 83–84; "Words to Be Spoken on the Law for Appropriating Money, After Giving a Little Introduction and Excuse," 1440.

133. *Discourses* 1.9, 219.

134. *Prince* 6, 25; 17, 64; and 24, 88–89; *Discourses* 3.11, 458.

135. *Prince* 3, 20.

136. *Prince* 7, 28.

137. *Prince* 9, 42.

138. According to Machiavelli, this is the case not only if one wants an empire like Rome, but even if one only desires a state which can maintain itself among adversaries.

139. *Prince* 6, 25.

140. *Discourses* 2.19, 217–19. Resonances can be heard here of Aristotle's depiction of women as "matter in need of form" and of women's contribution to the reproductive process as the "matter" or "material" for which the male supplies the "seed" or "principle." What mothers bring into being is thus ideologically appropriated from them and treated by man as his own doing just as the "whole" of the *polis* is regarded as supplying the meaning and integrity of its "parts." The parts are only the material for which political man supplies the form (Aristotelian version), or, the material (the people) lies limp and useless, in need of the man of *virtù* (Machiavellian version).

141. *Prince* 5, 23.

142. *Discourses* 3.9, 453.

143. *Discourses* 1.34, 268; 1.59, 319; and 2.15, 360–362.

144. See the discussion of the etymologies of matter and mother above.

145. *Prince* 5, 23.

146. Ibid., 31.

147. "Gratitude" is no minor theme in Machiavelli's political thought and it should now be clear why. Gratitude is linked to a construct of power in which the roots of power are meant to willingly give themselves over to another's purpose. See *Prince* 17, 62; *Discourses* 1.28–30, 255–261 and 1.59, 318; "Tercets on Gratitude or Envy" 740–744.

148. *Prince* 7, 31.

149. *Prince* 9, 39.

150. *Mandragola* 3.9, 800.

151. *History of Florence* 5.1, 1232.

152. *Discourses* 1.2, 197–99; see also 3.1, 319.

153. *Discourses* 2.24, 392–94.

154. Much ink has been spilled on the subject of the sources of Machiavelli's conception of *Fortuna*. (See, for example: Thomas Flanagan, "The Concept of *Fortuna* in Machiavelli," *The Political Calculus*; Vincenzo Ciofarri "The Function of Fortune in Dante, Boccacio and Machiavelli," *Italica* 24 (1947); Burleigh Wilkins, "Machiavelli on History and Fortune," *Bucknell Review* 8 (1959); J. G. A. Pocock, *The Machiavellian Moment: Florentine Political Thought and the Atlantic Republican Tradition* (Princeton: Princeton University Press, 1975); and H. R. Patch, "The Tradition of the Goddess *Fortuna* in Medieval Philosophy and Literature," *Smith College Studies in Modern Languages*, vol. 3, no. 4). That interest in this pagan goddess was current among poets, politicians, and literati of Machiavelli's milieu and was also prevalent among ancient and medieval minds is clear enough. Which of the various depictions of her most influenced Machiavelli's own rendition of the creature is less obvious, although it seems safe to choose Dante and Alberti over Aquinas and Aristotle. More significant is that Machiavelli was a sufficiently innovative and imaginative thinker to have constructed his own version of *Fortuna*. This means that we would do best to look within his writings for an understanding of what he took *Fortuna* to be and meant her to represent.

155. "Tercets on Fortune," 745–46.

156. "Life of Castruccio Castracani of Lucca," 552.

157. *History of Florence* 1.6, 1041, 1042.

158. *History of Florence* 3.23, 1177.

159. *Prince* "Dedication," 11.

160. *Letters*, 964.

161. *Prince* 25, 90.

162. "Tercets on Fortune," 747.

163. Ibid., 746.

164. Ibid., 747.

165. Ibid., 747.

166. Wood, "Machiavelli's Concept of Virtù," 171.

167. Machiavelli, in the History of Florence and elsewhere, makes frequent reference to times and places rife with internecine activity of too petty a sort to be called politics.

168. History of Florence 5.1.

169. "It is impossible for a republic to succeed in standing still . . . because if she does not molest some other, she will be molested, and from being molested rises the wish and the necessity for expansion; and when she does not have an enemy outside, she finds him at home, as it seems necessarily happens to all great states." Discourses 2.19, 379.

170. History of Florence 5.1, 1233; see also 1.39, 1079 and 5.1, 1284–85.

171. History of Florence 8.27, 1420–21.

172. Here is the way Machiavelli speaks of the Florentine peace of 1471: "There appeared in the city those evils that are usually generated in the time of peace, for the young men, more unrestrained than usual, spent without measure on dress, banquets and similar luxuries; and being without occupation, they wasted on gambling and whores their time and their property. Their ambition was to appear magnificent in their clothing, to use speech that was pithy and clever; he who most deftly nipped the others was the smartest and the most highly regarded." History of Florence 7.28, 1372.

173. Wood, "Machiavelli's Concept of Virtù," 170.

174. Ibid., 170.

175. Ibid., 170.

176. See John Geerken, "Homer's Image of the Hero in Machiavelli: A Comparison of Aretē and Virtù," Italian Quarterly 14, no. 53 (1970): 45–90.

177. History of Florence 1.19, 1057.

178. See La Mandragola (character of Lucrezia), Clizia (character of Clizia), and "The Snake Charmers."

179. See Clizia (character of Sofronia) and "Balfagor: The Devil Who Married."

180. Machiavelli seldom speaks of women in politics without reference to their disruptive status as sexual objects. In addition to the plays, see History of Florence 1.9, 1044; 1.20, 1058; 1.37, 38, 1076–77; and 2.3, 1084–85.

181. Again, see Clizia (character of Sofronia, who seeks to control her husband for purposes of her own power, not to obtain anything from him).

182. Ortega y Gasset insists that there is an etymological connection but that it runs the other way, i.e., that the first act was rape, then rapture. "The Sportive Origins of the State," History as a System, trans. H. Weyl (New York: W. W. Norton, 1962), 31.

5

The Root of the Mandrake

Machiavelli and Manliness

Mary O'Brien

Despite Plato's celebrated dictum that poets represent a menace to a well-run polity, male political theorists, in significant number, have shown a yearning to give aesthetic expression to their philosophies. Plato's own work is not only structured dramatically but is widely considered to have claims to literary eminence. Many men who were primarily poets also wrote political treatises, most notably Dante and John Milton. In the work of Jean-Jacques Rousseau, the line between philosophy and fable was a tenuous one, while for Friedrich Nietzsche it disappeared altogether. Samuel Taylor Coleridge fancied himself as a shrewd political commentator able to make sense of the Hegelian philosophy, and even the young Karl Marx wrote poetry. George Bernard Shaw, of course, wrote polemic in a number of prose forms, and in our own times, such diverse talents as Bertholt Brecht and Norman Mailer attempt to render politics in both philosophical and artistic terms.

Niccolò Machiavelli, widely credited with having turned traditional political philosophy into a modern political science, wrote comedies: it is one of these, *La Mandragola,* which will be considered here.[1] It may be thought a little odd that feminist criticism should find it in any way useful to spend time on a rather drearily unfunny comedy which is, moreover, profoundly misogynist. There are, however, resonances in the relation of Machiavelli's political theory and literary work which reflect on a question central to much contemporary feminist theory: the question of the separation of public and private life. This separation is not fanciful but is a concrete historical manifestation of both masculine subjective preoccupation with the dualism of human experience and the patriarchal practice which embodies this dualism in the political attempt to keep the private realm of necessity apart from the public domain of freedom. Hannah Arendt was perhaps the most eloquent modern apologist for this venerable dichotomy. She believed the separation to be under threat of extinction by the combined forces of the bourgeoisie and the proletariat and argued that only Machiavelli among the traditional greats of the discipline of political theory had a proper perception of the fact that the separation of the public and private realms is, in practice, the precondition of a rational and noble polity.[2] Arendt is correct in claiming Machiavelli as a staunch apostle of this ideological position. He never, however, spelled it out with the clarity which Arendt brings to her own phenomenology of the a priori dualism of the human condition. It must be said, moreover, that Machiavelli was a good deal more realistic than Arendt about the capacity of the public domain, properly constituted, to become the space in which fathers of families show forth their existential greatness. In fact, his major statements on the private realm and family life appear in his "literary" work, notably in *La Mandragola.* I therefore propose to examine Machiavelli's political works with a view to uncovering his estimation of the relation of family and polity, particularly with regard to his symbolic positing of this relation in the ambiguous concepts of *virtù* and *Fortuna.* The relation of domesticity and political praxis presented in *La Mandragola* can then be analyzed in terms not only of dramatic irony but of the deeper irony embedded in the ideology of patriarchal politics.

A word first about the mandragola, a poisonous plant of the nightshade family known in English as the mandrake, or man-dragon. It appears to have been a favorite with alchemists and herbalists and was always girt with superstition. The root was said to resemble a fetus and the plant to cry when pulled from the earth. Poets have found it symbolic, as in John Donne's *Song:*[3]

> Go and catch a falling star,
> Get with child a mandrake root,
> Tell me where all past years are,
> Or who cleft the Devil's foot;
> Thou, when thou return'st can tell me
> All strange wonders that befell thee
> And swear nowhere
> Lives a woman true and fair.

The symbolism lives on in Samuel Beckett's work *Waiting for Godot:*[4]

> Estragon: What about hanging ourselves?
> Vladimir: Hmm. It'd give us an erection.
> Estragon: (*highly excited*) An erection!
> Vladimir: With all that follows. Where it falls mandrakes grow. That's why they shriek when you pull them up. Did you not know that?
> Estragon: Let's hang ourselves immediately.

This superstitious vision of a mysterious biological force threatening the integrity of man's sexual potency and reproductive power is part of Machiavelli's "pragmatic" politics. His political work attempts to describe the theoretical and practical dimensions of an autonomous polity: his ideal politicians are an austere priesthood of the singleminded, able to practice a doctrine of the justification of means by ends without flinching from its more harrowing implications.[5] I will argue that Machiavelli believes that the major obstacle in the path to this problematic glory is, in both practical and symbolic terms, Woman. I will also argue that, from the standpoint of feminist politics, Machiavelli is correct: women do indeed reject the neurosis which sees nature as a cunning and powerful foe. Resistance to this pernicious doctrine, in which the endless defense of public and private violence as "necessary evils" is posited as necessary to the common good, is an essential part of feminist struggle. Feminists believe that the separation of the public and private realms does not merely institutionalize the dreams and realities of patriarchy: it ensures that politics *must* proceed from the violent exercise of power, an activity to which men are apprenticed in the private realm, inured to in popular culture, and practice as the dynamic of public life. Machiavelli's despair of overcoming and controlling the natural world was realistic within a patriarchal praxis. It is not, however, this dimension of "realism" in his thought to which male commentators have given attention. Machiavelli's "pragmatism" is generally interpreted as resting in the reality of power relations, perceived as immutable conditions of political life in general rather than of patriarchal politics in particular.

Polity and Family

The family, in late Renaissance Italy, was not merely a venerable social institution but was in the process of undergoing the change associated with the vanishing kinship relations which had underpinned the class structure of feudalism. Jacob Burckhardt doubtless exaggerates the extent to which bloodlines yielded to individual experience and performance.[6] Humanism no doubt believed, with Poggio, that there is no other nobility than that of personal merit,[7] but in practice, families which achieved power, whether by individual or collective endeavor, showed no tendency to abandon their progeny to their own individual excellence but kept the perquisites of power in the family. The Medici, Sforza, and Visconti families, for example, showed a hereditary durability which the Houses of Lancaster and York might well have envied. These families, whatever their origins, became and stayed powerful for long periods: hereditary power is not the prerogative solely of monarchs. Hereditary power remained the source of familial power and personal potency until men discovered the potentiality and potency of the "incorporation" (i.e., embodiment) of industrial wealth. Such wealth appears, happily for its possessors, to reproduce itself in wombless fecundity.

The abrasive tendencies to factionalism in family-based politics, examined and found tragic by Shakespeare in *Romeo and Juliet*, were a reality of political life in Machiavelli's time (1469–1527). The desire to establish family power invaded and frequently corrupted political life. Nowhere was this tendency more clearly demonstrated than in the papal practice of nepotism. Popes in those days did not often maintain office for too long a time, and they generally hastened to establish relatives in lucrative and powerful spots before death and deposition deprived them of re-source. Indeed, Machiavelli predicted gloomily that endeavors would be made to make the papacy hereditary.[8] As well as popes, merchant bankers and mercenaries became founding fathers of powerful families. Machia-velli did not care much for men in any of these occupational categories.[9]

In Florence, a long tradition of rendering the hereditary aristocracy politically impotent by "Ordinances of Justice" was undoubtedly a fine republican act and did much that was positive to widen the base of politi-cal life in the city state. The negative aspects, though, were formidable. The bourgeoisie were as patriarchal as the aristocracy. Family-based fac-tions persisted in conflict for more than a century, and the hatred of the Ordinances themselves by still vocal and often rich aristocrats was a source of considerable strife.[10] Machiavelli was well aware of the dangers to which a dissident and defeated aristocracy exposed republics, but the replacement of noble families by rich families was not a solution espe-cially relished by this "poor but patrician" secretary. Kinship seemed to Machiavelli to be a very destructive base for politics: he gave lip service to a norm of filial piety but rejected hereditary ties as the "most fallacious means of identifying the best men to rule."[11] Such was his dislike of the hereditary practice of leaving power—he is less specific about prop-erty—to "heirs and successors" that he advocated that the job of found-ing a republic, like the leadership of an army, was best done by "One man only."[12]

Machiavelli, steeped in the lore of republican Rome, considered that the longevity of a republic derived from its capacity to maintain the in-tegrity of public life in the teeth of all the tests which *Fortuna* could throw at it. He understood ideology and its workings, though he had no single word to describe it, and was appreciative of the political effective-ness of ideological hegemony. But in terms of the founding of republics, he quite specifically rejected Christian doctrines of original sin and pagan myths of primordial crime in favor of a practical and historical doctrine of political expediency, for which such notions as "sin" and "crime" are beside the point. His further rejection of kinship ties and heredity as grounds for the exercise of political power appears as a pragmatic response to realities of historical experience.

The domestic aspect of family life and its diverse social functions he viewed more ambivalently. He spoke briefly of "education," which he understood in quite broad terms encompassing what we now refer to as the socialization process.[13] He recognized some familial impact on the molding of character, but the main example he used—the insolence of the Appia—is a negative one and is contrasted unfavorably to "the goodness and gentleness displayed by an infinite number of *citizens*."[14] Private family life earns only a very brief chapter in *The Discourses*, and marriage arrangements introduce the chapter which expounds how women are liable to ruin states.[15] Machiavelli does advise the Prince to leave his subjects' wives and property alone, which can be interpreted as recommending some form of protection for family life; the effect is somewhat muted, though, by being immediately followed by the observation that "men forget more easily the death of their father than the loss of their patrimony."[16] *The Discourses*, in the probably incomplete form in which we have them, end on the theme of the disorderly effect which new families had on Rome.[17]

Family life, then, emerges in Machiavelli's thought as it appears in his experience; it is a three-level affair, with a certain amount of ambivalence in each. The first level is Machiavelli's admiring interpretation of Roman family life, which he sees as separated from political life; this view, however, owes more to myth than to history, and the private realm was still responsible for the decline of the republic. The second level is founded on his observation and experience of the political machinations of the powerful families of his own time, whose activities corrupt public life by virtue of nepotism, factionalism, and self-interest. On the household level, education is useful, for it is "of great importance whether a youth in his tender years hears any act praised or censured; this necessarily makes a lasting impression upon his mind, and becomes afterwards the rule of his life for all time."[18]

All of this, despite some inconsistencies, seems relatively straightforward. Two centuries later, Oliver Cromwell would repeat Machiavelli's basic message when he argued against hereditary power on the grounds that "who knoweth whether he may beget a fool or a wise man?"[19] Cromwell, however, still named his own foolish son Richard as his successor, but Machiavelli, a disgraced civil servant exiled to the privation of domestic life, did not have to face the problem of the legitimization of patriarchal power in personal terms. Yet the whole business cannot be understood simply as a response to actual events, historical and contemporary, for Machiavelli does not in fact let it rest there. He adds to the practical analysis a symbolic, indeed quite mystical conceptualization, which he expresses in terms of the existential struggle between two opposing forces that he calls *virtù* and *Fortuna*. The politician must serve an apprenticeship in this struggle, and only those who succeed in conquering *Fortuna* are fit to rule other men.

The exact meanings of *virtù* and *Fortuna* are not clear. I believe they are best understood as male and female. The negative, bad acts which boys must be taught to abhor are those acts repeatedly characterized by Machiavelli as "effeminate."[20] Thus, I propose that the appropriate translation for *virtù* is "manliness," which is quite consistent with Machiavelli's conceptualization in a way which transcends the mere opposition to effeminate. There is something cosmic in man's struggle with *Fortuna*, and something very familiar in the annals of the development of the theory and practice of male supremacy. Manliness is vigorous, thoughtful, prudent, passionate, aggressive, expansionary, and (regrettably), a scarce resource. Manliness is not self-seeking—and this is the ethical/mystical dimension—but is a transcendent service to the public weal. Effeminacy, on the other hand, is passive, unreasonable, unpredictable, given to luxuriousness and stay-at-home. Manliness can be explicated in terms not only of its *relation* to effeminacy, but also in terms of one of its own essential qualities: this is the ability for men to understand that "effeminacy" is but a pale personal reflection of a cosmic historical force called *Fortuna*. *Fortuna* embraces the irrational contrariness and unpredictability of the natural world as embodied in her handmaidens, women, and if great care is not taken in childraising, will produce effeminate men.

Attempts to locate the imprecision of the concept of *virtù* within *virtù* itself are doomed to failure, for there can be no manliness and no *virtù* unless woman is actively overcome. Male commentators who struggle with the concept rarely put this in quite these terms and would no doubt deprecate their crudity. In fact, the failure to understand Machiavelli's treatment of the man/woman dialectic arises from the well-known tension which Machiavelli's admirers feel in justifying the tougher implications of his theory of politics. John Plamenatz, for example, separates *virtù* into the categories of "heroic" and "civic" virtue, arguing that the first, the nasty bit, creates the conditions for the second, the nice bit.[21] Such apologetics for the means and end dilemma cannot be supported textually in a consistent way, for the tension which Machiavelli himself sets up is not within *virtù* but *between* *virtù* and *Fortuna*. Woman/nature/nurture challenges man/polity/violence in a primordial way which denies even the possibility of complementarity. *Fortuna*/woman challenges manliness to take her by force, to overcome and conquer her completely, to *control* her. The formulation of the encounter of manliness and femininity in chapter 25 of *The Prince* is explicitly and aggressively sexual. She can only be "conquered by force," a force exerted more effectively by the bold than the cold. This is not merely the roughest of wooing nor the conventional prelude to holy matrimony: it is, quite simply, rape.

Machiavelli is working in one sense on a symbolic level, but the history of culture/nature, mind/body, public/private dualism suggests a strong relation of this conceptualization to the historical struggles to create and defend patriarchal institutions. Traditionally, the institution of marriage has as one of its stabilizing functions the direction of the sex drive into socially useful channels, though history does not suggest that social structures have always fulfilled this functional imperative with spectacular success.

Machiavelli perceives with admirable clarity the vital need for the state to find ways of channeling the energies of citizens. He sees with equal clarity that energy creates, thrives on, and can overcome conflict.[22] He believes that conflict is that reality which makes politics necessary and necessarily utilitarian, but it is also that very necessity which sets up the potentiality for a man to be manly. Glory and utility are uneasy bedfellows, but manliness is both passionate and rational in Machiavelli's thinking. Prudent spontaneity and warm-blooded calculation are the apparent contradictions which pave the path to glory. This is why it is a path which, while it provides a backward perspective on history, cannot see where it is going. It cannot have an end, for an end would bring *stasis*, would cut off the possibility for action, and it is precisely in action that manliness shows itself forth. Manliness must constantly destroy and recreate its road to glory.

Manliness may create its own road, but it does not have to create its own obstacles. *Fortuna* does that; *Fortuna* constantly drives man abroad. This is because woman's place, home, is the place for the effeminate, those who are happy with petty competition and who evade conflict, who elevate family over polity, and who are willing to pay others to fulfill not only their responsibility, but also their destiny. "At home" is precisely that place where manliness cannot be at home. The most it offers is the release of sexual energy and the continuity of generation. Says Pico: "The brutes bring from their mother's body what they will carry with them as long as they live; the higher spirits are from the beginning, or soon after, what they will be forever."[23]

Mere biological continuity, from a patriarchal perspective, means nothing, and not just because blood, as Machiavelli remarks, is "necessarily modified by marriage."[24] Necessity and *Fortuna*, Felix Gilbert observes, are identical in Machiavelli's thinking.[25] The biological tie is a chain on manliness, but so, clearly are the *social* relations of reproduction. Family life is a very problematic affair, with the necessity of *Fortuna* and the contingency of paternity attendant on the cradle and the risk of women effeminizing the potentially manly. Paternity is therefore a duty to the polity and should aim to curb the dangerous seeds of *Fortuna*. Machiavelli favored an increase in population, believing Rome to have been more sensible than Sparta in this matter;[26] he also understood the need for some special stability to permit the proper education of the young. These are not just necessary functions, but are also tremendously dangerous imperatives. Stability and tranquillity enervate, and enervation breeds corruption.[27] Family life is shot through with natural and biological reality, and also with the messiness of affection and concern for individuals; it is subject to the mindless whims of *Fortuna* and her servant, Woman. In these circumstances, family and polity cannot be seen to stand opposed merely in an analytical or fatalistic way. "At home," the realm of women and their works, must be *actively* overcome, where necessary by force, as the precondition of the establishment of a public domain in which reason passionately prevails over necessity, unpredictability, and effeminacy. The separation of public and private exists historically in the development of Universal man, but the condition of that universality is the constant, violent maintenance of the rights of man and state to control the social relations of reproduction and the family, to overcome the soft seductiveness and passive destructiveness of women.

If this is a correct rendering of Machiavelli's view of the family, it must be noted that it bears significant relations to the realities of his times. Elected officers in Florence did not resign; they "went home" or, if disgraced, they were "sent home." Machiavelli himself was sent home in 1512, and his letters make it quite clear how unhappy this made him.[28] He was sent back to his marital family by a politically powerful family, the Medici. He appears to have been subjected to torture and then bored stiff, both of which were profoundly disquieting events. His vision of the relation of public and private life, however, is much more complex than a petulant complaint about his personal experiences. The contradictions involved transcend the psychological and personal realm and are perceived in the context of the existential and the historical. If in fact family life corrupts the very possiblity of heroism, then this conflict may be presented in dramatic terms as, indeed, it has been since classical times. Dramatically, one may discover that the dilemma is ultimately insoluble, that it is ultimately impossible for men to be manly. This is the tragic vision, the bleak life in which Creon's strength is unequal to family customs and in which Godot never "comes." On the other hand, drama may illuminate the way in which men act absurdly in the mistaken pursuit of private rather than public ends. This is the comic vision. Triviality and glory share a vulnerability to folly which makes the dualism of human existence as problematic as the arbitrary separation of family and polity, manliness and effeminacy, tragedy and comedy. It is of such folly which La Mandragola speaks, so it is worthwhile to discover what the play says.

The Private Realm as Comedy

Owing much to classical theater, the major debt of Italian Renaissance drama was to Rome. Shakespeare acknowledged this while poking fun at his over-awed and excessively imitative contemporaries. The words are given to Polonius: "the best actors in the world, either for tragedy, comedy, history, pastoral, pastoral-comical, tragical-historical, tragical-comical-historical-pastoral, scene indivisible, or poem unlimited: Seneca cannot be too heavy nor Plautus too light."[29]

Satirical though these words are, it is true, as Gilbert Highet points out, that drama cannot even be composed until its varieties and possiblities have been understood.[30] Only then can an age turn to creating something new within these forms. Machiavelli's contemporaries thought that he had created something new with La Mandragola.[31]

From a literary perspective, La Mandragola is a puzzling piece. Lord Thomas Babington Macaulay's famous accolade has been treated as a definitive judgment by many political writers.[32] Macaulay believed that had Machiavelli devoted himself to drama he would have produced a "salutary effect on the national taste." Given the sheer lewdness of La Mandragola, one might be forgiven for wondering about Macaulay's conception of the salutary and the tasteful.[33] What he is referring to is form and character; Macaulay's critical criteria are naturalism and believable characterization, and he finds the setting and characters of *La Mandragola* suitably true to life, which, insofar as "life" is patriarchally defined, it is.

Other critics have been less adulatory. Highet believes that the early promise of Italian drama "went sour with the plays of Machiavelli and Aretino, who took the structure, plot line and characters of classical comedy, modernized them, and added dirt"—dirt derived partly from their own minds and partly from medieval fabliaux.[34] Most of the great theatrical innovations—flats, *periaktos*, and raised stages—came after Machiavelli's time, and so the prologue of *La Mandragola* indicates a classical street scene in the Renaissance fashion. The three classic scenes—street with palaces for tragedy, street with shops and houses for comedy, and a woodland scene for the satyr play which the Renaissance would develop as pastoral—all of these were known by the turn of the century. Machiavelli also uses his street setting to permit and accelerate action and movement in the comedy.

The plot, too, is conventional, demonstrating that the staples of the dirty joke are depressingly enduring. They are all here: cuckolded husband, the tricky seduction of the chaste woman, her rapturous discovery that she likes it, the venal mother-in-law, the confusion of the genital and excretory functions, four-letter word furbishings, and the general triumph of the Penis Rampant. All of this is given a touch of legendary magic by the superstition inherent in the symbolism of the mandrake. The plot turns on twin axes: sexuality and manliness; fecundity and the uncertainty of paternity. One can easily sympathize with Carlo Goldoni's initial disgust at the lubricity of the piece, which he records in his memoirs, adding that he was "enchanted" by the characterization.[35]

The plot, which Machiavelli himself knows to be "slight," (*Prolog*, 117) cannot be simply ignored while one praises the characterization, however aesthetically satisfying such a procedure might be. The relation of plot to character and situation is sufficiently deft and rather zanily believable to integrate form and content. To divide the two is to make of *La Mandragola* an exercise in *imitatio* on the one hand and some kind of parable of *corruptio* on the other. *La Mandragola* has artistic limitations. Comedy, said Aristotle, imitates men who are inferior but not altogether vicious.[36] In *La Madragola* the wolfishness of the comedy is overstressed, and the bitterness of the prologue colors the characterization. For Machiavelli's contemporaries, this vicious underlay was probably concealed by their keener appreciation of topical allusions and word play,[37] but these very limitations are more salient to the characters than to the plot. Despite them, *La Mandragola* is a drama, not a smoking room anecdote nor a well-observed series of character sketches. Briefly, the plot concerns an old man, Nicia, whose wife, Lucrezia, is a model of virtue, but childless (for a summary, see Appendix A).[38]

Aristotle once remarked that what is right for a politician is not right for a poet.[39] "Right" or not, *La Madragola* has much in common with Machiavelli's political writing, though these latter are more poetical than the literary works are political. The first thing to be noticed about *La Madragola* is that the word "plot" can be taken quite literally. The whole piece is a well-structured and successful conspiracy. We know from *The Discourses* that Machiavelli regarded success in political conspiracy as rare: conspiracy "is understood to apply to a republic that is already partially corrupted; for in one not yet tainted by corruption such thoughts could never enter the mind of any citizen."[40]

The "comic" inversion in the play can be seen in the context of "Of Conspiracies," where Machiavelli warns that the prince who would guard himself against conspiracy must not harm his subjects' honor: "As to the attacking of men's honor, that of their wives is what they feel most, and after that their being themselves treated with indignity."[41]

Messer Nicia's foolishness tolerates both of these conditions. Yet he thinks that he is conspiring; he is too stupid to know that he is conspired against. The conspirators are performing in the play those very actions which, in *The Discourses*, cause conspiracies. This comic conspiracy, contrary to the fate foretold for most conspiracies in *The Discourses*, succeeds in the play. Cause and effect, as it were, are inverted in private affairs as opposed to public affairs.

This inversion gives form to the piece, but the political metaphor cannot be stretched too far: the real object of the conspiracy is Lucrezia's chastity, a private-realm virtue assaulted in terms of a metaphor which moves from conspiratorial to military activity. Lucrezia's virtue is a fortress to be taken, and fortresses "may or may not be useful according to the times."[42] Lucrezia has no friends, does not admit tradespeople to her house, and "has no maid or servant who's not afraid of her." The best fortress needs the love of the people, but Lucrezia not only has servants who are afraid of her, but a husband and mother who dislike her.[43] She is thus vulnerable, but Callimaco still could not seize upon her without her husband's connivance, and Nicia's stupidity and lust for paternity are undoubtedly Callimaco's greatest assets. They are not, however, enough; fundamentally, Lucrezia's vulnerability lies in her own virtue, as Timoteo, the priest, recognizes (3.9.800). The trouble with the marriage lies in its inversion: Lucretia dominates. Nicia not only stays "at home," he *wants* to stay at home: "I don't like to get off base" he says (1.2.782). Clearly this fortress has the wrong captain, but the "right" captain is impotent. The purpose of the play is to put manliness in command while *Fortuna* is transformed to her proper state of purely sensual being.

The ostensible siege is made necessary by Callimaco's lust. His sexual desire is irrepressible, and he feels his whole being to be at stake. The exaggerated monologues in which Callimaco expresses his desire (4.1, 4.4) are hyperbolic pastiches of great passion, which are rather well done. Callimaco is given the vocabulary of grand passion for the expression of mere lust. Yet for all this throbbing energy, his response is curiously oblique. He retains some prudence; no "off to storm the fortress" for him. He thinks at first to change Lucrezia's nature (1.1.781) by removing her from her fortress. That scheme is quickly abandoned when Ligurio points out that he might have opposition then (1.3.784). Attacking and over-coming the fortress is a better risk, and he is prepared to try anything, "even if it's strange, risky, injurious, disgraceful" (1.2.784). These are Princely words, if applied to the Public Good. Callimaco the manly is inverting public and private life. This may be owing to his age or his calling; the dramatis personae lists him as a "young merchant." The first may explain his impetuosity. The second may explain his method, for what he does is hire a mercenary to organize the attack. Callimaco vaunts his versatility, but it is not quite a model of humanist eclecticism.[44] He passes his time in study, amusement, and business (1.1.779). Renaissance humanists, inexact though that term may be, were united in despising business. The result of Callimaco's activities was that he had peace, no enemies, and the favor of all classes. In Machiavelli's terms, he lived in an enervating state of tranquillity. But one fears that this Callimaco, despite his posturing, is basically "effeminate." This is why he needs a mercenary to organize his attack on *Fortuna*. He is too lacking in manli-ness to perform this task himself. Here we have another public/private ambivalence. In his political writings, Machiavelli never tires of pointing out the futility for employing mercenaries for manly tasks, yet what is almost always disastrous in public affairs becomes ludicrously successful in an assault on the private domain.[45]

The ascription of the role of mercenary to Ligurio does not rest on the fact that he is hired help. The whole of Act 4, scene 9 is a farcical battle, complete with a roster of phony troops, a friendly enemy, a simulated scuffle, surrendered "arms" ("Give that lute here"), and military dialogue (see Appendix A).

The classical symbols of cuckoldry—horns and cuckoo—are lost on Nicia. He is fighting for his own dishonor. Yet Callimaco is something of a mercenary, too. He is being paid to fulfill Nicia's manly responsibilities: the prize is Lucrezia's body.

The conspiracy of Callimaco and Ligurio is a conspiracy of merchant and mercenary. "You and I have a natural affinity" Ligurio tells Callimaco (1.3.784). Indeed they have. By the end of the second act the conspiracy has been expanded to include Lucrezia's priest and her mother. Who will recruit them? Ligurio tells Callimaco: "You, I, money, our rascality, theirs" (11.6.792). Merchant, mercenary, church, and family are united by their corruption, and self-interest in a conspiracy of lust designed to overpower a virtuous woman.

By the end of the short first act, the natural affinity of Callimaco and Ligurio is established, and Ligurio is beginning to assert command. He has talked Callimaco out of his own scheme in favor of his own more dastardly plot. By the end of the second act, the web of conspiracy and deception has extended and Ligurio's authority is absolute:

> Cal.: Where do you want me to go now?
> Lig.: This way, that way, along this street, along that one. Flor-
>   ence is a big town.
> Cal.: (aside) This is killing me. (11.6.793)

This last line may be simply contiguous with Callimaco's extravagantly romantic vapors. It might be more subtle. The dialogue is not distinguished by subtlety, but Machiavelli does rather contemptuously suggest in the *Prolog* that some of his audience will not understand what is being said. In any case, the plot structure realizes the subtle implication, whether it is or is not intentional, that what is "killed" is Callimaco's independence, his ability to act autonomously, his *manliness*. "Effeminately," he calls to Ligurio: "Oh, don't leave me alone" (11.6.793).

This development constitutes the first ironic axis of the comedy:[46] I do not want to make equivocal distinctions between tragic and comic irony, as I agree with Northrop Frye that irony has its own movement and form. By the phrase "ironic axis" I want to convey the sense of *acted* inversion, the contradiction of intended end and experienced means which emerges visibly in the structure of the play but which is invisible to the protagonists. To this quite ordinary meaning, I wish to add the sense I am attempting to explicate between the play and the political writings. The "comic" inversion, the "funniness," is derived from Nicia as inverted citizen, Callimaco as inverted soldier, and Lucrezia as a chaste woman to be inverted to a harlot in the process of the action. Callimaco desires to show forth his manliness in the course of sexuality, but he can do so only by destroying his manliness. This is worked out dramatically in the first two acts. The second ironic axis is worked out in Acts 3 and 4. Here, Lucrezia surrenders her claim to virtue. Lucrezia is a strong woman. The overcoming of a strong position by brute strength or guile is not particularly ironic, and in Machiavelli's terms, is manly. It was a favorite ploy of the Romans for taking fortresses.[47] What is ironic is that those conventional bulwarks of family virtue, the parent and the priest, should be the agents of transforming family virtue to the rejection of family virtue. The only activity left to Callimaco is that of the stud, and Lucrezia's lack of effeminacy is remedied by her transformation to a whore, a true daughter of *Fortuna*.

These twin axes meld into one, formally and boisterously, in Act 5. A new, contemptuous conspiracy is formed, not against any individual but against the state of matrimony itself. Lucrezia has forgotten her desire for children in her desire for Callimaco. Instead of educating children in honor, she is educating Callimaco in ever more corrupt intrigue, teaching him "how we can be together at anytime without suspicion" (5.4.819). Callimaco has entered the fortress by a trick, but Lucrezia is still in command.[48] Lucrezia's transformation is complete, and her husband, ever ready with a curiously acute cliché, says to her that it is "as though you were born a second time" (5.5.819). Indeed, she has been; her biological birth has been transcended—she has no father—and redefined by masculine desire.

As for Callimaco, it is left to Fra Timoteo to define him with double entendre. "They are bringing out the prisoner" (5.1.815). Callimaco is the prisoner of his own desire, now controlled by the transformed Lucrezia, but he is also in a very real sense hopelessly in thrall to Ligurio. The latter will share with Callimaco the key to the downstairs loggia, courtesy of Nicia, "because they don't have women at home and live like animals" (5.6.820). This spavined lion and scruffy fox, one suspects, are going to be much more beastly at home with the Nicia family than anywhere else. Callimaco is patently in trouble with his mercenary. In any case, there is nothing to stop Ligurio from rejecting his *condotta* for a better one. Nicia is acting paymaster as the comedy closes, and Ligurio is already jogging his arm, telling him to remember to pay Siro (5.6.820).

Siro is an interesting and not entirely minor character, who does all the running about and finally runs off altogether (5.2.816). His master, Callimaco, knows him to be faithful but believes him to be something of a rascal (4.3.808). In fact, Siro is just as much of a rascal as his master desires him to be, and he has a well-articulated notion of good service: "I'm your servant, and servants ought never to ask their masters questions about anything or pry into their business, but when the masters themselves tell them, they ought to serve them faithfully; and so I've done and so I'm going to do" (1.1.779).

One may judge a Prince by his ministers, Machiavelli tells us, and where a minister is "competent and faithful" one can know his master to be wise.[49] So unwise is Callimaco that he does not know his own servant, spurns his advice (1.1.780), and never quite enlightens him as to the details of the plan (2.4.789). The more astute Ligurio spots Siro as "capable" and, with the connivance of Callimaco, takes him over, demonstrating again the identity of Callimaco and Ligurio: "When he gives you orders" says Callimaco, speaking to Siro and referring to Ligurio, "imagine that I am speaking" (4.5.809). Callimaco has handed over his manliness to a mercenary captain, and Siro obeys, although he has warned his master that Ligurio is "not reliable." Siro has also suggested that had Callimaco confided in him before they left France, he would have known how to advise him (1.1). Presumably, he would have advised him not to get involved in the absurd affair at all. Callimaco is a failed prince who does not know a good servant when he sees one. Machiavelli, the rejected secretary, has an axe to grind here.

Perhaps it is to read too much into the text to suggest this affinity between prince and adviser and master and servant, though a comparison between chapter 22 of The Prince and the relations of Callimaco and Siro is suggestive. It may be even more unlikely that Machiavelli put himself into his play as a member of the lower classes, but the difference Siro points out between the risk he takes and that of his master is wry enough: "I'll be in danger of my life and my master of his life and property" (2.4.789).

Machiavelli does plead "poverty" in the Prolog, and says he "plays the servant to such as can wear a better cloak than he can." Further, Siro is the only character not on stage at the end of the play, having "run away"

(5.2.816). He escapes the final corruption, and the sharp Ligurio sounds his epitaph: "Doesn't anyone remember Siro?" (5.6.821).

Ligurio himself had dismissed Siro with a quite gratuitous threat to "cut his throat." Siro is the good man who does the dirty work, keeps his mouth shut, and is humiliatingly rejected (and unpaid) for his pains. His is an invocative characterization.

The fact that the literary and political works of Machiavelli show thematic consistency is not, of course, remarkable. Nor is it surprising that this consistency is expressed in terms of paradox and irony. What is interesting from a feminist perspective is the fact that Machiavelli's dualism, expressed in terms of technique by the two different disciplines of theory and literature, is based upon a radical separation of public and private life which is perceived as quite fundamentally problematic. Whether the fairly persistent relationship of politics and literature reflects the problematics of patriarchal "overcoming" of nature, family, and women is a matter for further critical work. Machiavelli, an exceptional theorist in many ways, is almost unique in the annals of male-stream thought in his understanding of the fact that gender struggle is an essential substructure of history and that this fact has hard, cold consequences for the theory and practice of patriarchal politics. This dilemma cannot be seen merely as a result of Machiavelli's lack of economic sophistication, a sort of poetic substitute for a lack of understanding of class struggle. Marxist aesthetics could find in both the literary and political work sufficient evidence of the "degraded hero": Lukács' symbol of the ethical tensions between art and capitalism which appear in bourgeois literature.[50] Machiavelli's distrust of mercantilist families and the portrayal of Nicia and Callimaco as "merchants" might be interpreted as an early and acute comprehension of the process of transformation of merchants' capital to capital proper. Imaginative Marxists might see the servant Siro as a working-class consciousness antithetically posed against mercantilist corruption. However suggestive class analysis may be, however, it would have to be done inferentially, for Machiavelli's economics, derived from Sallust, are somewhat rudimentary.[51] But if the relations of production do not particularly excite Machiavelli, there can be no doubt that the social relations of reproduction are central to his political analysis. The struggle for an autonomous and scientific politics is a struggle in which political man, by whatever means he can devise, breaks free from the chains which bind him to biological and affective life. The fact that this precondition of polity tends to be dealt with on a literary rather than a theoretical level is a fact which, at the very least, presents feminist scholarship with a key to understanding one level of the ideological nature of male supremacy. It is only from a feminist standpoint and through a serious theoretical analysis of the process and relations of reproduction that the dialectic of Machiavelli's work can be uncovered.

I have argued elsewhere that the material base of the persistent dualism in patriarchal thought lies in the dialectical structure of human reproduction and the consequent differentiation of male and female reproductive consciousness.[52] The birth of a child is a double alienation: for women, a concrete experienced alienation mediated in living labor. For men, the alienation of the seed is a separation from nature, and from species continuity, an alienation which can only be sublated *culturally*; in Machiavelli's terminology, it is an alienation which must be "actively overcome." Paternity is fundamentally ideal; it is knowledge of process in general which cannot be particularized in the context of individual experience. Men are existentially passive toward and detached from the moment of birth: they participate only *potentially*, a participation which they have culturally defined as *potency*, yet potency is radically contingent. Male participation in reproduction is therefore understood *politically*; that is to say, in terms of a *right* to the child rather than in the value-creating reality of laboring to produce a child. This argument is supported by Machiavelli's transcendent realism, and my own analysis of the dialectics of reproduction in fact owes much to a careful reading of Machiavelli.

The dilemma which sends Machiavelli, the pragmatist, off to the physical/metaphysical confrontation of *Fortuna* and *virtù* may be stated thus:

I. Manliness is the crucial individual quality demanded by the tension between biological and civil society. Biological necessity, which takes as its cultural form the family, constantly threatens polity in several ways:

1. A tendency to effeminize young men in the course of a female-directed socialization process.
2. A tendency to fall back into the irrationality of biological reality, the natural world embedded in necessity, which creates the need for the family in the first place. Reproduction embodies a lack of certainty for all men, while sexuality and the *libido dominandi* undermine the certainties of rational lives: both reproduction and sexuality are resistant to control, by reason of their fundamental lack of reason.
3. Men cannot, indeed must not, fall for the obvious trap in the

simple solution presented in the notion of staying home and helping to socialize the children. Such a procedure would ef-feminize them further on the individual level; but they also must be free to create a public, collective realm in which ne-cessity may be superseded and its embodiment, the family, be firmly controlled by various politico/legal/militaristic processes which do not shrink from violence.

II. Polity is the crucial social structure required to produce and defend manliness as reasonable and just and therefore legitimately entitled to *control nature by the exercise of reason*. The strategy is to separate the realm of control—polity—from the realm of necessity—family. This cannot be a merely theoretical separation, for necessity/*Fortuna*/woman is as cun-ning as she is persistent, and children must keep on getting born. Con-stant vigilance is therefore necessary, a constant heroic fortitude which never lets up for a moment, incessantly and aggressively undertaking a life of angst and conquest. Pico's "higher spirits" must constantly remake themselves in action, be reborn continuously in a struggle which they are certain they have created for themselves and in which they are certain that they "make" themselves.

The irony of the first formulation is that the remedy must lie with the father, but he cannot attain exemplary manliness unless he leaves the battlefield of the domestic realm, where his male children need him, and fights his battles from "abroad." The primeval uncertainty embedded in his manliness destines him to a life of warfare. He can never wholly es-cape from the nature which is his mother's problematic gift to him; from the children whose paternity is in doubt if he leaves home; and from the sexual desire that lies ever in wait to trap and sap his manhood in uxoriousness.

The irony of the second formulation is that political man, having sepa-rated public and private, reason and passion, is left with little but undi-rected libido and a norm of aggression. He exchanges the integrative warmth of the hearth, with its intransigent contingency, for the cold but ironclad certainties of the Temple of Mars, where the rational drill of ends and means is clear but means must constantly bend to the enemy of chance which man never quite overcomes.

Isolated in this crude schematic way from its historical reality, the dilemma is so absurd that it cannot be expressed in anything but ideologi-cal or imaginative terms. In practice, men move from one realm to the other, and even Lorenzo the Magnificent, Machiavelli tells us, loved to play with his children. Yet *La Mandragola*, despite its earthiness, rests finally on the writer's sense of the irony of the iron men, who can ultimately deal with uncertainty only by the exercise of violence, while much vaunted "reason" rusts.

Reason, however, can also spawn intrigue, intricacy, and the general moral debilitation we see in the play, where Fortune and Nature are personified in fear and hope: "It's true that Fortune and Nature keep their account balanced. The more my hope has grown the more my fear has grown" (4.1.804).

One gives him courage, the other hope. *Fortuna* and nature are identical in their nonrationality. Necessity traditionally governs the domestic realm, and the domestic realm is traditionally the setting for comedy, and of course, it is the women's realm. But for Machiavelli, necessity is precisely that contingency which challenges and creates opportunities for manliness. The rules which govern the action in the play are general rules of human behavior. They are, however inadequately, institutionalized and, however inadequately, assert an exemplary moral code. For an autonomous politics transcending conventional morality, it would have to be demonstrated that experience and authority in the political realm differ substantively from that in the social realm, and patriarchy has defended political authority in this way. *La Mandragola*, if its relation to the political works has any validity at all, demonstrates exactly the opposite case. In neither literary nor political writings does the objective goal of the action provide the thrust of the action. "Objective goals"—Lucrezia's virtue or the good republic—are not goals but accidental foundations.[53] The goal is an abstraction—manliness—that can only be rendered concrete by social definition but, ironically, is inseparable from the family which it must transcend.

This, of course, is not to insist that known forms of family are the only possible means of regulating the social relations of reproduction, any more than mercantilism or capitalism are the only alternatives in regulating the relations of production. It is to insist, though, that political activity which seeks autonomy over and against the diversity of these relations is doomed to a self-destructive impotence, a pathos of manliness. Manliness, however understood, is radically one-sided and contingent in terms of human life-process. Machiavelli, whatever his status in a humanistic tradition, realized a peculiarly antihuman conception of politics in which manliness, divorced from humanity, finds its most apt expression in compulsive masculine militarism. The ultimate irony of the Man of Iron is that he cannot reproduce himself. He can only rust.

Notes

1. The translation by Allan Gilbert (*Works*, vol. 2) of *La Mandragola* has been used throughout this chapter, and references are placed in parentheses in the text, giving act and scene of the play and the pagination in this edition. Niccolò Machiavelli, *The Chief Works and Others*, 3 vols., trans. Allan Gilbert (Durham: Duke University Press, 1965). For a discussion of the dating of *La Mandragola*, see Sergio Bertelli, "When Did Machiavelli Write Mandragola?" *Renaissance Quarterly* 24, no. 3 (Autumn 1972): 317–26. The edition used for *The Prince and the Discourses* is Niccolò Machiavelli, *The Prince and the Discourses*, trans. Liugi Ricci (New York: Modern Library, 1950).

2. Hannah Arendt, *The Human Condition* (New York: Doubleday, 1959), 33.

3. Arthur Quiller-Couch, ed., *The Oxford Book of English Verse* (Oxford: Clarendon Press, 1939), 231–32.

4. Samuel Beckett, *Waiting for Godot* (New York: Grove Press, 1954), 8.

5. The most commonly quoted formulation is that of the Italian idealist philosopher, Benedetto Croce, who talked of Machiavelli's "austere and painful moral awareness" of the implications of such autonomy. Quoted by Frederico Chabod in *Machiavelli and the Renaissance* (London: Bowes and Bowes, 1958), xii.

6. Jacob Burckhardt, *The Civilization of the Renaissance in Italy* (New York: Washington Square Press, 1966).

7. Ibid., 218.

8. "History of Florence," in *Works*, 1:1063.

9. One of the most hasty and thorough practitioners of nepotism was Sixtus IV, whose activities demonstrate both the self-interested cooperation and distrustful factionalism of the papal, mercenary, and mercantile families. Sixtus, himself of low social origin, elevated his Rovere-Riario nephews to princedoms, including the marriage of one nephew to an obscure illegitimate daughter of the Sforza family, none other than Machiavelli's antagonist, Caterina. She later remarried into the Medici connection. For an account of these devious and very complex relationships, see Ernst Breisach, *Caterina Sforza, A Renaissance Virago* (Chicago: University of Chicago Press, 1967).

10. In one year (1393) Rinaldo opened the electoral rolls to the *grandi* because he needed their help and a few months later closed them again so that he could pronounce Cosimo de' Medici a member of the *grandi* and incapable of holding office. Cosimo was not neutralized, neither by this device, nor by his subsequent imprisonment and exile. As a contemporary remarked, the same golden bag which bought him out of prison would buy him in from exile. See C. C. Bagley, *War and Society in Renaissance Florence* (Toronto: University of Toronto Press, 1961), 127.

11. *Disc.*, 3.34, 509–10.

12. Ibid., 1.9, 138; 11.23, 394–96. See also *Prince*, 10, 37.

13. *Disc.*, 4.46, 535.

14. Ibid., 536 (my italics).

15. Ibid., 3.76, 488.

16. *Prince*, 17, 62.

17. *Disc.*, 4.44.

18. *Disc.*, 4.46, 535. The importance which Machiavelli also ascribed to the militia as a socializing agency is noted by Neal Wood in his Introduction to *The Art of War* (Indianapolis: Bobbs-Merrill, 1965), xxvii.

19. Quoted by Antonia Fraser in *Cromwell: The Great Protector* (New York: Dell, 1975), 664.

20. Examples are too numerous to be listed. See Wood on *ozio* in *The Art of War*, iv. In *Disc.*, 1.19, 172, Machiavelli unites the themes of heredity and effeminacy: a hereditary monarchy can lead to a city which is "effeminate and a prey to her neighbors." Chapter 2 of *The Prince* notes that hereditary monarchies are often stable, but as Rome can furnish no examples, Machiavelli notes only the House of Ferrarra. It was this same house which played perhaps the leading role in the development of theater in Renaissance Italy.

21. John Plamenatz, ed., *Machiavelli* (London: Fontana/Collins, 1972), 19.

22. For an account of the development of the concept of conflict as dynamic, see Neal Wood, "The Value of Asocial Sociability: Contributions of Machiavelli, Sidney, and Montesquieu," in Martin Fleisher, ed., *Machiavelli and the Nature of Political Thought* (New York: Atheneum, 1972), 282–307.

23. Quoted by Burckhardt, *The Civilization of the Renaissance in Italy*, 216.

24. *Disc.*, 4.46, 535.

25. Felix Gilbert, *Machiavelli and Guicciardini* (Princeton: Princeton University Press, 1965), 40–41.

26. Machiavelli approved the Roman custom of admitting strangers to citizenship. See *Disc.*, 2.3.

27. *Disc.*, 1.6, 127–29.

28. See especially letter No. 120: "I must discuss public affairs or be silent"; No. 225: "I love my native city more than my own soul"; and, of course, the justly famous and quite marvelous lived theater of No. 137 in which Machiavelli transports himself to Rome. *Letters*, 103, 249, 139–44.

29. *Hamlet*, 2.2.424. A reference to a proposed production of *La Mandragola* occurs in a letter to Guicciardini in 1525, which is signed "Niccolò Machiavelli, *Istorico, Comico et Tragico.*" Quoted by J. R. Hale, *Machiavelli and Renaissance Italy* (Harmondsworth: Penguin Books, 1972).

30. Gilbert Highet, *The Classical Tradition* (Oxford: Oxford University Press, 1970), 128.

31. Hale, *Machiavelli*, 138.

32. "Superior to the best of Goldoni and inferior only to the best of Moliere." Macaulay, Preface to *La Mandragola*, 48. Macaulay thinks Messer Nicia "the glory of the piece," comparing him with Shallow, Falstaff, Slender, Sir Andrew Aguecheek, Cloten, Osric, Patroclus, Calandrino, and Simon de Vila. Although Nicia is characterized as a crude typification in this analysis, this does not mean that he is presented without wit. To compare him with this list, however, is excessive.

33. Ibid., 50.

34. Highet, *The Classical Tradition*, 136.

35. Lewdness was popular not least among the clergy, who were fond of the bawdy tales of Plautus. Pius II is reported to have written a grossly indecent play before his elevation.

36. Aristotle, *On Poetry and Style*, trans. G. M. A. Grube (New York: The Liberal Arts Press, 1958), 10.

37. Jokes, Aristotle also notes, are "pleasant to those in the know: but do not seem felicitous" to those who are not. Ibid., 94.

38. This paper was written before publication of Hanna Pitkin's *Fortune Is a Woman* (London: University of California Press, 1984). Pitkin's fine analysis places *La Mandragola* firmly in the context of Machiavelli's dread of effeminacy.

39. Aristotle, *On Poetry and Style*, 55.

40. *Disc.*, 3.6, 431. "On Conspiracy"; see also *The Prince*, chapters 17, 18. Allan Gilbert notes in his translation how Ligurio guards against the revelation of this "comic conspiracy" at the end of Act 1: "The shortness of time and the business itself will keep him from discussing it, and there'll not be time to spoil our plan even if he does discuss it" (1.3, 785). He could have added the testing out of Timoteo (3.4), the throwing off-balance which Callimaco suffers from the unexpected complication (4.2, 816), and the general keeping of Siro in the dark.

41. *Disc.*, 3.3; 3.6, 412.

42. *Prince*, 20, 86.

43. *Prince*, 20, 80. "Therefore the best fortress is to be found in the love of the people."

44. Lévi-Strauss has argued that humanism as an ideology actually paves the way for dehumanization by virtue of its intransigent dualism (C. Lévi-Strauss, *Structural Anthropology*, vol. 2, trans. Monique Layton (New York: Basic Books, 1976), 41. For a feminist critique, see Geraldine M. Finn, "Understanding Social Reality: Sartre, Marx, and Lévi-Strauss," dissertation, University of Ottawa, 1981, 67–71.

45. An account of Machiavelli's view on mercenaries with its historical grounds is provided by C. C. Bayley. Mercenaries had and still have admirers. The two most famous equestrian statues of the Renaissance were erected in honor of *condottieri*. For a lavishly illustrated and circumspectly sympathetic account, see Geoffrey Trease, *The Condottieri: Soldiers of Fortune* (London: Thames and Hudson, 1970).

46. There is considerable conflict of opinion in literary circles about the nature and form of irony. See, e.g., the notion of irony as an essentially temporal dimension in Northrop Frye, *The Anatomy of Criticism* (New York: Atheneum, 1968).

47. *Disc.*, 2.32.

48. Machiavelli may have in mind here the Countess Sforza, a redoubtable woman said to have been prepared to sacrifice her children to avenge her husband (*Disc.*, 3.4, 430). Machiavelli in his diplomatic career encountered this formidable woman. See also Ernst Breisach, *Caterina Sforza*; *Disc.*, 3.6, 430. "History of Florence," 7, *Works*, 1149.

49. *Prince*, 22. It is instructive to read the whole chapter with an eye to Callimaco and Siro.

50. Marx's notion of form emerging from content is the basis of the aesthetic theory which George Lukács develops in *The Historical Novel*, trans. Hannah and Stanley Mitchell (Harmondsworth: Penguin Books, 1969). The distinction between "realized" and vulgar types used here owes much to Lukács, in the first case, and to Stalinist realism and Lucian Goldmann, in the second. However, Lukács's notion of "universal type" is not transferable to Renaissance comedy without a much more elaborate treatment than can be given here. He himself remarks, rather tantalizingly: "In comedy, the problem is somewhat different for reasons which cannot be explained here" (104). One of the reasons might be the encapsulation of time, which tends to deprive comedy of a historical dimension; another, the need for the inversion of reality to create the comic effect. The suggestion of "more adequate" typification relates to the placing of these characters outside of their "symbolic" context of trade, family, servant, and mercenary into a wider and therefore more adequate context.

51. Felix Gilbert points out that Machiavelli uncritically inherited from Sallust the notion of money as the root of all evil (174–75). The notion is not, of course, absent from the Christian tradition either.

52. Mary O'Brien, *The Politics of Reproduction* (London; Routledge & Kegan Paul, 1981), chapter 1.

53. *Disc.*, 2.2, 112; "Chance has given birth to these different kinds of governments among men."

6

Fortune Is a Woman—But So Is Prudence

Machiavelli's *Clizia*

Catherine H. Zuckert

Niccolò Machiavelli has long had a problematic reputation. Ever since *The Prince* was published—shortly after his death—his name has been more or less synonymous with evil. To call someone a Machiavellian is not a compliment. It's not everyone, after all, who counsels a prince to exterminate all members of the ruling family when he conquers a province or who praises generals like Hannibal for their marvelous cruelty. Machiavelli has not been without his defenders, of course. He himself was a Florentine republican, and scholars like Hannah Arendt and J. G. A. Pocock argue he tried to inspire his fellow citizens with the kind of military virtue possessed by the citizen-soldiers of the ancient Roman Republic. This defense, in terms of an attempt to revive republican virtue—or, more precisely, *virtù*—has, however gotten Machiavelli into trouble more recently. As the feminist critic Hannah Pitkin points out, the root of the word "virtue" (like the Latin *virtus* or Italian *virtù*) is *vir*, man. And, she argues, for Machiavelli this virtue can be maintained only by suppressing the feminine.[1]

In calling human excellence *virtue*, the Romans identified it with manliness. Virtue, in itself, represented a serious constriction of the Greek conception of human excellence as *aretē*, which is personified in Homer's *Odyssey* by a female demigoddess, daughter of Poseidon, who embodies wisdom, justice, and moderation. Like the Latin *virtus*, the ancient Greek word for courage, *andreia*, could be translated equally well by "manliness"—it also has "man," or *anēr*, as its root. However, for the Greeks courage was at most one of the cardinal virtues; it was not, as it became for the Romans, the core of virtue.

As Pitkin points out, moreover, Machiavelli did not merely take over or attempt to revive the Roman conception. His notion of *virtù* attributes much more importance to canniness, if not out-and-out fraudulence, than did the Roman *virtus*. Whereas the Romans glorified men who were willing to give their lives to defend the interests of the republic as a whole, Machiavelli praises princes and peoples able to maintain their independence. Because human beings are mortal, he recognized, they are always vulnerable, especially to the unexpected strokes or vagaries of fortune. It was, indeed, out of such a feeling of vulnerability or insecurity, Pitkin argues, that Machiavelli urged men not simply to try to control the power of the female goddess *Fortuna* but to suppress completely the feminine, associated as it is with weakness and dependency.

Pitkin takes the title of her book *Fortune Is a Woman* from a well-known passage in chapter 25 of *The Prince*, where Machiavelli observes:

> [I]t is better to be impetuous than cautious, because Fortune is a woman; and it is necessary, if one wants to hold her down, to beat her and strike her down. And one sees that she lets herself be won more by the impetuous than by those who proceed coldly. And so always, like a woman, she is the friend of the young, because they are less cautious, more ferocious, and command her with more audacity.[2]

Fortuna is, Pitkin admits, only metaphorically a woman; and she does not fault Machiavelli for attempting to assert human freedom by taking control of what would otherwise be left to chance. The problem lies in Machiavelli's characterization and treatment of women generally. As Pitkin observes, Machiavelli has very little to say in his political writings about the place or role of women, except to note in *The Discourses* that they can be a dangerous and disruptive element. The dirty underbelly or essentially inegalitarian foundation of Machiavellian politics in sexual oppression comes to the surface primarily in his literary works. In his plays and poems Machiavelli depicts women either as young, beautiful objects of desire or as older, ambitious competitors for power; in either case, he insists, masculine *virtù* requires that they be conquered and controlled.

If we turn to Machiavelli's play *Clizia*, however, we see that the cagey Florentine does not simply dismiss or demean women. On the contrary, in *Clizia*, Machiavelli presents a woman named Sofronia not merely as the rightful ruler of the household but as the embodiment of his new understanding of virtue. Because Sofronia exercises her *virtù* "behind the scenes," in private, in order to maintain her husband's good name and social position, she does not appear "in public" or at the end of the play to be a competitor, even though she proves in the play to be not merely his equal but his superior. (In *The Prince*, we should recall, Machiavelli also reminds his readers of the importance of maintaining appearances, especially with regard to religion.)

By presenting a woman as the embodiment of *virtù*, Machiavelli suggests that there is no essential difference between the sexes with regard to their potential for achieving human excellence.[3] In this way he appears to make way for—or even to be the founder of—what has become known as "liberal feminism." Machiavelli's denial of the importance of the difference between the sexes in and for politics points, moreover, to the fundamental thrust of his thought as a whole. In order to attach human beings more firmly to the goods of this world, he seeks to downplay, to privatize, if not entirely to suppress, human eroticism. Insofar as "the feminine" is associated with that which is desirable and beautiful, with that which lies beyond or transcends market exchange and the struggle to survive, with that which reminds us all of the limits of everyday human existence, Machiavelli tries to destroy it.[4] Because Machiavelli's plays bring to the fore his attack on the desire for that which transcends the life of the individual, reading the plays enables us to understand the fundamental character of his work as a whole. By calling our attention to the impotrance of these literary works, Pitkin has thus done us all a service.

Let me begin, then, by saying something briefly about the relation between Machiavelli's political writings and his plays, before I turn to a more detailed analysis of *Clizia*. To put it somewhat schematically: there is an important parallel to be drawn between the subject matter and general character of Machiavelli's major political writings, on the one hand, and the subject and character of his plays on the other; yet there is also an apparent difference between the political writings and the plays. Whereas in his political writings Machiavelli deals almost exclusively with public life, in his plays he depicts private affairs.

The parallel concerns the contrast between new and old. In the dedications to two, and only two, of his political writings, Machiavelli states that the work in question contains everything that he knows.[5] These dedicatory statements have long puzzled scholars, because the two books appear to be very different. In *The Prince* Machiavelli appears to be teaching magistrates how to acquire and maintain control, even tyrannical control, over other people; and in chapter 15 of that work Machiavelli explicitly states that he is presening a new moral teaching that, unlike the preachings of his predecessors, will prove to be practically effective. In *The Discourses*, on the other hand, Machiavelli presents a commentary on Livy's *History of the Roman Republic*. Rather than presenting a novel teaching to protential tyrants, he seems to be intent merely on reminding some young Florentine republicans of the wisdom of the ancients concerning both the desirability and the means of resisting tyranny.

Machiavelli's two plays present the same surface contrast. Whereas the plot of his best-known play, *La Mandragola*, is new or original with Machiavelli, *Clizia* is clearly a revival and adaptation of a play, *Casina*, by the Roman playwright Plautus, who himself explicitly revived and adapted a piece of so-called new comedy from ancient Athens. As in Machiavelli's major political writings, so in his plays, we seem to confront a marked contrast between an original product and a mere revival of the old.

Despite the contrast between the new and the old, there is a complementarity at work here. As his dedicatory statements indicate, in his political writings Machiavelli presents the same understanding of politics from two somewhat different vantage points. In *The Prince* he argues that the best way for a prince to secure his own power is to secure the interests of his people. He will maintain their support if, and only if, he leaves their property and their women (or their honor) alone. In *The Discourses* Machiavelli shows that people need leaders or princes to secure their liberty and goods. There are, in other words, no princes without peoples and no peoples without princes; these are two poles or views of the same political phenomenon.

Likewise with regard to the plays. Although *La Mandragola* appears to be original and *Clizia* a mere revival, both involve, to a certain extent, a retelling of the story of Lucretia. And it is in the story of Lucretia that the congruence between Machiavelli's plays and his political writings makes itself apparent.

Lucretia, a young and beautiful Roman matron, was raped by the son of the Tarquin king when her husband was away at war. If she did not accede to his wishes, Sextus told her, he would kill her and a male slave, put them in bed together, and say that he had found them there. If she accused him before her husband, he would deny any wrongdoing. There would be no signs of a struggle; he had, after all, not had to use any force. Contrary to his expectation, however, when Lucretia's husband, Brutus, returned home, she first told him what happened and then plunged a dagger into her chest to prove that she thought she had been fatally dishonored. Taking up the bloody dagger, Brutus led a successful rebellion against the Tarquin monarchy. Thus, according to the legend, the Roman Republic was established to avenge the honor of a woman.

There are several things to be said about the story of Lucretia and its significance in Machiavelli's works. First, in *The Discourses* (3.5) Machiavelli dismisses this account of the origins of the Roman Republic.

> Tarquin was driven from Rome, not because his son Sextus had violated Lucretia, but because he had disregarded the laws of the kingdom and governed it tyrannically; having deprived the Senate of all authority, which he appropriated to himself, and having diverted the funds intended for the improvement of the public places . . . to the construction of his own palace . . . [a]nd not content with having incurred the enmity of the Senate, he also aroused the people against him, unlike his predecessors, by obliging them to perform all sorts of mechanical labor. So that, having disgusted all Rome by his many acts of cruelty and pride, he disposed the minds of the Romans to revolt against him on the first occasion that might offer. And if the incident of Lucretia had not occurred, some other would have produced the same effect.[6]

In a later chapter of *The Discourses* (3.26) titled "How States Are Ruined on Account of Women," Machiavelli makes the same observation; disputes concerning women provide the occasion, but only the occasion, for the outbreak of more fundamental conflicts between parts of the city.[7] Men do avenge wrongs to their wives, he admits, but they do so for the sake of maintaining their own honor. Eros, or love, is *not* a politically important passion, as Machiavelli sees it.

If we turn now to his retellings of the story of Lucretia in his plays, we seem to see the same understanding at work. In the first place, both *La Mandragola* and *Clizia* are comedies. As Machiavelli presents it, the story of Lucretia is not tragic; if anything, he suggests, her reaction to the rape is exaggerated and hence ridiculous. In the second place, both comedies depict purely domestic affairs. In his plays as in his political prose, Machiavelli presents love as a purely private—that is, politically irrelevant—passion. The animating force in people's private or domestic lives might thus appear to be different from the passions that move them to act in public. But, I shall argue, in his plays Machiavelli shows that human beings act, and ought to act, according to the same principles in private that he argues in his political writings should guide public life. In both cases, Machiavelli shows, immediate desires like love need to be disciplined by considerations of one's long-term interest in maintaining one's estate and reputation.

The Two Comedies

Let us look, then, at Machiavelli's two plays (for summaries, see Appendices A and B).[8]

In *La Mandragola*, Ligurio is clearly a Machiavellian character. In the new regime he founds, everyone gets what he or she wants—that is, the common good is achieved—under, and only under, two conditions. First, all parties must give up their attachment to traditional notions of virtue—masculine and feminine, ancient and Christian, courage or manliness as well as chastity. Second, and equally important, they must satisfy their desires in ways that maintain public propriety. If the arrangement in Nicia's household were publicly revealed, no one would be happy—Nicia would not get his heir, Lucrezia would lose her reputation, Callimaco would lose his access to her, and Ligurio would surely lose his support.

This need to take account, not only of one's own reputation and estate, but also the name, social standing, and property of others is emphasized even more strongly in *Clizia*. In *Clizia*, however, the Lucretia theme
is rather muted. At one point both in Machiavelli's play and in its Latin
source, the title character is said to be running about crazed, brandishing
a sword and threatening to kill both the master of the house (who intends
to marry her to a servant so that he himself can have his way with her)
and his servant-accomplice. In neither case, we note, does she threaten
to kill herself. Machiavelli might well think that by threatening to strike
those who would wrong her rather than stabbing herself, she is taking a
more sensible course of action than her Roman predecessor. Neither
Clizia nor Plautus's Casina saves her honor by threatening or using force,
however. The story of her crazed behavior is merely a story—part of a
ruse designed by the wife to shame her husband out of a disreputable
passion and so to salvage the honor or respectability of everone concerned. One should remember, of course, that the point of the original
Lucretia story was that by killing herself she maintained not only her own
honor—or reputation for principle—but also her husband's. Moreover,
her act provided the occasion for, if it did not literally cause, the overthrow of a tyranny and the founding of a free republic. That story is,
moreover, from Machiavelli's point of view, merely a story that conceals
the true causes of later events. In *Clizia*, we will see, Sofronia directs the
course of events to maintain the reputation of everyone in the household,
but her role would not, except for Machiavelli's play, be publicly visible
or known.

Machiavelli introduces the issues raised by the story of Lucretia rather
indirectly in Act 1 of *Clizia*. Nicomaco's son Cleandro (whose name
means "man of the muse") is also in love with Clizia. He complains to a
friend, Palamede, that both his father and his mother stand in the way of
his satisfying his desire for the beautiful young girl. Cleandro hopes his
friend will help him, but Palamede responds to Cleandro's tale of woe by
observing that he has learned to avoid three sorts of people: singers who
burst into song in the middle of a conversation, old men who wander off
into every church they see to say their paternosters, and lovers who complain so of their afflictions that one can't help but pity them. Palamede
is named after a soldier in the Trojan War, which, like Brutus's rebellion
against the Tarquins, was not only purportedly fought to avenge the
honor of a woman but also resulted in the destruction of a patriarchal
monarchy. Celebrated in not one, but two, epic poems, the Trojan War

was also, according to legend, indirectly responsible for the founding of Rome. What Palamede has apparently learned from reflecting on the experience of his namesake—or, perhaps, from intervening history—is to avoid poets (those who celebrate such wars and create legends), piety (propagated by the poets and rooted as it is in the fear of death), and love. Having listened to Cleandro's account of his woes and frustration, Palamede therefore flees, never to return. He does not want to be an ancient hero like Achilles, to suffer and ultimately to die for the love of a friend, to be compensated, if at all, by having his story told by poets to later generations.

Since neither Machiavelli's *Clizia* nor its Roman source, *Casina,* is exactly popular reading, it may prove useful to review the plot before inquiring about the significance of some of the changes Machiavelli made to the original and, finally, to reflect on the meaning of the play as a whole (see Appendix B).

Both in *Casina* and in *Clizia* a relatively wealthy family takes in as a ward a little girl of unknown parentage and raises and educates her. Machiavelli made at last four changes in the basic story, however, all of them quite significant. First, as he reminds his audience in the prologue, he has transposed the events that first occurred in Athens to a Florentine setting. He has chosen to do this, first, because ancient Athens is now in ruins. Something about that regime did not last, he reminds us. Florence may be at least potentially the site of the establishment of a more lasting democratic or, in Machiavelli's terms, "republican" polity. Machiavelli does not, he indicates, simply want to revive or repeat the old. Second, he tells us, he has chosen the Florentine setting because his audience understands Italian but not Greek. By reminding us of the difference in language at the very beginning, Machiavelli alerts careful readers—or auditors—to the double meaning of his heroine's name. In Italian, the word *sofronia* is connected with suffering; Sofronia suffers or, as her husband Nicomaco suggests in Act 2, she causes suffering by insisting that people suppress their own desires and submit to the will of God. When we first meet her in Act 2, she is going to church. Understood in an Italian context, Sofronia seems, at least on the surface, to be an embodiment of Christian virtue. She wishes to protect her ward Clizia's chastity, but she submits, at least apparently, to the will of her masters, both earthly and divine. Understood in terms of its Greek roots, however, Sofronia's name is associated with the classical virtues of *sophrosynē* (or moderation) and *phronēsis* (or practical reason). As we shall see in the play, Sofronia does, in fact, embody a certain kind of practical wisdom; and she finally succeeds in enforcing a certain amount of self-control on all members of her family. As a result, at the end she is recognized as the rightful ruler or governor of the household by her husband, Nicomaco. The prudence and moderation Sofronia displays are, however, quite different from the virtues extolled by ancient authors. They are, rather, elements of the virtuosity, or *virtù*, through which Machiavelli suggests an apt ruler can realize the self-interest of all the individuals in a community and so, in sum, the common good. Thus in Machiavelli's comedy *Clizia*, not a man, but a woman, embodies *virtù*.[9]

Sofronia plays a larger role in *Clizia* than the wife, Cleostrata, had in *Casina* because of the third change Machiavelli made. In *Casina* the father sends his son and rival away; we never see him onstage. In the Machiavellian version it is Clizia, not Cleandro, who remains offstage throughout the play. Sofronia keeps the girl locked up to protect her modesty—both her reputation and her chastity or feminine virtue. The effect on both of these changes—namely, the setting and which character is sequestered from view—is to elevate not merely the status of women but also the moral tone of the play as a whole.

The differences between Machiavelli's comedy and its Roman source, with respect to both the presentation of women and the moral of the story, are evident from beginning to end. In the prologue to *Casina* Plautus suggests that once she is married, Casina will become a whore; and in the epilogue he promises to reward all men who applaud his work with as many mistresses as they desire. (So much for the superior morality—or "virtue"—of the Romans.) In the prologue to *Clizia* Machiavelli states that "the author of this comedy" will be "sorely distressed if [his audience] were to find . . . that it contained any indecency. . . . Comedies were invented," he observes, "to be of use and of delight." Their use is in teaching, especially the young, by presenting examples of "the avarice of an old man, the frenzy of a lover, the deceit of a servant, the greed of a parasite, the indigence of the poor, the ambition of the rich, the wiles of a whore, and the bad faith of all men."[10] In order to delight, however, comedies must make their audiences laugh, and "that cannot be done while keeping our speeches grave and austere." But Machiavelli does not claim to have transformed an X-rated ancient pornographic play into G-rated family entertainment. He has, in effect, made it into an R-rated fine-arts film with a serious message embedded in a lot of good jokes. To ferret out the moral of his story, however, we need to look at a fourth change Machiavelli made to his source.

In her attempt to stop the father in *Casina*, the mother takes her son's part by seeking to marry the girl to a household slave who will give the son the same opportunity to frolic adulterously that the father had secured from his bailiff. Like the goddess Juno to whom she is compared, Cleostrata appears to be more concerned about the affront to her own marriage or attractiveness than she is about guarding the girl's virginity or her son's morals. In *Clizia*, on the other hand, Sofronia tells her son Cleandro that she has no more sympathy for his lecherous desires than she does for his father's. If the choice were simply between letting the father or the son have the girl, Sofronia would stop opposing Nicomaco.

Finding the realization of his desires opposed by both his mother and his father, in *Clizia* Cleandro on more than one occasion bemoans his bad fortune. Machiavelli thus has an opportunity to introduce a serious theme from his political writings in comic form. In what seems to be a parody of Machiavelli's own statement in chapter 25 of *The Prince* about Fortune's favoring the young, Cleandro twice complains that the goddess has forsaken the youth she is supposed to like and granted her favors to the old man. What Machiavelli shows in the denouement is that the young may in fact enjoy good fortune, but only if their elders have previously taken appropriate steps or precautions to ensure it.

Once again the contrast between Machiavelli and his source makes the point stand out. In both *Casina* and *Clizia*, the son does finally get to marry the maiden. But in *Casina* the happy resolution appears to be *deus ex machina*, merely the accidental product of good luck or chance; it is not a result of anything anyone did or said in the play itself. In the epilogue we are told that Casina proves to be the daughter of a citizen of Athens, so the son can marry her. In *Clizia* the girl proves to be the daughter of a wealthy Neapolitan who at the end of the play gratefully agrees to marry her to the son of the family that took in his child and educated her. Had he found his daughter married to a no-good servant, as both Nicomaco and Cleandro wanted, Raymondo would hardly have been so grateful or agreeable. In *Clizia* Cleandro's good fortune or happiness in the end is thus a direct result of his mother's precautions, her preventing both father and son from satisfying their amorous desires immediately—and foolishly.

In chapter 25 of *The Prince*, before Machiavelli compares fortune to a woman, he compares it to a river. Just as a stream may wreak havoc and

destruction by overflowing its banks and flooding the surrounding coun-
tryside if people do not take precautions against it by building dikes, so,
he suggests, the power of Fortune, which cannot simply be controlled or
suppressed, can and must be channeled. We ought then to ask: What are
the dikes Sofronia builds or the precautions she takes to channel the
power of fortune in *Clizia* so that it has beneficent rather than detrimen-
tal effects?

To find out, we have to look in more detail at Sofronia's contest with
her husband, Nicomaco. She is on her way to church when we first see
Nicomaco accost her in the street. As Machiavelli advises his prince to
do, Sofronia keeps up an appearance of faith; but she does not rely on
God, his representatives, or mere good fortune to take care of her interests. On the contrary, she has several contingency plans that she can
adopt depending upon the circumstances. Nicomaco first suggests that
they resolve their dispute by selecting a mediator—the friar Timoteo, for
example, whose prayers worked a miracle by causing the sterile wife of
Nicia Calfucci, Madonna Lucrezia, to become pregnant. But Sofronia
smartly responds that it does not take a miracle for a friar to get a woman
pregnant: "It would be a miracle if it were a nun!"[11] Sofronia does not
want to appoint a mediator, because she does not want to let anybody
outside the family know about her husband's disgraceful behavior. But
when her son tells her that his father has resolved to give Sofronia her
dowry back and send her packing and that he will have Clizia married
that evening or burn the house down, Sofronia agrees to try two means
of solving their dispute within the family itself (see Appendix B).[12]

What, you might ask, is the point of this complicated story? The point
is, first, that in *Clizia* Machiavelli presents a woman as the embodiment
of the practical wisdom or *virtù* it takes to rule. *Virtù* may include knowledge of the need to use force upon occasion, but it is not in itself a matter
of force or physical strength. It is more a form of foresight that, as such,
can be exercised by a woman as well as by a man. But what, we then
ought to ask, is the specific character of the foresight, prudence, or *virtù*
Sofronia displays?

At one point in the play Cleandro observes that he is opposed by his
mother's "ambition."[13] She tries to prevent both her husband and her
son from acting on their amorous desires in order to maintain the family
name and estate. She is thus shown to act on the basis of the only two
considerations that Machiavelli suggests, in his political writings, do, and
ought to, concern political men: their own glory and wealth. She acts, in

other words, on the basis of her own self-interest. But, it turns out, her self-interest coincides with the long-term self-interest of her husband and son as well. If Nicomaco had succeeded in marrying his ward to his servant to satisfy his own desires, he would have made himself subject to ongoing blackmail by that servant. Even at his worst, Nicomaco retains some concern for keeping up appearances; he does not, after all, like Jove, simply rape Clizia in disguise. Nicomaco tries to satisfy his desire under cover—and that desire, I might add, is not simply for Clizia. It is also to be himself a young lover again. If Clizia were to have a child under this arrangement, Nicomaco would certainly leave some, if not all, of his estate to it. As both Sofronia and Cleandro see, the consummation of Nicomaco's clandestine affair would thus harm the son's interests in two different respects. However, if Cleandro himself were either to marry, or to have an affair with, Clizia, he would also harm his own interests. If he married her, a fatherless girl, he would sacrifice the dowry he has a right to expect; if had an affair with her, he would arouse his father's jealousy and enmity. In opposing the desires of her husband and son, Sofronia does not seem, like Cleostrata, to be concerned with the potential insult to her own person, her husband's lack of faith, or her son's morals so much as with the effects of their foolish acts on the family's reputation and economic interests. The *virtù* she exemplifies constitutes a kind of self-restraint, but it is not self-restraint or moderation exercised for its own sake; it is self-restraint exercised for the sake of acquiring and maintaining position and property. It is not, in other words, the same as the ancient virtue *sophrosynē*. Sofronia is able to play on the credulity of others, and to exercise foresight, because she sees that although they may be temporarily seized by an immediate desire, other people are fundamentally moved by the same two concerns that animate her. She could not embarrass Nicomaco into submission if he did not care about his appearance in the eyes of others; nor could she restrain Cleandro if he were completely unconcerned about his inheritance or estate.

Both in private and in public, both in his plays and in his political writings, Machiavelli suggests that it is foolish to act on the basis of one's immediate impulses or "love" instead of calculating one's long-term self-interest. And there is more to his denigration of love as a motive of human action than may first appear. In a speech Machiavelli added to the original story, Sofronia tells us that before Nicomaco became infatuated with Clizia, he had been an admirable husband, citizen, and father. "He used to be a serious, resolute, considerate man," Sofronia says.[14]

Under the influence of love, however, Nicomaco becomes a tyrant. When Sofronia opposes his desires, he threatens to destroy the family by sending her packing. He *will be master* of his own house, he insists to his son. If the marriage does not occur that very night, Nicomaco threatens, he will destroy his own estate by burning down the house. In the name of love, he is willing to sacrifice not merely his own legitimate son but the entire family, his chosen people, one might say, in favor of a child he has by a virgin purportedly married to another, more lowly man.[15] In the name of love, he proposes to act like God.

According to the ancient Greek philosophers Xenophon and Plato, tyrants were, essentially, great lovers. They not only wanted to have everything they might desire; they also wanted, above all, to be loved themselves. Put simply, they wanted to be gods. Human love is, in other words, an expression of an essentially unsatisfiable desire on the part of human beings to overcome the limitations imposed by their morality. That desire is at the root not merely of procreation, but also of piety, the worship of gods (which, Aristotle suggests [*Politics* 1252b25], are mere projections of human desire), philosophy understood as love of the eternal truth, and tyranny.

Because human beings are mortal, Machiavelli suggests, they will not achieve satisfaction or peace so long as they act primarily on the basis of eros. If human beings are to avoid continual conflict and tyranny, the contests and wars to which, the poets tell us, love gives rise, eros must be domesticated. That is, it must be kept strictly within the private sphere. Even within the household, man's essentially unsatisfiable eros must be subordinated to, and disciplined by, an attachment to the more external and transient, but humanly attainable (because humanly produced), goods of reputation and estate. Whereas Aristotle traces the origin of the political association to the family, we might observe, Machiavelli does not. Both the relations Aristotle says constitute the family—the procreative relation between male and female and the foresighted, but despotic, control of the master over the slave—are expressions of human eros, as Machiavelli sees it. Neither can, therefore, provide a stable foundation for an ordered community, private or public. Because they are mortal, human beings are essentially changeable; and because they are essentially changeable, their attachment to any particular object or person cannot be relied on any more than can their word or "faith." Rather than try to build a community on the basis of love and trust, Machiavelli thus urges, we must found it on the one unchanging characteristic of all human beings: their attachment to their own lives, property, and standing in the eyes of others. As he states in the song with which he concludes the first acts of both *La Mandragola* and *Clizia*, "Mix'd death and life [i.e., mortal], no man can know . . . heaven's greatest virtue, love undying . . . [which leads us to] flee our welfare as from error, and think more of our lover than [of] self."[16]

The emphasis on the fundamental importance of self-interest and reputation both in Machiavelli's plays and in his political writings leads me, however, to one final reflection. You may have noticed that in *Clizia* Machiavelli presents himself, or at least his namesake, Nicomaco, as an old lover, not to say a fool. There is, perhaps, a biographical reason for this; at the time the play was produced—and it was produced during Machiavelli's lifetime—he was having a well-known affair with an actress in Florence.[17] I suspect he had another reason, however, for making the libidinous Florentine in *Clizia* his namesake. Nicomaco had been a highly regarded man who had taken care of his business, both public and private, and taught his son about human affairs by using examples both ancient and modern; he was, in other words, much like Machiavelli himself. Nicomaco was willing, however, to give up his social standing and reputation for the sake of his love. Machiavelli had not yet published *The Prince* when the first version of *Clizia* was produced, but I suspect he had an inkling of the effect the former would have after his death. Machiavelli himself was, I thus submit, also a man willing to sacrifice his good name—to be called a devil and teacher of evil—in order to benefit future generations by teaching them how better to order their affairs, both public and private. But whether Machiavelli's expressed understanding of human nature takes proper account of his own magnanimity and self-sacrifice is a good question indeed.[18]

Notes

1. Hannah Fenichel Pitkin, *Fortune Is a Woman* (Berkeley and Los Angeles: University of California Press, 1984).

2. Niccolò Machiavelli, *The Prince*, trans. Harvey C. Mansfield Jr. (Chicago: University of Chicago Press, 1985), 101.

3. Machiavelli makes this point most dramatically in *Discourses* 3.6 when he relates the story of Mistress Catherine, wife of Count Girolamo. When the citizens of Forlì killed the count and took his wife and children prisoner, the countess promised to go to the citadel and arrange to have it turned over to the rebels, who continued to hold her children hostage. Once inside the citadel,

however, she reproached the citizens for killing her husband and threatened them with vengeance. To show that she did not care about the fate of her children, she exposed her sexual parts and said that she was capable of having more. So much for feminine modesty and delicacy, to say nothing of the maternal instinct. Like Catherine, Machiavelli suggests, women often use stereotypical images to enable them to get what they want in a quite unstereotypical fashion.

4. Cf. Leo Strauss, *Thoughts on Machiavelli* (Glencoe, Ill.: Free Press, 1959), 17.

5. Cf. Friedrich Nietzsche, *The Gay Science*, trans. Walter Kaufmann (New York: Vintage, 1974), paragraph. 60; Simone de Beauvoir, *The Second Sex* (New York: Random House, 1952), 139–91.

6. Quotations from *The Discourses* are based on a comparison of *Discourses*, trans. Leslie J. Walker (New York: Penguin, 1974) with a literal translation in manuscript form by Harvey C. Mansfield Jr. and Nathan Tarcov, and *Discorsi sopra la prima deca di Tito Livio: Tutte le opere* (Florence: G. Barbera Editore, 1929), 53–262.

7. Arlene Saxonhouse gives a similar account of the import of this chapter in "Niccolò Machiavelli: Women as Men, Men as Women, and the Ambiguity of Sex," in *Women in the History of Political Thought: Ancient Greece to Machiavelli* (New York: Praeger, 1985), 162–66.

8. Quotations from *Clizia* and *La Mandragola* are based on a comparison of the J. R. Hale translation in *The Literary Works of Machiavelli* (London: Oxford University Press, 1961) and the bilingual edition by David Sices and James B. Atkinson of *The Comedies of Machiavelli* (Hanover, N.H.: University Press of New England, 1985).

9. As Hannah Pitkin herself notes somewhat ironically, the Italian word *virtù* is, like the Italian word *fortuna*, "of feminine gender." Pitkin, *Fortune*, 131 n. 103.

10. Hale, *Literary Works*, 68; and Sices and Atkinson, *Comedies*, 282–85.

11. Hale, *Literary Works*, 84; and Sices and Atkinson, *Comedies*, 314–15.

12. In *Discourses* 3.6 Machiavelli states that one of the many ways a conspiracy is discovered is that a conspirator tells a wife or child or some indiscreet person about it. For example, Dinnus, one of the conspirators with Philotas against Alexander, confided the plot to Nicomachus, a lad of whom he was enamored, who told it to his brother Ciballinus, who at once communicated it to the king. In *Clizia* the boy's Italian namesake Nicomaco conspires and is overheard by his son. As Arlene Saxonhouse points out in "Niccolò Machiavelli," Machiavelli loves inversions.

13. Hale, *Literary Works*, 118; and Sices and Atkinson, *Comedies*, 390–91.

14. Hale, *Literary Works*, 84–85; and Sices and Atkinson, *Comedies*, 316–19.

15. The God of Scripture was apparently more moral than the philandering deity of the pagans, to whom the father explicitly compares himself in *Casina*. But in the association he draws between Nicomaco and the Father in Heaven, Machiavelli intimates that this God, too, is a tyrant—or, really, a projection of the tyrannical character of human desire. He demands absolute obedience to his will, and he is willing to sacrifice his only begotten son—out of love, or perhaps the desire to be loved, i.e., worshiped.

16. *Mandragola* in Hale, *Literary Works*, 17; and Sices and Atkinson, *Comedies*, 180–81. *Clizia* in Hale, *Literary Works*, 78; and Sices and Atkinson, *Comedies*, 302–3.

17. Sices and Atkinson, *Comedies*, 23.

18. Cf. Strauss, *Thoughts*, 289–90 and 294–98.

7

Machiavelli and the Citizenship of Civic Practices

R. Claire Snyder

There cannot be good laws where armies are not good, and where there are good armies, there must be good laws.

—Machiavelli, *The Prince*

Niccolò Machiavelli's work forms a quintessential example of the Citizen-Soldier ideal in civic republicanism. Within the civic republican tradition, the Citizen-Soldier ideal is absolutely central for several reasons. In the first place, it links the two realms in which a republic must remain free and autonomous: It links the civic realm, in which republican citizens govern themselves for the common good, with the civic militia, through which citizen-soldiers protect their liberty and autonomy from the threat of external enemies. As we shall see, the Citizen-Soldier constitutes a normative ideal that necessarily entails a commitment to a set of republican political principles, including liberty, equality, fraternity, the rule of law, the common good, civic virtue, and participatory citizenship.

The Citizen-Soldier ideal forms the centerpiece of what I call a *citizenship of civic practices*. According to this model, individuals actually *become* citizens as they participate together in civic practices, traditionally including those of the civic militia. More specifically, within the civic republican tradition, "citizen" is not a prepolitical identity. Individuals are not "citizens" simply by virtue of the fact that they live within certain borders (*ius solis*) or because they have a particular class or ethnic heritage (*ius sanguinis,* or what could be called the *citizenship of blood*). Instead, engagement in civic practices *produces* a common civic identity; it constitutes diverse individuals as citizens. Never finally achieved, citizenship must be constantly constructed and reconstructed through engagement in civic practices. And traditionally, participation in the civic militia formed the main practice through which citizenship was constructed.

Both virtues and vices characterize the citizenship of civic practices. On the one hand, through participation in the civic milita individuals become citizen-soldiers as they learn patriotism, selflessness, and fraternity, all of which coalesce into civic virtue. On the other hand, these same martial practices can teach citizen-soldiers the vices that form the flip sides of these same virtues: Patriotism becomes conquest, selflessness conformity, and fraternity chauvinism. And instead of civic virtue, we get the other half of Machiavellian *virtù*: a combative *armed masculinity*. As we shall see, within the Citizen-Soldier tradition, the creation of participatory citizenship historically entails both an enemy and the denigration of femininity. While any version of the citizenship of civic practices will produce vices as well as virtues, when service in the civic militia forms the primary civic practice constitutive of citizenship, the vices are more prominent. Because of the centrality of the Citizen-Soldier ideal to Machiavelli's vision, his republican virtues are inextricably linked to a corresponding set of vices.

The Republican Reading of Machiavelli

The argument that the Citizen-Soldier ideal stands at the very center of Machiavelli's theoretical framework depends upon a republican reading of Machiavelli. However, not all political theorists see Machiavelli as a republican theorist.[1] The debate over the political orientation of Machiavelli's work grows out of the apparent contradiction between the autocracy of *The Prince* and the republicanism of *The Discourses*. Those who focus primarily on *The Prince* doubt Machiavelli's commitment to republicanism. For example, Leo Strauss and Harvey Mansfield consider Machiavelli a "teacher of evil."[2] Other scholars see Machiavelli as an advocate of imperialism and conquest[3] and/or as a protofascist.[4] Many great German thinkers, such as Fichte, Hegel,[5] Herder, Ranke, and Meinecke, stress the role *The Prince* played—for better or for worse—in the emergence of nationalism during the nineteenth century.[6] Often critics of Machiavelli bolster their claims by summoning up the long history of outrage over Machiavelli's work.[7] Still another school of thought stresses that regardless of his intent, Machiavelli divorced politics from morality and so in this way ended up justifying pure power politics, realpolitik.[8] Some believe Machiavelli did not actually advocate power politics but simply presented a technical study of how politics works.[9] Others argue that he was in fact tortured over the necessity of doing evil for the sake of good.[10] Nevertheless, in opposition to these views of Machiavelli, an increasingly huge body of scholarship emphasizes the strong republican themes present in Machiavelli's oeuvre, particularly in *The Discourses*.[11] These readers of Machiavelli explain *The Prince* in a variety of ways.[12] The fact that Machiavelli was a lifelong advocate of civic republicanism in practice provides additional evidence for many republican readings of his theoretical work.

My reading of Machiavelli builds on the large body of scholarship that portrays him as a republican theorist, and this chapter discusses Machiavelli's republican ideals in depth. My focus on the Citizen-Soldier ideal in Machiavelli's work bolsters arguments that see *The Prince* as providing instructions that, if followed, would lay the groundwork for the transition from a monarchy to a republic.[13] This reading relies upon the famous last chapter of *The Prince*, in which Machiavelli states the following:

> If then, your glorious family resolves to follow the excellent men I have named who redeemed their countries, she must *before all other things, as the true foundation of every undertaking, provide herself with her own armies*, because there cannot be more faithful or truer or better soldiers. And though each one of them is good, they will become better if united, when they see themselves com-

manded by their own prince and by him honored and maintained. It is necessary, therefore, for her to prepare such armies in order with Italian might to defend herself against foreigners.[14]

Here Machiavelli advises the prince to arm his subjects. In so doing, he advises the prince to lay the foundation for a republic because—as we shall soon see—Machiavelli considered engagement in martial practices as constitutive of republican citizenship and thus as the foundation for a republic.

My ultimate claim is that Machiavelli presents a dialectical vision in which republican ideals and the heroic ethic are reconciled in the figure of the Citizen-Soldier. That is to say, while ostensibly contradictory, Machiavelli's republican citizenship and his emphasis on the heroic ethic—glory, grandeur, and conquest—come together in the figure of the Citizen-Soldier and form a package of interconnected virtues and vices. My reading builds on the work of Mark Hulliung, who begins to get at this dialectic in his book *Citizen Machiavelli:* "If, as we have argued, a Machiavellian potentiality always inhered in the republican tradition, the secondary literature errs in dwelling solely on the 'idealism' of civic humanism and in contrasting it with the so-called 'realism' of Machiavelli."[15] According to Hulliung's rendition, the civic humanists were always champions of the heroic ethic of glory.[16] Hulliung seems to be proffering a dialectical reading when he argues that Machiavelli insisted "that republics and conquest go hand in hand." Criticizing the republican readings of the Florentine, Hulliung argues that

> it is not enough to bridge the gap between the *Prince* and the *Discourses* or to point to Machiavelli's republican progeny in order to make a case for an un-Machiavellian Machiavelli. At this point the standard interpretation of Machiavelli ends when it is precisely at this point that it should begin. Why did Machiavelli favor republics over monarchies? *If the answer may be phrased in terms of liberty, it may equally well be phrased in terms of power,* for his constant principle is that the greatest triumphs of power politics are the monopoly of free, republican communities. The standard scholarly interpretation of Machiavelli is therefore revisionist; it deletes all that is most striking and shocking in his thought; it is Machiavelli expurgated.[17]

However, Hulliung backs away from a dialectical reading. That is, while Hulliung rightly restores the heroic ethic of heroism, glory, and conquest to the center of Machiavelli's work, in so doing he shortchanges the civic republican aspects, which, as I will demonstrate, are equally central.[18] What Hulliung ultimately does is subordinate Machiavelli's advocacy of republicanism to his desire for *grandezza* and *gloria*. What I am suggesting, on the other hand, is that for Machiavelli the two sets of ideals are equally important and that he synthesizes them through his articulation of the Citizen-Soldier.

Within Machiavelli's oeuvre the heroic ethic and the commitment to civic republican principles—liberty, equality, fraternity, the rule of law, the common good, civic virtue, and participatory citizenship—come together in the figure of the Citizen-Soldier. That is to say, the benefits of republicanism can be obtained only for citizens of a particular republic, and these individuals must constitute themselves as citizens in opposition to an enemy against which they prepare to fight. In other words, to the extent that the Citizen-Soldier ideal forms the foundation of civic republicanism, this tradition presents a framework in which its virtues— including patriotism, selflessness, fraternity, civic virtue, and participatory citizenship—are intertwined with its vices—conquest, conformity, chauvinism, armed masculinity, and exclusion. Thus Hannah Pitkin is correct when she states that Machiavelli is "both a republican and something like a protofascist."[19] While the interconnection of virtues and vices always exists within civic republicanism, it exists to a much greater extent when martial practices are privileged over other possible forms of civic practices.

Uniting the Republic in Theory

The ideal of the Citizen-Soldier stands at the very center of Machiavelli's republican theory because it unifies his political understanding, which, in Pitkin's words, "consists of a set of syntheses holding in tension seemingly incompatible truths along several dimensions." The figure of the Citizen-Soldier embodies the linkages between the civic realm and the militia, citizenship and armed masculinity, civic virtue and *virtù*, republican ideals and militarism. Pitkin argues that many of the apparent contradictions in Machiavelli's thought come from the unraveling of these syntheses. However, "even when he loses the syntheses," she argues, "he is a better teacher than many a more consistent theorist, because he refuses to abandon for very long any of the aspects of the truth he sees."[20]

The Citizen-Soldier forms the linchpin in Machiavelli's dialectical edifice. First and most democratically, the Citizen-Soldier fuses the militia to the civic realm of republican self-rule. The soldier who risks his life to defend the republic is also the citizen who participates in forming laws for the common good. Both halves of the Citizen-Soldier ideal are equally important: Citizen-soldiers fight to defend their ability to govern themselves for the common good through the rule of law. In other words, the Citizen-Soldier ideal does not mean simply that citizens constitute the military. Normative rather than empirical, the Citizen-Soldier embodies a commitment to civic republicanism, complete with all its ideals: liberty, equality, fraternity, the rule of law, the common good, civic virtue, and participatory citizenship.

Second, the Citizen-Soldier ideal represents the fusion of armed masculinity onto republican citizenship. That is to say, service in the civic militia plays a key role not only in the constitution of republican citizenship but also in the construction of armed masculinity, of what it means to be a man. Through engagement in martial practices, individuals become citizen-soldiers, as they acquire *virtù*, a central concept in Machiavelli's work and one that crystallizes the traditional fusion of masculinity onto citizenship within civic republican tradition. *Virtù* has two meanings in Machiavelli's oeuvre. In the first place, it means civic virtue, the placing of the common good before individual self-interest, a necessary prerequisite to republican self-rule. At the same time, however, *virtù* means the virile action necessary to the domination of *Fortuna*, action which, as we will see, constitutes a combative form of armed masculinity formed in opposition to a denigrated femininity. Service in the militia teaches *virtù* in both its senses.

Third, the Citizen-Soldier, exemplar of *virtù*, embraces a form of citizenship that is simultaneously republican and militaristic. The republican Citizen is also the Soldier, and every Soldier requires an enemy against which he must prepare to fight. The militarism inherent in the ideal of the Citizen-Soldier plays a key role in unifying the republic as it prepares to defend itself against external enemies and consequently helps prevent the emergence of internal factions. It provides a venue through which citizens of superior ability can serve the republic. And it plays a vital role in the production of armed masculinity.

Linking "Good Laws and Good Armies"

The Citizen-Soldier ideal connects the civic realm of legislation to the civic militia, a connection Machiavelli emphasizes in his famous demand for both "good laws and good armies." Both "good laws"—aimed at the common good and created through the participation of citizens—and "good armies"—made up of all citizens and organized as a civic militia—are necessary to the creation and maintenance of a republic. In both *The Prince* and *The Discourses* Machiavelli stresses that "good laws and good armies" are "the principal foundations of all states"—princedoms as well as republics: "And because there cannot be good laws where armies are not good, and where there are good armies, there must be good laws, I shall omit talking of laws and shall speak of armies."[21] While I would insist that civic participation in legislation is no less important to Machiavelli's republicanism than is participation in the civic militia, taking Machiavelli at his word I begin with his discussion of the necessity of good armies.

Machiavelli emphasizes the need for good armies for several reasons. In the first place, the continued existence of a republic depends quite directly on good armies. That is to say, every state needs good armies because—at least in Machiavelli's world—all states are vulnerable to attack from competing states.[22] Machiavelli knew very well that a republic is a very fragile entity that must be carefully nurtured and defended. Although for the first third of the fifteenth century "Florence was a genuine republic"—albeit one that restricted citizenship to an elite group of wealthy, powerful men[23]—by the time Machiavelli wrote his political theory of republicanism, the Florentine republic was merely a memory.[24] Thus, he recognized the precariousness of republican government and its vulnerability to both external and internal threats. Only an armed state can protect itself from foreign conquest and thus maintain its republican ideals.

In fact, many scholars emphasize that military threats from northern Italy and France played a key role in the reemergence of the theory of civic republicanism during the fifteenth century. Although Florence had a tradition of self-government, it was not until the fifteenth century that theoretical justification of republicanism began to emerge. By that point the Florentine republic was being threatened by princedoms and dukedoms to the north. As Hans Baron has demonstrated, around the year

1400 this threat to their way of life led Florentines to begin to think self-consciously about their political practices and to define themselves in connection with the ancient republics rather than with the Empire.[25] In other words, civic republicanism's reemergence as a theory came out of the Florentine attempt to solidify its identity in the face of the threat of external enemies.

Second, for Machiavelli good military organization means a civic militia made up of all citizens: "An army evidently cannot be good if it is not trained, and it cannot be trained if it is not made up of your subjects. Because a country is not always at war and cannot be, she must therefore train her army in times of peace, and she cannot apply this training to other than subjects, on account of the expense."[26] History reveals, he argues, that disarming the people leaves states vulnerable to conquest.[27] And border guards are not enough. States that "make some little resistance on their boundaries" have "no recourse" when

> an enemy has passed them. . . . And they do not see that such a way of proceeding is opposed to every good method. The heart and the vital parts of a body should be kept armored, and not the extremities. For without the latter it lives, but when the former is injured, it dies; and these states keep their hearts unarmored and their hands and feet armored. What this error has done to Florence has been seen and is seen every day; and when an army passes her boundaries and comes within them close to her heart, she has no further recourse.[28]

Thus, the defense of the republic absolutely requires an armed populace.[29]

Moreover, a civic militia made up of all citizens helps maintain peace, preserve liberty, and minimize the possibility of tyranny. Hired mercenaries or foreign auxiliary armies cannot be trusted to protect a state of any type: "mercenary forces never do anything but harm."[30] In the first place, Machiavelli argues that a civic militia has no interest in continuing a war unnecessarily. Professional soldiers do. They "are obliged either to hope that there will be no peace, or to become so rich in time of war that in peace they can support themselves."[31] Because they are not professionals, citizen-soldiers do not expect anything from war, "except labor, peril, and fame." Instead of wanting to remain at war, they wish "to come home and live by their profession." In Machiavelli's words, the citizen-soldier "when he was not soldiering, was willing to be a soldier, and when he was soldiering, wanted to be dismissed" (576). A citizen-soldier "will gladly make war in order to have peace," but "will not seek to disturb the peace in order to have war" (578). Thus the ideal of the Citizen-Soldier should decrease the chances of war, not increase them.

The use of professional soldiers also puts the republic at risk of being tryannized by them. When wars are finished, mercenaries and auxiliaries exist by "exacting money from the cities and plundering the country" (574). On the other hand, Machiavelli argues,

> no great citizen ever presumed . . . to retain power in time of peace, so as to break the laws, plunder the provinces, usurp and tyrannize over his native land and in every way gain wealth for himself. Nor did anybody of low estate dream of violating his oath, forming parties with private citizens, ceasing to fear the Senate, or carrying out any tyrannical injury in order to live at all times by means of warfare as a profession. (575–76)

Moreover, when professional soldiers become tyrants, an unarmed citizenry has no recourse.

Furthermore, not only do mercenaries and auxiliary armies pose the threat of plunder, tyranny, and perpetual war, they also make bad soldiers because the only true inspiration for fighting is the protection of one's own liberty. Mercenaries and auxiliaries "are useless and dangerous; . . . they are disunited, ambitious, without discipline, disloyal." While mercenaries are "valiant among friends, among enemies [they are] cowardly." Consequently,

> in peace you are plundered by them, in war by your enemies. The reason for this is that they have no love for you nor any cause that can keep them in the field other than a little pay, which is not enough to make them risk death for you. They are eager indeed to be your soldiers as long as you are not carrying on war, but when war comes, eager to run away or to leave.[32]

There is a tremendous difference, Machiavelli argues, between "an army that is satisfied and fights for its own glory and an army that is ill disposed and fights for some leader's ambition."[33] Men will willingly and courageously risk their lives only to defend their own liberty:

Nothing made it harder for the Romans to conquer the people around them and part of the lands at a distance than the love that in those times many peoples had for their freedom, which they defended so stubbornly that never except by the utmost vigor could they be subjugated. We learn from many instances in what perils they put themselves in order to maintain or regain that freedom, and what revenge they wreaked on those who took it from them.[34]

J. G. A. Pocock puts it nicely when he says, "the paradox developed in Machiavelli's argument is that only a part-time soldier can be trusted to possess a full-time commitment to the war and its purposes."[35] Thus only a civic militia can be relied upon to defend a republic.

It is important to note here that when citizen-soldiers fight to defend their republic and their ability to govern themselves through the formation of manmade laws, they fight for a secular political order. Civic republicanism emerged in the fifteenth century in direct opposition to a Christian worldview and political order.[36] As Pocock explains, the revival of Aristotelianism and the revaluation of history led to a break with the medieval Christian "scholastic-customary" framework and a rediscovery of citizenship. The reemphasis on the importance of time and the deliberative and creative powers of the human mind in both the intellectual movement of civic humanism and the political movement of civic republicanism constituted an attack on the medieval Christian worldview, with its traditional, hierarchic view of society, and on the structures of monarchy and aristocracy it justified: Citizenship requires liberty rather than subjection to tradition, equality rather than hierarchy and rank, fraternity rather than paternity and filiality, and autonomy rather than obedience to natural God-given law and dependence upon natural superiors. Pocock states it baldly: "Machiavelli unequivocally prefers the republic to revealed religion."[37] Citizen-soldiers fight to protect their secular political order and civic ideals. They do not fight for God and His revealed Truth.

Creating Virtù: A Common Good for Manly Citizen-Soldiers

Besides being necessary to the continual existence of a republic, the practices of the civic militia are absolutely essential to Machiavelli's citizenship of civic practices because they play a key role in the *creation* of masculine citizen-soldiers out of male individuals. That is, for Machiavelli masculinity requires soldiering, and soldiering must be linked to citizenship. Participation in martial practices simultaneously constructs all three characteristics. The interrelated constructions of masculinity, soldiering, and citizenship come together in Machiavelli's concept of *virtù*, which is produced directly by engagement in martial practices.

The Citizen-Soldier ideal embodies Machiavelli's concept of *virtù*, a concept that connects the civic realm to the civic militia and fuses armed masculinity to citizenship. *Virtù* has a dual meaning in Machiavelli's work, and citizen-soldiers must possess *virtù* in both senses.[38] In the first place, civic republicanism requires a sense of *civic virtue*, defined as the characteristic whereby individuals place the common good ahead of individual self-interest.[39] In Quentin Skinner's words,

> a self-governing republic can only be kept in being . . . if its citizens cultivate that crucial quality which Cicero had described as *virtus*, which the Italian theorists later rendered as *virtù*, and which the English republicans translated as *civic virtue or public-spiritedness*. The term is thus used to denote the range of capacities that each one of us as a citizen most needs to possess: *the capacities that enable us willingly to serve the common good, thereby to uphold the freedom of our community*, and in consequence to ensure its rise to greatness as well as our own individual liberty.[40]

This is not to say that the common good stands opposed to individual interests. To the contrary, by definition the common good includes the good of each individual.[41] However, government for the common good does constitute an alternative both to a system of rule based on balancing individual interests (such as liberalism) and to rule based on one particular interest that stands opposed to the common good (such as tyranny).

Within the Citizen-Soldier tradition, service in the civic militia plays a key role in the creation of civic virtue, a necessary prerequisite to the willingness to make laws aimed at the common good. According to Skinner, "a leading theme of Book II of Machiavelli's *Discorsi*" is that "the martial values," including "courage and determination to defend [the] community against the threat of conquest and enslavement by external enemies," constitute the capacities citizens need to possess in order to uphold the common good, ensure greatness, and protect the liberty of both the community and the individuals who compose it.[42] Participation in the civic militia requires soldiers to act together for the common good and to sacrifice particular goods to universal ends. In this way military service forms a type of civic education that teaches individuals to act together for the common good during civic legislation. And in this way civic and martial virtue are interconnected. As Pocock explains, "[I]t may be through military discipline that one learns to be a citizen and to display civic virtue."[43] In other words, soldiering privileges certain *virtues* that become attached to citizenship—among them courage, selflessness, fraternity, and patriotism. These virtues force the citizen to rise above his own particular interests and to think of the good of the community as a whole. Thus, within the Citizen-Soldier tradition in general and in Machiavelli's work in particular, martial virtue plays a central role in the construction of civic virtue.

But while civic virtue grows out of martial virtue, martial virtue necessarily presupposes civic virtue: The willingness to self-sacrifice presupposes an identification with the republic. As Pocock argues, the citizen's desire to defend his life in the republic guarantees he will be virtuous in battle.[44] Citizen-soldiers fight to defend their liberty, equality, fraternity, their laws aimed at the common good, and their participatory citizenship. Only the love for one's *patria* and the ideals it represents allows for the possibility of self-sacrifice. Thus, for Machiavelli, the civic militia with its martial virtue is inextricably linked to the realm of civic legislation with its civic virtue by the ideal of the Citizen-Soldier.

The second meaning of *virtù* in Machiavelli's work is *virile political action*, which is directly related to traditional understandings of *masculinity*. As Pitkin explains, *virtù* means "energy, effectiveness, virtuosity" and "derives from the Latin *virtus*, and thus from *vir*, which means 'man.' *Virtù* is thus manliness, those qualities found in a 'real man.'"[45] Machiavellian *virtù* connotes a form of armed masculinity that stands opposed to "*effeminato* (effeminate), . . . one of his most frequent and scathing epithets."[46] The republican citizen characterized by armed masculinity acquires *virtù* as he battles *Fortuna*, a concept Machiavelli understood as feminine.[47] To quote Machiavelli:

> I conclude then (with Fortune varying and men remaining stubborn in their ways) that men are successful while they are in close harmony with Fortune, and when they are out of harmony, they

are unsuccessful. As for me, I believe this: it is better to be impetuous than cautious, because *Fortune is a woman and it is necessary, in order to keep her under, to cuff and maul her.* She more often lets herself be overcome by men using such methods than by those who proceed coldly; *therefore always, like a woman, she is a friend of young men, because they are less cautious, more spirited, and with more boldness master her.*[48]

Feminine Fortune can be mastered only by an *armed masculine virtù.*

For Machiavelli, engagement in virile martial practices is necessary for the construction of armed masculinity. In other words, armed masculinity does not exist naturally in male individuals. Instead, it must be *produced.* "Pondering, then, why it can be that in those ancient times people were greater lovers of freedom than in" his times, Machiavelli concludes that the difference comes "from the same cause that *makes men now less hardy.*" That is to say, "this [Christian] way of living, then, *has made the world weak and . . . effeminate.*" Christians are effeminate because they do not engage in virile martial practices. On the other hand, pagans were manly because they were "fiercer in their actions" than the Christian males. Pagan sacrifices were "magnificent, . . . full of blood and ferocity. . . . [And] this terrible sight *made the men resemble it.*" In contrast to this, Christianity has made men effeminate by "glorif[ying] humble and contemplative men rather than active ones."[49] Clearly, Machiavelli did not consider armed masculinity a naturally occurring characteristic of male individuals. To the contrary, it must be constructed through participation in the fierce, bloody, and magnificent actions required during military service. Furthermore, Machiavelli constructs his manly *virtù* not only through struggle against a *Fortuna* considered feminine but also in opposition to a Christianity also considered feminine. In other words, *virtù* is both manly and secular. As Hulliung puts it,

> Arrayed on one side are the pagan virtues: *virtus,* glory, grandeur, magnificence, ferocity, exuberance, action, health, and manliness; on the other side are the Christian virtues, humility, abjectness, contempt for human things, withdrawal, inaction, suffering, and disease—and the upshot of these Christian 'virtues,' he concludes, is the womanish mankind of postclassical times, whose histories are as ignoble as Rome's was noble.[50]

And as Hulliung puts it, in Bonnie Honig's words,

> Machiavelli seek[s] in *virtù* a manly alternative to what [he] de-
> scribes as the feminizing, enfeebling and immobilizing virtue of
> Christianity. . . . *Virtù* for Machiavelli is a political excellence,
> connected with the greatest of all worldly rewards, glory. . . .
> Machiavelli criticizes virtue because its otherworldliness turns
> men away from the grandest of human worldly endeavors and sab-
> otages the enterprise of politics.[51]

In short, the second meaning of Machiavellian *virtù* is a combative, secular armed masculinity, constructed in fierce opposition to femininity.

In laying out the dual meaning of the term *virtù* in Machiavelli's
oeuvre, I want to suggest that there is not one "civic *virtù* of Machiavelli's
Discourses—the excellence of a citizen in a republic"—and a "rather different princely *virtù* of *The Prince*," as Honig asserts,[52] but rather that the
two meanings are unified by the ideal of the Citizen-Soldier. The civic
virtue of the citizen and the combatively masculine action of the soldier
come together in a figure that exhibits both characteristics at once. Put
differently, engagement in the martial practices of the civic militia simultaneously creates citizens with civic virtue, soldiers who display manly
virtù, and men who acquire their armed masculinity in opposition to a
denigrated femininity. Consequently, Machiavelli's Citizen-Soldier ideal
fuses together soldiering, masculinity, and citizenship.

Because "masculinity" is socially constructed rather than rooted in
nature, it can never be secured finally. As a consequence, "femininity"—
masculinity's "excess and remainder"[53]—always poses a threat to republican citizen-soldiers. Pitkin lays out four reasons for this. First, the
seductive power of young women as sex objects "threatens a man's self-
control, his mastery of his own passions." Second, women's erotic power
"threatens to infect him with feminine softness." Third, men often suc-
cumb to the temptation to violate the chastity of another man's woman,
which is one sure way to create political opposition and division. As
Machiavelli says, men will tolerate most things as long as they "'are not
deprived of either property or honor,'" and, for him, women constitute
both. And fourth, women threaten republican citizenship by "weaken[ing]
the manly self-control of citizens . . . [which] tends to privatize the republican citizen, drawing him out of the public square and into the bedroom."[54] In other words, femininity threatens the masculine citizen-

soldier's ability to govern himself through legislation aimed at the common good, because it fuels his passions, privatizes him, and disrupts his ability to unite with other men, all of which interfere with the creation of civic virtue. Furthermore, these three things plus the stimulation of feminine softness within him hinder his cultivation of the martial virtues.

Because the Citizen-Soldier constitutes himself in opposition to "femininity," Machiavelli's normative republican vision requires the exclusion of feminine individuals, that is, women.[55] Moreover, it demands that citizen-soldiers stomp out any so-called "feminine" feelings that might exist within themselves. Consequently, as Pitkin argues, Machiavelli

> juxtapose[s] men, autonomy, adulthood, relations of mutuality, politics, the *vivere civile*, human agency in history, and humanness itself, on the one side, to women, childhood, dependence, relations of domination, nature, the power of environment and circumstance, instinct, the body, and animality, on the other. Human autonomy and civility are male constructs painfully won from and continually threatened by corrosive feminine power. Male ambition and human sexuality, however, play ambiguous roles in this struggle, sometimes aiding and sometimes threatening the men. Indeed, the men themselves are ambivalent about the struggle; . . . feminine power seems to be in some sense inside the men themselves. *Only ferocious discipline and terrifying punishments can secure them in the male enterprise of becoming human and autonomous.*[56]

"Masculinity" is never a fait accompli; it must be continually constructed and reconstructed through ferocious military discipline and virile actions. And because of the combative nature of the Citizen-Soldier's masculinity, as Wendy Brown rightly argues, his "construction of manliness . . . entails not mere opposition to but conquest of woman."[57] "Femininity" constitutes a profound danger to a tenuously constructed armed masculinity. Only continual engagement in martial practices can ward off the feminine threat that exists not only outside men but within them as well. In short, the entire structure of Machiavelli's civic republicanism is erected upon the denigration of femininity in all its manifestations.

Soldiering plays a key role in the creation of both armed masculinity and citizenship in Machiavelli's work; it is the solder that fuses armed masculinity onto citizenship. However, soldiering, Machiavelli tells us, does not come naturally either to men or to citizens. Instead, good soldiers must be *created* through the right institutional context; discipline and training are absolutely essential to this process. Princes and republics that lack their own soldiers "ought to be ashamed," he argues. Using the example of Tullus, Machiavelli argues that the lack of soldiers "comes not from a lack of men fit for warfare but from their own error, because they have failed *to make their men soldierly.*"[58] Tullus' ability was "so great" that "under his direction he immediately made [his men] into very excellent soldiers. So it is truer than any other truth that *if where there are men there are not soldiers, the cause is a deficiency in the prince* and not a deficiency in the position or nature of the country." Warriors, Machiavelli concludes, could exist "in every . . . region where men are born, *if only* there is someone who can *direct them toward soldiership.*"[59] In *The Art of War* Machiavelli says that "ancient examples show that in every country training can *produce* good soldiers, because where nature fails, the lack can be supplied by ingenuity, which in this case is *more important than nature.*"[60] Likewise, in *The Prince* Machiavelli argues that

> if, in so many convulsions in this land and in so much warfare, Italy's military vigor always seems extinct, . . . the cause is that her old institutions were not good, and no one has been wise enough to devise new ones; and . . . in Italy there is no lack of matter on which to impose any form; there is great power in the limbs, if only it were not wanting in the heads.[61]

Clearly, for Machiavelli, the practices of the civil militia play a central role in the actual *production* of manly soldiers.

Soldiering, however, must be connected to citizenship. Machiavelli connects the civil militia directly to the sphere of civic realm in which republican citizens form good laws, when he emphasizes that liberty is the primary underpinning for good armies. "Wherever there are good soldiers," he argues, "there must be good government."[62] This is true because soldiers can be good only when they are protecting their liberty, which can be established and maintained only through good government. That is, Machiavelli believes that liberty must be created through and nurtured in a context of good laws. Good laws both produce and protect liberty by limiting arbitrary power: "To republics, indeed, harm is done by magistrates that set themselves up and by power obtained in unlawful ways, not by power that comes in lawful ways."[63] Good armies require good laws.

Machiavelli argues that only within the context of republican institutions, such as the civic militia and the rule of citizen-authored law, can individuals become citizens. That is, when Machiavelli states that "laws make [men] good,"[64] he argues that outside of the context of law, men can easily slip back into their baser selves:

> As is demonstrated by all those who discuss life in a well-ordered state—and history is full of examples—it is necessary for him who lays out a state and arranges laws for it to presuppose that all men are evil and that they are always going to act according to the wickedness of their spirits *whenever they have free scope*.[65]

That is why Machiavelli favors the rule of law over the rule of men: "Absolute authority in a very short time corrupts the matter and makes itself friends and partisans."[66] For this reason Machiavelli cautions against the long-term delegation of power from the citizens to a magistrate. Although republics should empower a group of citizens to make executive decisions when quick decisions are needed, and so the necessarily slow deliberative process cannot be used, republics must be careful not to delegate this power for long periods of time because "when free authority is given for a long time—that is, for a year or more—it will always be dangerous and will produce good or bad effects according as those to whom it is given are bad or good."[67] And of course whether they are bad or good depends on whether they are able to use power to advance their own particular interests at the expense of the republic.

Partisanship within a republic is problematic because it causes individuals to place private ambition over public good and so compromises the process of legislation for the common good. Citizens in a republic must rule "wholly for the benefit of the state and [should] not in any respect regard private ambition."[68] *Public* citizenship means ruling for the common good, and ruling for the common good constitutes public citizenship. Both are possible only in a republic:

> Without doubt this common good is thought important only in republics, because everything that advances it they act upon, and however much harm results to this or that private citizen, those benefited by the said common good are so many that they are able

to press it on against the inclination of those few who are injured
by its pursuit. The opposite happens when there is a prince; then
what benefits him usually injures the city, and what benefits the
city injures him.[69]

Not ruling for the common good causes great disorder, while doing so
leads to greatness and increased wealth for the republic.[70]
Machiavelli believes that given the right republican institutional context, human beings can rise above their own narrowly defined self-interests and rule themselves for the common good.[71] Although he holds a
cynical view of human nature, as a whole his writings reveal his belief
that republican institutions and civic participation can successfully transform selfish individuals into citizens. While he frequently refers to "the
nature of men" as "ambitious and suspicious," as unable to "know how
to set a limit on its own fortune,"[72] as "insatiable" and therefore always
discontented,[73] as shortsighted, vengeful, and ungrateful, he believes that
in the context of the rule of law these self-interested men can become
republican citizens. Arguing "against the common opinion" that insists
on the need for princely rule because "the people, when they are rulers,
are variable, changeable, and ungrateful," Machiavelli argues that in the
context of the rule of law, the people can rule themselves better than a
prince: "A people that commands and is well organized will be just as
stable, prudent, and grateful as a prince, or will be more so than a prince,
even though he is thought wise." Moreover, "a prince set loose from the
laws will be more ungrateful, variable and imprudent than a people. . . .
The variation in their actions," he argues, "comes not from a different
nature—because that is the same in all men, and if there is any superiority, it is with the people—but from having more or less respect for the
laws under which both of them live."[74] Thus, for Machiavelli the key
determinant of how men will behave is the context of political institutions within which they live; men's actions are not necessarily driven by
"human nature." While without the rule of law, men will interact only
on the basis of power and self-interest, under the rule of law, men are
capable of governing themselves in accordance with the common good.
    In fact, Sebastian de Grazia argues that Machiavelli's contention that
naturally selfish individuals can still govern themselves for the common
good marks his break with ancient philosophy:

>   In our philosopher's world men do not have an inherent impulse
>   toward the common good. Quite the reverse. These wicked and

unruly men are not just a few: they comprise mankind. . . . This is Niccolò's third major contribution to political philosophy: the vision of a world in which rational brutes must reach the common good. Binding a permanent, state-prone, or political and social, human nature to the end of a good-in-association, or the common good, was a triumph of ancient political philosophy. Niccolò snaps the link of nature and end. The common good is still the goal but no longer do men reach it naturally.[75]

Born rational brutes, (male) individuals are *capable* of governing themselves for the common good, *but only in the context of participatory republican institutions*.

On this point my reading differs from the one presented by Wendy Brown in *Manhood and Politics*. In contradistinction to Brown, who stresses that Machiavelli's work emphasizes the "immutable characteristic of man,"[76] I would argue that for Machiavelli, man's "second nature" is much more important than any essential human nature. While Brown declares that "Machiavelli harbors no illusions about the usefulness of a political theory based upon 'men as they might be' rather than men as they are or can be," I would argue that Machiavelli does in fact offer a vision of how men could be *given the right republican institutions*. More specifically, Brown uses the following passage to emphasize the "animality" Machiavelli attributes to human nature:

> What great difficulty *a people accustomed to living under a prince* has later in preserving its liberty, if by any accident it gains it. . . . And such difficulty is reasonable because *that* people is none other than a brute beast which, though of a fierce and savage nature, has always been cared for in prison and slavery. Then if by chance it is left free in a field, since it is *not used to* feeding itself and does not know the places where it can take refuge, it becomes the prey of the first one who tries to chain it.[77]

In opposition to Brown's usage, I would stress that this passage emphasizes not man's "immutable" human nature but rather the importance of political institutions in reconstructing the "nature" of man. That is, "people accustomed to living under a prince" have not been transformed into citizens capable of ruling themselves through participation in civic and martial practices. For Machiavelli these practices are critically important, precisely because only they can construct citizens out of ambitious, self-interested individuals.

In other words, Machiavelli espouses a citizenship of civic practices in which a man never finally *becomes* a citizen, in the sense that he will always think and act in terms of the common good. Outside of republican institutions—such as the rule of citizen-authored law and the civic militia—which require him to behave as a citizen, he will cease to be one. Hence, the process of becoming a citizen is never finished. Citizens must be constantly re-produced through engagement in civic practices. For Machiavelli, participation in the twin practices of civic republicanism—in both the civic militia and civic legislation—actually *produces* masculine citizen-soldiers out of male individuals. That is why only a republic contains citizens.

This citizenship of civic practices contrasts with two other conceptions of citizenship: *ius solis* and *ius sanguinis*—or what I call the *citizenship of blood*. This latter concept bases citizenship on common bloodlines and so to members of a particular ascribed group. With his positive appeal to the integration of new people into a republic—whether by choice or by force—Machiavelli clearly rejects the idea that citizenship should be based on common blood. He is not interested in securing citizenship only for those with Italian blood or noble blood. On the other hand, Machiavelli does not define citizens as any group of individuals living within a particular bounded territory. For instance, individuals living within particular borders but under the rule of a prince are called subjects, not citizens. Hence, Machiavelli does embrace a citizenship of civic practices that requires participation in self-rule and in the civic militia. To be a citizen in a civic republic, one must constantly act as a citizen; the category of "citizen" is never finally consolidated.

In other words, implicit in Machiavelli's vision is a performative understanding of both civic and gender identity. Gender and citizenship are not prepolitical categories. That is to say, there are not "men," "women," and "citizens" who then choose whether or not to engage in political action. When Brown argues that "manhood constructs politics," she is arguing that prepolitical, cultural understandings of "manhood" directly affect the shaping of politics because men make politics.[78] In this configuration, manhood preexists politics. My analysis is slightly different. Instead of viewing "men," "women," and "citizens" as prepolitical categories, I contend that both citizenship and gender are constituted through engagement in particular practices—civic and martial practices for men and domestic practices for women. Consequently, we cannot simply state with Jean Bethke Elshtain that "Machiavelli's politics eliminates women by definition from the most important field of citizen involvement, military exploits,"[79] for this would assume that for Machiavelli gender identity preexists politics. Instead, we must recognize that manhood for Machiavelli is actually constituted through engagement in politics. In other words—turning Brown on her head—politics constructs manhood.

The idea that gender is performatively constructed rather than rooted in nature is important for democratic and feminist theorists because it allows for the possibility of change. Ironically, despite the thoroughly masculine character of Machiavelli's Citizen-Soldier, his implicitly performative understanding of citizenship—his citizenship of civic practices—actually allows us to imagine the possibility of including female individuals as citizens. That is, if men were *naturally* more capable of autonomy and mutuality than women, then the possibility that women could ever become autonomous republican citizens would be profoundly problematical. However, this is not Machiavelli's argument. As I have demonstrated, Machiavelli does not argue that men are naturally autonomous and capable of mutuality. In fact, Machiavelli repeatedly stresses that it is only within a carefully constructed context of always-fragile republican institutions that men are able to transcend their ambitious, power-seeking, self-interested behavior and learn to become autonomous republican citizens capable of mutuality. And although many scholars have shown that Machiavelli considered only men capable of achieving autonomy and political mutuality, he did not argue that men are naturally that way. On the contrary, Machiavelli argues that men become citizens capable of autonomy and mutuality only through participation in civic and martial practices. Furthermore, this constitution of masculine citizens is never finally completed because once the civic republican context is ruptured, men revert back to being self-interested power-seekers. Outside of the practices that produce republican masculinity, "men" become effeminate.[80]

What I am suggesting, then, is that if men's natures are subject to social construction through political practice, then so are women's. Women are not essentially more dependent, natural, and corporeal than men. To the contrary, they remain that way—partly at least—because of exclusion from civic and martial practices. Consequently, the citizenship of civic practices contains the democratic potential of including female individuals in republican citizenship: Perhaps female individuals could become republican citizens alongside "men" *if* they began to engage in the same civic and martial practices. At the same time, however, as we will see, the democratic potential of the citizenship of civic practices is undermined when the primary civic practice constitutive of citizenship is service in the civic militia, because the martial practices inherent in the civic militia produce a particularly combative form of armed masculinity that ultimately undermines the mutuality entailed in the idea of republican citizenship.

Identity out of Diversity

One of the most democratic aspects of the citizenship of civic practices is the construction of politically equal citizens out of diverse individuals. The practices of citizenship assume a certain amount of political equality among those to which it is extended. That is to say, ideally, all citizens should be included in the process of self-rule. In Rome, Machiavelli tells us,

> A Tribune, and any other citizen whatever, had the right to propose a law to the people; on this every citizen was permitted to speak, either for or against, before it was decided. This custom was good when the citizens were good, because it has always been desirable that each one who thinks of something of benefit to the public should be permitted to state his opinion on it, in order that the people, having heard each, may choose the better. (242)

Political equality is essential to civic legislation because power imbalances compromise the possibility of ruling for the common good. In Rome, Machiavelli continues, "when the citizens became wicked" and thus concerned only with their own self-interest, civic legislation "became very bad, because only the powerful proposed laws, not for the common liberty but for their own power, and for fear of such men no one dared to speak against those laws. Thus the people were either deceived or forced into decreeing their own ruin."[81] Thus, without political equality civic legislation cannot occur, and without civic legislation there can be no citizenship.

Machiavelli argues that republican self-rule is superior to autocracy. In comparing the rule of the people to the rule of princes, Machiavelli argues that

> as to judging things, very seldom does it happen, when a people hears two men orating who pull in opposite directions, that if the two are of equal ability, the people does not accept the better opinion and does not understand the truth it hears. And if in matters relating to courage or that seem profitable, as we said above, it errs, many times a prince too errs as a result of his own passions, which are many more than those of the people. It also appears that in choosing magistrates a people makes far better choices than a prince, nor will a people ever be persuaded that it is wise to put into high places a man of bad repute and of corrupt habits—something a prince can be persuaded to do easily and in a thousand ways.[82]

Citizens are more likely to rule for the common good and appoint qualified magistrates and less likely to govern according to passion and whim than are princes.

While Machiavelli stresses the need for *political* equality, however, he does not call for the elimination of all differences. In fact, not only does diversity exist, but it constitutes one of the benefits of republican government: "Thence it comes that a republic, being able to adapt herself, by means of the diversity among her body of citizens, to a diversity of temporal conditions better than a prince can, is of greater duration than a princedom and has good fortune longer."[83] There exist, Machiavelli argues, in every republic "two opposed factions, that of the people and that of the rich."[84] He goes on to insist, moreover, that in Rome it was precisely the differences between the nobility and the people that formed "a first cause" in keeping "Rome free." That is to say, although noisy, he argues, "those dissensions" brought "good effects."[85] More specifically, those dissensions in Rome did not cause "bloodshed" and were not "injurious" because of "honorable conduct" rooted in "good education," which was rooted

> in good laws; good laws in those dissensions that many thoughtlessly condemn. For anyone who will properly examine [the outcome of these dissensions] will not find that they produce any

exile or violence damaging to the common good, but rather laws
and institutions conducive to public liberty.[86]

In other words, the diversity of views considered when all citizens participate leads to the creation of good laws. And the process of participating
in the formation of these laws contributes to the constitution of republican citizens out of diverse individuals. Thus, Machiavelli envisions *political* equality that allows for diversity.[87]

Moreover, governing for the common good does not annihilate individuality, but to the contrary actually creates citizens out of diverse individuals. De Grazia argues that Machiavelli's conception of the common
good locates "the benefit not on the community considered as an abstract
whole, but on its members as individuals (each one) or as superior numer-
ically (the most)."[88] Pitkin too stresses that Machiavelli's common good
requires neither "a selfless merging" nor "submission to . . . repressive
discipline." Instead, his republic

> offers each Citizen, each class of Citizens, the genuine possibility
> of fulfilling individual needs, pursuing separate interests, express-
> ing real passions; it does not depend on sacrifice, either voluntary
> or enforced. Yet the selfish and partial needs, interests, and pas-
> sions brought into the political process are transformed, enlarged,
> brought into contact with the conflicting needs, interests, and
> passions of other Citizens and ultimately redefined collectively in
> relation to the common good—a common good that emerges only
> out of the political interaction of the Citizens.[89]

The Citizen, she argues, can develop *virtù* only in the "actual experience
of citizen participation. Only in crisis and political struggle are people
forced to enlarge their understandings of themselves and their interests."[90] Participation in the process of legislating for the common good
leads not only to good laws but also constitutes diverse individuals as
citizens.

The important point here is that while in Machiavelli's world, republican citizenship was in fact restricted to an elite group of men, within this
group differences existed. In other words, although from the outside the
group seems very homogeneous—especially from a late-twentieth-
century perspective—class differences existed and, moreover, the people
included in the group no doubt believed themselves to be a diverse group

of unique individuals with often conflicting desires. This view of civic republicanism offers us the possibility of imagining the creation of political equality out of a much greater diversity of individuals and the forging of a citizenship of civic practices that does not annihilate differences.

Nevertheless, though Machiavelli insists that differences among citizens contribute to a well-governed republic, he also cautions that these differences can be destructive when they lead to the formation of factions. Because of natural inequalities of ability some men will achieve greater reputations than others. Unless harnessed to serve the public good, men of superior ability could destroy a republic. Reputation should be regulated, so that "citizens will get repute from popularity that aids and does not injure the city and her liberty."[91] In other words, reputation should be gained and honors given for deeds that benefit the common good. Reputations "gained in private ways"—by "conferring . . . benefits on various private persons, by lending them money, marrying off their daughters, protecting them from the magistrates, and doing them similar private favors"—"are very dangerous and altogether injurious" because these acts "make partisans of their benefactors and give the man they follow courage to think he can corrupt the public and violate the laws."[92] Large differences of wealth and power can destroy a republic. In sum, although diversity and natural inequalities in ability can contribute to the health of a republic, these differences can become divisive and lead a republic to ruin. To stave off this possibility, there must be political equality among citizens and publicly acclaimed ways for men with superior abilities to serve the common good. There must also be political equality established and maintained through the rule of law to prevent individuals from exercising arbitrary power.

That is to say, the struggle of diverse individuals to act together for the common good both invigorates and threatens the existence of a civic republic. Honig emphasizes this in her discussion of Machiavelli. As she explains it, Machiavelli stressed that insatiable human desires "cannot be extirpated but they can be held in a creative and productive tension." Only the "perpetuity of [the] struggle" between the nobles and the people "and the institutional obstacles to its resolution, prevent any one party from dominating and closing the public space of law, liberty, and virtù."[93] Republicanism necessarily entails struggle and dissension as diverse individuals act together. While this always involves risk, it also keeps a republic vibrant.

Republican Ideals and Militaristic Conquest

Machiavelli argues that preparing for war helps unify citizens for the common good: "The disunion of republics usually results from idleness and peace; the cause of union is fear and war."[94] War facilitates civic republicanism in three ways. In the first place, as I have been arguing, participation in the civic militia creates citizen-soldiers out of diverse individuals. In other words, by serving together in the civic militia, individual males achieve a sense of patriotism, selflessness, and fraternity, and they gain a common civic identity. Preparing for war provides a venue through which individuals can act together for the common good and so become citizens. And the existence of a common enemy helps prevent the formation of factions within a republic. Put differently, preparing for war keeps the focus on what citizens have in common and places the enemy outside of the republic's borders rather than within them.

Second, being at war allows men of superior ability both to serve the republic and to achieve personal glory as military officers. Republics, Machiavelli tells us, tend to "show this defect":

> They pay slight attention to capable men in quiet times. This condition makes men feel injured in two ways: first, they fail to attain their proper rank; second, they are obliged to have as associates and superiors men who are unworthy and of less ability than themselves. This abuse in republics has produced much turmoil, because those citizens who see themselves undeservedly rejected, and know that they can be neglected only in times that are easy and not perilous, make an effort to disturb them by stirring up new wars to the damage of the republic. When I consider possible remedies, I find two: the first is to keep the citizens poor, so that, when without goodness and wisdom, they cannot corrupt themselves or others with riches; the second is to arrange that such republics will continually make war, and therefore always will need citizens of high repute, like the Romans in their early days.[95]

As Honig puts it,

> if a republic's energies are not expended in war, they turn inward. If legitimate, institutional avenues of expression are not available, instincts and ambitions will seek other avenues of expression, and

the result will be destabilizing conspiracies and the eventual overthrow of the regime.[96]

A civic militia constantly preparing for war helps republics maintain
unity by providing a way of rewarding talented men in accordance with
the common good. Thus, militarism channels the constant struggle that
both invigorates and threatens the republic into service for the common
good.

And third, the waging of war is necessary to the construction of Machiavelli's armed masculinity. In his words, "[I]f heaven is so kind to [a city]
that she does not have to make war, the effect might be that ease would
make her effeminate or divided; these two things together, or either
alone, would cause her ruin."[97] Soldiering is essential to the constitution
of armed masculinity for Machiavelli. Soldiering simultaneously produces
armed masculinity and republican citizenship and melds the two into
one.

At first glance, Machiavelli's suggestion that "republics [should] continually make war" seems to contradict one of his main justifications for
the Citizen Soldier ideal. As discussed earlier, Machiavelli argues that
one of the important characteristics of the civic militia is that citizen-
soldiers are less likely to wage war than professional soldiers and that men
of superior ability can cause problems for a republic by "stirring up new
wars." Now we see that he also advocates continual preparation for war
as a way of preventing the latter problem and unifying the republic: "Because a country is not always at war and cannot be, *she must therefore train
her army in times of peace.*"[98] Although citizen-soldiers "will not seek to
disturb the peace in order to have war,"[99] they must constantly prepare
for war.

To resolve this paradox, Machiavelli uses the ideal of the Citizen-Soldier dialectically to reconcile republican citizenship with militarism. Preparing to fight external enemies imbues citizen-soldiers with patriotism,
selflessness, fraternity, civic virtue, and civic participation, as well as
armed masculinity. Unfortunately, along with these virtues come the
vices of conquest, conformity, chauvinism, combativeness, and exclusion.
Machiavelli's republican citizens need to prepare for war. With his Citizen-Soldier, Machiavelli attempts to balance republican ideals with the
heroic ethic. He does not subordinate one to the other. So while Hulliung mistakenly argues that Machiavelli puts republicanism in the service
of conquest, de Grazia also errs when he argues that our theorist places

conquest in the service of republican ideals.[100] De Grazia might be right that "Niccolò is not a militarist at heart," but his Citizen-Soldier is both a republican citizen and a militaristic soldier. Embodying *virtù* in both senses—civic virtue and armed masculinity—the Citizen-Soldier synthesizes a variety of oppositional ideals in Machiavelli's work, including civic republicanism and militarism.

Machiavelli values the heroic ideal. That is why, as Hulliung points out,

> of all republics past and present to choose from, it was the world-conquering Roman republic that arrested Machiavelli's attention. The ancient model he admired and hoped to reproduce in modern times was none other than that singularly expansionary, singularly successful Roman republic whose way of life had been the fulfillment of *virtus*, and ethic of glory, grandeur, and heroism.[101]

But at the same time, as Pocock explains, the continued existence of the republic also requires an internal commitment to republican ideals: "The republican can dominate *Fortuna* only by integrating its citizens in a self-sufficient *universitas*, but this in turn depends on the freely participating and morally assenting citizen. The decay of citizenship leads to the decline of the republic and the ascendancy of *Fortuna*."[102] That is, it would mean the end of both republican ideals and the heroic ethic. One of the reasons Machiavelli supported republicanism and the civic militia is because it allowed for the greatest development of *virtù*—in both its senses.

As is often the case, however, Machiavelli's impressive dialectical synthesis did not withstand realpolitik. His work gave birth to the idea of raison d'état and so played a key role in the emergence of nationalism. In this case, the republican ideals dropped out but the militarism did not. Friedrich Meinecke explains this phenomenon as follows:

> It has been the fate of Machiavelli, as of so many great thinkers, that only one part of his system of thought has been able to influence historical life. . . . His ideal of *virtù* soon faded . . . and with that too the ethical aim of his statecraft. . . . Generally speaking he was seen first and foremost as having prepared the poison of autocracy; as such, he was publicly condemned and secretly made use of. . . . The chief thing was, however, that the idea of political

regeneration was altogether beyond the capabilities and the
wishes of the peoples and the rulers of the time, and hence it fell
to the ground. . . . Machiavelli's ancient heathen idealism of the
State was no longer understood by the men of the Counter-Reformation period. . . . But they very well understood the ancient
heathen realism of his statecraft.[103]

Meinecke traces the evolution of Machiavelli's politics as it slowly transformed into a justification for German nationalism in the early twentieth
century.[104]

In an attempt to defend Machiavelli against the charges that his theory
played into the emergence of nationalism, Maurizio Viroli argues that
Machiavelli advocated patriotism rather than nationalism. Viroli defines
patriotism as the love of the political institutions, laws, and way of life
that sustains the common liberty of the people. Political in orientation,
it involves a charitable love of the republic. Nationalism, on the other
hand, posits a spiritual unity, a cultural and linguistic oneness or homoge-
neity among the people. It requires unconditional loyalty and mixes love
with pride and fear.[105] But while Viroli rightly distinguishes between patriotism and nationalism, he wishes away the slippage that easily occurs
between the two tendencies: Machiavelli theorized patriotism but
spawned nationalism. And this is no accident. So while I share Viroli's
desire to foster patriotism while condemning nationalism, my understanding of Machiavelli's project reveals that the two go hand in hand.
Moreover, when Machiavelli made martial practices the foundation for
his republican citizenship, he exacerbated the vicious flip sides of the
virtues he was primarily trying to create.

Nevertheless, because of the dialectical nature of his theory, Machiavelli's legacy is appropriately dual. On the one hand his theory did indeed
undergo what Meinecke calls a "sinister development" as its dialectical
edifice collapsed into "Machiavellianism" and then evolved into nationalism[106]—complete with its own virtues and vices. On the other hand,
however, Machiavelli's theoretical vision also forms the origins of what
Pocock refers to as "the Atlantic republican tradition" that culminated
in the American and French Revolutions. This tradition retains Machiavelli's commitment to the cluster of republican ideals: liberty, equality,
fraternity, the rule of manmade law, the common good, civic virtue, and
participatory citizenship. And we will soon see to what extent the traditional vices continue to live on within this tradition as well. So the

dialectical nature of Machiavelli's thought produces two divergent traditions—one more virtuous and one more vicious—each of which entails its own interrelated sets of virtues and vices.

I end with two conclusions and two questions. First of all, based on my reading of Machiavelli it seems that to the extent that the citizenship of civic practices privileges martial practices over other possible forms of civic action, the vices of this tradition will be amplified. Due to its militaristic nature, the Citizen-Soldier ideal has two major flaws. In the first place, it requires the presence of an enemy. As Brown puts it, Machiavellian "politics is utterly dependent upon the presence of an enemy, it is at all times a fight, and dissolves when opposition is not present or is too weak to inspire consolidated struggle."[107] The invocation of an enemy for the purposes of fostering republican citizenship brings out the vicious side of the Citizen-Soldier tradition. Constant preparation for combat against an enemy does indeed facilitate the creation of republican citizenship but at an undemocratic price. Preparing for war renders citizen-soldiers patriotic as it fuels their desire for conquest. Citizen-soldiers selflessly serve the republic, but the cause of war exerts pressure on them to conform. Military service necessarily requires both feelings of fraternity and feelings of superiority toward the enemy—chauvinism. So, to the extent that the militaristic practices make up the civic practices constitutive of citizenship, the vices of civic republicanism will be strengthened. Question number one: Would a broader, less combative variety of civic practices produce the virtues of republican citizenship, while minimizing its related vices?

Secondly, as we have seen in our discussion of Machiavelli, martial practices play a key role in the constitution of both armed masculinity and republican citizenship within the Citizen-Soldier tradition; soldiering forms the link that fuses masculinity onto citizenship. Moreover, the combative nature of the armed masculinity produced by this tradition results in the denigration of femininity and all the values traditionally associated with it. At the same time, however, because within the citizenship of civic practices both masculinity and citizenship are politically and socially constructed, the possibility remains of reconstructing traditional configurations of gender and citizenship. This leaves us with our second question: What would happen if women began to engage in civic practices that produce masculine citizen-soldiers?

Notes

1. All Machiavelli citations are from *Machiavelli: The Chief Works and Others*, 6 vols., trans. A. Gilbert (Durham: Duke University Press, 1965). For a good overview of the debates, see Mark Hulliung, *Citizen Machiavelli* (Princeton: Princeton University Press, 1983), chap. 1. Four good older surveys are Hans Baron, "Machiavelli: Republican Citizen and Author of the *Prince*," *English Historical Review* 76 (1961): 217–53; Richard C. Clark, "Machiavelli: Bibliographic Spectrum," *Review of National Literatures* 1 (1970): 93–135; Eric Cochrane, "Machiavelli: 1940–1960," *Journal of Modern History* 33 (1961): 113–36; and John H. Geerken, "Machiavelli Studies Since 1969," *Journal of the History of Ideas* 37 (1976): 351–68.

2. For Leo Strauss's original argument see his *Thoughts on Machiavelli* (Glencoe, Ill.: Free Press, 1958). For a defense of Strauss, see Harvey C. Mansfield Jr., "Strauss's Machiavelli," *Political Theory* 3 (1975): 372–84. For J. G. A. Pocock's criticism see "A Comment on Mansfield's 'Strauss's Machiavelli,'" *Political Theory* 3 (1975): 385–401.

3. Hulliung, *Citizen Machiavelli*.

4. Alfred von Martin, *Sociology of the Renaissance* (New York: Harper and Row, 1963), 65–70.

5. G. W. F. Hegel, *Hegel's Political Writings*, trans. T. M. Knox (Oxford: Clarendon Press, 1964), 219–29. See Shlomo Avineri's commentary in *Hegel's Theory of the Modern State* (Cambridge: Cambridge University Press, 1972), 53–54.

6. For overviews of these interpretations, see Baron, "Machiavelli," 219; Ernst Cassirer, *The Myth of the State* (New Haven: Yale University Press, 1946), 121–25; and Clark, "Machiavelli," 101. See Friedrich Meinecke's discussion of Hegel, Fichte, and Ranke in *Machiavellism: The Doctrine of Raison d'État and Its Place in Modern History*, trans. Douglas Scott (New Haven: Yale University Press, 1957), 343–91.

7. For discussions of sixteenth- and seventeenth-century condemnations of Machiavelli and his more favorable eighteenth-century reception, see Baron, "Machiavelli," 217–21; Cassirer, *The Myth of the State*, 116; and Clark, "Machiavelli," 98–101.

8. For examples, see Jean Bethke Elshtain, *Public Man, Private Woman: Women in Social and Political Thought* (Princeton: Princeton University Press, 1981), 92–99; Max Lerner, introduction to *The Prince and the Discourses* (New York: Random House, 1950); and Harvey C. Mansfield Jr., *Machiavelli's Virtue* (Chicago: University of Chicago Press, 1996).

9. Cassirer, *The Myth of the State*.

10. See Benedetto Croce, *Politics and Morals*, trans. Salvatore J. Castiglione (New York: Philosophical Library, 1945), and Maurice Merleau-Ponty, "A Note on Machiavelli," *Signs*, trans. R. C. McCleary (Evanston: Northwestern University Press, 1964), 211–23.

11. Important republican readings of Machiavelli's work include Sebastian de Grazia, *Machiavelli in Hell* (New York: Vintage Books, 1989); Hannah Fenichel Pitkin, *Fortune Is a Woman: Gender and Politics in the Thought of Niccolò Machiavelli* (Berkeley and Los Angeles: University of California Press, 1984); J. G. A. Pocock, *The Machiavellian Moment: Florentine Political Thought and the Atlantic Republican Tradition* (Princeton: Princeton University Press, 1975); and Quentin Skinner, *Machiavelli* (Oxford: Oxford University Press, 1981). For a recent discussion of various aspects of Machiavelli's republicanism, see *Machiavelli and Republicanism*, ed. Gisela Bock, Quentin Skinner, and Maurizio Viroli (Cambridge: Cambridge University Press, 1993).

12. For example, Baron argues that "instead of looking at the *Prince* and the *Discourses* as two complementary parts of one harmonious whole, we would indeed do better to reconsider what to earlier generations had seemed to be so manifest: that Machiavelli's two major works are in basic aspects different and that the *Discourses* have a message of their own." See "Machiavelli," 217–53. Allan H. Gilbert sees *The Prince* as a realpolitikal means to a republican end. See his *Machiavelli's*

Prince and Its Forerunners (Durham: Duke University Press, 1938) and his introduction to *The Prince and Other Works* (New York: Hendricks House, Farrar, Straus, 1946). Meinecke argues that "the contrast between the monarchist bias in the *Principe* and the republican tinge of the *Discoursi* is only apparent. The quantity of *virtù*, which existed in a people, was the factor that decided whether a monarchy or a republic was the more suitable." See *Machiavellism*, 43.

13. For example, de Grazia argues that "a staunch republican, [Machiavelli] is convinced that the times require extraordinary measures taken by one man alone. His republicanism has no theoretical problem accommodating one-generation, one-alone leadership if it will lend life to the republic." See *Machiavelli in Hell*, 240. Meinecke argues that Machiavelli's "republican ideal therefore contained a strain of monarchism, insofar as he believed that even republics could not come into existence without the help of great individual ruling personalities and organizers. He had learnt from Polybius the theory that the fortunes of every State are repeated in a cycle, and that the golden age of a republic is bound to be followed by its decline and fall. And so he saw that, in order to restore the necessary quantum of *virtù* which a republic had lost by sinking to such a low point, and thus raise up the State once again, there was only one means to be adopted; namely, that the creative *virtù* of one individual, of one *mano regia*, one *podesta quasi regia* (*Discourses*, 1.18, 55), should take the State in hand and revive it. Indeed he went so far as to believe that for republics which were completely corrupt and no longer capable of regeneration, monarchy was the only possible form of government. Thus his concept of *virtù* formed a close link between republican and monarchical tendencies, and, after the collapse of the Florentine Republic, enabled him without inconsistency to set his hopes on the rule of the Medici, and to write for them the Book of the Prince. In the same way it made it possible for him immediately afterwards to take up again in the *Discorsi* the strain of republicanism, and to weigh republic and monarchy against one another." See *Machiavellism*, 31–33.

14. Machiavelli, *Prince*, chap. 26, 95, emphasis mine.

15. Hulliung, *Citizen Machiavelli*, 25.

16. Ibid., 19.

17. Ibid., 5, emphasis mine.

18. Hulliung begins by arguing that "'civic humanism,' as formulated by contemporary scholars, errs in de-emphasizing or even expurgating the vital notions of *grandezza* and *gloria* from the republican tradition"—values that he suggests were always there. But he ends by attacking the commitment to republican ideals in Machiavelli's thought: "the political significance of speech and rhetoric has been overemphasized" in republican readings of Machiavelli and so now needs to "suffer a certain demotion in contemporary scholarship." *Citizen Machiavelli*, 21.

19. Pitkin, *Fortune Is a Woman*, 4.

20. Ibid., 285.

21. Machiavelli, *Prince*, chap. 12, 47.

22. "War is inescapable. . . . The need for a common defense against other men . . . arises at the dawn of mankind and remains day and night." De Grazia, *Machiavelli in Hell*, 166.

23. Pitkin, *Fortune Is a Woman*, 14.

24. See Pocock, *Machiavellian Moment*, and Pitkin, *Fortune Is a Woman*, for a more detailed history.

25. Hans Baron, *The Crisis of the Early Italian Renaissance*, 2d ed. (Princeton: Princeton University Press, 1966).

26. Machiavelli, *Discourses*, 3.31, 500.

27. Machiavelli, *Discourses*, 2.30, 410.

28. Ibid., 410–11.

29. For a historical discussion of Machiavelli's practical attempts to organize a militia, see C. C. Bayley, *War and Society in Renaissance Florence* (Toronto: University of Toronto Press, 1961), 240–67.

30. Machiavelli, *Prince*, chap. 12, 48.

31. Machiavelli, *Art of War*, I, 574.

32. Machiavelli, *Prince*, chap. 12, 47. Machiavelli also argues in *Discourses* 1.43 (286) that mercenaries are "useless" because they have "no other reason that holds them firm than the little pay you give them. This reason is not and cannot be enough to make them faithful or so much your friends that they are willing to die for you."

33. Machiavelli, *Discourses*, 1.43, 286.

34. Machiavelli, *Discourses*, 2.2, 328.

35. Pocock, *Machiavellian Moment*, 200–201.

36. See Pocock, *Machiavellian Moment*, 51–52.

37. Pocock, "A Comment on Mansfield's 'Strauss's Machiavelli,'" 390. See also de Grazia, *Machiavelli in Hell*, 216. Cassirer agrees: "In [Machiavelli's] theory all the previous theocratic ideas and ideals are eradicated root and branch." However, despite his rejection of Christianity, Cassirer argues, Machiavelli "never meant . . . to separate politics from religion. He was an opponent of the Church but he was no enemy of religion. He was, on the contrary, convinced that religion is one of the necessary elements of man's social life. But in his system this element cannot claim any absolute, independent, and dogmatic truth. Its worth and validity depend entirely on its influence on political life. By this standard, however, Christianity occupies the lowest place. For it is in strict opposition to all real political *virtù*. . . . A merely passive religion, a religion that flees the world instead of organizing it, has proved to be the ruin of many kingdoms and states." *The Myth of the State*, 138.

38. Pocock, *Machiavellian Moment*, 157, 193.

39. For an oppositional discussion of virtue in Machiavelli, see Mansfield, *Machiavelli's Virtue*, 6–52. For example, Mansfield asserts the "classical republican interpretation[s] . . . understand Machiavelli's virtue admiringly as self-sacrifice for the common good of the republic. That it is not" (xv).

40. Quentin Skinner, "The Republican Ideal of Political Liberty," in Bock, Skinner, and Viroli, *Machiavelli and Republicanism*, 303, emphasis mine.

41. De Grazia, *Machiavelli in Hell*, 176.

42. Skinner, "The Republican Ideal of Political Liberty," 303.

43. Pocock, *Machiavellian Moment*, 201.

44. Ibid., 203.

45. Most scholars agree with this derivation of the term *virtù*. For an oppositional view, see Mansfield, who denies that Machiavelli's virtue comes from ancient or Roman understandings of manliness. *Machiavelli's Virtue*, 36–37.

46. Pitkin, *Fortune Is a Woman*, 25. For similar arguments see Hulliung, *Citizen Machiavelli*, 29, and Wendy Brown, *Manhood and Politics: A Feminist Reading in Political Theory* (Totowa, N.J.: Rowman & Littlefield, 1988), 90.

47. For an in-depth and nuanced exploration of this issue, see Pitkin, *Fortune Is a Woman*.

48. Machiavelli, *Prince*, chap. 25, 92.

49. Machiavelli, *Discourses*, 2.2, 330–31, emphasis mine.

50. Hulliung, *Citizen Machiavelli*, 68.

51. Bonnie Honig, *Political Theory and the Displacement of Politics* (Ithaca: Cornell University Press, 1993), 68–69.

52. Ibid., 230.

53. Ibid., 3.

54. Pitkin, *Fortune Is a Woman*, 117–18.

55. Brown makes a similar argument in *Manhood and Politics*.

56. Pitkin, *Fortune Is a Woman*, 136, emphasis mine.

57. Brown, *Manhood and Politics*, 88.

58. Machiavelli, *Discourses*, 1.21, 246, emphasis mine.

59. Ibid., 247, emphasis mine.

60. Machiavelli, *Art of War*, I, 581, emphasis mine.

61. Machiavelli, *Prince*, chap. 26, 94.

62. Machiavelli, *Discourses*, 1.4, 202.
63. Machiavelli, *Discourses*, 1.34, 267.
64. Machiavelli, *Discourses*, 1.43, 201.
65. Ibid., emphasis mine.
66. Machiavelli, *Discourses*, 1.35, 270.
67. Machiavelli, *Discourses*, 1.34, 268.
68. Machiavelli, *Discourses*, 3.22, 482.
69. Machiavelli, *Discourses*, 2.2, 329.
70. Machiavelli, *Discourses*, 1.49, 296.
71. See Pocock, *Machiavellian Moment*, 193.
72. Machiavelli, *Discourses*, 1.29, 257.
73. Machiavelli, *Discourses*, 2.1, 323.
74. Machiavelli, *Discourses*, 1.58, 315.
75. De Grazia, *Machiavelli in Hell*, 269–70.
76. Brown, *Manhood and Politics*, 73.
77. Machiavelli, *Discourses*, 2.16, 235, emphasis mine. Also see Brown, *Manhood and Politics*, 74.
78. Brown, *Manhood and Politics*.
79. Elshtain, *Public Man, Private Woman*, 98.
80. Machiavelli, *Discourses*, 1.21, 247; 3.36, 510.
81. Machiavelli, *Discourses*, 1.18, 242.
82. Machiavelli, *Discourses*, 1.58, 316.
83. Machiavelli, *Discourses*, 3.9, 453.
84. Machiavelli, *Discourses*, 1.4, 203.
85. Ibid., 202.
86. Machiavelli, *Discourses*, 1.4, 203.
87. Pitkin stresses this point in *Fortune Is a Woman*, chap. 4.
88. De Grazia, *Machiavelli in Hell*, 192.
89. Pitkin, *Fortune Is a Woman*, 93.
90. Ibid., 96.
91. Machiavelli, *Discourses*, 3.28, 492.
92. Ibid., 493.
93. Honig, *Political Theory and the Displacement of Politics*, 70. See Machiavelli, *Discourses*, 2. Preface; I.vi. and "Homer's Contest," 36–37.
94. Machiavelli, *Discourses*, 2.25, 399.
95. Machiavelli, *Discourses*, 3.16, 469.
96. Honig, *Political Theory and the Displacement of Politics*, 71. See also Hulliung, *Citizen Machiavelli*, 26.
97. Machiavelli, *Discourses*, 1.6, 211.
98. Machiavelli, *Discourses*, 3.31, 500, emphasis mine.
99. Machiavelli, *Discourses*, 1, 57–58.
100. Hulliung, *Citizen Machiavelli*, 36; de Grazia, *Machiavelli in Hell*, 172.
101. Hulliung, *Citizen Machiavelli*, 5–6.
102. Pocock, *Machiavellian Moment*, 56. Hulliung argues similarly: "While the individual excellence of the prince may be admirable, the greatest feats of heroism are collective and popular in nature. In its democratic form, *virtus* taps the potential greatness of the common man, his willingness to fight and die for his country, and can claim as its due meed of glory the conquest of all other republics." *Citizen Machiavelli*, 5–6.
103. Meinecke, *Machiavellism*, 44–45.
104. See also Cassirer, *The Myth of the State*, 140–41.
105. Maurizio Viroli, "The Meaning of Patriotism," paper presented at the Walt Whitman Seminar, Rutgers University, New Brunswick, N.J., 1 February 1994.
106. Meinecke, *Machiavellism*, 410.
107. Brown, *Manhood and Politics*, 115.

8

The Seriously Comedic, or Why Machiavelli's Lucrezia Is Not Livy's Virtuous Roman

Melissa M. Matthes

The Seriously Comedic

In a letter to Vettori, Machiavelli describes the relationship between the comedic and the serious in their correspondence:

> Anyone who saw our letters, honored friend, and saw their diversity, would wonder greatly, because he would suppose now that we were grave men, wholly concerned with important matters, and that in our breasts no thought could fall that did not have in itself

> honor and greatness. But then, turning the page, he would judge
> that we, the very same persons, were light-minded, inconstant,
> lascivious, concerned with empty things. And this way of pro-
> ceeding, if to some it may appear censurable, to me it seems
> praiseworthy, because we are imitating Nature, who is variable;
> and he who imitates her cannot be rebuked.[1]

While ostensibly commenting on the variability in his correspondence,
Machiavelli is also implicitly offering a justification for writing comedy as
well as political treatises: he is simply imitating Nature. Yet it is a rather
peculiar, indeed, "Machiavellian" conception of Nature that he has in
mind. Machiavellian Nature is not ordered, determined, and stable; it
is variable, contingent, an inevitable process of change. Indeed, part of
Machiavelli's sense of humor derives from mocking those fools who mistakenly believe Nature is staid and who fail to accommodate her whimsy.

Thus, Machiavelli's comedies, particularly La Mandragola, are themselves articulations of this interplay between the serious and the comedic.
La Mandragola, obviously, represents the comedic element of his political
writings. But the play also enacts a relationship between the serious and
the comedic: it is a comedy with a serious political element as well as a
serious political argument presented in a comedic medium.

La Mandragola is both engaged with the New Plautine comedy of the
period and implicitly a critique of it. The principal elements of the New
Comedy formula are present: the lover(s) blocked by interested elders or
others, escape or hiding within or without the city enclosing an ordered
society, and an eventual harmonious reconciliation.[2] In Machiavelli's
play, however, there are two significant divergences. First, unlike most
Plautine comedies, there is no deus ex machina or marvelous discovery to
create a happy resolution. The only forces propelling the plot are those
of human ingenuity and opportunism. Characters achieve their goal because of their own wit or scheming.

Second, unlike the traditional Plautine plot line, the seemingly happy
resolution of Machiavelli's comedy conceals narrative duplicity. In the
end, the course of events as perceived by some of the dramatic characters
is not the real course of events as understood by the audience of La Mandragola. The audience and several of the stage characters share the knowledge of a secret kept from other members of the play's society: all has
not been revealed at the end. There is a discrepancy between the two
simultaneous stories unfolding and supposedly settled in the fifth act.

One ending is the harmonious closure of New Comedy, the happy resolution of the play: Nicia can anticipate the arrival of his much-sought-after heir, and Callimaco has made Lucrezia his lover. The other ending is an unfinished contingent plot: Nicia has unwittingly authorized his own continued cuckolding by offering a key to his home to both Ligurio and Callimaco; he remains unaware of their role in the plot. And Lucrezia, by paying the Friar a purseful of money, seems implicitly to be asking for the continued sanction of her adultery. Her conversion has been complete but unrevealed. She and Ligurio remain the only dramatic characters who are aware of all of the machinations of the others. Thus, this second ending is unstable, requiring assiduous attention to the mutability of fortune. The comedy thus has an unresolved ending with the potential for the resolution not to remain happy.

With this incomplete ending, however, Machiavelli creates an ideal vehicle for the edification of the audience's political judgment. The humor of the play invites the audience to laugh with the conspirators, to identify with the wits (Ligurio and Lucrezia) rather than with the buffoon (Nicia). As a result, at the conclusion the audience is placed in a position of complicity: "What we, the viewers, agree to silence is our awareness that events at the 'end' are not closed back in a great circle that creates a renewed social harmony but one that opens onto vistas of disruption and deception . . . the play is more cynical than carnivalesque."[3] The audience's identification and collusion is not simply an object lesson in Machiavellian politics; it is a participatory event. The comedy makes the audience actors in its world. From the prologue—"May you be tricked as she was"—to the ending—"Who wouldn't be tickled?"—the audience is invited in. And for Machiavelli, the audience's identification with the machinations of the protagonists is the necessary catalyst for political action.

Consider, in this regard, several letters Machiavelli wrote to Vettori in 1513 in which he asserts that the reason the Swiss have become a force to be feared is because they have begun to imagine themselves as Romans.[4] Machiavelli perceives a contagion here between imagination and reality: "I believe that as Nature has given each man an individual face, so she has given him an individual disposition and an individual imagination. From this it results that each man conducts himself according to his disposition and his imagination."[5] Unable to change their dispositions, Machiavelli thus strives for influence over men's imaginations. And comedy presents a powerful medium. The laughter of comedy, with its destabilization of traditional forms and its sense of transgression, creates in the audience a sense of being unbalanced and thus open to possibilities. And it is then that Machiavelli's lesson begins.

The most difficult moment in leading people to political action, according to Machiavelli, is getting them to conceive of themselves as political actors. He is confident, however, that once they imagine themselves as republicans, the republican process itself will actually make them so; what they lack in nature, artifice, in the form of the law and institutions, will augment.[6] It is as if Machiavelli knows that men are not republican by disposition but hopes that the process of imagining themselves as such will make them so.[7] Machiavelli needs only to spur the people's desire, not change their nature. Words, not steel, he believes, will suffice to recall them to their imagined republican selves.

And so La Mandragola becomes a source of political edification. Its invitation to the audience, its seduction of their laughter, induces identification with those characters who behave as Machiavelli deems necessary for political action. The instability of the ending necessitates judgment; the play does not end with a packaged didactic lesson. There is no satisfied catharsis that the world is ordered and stable; rather the audience's nervous laughter at the unfinished ending is an implicit acknowledgment of a Machiavellian worldview. Constant vigilance and agility is required to maintain one's place on the wheel of fortune.

So while the content of the comedy is ostensibly a reinterpretation of Livy's tragic rendition of the story of the rape of Lucretia (as the remainder of this chapter will detail), Machiavelli's sense of humor—laughter generated by human ingenuity rather than the marvelous, his enjoyment of narrative duplicity rather than happy endings—illuminates as much about his serious political argument as his reconfiguration of the story itself.

Why Lucrezia Is Not Livy's Noble Roman Matron

The most significant textual justification for a parallel reading of La Mandragola and Livy's Early History of Rome lies in how the mandrake works. Tellingly, the mandrake functions in Machiavelli's play in much the same way as Lucretia's rape and suicide function in Livy's version. The mandrake, like the rape, is both a poison and a cure.[8] Just as Lucretia's body enacted the founding through her contamination by Tarquin (tyranny) and her expunging of this pollution through her suicide (the founding), so the mandrake both poisons Lucrezia, requiring "someone to sleep with her right away . . . to draw off all the poison of the mandrake after one night"[9] *and* cures her, thus enabling her to conceive; "There is nothing more certain to make a woman conceive than to give her a potion made with the mandrake root" (2.6, 195).

As a result, Lucrezia is positioned both to purge the society, having inhaled its contaminants, and to restore it to health. Machiavelli echoes this process in *The Discourses:* "For in nature as in simple bodies, when there is an accumulation of superfluous matter, a spontaneous purgation takes place, which preserves the health of the body" (2.5). Interestingly, like her predecessor's, Lucrezia's downfall and contamination results from the carelessness of her kinsfolk. In both versions, it is the bragging of a relative that ignites the plot: in Livy's, Lucretia's husband brags about her virtue; and in Machiavelli's, a cousin traveling abroad does so. In *La Mandragola* Lucrezia is further polluted by the corruption of those around her: her husband, Nicia; her mother, Sostrata; and her confessor, Fra Timoteo.

Machiavelli also reflects on and satirizes the motif of paternity that Livy suggests with Brutus's kiss of Mother Earth. *La Mandragola,* too, is preoccupied with images of conception, birth, and motherhood. The primary impetus for Nicia's cuckolding is his own desire to have an heir. Here Machiavelli, like Livy, highlights male anxiety about feminine power and the difficulty of guaranteeing the birth of a republic. Just as a man can never guarantee the paternity of his children, so a political founder cannot guarantee the success of his republic. While Livy suggests solo male procreation and implicit renunciation of the feminine as a resolution, Machiavelli advises seduction of the feminine. Obviously, there is no certainty of paternity in *La Mandragola* when Nicia is cuckolded by Callimaco. Certainty of paternity, like final domination of *Fortuna,* is impossible. It is interesting to note, too, that the paternity of feminine power is itself ambiguous for Machiavelli. In his poem "Fortune," written to Soderini, Machiavelli writes:

Whose daughter she might be, or from what seed Nobody knows;
    Only one thing is sure:
    Her might can make Jove, too, watch out in dread.[10]

Lucrezia's own paternity is unspecified in *La Mandragola*. Her father is neither present nor mentioned, and her mother is presumed to have been promiscuous in her youth.[11] This absence of paternal authority grants a suprising autonomy to femininity in the play.

Nonetheless, while paralleling Livy's version in several interesting ways, Machiavelli's story is more engaging in its differences. In Livy's account the rape of Lucretia highlights how a private transgression has public, political reverberations. Lucretia's private violation and suicidal confession reveals, in part, a cultural secret. In Machiavelli's account, however, there is no such distinction between the public and private or any such seeming revelation. All there is for Machiavelli's Lucrezia is politics and the realm of appearances. What concerns Machiavelli is not the distinction between, or violation of, the public and private spheres, but rather the politicization of virtue. In his domestic comedy, Machiavelli tries to demonstrate the necessity of making private morality answer to public necessity, rather than vice versa.

Lucretia forfeits her chastity in order to ensure her status as citizen. Through her seduction the possibility for the republican founding is conceived; her participation is integral to the founding's success. Her private immorality serves a public good. Being a good citizen necessitates her willingness to act against the principles of private, and in this case Christian, morality. Lucrezia is willing to do this and thus personifies an ideal Machiavellian political actor.

Another important distinction between the two versions is announced in the very frontispiece of *La Mandragola*. The frontispiece is the image of the classical centaur except that instead of holding the usual arrow, he is serenading with a violin, suggesting that persuasion, "sweet nothings," not force, will determine the outcome of the play. The stage is set for Machiavelli's belief that often cunning and fraud, even seduction, are more effective than force (*Discourses* 2.13).

In contrast, the dagger is the pivotal symbol in the Roman version. Tarquin menaces Lucretia with a knife, Lucretia kills herself with a dagger, and Brutus swears upon the same knife to drive the Tarquins from Rome. The only dagger in *La Mandragola* is the pathetic stick Nicia arms himself with just as he arranges for his own cuckolding: "He's wearing a little cloak that does not cover his ass. What the hell does he have on his head? He looks like a cross between an owl and a monk, and down below he has a little blade sticking out."[12]

Also suggestively, Nicia's "little blade" is Machiavelli's not-so-subtle allusion to the diminishing masculinity of his compatriots, resulting, in part, from the enervating influence of the Catholic Church: "Though it may appear that the world has grown effeminate, and Heaven has laid aside her arms, this without doubt comes chiefly from the worthlessness of men who have interpreted our religion according to sloth and not according to vigor" (*Discourses* 2.2). Pagan religion, in contrast, was full of pomp and magnificence. The pagans cultivated worldly glory rather than the humility and contemplative life of Christianity. Nevertheless, Machiavelli defends Christianity as the victim of "false interpretation." Christianity does not create effeminate men, rather it is the result of "worthless men" who have misunderstood what Christianity intends: "For if they consider that it [Christianity] allows us the betterment and the defense of our country, they would see that it intends that we love and honor her and prepare ourselves to be such that we can defend her" (*Discourses* 2.2). Thus, Machiavelli does not discount the importance of religion to the political,[13] only interpretations of religion that render men unfit political actors. The contrast evoked between the spectacle of Nicia's "little blade" and that of Brutus's heroic retrieval of the dagger from Lucretia's breast demonstrates just how unfit Machiavelli imagines this misinterpretation of Christianity has rendered Renaissance men.

Nonetheless, while in some respects highlighting Florence's deficiencies in comparison with her Roman ancestor, Machiavelli's rewriting of Lucretia's rape is simultaneously a reconfiguration and contestation of Roman authority. Machiavelli's rewriting allows for the possibility of political action without the tyranny of Roman authority. Machiavelli wants to maintain in some form both Roman authority and its innovation. As Hanna Pitkin notes, it is unclear when one strives to imitate the Romans whether one imitates *them* or their capacity for innovation.[14] Machiavelli's compromise is echoed by Hannah Arendt when she asserts about the American founding that its authority was the "authority of reconstitution itself; an authority inherent in its own performances."[15] That is, republican authority must be exercised in a way that further politicizes the people rather than in a way that renders them quiescent. And that is exactly what Machiavelli's rendition of the founding in *La Mandragola* does. His revision demonstrates the capacity for the founding to be amended and augmented. Set in contemporary Renaissance Italy rather than in ancient Rome, the play sets the beginning, the possibility for founding, in the present. Foundation is, as it were, continuous foundation. This maintenance of Roman antiquity is achieved through an augmentation that takes place by way of translation.[16] Machiavelli maintains the authority of Rome through a rendition, a translation of a traditional story, Livy's story of the rape of Lucretia. And this translation is manifest, in part, in the way in which in Machiavelli's account, Lucretia's rape becomes not only bloodless but consensual.

In contrast to the comedy, however, the founding stories that Machiavelli recounts in The Discourses and The Prince each involve violence—Romulus kills Remus; Verginia is slain by her own father; and Tarquin rapes Lucretia. Nonetheless, oddly, Machiavelli remains confident that the Italian republic he is seeking to renew can be renovated without violence. Apparently, Machiavelli believes that words will be sufficient to renew the republic since the Florentine people are not entirely corrupt: "For a licentious and mutinous people may easily be brought back to good conduct by the influence and persuasion of a good man . . . words suffice to correct those [defects] of the people whilst those of the prince can only be remedied by violence" (Discourses 1.58). When trying to dislodge a corrupt prince, violence is necessary; but when attempting to reform a wayward people, words (and spectacle) are sufficient. Persuasion, not force, founds the republic. For it is easy to persuade the people initially, but more difficult to "keep them in persuasion. And so it is necessary to order things so that when they no longer believe, they can be made to believe by force."[17] Machiavelli's advice to innovators is not only to begin with persuasion and to use force only when necessary, but also "to order things so that when they no longer believe, they can be made to believe" (Prince 7). In other words, for Machiavelli, even force works rhetorically as persuasion. It too must be staged.

Although Machiavelli does occasionally seem preoccupied with force and the "armed citizen," close examination of his discussions of force often exposes his focus on the "reputation of force,"[18] the "display of power," and "appearing to trust one's citizens."[19] His reliance is rather on how force is narrated—what is said about one's ability, how that force appears and is later remembered. It is interesting to note in this regard that Machiavelli is credited with being the first to organize a military parade.[20] Apparently, after establishing the citizen militia in Florence in 1506, Machiavelli arranged a parade through the streets of Florence. For Machiavelli, spectacle and narrative are the materiality of power and of the real.

It is possible to have a bloodless revolution, Machiavelli asserts, when the new government is established by the consent of a large group of people (*Discourses* 3.6). As an example, he cites the expulsion of the Tarquins as a transition from slavery to liberty in which "no one else suffered injury" except for the chiefs of state. On the other hand, if a government originates in violence, there is, of course, not only the violence of the revolution but also the threat of continued violence as a result of the desire for revenge by those injured by the establishment of the new government. Yet how can Machiavelli name the expulsion of the Tarquins "bloodless" when Lucretia is raped and commits suicide? What does he mean that "no one else suffered injury" when Lucretia dies as a result of her violation?

Elsewhere in *The Discourses* Machiavelli refers to "what happened to Lucretia" as both an "accident"[21] and an "excess."[22] While he acknowledges that her rape was a catalyst for the founding, he insists it was not a necessary one:

> Tarquin was driven from Rome, not because his son Sextus had violated Lucretia, but because he had disregarded the laws of the kingdom and governed it tyrannically. . . . If the accident of Lucretia had not occurred, some other would have produced the same effect; for had Tarquin conducted himself like the previous kings, when his son Sextus committed that crime, Brutus and Collantinus would have appealed to Tarquin for vengeance against Sextus, instead of stirring up the Roman people as they did. (*Discourses* 3.5)

Here, apparently, is the misogynist Machiavelli who seems to have earned every feminist invective against him. He expresses no moral outrage about the rape; and his silence, indeed, his interpretation of Lucretia's violation in terms of political expediency, is quintessential "evil Machiavel." What seems to matter to him is only how events correspond with the demands of political life. Yet is it sheer misogyny and opportunism that motivates Machiavelli's reading of Lucretia's rape? How does the "accident of Lucretia" figure politically in Machiavelli's conception of foundings?

First, Machiavelli's discussion of the expulsion of the Tarquins is found in a chapter titled, "What Causes a Kingdom to Be Lost by a King Who Has Inherited It." Apparently, for Machiavelli, unlike Livy, the Tarquins are not usurpers but inheritors of the state. And thus to them he repeats advice that he gives in *The Prince:* "Princes should know, then, that they begin to lose their positions at the hour when they begin to break the law and those old ways and customs under which for a long time men have lived" (*Discourses* 3.5).

The *political* principle at work in this chapter is that the ruler can maintain his power only with the concurrence of the people. Tarquin was driven out because he had "deprived Rome of all the liberty which under the other kings she had preserved." If Tarquin had lived like other kings, Brutus and Collantinus would have come to him for vengeance against Sextus rather than inciting rebellion against his father's rule. Instead, they incite revolution, for Tarquin has not demonstrated that he is a friend of the people who, like Brutus, would be willing to sacrifice his own sons for their preservation.[23] According to Machiavelli, Tarquin has incurred the people's wrath by reducing them to unsavory chores: "For he roused the populace as well against him, making them labor at lowly tasks, very different from those in which his predecessors had employed them" (*Discourses* 3.5).

In constrast, Livy notes that while Tarquin used the poorer classes to build the temple in Juno, the laborers thought it "an honorable burden with a solemn and religious significance and they were not, on the whole, unwilling to bear it."[24] While Livy does note that the laborers were not as willing to be involved in some of Tarquin's more labor-intensive projects, he nowhere suggests that this "menial work" led to rebellion. For Livy, most of the injuries that Tarquin inflicts are against the Senate, not the people. In contrast, for Machiavelli it is because of Tarquin's violation of the people that he is driven from Rome in a bloodless revolution initiated with the consent of the people. And this, for Machiavelli, is the most important aspect of the rape of Lucretia and the expulsion of the Tarquins: the *consent* of the people for the founding. Here also is to be found a challenge (if not justification) for the overt misogyny of Machiavelli's formulation of "the excess against Lucretia."

The desire that ignites the expulsion, for Machiavelli, is not the excessive one of Sextus but rather the desire of the people to be well governed, as he notes in the same chapter, "For when men are well governed, they do not seek for nor wish any other liberty" (*Discourses* 3.6). It is the people's desire which spurs the founding and to which Machiavelli is most attentive. The foundation of the republic is the people, and this is his *political* reason for diminishing the significance of the rape of Lucretia. For Machiavelli, to highlight the link between the rape and the founding, as Livy does, is to locate the republican founding with the Senate/nobles rather than with the people.

It is noteworthy that one of Machiavelli's few overt disagreements with Livy concerns the nature of the people: "Titus Livius as well as all other historians affirm that nothing is more uncertain and inconstant than the multitude. . . . But as regards prudence and stability, I say that the people are more prudent and stable and have better judgment than a prince" (*Discourses* 1.58). For Machiavelli, there is nothing by nature that prevents the people from being both good judges and good governors of themselves. Although Machiavelli does not deny the importance of the founder, the consent of the people is pivotal to the founder's success.

At work also in this discussion of the people's nature is Machiavelli's reconfiguration of Roman authority. As Arendt notes, Roman authority (*auctoritas*) was constituted by a trinity of authority, religion, and tradition: "Members of the Senate, the elders or *patres* (fathers) were endowed with authority which had been obtained by descent and by transmission (tradition) from those who had laid the foundations for all things to come, the ancestors, whom the Romans called *maiores* (founders)."[25] Machiavelli's rendition of the expulsion of the Tarquins is an attempt to redraw the line of descent for this founding authority from the Senate to the people. For Machiavelli, both power and authority rest with the people; they are their own founders. Consequently, Machiavelli highlights consent, specifically the consent of the people, not the rape of Lucretia, in his account. Indeed in Machiavelli's bloodless, consensual version of the founding story, *La Mandragola*, Lucrezia is neither raped nor does she commit suicide. Rather, she gives her reluctant assent to adultery (5.5, 269) (for summary, see Appendix A).

The comedy's conspiracy to obtain Lucrezia's "consent" parallels the consent of the people necessary for the founding of the republic. In *La Mandragola* Lucrezia is the embodiment of the people, able to judge the common good and to adjust her actions accordingly. Her consent to Ligurio's scheme is what enables one dimension of the happy resolution of the comedy, the founding of a new domestic order.

Seduction in the Realm of Appearances

The word *mandragola* in Italian refers to the phallic-like root of a plant presumed to have not only magical powers but also the quality of an aphrodisiac. Tellingly, the mandrake potion in the play is a ruse; it is never administered. Ostensibly, Lucrezia will conceive, not because of a magic potion, but because of the heated passion of her young lover. In fact, there are several insinuations in the play that Lucrezia's husband is either impotent or a homosexual.[26] Moreover, the mandrake potion, if taken, is fatal to men (the first man to have sex with a woman treated with the potion dies), while the woman remains unaffected.[27] This is perhaps testament to the battle Machiavelli perceives between masculinity and femininity as well as between their respective counterparts, *virtù* and *Fortuna*. Nevertheless, it remains a battle without an obvious resolution in either *La Mandragola* or elsewhere in Machiavelli's writings.

Significantly, Machiavelli does not deny women's sexual and reproductive powers in *La Mandragola* (Lucrezia does live to give birth to a child).[28] Nonetheless, the mandrake could easily be read as a manifestation of Renaissance men's anxieties about feminine power; Machiavelli's characters overcome feminine power because the mandrake is only a ruse! However, although the mandrake may be a ruse, the play demonstrates that feminine power is not; rather, feminine power is potent in the world of appearances. The mandrake "works" because in Machiavelli's world, appearances have become the real.

Although Lucrezia is heralded in the prologue as "fit to govern a kingdom," she never appears alone onstage or leaves the interior of her home or the church. She, like the other Machiavellian actor, Ligurio, has no soliloquies, and we know of her primarily through the mouths of men.[29] Thus, Lucrezia's seduction is complicated by the fact that the audience only learns of her compliance from her would-be rapist, Callimaco. We are left to judge from appearances, by her willingness at the end of the comedy to play hostess to Callimaco in her home and to pay the friar a purse full of money for his blessing on her pregnancy. What is significant about Lucrezia is not her rape but the spectacle the dilemma her rape or seduction poses.

What *is* integral is appearances. For seduction is nothing if not a play on the appearance of things; seduction does not try to dispel appearance for the sake of a reality beyond.[30] Rather, seduction is a mastery of signs. As Jean Baudrillard develops, "To seduce is to die as reality and to reconstitute oneself as illusion."[31] Seduction is play, a challenge, a strategy of appearances. And thus for Machiavelli, seduction, not rape, is the ideal metaphor for political action.[32]

An absolute, like rape, is illicit in Machiavellian politics because it is irresistible. This interpretation counters that of some who have argued that Machiavelli's *La Mandragola* makes a mockery of the reality of rape, that his revision of Livy's story argues against the very possibility of rape.[33] Yet, Machiavelli's Lucrezia is seduced, rather than raped, *because* Machiavelli recognizes the irreversibility of rape and wants to suggest a conception of political action less contingent, ironically, on violence and a literal determinism. "God, self-evident truths, natural law are all despotic because they are irresistible. And because they are irresistible, they do not persuade to agreement, they command to acquiescence."[34] Rape, too, is a command; seduction, however, is for Machiavelli quintessentially political. What Machiavelli reveals through his strategy of seduction is that politics, too, is about appearances, about the instability and disruption of the distinction between appearance and reality.

Seduction suggests also the contingency of political action, the uncertainty of outcome and the continual need to adjust to the vicissitudes of circumstances. Through his strategy of seduction, Machiavelli deploys not only a certain kind of femininity but also a form of mutuality necessary for political action. For Machiavelli politics is always agonistic. Yet he finds something other than violence and danger in struggle.[35] Rather than condemning tumult and conflict, he praises them for their ability to preserve the republic: "For whoever will carefully examine the result of these agitations will find that they have neither caused exiles nor any violence prejudicial to the general good, and will be convinced even that they have given rise to laws that were to the advantage of public liberty" (*Discourses* 1.4). Conflict is a sign of the vitality of politics. Political action is about negotiation and accommodation, not about strict adherence to given principles. Without motion, without dissension, there would be no politics. Thus, a political actor inattentive to the changing whims of *Fortuna* would have little political power; one must recognize where one is on the wheel of fortune and leap accordingly.

It is this relationship of contest that Machiavelli urges between political actors and feminine power: political actors must engage with the feminine but still maintain their masculinity; they must be attentive to *Fortuna*'s power but build the dikes to contain her dominion. *Fortuna*, like Lucrezia, must also be seduced, not raped. For she, as the feminine principle of political action, cannot be completely dominated or annihilated. As Machiavelli begrudgingly acknowledges, "She is the arbiter of one half of our actions but she still leaves the control of the other half, or almost that, to us."[36]

Although Machiavelli uses the language of conquest—"if you wish to master her, to conquer her by force"[37]—this is followed immediately by the reminder that "it can be seen that she *lets* herself be overcome by the bold rather than by those who proceed coldly."[38] Again, even the contrast with those who proceed *coldly* intimates the alternative of passion and heat, the strategy of seduction. The relationship that political actors have with *Fortuna* is one of interminable seduction. They must constantly anticipate her desires, prepare for her arrival, and adjust themselves to her whims.

Like Lucrezia, who is seduced because of others' preparedness ("your cleverness, my husband's stupidity, my mother's silliness, and my confessor's guile"), so too *Fortuna* is seduced and domesticated by man's preparedness: "Where Fortune is concerned: she shows her force where there is no organized strength to resist her; and she directs her impact where she knows that dikes and embankments are not constructed to hold her. . . . It does not follow that when the weather is calm we cannot take precautions with embankments and dikes, so that when they rise up again the waters will be channelled off or their impetus will not be either so unchecked or so damaging."[39] And this is part of the paradox of the feminine for Machiavelli. Although his images of women are riddled with sexual violence, in his political narrative it is the feminine that ultimately makes politics possible. Indeed, he suggests that it is the spectacle of the feminine that will bring the people back to themselves and thus enable the founding.

Nonetheless, although this strategy of seduction grants a certain recognition to the feminine other in the form of *Fortuna*, seduction is not without its own hierarchy of domination. That is, it is one thing for the feminine other to *yield* as *Fortuna* does, and quite another for her to demand what she wants. Yet there is still another complication. *Fortuna* yields because of the ability of the political actor to make a spectacle of himself; he considers how his power will be perceived and adjusts himself accordingly. For Machiavelli this capacity to see oneself as others do enables one to formulate an understanding of power. As Merleau-Ponty has noted, "Power bears a halo about it, and its curse is to fail to see the image of itself it shows to others."[40] In the case of the prince, he must learn to see himself from the perspective of the people and to alter his image accordingly.

Like Lucrezia's seduction, which suggests a process of founding rather than its one-time inauguration, so as theatre, *La Mandragola* is a ritual reenactment of the origin, repeated endlessly with each performance. This reenactment purifies contaminants from the society and solidifies communal bonds. And Machiavelli uses a medical lexicon to suggest the purification: "Every day some ill humors gather which must be cured."[41]

Spectacles, as Machiavelli reminds us throughout *The Prince* and *The Discourses*, help to bring the people back to themselves; because of memory lapses, the people may forget their founding principles and need to be reminded of them.[42] Ironically, for Machiavelli it is spectacle, not action, that brings the people back. Remembrance itself is a kind of seduction; recollection and temptation are twin impulses. The recollection of the past, manifested though spectacle, sparks a desire for imitation. Re-presentation of the past seduces political actors in the present. Thus, Machiavelli is careful about what he represents. Because there is a contagion effect about recollection, Machiavelli does not want to represent the most violent renditions of the past—the initial fratricide of Remus or the sexual violation of Lucretia.

For Machiavelli, the ability to make a spectacle of oneself is the mark of a successful prince. This capacity to see oneself as others do enables one to formulate an understanding of perspective. The prince can see himself from the perspective of the people and alter his image accordingly. This formulation is Machiavelli's rather clever satire of the mirror of princes literature. Concurrently, Machiavelli subverts the conception of the object of the look as always already feminized and passive. Here he—or in the case of Lucrezia, she—who is most attentive to being looked at, has the most power. Lucrezia, like the prince, is a political actor, orchestrating her appearance, controlling how she is looked at.

In some respects, Lucrezia is the prototypical Machiavellian political actor. She adjusts when the circumstances demand,[43] seizes *Fortuna,* and uses deception to achieve her ends. Upon her is Machiavelli's hope for the success of the play pinned: "How fortunate if you could be tricked in the way she was!"[44] Lucrezia is the embodiment of dissimulation *and* she reveals reality for what it is. Foremost, she is not what she seems—she proves through the course of the play that she is neither as chaste nor as naive as the other characters presume. She personifies dissimulation. Yet this dissimulation is reality; reality is not what it seems, and Machiavelli is continually urging political actors to be attentive to the duplicity of appearances and the fallacy of their judgments.

Quite interestingly, Lucrezia, and the Renaissance feminine in general, personify what Froma Zeitlin identifies as the paradox of theater: "While theatre resorts continually to artifice, as it must, to techniques of make-believe that can only resemble the real, it can also better represent the larger world outside as it more nearly is, subject to the deceptions, the gaps in knowledge, the tangled necessities, and all the tensions and conflicts of a complex existence."[45] Lucrezia reveals to the male character that the world is other than he originally imagined it and that he cannot ultimately control it. For example, although the bragging of one of her relatives and the desires of Callimaco ignite the plot, they both ultimately lose control of the narrative. Although Callimaco achieves his desired end, he does not control the machinations that drive the plot; Ligurio, and, eventually, Lucrezia do.

Clearly, political actors do not exercise control over the unfolding of events. What they *can* control, however, is how they respond to changing circumstances. At some level, *La Mandragola* is a story demonstrating that because men cannot control the effects of either their words (i.e., the brag) or their acts, they must learn how to change themselves according to how their words and acts are construed by others; they must change themselves as circumstances change. They must learn how to seduce the feminine *Fortuna*. Thus, Lucrezia is a "lesson" to men. She is Machiavelli's invitation to political actors to dissimulate. Moreover, Lucrezia shows men that the world is not as they imagined it to be. For example, she reveals to the characters of the play (and to the audience) that she is not as chaste as they presumed; in fact, she is relatively willing to be deceived herself and to conspire in adultery. But her conversion is not because she is corrupt, as some have suggested,[46] but because she is astute. She is adapting to circumstances, seizing opportunity before *Fortuna* passes by and only her bald head is visible.[47]

Lucrezia embodies the complexities appearance poses for Machiavellian politics—not only the indeterminability of seeming and being, but also the imporance of being able to determine when to use force and when persuasion. Although Machiavelli's Lucrezia does not kill herself, she performs a similar narrative function to Livy's Lucretia. She controls how her story is told, how she is read. As spectacle, Lucrezia teaches to other male characters and spectators of the play how to be men, specifically, how to be successful, autonomous, political actors. She highlights the need for the other in order to know oneself, and she attests to the complexities and ambiguities implicit in achieving manhood. It is the spectacle of the female body, again, both literally and metaphorically, that constitutes the initial political "we." Lucrezia is testament to both Machiavelli's fascination with the power of *Fortuna* and the feminine, and his fear of her devastating power and influence.

For Machiavelli, men and women are sexual antagonists, just as are *virtù* and *Fortuna*. But this struggle with the enemy can aggrandize oneself and ensure one's own success. Throughout book 2 of *The Discourses*, Machiavelli details "How Rome Became Great by Ruining Her Enemies." Rome was able to become powerful through struggle, partially, as Machiavelli elaborates, because she fought *without* annihilating or completely impoverishing the conquered country. In a parallel vein, as demonstrated through *La Mandragola*, antagonism with *Fortuna* as well as with femininity enriches male *virtù*. Women serve as worthy enemies who augment men's *virtù*; contestation and struggle with women both teaches men and empowers them. And, as a "worthy enemy," Machiavelli grants women, as personified by *Fortuna*, autonomous power. She does, after all, still control half of men's actions.

For Machiavelli, stability is ephemeral, and politics itself is about the contestation of meaning. Politics means manipulating appearances in order to achieve a desired end. Machiavelli embraces the dilemma of the instability of each to the other and articulates a politics that assumes the mediation of appeearances and adjusts itself accordingly. This antagonism and reconciliation is personified in Machiavelli's articulation of the relationship between *virtù* and *Fortuna*. Machiavelli is the realist who recognizes the "real" as the realm of appearances.

Focusing on Machiavelli's theatrical texts foregrounds what risks neglect in traditional formulations of realism. For Machiavelli, power is not simply about domination, empire, and glory; rather, Machiavelli's Renaissance relationship to the Roman republican tradition (primarily through Livy) articulates his celebration of contestation rather than domination, of the people rather than empire, and of the common good as well as of glory. These themes are most fully developed in Machiavelli's theater, where he both imitates and innovates the Romans, where he repeats and rewrites history and where he re-presents reality in the realm of appearances.

Finally, the story of the rape of Lucretia raises the theme of violence in Machiavelli in a register other than that of competing state and self-interests. The story of the rape suggests, first, the violence of any beginning, the problem of asserting command before the principles of that authority are secured. Yet Machiavelli's rendition of the story, in which Lucrezia is not raped but seduced, suggests that neither politics nor political foundings rest solely on force. Secondly this pivotal story of the founding implies that politics does not enjoy the autonomy on which political realism would like to insist. In fact, the play details the ways in which political power is inscribed in the body; in other words, Machiavelli's plays take quite seriously the metaphor of the "body politic." Notions of masculinity, of femininity, and of sexuality are revealed as integral to the founding as well as to the maintenance of politics. The domestic comedy of *La Mandragola* is, in part, a recognition that political power does not exist solely in the relations between states or in the relation between the state and the citizen, but rather that power also asserts itself through imposing interpretative grids on the human body, particularly in constructions of masculinity and femininity.

Notes

1. Letter to Vettori, no. 159 in *Machiavelli: The Chief Works and Others*, ed. and trans. Allan Gilbert (Durham: Duke University Press, 1989), 2:961.

2. Jackson Cope, *Secret Sharers in Italian Comedy: From Machiavelli to Goldoni* (Durham: Duke University Press, 1996), 5.

3. Ibid., 5.

4. See, for example, Letters no. 131, August 10, 1513, and no. 134, August 26, 1513, in *Chief Works and Others*, 2:915–21 and 922–26.

5. No. 116, "Letter to Soderini, January 1512 (1513)," in *Chief Works and Others*, 2:895–97.

6. See, for example, *Discourses*, 1.58 in *Chief Works and Others*, "And if princes show themselves superior in the making of laws, and in the forming of civil institutions and new statutes and ordinances, *the people are superior in maintaining those institutions, laws, and ordinances*, which certainly places them on a par with those who established them" (italics mine).

7. It is for this reason that Machiavelli disagrees with Livy and other ancient writers regarding the nature of the people. While Livy asserts that the multitude are inconstant, Machiavelli insists that the defect is not in the nature of the people themselves, but is a function of each person's response to the law: "The difference in their [the prince's and the people's] conduct is not due to any difference in their nature (for that is the same, and if there be any difference for good, it is on the side of the people); but to the greater or less respect they have for the laws under which they respectively live" (*Discourses* 1.58). In addition, "a licentious and mutinous people" can be brought back to good conduct by the persuasion of a good man. An evil-minded prince, on the other hand, can only be overcome with violence.

8. For an extended discussion of Lucretia as *pharmakons* see Ronald L. Martinez, "The Pharmacy of Machiavelli: Roman Lucretia in *Mandragola*," in *Renaissance Drama as Cultural History: Essays from Renaissance Drama 1977–1987*, ed. Mary Beth Rose (Evanston: Northwestern University Press, 1990), 31–73.

9. *La Mandragola* 2.6, in *The Comedies of Machiavelli*, ed. and trans. David Sices and James B.

Atkinson (Hanover: University Press of New England, 1985), 197. Citations in the text hereafter are from this edition.

10. "The Capitoli," in *Lust and Liberty: The Poetry of Machiavelli*, trans. Joseph Tusiani (New York: Obolensky Press, 1963), 113.

11. Theodore Sumberg, "*La Mandragola*: An Interpretation," *Journal of Politics* 23 (1961): 327.

12. *La Mandragola* 4.8. This image also clearly mocks Nicia's sexual impotence in the same way that the dagger invokes Tarquin's potency.

13. See, for example, *Discourses* 1.11: "And whoever reads Roman history attentively will see in how great a degree religion served in the command of the armies, in inspiring the people and keeping men good, in making the wicked ashamed."

14. Hanna Fenichel Pitkin, *Fortune Is a Woman: Gender and Politics in the Thought of Niccolò Machiavelli* (Berkeley and Los Angeles: University of California Press, 1984), 88.

15. Hannah Arendt, *On Revolution* (New York: Viking Press, 1963), 202.

16. Jacques Derrida, "Deconstruction in America: An Interview with Jacques Derrida," *Critical Exchange* 17 (1985): 24–25.

17. *The Prince*, in *Chief Works and Others*, 26.

18. See, for example, *Discourses* 1.19 and 2.14, where Machiavelli gives numerous examples of the necessity for kings often to wage war in order not "to appear effeminate . . . and be esteemed little" and "because the zeal of the prince's friends will be chilled on seeing him *appear* feeble and cowardly" (my emphasis). In fact, Machiavelli goes so far as to say in 2.31: "I do not mean to say by this, however, that arms and force are never to be employed, but that they should be reserved as *the last resort* when other means fail" (my emphasis).

19. This is ostensibly Machiavelli's argument when he discusses the injuries of relying upon fortresses. His critique centers not so much on their advantage or disadvantage in a specific battle plan as on how their use *appears* to others and what it *seems* to suggest about the prince's confidence in the valor of his own citizens. Here Machiavelli prefers to depend more on the goodwill of the citizens than on the strength of citadels.

20. Roberto Ridolfi, *The Life of Machiavelli*, trans. Cecil Grayson (Chicago: University of Chicago Press, 1963), 88.

21. "E se lo accidente di Lucrezia non fosse venuto, come prima ne fossenato un altro" (*Discourses* 3.5).

22. "E come si è veduto in questra nostra istoria, l'eccesso fatto contro a Lucrezia tolse lo stato ai Tarquinnii" (*Discourses* 3.26).

23. Harvey J. Mansfield, *Machiavelli's New Modes and Orders: A Study of the Discourses on Livy* (Ithaca: Cornell University Press, 1979), 314–16.

24. Titus Livy, *The Early History of Rome*, trans. Aubrey de Selincourt (New York: Penguin, 1978), 1.57.

25. Hannah Arendt, "What Is Authority?" in *Between Past and Future: Eight Exercises in Political Thought* (New York: Penguin Books, 1961).

26. Consider, for example, Nicia's early remarks that Lucrezia is always cold at night and is found on the floor praying on her knees, and his own rather keen interest in "checking" the anatomy of his "victim" in order to be certain that it is sufficient and functional.

27. Martinez, "The Pharmacy of Machiavelli," 67–68.

28. In *Clizia* there is a reference to the birth of a child to Lucrezia and Callimaco through the miracle of the prayers of Friar Timoteo: "Don't you know that through his [Friar Timoteo's] prayers the wife of Messer Nicia, Madonna Lucrezia, who was sterile, became pregnant?" (Nicomaco to his wife, Sofronia, 2.3).

29. Of course, part of the reason that she is rarely on stage is that the part of Lucrezia would have been played by a young male actor. Apparently, the ability of a man to portray "the most beautiful woman in Italy" strained even Renaissance credulity.

30. Jean Baudrillard, *Seduction*, trans. Brian Singer (New York: St. Martin's Press, 1990).

31. Ibid., 69.

32. John Forrester notes, for example, that "seduction, unlike rape, has a positive and a negative face . . . rape is punctual, instantaneous, involving not only physical violence, but temporal violence. Seduction is interminable, and even the spiritual rapists may imitate this interminability through their endless repetition" ("Rape, Seduction and Psychoanalysis," in *Rape: An Historical and Social Enquiry*, ed. Sylvanna Tomaselli and Roy Porter [Oxford: Basil Blackwell, 1989], 82).

33. See Jean Bethke Elshtain, *Public Man, Private Woman: Women in Social and Political Thought* (Princeton: Princeton University Press, 1981); and Mary O'Brien, "The Root of the Mandrake: Machiavelli and Manliness," in *Reproducing the World: Essays in Feminist Theory* (San Francisco: Westview Press, 1989), 103–26.

34. Arendt, *On Revolution*, 202.

35. Maurice Merleau-Ponty, "A Note on Machiavelli," in *Signs*, trans. Richard C. McCleary (Evanston: Northwestern University Press, 1964), 211.

36. *The Prince*, chap. 25.

37. Ibid.

38. "E si vede che la si lascia più vincere da questi, che da quelli che freddamente procedono" (ibid.).

39. Ibid.

40. Merleau-Ponty, "A Note on Machiavelli," 216.

41. Ibid.

42. See Melissa M. Matthes, *The Rape of Lucretia and the Founding of Republics* (University Park: Pennsylvania State University Press), chap. 3, for a full development of this theme.

43. Nonetheless, her transformation is probably not as rapid as Callimaco believes; Nicia revealed earlier that Lucrezia had already been deceived by a friar who tried to take advantage of her while she was saying her novenas. Indeed, Lucrezia was probably never as naive as the men believed.

44. *La Mandragola*, Prologue.

45. Froma Zeitlin, "Playing the Other: Theater, Theatricality and the Feminine in Greek Drama," *Representations* 11 (Summer 1985): 79.

46. See Susan Behuniak-Long, "The Significance of Lucrezia in Machiavelli's *La Mandragola*," *Review of Politics* (Spring 1989): 264–80.

47. In one of Machiavelli's poems, he reiterates the popular image of *Fortuna* as bald from behind: "The back of my head is utterly shorn / In vain, therefore, men try to grab me, when / I pass them by, or if around I turn" (*Lust and Liberty: The Poetry of Machiavelli*, 128).

9

Rhetoric, Violence, and Gender in Machiavelli

Cary J. Nederman and Martin Morris

Feminist readers of Machiavelli have long noted the significance of the "economy of violence" in his work. His emphasis on force, strength, and military prowess—all aspects of his central value, *virtù*—points to an exclusionary attitude toward women as fully civic and political creatures. As Jean Bethke Elshtain has observed, "Machiavelli's politics eliminates women by definition from the most important field of citizen involvement" (Elshtain 1981, 98; see 95–98 for the "economy of violence").

Versions of this paper were presented at the Canadian Political Science Association meeting, Québec, May 2001; and at the American Political Science Association meeting, Philadelphia, August 2003.

Perhaps most notoriously, Machiavelli's personification of *Fortuna* as a woman who must become the object of violence in order to be mastered suggests a deep-seated gender bias in his theory. One can hardly dispute Hanna Fenichel Pitkin's assertion that, according to Machiavelli's understanding, the world is "run by a large senior, female person who holds men in her power to a greater or lesser extent" and who is "threatening to men, to manliness, to politics and the *vivere civile*" (Pitkin 1984, 165). For Machiavelli, the feminine is a source of fear that requires a forceful response.

This chapter attempts to extend feminist insights about Machiavelli's economy of violence by examining its rhetorical dimension. It has now become commonplace to acknowledge the importance of the classical rhetorical tradition for his thought (Rebhorn 1988; Kahn 1994; Viroli 1998, 73–113). Certainly, Machiavelli's education included a careful study of not only the techniques of the ancient masters of rhetoric but also the theories of language and society proposed by authors such as Cicero. Most notably, the gendered aspect of rhetoric in Machiavelli's thought is revealed in how violence versus eloquence plays out in his account of *Fortuna*. Our view, simply put, is that Machiavelli's treatment of *Fortuna* problematizes the classical rhetorical distinction between force and debate—a distinction that Machiavelli challenges without real explanation in many of his writings. Why can't *Fortuna* be persuaded? Why must "She" be violently abused? How does the question of the violence to *Fortuna* frame Machiavellian politics? We argue first that Machiavelli's insistence upon rational discourse as the basis for fully civil life, in conjunction with his reduction of *Fortuna* to a feminized, naturalistic, and hence derationalized power, reinforces the antifeminist features of the economy of violence. We shall support this claim by considering the classical rhetorical distinction between force and debate, then by turning to Machiavelli's own rhetorical politics, and finally by contrasting his conception of discourse with his treatment of *Fortuna*. Second, we argue that the tension thus revealed in Machiavelli's rhetorical republicanism is associated with his inadequate approach to the intersubjectivity of the republican political realm grounded in the use of speech and reason. We draw on the work of Jürgen Habermas in order to underline the relevant philosophical positions in the classical rhetorical tradition that allow for a feminist corrective to these inadequacies.

Rhetoric and Violence

The quintessential statement in classical rhetoric of the distinction between eloquent speech and political violence was made by Cicero. In
his view, the glorification of armed conflict amounts to a denigration of
characteristically human qualities in favor of a bestial nature: "There are
two ways of settling a dispute: the one, by discussion, the other, by force;
and since the former is proper to human beings, the latter to the brute,
we may resort to force only when discussion is not possible" (Cicero
1913, I.34). In other words, violence is inconsistent with distinctively
human nature; it reflects the animalistic side of our existence. Hence
peaceful harmony is the true natural condition of humanity, according
to Cicero. If we draw upon our rational and linguistic capacities—those
characteristics with which we are born and that we share in common
with the gods (I.22–27)—we will be able to settle all disputes and govern
ourselves without recourse to violence. "The only rationale for going to
war, therefore, is that we may live in peace (*pax*) uninjured" (I.35). Cicero believes that Rome, at least as long as it was under "temperate" republican rule, followed policies consonant with this principle: armed conflict
was pursued only as a last resort, when negotiations had proved ineffective at settling dispute. Vanquished enemies were not generally enslaved
or slaughtered, but were (like Cicero's own ancestors) extended Roman
citizenship and permitted to exercise political rights within the republic
(I.35–38). It is only by adopting such policies, Cicero believes, that the
goal of concord may be achieved.

Cicero's condemnation of violence and praise for reasoned speech are
clearly rooted in his fundamental philosophical precepts. He propounds
an idea of human nature conceived in terms of the native powers of
reason and speech: "Nature through reason reconciles man with man by
means of speech" (I.12). The primacy accorded to reason and speech
reflects the fact that these powers stimulate "the processes of teaching
and learning, of communicating, discussing and reasoning [that] associate
men together and unite them into a sort of natural fraternity" (I.50). In
Cicero's view, intellect and language may be regarded as nature's method
of endowing the human species with the capacity it needs to survive
(I.11). For from social contact emerges the full range of political and
economic relationships through which men sustain and support themselves:

> Without the association of men, cities could not have been built or peopled. In consequence of city life, laws and customs were established, and then came the equitable distribution of private rights and a definite humane spirit and consideration for others, with the result that life was better supplied with all it requires, and by giving and receiving, by mutual exchange of commodities and conveniences, we succeed in meeting all our wants. (I.15)

In effect, the result of natural human sociability is the preservation and protection of the species. The powers of speech and reason alone render possible all the advantages of political and economic association. Yet it is not strictly in order to satisfy their physical needs, but instead because of their native linguistic and rational faculties, that human beings seek out fellowship with one another and congregate in communities. Their coming together into society is therefore not reducible to an instrumentalist or functionalist reason. The material sustenance and foundation of their lives is itself produced by and a condition of the natural cooperative mutuality of speaking and doing together. The fully satisfying life of the city can be realized only with the flourishing of these natural capacities of linguistically mediated intercourse and exchange.

The rational and linguistic features of human nature thus explain, for Cicero, the origins of social organization. He postulates people in a primordial condition where they lead a scattered, brutish existence devoid of intellect, religion, family, and law (Cicero 1949, I.2). But these primitive creatures also harbor the powers of speech and reason, which naturally impel them to be sociable (Cicero 1942, I.32–33). Speech, in particular, is crucial to human association, insofar as "it does not seem possible that a mute and voiceless wisdom could have turned human beings suddenly from their habits and introduced them to different patterns of life" (Cicero 1949, I.3). The realization of humanity's social sentiments required, however, the guidance of a wise and eloquent man, by whose instruction others discovered and improved their own rational and discursive capabilities. Through the persuasion of this especially skilled individual (Cicero 1942, I.31), his fellow creatures exchanged their solitary existence for a social one. At his behest, they learned useful and honorable occupations, assembled into cities, obeyed voluntarily the commands of others, and observed law; in sum, "he transformed them from wild savages into a gentle and kind folk" (Cicero 1949, I.2). All of these developments Cicero emphatically premises on the natural ability of speech coupled with reason: not merely does rational discourse sepa-rate man from lesser animals, but it renders possible the mutual under-standing through which the sacrifices and burdens of human association may be explained and justified. In the absence of reason combined with eloquence, none of the blessings of social and political community could be acquired.

It is worthy of note that violence and force play no role in the process of social formation depicted by Cicero—indeed, coercion seems antithet-ical to his account. Political order rests on the rational agreement of the masses to the eloquent persuasion of their leaders, not on intimidation and threats of injury. Otherwise, no social order could be just, since jus-tice itself requires for Cicero the absence of harm (Cicero 1913, I.20). Cicero underscores the incompatibility of violence and mature human civilization in *Pro Sestio*. He begins by repeating the familiar formula of social origination:

> There was a period of evolution . . . when man led a solitary and nomadic existence, and his possessions were what he could grasp for himself by brute force, murder, and violence, and keep if he was able. It was due entirely to some early men of genius and wisdom, who realized the extent of humanity's capacity to learn, that these scattered creatures were persuaded to congregate and were thereby brought from a state of savagery to the rule of justice and civilization. (Cicero 1958, 91)

Having described the transformation of human existence from disorder to order—the process of the creation of republican rule—Cicero concludes, "[n]ow the chief distinguishing feature between that early crude existence and this later civilized life that I have described lies in the difference between the rule of law and that of force. If you will not have the one, you must have the other" (92). When people live according to law, which is itself a product of a rationally arranged public sphere, they are living in a manner most consistent with true human nature. When they live in a violent manner, beyond and outside the law, they are in effect living not as human beings, but as beasts, in denial of their capacities for reason and speech and bereft of all the benefits of peaceful community that flow thence.

Hence the use of physical force may on occasion remain a necessity for civilized human beings, but it can never really be a virtue, according to Cicero. If we realize most completely our natural humanity when we demur from physical force, then virtue itself (which Cicero defines as "reason perfected, which is certainly in accord with nature" [Cicero 1928, I.5]) may never be said to partake of that which is unnatural. His preference for reasoned public debate seems to mirror the philosophy of life that is often regarded to be quintessentially Ciceronian: *otium cum dignitate* (Cicero 1958, 98). This phrase has been subjected to many different interpretations (Cumming 1969, 1:254, 1:276–77; Wood 1988, 197–99). However we understand these watchwords, they suggest that no true virtue is ever to be found in violence or combat. If *otium* (alternately translated as repose, leisure, or peace) is the proper condition of human existence, then people in their natural state must abjure the fury of armed conflict, which is antithetical to the good order and harmony implied by *otium*. By contrast, *otium* is perfectly consistent with statesmanship, since the role of the civic leader is to keep and guarantee the peace in a manner consonant with justice. The goal of the statesman is precisely *otium cum dignitate;* the phrase encapsulates the rightful end of the republic as a whole, as well as of its individual citizens. Although the statesman must involve himself in verbal duels and complex plots, these have but one purpose: to strengthen the public welfare of the community itself. It follows, therefore, from this Ciceronian logic, that physical force has no place in politics and that armies ought to be strictly subordinated to civilian leaders and to the entire citizen body.

Machiavelli's Rhetorical Republicanism

It is well known that one of the central themes of Machiavelli's *Discourses* is the defense of the view that the popular elements within the community form the best safeguard of civic liberty as well as the most reliable source of decision-making about the public good (Hulliung 1983, 32–35). In particular, Machiavelli contrasts the constancy and trustworthiness of the people, who are often accused of fickleness and ineptitude, with the improbity of the nobility, who are commonly regarded to be the "natural" leaders of a republic. What permitted Rome to avoid public corruption and to extend its empire for so many centuries, Machiavelli believes, was precisely the fact that ordinary citizens demanded and were accorded such a large hand in public determinations. The people thus thwarted the use by patricians of public power to pursue private interests. The apparent "tumults" between the popular and elite segments of the Roman population were in fact the key to Rome's success (Machiavelli 1965, 200–203).

Machiavelli's praise for the role of the people in securing the republic is supported by his confidence in the generally illuminating effects of public speech upon the citizen body (Nederman 2000, 262–67). Near the beginning of Book I of *The Discourses*, he notes that some may object to the extensive freedom enjoyed by the Roman people to assemble, to protest, and to veto laws and policies. But he responds that the Romans were able to maintain liberty and order because of the people's ability to discern the common good when it was shown to them. At times when ordinary Roman citizens wrongly supposed that a law or institution was designed to oppress them, they could be persuaded that "their beliefs are mistaken . . . [through] the remedy of assemblies, in which some man of influence gets up and makes a speech showing them how they are deceiving themselves. And as Tully says, the people, although they may be ignorant, can grasp the truth, and yield easily when told what is true by a trustworthy man" (Machiavelli 1965, 203). The reference to Cicero (one of the few in *The Discourses*) confirms that Machiavelli has in mind here a key feature of classical republicanism: the competence of the people to respond to and support the words of the gifted orator when he speaks truly about the public welfare.

Machiavelli returns to this theme and treats it more extensively at the end of Book I. In a chapter intended to demonstrate the superiority of popular over princely government, he argues that the people are well ordered, and hence "prudent, stable, and grateful," so long as room is made for public speech and deliberation within the community. Citing the formula *vox populi, vox dei*, Machiavelli insists that "public opinion is remarkably accurate in its prognostications. . . . With regard to its judgment, when two speakers of equal skill are heard advocating different alternatives, very rarely does one find the people failing to adopt the better view or incapable of appreciating the truth of what it hears" (316). Not only are the people competent to discern the best course of action when orators lay out competing plans, but they are in fact better qualified to make decisions, in Machiavelli's view, than are princes. For example, "the people can never be persuaded that it is good to appoint to an office a man of infamous or corrupt habits, whereas a prince may easily and in a vast variety of ways be persuaded to do this" (316). Likewise, should the people depart from the law-abiding path, they may readily be convinced to restore order: "For an uncontrolled and tumultuous people can be spoken to by a good man and easily led back into a good way. But no one can speak to a wicked prince, and the only remedy is steel. . . . To cure the malady of the people words are enough" (317). The contrast Machiavelli draws is stark. The republic governed by words and persuasion—in sum, ruled by public speech—is almost sure to realize the common good of its citizens; and even should it err, recourse is always open to further discourse. Nonrepublican regimes, because they exclude or limit discursive practices, ultimately rest upon coercive domination and can only be corrected by violent means.

Fortune and Violence

The republican public sphere, then, is a realm of rational discussion for Machiavelli—precisely the opposite of monarchies and principalities, whose goal is security rather than liberty (Nederman and Gomez 2002). Accordingly, those who are included within the citizen body must be confined to those who are capable of reasoned speech and who thus eschew violence among themselves. It is true that Machiavelli upholds the necessity of a citizen militia and of class strife as preconditions of a free republic. But such factors do not amount to a justification of internecine civic violence or the coercive character of social institutions. The best sort of city, one in which men live freely, requires a foundation in rational discourse.

The enemy of civil order, in turn, is *Fortuna*, a concept whose meaning for Machiavelli has been widely debated without a very satisfactory resolution. We cannot begin to rehearse these discussions at present. Suffice it to say that *Fortuna* raises problems about Machiavelli's religious and cosmological beliefs, as well as about his ideas of human nature and action. Scholars have commonly noted that his treatment of *Fortuna* stands at considerable distance from traditional classical and Christian views of the subject (Patch 1922, 226–27; Vatter forthcoming). Where conventional representations regard *Fortuna* to be a mostly benign, if fickle, source of human goods and evils, Machiavelli's goddess is a malevolent and uncompromising fount of human misery, affliction, and disaster. While human *Fortuna* may be responsible for such success as human beings achieve, no man can act effectively when directly opposed by the goddess (Machiavelli 1965, 407–8).

Machiavelli's most famous discussion of *Fortuna* occurs in chapter 25 of *The Prince*, in which he proposes two analogies for understanding the human situation in the face of events. Initially, he asserts that *Fortuna* resembles "one of our destructive rivers which, when it is angry, turns the plains into lakes, throws down the trees and buildings, takes earth from one spot, puts it in another; everyone flees before the flood; everyone yields to its fury and nowhere can repel it." Yet the furor of a ranging river does not mean that its depredations are beyond human control: before the rains come, it is possible to take precautions to divert the worst consequences of the natural elements. "The same things happen about *Fortuna*," Machiavelli observes: "She shows her power where *virtù* and wisdom do not prepare to resist her, and directs her fury where she knows that no dykes or embankments are ready to hold her" (Machiavelli 1965, 90). *Fortuna* may be resisted by human beings, but only in those circumstances where "*virtù* and wisdom" have already prepared for her inevitable arrival.

Machiavelli reinforces the association of *Fortuna* with the blind strength of nature by drawing a connection directly to the goddess's gender. Commenting that success depends upon appreciation of the operational principles of *Fortuna*, he explains that his own experience has taught him that "it is better to be impetuous than cautious, because *Fortuna* is a woman and it is necessary, in order to keep her under, to beat and maul her." In other words, *Fortuna* demands a violent response of those who would control her. "She more often lets herself be overcome by men using such methods than by those who proceed coldly," Machiavelli continues, "therefore always, like a woman, she is the friend of young men, because they are less cautious, more spirited, and with more boldness master her" (92). The feminine identity of *Fortuna* demands an aggressive, even violent response, lest she take advantage of those men who are too retiring or effeminate themselves to dominate her. Machiavelli's association of womanhood with nature is one familiar to feminist critics, as is his doctrine that such abject/objectified "otherness" requires regularization at the hands of masculine normalization.

These dual themes of the domination of nature and the physical mastery of woman are reinforced by Machiavelli's less well-known poem, "Tercets on Fortune." In this short work, the gendered aspect of *Fortuna* receives greater attention than in *The Prince*, yet the connection to nature (in the form of the "rapid torrent") is also reiterated (748). *Fortuna* is implicated by Machiavelli in a dialectic of violence. On the one hand, she is the source of human misery: "You should not dread other wounds than her blows, because this shifting creature often and by habit resists with the greatest might where she sees that nature is strongest. Her natural power for all men is too strong and her reign is always violent" (745), and "[y]ou cannot trust yourself to her nor hope to escape her hard bite, her hard blows, violent and cruel" (747). *Fortuna* attacks human beings in a wanton and entirely unpredictable way; she is, in effect, a wild animal, incomprehensible to those who try to treat her on human terms. On the other hand, she is not beyond manipulation by the man who ably interprets her ways and applies his knowledge to the goal of domination. "If *virtù* still greater than hers does not vanquish her," then *Fortuna* will prevail (745). Yet this is not the inevitable result. "We well realize how much he pleases Fortune and how acceptable he is who pushes her, who shoves her, who jostles her" (748–79). Violence begets violence: if she is forceful with human beings, then the appropriate response is to adopt her stratagems. A bold man, unafraid to meet *Fortuna* on her own terms, stands at least a chance of victory.

Machiavelli's remarks point toward several salient conclusions about *Fortuna* and her place in his intellectual universe. Throughout his corpus, *Fortuna* is depicted as a primal source of violence (especially as directed against humanity) and as antithetical to reason. Thus, Machiavelli replicates the classical insistence that force and rational discussion are incommensurable forms of activity. *Fortuna*'s irrationality, demonstrated by her fickle treatment of human beings, is at the same time simply the token of a violent character. On these very grounds, *Fortuna* is insusceptible to the techniques of rhetorical persuasion and eloquence. No amount of honeyed or reasoned speech can compel *Fortuna* to "come to her senses," because the basis of her existence is overwhelmingly violent. Words will never suffice as a means of controlling *Fortuna*: people, if they have any hope of turning the goddess to their bidding, must act directly to resist her machinations. And that active response to *Fortuna* must itself be of a violent sort. The nature of the goddess demands that, since she cannot be reasoned with, she must be treated roughly and forcefully, without showing her any of the respect that a citizen must show toward his fellows as a consequence of their common *vivere civile*. In our response to *Fortuna*, then, our success requires that we set aside the distinctively human aspects of our nature and become bestial. No other reaction than beating and mauling is possible in the face of such an angry, menacing, and entirely implacable force devoid of speech and reason.

Rhetoric, Force, and Gender

Machiavelli's "machismo" in the face of *Fortuna* thus registers a tension in his thought that feminists need to deconstruct. The question that may now be posed is this: is the gendered nature of Machiavelli's treatment of *Fortuna* somehow a *product* of his failure to deal adequately with the intersubjectivity of the political realm that is demanded by his commitment to popular sovereignty? We believe it is. The feminine figure of *Fortuna* is more than a literary device used by Machiavelli to demonstrate the unpredictable character of politics, which then sets up this moment of his advice to princes. It is also more than simply an expression of the sexism of Machiavelli's patriarchal society. The gendered violence Machiavelli introduces into his political theory at this moment marks his attempt to find a legitimate place for force and coercion that will complement rather than undermine a political sphere in which "words are enough" to solve problems. What Machiavelli lacks is an adequate purchase on the binding force immanent to words or language use itself, which threatens his particular articulation of the republican rhetorical ideal. His response to *Fortuna* is one possible outcome of this more general deficiency—possible, rather than determinate, because the sexual violence is also historically contingent on the discursive production of sexual difference and the underlying power relations that generate it (Butler 1990; Foucault 1980). Without fully addressing the binding force of language itself in the political realm, Machiavelli displaces the residual violence of his rational speech onto a feminized, irrational other.

Our argument is thus not that Machiavelli's use of the sexual metaphor is entirely contingent on the historical context or, closely related to this, that he adopts it with his intended audience in mind. This would in effect negate the feminist analysis of this figure by treating the sexual violence directed at *Fortuna* as simply a literary device (the view of Balaban 1990). Nor is our position quite the opposite: that this violence is necessarily generated by his failure to think the political in terms other than the instrumental, which, following a Weberian and Freudian reading of Machiavelli, requires that a modern, feminized other be subjected

to a modern, manly *virtù* (see McIntosh 1984, 194–95). Certainly Machiavelli represents a modernizing turn in Western political theory with the
instrumentalism that permits his economy of violence. However, our
considerations above point to Machiavelli's clear commitment to a republican politics of popular sovereignty that relies on the people's capacity
to judge among competing attempts to persuade by the public use of
speech. This cannot be subsumed under an instrumentalist approach.
What we wish to raise instead is the question of a distinct social force that
inheres in language use itself, even in the rational argument preferred for
public decision-making. It is a rather more obscure force than outright
coercion, a force that Machiavelli fails to recognize, and for this reason
allows a violent force to irrupt into his text as his response to *Fortuna*.

As we have seen, Machiavelli implicitly challenges the strict distinction between speech and violence established by the Ciceronian rhetorical inheritance. Cicero distinguishes the virtuous sociality of republican
rule based on rational, eloquent speech from the unnatural social force
of violence that he believes ought not play any role in legitimate public
affairs. Machiavelli undermines this division even while seeking to affirm
the priority of a republican *virtù*. His inclusion of violence in the normal
or ideal public sphere excludes and violently maltreats the identity of
one group that is an interested party of the political society. For how
could women not be part of the social contact and association that, for
Cicero, launches human development toward justice and civilization?
Natural association assumes natural as well as social reproduction. Feminists have long argued that the work of social reproduction done by
women is undervalued and ignored in the history of political thought. So
it is here. Only by explicitly excluding women from the key moments of
social formation (i.e., "It was due entirely to some early men of genius
and wisdom") can this fact be suppressed. By not mentioning or including women in the political participation of city life and its development,
Cicero is thus also implicated in this contradiction of the republican
"reconciliation" of men with men. In Machiavelli's work, the contradiction is given expression directly by the association and comparison of
woman—a gender category, which is not simply a "given"—with the
cycles of irrational, natural violence, an association and comparison that
now invites an equally violent and speechless response.

Recall that Cicero emphasizes the "natural fraternity" of human beings
arising from "teaching and learning, . . . communicating, discussing and
reasoning." With this, Cicero articulates a principle, but also an empiri-

cal observation based in his own historical time, including the interpretation of existing traditions of legal and political thought and practice.
What he seeks to do here is draw on the social power that inheres in these
communicative activities for *politics*—in explicit contrast to violence or
force. This effort receives emphasis by his association of *otium* with the
good order and harmony of the political sphere. It suggests for him the
most compelling account of the social bonding required for stable, cooperative relations among the citizens of a republic. Violence is completely
excluded from this bonding activity. It is thus because women do not yet
participate equally in the political realm, despite being equally involved
in "natural" social formation and being able in principle to be party to
"teaching and learning, . . . communicating, discussing and reasoning,"
that a certain violence of exclusion is enacted. Machiavelli aggravates
this violent exclusion to the extent that women's possible protests against
or resistance to the political power of men should in fact be opposed with
strategic violence. For if woman may be legitimately likened to a raging
torrent or irrational force of nature—with all the disruptive and destructive social effects this implies—then accordingly she may be beaten into
submission when she challenges the proper order of the affairs of man.
Here Machiavelli undermines the rhetorical republican ideal most directly.

Speech, Power, and the Social Bond

Yet the republican rhetorical tradition, as represented here by Cicero and
Machiavelli, may not be entirely discredited by this feminist critique. The
importance of a "natural fraternity" immanent to the use of speech and
reason, which forms the philosophical core of Cicero's political view,
represents a social power that is in principle inclusive of all full citizens
of the city. The universal orientation that can be found here in the communicative power of speech and reason has been taken up again recently
by Jürgen Habermas and it is worthwhile to consider the intersection of
his thought with this aspect of the rhetorical tradition and the problems
under consideration.[1] For Habermas, communicative power resides in
the socially "bonding or binding" effect that coordinates the speech of
speakers and hearers when they raise and redeem validity claims in
linguistically mediated communication that is oriented toward mutual

understanding and agreement. The communicative aspect of the republican rhetorical tradition that sought to identify the specific political brotherhood forged by the public use of speech and reason finds an equivalent in Habermas's theory of the socially bonding power of language use. This universal operation of language use claims at least a gender-neutral possibility that might provide a corrective to the exclusions and violence articulated by Cicero and Machiavelli.[2]

Without reconstructing Habermas's position in detail, we may summarize the aspects of his approach relevant to our concerns. In short, Habermas's claim is that speech is always also an action (following the speech pragmatics of J. L. Austin and John Searle, among others), and that the communicative content enacts a special motivation to produce or reproduce shared worlds of knowledge, meaning, and valid norms. Following a theme central to the tradition of rhetoric, an utterance can be said to "do" something when it achieves a material effect on its audience—powerful oratory persuades listeners to accept a speaker's views, to follow voluntarily rules made by others, and so forth. Put simply, the general notion of the material power of language use is taken up in various ways in twentieth-century pragmatic linguistic philosophy as a universal aspect of speech action. Speaking and hearing both "do" things under the dynamic conditions of language use. The most important material effect that interests Habermas is the distinctive rational bonding capacity of language use. This effect is achieved precisely through the structure and practice of intersubjective recognition of claims to validity. Formal recognition of validity claims occurs today most clearly in academic argumentative discourse, where the responsibility for proposing valid claims and responding rationally is ostensibly most pure. But this recognition of and responsibility for validity is also found in communicative exchange at the level of everyday speech. Everyday action within a communicative context always requires some interpretive effort—negotiations of shared meaning, assessment of the action context, selection of appropriate norms of behavior, and so forth. It is because at a crucial level all human communicative expression requires interpretation that Habermas can claim that the dynamics of language use deserve a central place in any account of social power. In short, the constant and "natural" need for interpretation always involves speakers and hearers in an ongoing process of raising and redeeming validity claims that constitutes the material substrate of language use. Intersubjective recognition via language is part and parcel of the processes of social reproduction at the levels of individual and collective in the human "lifeworld" itself (and indeed cannot be avoided by a speaker without risking individual pathologies associated with his or her removal of social interaction as such) (Habermas 1984; Habermas 1992, 149–204).

The rational assumption of the validity claim is that reasons must always be able to be given that demonstrate the validity of a claim to the satisfaction of all those concerned. Recognizing a validity claim thus entails that, in principle, valid reasons can be given and, further, that both speaker and hearer, in principle, are able to agree that the conditions for a claim's validity have been satisfied. This is the meaning of the binding rational nature of communicative action:

> A speaker can *rationally motivate* a hearer to accept his speech act offer because—on the basis of an internal connection among validity, validity claim, and redemption of a validity claim—he can assume the *warranty* [*Gewähr*] for providing, if necessary, convincing reasons that would stand up to a hearer's criticism of the validity claim. Thus a speaker owes the binding (or bonding: *bindende*) force of his illocutionary act not to the validity of what is said, but to *the coordinating effect of the warranty* that he offers: namely, to redeem, if necessary, the validity claim raised with his speech act. (Habermas 1984, 302)

The binding/bonding power of communicative action is drawn from the "illocutionary force" identified by speech act theory that is brought into play in the linguistically mediated action of reaching understanding and agreement. Habermas wishes to place at center stage the rational force of argumentation as that which offers a better orientation for political rule (and, more broadly, participation) than nonargumentative forms such as mere coercion or outright violence. Argumentation, Habermas writes, "sets in motion a *co-operative* competition for the better argument" where "the goal of a communicatively reached agreement unites the participants from the outset" (Habermas 1998, 44).

In a parallel to the classical view of the incommensurability of rational discussion and force, such communicative power is to be sharply distinguished from strategic or instrumental power. Strategic or instrumental action is oriented to the egological success of the speaker rather than the mutual understanding and agreement of speaker and hearer, and thus seeks to coordinate action through empirical rather than normative effects. Action oriented toward success is empirical because a speaker achieves his or her effect on the hearer through sanctions, threat or reward, manipulation, coercion, or violence. The bonds established through such action cannot be motivated by the acceptance or rejection of claims to validity (what Habermas means by rational motivation) but only by inducement or coercion (the empirical). By contrast, communicative action coordinates speakers and hearers normatively by enjoining them in a practical, cooperative effort aimed at reaching consensuses—and such consensuses can concern the existence of objective facts about the world, appropriate norms of intersubjective relations, or the sincerity of subjective expressions (relating to the three "worlds" of human experience) (Habermas 1987, 113–97). Rational motivation, distinguished from empirical motivation, thus relies on this special force of validity, which Habermas sees as the essential power underlying the democratic polity and the basis for his faith in the possibilities of popular self-government (Habermas 1997).

This indicates an important similarity between Habermas's approach to the distinction between speech and coercion and that found in the rhetorical republicanism of Cicero and Machiavelli. From a Habermasian perspective, however, the problem of *Fortuna* can be addressed through the recognition of the contingency of *all* valid claims, which is meant to apply just as much to claims about the objective world ("nature") as the social and subjective worlds. In the absence of natural law or metaphysical or religious foundations for determining the validity of knowledge about the world or the validity of law, knowledge and law must acquire validity from the actions of the people who come to respect or hold the beliefs of the laws. In the rhetorical republican tradition, the people recognize the validity of the law with the guidance supplied by great statesmen. This guidance must be ongoing precisely because all action is open-ended and any established or existing conditions may change, sometimes without warning. Thus there must be an *actual* achievement of agreement among the people, not simply a de facto agreement. A de facto agreement or assent from the people may be imposed through coercion or manipulation; what is important in the rhetorical tradition is that the people be *convinced* through speech and reason. Now, the nature of this conviction differs in significant ways from the kind of conviction attached to the recognition of validity claims theorized by Habermas. However, what we wish to draw attention to here is only the clear difference between a de facto or forced agreement and one that is achieved through the liberty of the people (in the ancient sense). The very possibility of *reaching* consensuses rationally rather than simply attaining or reproducing them through strategic or instrumental action assumes a contingency and indeterminacy to human affairs that requires the active, free participation of the people. Consensus in this sense is not undermined by the contingency of validity; indeed, it presupposes it.

Fortuna cannot be convinced like rational human beings because she is a natural force external to human affairs. Machiavelli believes men must treat natural contingency forcefully since they cannot reason with the blind, irrational violence of "wild" nature. Yet men may also reason together about the facts of "wild" nature, and agree among themselves as to what may be the best course of action to deal with a natural challenge given the available knowledge. This kind of reasoning, whether guided by a great statesman or not, is just what citizens are intended to do when speech and reason are used to decide on or assent to appropriate laws. The illegitimate move Machiavelli makes is precisely assimilating natural contingency to social and political contingency, which allows him to treat all in the same way. Contingency and indeterminacy need not be dealt with by collective aggression embodied in the state if such factors are recognized among the very *conditions* of rational decision-making mediated by speech.

The unpredictability and contingency of political affairs can in this way present itself as a happy situation—even though actual outcomes may produce calamity and suffering for some—because the fact of uncontrollable future states of affairs *demands* ongoing discussion, argument, and contestation on the part of citizens in a republic (or, in Habermas's case, a constitutional democracy). There is no good reason, from a republican or a Habermasian perspective, why the existence of unpredictable and uncontrollable events requires *only* a strategic, violent response. In particular cases, such a response may be appropriate, but it would be a course of action to which all citizens should be a party. In other words, a distinction must be drawn between the advent of unpredictable, sometimes disruptive or violent occurrences in *nature* and those that have *social* origins. Machiavelli already approves of the intermittent venting of the polity's "ill humors" in the conflict of plebeian and noble classes from which the Roman republic drew strength. While there may be no way to avoid calculated, strategic violence when faced with a real or potential natural event that poses a threat, the possibility of threats to "maintaining one's state" presented by social forces can, in principle, always be addressed through decision-making processes based on speech and reason, or, in Habermas's vocabulary, rational discussion oriented toward agreement. The difference between natural and social unpredictability is a distinction Machiavelli does not draw sharply enough, but it is decisive in order to adequately account for intersubjective and intergroup relations in a republican polity.

The conclusion with respect to our discussion of Machiavelli and his antifeminist treatment of *Fortuna*, therefore, is that there is also no good reason why women should necessarily be equated with irrational, unpredictable violence according to the rhetorical republican model. For even if women raise issues disturbing or disruptive to the settled virtues established in the republican polity, such disturbances and disruptions ought to be treated at least in the same way as Machiavelli treats the "tumults" of class conflict: as a healthy, appropriate aspect of republican rule.

Notes

1. There are, of course, substantial differences between classical republicanism's privileging of rhetoric and Habermas's modern approach to argumentation, public debate, and deliberation. In particular, the stress on the emotional effects of rhetorical acts that one finds in Machiavelli's *Discourses* is clearly at odds with the cognitive value of rational deliberation in Habermas's model. Without denying the importance of such differences in any detailed consideration of the two positions, we wish to set these aside for the purposes of the present chapter in order to focus on our central contrast of reasoned speech and violence. Further research is needed concerning the material effects of language use in order to draw out and assess these differences and contrasts between classical rhetoric and modern deliberative models.

2. See Nancy Fraser, *Unruly Practices: Power, Discourse, and Gender in Contemporary Social Theory* (Minneapolis: University of Minnesota Press, 1989), 113–87, for a sympathetic feminist critique of Habermas that also attempts to develop Habermasian themes useful to feminism.

References

Balaban, Oded. 1990. "The Human Origins of *Fortuna* in Machiavelli's Thought." *History of Political Thought* 11: 21–36.

Butler, Judith. 1990. *Gender Trouble: Feminism and the Subversion of Identity*. New York: Routledge, 1990.

Cicero, Marcus Tullius. 1913. *De officiis*. Ed. Walter Miller. Cambridge, Mass.: Harvard University Press.

———. 1928. *De legibus*. Ed. C. W. Keyes. Cambridge, Mass.: Harvard University Press.

————. 1942. *De oratore*. Ed. E. W. Sutton and Harris Rackham. Cambridge, Mass.: Harvard University Press.

————. 1949. *De inventione*. Ed. H. M. Hubbell. Cambridge, Mass.: Harvard University Press.

————. 1958. *Pro Sestio*. Ed. R. Gardner. Cambridge, Mass.: Harvard University Press.

Cumming, Robert Denoon. 1969. *Human Nature and History*. 2 vols. Chicago: University of Chicago Press.

Elshtain, Jean Bethke. 1981. *Public Man, Private Woman: Women in Social and Political Thought*. Princeton: Princeton University Press.

Foucault, Michel. 1980. *The History of Sexuality*. Vol. 1. New York: Vintage Books.

Fraser, Nancy. 1989. *Unruly Practices: Power, Discourse, and Gender in Contemporary Social Theory*. Minneapolis: University of Minnesota Press.

Habermas, Jürgen. 1984. *The Theory of Communicative Action*. Vol. 1. Trans. Thomas McCarthy. Boston: Beacon Press.

————. 1987. *The Theory of Communicative Action*. Vol. 2. Trans. Thomas McCarthy. Boston: Beacon Press.

————. 1992. *Post-Metaphysical Thinking: Philosophical Essays*. Cambridge: MIT Press.

————. 1997. "Popular Sovereignty as Procedure." In *Deliberative Democracy: Essays on Reason and Politics*, ed. James Bohman and William Rehg. Cambridge: MIT Press.

————. 1998. *The Inclusion of the Other: Studies in Political Theory*. Trans. William Rehg. Cambridge: MIT Press.

Hulliung, Mark. 1983. *Citizen Machiavelli*. Princeton: Princeton University Press.

Kahn, Victoria. 1994. *Machiavellian Rhetoric*. Princeton: Princeton University Press.

Machiavelli, Niccolò. 1965. *The Chief Works and Others*. 3 vols. Trans. Allan Gilbert. Durham: Duke University Press.

McIntosh, Donald. 1984. "The Modernity of Machiavelli." *Political Theory* 12: 184–203.

Nederman, Cary J. 2000. "Rhetoric, Reason, and Republic: Republicanisms—Ancient, Medieval, and Modern." In *Renaissance Civic Humanism: Reappraisals and Reflections*, ed. James Hankins. Cambridge: Cambridge University Press.

Nederman, Cary J., and Tatiana V. Gomez. 2002. "Between Republic and Monarchy? Liberty, Security, and the Kingdom of France in Machiavelli." *Midwest Studies in Philosophy* 26: 82–93.

Patch, Howard R. 1922. *The Tradition of the Goddess Fortuna in Medieval Philosophy and Literature*. Smith College Studies in Modern Languages, vol. 3, no. 4. Northampton, Mass.: Smith College.

Pitkin, Hannah Fenichel. 1984. *Fortune Is a Woman: Gender and Politics in the Thought of Niccolò Machiavelli*. Berkeley and Los Angeles: University of California Press.

Rebhorn, Wayne A. 1988. *Foxes and Lions: Machiavelli's Confidence Men*. Ithaca: Cornell University Press.

Vatter, Miguel E. Forthcoming. "Fortuna in the Republican Tradition of Politics." In *Lessico Repubblicano*, ed. Maurizio Viroli.

Viroli, Maurizio. 1998. *Machiavelli*. Oxford: Oxford University Press.

Wood, Neal. 1988. *Cicero's Social and Political Thought*. Berkeley and Los Angeles: University of California Press.

10

Beyond *Virtù*

John Juncholl Shin

In the *Florentine Histories*, Machiavelli offers the following critique of the leaders of Florence, couched as an opinion voiced by the Florentine citizens after a military defeat:

> Look at how their advice has been exposed and to what end they were moving: not to defend freedom, which is their enemy, but to increase their own power, which [*Dio*] has justly diminished. They have burdened the city not only with this campaign but with many, because the one against King Ladislas was like this

one. To whom will they now turn for help? To Pope Martin, who
was torn apart by them out of regard for Braccio? To Queen Giovanna, whom by abandoning they had made to throw herself into
the lap of the king of Aragon? (*Florentine Histories*, 151–52; hereafter *FH*)[1]

By satirically postulating that the leaders could now turn for help to other
presumably ineffectual leaders such as Pope Martin and Queen Giovanna
of Naples, Machiavelli implies that the leaders have become less than a
pope or a woman. The use of Pope Martin in this passage is consistent
with Machiavelli's critique of the Vatican as an incompetent principality
that causes trouble for its neighbors and is responsible for the chaos in
Italy (e.g., *PD*, 149–53). The use of Queen Giovanna in this passage is
consistent with Machiavelli's caution against women in politics (e.g., *PD*,
188–89).

    However, on a deeper level, Machiavelli's discussion of Queen Gio-
vanna isn't about women at all. Rather, it is about defining the contours
of masculinity while claiming to criticize women. To Machiavelli, Queen
Giovanna is not a historical reality but a rhetorical device. For starters,
her presence in this passage, and in other places in the *Florentine Histories*, creates a puzzle. By Machiavelli's own accounts, Queen Giovanna was
far from being an ineffectual leader whose incompetence caused trouble
for her own state and for Italy. Rather, she was a skillful leader and diplomat. She retained control of Naples when her soldiers switched their
loyalty to her husband (*FH*, 48). When her army deserted her because of
her disagreement with the pope, she manipulated the kings of Aragon
and France into letting her use their forces (*FH*, 48–49, 136). This was
quite a feat of diplomacy, since, unlike other states that relied on foreign
powers and auxiliary forces, Naples remained independent and relatively
prosperous during Giovanna's reign. She didn't fail her people when she
chose to "throw herself into the lap of the king of Aragon." Instead of
being a misguided move arising from desperation, her tactic was a shrewd
response to the harsh realities of Italian politics and positioned Naples as
a key element in the Italian balance of power. Her diplomatic balancing
act was so superb, in fact, that her death caused an immediate eruption
of warfare in Italy among powers vying for her territory (*FH*, 190ff.). Not
only should Machiavelli have commended her as a successful example of
a prince who maintained her *stato* (see Hexter 1973), but he also could
have used her as an example of an audacious actor who fought against

Fortuna. She was a true prince with *virtù*, embodying all the qualities of "masculine" excellence necessary for success.

Why, then, does Machiavelli use Queen Giovanna as a symbol for ineffective leadership? From one vantage point, obviously, Machiavelli's distrust of women leads him to miss out on an opportunity to demonstrate the intricacies of *virtù* by pointing to Giovanna's skills and audacity. We can easily add Machiavelli to the long list of political theorists who rendered their visions inconsistent and perhaps even invalid by writing off one half of the human population. From another, however, the damage done to *virtù* through his neglect of Giovanna is intolerable even from Machiavelli's own perspective. What message are we to get from Machiavelli's story of a woman who had the qualities Machiavelli advocates in *The Prince,* which led to action, achievement, authenticity, and success—qualities that Machiavelli associates with the word *virtù*—who is then criticized as not good enough? What are men, Machiavelli's intended readers, to do if on the one hand they are told to be *virtuosi* but then are told that *virtù* makes them only as good as a contemptible woman? Machiavelli's message must go beyond *virtù* itself to be internally consistent, and his misogyny may have a systematic role after all.

In this chapter I will argue, first of all, that Machiavelli's discussions of women are not about women at all, but about qualities a man should have, or "masculinity." I believe the examples Machiavelli makes of Giovanna and similar women in history directly serve his overall project of defining masculine citizenship. Second, I will argue that Machiavelli's masculinity does not only entail activity, achievement, authenticity, and success—again, *virtù*—but also passivity, dependence, and abstractness, qualities I call "functionality," because Machiavelli believes that men must function in the name and service of an abstraction outside themselves. In the following section, I will define functionality-as-masculinity through a discussion of masculine abstraction framed by object relations theory and through a brief reading of Descartes. Next I will read *The Prince* and Machiavelli's short story *Belfagor* from the perspective of ordinary men, the intended readers of *Belfagor.* This will show that the heroes of *The Prince* and *Belfagor* are special not in their possession of *virtù*, but in their willingness to act as passive servants of the nation. I will then conclude with a discussion of women in Machiavelli's writings to show that they are, in the end, men in disguise, serving as examples of people who had *virtù* but did not use it functionally, and are therefore detestable and "effeminate" in Machiavelli's view.[2]

By distinguishing between *virtù* and functionality, I depart from the bulk of the literature on Machiavelli and masculinity, which focuses on *virtù* as the sole encapsulation of Machiavelli's masculine ideal. Hanna Fenichel Pitkin provides the most complex and comprehensive represen- tation of this view in *Fortune Is a Woman*. Pitkin examines the competing images of the fox, the lion, the founder, and the citizen, the last being the most feasible and desirable in Machiavelli's view:

> Although the Citizen is, like the fox and the Founder, an image of manhood, it embodies *virtù* in a fundamentally different way. For, both fox and Founder have *virtù* through their personal, indi- vidual autonomy, understood as needing no others, having ties to no others, acting without being acted upon. For the Citizen, by contrast, *virtù* is sharing a collective autonomy, a collective free- dom and glory, yet without loss of individuality. *Virtù* is systemic or relational. Thus it not merely is compatible with, but logically requires, interaction in mutuality with others like oneself. (Pitkin 1984, 81)

Pitkin's conception of citizenly *virtù* requires a transcendence into collec- tive life without the negation of the individual (282). *Virtù* is necessarily an individual quality as well as a collective achievement.

Functionality, unlike citizenship, however, requires the negation of individual life, including citizenly *virtù*, and places the abstract needs of the collectivity above all other concerns. There are residual benefits of functionality such as glory and the satisfaction that comes with success. Yet, in the end, Machiavelli demands the absolute sacrifice of the individ- ual for the sake of the collectivity not as a concrete collection of individ- ual actors but as an abstraction that wills and acts independently of its constituent parts. Within functionality and within the abstract collectiv- ity served by functionality, citizenship is not possible. Indeed, individual action and individual qualities are irrelevant in consideration of func- tionality; functionality is not an extension of *virtù*, but an entirely sepa- rate criterion for masculinity. "Effeminacy," or the failure to be fully masculine, then, entails not the failure to acquire *virtù*, but the failure to understand this vision of abstract collectivity, the inability to accept the almost divine, independent, and transcendent existence of the collectiv- ity as such.

A Critique of Masculinity

This chapter builds on feminist critiques of political theory that use object relations theory to locate in male sexuality certain problematic elements of political identity. These elements can be collectively called "abstraction," the tendency of male political theorists to argue that political subjectivity must entail the separation of the subject from the object, the masculine from the feminine, the action from the body, and so forth. Object relations theory postulates that this stems from the way differentiation—the process of acquiring gender identity—takes place when the primary caretaker is a woman. In such a condition, a boy must come to equate his gender identity with the separation from and opposition to "the other," creating the need to deny his own body so that his dependence on his caretaker can be denied. This also creates the need to define himself as a "subject" in opposition to the "object" world. Jane Flax, in particular, argues that this tendency shows up in Descartes' denial of the body and social interaction in his epistemology, and in the absence of childhood, a state of dependence, in the "State of Nature" theories of Hobbes and Locke (Flax 1980). Jessica Benjamin takes a further step in pointing to men's need for separation and clear boundaries to explain Hegel's exposition of master-slave relationships and Weber's concept of "rational violence" (Benjamin 1980).

I will address two difficulties with this object relations approach. First is the fact that there is no single masculinity. Notions of masculinity vary from culture to culture and time to time, and masculine abstraction may be a phenomenon specific to modern Western European cultures and other cultures influenced by them. As Nancy Chodorow concedes in *Feminism and Psychoanalytic Theory*, arguments about sexuality resting on the structure of women-as-primary-caretaker, an almost universal phenomenon, have never been adequate (Chodorow 1989, 6–8). We need also to account for the ways in which different cultural and institutional structures result in different masculine and feminine identities. If object relations theory is to realize its strengths as an explanatory theory, we must take note of its very premise, that individual development occurs in relation to and interaction with others. Accounting for the development of masculine identity, then, requires accounting for the context of the psychological process, and is therefore as much a historical and anthropological task as it is a psychoanalytic task (e.g., Pitkin 1984, 173–229). I hope to contribute to this development by pointing to the fact that in Machiavelli we see not one but three different images of masculinity: 1) the image of Christian-moral-virtuous man, quickly dismissed and denounced by Machiavelli as weak and "effeminate"; 2) the image of Roman Republican citizen-soldier-statesman hailed by Machiavelli and encapsulated in the word *virtù*, an image that, unfortunately for Machiavelli, is imaginary and extinct; and, finally, 3) the image of functional-abstract masculinity that emerges in Machiavelli's attempt to reinstate the Roman image. The presence of these competing images of masculinity suggests that Renaissance Florence in Machiavelli's time marks a moment of transition in concepts of masculinity. Thus, the modern Western concept of masculinity is a historical product rather than a structural necessity.

The second difficulty with object relations theory is its focus on the instability of masculine identity, captured especially in Benjamin's description of violence, sexual or rational, as an unstable ego's tantrumatic test for boundaries (Benjamin 1980, 59–64). Compelling as Benjamin's argument may be, it does not satisfactorily explain why abstract rationality remains so deeply entrenched. It is one thing to say that these troubled, tantrumatic, violent souls find some solace through the exclusion of women from the public spheres. It is quite another to account for the fact that men seem to deal with one another in the public spheres with some degree of peace and harmony, and then return home to the private spheres in which they are entirely dependent on women's work and emotional support. If we focus on abstract rationality as an individuating tendency, a force that separates men from women and men from men, we arrive at an image of the social/epistemological world in which men are always at war. This is not a satisfactory image in that 1) the modern world isn't always in a state of war; and 2) no men—no one—would want to remain in such a state. Men would soon opt for a way out, even if this process entailed the abandonment of individuality, rationality, and separation. Something in the public sphere must also supply enough solace so that, for the most part, their psyches remain at peace.

The desire to opt out of the individuated world of masculine abstraction can be clearly seen in Descartes' infamous *Discourse on Method*, the treatise that postulates the existence of *cogito*, the independent, disembodied generator/holder of knowledge. As Jane Flax points out, *cogito* is the purest instance of masculine abstract rationality, acting in the absence of a viable physical reality, without sensory perceptions worthy of trust, and without the need for nourishment or companionship (Flax 1980, 27; see also Harding 1986, 133). Everything must be denied—even the existence of other human beings and of the world—save for the existence of a thinking, knowable self. *Cogito* can thus think, know, and exist in the absence of any other being, physical or otherwise, and is secure in the safety of absolute independence and isolation.

Cogito can do so, that is, with the glaring, and often underexamined, exception of his dependence on God:

> Following this, reflecting on the fact that I had doubts, and that consequently my being was not completely perfect, for I saw clearly that it was a greater perfection to know than to doubt, I decided to inquire whence I had learned to think of some thing more perfect than myself; and I clearly recognized that this must have been from some nature which was in fact more perfect . . . ; and because it is no less contradictory that the more perfect should proceed from and depend on the less perfect, than it is that something should emerge out of nothing, I could not hold it from myself; with the result that it remained that it must have been put into me by a being whose nature was truly more perfect than mine and which even had in itself all the perfections of which I could have any idea, that is to say, in a single word, which was God. (Descartes 1968, 54–55)

Bear in mind that *cogito*'s declaration of "I think, therefore I am" (53) follows a state of despair, the state of radical doubt, which *continues* after this declaration. To know without doubt of one's existence was just the beginning of a solution to the dilemma that, once in denial of his corporeal-sensory reality, *cogito* was completely lost and without the ability to know anything at all. Therefore, *cogito* had to face the fact that his quest for certainty—analogous to a boy's quest for individuated identity—had landed him on a path to nowhere—analogous to a boy's abstracted, tantrumatic state of war. *Cogito* longs for an escape from this world of instability, and this longing is fulfilled by the presumed existence of a being that originated this longing, or God.

Furthermore, God's gift of *cogito* isn't for Descartes' exclusive use. The ability to know of God's perfection and "to be myself infinite, eternal, immutable, omniscient, all-powerful, and finally to have all the perfections that I could observe to be in God" (56) is shared among *all* rational beings—the operative phrases are "we," "our mind," and "our use" (80). While Descartes fundamentally remains skeptical of other individuals' ability and willingness to correctly acquire *cogito* (77, 81–87), *cogito* offers the best hope yet of communicating and cooperating with other individuals. In fact, Descartes needs others more than ever, and desires "to show in [this treatise] so clearly the use the public could derive from it, that I would oblige all those who wish for the general well-being of men, that is to say, all those who are truly virtuous and not simply in appearance or who merely profess to be so, both to *communicate* to me the experiments they have already made and to *help* me to investigate those which remain to be done" (81; my emphases). Once the other knowers also acquire *cogito*, and thus have faith in God, they no longer threaten Descartes' ability to know the truth. With God's mediation, knowledge can be shared across individuals with *cogito*, and knowledge can be accumulated over time. Rather than an isolated, lonely creature, *cogito* is a social animal; he needs communication and cooperation to expand his knowledge. What is more, *cogito* can come to terms with his own mortality, and his need for the others can be regrounded in his physical reality.

> The other reason which has compelled me to put pen to paper is that, becoming daily more and more conscious of the delay which my plan of self-instruction is suffering, owing to the vast number of experiments which I need to make, and which it is impossible for me to do without help from others, although I do not flatter myself so much as to hope that the public will take a great share in my interests, I am yet unwilling to default so much in my own cause, as to give those who will *survive* me reason to reproach me one day for not having left them many things in a much better state than I have done, if I had not too much neglected to acquaint them of the ways in which they could have contributed to my designs. (88–89; my emphasis)

Corporeal reality, even death, no longer threatens *cogito*'s quest for perfection, and men can now not only safely converse with one another, but also safely come home to the dinners prepared by their mothers and wives. *Cogito*'s mortality, and the vastness of God's truth, makes the need for cooperation all the more urgent. Thus, while abstraction forces *cogito* into a state of absolute isolation and despair, it also presents the solution in the guise of an absolute knower, God, whose grandness in fact makes collective knowledge mandatory. Even the seemingly individualist, self-sufficient *cogito* must function in service of an abstract knower, and without this functional relationship to God collective knowledge is not possible.

In contrast to object relations theory's argument, Descartes' epistemology does not end with the isolated, lonely world of *cogito* in denial of everything. Through *cogito*'s forlorn denial, Descartes comes into communion with God; then, through *cogito*'s trust in God, Descartes comes into contact with the other knowers. Descartes' final aim is therefore not isolation as such, but a special kind of social epistemology that can be achieved through isolation and abstraction, a conception of knowledge as a collective enterprise undertaken by individuals abstracted from their physical existence. *Cogito* is so abstracted and so dependent on God, in fact, that these individuals can ignore and be safe from their physical existence. Knowledge, then, exists outside these individuals, and can be kept safe from mortality. Without this abstract community of knowers, knowledge perishes with the individual. With an abstract community of knowers, however, knowledge is permanent and progressive.

Similarly, believing *virtù* alone cannot be the path to greatness, Machiavelli introduces *Dio*, an absolute deity, and the nation, a unit of collective action. *Dio* is the patron deity of the nation; the nation is a collection of human beings special in its ability to shape history, much as Descartes' rational science is capable of shaping knowledge. So long as action, statecraft, and history remain the arenas of individual action, Machiavelli believes, nothing worthy of note will ever be done, for all individuals, acting alone or together, are subject to the whims of their circumstances, or *Fortuna*. Through his trust in *Dio*, Machiavelli attempts to make human action meaningful and accumulative, just as Descartes makes human knowledge meaningful and accumulative through his trust in God. To this end, of course, even *virtù* is not an absolute ideal but an instrumental skill that must be deployed or not deployed as demanded by circumstances.

One of the difficulties of feminism has been to pry men out of the comfortable positions of power they have held. I believe object relations theory is a useful tool in explaining to men that their positions are not very comfortable after all. Yet object relations theory is not a sufficient tool to convince men to yield, because their position is far more comfortable than the theories of ego-boundary instability suggest. My exposition of Machiavelli is intended to break through this deadlock and reach at the very source of men's resistance to change—to explain why men feel frustrated and complain about the pain of being male and yet would not give up any of it at any price. Many have condemned Machiavelli for his denial of Christian-moral virtues, and have seen in his *virtù* either heartless, instrumentalist monstrosity or an unattainable ideal (Skinner 1981, 1; Brown 1988, 86–90; Pitkin 1984, 281–82). Yet men seem to have settled in comfortably with their role as functional dependents of abstract collectivities that dispense political power. Men hold power not because of their independence, but because of their dependence on the abstract actor. I call this state of dependence "functionality." Functionality, not *virtù*, defines masculinity in Machiavelli's writings, and defines male privilege in the modern world.

The Prince and Belfagor

My search for masculine functionality begins with *Belfagor*, which provides a counternarrative to *The Prince*. The plot of *Belfagor* can be broken down into three parts. In the first part, Belfagor, the arch-devil, is dispatched to Florence by Lucifer to verify the claims made by men coming to the underworld that their corruption is due to marriage. There, he marries Onesta Donati, who abuses Belfagor to no end and bankrupts him through her spending habits and her brothers' incompetence. Belfagor is finally forced to flee Florence in fear of creditors. In the second part, Belfagor meets Gianmatteo, an ordinary farmer, and promises him wealth in return for hiding Belfagor from the creditors. Gianmatteo helps Belfagor, who rewards Gianmatteo through a scheme of deception. Belfagor possesses daughters of rich families so that Gianmatteo might perform some perfunctory exorcist rituals, whereupon Belfagor leaves them and Gianmatteo collects the exorcist's fees. Belfagor then considers his debt to Gianmatteo repaid and tells Gianmatteo never to interfere with his future ventures. In the third part, however, instead of returning to the underworld with his findings, Belfagor possesses the daughter of the King of France. The king uses his power to enlist Gianmatteo's service with the threat of death. Gianmatteo appeals to Belfagor to save his life, but Belfagor refuses. Here, Gianmatteo comes into his own and devises a plan to save his life and defeat the arch-devil. He creates a large spectacle in the city square, with the Belfagor-possessed princess as the centerpiece.

Then, with a terrible din that startles Belfagor, Gianmatteo announces that Onesta, Belfagor's wife, is coming to get him, and Belfagor flees to the underworld in terror. Gianmatteo returns home, richer and quite proud of his victory.

The explicit message of *Belfagor* is that the men were right, that women do corrupt men and are sources of evil in this world. Yet Onesta's extraordinary evil and Belfagor's extraordinary flair for self-defeat suggest that the moral of the story, in fact, concerns not the evils of women, but the folly of the likes of Belfagor. In his retreat home, Belfagor carries with him false information concerning women—since not all women are like Onesta—that will result in the vindication of men who, like Belfagor, have no one to blame but themselves. It is clear from the story and the tone of the narration that Belfagor failed not only as a Florentine patriarch and merchant and as a devilish seducer of the innocent, but also in his most important role, as a truth-seeking envoy of the underworld. Belfagor fails as a man because he fails to serve the needs of his nation, and his failure to serve his nation functionally is contrasted with Gianmatteo's ability to do so despite his lack of *virtù*.

One of the striking aspects of *Belfagor* is the similarity Machiavelli creates between Belfagor, the protagonist of *The Prince*, and Lorenzo de' Medici, to whom *The Prince* was eventually dedicated.[3] If Lorenzo was to take comfort in *The Prince*'s praise of an instrumentalist, realist prince, *Belfagor* presents a similar character in Belfagor, but this time as a loser. Belfagor appears in Florence with impressive wealth and a large entourage in tow, and such was Lorenzo's triumphant return to Florence. Belfagor claims to be a native of a foreign land, Spain, whence Lorenzo's auxiliary allies came. Belfagor's wealth is of artificial origins, created not by his efforts but by the power of the underworld. Lorenzo's power rested upon his family's wealth and power and the support of foreign armies, not upon his own doings. Furthermore, like the prince of *The Prince*, Belfagor has no regard for morality. Not only does he flee the town to escape his financial responsibility, but he recruits the initially innocent Gianmatteo into an adventure in deception-for-profit. He then repays Gianmatteo by tricking him into an impossible situation. Belfagor is the ultimate fox, even more dangerous because, as a devil, he has the power of the lion as well.[4] Yet this foxy nature leads to Belfagor's own defeat, as he falls into the very trap he set for Gianmatteo. A fox does not a prince make.

Belfagor, as a fox, also understands the importance of spectacle. He squanders a great deal of his wealth "to aim at reputation and consideration among mankind." (*Belfagor*, 15; hereafter *B*) In this Onesta excels, too, as she puts Belfagor through "follies and extravagances into which he ran in order to gratify her taste for dress, and every article of the newest fashion," and, "being resolved not to be outshone by her acquaintance, [Onesta] insisted that [Belfagor] should exceed them all in the richness of their feasts" (*B*, 18). Better yet, it was when Belfagor "began to enter into all the pomps and vanities of the world" that he fell in love with Onesta, allowing himself to be subjected to her abuse (*B*, 15). Belfagor is the most like the instrumentalist-specularist prince of *The Prince* and like Lorenzo at the moment he is the most like, and the most vulnerable to, Onesta. Belfagor's taste for reputation renders him an "effeminate" slave. Even his power to create reputation and illusion renders him a slave. Lorenzo should not expect much more.

The Prince and Gianmatteo

If Belfagor mirrors the ugly side of Lorenzo, Gianmatteo mimics the positive side of the prince. The fact that Gianmatteo faced *Fortuna* squarely and won, of course, is the highlight of his similarity with the prince. Stuck between Belfagor, with his devilish powers, and the king of France, with his earthly powers, Gianmatteo has no easy way out of his situation. Only by thinking for himself and risking his life can he "return triumphantly home" (*B*, 32). Gianmatteo successfully follows *The Prince*'s suggestions to be bold and audacious (*PD*, 94). In this sense, Gianmatteo achieves *virtù* without the specific skills required of the fox and the lion, but still in the way of the fox and the lion, through a brilliant strategy worthy of the ancient greats.

However, if we consider this aspect alone, no real distinction can be made between Gianmatteo's *virtù* and Belfagor's. Belfagor, too, faces *Fortuna* when Onesta squanders his wealth, and when, to make matters worse, his financial ventures with Onesta's brothers result in failure. One might call his flight from Florence a cowardly move, but Belfagor is nonetheless resourceful in his ability to deal with this contingency. If he had not faced *Fortuna* squarely, he would not have recruited Gianmatteo and escaped the creditors' pursuit. This suggests that defying *Fortuna* alone does not make one a "man."

Instead, the real difference between Belfagor and Gianmatteo comes from the source of Gianmatteo's ultimate success: his appeal to the people of France. To expel Belfagor from the princess's body, Gianmatteo asks the king to set up a stage in the town center. The king and other important political and religious figures enter with as much pomp and ceremony as possible, and are seated as the audience. The stage is also surrounded by a great crowd of the ordinary subjects of the king, as well as an army of musicians (B, 28–30). Gianmatteo, in effect, combines all the trappings of a proper political unit into an ad hoc political community. The historical mission of this community is a little silly and temporary—to create noise and spectacle in order to disorient Belfagor just enough to make Gianmatteo's delivery of the punch line effective. Until Gianmatteo declares that Onesta is coming to get Belfagor, the spectacle only amuses Belfagor, making him more resolute. Yet it is important to note that without this community, even if it was a community-as-spectacle, Gianmatteo's plan would not have worked. It is only because this senseless display of community creates mystery and curiosity in Belfagor's mind that the subsequent strike of noise made by the musicians is capable of confusing him. Without Belfagor's attention and curiosity, the noise would have had little effect. Furthermore, without the noise that really startled and confused Belfagor, Gianmatteo's claim that Onesta was coming would have been laughed off. When Gianmatteo landed on the idea of invoking Onesta to remove Belfagor, he must have recognized that the plan was by itself ineffective. Belfagor would have seen through it. Even Onesta's actual presence might not have really frightened him. It was Gianmatteo's genius, therefore, to use the power of public spectacle to turn his clever idea—a personal property—into political power.

Granted, Gianmatteo does little more than stage a show to save the life of a single person—not the princess's, but his own—but Machiavelli's imagery here comes from a more powerful origin. Gianmatteo's stage direction turns a city square with a woman in its center into a symbol of political mobilization. This image comes from no less a source than the legend of the foundation of the Roman Republic, as told by Livy (Livy 1971, 96–101). The legend is that of Lucretia, which also serves as the basis for Machiavelli's play *La Mandragola*. Lucretia, a noblewoman, is raped by the son of a ruthless tyrant of Rome. After exhorting her relatives to take revenge on the tyrant's family,[5] she commits suicide. Her relatives, led by Junius Lucius Brutus, display her fallen body in the public square to mobilize the city against the tyrant, and go on to found the venerable Roman Republic. Albeit in farcical forms, Gianmatteo's little scheme resonates with the image of the Lucretian revolutionaries in one important respect: private tragedy is transformed into a matter of public action. Gianmatteo's solution to his little dilemma is to use forces beyond his own capacity to consolidate the power of the many, and to himself become a leader of this power. He is not only a strategist and a doer: He is also a leader, and a mobilizer of public power. In this regard, Gianmatteo resembles and in fact exceeds the prince of *The Prince*; he is a founder *and* a citizen.

Dio and the Fools

However, there is a catch. Gianmatteo, at the end of *Belfagor*, does not remain in France. He does not remain a public mobilizer, but returns home with the appropriate fees for his service. It is true that his little political community was little more than, literally, a theater, and there was no reason for it to remain in force once Belfagor left. It is also true that Gianmatteo had no interest in staying in France as a citizen or as a founder. He just wanted to save his life and retire in comfort. Yet, we must ask, if Gianmatteo is to be comparable to the prince, why should he be removed from the French pseudo-republic, while the prince seems to go on to bigger and better things? Here we begin to see the problematic nature of the role that both Gianmatteo and the prince play as men.

Chapter 25 of *The Prince*, on *Fortuna*, begins not as a discussion only of the feminine *Fortuna*, but also of the masculine *Dio*: "It is not unknown to me how many have been and are of opinion that worldly events are so governed by [*Fortuna*] and by [*Dio*], that men cannot by their prudence change them, and that on the contrary there is no remedy whatever, and for this they may judge it to be useless to toil much about them, but let things be ruled by chance" (*PD*, 91). Obviously, this opinion annoys Machiavelli. Chapters 24 and 25 are devoted to arguing that successes and failures come not by chance but by the merits and shortcomings of the actors, especially the princes. Chapters 25 ends with the passage on the need to be bold, fierce, and audacious (*PD*, 89–94). However, in all this discussion, "rule by chance" is not personified in both *Fortuna* and *Dio*, as in the opening passage of chapter 25, but only in *Fortuna*.

When Machiavelli mentions two issues and discusses only one, we can

be sure that he will return to the other.[6] *Dio*, in fact, makes his appearance in the next chapter, the final chapter of *The Prince* on the unification of Italy. Here, *Dio* takes on a persona very different from *Fortuna*.
In contrast to *Fortuna*, who is fickle, unreliable, and untrustworthy, *Dio*
presents a sense of purpose. The very idea of the unification of Italy,
Machiavelli argues, is *Dio*'s own design (*PD*, 95). Also, in contrast to
Fortuna, who must be coerced and defied, *Dio* is presented as a force that
cannot and must not be opposed: "Besides this, unexampled wonders
have been seen here performed by [*Dio*], the sea has been opened, a cloud
has shown you the road, the rock has given forth water, manna has
rained, and everything has contributed to your greatness, the remainder
must be done by you. [*Dio*] will not do everything, in order not to deprive
us of free will and the portion of the glory that falls to our lot" (*PD*, 96;
my emphasis). What *Dio* prepares, the prince must finish: He must take
full advantage of the opportunities provided by *Dio*. Here we see that the
prince is but an instrument of *Dio*, and is allowed a degree of independence only as a marginal benefit for his participation in *Dio*'s plan. This
is in stark contrast to the discussion of *Fortuna*, whose will must be bent
to fit the prince's will and who must be seduced by force. The prince is
still exhorted to act, but now he must act not to fulfill his own desires,
but in accord with the will of an entity greater than himself. Masculine
action, therefore, is defined not only by defiance of the feminine, but also
by functional conformity to a greater role, which is *Dio*'s will.

By invoking the Christian deity's name, Machiavelli does not ask the
prince to lead a moral crusade on behalf of the Catholic Church. Far from
it, as the task at hand requires that the power of the Catholic Church be
superseded by the power of Lorenzo's family—not a difficult task given
that the Church is headed by a member of the Medici, a fact noted in
this chapter (*PD*, 95). The supplicant before *Dio*, rather, is the nation of
Italy: "Behold how [Italy] prays [*Dio*] to send some one to redeem her
from this barbarous cruelty and insolence. Behold her ready and willing
to follow any standard if only there be some one to raise it. There is
nothing now she can hope for but that your illustrious house may place
itself at the head of this redemption, being by its power and [*Fortuna*] so
exalted, and being favoured by [*Dio*] and the Church, of which it is now
the ruler" (*PD*, 95). Here Italy becomes the primary abstract actor to
which *Dio* himself, the Medici family, the Catholic Church, and *Fortuna*
become obedient servants. Although *Dio* appears to be the most active
and willful actor, he recognizes the primacy of Italy's wishes. For the sake

of Italy, even *Fortuna* pledges her cooperation. The Catholic Church takes its proper place, not as a renegade principality causing chaos and weakness in Italy, but as a representative of *Dio*'s—and indirectly Italy's—will. As *Dio*'s instrument, and with *Fortuna* and the Catholic Church as his cheerleaders, Lorenzo is the nation's instrument, a mere tool fulfilling Italy's wishes. Lorenzo must obey.

So the prince's seeming passivity and insignificance before *Dio* is linked with the nature of the task. In matters concerning the nation, the prince is a functional tool, not an audacious, willful actor. Likewise, Gianmatteo becomes a hero only so that he can resolve a matter of national emergency. Belfagor's possession of the daughter of the king of France, in contrast to his possession of the daughters of a Florentine merchant and the king of Naples, is a crisis of a political unit greater than a private person or of a small city. In this role as a national hero, however, Gianmatteo and the prince are not to be understood in terms of their private will, but their passivity. Gianmatteo chooses to cooperate with Belfagor in the first two instances of possession, acting as an apprentice fox with fledgling *virtù*. In the last occasion, however, he is forced by the power of the king—with the threat of death—to participate. He recruits the nation to save his life, but, more importantly, Gianmatteo was recruited by the nation first. His heroism—that is, his masculinity—comes from the passivity of his situation. He is not a man until he submits to the nation and performs its will. Belfagor, who acts upon his own will rather than the task assigned to him by his nation, the underworld, is not only a failure, but less than a man, a victim not only of *Fortuna* but also of Onesta, a "mere" woman. Gianmatteo, by contrast, is a hero for having acted upon the will of a nation, but he is also rendered insignificant once the task was completed. He derives personal satisfaction from his success, and his name may be remembered in glory, but the fact remains that he is but a tool, and such satisfaction and glory are a small payment for a job well done, "a portion of the glory that falls to our lot" (*PD*, 96). The ultimate glory and success belong to the nation, not to the heroes. Their role is merely functional.

Therefore, the primary actor of *The Prince* and *Belfagor* alike is the nation, an abstract entity. The heroes, who act seemingly for their own benefit, do so in service of the abstract actor. The heroes' greatness stems from the nation's greatness and the heroes' functional passivity. Machiavelli thus creates a world in which political subjectivity lies primarily with an abstract entity, and only secondarily and indirectly with men.

The difficulty of referring to Italy as if it were a unified actor is obvious throughout *The Prince* where Machiavelli repeatedly makes note of Italy's fragmented state of affairs. Nevertheless, what interests Machiavelli is the creation of such a unified entity in Italy, and this is Lorenzo's task, so that like France, Rome, and other movers of history, Italy, too, can leave its own mark.

So must Lorenzo dedicate himself to following Italy's wishes. His greatness, his success, his boldness, and his audaciousness—everything that makes Lorenzo *virtuoso*—are meaningless unless he uses them for the good of the Italian nation. Lorenzo is a private hero, subject to the whims of *Fortuna*, as long as he acts on his own behalf. Gianmatteo, similarly, is an insignificant nobody if he doesn't put his cleverness toward building the political. It matters not, conversely, how stupid, immoral, and worthless they may be as human beings, as long as Gianmatteo and Lorenzo participate in the greatness of the political. This is the way, and the only way, greatness may be attained. This is the way Gianmatteo may be rendered likeable at all. When Machiavelli says "I love my native city more than my own soul," (*Letters of Machiavelli*, 249) he suggests that he is willing to abandon not only his virtue, and thus his soul, but also his *virtù*, for the sake of Florence, just as Lorenzo is asked to do for Italy and Gianmatteo for France.

Machiavelli thus reconciles the ancient *virtù* of republican soldier-citizen-founders, the heroic and capable men of Greek and Roman legends, with the desperate, ruthless need of his own political reality. The only way men can be considered great is to dedicate their virtue and *virtù* alike to the nation, to be functional as well as *virtuosi*. Otherwise, they may become, like Belfagor, detestable and "effeminate." Better yet, Machiavelli teaches them to be specular, to worry themselves with reputation, to be deceptive, to appear immoral as situations demand, and to wield their power ruthlessly—stripping them of all the qualities that made them admirable, leaving them only with their audaciousness and their destructive powers—so that they may achieve the dream of a unified Italy all the more quickly.

Women's *Virtù*, Lost and Found

We can in this light reevaluate Machiavelli's treatment of Queen Giovanna and other women of history. The irony is that, as I pointed out,

Giovanna is an audacious actor, a true prince, and yet Machiavelli treats what I have described as Giovanna's assets, her ability to maintain the balance of power in Italy in her own and her city's favor, as her liability. It was not enough to Machiavelli that Giovanna was skillful and audacious. Rather than praising her for opposing the pope head on, at a considerable risk to herself and her city (*FH*, 45), Machiavelli criticizes Giovanna on the basis of the *consequences* of her *virtù*. He notes that her death— precisely because of her *virtù*—leads to the eruption of warfare in Italy and eventually to the decline of the stabilizing forces of the peninsula, the Venetian and Florentine Republics (*FH*, 205ff.). It appears as if Giovanna is thus held responsible for events far beyond her control, and far in excess of what Machiavelli requires of any other actors. She receives no credit, but all the blame, for her *virtù*.

Similar patterns emerge from Machiavelli's treatment of other women politicians in the *Florentine Histories*. He blames Queen Rosamund for the fall of the Longobards' hegemony in Italy (*FH*, 18–19), and blames an unnamed Donati widow for the eruption of a Guelf-Ghibelline conflict in Florence (*FH*, 55). In each of these cases, we can with little difficulty find instances of Machiavellian *virtù*, as these women audaciously used deception, conspiracy, specularity, and manipulation to further their own causes. In fact, Queen Rosamund and the Donati widow were both motivated not for their own benefit but the benefit of their greater social units. Rosamund acted for her native nation, which was defeated and absorbed by the Longobards, only to be insulted when her Longobard husband drank out of her father's skull. The Donati widow acted for the consolidation of her family's alliances with other families; she, in a manner of speaking, practically founded the Guelf party (*FH*, 56). These women, even though they were mere matrons and were unable to establish absolute dominion as princes, obviously loved their communities more than themselves.

However, despite their motives, which exceeded mere selfishness, Machiavelli emphasizes the fact that these women's actions, while beneficial to their own clans, engendered chaos in a greater, more abstract unit. The Donati widow's actions, while undoubtedly political and successful as far as her clan was concerned, resulted in factionalism in the greater unit, the city of Florence. Giovanna's actions, while beneficial to her city, resulted in warfare and decline in the greater unit, the nation of Italy. The problem with Rosamund's failure is not her failure in itself, but the consequent loss of Italy's chance at remaining a unified and formidable nation. In every case, the women are blamed not for failing to be *virtuosi* enough,[7] but for sacrificing the greater for the sake of the lesser, for using their *virtù* incorrectly. In this way, Machiavelli's misogyny does not end with a critique of femininity, but refines masculinity by emphasizing the importance of the abstract units rather than that of quality, action, or success. To be unlike these women is to be more masculine, which is to be more like Gianmatteo and less like Belfagor; skill, audaciousness, and all other qualities of *virtù* are unimportant when the consequences of one's actions are concerned. In fact, such qualities must be used, sacrificed, and even abandoned for the sake of the greater. Otherwise, the actor, no matter how *virtuoso*, is rendered "effeminate."

The solution to the puzzle of Giovanna and other *virtuosi* women is this: they are, indeed, *virtuosi*, but they are not fully masculine. Giovanna is perhaps as admirable as any man—willful, successful, and certainly more capable than Gianmatteo, a mere peasant. Giovanna does not even quite fit Machiavelli's claim that women, by arousing men's sexual desires, cause dissention and bring states to ruin (*PD*, 488–89; Pitkin 1984, 110–22); her friends and enemies desired not Giovanna as a sexual object, but her dominion over Naples. To be sure, Giovanna loved her native city as much as Machiavelli loved his, and, in favorable contrast to Machiavelli, could actually bring greatness to her city. Nevertheless, Giovanna failed in one critical sense: she did not serve *Dio*, and hence the nation.

In short, these women, as Machiavelli describes them, are imaginary entities. His portrayals of women serve only as a point of contrast, a "mirror" that reflects only part of ideal masculinity and thereby affirms what the whole of masculinity must be. Machiavelli imbues women with capacity and incapacity in the same way he imbues men with *virtù* and functionality, not as a way of describing women, but as a way of creating men. Thus women only negatively, through their lack, indicate what Machiavelli believes men must have. By attributing women with *virtù*, and then emphasizing their lack of functionality, Machiavelli argues that men must be wary of attaining *virtù* alone, that men must balance their *virtù* and functionality to be considered truly great.

To the extent that Machiavelli wrote *The Prince* to reimagine the citizen-soldier masculinity of the Roman Republic so that his nation could be saved, *The Prince* is a tragedy, a failed attempt to reconstruct masculinity. The same crisis that compelled Machiavelli to recover *virtù* also forces him to then sacrifice his men's individual *virtù* for the sake of political unity. Political actors are allowed to be political, and thereby masculine, only by creating an abstract actor on whose behalf they can act, and for whose sake they must sacrifice themselves. Without a unified Italy, Lorenzo's *virtù* means nothing.

Ultimately, however, men can find comfort by being functional to the abstract actor. This abstract actor, while negating both virtue and *virtù*, provides the political actors with hope, power, future, and an arena of action. The tragedy of *The Prince* is therefore itself the solution to the tragedy of masculinity. The political world occupied by men of virtue and *virtù* is cynical and desperate. By contrast, the political world of functional masculinity is powerful and hopeful. It provides the stability of ego-boundary that is lacking in the tantrum-throwing sadists described by Benjamin. There is no need for men to struggle for ego-boundary stability in Machiavelli's world, which has become our world, because it can be achieved through the total surrender of selfhood.

Some authors writing in the field of men's studies have argued that the idea of patriarchy, of men's power, is a myth. Warren Farrell, in particular, has argued that the disposability of men is a proof that men do not hold power (Farrell 1993). On the contrary, I have shown that, in Machiavelli's writing, disposability, or, more precisely, the ability and willingness to dispose oneself, is a precondition for admittance into positions of masculine power. The difficulties of masculinity—the pain of differentiation, Oedipal struggles, ego-boundary instability, and so forth—are nothing more or less than a hazing process that, under the guise of "making sure that they are masculine enough," ensures that men, once admitted into the circle of power, would be loath to leave. The pain of masculinity is, in turn, only one of many acts of violence committed by the apparatus of masculine power. The state, the military, the family, and other alleged arenas of male disposability are also arenas of patriarchy. These institutions, even when directed against men, are also directed *by* men. Their acts of violence against men, therefore, serve the same purpose as violence against women and other groups constituting "the other." That is, while violence keeps "the other" in positions of subordination, it pressures men to stay within the fold of power as insurance against falling victim to other violence. Once they commit themselves to the power apparatus, men need not fear any longer, much as the prince no longer fears the loss of his virtue, his *virtù*, or even his life once he is ensured a share of the glory of his nation. Of course, such a possibility is closed to "the other." Terror works both ways, but power does not.

The achievement of gender equality therefore requires the dissociation of male identity from masculine-functional identity—the rejection of the argument that being a man necessarily entails functionality and membership. Machiavelli's writings, I have shown, contribute to the construction of male identity as masculine functionality. This is an understandable response to the political and social realities of his time, an attempt to edify and maintain during a time when everything, including Machiavelli's own life, appeared to be falling into chaos. To counter Machiavelli, perhaps, we need to foster an environment for our children—particularly our sons—in which they are protected from masculine hazing and other assaults that create a sense of crisis and instability, the assaults that recreate the *Story of O* in our own homes.

Notes

1. See also *The Prince and The Discourses*, trans. Luigi Ricci (New York: Random House, 1950), 46; hereafter *PD*.

2. In this chapter, the words "maleness" and "femaleness" and their cognates refer to qualities argued to be common (Kantian *Sein*) among individuals who are physically male or female (generally referred to as "sex"). Such qualities can be acquired, inherited, or nascent. The words "masculinity" and "femininity" and their cognates refer to qualities argued to be desirable (Kantian *Sollen*) for individuals who are socially male or female (referred to as "gender"). Feminine qualities may not necessarily be opposed to or exclusive of masculine qualities. By contrast, the word "effeminacy" refers to qualities argued to be opposed to and exclusive of masculine qualities and/or to the state of lacking masculinity. "Effeminate" qualities may not necessarily be compatible with or inclusive of feminine qualities. "Men," "women," "boys," and "girls" refer to gendered individuals, who, of course, may or may not have any, some, or all of these gender-related qualities. The word "virtue" refers to moral-ethical goodness and qualities relating to excellence in a general sense. The word *"virtù"* is used as Machiavelli uses it, generally denoting qualities of masculine excellence, specifically denoting personal qualities relating to the ability to succeed (esp. in the *Florentine Histories*, trans. Lauren F. Banfield and Harvey C. Mansfield Jr. [Princeton: Princeton University Press, 1988]), willingness to act (esp. in *The Prince*), and military skills (esp. in *The Art of War*, in *Chief Works and Others*, ed. and trans. Allan Gilbert, 3 vols. [Durham: Duke University Press, 1989], 1:561–726). It also denotes political leadership and qualifications as a citizen.

3. I use "Lorenzo" to refer to Machiavelli's imagined reader of *The Prince*, and "the prince" to refer to the ideal prince portrayed in *The Prince*. *The Prince* was, in fact, originally addressed to Giuliano de' Medici, the brother of Pope Leo X (Giovanni de' Medici), who had subdued Florence. Giuliano was expected to rule Florence or all of Northern Italy by the Pope's appointment. Machiavelli hoped that Francesco Vettori, employed by the Medici as ambassador to Rome, would show *The Prince* to Giuliano. When Lorenzo de' Medici, Giuliano's nephew, arrived as the ruler of Florence instead, the dedication was changed to Lorenzo, who apparently never would read *The Prince*. See Sebastian de Grazia, *Machiavelli in Hell* (Princeton: Princeton University Press, 1989), 32–44; Max Lerner's introduction to *PD*, xxx. The lesson of this history, as de Grazia points out, is that Machiavelli's advice and exhortations are addressed to the house of Medici as a whole rather than any

individual member that happens to rule Florence (de Grazia 1989, 43). We can likewise assume that anyone who can carry out Machiavelli's hopes in the final chapter of *The Prince* will do—a qualification that Cesare Borgia had so recently failed to fulfill (de Grazia 1989, 43–44; *PD*, 95).

4. See Hanna Fenichel Pitkin, *Fortune Is a Woman* (Berkeley and Los Angeles: University of California Press, 1984), 25–51, for a discussion of Machiavelli's notion of the fox and the lion as imperfect slices of masculinity.

5. To whom, incidentally, Lucretia's husband and Brutus were both related (Titus Livy, *The History of Rome from its Foundation*, Books 1–5, in *The Early History of Rome*, trans. Aubrey de Selincourt [Harmondsworth: Penguin Books, 1971], 72, 96–97).

6. E.g., chapters 12 and 13 on mercenaries and auxiliaries, respectively (*PD*, 44–53).

7. I use the masculine plural here since the point is that, by Machiavelli's standards, these women are, in fact, "man enough" as far as their *virtù* is concerned, and since Machiavelli may take *virtuose* to mean something different.

References

Benjamin, Jessica. 1980. "The Bonds of Love: Rational Violence and Erotic Domination." In *The Future of Difference*, ed. Hester Eisenstein and Alice Jardine, 41–70. New Brunswick, N.J.: Rutgers University Press.

Brown, Wendy. 1988. *Manhood and Politics*. Totowa, NJ: Rowman & Littlefield.

Chodorow, Nancy Julia. 1989. *Feminism and Psychoanalytic Theory*. New Haven: Yale University Press.

De Grazia, Sebastian. 1989. *Machiavelli in Hell*. Princeton: Princeton University Press.

Descartes, René. 1968. *Discourse on Method and the Meditations*. London: Penguin Books.

Farrell, Warren. 1993. *The Myth of Male Power*. New York: Berkley Publishing.

Flax, Jane. "Mother-Daughter Relationships: Psychodynamics, Politics, and Philosophy." In *The Future of Difference*, ed. Hester Eisenstein and Alice Jardine, 20–40. New Brunswick, N.J.: Rutgers University Press.

Harding, Sandra. 1986. *The Science Question in Feminism*. Ithaca: Cornell University Press.

Hexter, J. H. 1973. *The Visions of Politics on the Eve of the Reformation: More, Machiavelli, and Seyssel*. New York: Basic Books.

Livy. 1971. *The History of Rome from its Foundation*, books 1–5. In *The Early History of Rome*, trans. Aubrey de Selincourt. Harmondsworth: Penguin Books.

Machiavelli, Niccolò. 1950a. *The Prince*. In *The Prince and The Discourses*, trans. Luigi Ricci, 3–98. New York: Random House.

———. 1950b. *The Discourses*. In *The Prince and The Discourses*, trans. Luigi Ricci, 99–540. New York: Random House.

———. 1954. *Belphagor* [*sic*]. London: Rodale Press.

———. 1961. *Letters of Machiavelli*. Trans. Allan Gilbert. Chicago: University of Chicago Press.

———. 1988. *Florentine Histories*. Trans. Lauran F. Banfield and Harvey C. Mansfield Jr. Princeton: Princeton University Press.

Pitkin, Hanna Fenichel. 1984. *Fortune Is a Woman: Gender and Politics in the Thought of Niccolò Machiavelli*. Berkeley and Los Angeles: University of California Press.

Skinner, Quentin. 19891. *Machiavelli*. New York: Hill and Wang.

11

Machiavelli, Civic Virtue, and Gender

Vesna Marcina

The republic or polity was in yet another sense a structure of virtue: it was a structure in which every citizen's ability to place the common good before his own was the precondition of every other's, so that every man's virtue saved every other's from [corruption].

—J. G. A. Pocock, *The Machiavellian Moment*

Fluidity dominates Machiavelli's vision of world affairs. . . . Men can become—indeed often must become—beasts, private citizens can become rulers, men can become women, and women . . . can be "fit to govern a nation."

—Arlene Saxonhouse, *Women in the History of Political Thought*

The different ways that feminist scholars deal with the canon have led to two different conclusions about Machiavelli. On the one hand, Hanna Fenichel Pitkin argues that one of the persistent themes in Niccolò Machiavelli's works is the construction of manhood.[1] In this construction, he often juxtaposes *virtù* with a feminized virtue as it appears in *Fortuna* or in effeminate (weak, passive, dependent) men. As a result, "*virtù* is thus manliness, those qualities found in a 'real man.'"[2] For Pitkin, Machiavelli accomplishes the celebration of men and manhood at the expense of women and womanhood.

On the other hand, other scholars assert that Machiavelli tends to systematically transgress the boundaries between what we consider to be oppositions: good and bad, virtue and vice, man and woman. Unlike Pitkin, Bonnie Honig argues that for Machiavelli "true manliness means the capacity to cross-dress, to put on the accoutrements of the truest . . . woman."[3] We need only to look at the relationship between *virtù* and *Fortuna* to evidence her claim. The prince who possesses *virtù* must learn to imitate *Fortuna*.

Taken together, Pitkin's and Honig's positions suggest that the status of gender in Machiavelli's political thought remains unsettled. I hope to shed some light on that status by utilizing the two dominant feminist interpretive strategies: examining both woman/women and gender. First, I examine the women Machiavelli writes about; second, I interrogate his concept of civic virtue to uncover its gendered meanings. I argue that Machiavelli's concept of civic virtue requires gender-bending—namely, that his civic virtue is less masculine and exclusionary than traditionally perceived. I suggest that the implications of his requirement are serious: the political inclusion of women in his republic even if he never imagined women as full republican citizens. I thus hope to confirm the need to reread and reevaluate the canon from a feminist perspective.

This chapter proceeds in three sections. First, I examine the feminist scholarship on Machiavelli, which, as mentioned above, is largely critical of his project. This review of feminist literature situates my work within existing scholarship and notes the problems of the work of those, specifically Saxonhouse, with whom I am aligned as a feminist scholar. Second, I turn to the Italian Renaissance debate on women and suggest that if we reread Machiavelli in the context of this debate (with which he may have been familiar), some of what he writes about women can be seen in a more favorable light. Although Machiavelli never writes a categorical defense of women, some of his examples fall squarely, and sometimes not so squarely, within this tradition. Third, I argue that if his conception of civic virtue is inclusive then so may be his conception of citizenship. Women are not necessarily excluded from republican citizenship. It is to the feminist critique of Machiavelli that we now turn.

The Feminist Critique of Machiavelli

Virtù and *Fortuna* are central concepts in both *The Prince* and *The Discourses*,[4] and are a source of condemnation among feminist critics. Pitkin provides the standard interpretation of the gendered character of these concepts in Machiavelli.[5] Their gendered quality requires almost no elaboration: *virtù* is a masculine ideal, while *Fortuna* is a feminine one. "Though it can sometimes mean virtue, *virtù* tends mostly to connote energy, effectiveness, and virtuosity"—qualities that belong to "the real man." Civic virtue, the *virtù* of *The Discourses*, on the other hand, belongs to the (male) citizen in a republic.[6] In the principality, the prince may be the only person to possess *virtù*. In the republic, all citizens must possess *virtù*. While these two concepts differ in substance, they both serve the same goal: the preservation of the state. *Fortuna*, the goddess, threatens both; she represents chance, that which potentially destabilizes a political entity, whether principality or republic. *Virtù* must be exercised over *Fortuna* to control her. In fact, in the infamous chapter 25 of *The Prince*, Machiavelli recommends to the prince to beat her.

Pitkin writes that "[t]he themes are political and public, yet the imagery in which they are expressed is often personal and sexual. Political power and military conquest are eroticized, and eros is treated as a matter of conquest and domination." Essentially, she argues that the struggle between *virtù* and *Fortuna* symbolizes Machiavelli's preoccupation with the struggle between his own manhood and the threat womanhood poses to it. After all, "if *virtù* is Machiavelli's favorite quality, *effeminato* is one of his most frequent and scathing epithets. Nothing is more contemptible or more dangerous for a man than to be like a woman or for that matter, a baby or an animal—that is passive and dependent."[7]

Other feminist works on Machiavelli come to largely the same conclusion. Jean Bethke Elshtain argues that Machiavelli militarizes republican citizenship by fusing the ideal of the citizen with that of the soldier.[8] As a result, women become excluded from participating in political life, for they cannot meet the requirements of the citizen-soldier. In other words, women are not nor can they become citizens in Machiavelli's republic as he theorizes citizenship. Similarly, R. Claire Snyder argues that Machiavelli, as a participant in the citizen-soldier tradition, constructs citizenship by relying on a "particularly combative form of *armed masculinity*"—an armed masculinity that ultimately closes the door (even if it remains unlocked from Snyder's perspective) to women's citizenship in Machiavelli's republic. In Snyder's words, "the combative nature of the armed masculinity produced by this tradition results in the denigration of femininity and all the values traditionally associated with it."[9]

Wendy Brown argues that Machiavelli's vision of politics is wholly a masculine one. While Machiavelli denies the value of political theory before him by bringing the body back into politics, "the body that gains *entrée* in Machiavellian politics is without qualification a male, extremely 'macho' one." For example, this body "seeks power over others, beats, rapes, displays, unfeelingly seduces, and plunders."[10] In other words, *virtù* is a masculine ideal: "*Virtù* is the paradigmatic symbol of manhood; exercised to its fullest, it rids man of all softness in himself and all dangers of being enveloped, overcome, or seduced by the goddess who would undo or enslave him." Consequently, *Fortuna* is a woman; she represents female power. And while this power is not passive or dependent, it is wholly distinct from male power and unavailable to men.[11]

Brown and Pitkin essentially agree that the female image of *Fortuna* is a strong and powerful, albeit subversive one. Yet neither acknowledges that the boundary between *virtù* and *Fortuna*, between masculine and feminine, is unpoliced. In other words, a distinction certainly exists for Machiavelli, but its boundaries are crossable. While the interpretations of Pitkin, Elshtain, Brown, and Snyder are not entirely mistaken, neither are they entirely correct. In the words of Bonnie Honig: "Indeed, in spite of Machiavelli's reliance on the gendered opposition to structure his depiction of feminine [F]ortuna and masculine *virtù*, the relation between the two turns out to be less adversarial and oppositional than indebted and mimetic. The highest overall excellence of Machiavelli's man of *virtù* is his ability to be like [F]ortuna, to be as capricious, unpredictable, and wily as she." Honig further suggests, "Machiavelli's man of *virtù* is less thoroughly masculinized than he is often taken to be,"[12] thus substantially agreeing with Saxonhouse's conclusions. Saxonhouse convincingly argues that substantial gender-bending occurs in Machiavelli's works. What Machiavelli does in his works is turn "good into bad, bad into good, virtue into vice, men into women, and women into men—or, more precisely, he makes the difference between what had been opposites so ambiguous that we can no longer tell good from bad or women from men."[13]

In short, from Machiavelli's perspective, the man who truly possesses *virtù* is the one who knows how and when to act like *Fortuna*. In fact, *Fortuna* is a dominant force, a force to be reckoned with, in Machiavelli's works.[14] After all, one man's *virtù* is another man's *Fortuna*.[15] Gender, to borrow Saxonhouse's words, becomes ambiguous;[16] gender in Machiavelli is simply not as clear cut as Pitkin, Elshtain, Brown, and Snyder suggest. Masculine and feminine qualities, powers, and virtues may be distinguished, but they do not constitute uncrossable boundaries for Machia-velli. "Men must . . . become women in their capacity to be *fickle*. They must learn from the female Fortuna."[17] Thus, the lessons *Fortuna*, the goddess, offers are priceless to the one who seeks *virtù*.

This chapter seeks to support and extend Saxonhouse's conclusion since she provides but one example of a traditionally feminine quality—fickleness—that the successful prince should imitate. Saxonhouse's lim-ited conclusion is not surprising since she focuses exclusively on the *virtù* of the one, not the many, and since she takes for granted that the concept is uniform throughout Machiavelli's work. To put it another way, her assumption of uniformity precludes her from seeing the gender-bending characteristics in the republican Machiavelli who moves beyond the *virtù* of the one to the *virtù* of the many.

My analysis of gender in Machiavelli will focus on civic virtue and thus civic republicanism as it appears in *The Discourses*. My goal is to illustrate, by showing that civic virtue is potentially an inclusive concept, that in fact women can be incorporated as citizens into Machiavelli's vision of the republic. Thus, I build on Saxonhouse's interpretation and fortify the gist of her argument by extending it to Machiavelli's project in *The Discourses*. I also take issue with Pitkin's unilateral interpretation of gender in Machiavelli. The following section provides the foundation for my argument by exploring the context in which Machiavelli wrote: the debate on women in the Italian Renaissance.

Querelle des Femmes

The *querelle des femmes* refers to the four-century-long literary debate on women sparked in the late Middle Ages by a Parisian, Christine de Pisan, who decided to respond to what she perceived as pervasive misogyny in the dominant tradition of ancient and medieval texts. In her *Book of the City of Ladies*, first circulated in 1405, she defends women and the femi-nine and envisions an ideal community by, for, and of women.[18] The literary debate quickly gained momentum with the appearance of Pizan's book and spread through Europe until mid-Renaissance. During this pe-riod, the *querelle des femmes* saw many authors, both men and women, defending women or specifically feminine qualities or both against the dominant tradition that thought women intellectually, ethically, morally, and physically inferior to men. Of course, political, economic, and social inferiority followed from the judgments of the dominant tradition. Several Italian medieval and Renaissance authors participated in the defense of women against the dominant tradition, including Boccaccio, Ariosto, Castiglione, Capella, Cornazzano, Vespasiano, Goggio, Strozzi, Sabadino, and Modereta Fonte. Most of these authors wrote in the late fifteenth to early sixteenth centuries.[19]

Pamela Benson argues that Renaissance defenses of women can be divided into two separate models: women in the first model are "independent" and in the second are "interdependent."[20] The first model defends women by arguing that they are as capable as men; they can and do possess masculine qualities. I call this the "women as men" model, in which women can be expected to perform as well as men, to exhibit the same qualities as men, and to act like men in like situations. According to this model, woman can be masculine and can compete with men on equal terms. The second model defends women by celebrating, rather than denigrating, stereotypically feminine qualities. The second model essentially transforms feminine liabilities into assets.[21] I call this the "women as women" model, where women are as capable as men because of the various specifically feminine qualities they possess. Women need not possess stereotypically masculine qualities or act in stereotypically masculine ways according to this model because feminine traits and acting in feminine ways are just as valuable. Both of these models function on the basis that various qualities and traits are coded as masculine or feminine. The former claims that masculine-coded traits are not exclusively male. Women can and do act masculinely. The latter argues that feminine-coded traits are as valuable as masculine ones: feminine qualities complement masculine qualities. According to Benson, authors within the defense tradition often employ both models to varying degrees.

In Machiavelli's work, we see clear examples of the first model. The few women he celebrates in his works are often more masculine than feminine. We also see less clear examples of the second model: instances where Machiavelli celebrates feminine qualities, but not women. For example, the successful new prince should learn how and when to act like *Fortuna*: he should learn to be fickle, changing, and unpredictable, otherwise he cannot expect to be a new prince for very long. Both models, as discerned in Machiavelli, correspond to a common theme of the Renaissance: gender-bending. Scholars argue that self-fashioning was a prominent phenomenon during this period. An individual of this period would use his or her outward appearance—hairstyle, clothing, and manners—to express him- or herself. But "the much-acclaimed Renaissance self-fashioning goes hand in hand with playful and creative experimentation with gender distinction";[22] thus self-fashioning often meant gender-bending.

The following section explores the employment of the two models used in the defense of women by the gender-bending Machiavelli. Perhaps this begs the questions: Was Machiavelli aware of the debate? And did he participate in it? I do not claim that Machiavelli actually partook in the debate, but merely that he might have been influenced by it. As we shall see, both models appear in his works, which suggests that he was at the very least familiar with Italian defenses of women. Machiavelli was writing at the height of the debate and may have been exposed to the views of authors engaged in this controversy. In fact, in a letter he wrote to Lodovico Alamanni dated December 17, 1517, he praises *Orlando Furioso* by Ariosto, a prominent work in the Italian defense tradition.[23] In a letter to Vettori dated February 25, 1514, in a letter to Guicciardini dated May 17, 1521, and in *The History of Florence*, he refers to the author Boccaccio, another conspicuous defender of women, and to his works.[24] It is possible that Machiavelli was exposed to the debate through these works, and his own work may parallel both defense models to some degree. Let us take a look now at his use of the first, "women as men" model.

Women as Men

The first model defends women by arguing that they can and often do possess traditionally masculine qualities: the female sex adopts the male gender. While Machiavelli never explicitly engages in a defense of women in his works, he does use examples of women who act like men to illustrate the historical lessons he advances. In other words, Machiavelli uses women as exemplars of the political lessons he wishes to teach. He uses women as model political actors. He may not do this often, but the fact that he does it at all is important.[25] At the very least, he indirectly provides a defense of women that accords with the first model of the Italian defense tradition.

Perhaps the most noted examples are those of Madonna Caterina in

The History of Florence and in his chapter on conspiracies in *The Discourses on Livy*.[26] Machiavelli uses the example of the countess because she took revenge against her husband's conspirators by conspiring against them. According to Machiavelli, her desire for revenge and her consequent actions should have been foreseen by the conspirators (*Discourses*, 3.6; hereafter *D*). She, in fact, assumed a military role as she commanded the defense of her city while the conspirators held her children hostage.[27] She did so by persuading the conspirators who had killed her husband to allow her to go into the fortress, which they still needed to secure for the success of their enterprise. She assured the conspirators that she would deliver them the fortress by leaving her children with them. As soon as she entered, she broke her promise: she threatened the conspirators with death and torture for murdering her husband. When the conspirators threatened her children, she replied that she could still bear more. In the end, she recovered her state and avenged the death of her husband.[28] Indeed, of all the Sforza family members, the Countess was the only one to effectively use the fortress according to Machiavelli (*Prince*, 20; hereafter *P*). Machiavelli warns would-be conspirators of the dangers involved in their enterprise, dangers that Madonna Caterina, acting more masculinely than femininely, illustrates well (*D*, 3.6).

In the same discourse on conspiracies, Machiavelli describes the audacity (*l'audacia*) of Epicharis, a mistress of Nero who conspired against him. Here he also describes Marcia, a concubine, who successfully conspired against Commodus and killed him with the help of her two partners after she learned that he was planning to have her killed (*D*, 3.6). That Machiavelli uses so many examples of women in his section on conspiracies is significant. Throughout his works, Machiavelli openly gives advice to the weak on how to become strong and, once strength is achieved, how to stay strong. More importantly, Machiavelli argues that there is no enterprise "more dangerous or more bold" than conspiring against a prince (*D*, 3.6). Conspirators, then, regardless of whether they are men or women, possess great *virtù*.

In *The Prince*, Machiavelli uses Dido as a model for the new prince (*P*, 27). In Virgil's *Aeneid*, Dido builds Carthage; she is the skillful founder and leader of a nation. For Machiavelli, Dido imparts the lessons of the danger involved in establishing a new state and the need for cruelty when doing so. She affirms Machiavelli's claim that the new prince cannot escape the use of brutality in his, or in this case her, endeavor: "The harshness of things and the newness of the kingdom compel me to contrive such things, and to keep a broad watch over the border" (*P*, 28). Dido thus upholds Machiavelli's notion of necessity. In *The Discourses*, he further describes Dido's ability to seize a new territory "with art" and maintain it "by way of friends and confederates" (*D*, 2.8).

In his most celebrated play, *La Mandragola*, Machiavelli has Ligurio say of Nicia: "I don't believe there's a stupider man in the world than this fellow; yet how Fortune has favored him! He's rich; he has a beautiful wife, virtuous, courteous, and fit to rule a nation."[29] Lucrezia, Nicia's wife, is a woman who can rule a nation. Though this statement is made in a dramatic work, rather than in the typical political treatise, Machiavelli's claims concerning Lucrezia accord with the previous examples and the first model of women as men.

Lest we forget how strong, powerful, violent, and masculine *Fortuna* can be, let us turn to a final example of Machiavelli's gender-bending. In his "Tercets on Fortune," Machiavelli writes: "Yet you cannot therefore trust yourself to her nor hope to escape her hard bite, her hard blows, violent and cruel."[30] *Fortuna* herself is often more masculine than feminine.

What conclusions can be drawn from the women as men model? This model does not really open the door to women writ large in Machiavelli's republic, but merely affirms Machiavelli's gender-bending by pointing to unusual or exceptional women, women who act more like men when they can and do participate in politics. Some women may, in fact, possess the quality of real men, *virtù*, and thus succeed in political life. In short, Machiavelli commends women who display masculine qualities; Machiavelli praises manly women. What the first model shows is that there is room for women who act like men in Machiavelli's vision of politics. On the other hand, the second model does open the door to women's participation across the board. This model, however, to which we now turn, is slightly more complicated than the first.

Women as Women

Machiavelli does not celebrate women qua women. What Madonna Caterina, Dido, and the other women discussed above show is that Machiavelli makes no hesitation to use women as illustrative models, but they are distinct examples of women as men: women exhibiting masculine traits, engaging in masculine activities, acting like men. Although Machiavelli does not celebrate women qua women, we cannot conclude that he does not celebrate feminine qualities. In other words, Machiavelli may not praise individual feminine women, but that alone does not rule out the possibility that he celebrates feminine traits. How could Machiavelli praise the feminine without praising women? Let's take a second look at Saxonhouse. She provides an instance of his celebration of a particular trait that Machiavelli's time considered feminine: a successful prince must mimic *Fortuna*. He must learn to be fickle, change as the situation necessitates, mutate according to the demands of the time. If a new prince can accomplish this, then he will be successful. After all, one man's *virtù* is another man's *Fortuna*. My question is: Can we find no other indications of Machiavelli's praise of the feminine? Answering this question requires an analysis of one important concept in Machiavelli's republican works: civic virtue.

Civic Virtue

Civic virtue is the quality par excellence in republican political actors. What does this concept mean for Machiavelli? Indeed, its meaning is complicated, as we shall see. Civic virtue, for Machiavelli, is the primacy of the common good over the private interests of the individual, and the key to founding and maintaining a republic. This is not to say, however, that the common good is antithetical to private interests. The two can and do coincide in many cases. Problems arise when citizens pursue their personal interests at the expense of the common good: problems arise when the two do not coincide. In these cases, the question then becomes which will a citizen pursue? Civic virtue means that the citizen will pursue the common good at all costs, even when private interests are not served.

Perhaps the best way to get at the meaning of civic virtue for Machiavelli is to examine his concept of corruption. Often, Machiavelli speaks of civic virtue by way of a reference to its absence, a common theme in *The Discourses*. Where there is no civic virtue, there is corruption. Even where civic virtue exists, corruption is an ever-present danger. Corruption of citizens and rulers occurs when they place their individual, private interests before the common good, thus causing the collapse of a good state. For example, the three forms of state, principality, aristocracy, and democracy, are "so easily corrupted that they too become pernicious" and fall into three corrupt counterparts, tyranny, oligarchy, and anarchy. Good states are good because they are composed of political actors who are "more prudent and more just," who act "according to the laws ordered by them, placing the common utility before their own advantage" (*D*, 1.2). Good states become corrupt because, as time and authority pass to the next generation, the opposite occurs, where their citizens are neither prudent nor just, and the cycle of decline begins. The unfortunate fact that Machiavelli apprehends is that citizens and rulers inevitably place their private interests before the common good, thus causing their own and their city's demise. Principalities then slip into tyranny because of corruption; the tyranny is overthrown by aristocrats who form an aristocracy, which slips into oligarchy; the people overthrow the oligarchy and form a popular state that quickly slips into anarchy, at which point the cycle begins anew.[31] "[S]umptuousness and lasciviousness," "avarice," "ambition," "usurpation," and "license" reign in these corrupt regimes (*D*, 1.2).

Machiavelli's goal is to stop the continuous movement from good to corrupt state. The republic is meant to meet this goal. A republic stops the cycle because it combines the best of the three types of governments and addresses the problems of time, i.e., preservation and corruption, by eliminating the dangers inherent in each of the governments alone (*D*, 1.2). A republic, then, is part principality, part aristocracy, and part democracy: It is a mixed government. But a mixed government is not only meant to serve a "checks and balances" function as we understand it in its modern, American sense. First, a mixed government for Machiavelli addresses the problem of corruption by erecting a structure conducive to the cultivation of civic virtue by getting people, that is, ordinary citizens, involved in the political process. Second, a mixed government provides flexibility when necessary since it can adapt to changing circumstances. For example, when a crisis necessitates a swift response, a prince alone can act quickly since there are no restraints built into this office.[32] A republic recognizes this necessity and allows for such princely responses, yet does not rely solely on the prince for its preservation. A republic relies on the prince in crisis situations alone.[33] This guarantees a longer life for the republic because a prince along with his heirs too easily grow corrupt, whereas a mixed government fosters civic virtue and provides flexibility.

Further, rulers of corrupt states "are worthy of reproach" (*D*, 1.10).

Caesar, Nabis, Phalaris, Dionysius, and the like are criticized as founders of tyranny. Machiavelli writes of Caesar:

> Nor should anyone deceive himself because of the glory of Caesar, hearing him especially celebrated by the writers; for those who praise him are corrupted by his fortune and awed by the duration of the empire that, ruling under that name, did not permit writers to speak freely of him. But whoever wishes to know what the writers would say of him if they were free should see what they say of Catiline. Caesar is so much more detestable as he who has done an evil is more to blame than he who has wished to do one. He should also see with how much praise they celebrate Brutus, as though, unable to blame Caesar because of his power, they cele- brate his enemy. (D, 1.10)

Caesar exemplifies the ruler who founds a tyranny and thus deserves our condemnation. Rulers who found tyrannies rather than republics do not "perceive how much fame, how much glory, how much honor, security, quiet, with satisfaction of mind, they flee from by this policy; and how much infamy, reproach, blame, danger, and disquiet they run into" (D, 1.10). They deserve blame for not eliminating rancor, license, and ambi- tion when the opportunity presented itself. Caesar, again, is Machiavelli's prime example: rather than reorder a corrupt city, he chose to spoil it entirely and exchange a great "opportunity for glory" for "sempiternal infamy" (D, 1.10). Caesar did not submit his desire to dominate to the common good and thus destroyed the republic and its free way of life. The (manly) desire to dominate is among the most dangerous in a republic.

Not only did Caesar fail to achieve glory in Machiavelli's eyes, he sacrificed his life for an utterly selfish endeavor. After all, Caesar's greatest danger came from within his tyrannical state. What usually causes men to conspire against a prince (or tyrant) is their desire to free their father- land from his grips. In fact, "nor can any tyrant guard himself from [con- spiracies] except by laying down the tyranny" (D, 3.6). Brutus attempted to free Rome from Caesar's yoke and reestablish the Roman republic be- fore it was too late. His civic virtue, his "authority and severity," thus became articulated in Caesar's assassination (D, 1.17). Of course, his attempt to reassert the republic was unsuccessful in the end, as, according to Machiavelli, Caesar had thoroughly corrupted the people, but Machia- velli praises Brutus nonetheless.

Founders must establish a well-ordered polity by writing constitutions and laws that encourage and enforce civic virtue among political actors (D, 1.2). The prudent founder, "who has the intent to wish to help not himself, but the common good," orders a republic so that political power is shared (D, 1.9). Rulers, as they exhibit their own civic virtue, provide political and military leadership and serve as inspirational role models to the citizens of a republic (D, 3.1). Both founders and rulers must write good laws and renovate them when necessary to coerce the citizens to possess civic virtue and thus maintain the republic (D, 1.3, 3.1). They must provide a civic religion to foster civic virtue among the citizens (D, 1.2). Coercion and fear of punishment, Machiavelli argues, are among the best ways to instill civic virtue in citizens who have yet to learn its importance. Rulers must work to repel envy among citizens, by violence if necessary (D, 3.30). As well, rulers must learn to step down from their political and military commands to avoid the dangers that accompany their prolongation, specifically the danger that the loyalty of citizens may be diverted from the republic to an individual (D, 1.34). Cincinnatus, who refused the extension of his rule as consul, is Machiavelli's foremost example of this trait: if his "goodness and prudence" had existed in all of Rome's citizens, the cause of Rome's ruin would have been eliminated (D, 3.24). If founders and rulers are successful on these counts, then they will have taken care of their internal affairs. But what about external affairs? Rulers must also work to prevent foreign domination of their city since the threat of being conquered is always a threat to liberty. They accomplish this by pursuing foreign domination themselves (D, 2.19). If founders can establish a well-ordered polity and rulers can condition internal and external forces, then they will have led their city to greatness (D, 3.1). So we see that founding and leading a republic are not easy tasks, but require extraordinary ability and effort, personal sacrifice, and cruelty, if necessary. The civic virtue of founders and rulers requires a delicate balance between its competing fundaments. Ultimately, founders and rulers must submit their ambition to the common good and teach others to do so as well.

But it is not merely founders and rulers who are judged by the criterion of civic virtue. Citizens, too, must privilege the common good over their own private interests, although in this case the two are far more likely to be aligned. Nonetheless, citizens must often be taught the lessons of civic virtue. After all, kingdoms, which depend solely on the virtue of the one, fail for a very simple reason: "princes are of short life" (D, 1.11). Once the virtuous prince dies, his corrupt heirs take over and the cycle of corruption begins. Thus a republic requires not "one prince who governs prudently while he lives, but one individual who orders it so that it is also maintained when he dies" (*D*, 1.11). Once the state is ordered as a republic, it is the many who play the role of maintaining it: "the thing itself is ordered to last long . . . if it remains in the care of the many and its maintenance stays with the many" (*D*, 1.9). Citizens are ultimately entrusted with maintaining the republic, and they accomplish this enormous task in different ways. Some serve as soldiers and prevent the external threat to freedom from foreigners (*D*, 2.2). Since they refuse to be dominated by would-be tyrants, they should be charged with protecting the freedom of all citizens. And they should guard the republic's freedom by publicly accusing individuals who would threaten it (*D*, 1.5, 1.7). The republic further orders the participation of the many by providing an arena in which citizens can propose laws and deliberate before a judgment is reached (*D*, 1.18). Machiavelli assumes that the citizens possess civic virtue in each of these cases. If they do not, he suggests that it is up to rulers to instill civic virtue in them, as discussed above.

For Machiavelli, founders, rulers, and citizens alike must submit to the common good in a republic. Civic virtue as it applies to citizens also applies to rulers: each must favor common interests over personal ones. Thus, civic virtue requires submission to the common good and dependence on others to submit to the common good as well. Otherwise the republic grows corrupt. Of course, the means of accomplishing the common good for different political actors may differ, but the end does not: civic virtue dictates the individual's submission to the common good and dependence on others to do the same. Machiavelli acknowledges that this is a difficult endeavor and endorses the use of extraordinary measures to ensure that the common good prevails. Why, for example, does Scipio deserve our praise according to Machiavelli? He writes: "For after the defeat that Hannibal had given to the Romans at Cannae, many citizens gathered together and, terrified for their fatherland, agreed to abandon Italy and move to Sicily. Hearing this, Scipio went to meet them and with naked steel in hand constrained them to swear they would not abandon the fatherland" (*D*, 1.11). Scipio, because of his concern for the common good of Rome, forces his fellow citizens to stay and fight. His *virtù* resides in his submission to the common good and his attempt to ensure that his fellow citizens do the same, for he knows he cannot succeed without them. He depends on them. But his *virtù* also resides in vigilance and aggressiveness. After all, it is "with naked steel in hand" that he convinces his fellow citizens to swear they would not abandon Rome.

The citizens in this instance are not praiseworthy because they were willing to abandon their fatherland to protect themselves. Machiavelli argues that individuals often become "cowardly and weak" when they begin to think of their own personal danger in such situations (D, 1.57). What this shows is that, for Machiavelli, civic virtue is so important in a republic that the use of fear and force are justified to maintain it if necessary. Of course, the republic itself is meant to foster civic virtue in political actors, but if it fails, if times become particularly difficult as this example illustrates, commentators agree that Machiavelli is willing to resort to force when necessary.

Although this example illustrates Scipio's *virtù* and not that of the citizens, Machiavelli does enumerate reasons why citizens deserve praise. They help preserve the republic and maintain freedom by submitting to the common good, though their submission often requires less of them than it does the nobles because Machiavelli largely equates plebeian desires with the common good. For example, the plebeian desire not to be dominated by others is so great that citizens will take greater care in guarding everyone's freedom as a result of that desire (D, 1.5). This is an example in which the desire of the many, namely not to be dominated, coincides with the common good of the republic, namely liberty, as long as the many are not corrupt. According to Machiavelli, the many not only guard their own individual freedom, but the freedom of all citizens.

What is striking about civic virtue as outlined here is its twin requirement of submission and dependence. Civic virtue depends on these traits in political actors: citizens must submit to the common good for the success of the republic and they have no choice but to depend on others to resist corruption. While Machiavelli never explicitly addresses these concepts—the terms do not figure in his writings—the general ideas nonetheless appear in his works. The themes of submission and dependence both figure in his examples of republican citizenship, as the following examples illustrate. First, Scipio, as previously discussed, nicely illustrates both submission and dependence as a function of his civic virtue. He submits his self-interest, and ultimately he is willing to submit his life, in the name of Rome, and he needs his fellow citizens to do the same. He depends on his fellow citizens. Second, the case of Manlius Capitolinus illustrates the submission of the citizens to the common good. After the Roman people rightly condemned Manlius to death, they actually missed him. In the words of Livy: "After there was no danger from him, desire for him soon took hold of the people" (D, 1.58). And yet Machiavelli suggests, "if Manlius had been resuscitated among so much desire, the people of Rome would have given the same judgment on him as it did when it condemned him to death" (D, 1.58). In other words, despite the fact that they missed him, they would not have changed the penalty. The people, ordinary citizens, thus submit their private desires to the common good. Third, in a chapter of The Discourses titled "That a good citizen ought to forget private injuries for the love of his fatherland" (D, 3.47) Machiavelli discusses the case of Fabius, who named Papirius Cursor as dictator despite the personal injuries the latter caused to Fabius. For Machiavelli a good republican citizen, like Fabius, submits "private hatreds" to the "public benefit" (D, 3.47). Last, Cincinnatus submits his private interests to the common good as a function of his civic virtue. To the surprise of those around him, he steps down from his post as military dictator. Certainly, he could have advanced his own interests in this post, but he submits to the common good instead by not overextending the term of his leadership. So we see that submission is a prominent theme in Machiavelli's examples of republican citizenship.

Dependence is a more prominent theme than submission in Machiavelli's discussion of corruption. Corruption occurs when citizens place their private interests above the common good. Citizens depend on one another to resist corruption. Once they cease to do so, the republic is in danger, which is precisely the reason the republic structures civic virtue and hence mutual dependence. Individuals rely on others for their well-being vis-à-vis the well-being of the community. Citizens rely not only on themselves but on other citizens to maintain their way of life, a free way of life birthed by the republic. Consider, for instance, Scipio's dependence on his fellow citizens. Thus we see that both submission and dependence are integral characteristics of the public self in Machiavelli's republic.

Pitkin agrees that though the term does not actually appear, the theme of dependence does: "dependence appears with obsessive persistence in all his works." However, in Pitkin's interpretation, "[d]ependence is characteristic of women, children, and animals; for men it is despicable and dangerous." I argue that while dependence may be a traditionally feminine characteristic, as Pitkin suggests, it is not limited to women in Machiavelli's works. There are cases, perhaps limited to his republic, when it is *not* "despicable or dangerous" for men to be submissive or dependent. Even though her examples clearly demonstrate Pitkin's claim, the status of dependence in Machiavelli's works is less consistent than she portrays. For example, according to my argument, the republic is a ·structure that forces its citizens, male and female alike, to depend on each other's civic virtue. The republic structures mutual dependence. But for Pitkin, "what men and states must avoid at all costs is resembling women."[34] I argue that the latter is an overstatement of the case.

This is not to say that Pitkin's characterization of gender in Machiavelli's thought is without foundation. Machiavelli sometimes writes of effeminate men, cities, or republics (*D*, 1.6, 1.19, 1.21, 2.2, 3.10, 3.46). And he often characterizes feminine qualities in negative ways. But, as I show in this chapter, he is less consistent than Pitkin presents and as a result more woman-friendly than she is willing to acknowledge. One needs only to consider that Machiavelli's politics are open to women who act like men to see that his consistency on this score is questionable. Of course, one may still argue that generally Pitkin is correct: Machiavelli's treatment of women often accords with her interpretation. However, I would like to move beyond his treatment of women to discuss the fundaments of his concepts, their implications, and their relationship to one another. This interpretive strategy—focusing on the gendered character of the concepts themselves—reveals a potentially inclusive Machiavelli. On this score, his concept of civic virtue is significant in that it requires gender-bending of citizen-men. The crux of the difference, then, between Pitkin's interpretation and mine is that we use different interpretive strategies. I hope to show that we need both strategies to illustrate how complicated gender difference becomes in his works.

Maurizio Viroli likewise disagrees with Pitkin on this matter. Pitkin, in her analysis of a letter to Vettori, concludes that Machiavelli despises the (feminine) characteristic of dependence in men.[35] Viroli argues that Pitkin "overlooks the fact that what Machiavelli is urging his friend Vettori to do [in this letter] is to abandon himself to love . . . to give up autonomy and become fully dependent, indeed to become a slave" to a woman. Put differently, what Pitkin does in this instance is take Machiavelli's statement concerning dependence out of context. In Viroli's analysis, "[d]ependence and abandonment to the love of women are . . . the best conditions of men's life" for Machiavelli, and he would happily trade his autonomy for love.[36] In short, for Viroli, dependence appears in

Machiavelli's writings in a more favorable light than Pitkin would have us believe.

My claim differs from Viroli's, but is also at odds with Pitkin's. I suggest that the republic requires civic virtue among its citizens, which turns upon submissive and dependent behavior. Submission and dependence are traditionally coded as feminine traits (as Pitkin argues), but in Machiavelli's republic they are required of his male citizens. Machiavelli's notion of civic virtue, then, requires gender-bending of his citizen-men. Machiavelli's citizens must submit their manly ambition to the common good since one of the most dangerous threats to the republic and its free way of life comes from men's desire to dominate others—women do not pose such a threat (D, 1.5).

So male citizens engage in gender-bending in Machiavelli's republic, and princes must also gender-bend to achieve success. The question becomes whether his politics are open to women. We have seen that Machiavelli's politics are certainly open to specific women who act like men, as Saxonhouse clearly establishes. Consider Madonna Caterina and the other women he specifically discusses. We must ask, then, whether or not women in general can become citizens in his republic. If, in fact, Machiavelli requires his male citizens to act, in a certain sense, submissively and dependently, and these are traditionally marked as feminine qualities, then there is no reason to exclude women from republican citizenship as long as women can also meet its masculine qualities. Of course, submission and dependence do not represent the whole of civic virtue, but they do represent two significant fundaments. Vigilance and aggressiveness appear as two more fundaments of civic virtue, as discussed above . So my claim is that Machiavelli expects gender-bending of his male citizens, which ultimately opens the door to women's participation. Let's explore this in more detail.

Women as Republican Citizens

Machiavelli may not have directly participated in the Italian defense tradition, but we can find a defense of women in his works. He makes no hesitation to use women as historical examples when they act like men and when these acts coincide with the lessons he wishes to teach. Whether Machiavelli praises feminine qualities is another story. His discussions of *Fortuna* suggest that he is willing to praise some qualities. Likewise, his examples of virtuous republican citizens suggest that submission and dependence, both "feminine" traits in Machiavelli's time, are considered fundaments of civic virtue. Political actors in republics—founders, rulers, and citizens—must submit their private interests to the common good if necessary. They depend on their fellow citizens to do the same. Citizens must engage in gender-bending, bringing their feminine-coded behaviors to the fore for the good of all. Otherwise, the republic becomes corrupt and soon ceases to exist entirely. And even though feminists criticize both Machiavelli and civic republicanism, the republican Machiavelli deserves a second look. If civic virtue means that citizens act submissively and dependently and the republic fosters these behaviors, then Machiavelli does not entirely deserve the infamy among feminists that he receives. I suggest that Machiavelli envisions a structure of governing that privileges some feminine-coded traits for the sake of civic virtue. The question that remains is whether women can become citizens in his vision of the republic. I argue that Machiavelli's citizens, regardless of their sex, must act like men *and* women. As the virtuoso prince mimics *Fortuna*, the male republican citizen displays some feminine-coded traits. For Machiavelli, citizen-men must exhibit both masculine and feminine traits for the republic to succeed. If this is the case, then women can certainly be incorporated as citizens into the republic without altering Machiavelli's recommendations. Perhaps it is time to take Machiavelli's praise seriously. Since Machiavelli's vision of republican citizenship is not wholly masculine, his theory of republican democracy is not inherently sexist. Citizenship need not exclude women in his republic.

However, one may argue that just because Machiavelli expects men to act in ways that are stereotypically associated with women on occasion, it does not follow that women can be easily incorporated into his republican theory. Let us turn to the potential objections to my claim. For example, how should we respond to the criticism that Machiavelli never explicitly discusses the topic of women as republican citizens? Pamela Benson argues that although the defense tradition as a protofeminist position attempted to elevate the status of women, its authors stopped short of the conclusions their arguments seem to warrant, the conclusions that nineteenth- and twentieth-century feminists do reach, that women are fully equal citizens.[37] Machiavelli, like the Italian Renaissance defenders of women, puts the arguments in place for including women in his polity, even though he does not draw the logical conclusion.

One could object that the submission and dependence of republican citizens are different from the traits of the same name traditionally ascribed by men to women. If that is the case, then we must ask whether or not the traits are similar enough. I would argue that even if they are different in some respects, the phenomenon itself is the same even thought the object of submission is different in each case. In Machiavelli's *Discourses*, citizens rightly submit to the republic. At the time he wrote, women were expected to submit to their husbands. In both cases, the act itself, the act of submission, is the same. Let's take a moment to establish this to be the case. There are important differences between a republic and a family, which I do not wish to erase. However, I would like to *privilege* the similarities. Machiavelli theorizes citizenship in a way that makes necessity an important feature of a republic. Necessity is instrumental in making citizens do what they may not otherwise do: submit to the common good of the republic. Yet unlike many republican thinkers, Machiavelli does not necessarily want to eliminate or transform a citizen's self-interest.[38] According to Machiavelli, private interests may or may not coincide with the common good, and the ideal citizen submits his private interests to the common good even when the two do not coincide. The republican structure intends to foster this type of behavior in its citizens by reminding them that the republic is not merely an abstract entity; the republic is in fact one's fellow citizens. Necessity is an important feature of a family as well. Husbands and wives, for example, often submit their personal interests to the family out of necessity, especially when there are children involved. Children often force parents to act in ways they may not otherwise. Ideally, husbands, wives, sons, and daughters must think not only of themselves, but also of their fellow family members— the way that a republic's citizens must think not only of themselves, but also of their fellow citizens. In both the family and the republic, the self-interest of various individuals may or may not coincide with the common good of the greater entity. Neither a republic nor a family denies the existence of self-interest, neither wishes to transform self-interest, but both require that individuals submit their self-interest to the greater good if necessary. Both require that individuals take account of others.

What about dependence? Citizens depend on one another to submit to the common good for the survival of the republic. And when Machiavelli wrote, women were dependent on their husbands and families for their survival. Again, the act itself is the same in each case. Some might object that perhaps what we have in the case of republican citizens is in fact interdependence as opposed to the total dependence of women and wives. But is this really the case? Or are the two, in fact, similar? My answer is yes. The family is a structure in which husbands depend on their wives and wives depend on their husbands in different ways; perhaps the dependence of wives should more appropriately be called interdependence since the relationship is in fact reciprocal, though this aspect often remains hidden. Feminists insightfully argue that the seemingly differing status of men and women in marriage simply denies the reciprocity and hides men's dependence in such a relationship. After all, "few people would disagree with the statement that marriage involves . . . *mutual vulnerability and dependence*."[39]

One could also object that Machiavelli makes no serious exploration of women as political actors: He simply does not take women seriously as potential forces for political good. After all, he titles one chapter "How a state is ruined because of women" (*D*, 3.26). If women are the cause of a state's ruin, how could they possibly be incorporated into the state as citizens? If women are represented by *Fortuna*, how could the republic accommodate them? This objection argues that for Machiavelli women are the unknowable; they are chance; they are that which destabilizes a polity. This poses an interesting problem, as Saxonhouse notes, because the cases Machiavelli uses do not actually support the conclusion that women led to the downfall of a state.[40] For instance, Machiavelli cites Lucretia, Virginia, and the incidents in Ardea to support his claim.[41] Yet in earlier chapters, Machiavelli dismisses the charges levied against Lucretia and Virginia (*D*, 3.2, 1.40, 1.44, 1.57). Saxonhouse explains that Machiavelli (a) corrects those who make the charges against the women, and (b) argues that the two women are merely indications of political misrule and did not actually cause the ruin of the states.[42] Saxonhouse is correct. In fact, Machiavelli does more than dismiss the charges and correct the historical record, he argues that the results of these incidents caused the destruction of corrupt states, whose ruin was worthy of celebration. When the Ten fell after Virginia's death, Machiavelli argues, "Rome was brought back to the form of its ancient freedom" (*D*, 1.40). And Tarquin the Proud would have been expelled, according to Machiavelli, regardless of Lucretia's rape since "he had broken the laws of the kingdom and governed it tyrannically" (*D*, 3.5). He does not celebrate the women in these cases, but he does celebrate the fall of the rulers. So the objection that women cannot be part of politics overstates its case and discounts evidence to the contrary.

It might also be objected that my argument ignores an important element of the republic, civic virtue, and citizenship: the military. Clearly, the military plays an integral role for the republican Machiavelli. The military, war, and like concerns compose a significant portion of *The Discourses*. He devotes numerous chapters to the importance of citizen armies for both republics and kingdoms. In fact, the vigilance and aggressiveness associated with soldiering are two more fundaments of civic virtue. We must ask: Why is military service important? There are several reasons, but perhaps Machiavelli's most important argument is that military service is valuable because it teaches citizens—i.e., men—the lessons of civic virtue (*D*, 2.17). Combat, he argues, provides ample opportunity for men to be virtuous. If military service is such an important element of citizenship in a republic, then what of women? What is the schoolroom for women? Isn't the ideal citizen a soldier? My response to this objection is twofold. First, if Machiavelli expects men to possess masculine and feminine traits, then is it unreasonable to expect women to possess both as well? In the United States, women soldiers fight for the right to engage in combat along with their male counterparts. These women have expressed their desire to defend their country; they are willing to sacrifice their lives for their nation; they have clearly expressed their civic virtue. This contemporary example illustrates not only the reasonableness of expecting women to act like men, but its reality. Perhaps this example is anachronistic and would not apply to the conditions of early modern warfare, but Madonna Caterina, whom Machiavelli discusses on more than one occasion, and Joan of Arc, whom Machiavelli ignores, successfully assumed military roles during times relevant to Machiavelli's writings. Further, Machiavelli seems to think that some women can and do act like men (see the "women as men" model above). Second, we must acknowledge that military service is not the only means of teaching citizens the lessons of civic virtue. Machiavelli lists other valuable methods, such as civic religion, education, and inspiration from exemplary leaders (*D*, 1.4, 1.11, 3.1). So even if women (and men) are citizens, but not soldiers, they can and will learn the lessons of civic virtue in his republic. In fact, the real experiences of many women parallel this phenomenon: in the context of the family, they learn the lesson of something like civic virtue well as they learn to submit their personal interests to the common good of the family. The same holds true for men. That Machiavelli does not acknowledge such (private) examples in his writings does not undermine their usefulness for the point at hand.

Finally, it might be objected that I ignore Machiavelli on the topic of submission to the Church, an omission that undermines my argument that the republic structures submission and that submission constitutes a fundament of civic virtue. Yet one could argue that Machiavelli clearly loathes submission and submissive behavior. One need only to look at his discussion of the Church to substantiate this claim, for Machiavelli condemns the Church because it demands submission (D, 1.12). If he does not condone submission to the Church, how could he condone submission to the republic?

The true question then becomes whether Machiavelli rejects submission per se or submission to the Church. There is substantial evidence to support the interpretation that Machiavelli thinks that the Church is the cause of Italy's ruin (D, 1.12). However, the reason for this ruin was not because of submission per se but because the Church diverted the loyalties of the citizens from their appropriate locus, the republic. By loyalty I mean allegiance or attachment. In the above comparison, both church and state demand loyalty, of which submission is one condition. The Church itself demands loyalty from its members and thus rivals the state (D, 1.12). Machiavelli's solution to the problem of religion and politics is to identify religion as a potential tool for politics, a criterion the Catholic Church did not meet since it reversed the relationship: religion first, politics second. Thus, as Isaiah Berlin argues, part of Machiavelli's project is not only to achieve the emancipation of politics from religion, but also to achieve the triumph of politics over religion—at least as far as power is concerned and at least as it existed in his day.[43]

Conclusion

Many find Machiavelli disturbing: Some call him wicked and evil,[44] while others argue that he is merely describing the world as it is, not as it should be.[45] Yet attempts to resurrect the republican Machiavelli have tried to chip away at his notoriety.[46] In any case, feminists tend to judge Machiavelli and his works as part of a much larger philosophical tradition that marginalizes women and the feminine. My argument is that the earliest feminist conclusion about Machiavelli, while largely accurate, overstates its case and discounts the nuances of his central concepts. Machiavelli's works largely accord with the Italian Renaissance tradition of the defense of women. Machiavelli, to different degrees, employs both the "women as men" and "women as women" models that this tradition embraces in his own writings. He uses women to exemplify the historical lessons he wishes to advance and he celebrates some feminine-coded qualities. Gender-bending is a prominent theme in Machiavelli's thought. From his gender-bending flows a potentially inclusive vision of a republic. Machiavelli's republic structures submissive and dependent behavior in his (male) citizens as a function of their civic virtue. So civic virtue is less masculine than we tend to think. Machiavelli expects men to possess both masculine- and feminine-coded traits; he expects gender-bending of his male citizens. Is it asking too much to expect the same of women? I think not. So Machiavelli's republicanism is not inherently sexist.

But why should feminists care whether or not we can salvage Machiavelli? Is this canonical author even worth saving? We should reread Machiavelli because he can be useful to feminists in different ways. First, if we take seriously that civic virtue, the quality of the good citizen, requires submission and dependence to the common good, then we have found an inconsistency in Machiavelli's works, for he often associates the two traits with women or Christianity in a pejorative sense. Yet when his concept of civic virtue invokes submission and dependence, there is no negative connotation. What are we to make of this? Machiavelli's works can be used to illuminate a genealogical study of submission and dependence, their gendered associations, and their value connotations.[47] Such a concept analysis would further help to uncover the ways in which gender plays a key role in assigning value to an activity and may ultimately help to undermine stereotypes.

Second, if we reread his work while reevaluating feminist judgments of him, Machiavelli points us toward an alternative conception of democratic citizenship. We might think that his conception appears rather traditional within republican thought where the citizen-soldier is a common ideal. But if we look beyond his ideal of the citizen-soldier to his concept of civic virtue, we find several competing fundaments including vigilance, aggressiveness, submission, and dependence. These are traditionally gendered qualities for Machiavelli *and* for us, ultimately composing an unusual mix. Machiavelli's requirement of civic virtue from all citizens means requiring gender-bending of all citizens. Citizenship becomes a site of political action as Machiavelli asks citizens to perform in different (gendered) ways at different times. Machiavelli may have been referring to citizen men, but civic virtue's requirement of gender-bending opens the door to women as well.

However, there are risks in embracing Machiavelli and his conception of citizenship. Would women even want to be included in Machiavelli's republic? Submission and dependence may open the door to women's participation, but are these grounds upon which we want to forge our inclusion? Probably not. And this is why I suggest that Machiavelli points us toward, rather than provides us with, an alternative conception of democratic citizenship, an alternative based on both "manly" and "womanly" virtues.

So we can learn some useful lessons from Machiavelli even if we choose to revise or ultimately abandon his vision of the republic and its citizens. In treating civic virtue as a quiver for different, sometimes antithetical arrows, I hope to illustrate that women are not precluded from Machiavelli's republican political thought. Indeed, Machiavelli requires his male citizens to act in masculine *and* feminine ways. If male citizens are required to gender-bend in Machiavelli's republic, then by implication the door opens to female citizens. Women may become citizens in Machiavelli's republic.

Notes

1. Hanna Fenichel Pitkin, *Fortune Is a Woman: Gender and Politics in the Thought of Niccolò Machiavelli* (Berkeley and Los Angeles: University of California Press, 1984).

2. Ibid., 25.

3. Bonnie Honig, *Political Theory and the Displacement of Politics* (Ithaca: Cornell University Press, 1993), 16.

4. Niccolò Machiavelli, *The Prince*, in *Chief Works and Others*, ed. and trans. Allan Gilbert, 3 vols. (Durham: Duke University Press, 1965), vol. 1. Text citations of *The Prince* refer to chapters. Machiavelli, *Discourses on Livy*, trans. Harvey C. Mansfield and Nathan Tarcov (Chicago: University of Chicago Press, 1996). Text citations of *The Discourses* refer to book and chapter.

5. Pitkin, *Fortune Is a Woman*.

6. Ibid., 25, 80.

7. Ibid., 25.

8. Jean Bethke Elshtain, *Public Man, Private Woman: Women in Social and Political Thought* (Princeton: Princeton University Press, 1981), chap. 2.

9. R. Claire Snyder, *Citizen-Soldiers and Manly Warriors: Military Service and Gender in the Civic Republican Tradition* (Lanham, Md.: Rowman & Littlefield, 1999), 31, 38. It is important to note that Snyder is far more optimistic regarding the inclusive potential in Machiavellian citizenship than

other feminist political theorists. However, she suggests this potential is undermined by Machiavelli's insistence on a civic militia in which citizens learn how to be masculine.

10. Wendy Brown, *Manhood and Politics* (Totowa, N.J.: Rowman & Littlefield, 1988), 9.

11. Ibid., 88, 90, 91.

12. Honig, *Political Theory and the Displacement of Politics*, 16.

13. Arlene Saxonhouse, *Women in the History of Political Thought* (New York: Praeger, 1985), 151.

14. Ibid., 155, 156.

15. An example illustrates this point: A prince must exercise his *virtù* to remain a prince, while a conspirator also exercises his *virtù* to topple the prince and replace him. From the perspective of the prince, the conspirator is *Fortuna*, and yet the conspirator is merely exercising his *virtù*.

16. Saxonhouse, *Women in the History of Political Thought*, 151.

17. Ibid., 156; my emphasis.

18. Christine de Pisan, *Book of the City of Ladies*, trans. Earl Jeffrey Richards (New York: Persea, 1982).

19. The works of all of these authors were available during Machiavelli's lifetime with the exception of Fonte, whose work did not appear until the late sixteenth century.

20. Pamela Benson, *The Invention of the Renaissance Woman: Female Independence in the Literature and Thought of Italy and England* (University Park: Pennsylvania State University Press, 1992), 5.

21. Ibid., 4.

22. Maryanne C. Horowitz, "Introduction: Playing with Gender," in *Playing with Gender: A Renaissance Pursuit*, ed. Jean R. Brink, Maryanne C. Horowitz, and Allison P. Courdert (Urbana: University of Illinois Press, 1991), ix.

23. Machiavelli, *Lettere Familiari* (Florence: E. Lisio, 1883), letter 166.

24. Machiavelli, *Lettere Familiari*, letters 144, 179; Machiavelli, *The History of Florence*, in *Chief Works and Others*, vol. 3, book 2, chap. 42.

25. To argue that Machiavelli's celebration of women is a form of tokenism is to suggest that Machiavelli included these women in his works for reasons other than their usefulness for the project at hand.

26. As Florentine Secretary, Machiavelli was sent to meet and negotiate with the Countess in 1499. Pulver describes it as Machiavelli's "first really difficult mission" given the Countess' reputation: "Her determination was more than masculine, and her fearlessness almost proverbial." Jeffrey Pulver, *Machiavelli: The Man, His Work, and His Times* (London: Herbert Joseph, 1937), 76–77.

27. Margaret L. King, *Women of the Renaissance* (Chicago: University of Chicago Press, 1991), 158.

28. Machiavelli, *The History of Florence*, book 8, chap. 42.

29. Machiavelli, *La Mandragola*, in *Chief Works and Others*, vol. 2, I.3.

30. Machiavelli, "Tercets on Fortune," in *Chief Works and Others*, vol. 2, lines 106–8.

31. Compare Machiavelli's assessment with Polybius's analysis of regime cycles in his *Rise of the Roman Empire* (New York: Penguin, 1979).

32. Compare the prince with the aristocratic portion of the government, whose restraint lies in the fact that it is composed of several individuals. This means that one person cannot act alone; all must act in concert, which requires time, deliberation, and persuasion, among other things.

33. That is, once it has been founded. The republic cannot found itself; it requires a founder, a virtuous prince, to establish it.

34. Pitkin, *Fortune Is a Woman*, 19, 22, 110.

35. Ibid., 22.

36. Maurizio Viroli, *Machiavelli* (Oxford: Oxford University Press, 1998), 29.

37. Benson, *Invention of the Renaissance Woman*, chap. 1.

38. Compared to a republican like Rousseau, who wants to see particular wills fade away into the general will, Machiavelli begins to look liberal on this count.

39. Susan Moller Okin, *Justice, Gender, and the Family* (New York: Basic Books, 1989), 138.

40. Saxonhouse, *Women in the History of Political Thought*, 163.

41. Sextus, son of Tarquin the Proud who ruled at the time, raped Lucretia. Shortly after this incident, Lucretia committed suicide in order to preserve her own and her husband's dignity, and Tarquin the Proud was expelled from Rome. Virginia was killed by her father so she would not have to marry Appius, one of the Ten, who fell in love with her and would have taken her by force. The Ten fell shortly thereafter. In the city of Ardea, a wealthy woman received proposals from a plebeian and a noble. Her tutors and mother disagreed on whom she should marry. Armed conflict resulted between the plebs and the patricians as a result of this incident.

42. Saxonhouse, *Women in the History of Political Thought*, 163.

43. Isaiah Berlin, *Against the Current* (Princeton: Princeton University Press, 2001), 71.

44. Leo Strauss, *Thoughts on Machiavelli* (Chicago: University of Chicago Press, 1958).

45. Ernst Cassirer, *The Myth of State* (New Haven: Yale University Press, 1946).

46. J. G. A. Pocock, *The Machiavellian Moment* (Princeton: Princeton University Press, 1975); Quentin Skinner, *Machiavelli* (Oxford: Oxford University Press, 1981).

47. See Nancy Fraser, *Justice Interruptus: Critical Reflections on the "Postsocialist" Condition* (New York: Routledge, 1997), for her genealogy of economic dependence.

References

Benson, Pamela. *The Invention of the Renaissance Woman: Female Independence in the Litera-ture and Thought of Italy and England.* University Park: Pennsylvania State University Press, 1992.

Brown, Wendy. *Manhood and Politics.* Totowa, N.J.: Rowman & Littlefield, 1988.

Cassirer, Ernst. *The Myth of State.* New Haven: Yale University Press, 1946.

Elshtain, Jean Bethke. *Public Man, Private Woman: Women in Social and Political Thought.* Princeton: Princeton University Press, 1981.

Fraser, Nancy. *Justice Interruptus: Critical Reflections on the "Postsocialist" Condition.* New York: Routledge, 1997.

Honig, Bonnie. *Political Theory and the Displacement of Politics.* Ithaca: Cornell University Press, 1993.

Horowitz, Maryanne C. "Introduction." In *Playing with Gender*, ed. Jean R. Brink, Mary-anne C. Horowitz, and Allison P. Courdert. Urbana: University of Illinois Press, 1991.

King, Margaret L. *Women of the Renaissance.* Chicago: University of Chicago Press, 1991.

Machiavelli, Niccolò. *Lettere Familiari.* Florence: E. Lisio, 1883.

———. *Tutte le Opere Storiche e Letterarie di Niccolò Machiavelli.* Ed. Guido Mazzoni and Mario Casella. Florence: G. Barbera, 1929.

———. *Chief Works and Others.* 3 vols. Ed. and trans. Allan Gilbert. Durham: Duke University Press, 1965.

———. *Discourses on Livy.* Trans. Harvey C. Mansfield and Nathan Tarcov. Chicago: University of Chicago Press, 1996.

Okin, Susan Moller. *Justice, Gender, and the Family.* New York: Basic Books, 1989.

Pitkin, Hanna Fenichel. *Fortune Is a Woman: Gender and Politics in the Thought of Niccolò Machiavelli.* Berkeley and Los Angeles: University of California Press, 1984.

Pizan, Christine de. *Book of the City of Ladies*. Trans. Earl Jeffrey Richards. New York: Persea, 1982.

Pocock, J. G. A. *The Machiavellian Moment*. Princeton: Princeton University Press, 1975.

Polybius. *Rise of the Roman Empire*. Trans. Ian Scott-Kilvert. New York: Penguin, 1979.

Pulver, Jeffrey. *Machiavelli: The Man, His Work, and His Times*. London: Herbert Joseph, 1937.

Saxonhouse, Arlene. *Women in the History of Political Thought*. New York: Praeger, 1985.

Skinner, Quentin. *Machiavelli*. Oxford: Oxford University Press, 1981.

Snyder, R. Claire. *Citizen-Soldiers and Manly Warriors: Military Service and Gender in the Civic Republican Tradition*. Lanham, Md.: Rowman & Littlefield, 1999.

Strauss, Leo. *Thoughts on Machiavelli*. Chicago: University of Chicago Press, 1958.

Viroli, Maurizio. *Machiavelli*. Oxford: Oxford University Press, 1998.

12

Rethinking Machiavelli

Feminism and Citizenship

Jane S. Jaquette

In the realist tradition, the conviction that individuals are violent and aggressive by nature justifies the concentration of power in the hands of the state. Machiavelli is seen as an important architect of this approach. By arguing that men are evil by nature (which differs from the classical view that men do evil out of ignorance)[1] and by asserting that princes may have to commit political acts that would be considered immoral in private life, Machiavelli is said to have made politics a separate sphere, "beyond good and evil."[2] His cold detachment combined with his assertion that human affairs take similar courses in all times and places has contributed to the view that Machiavelli was the first to treat politics scientifically and the first to discover the "laws of human behavior."[3]

Feminists have used these conventional interpretations as the basis for criticism of Machiavelli. They fault Machiavelli for splitting the public from the private, making politics an arena "where terms like 'power, force, coercion and violence' structure political action and consciousness."[4] By dismissing all that is "feminine" as cowardly and unworthy, feminists argue, Machiavelli reveals his misogyny and narrows the range of the political. With Machiavelli, the classical concept of virtue loses its meaning and *virtù* becomes synonymous with the male urge to dominate.

Feminists have also focused on the ways Machiavelli militarizes both international and domestic politics. Although some praise him as a theorist of republicanism, others point out that Machiavelli's republics must expand to survive, making war inevitable. By arguing that citizens should also be soldiers, he seems to make military service a prerequisite for citizenship. Finally, as "first scientist," Machiavelli is implicated in the gender and science debate, and stands accused of helping to construct a form of knowledge that men have used to dominate both women and nature.[5]

This chapter argues that such interpretations are often based on partial readings of Machiavelli's texts, and that it is time to recover Machiavelli as an interlocutor rather than a foil for feminist theory. I maintain that Machiavelli does not develop general laws of human behavior, or find all men evil, or separate the male sphere of politics from the domestic world of women.[6] Instead, I contend, Machiavelli sees the two realms as virtually indistinguishable, with elements of realpolitik and compassion in both. He recognizes that women have the *virtù* to rule and, in his two most famous plays, he assigns the role of the prince to a woman. Despite his scorn for the "feminine," Machiavelli trains his prince in the art of deception, a quintessentially feminine form of power.[7]

To many, Machiavelli's famous metaphor—that Fortune is a woman and she must be "taken by force"—simply makes overt his patriarchal attitudes.[8] But I will argue that Machiavelli engaged women rather than fleeing them, as Susan Bordo has argued of Descartes as representative of Enlightenment philosophers.[9] Unlike political theorists from Plato to Rousseau, Machiavelli does not set reason against the passions. This choice radically changes the debate about femininity and political aptitude and challenges both the classical and the Christian rationales for excluding women from politics, although Machiavelli may seem to erect a different barrier by making the soldier a model for the citizen.[10]

The feminist tendency to take the moral high ground makes Machia-velli a tempting target; since his own time, Machiavelli has been de-scribed as the incarnation of evil. But Machiavelli has his defenders, from those who see him as a champion of republicanism to those, like Isaiah Berlin, who argue that he is setting classical values against the Christian "virtues," which he found unsuited to the organization of political life. To Berlin, Machiavelli is modern in his realization that men can pursue goals that are equally valid but morally incompatible with each other,[11] a move that both undermined all rationalist positions and recognized con-flict as a permanent part of the human condition.[12] Building on this ob-servation, John Pocock and Hanna Fenichel Pitkin both argue that Machiavelli anticipated the contemporary ideal of a pluralist political community.

Machiavellian "Men"

Machiavelli is said to have identified laws of human behavior because he saw men "as they really are," that is, as cowardly in the face of power, aggressive toward the weak, and self-interested. This image, however, ig-nores the important differences Machiavelli found among men, though he does in fact sometimes generalize, calling them "ungrateful, voluble, dissemblers, anxious to avoid danger and covetous of gain," "selfish," and easily deceived.[13]

But for Machiavelli, humans are not evil so much as *unreliable*. "As long as you benefit them," Machiavelli tells the prince, "they are entirely yours." They promise to support you "when the danger is remote," but when they are called on to fulfill their promises when danger is near, "they revolt." It is because he cannot count on his subjects' loyalty or gratitude that the prince must both use force and maintain his reputation as a ruler who is prepared to do so. As Machiavelli advises the prince, "love is held by a chain of obligation which, men being selfish, is broken whenever it serves their purpose; but fear is maintained by a dread of punishment that never fails."[14]

To establish his power and rule effectively (and these are not always the same), the prince cannot rely on vague generalizations about all peo-ple; he must understand their differences in order to anticipate how they will act. People have different personalities, which for Machiavelli are produced by several factors: the balance of humors in the body; whether one belongs to the *grande* or the *popolo*; one's family history. Most important, individuals can be expected to act differently depending on "the times," that is, the degree of political *virtù* or decay present in a given political community.

People are not naturally violent. If that were the case, it would be unnecessary for Machiavelli to school the prince in the uses of force and to steel the prince's will against moral doubts. Machiavelli's instrumentalism entails what Sheldon Wolin describes as an "economy of violence," which balances the costs of force against the value of the ends for which it is used. In this calculus, fraud is often a more efficient way to achieve the prince's goals than force. And although Machiavelli thinks a prince who seeks power for its own sake may succeed, he will never be honored.[15] A prince drunk on his own power will forget what it is for.

Cyclical History and the Politics of Innovation

In his introduction to *The Discourses*, Machiavelli laments his contemporaries' lack of willingness to learn from the past, and blames the "proud indolence [*ozio*] which prevails in most of the Christian states" as the source of this neglect.[16] Borrowing from Polybius, he develops a cyclical theory of how states rise and fall. But unlike Polybius, Machiavelli believes that whatever their form—rule by one, by the few, or by the many—states will never reach equilibrium.[17] The natural order is flux.

Machiavelli thus calls on the prince to act boldly to reverse the cycle of history in a decaying society. For this reason, his focus is on the challenges facing a "new," not an established, prince. The new prince is by definition a usurper who is trying to alter a country's habits and customs and therefore cannot rely on them for his authority. "[D]isorders spring at first from a natural difficulty which exists in all new dominions," Machiavelli writes, where the "inevitable harm inflicted on those over whom the prince obtains dominion" is resisted and resented. Nor can the prince expect loyalty from those who invited him in: you cannot "maintain the friendship of those who have helped you to obtain this possession," Machiavelli warns, "as you will not be able to fulfill their expectations."[18]

To Pocock, the new prince is an innovator in an even more profound sense. The collision between Machiavelli's cyclical understanding of history with the linear but eschatological Christian view of time produced a new concept of history as linear and secular, Pocock argues. Where the Christian notion of linear history only made sense at the "end of time," Machiavelli thinks man is capable of intervening in history in the here and now. Machiavelli goes against Christian tradition by favoring the *vita activa* over the *vita contemplativa*, that is, human action over the passive acceptance of "God's plan."[19]

Thus what is truly new about Machiavelli's prince is that he is expected to act "in time" for openly secular, fully political ends. In rejecting what Jean Bethke Elshtain calls "the womanly virtues" of Christianity,[20] Machiavelli also rejects the traditional Christian understanding of history and changes the individual's relation to the polity,[21] arguably a necessary step in the development of the secular, ultimately democratic state. As Pocock observes, "a customary community in one corner of an eternal order is not a republic of citizens."[22]

Pocock's analysis enables us to see the possibility of a sophisticated rationale for the use of force. Because the prince is acting "in time," against uncertainty, he is a "man in a hurry" who cannot wait for history to reveal its plan. He must act decisively. Pocock argues that instead of contrasting *Fortuna* and *virtù* in the classical tradition as "disorder" and "balance," Machiavelli differentiates them as "uncertainty" and "innovation." The new prince cannot control what will happen, nor can he rely on God's intervention. He can try acting with prudence, but in times of uncertainty *Fortuna* does not always reward prudence, but rather the individual who seizes the initiative.

Feminist Critiques: Public versus Private?

The feminist litany against Machiavelli is long: he separates the public and the private (keeping "the private realm of necessity apart from the public domain of freedom"),[23] rejects the "feminine," prescribes a hypermasculine version of power as the basis of the state, and militarizes citizenship.

Machiavelli does separate the public from the private in one sense with which feminists and progressives can readily identify and may find acceptable: he distinguishes the public good from the pursuit of private interests. When the motives of citizens become particular and selfish, and this often happens among the nobles, the public good suffers and *virtù* is absent.[24] Frivolous and wasteful consumption is a sign of decay in Machiavelli's literary works, where men often try to meet their wives' demands to "keep up with the Joneses" rather than acting sensibly, as is true of Rodrigo and his domineering wife in Machiavelli's "Tale of Belfagor."[25]

But Machiavelli makes neither the Greek nor the modern distinction between the household and the political world. The Greeks separated the household (*oikos*) from the political realm because they believed the family was "a threat to political life."[26] The modern distinction emerged when the Industrial Revolution separated household from factory production, making the economy part of the "public" sphere and the home a "haven."[27] By contrast, Machiavelli does not divide the family from the state. Families are essential to his political analysis, perhaps because, in Florence as in the other Italian city-states of the late Renaissance, the competition among elite families was the very stuff of politics.[28]

One example of Machiavelli's blurring of the line between public and private is his obsession with conspiracies, which are played out as domestic dramas. In one memorable case, the Emperor Commodus discovers a plot against him; he draws up a list of the conspirators and puts it under his pillow, where his favorite child finds it. A concubine, seeing the child with the list, takes it from him—and runs to tell her co-conspirators so they can kill Commodus before they are killed by him. Machiavelli argues that the domestic dimension of most conspiracies, unlike in the example of Commodus, usually works in the prince's favor. Because the plotters often confide their plans to a "wife or child" or discuss them where a servant can overhear, it is difficult to keep conspiracies secret, so the prince can more easily discover and thwart them.[29]

Some of the most memorable scenes in *The Prince* are Machiavelli's examples of how successful rulers tricked and then killed their rivals. These ruses are usually set in "private" spaces. In a typical case, the prince calls his enemies to a banquet; when the rival group is assembled, the prince's retainers lock the doors and take the "guests" by surprise, killing them all in a single stroke.[30]

Public or private, violence can be an efficient means to power for the "new" prince who is most vulnerable to challenge from others who feel themselves equally able to rule because they too come from the ruling families of a city. Because they rely on trust, Machiavelli's examples of the successful use of force also involve deception; they are as likely to occur within the household as in the piazza. Machiavelli also equates families and politics when he counsels the prince that it is important to know the family histories of potential supporters and enemies because "the same family in a city always preserves the same characteristics."[31] By this he means that elite families' alliances and political proclivities do not change very much over time, allowing the prince to anticipate potential sources of opposition and support.[32]

In some cases, Machiavelli does seem explicitly to exclude women from politics. In *The Discourses*, Machiavelli notes that "women have been the cause of great dissensions," citing Aristotle's observation that "one of the first causes of the ruin of tyrants [is] the outrages committed by them on the wives and daughters of others, either by violence or seduction." Feminists have taken this to mean that Machiavelli does not think that women have a place in politics, and that he sees women as men's property. But a closer reading suggests that Machiavelli is making a practical observation about how the world works, and that men's lack of control over their own actions, not women's unsuitability to politics, is the problem. He urges the prince not to engage in the practice of sexual familiarity with the wives and daughters of his subjects. In this case as in others, Machiavelli counsels self-restraint.[33]

Many would argue that the most important public/private distinction in Machiavelli's thought is the line he is said to draw between public and private ethics, asserting the "autonomy" of politics from other spheres of life. But Pitkin, often a tough critic of Machiavelli, argues against this interpretation. Citing Machiavelli's love of paradox,[34] she writes that "Machiavelli does indeed say that what is morally good in normal life may have terrible consequences in the long run and on the larger scale, especially in corrupt or immoral times. Apparent kindness may turn out to be cruel, and apparent generosity may have different consequences with public or private funds. But such claims do not amount to making politics a distinct realm with a special morality, or with none." Instead, Pitkin suggests, "[t]he rules of conduct for private life displayed in Machiavelli's fiction and his letters are much the same as those advanced for public life in his political theory."[35]

The Prince Has No Gender

Machiavelli's plays were much better known to his contemporaries than his political works and, along with his letters and poems, they too reveal his views of women. Two provocative illustrations are provided by his most successful plays: *La Mandragola* and *Clizia*. Both show the continuity between public and private in Machiavelli's thought and both raise larger political and social themes while giving the reader a lively sense of bourgeois life in early sixteenth-century Florence.[36]

Commentators have advanced the argument that Machiavelli identifies with one or another male character in these plays. I suggest, however, that Machiavelli's "hero" in each is a woman, and that both plays are written to make the audience more familiar with the moral and practical issues that the "new" prince must face. The plays not only satirize Florentine life but defend Machiavelli's unconventional approach to moral action, particularly his realist recognition that "bad" acts can bring about "good" ends. In both plays the female protagonist relies on deception and commits an "immoral" act that preserves her family and, in metaphorical terms, the state.

The case of *Clizia* is straightforward. Written in about 1524, late in Machiavelli's life, *Clizia* is based on a classical play by Plautus, and it begins with the dilemma Plautus poses, although Machiavelli gives it a moral point that is lacking in the original (for a summary, see Appendix B). From the beginning, Sofronia dominates the action and frames the moral message of the play. Machiavelli makes it clear that Sofronia wants to renew the family's *virtù*.[37] Like the state before it becomes corrupt, Nicomaco before his affection for Clizia was a man of *virtù*, aware of history and of his role as an example to his son and other members of the family.

But, Sofronia says, "since he's had this girl on the brain, his affairs have been neglected, his farms are decaying, his trade is going to ruin." The servants and his son, Cleandro, have "lost all respect for him," and because he is not providing a good example, "they all do as they like."[38] A state in which people "all do as they like" is a state that has fallen into what Machiavelli calls "license," where individuals only pursue private interests and disregard the common good.

When Sofronia is unable to convince Nicomaco to postpone Clizia's wedding to Pirro, his servant, so that he may himself sleep with Clizia, she first looks to *Fortuna* as an ally, suggesting that she and Nicomaco draw names to see which servant will be paired with Clizia. But when Pirro's name is drawn, Sofronia does not give up: she dresses a third servant in Clizia's clothes and puts him under the sheets so that, when Nicomaco climbs into bed, he will try to seduce the servant, mistaking him for Clizia. The switch succeeds, and the old man is rebuffed. After being "publicly" embarrassed before the family and his neighbors,[39] Nicomaco readily agrees to return to his former self. At the last moment, Clizia's real father appears, proving her to be of noble descent and removing all barriers to a marriage with Cleandro.

Some have argued that the fact that Clizia herself never appears on stage is an indication of Machiavelli's contempt for women. Catherine Zuckert argues the opposite, that Clizia's absence raises the moral tone of the play, and turns the audience's attention away from ribald jokes about Clizia's chastity to the issues of Sofronia's choices and Nicomaco's virtue. The hero of the play is clearly Sofronia, to whom Machiavelli assigns the key attributes he wishes his prince to cultivate.[40] Unable to rely on *Fortuna*, Sofronia acts boldly and, working against time, a touch that Pocock would appreciate, she resorts to deception and restores the "state" and its "citizens" to virtue.

La Mandragola, or *The Mandrake Root*, was written earlier, in 1518. It is a more original play, with a plot based on "an ingenious and crude practical joke of the sort familiar to generations of readers of the Florentine *novelle*,"[41] though Machiavelli makes something quite different of it (for a summary, see Appendix A).[42] The family is renewed, its future guaranteed by the expected birth of an heir.

Pitkin asks with whom Machiavelli identifies in *La Mandragola*, and answers that it cannot be Nicia (despite the fact that Nicia is a pun on Niccolò),[43] nor Callimaco (who initiates the action but seems not very bright). She concludes that it must be Callimaco's friend Ligurio because he, like Machiavelli, is the cunning adviser to a reluctant prince.[44] "Machiavelli seeks to manipulate the prince into seizing power—both for the prince's glory and the good of Italy. If he were to succeed, the prince would get the actual power just as Callimaco gets the girl: poor, despoiled Lady Italy as she appears in the last chapter of *The Prince*, eager to receive him so that on her he may father a new state and perpetuate his name." But, she asks, if Ligurio is so smart, why doesn't he get Lucrezia instead of serving Callimaco? Perhaps, she speculates, Ligurio embodies Machiavelli's own sense of frustration about being an adviser to princes, one whose advice is often spurned. Or perhaps Ligurio's reward is the "gratification" he gets from "outsmarting all the others."[45]

Having decided on Ligurio, Pitkin develops the thesis that he is Machiavelli's "fox," in Italian *furbo*, "one who has skill in employing ruses that are usually, but not necessarily, dishonest." The *furbo* may be "scrupulously moral in his relation with family and friends, yet take pride in his ability to cheat someone outside his intimate circle." Pursuing this notion further, she asks whether Machiavelli is not the "consummate" fox, "disparaging himself and flattering others," concealing himself—and, "in his cleverness, in danger of losing . . . his real self."[46]

Turning to Lucrezia, Pitkin finds Machiavelli's characterization of her "inconsistent." On the one hand, Lucrezia is "the paragon of virtue and chastity," and "when she is told of Ligurio's plan, she objects to the 'sin' and 'shame' of it" and to the "idea of taking an innocent man's life." But she is then transformed "after one night . . . into a resolute and competent adulteress." Comparing her to the Roman Lucretia—who nobly commits suicide when she is raped, bringing about the overthrow of the Tarquin kings and the founding of the Republic—Pitkin concludes that Machiavelli is "playing out as farce, in family life, what Livy relates as tragedy in . . . Roman political life." In Machiavelli's version, the taking of Lucrezia does not lead to renewal, but only to "the birth of a child in a world that remains as corrupt as before." And "[t]hough the cuckolded husband tells Lucrezia after her adulterous night that 'it's exactly as though you were born a second time,'" Pitkin states firmly that "no regeneration—either Christian or classical—has taken place."[47]

I think Pitkin is right to emphasize the significance of deception in Machiavelli's view of power, but wrong to reject Lucrezia as the character with whom Machiavelli most identifies.[48] Pitkin seems to prefer the classical distinction between public and private, so a "family farce" is by definition no place for heroic action. But she is also put off because Lucrezia (unlike the Roman Lucretia) has sacrificed her claim to virtue by taking up with Callimaco, and by not taking her own life.

Mary O'Brien, commenting from an ecofeminist standpoint in her chapter on Machiavelli in *Reproducing the World*, is similarly offended. She describes Callimaco as exploiting Lucrezia's moral virtue (her trust in her mother and in her confessor) to gain entry to the "fortress" of her sexual virtue. Although she describes Lucrezia as "still in command" after Callimaco has "raped" her, O'Brien characterizes Lucrezia's sexual response to Callimaco as an "insatiable, voluptuous lust" and summarily pronounces her lost: "her virtue sinks beyond a trace." To O'Brien, Lucrezia's "rebirth" is a negative transformation: she has been "redefined by masculine desire."[49]

The parallel with the historic Lucretia does suggest a different order of virtue. But I would argue that Machiavelli and his audiences were well aware of the historical and moral distance between Rome and Florence, although Machiavelli had not relinquished hope that strong leadership could bring political renewal to Florence.[50] His dramas were intended to educate the public in ways that would make that more likely. He certainly satirized Florence and himself in the characters of Nicia and Nicomaco. But his letters, poems, and his own life show that chastity for women was not the moral issue for Machiavelli that we assume it to be.[51] Neither Machiavelli nor his audience finds it strange that Lucrezia would have sexual desires of her own.[52]

Sofronia and Lucrezia both use deception to save the family/state.[53] Giulio Ferroni suggests that La Mandragola also teaches another Machiavellian lesson: to succeed, the prince must adapt to what Fortuna brings. As Machiavelli writes,

> No man is found so prudent as to be able to adapt himself to [changes in time and circumstance], either because he cannot deviate from that to which his nature disposes him, or else because having always prospered by walking in one path, he cannot persuade himself that it is well to leave it; and therefore when it is time to act suddenly, does not know how to do so and is ruined; for if one could change one's nature with time and circumstances, fortune would never change.[54]

If, instead of seeing Callimaco as the prince and Ligurio as his Machiavelli-like advisor, we make Lucrezia's ability to "change her nature with time and circumstance" a positive focal point, as Ferroni suggests, she is no longer "inconsistent," "poor," or "despoiled." Once Lucrezia learns of the mandrake from her mother and the Friar, she takes control of the action.[55] Lucrezia is not raped; she makes the decision to take the potion and to sleep with someone not her husband, who vows to marry her "when God has other plans for" Nicia. Lucrezia explicitly acknowledges the role of Fortuna, deciding when she finds Callimaco in her bed that "some divine influence has willed this." By being open to change, and acting on her new assessment of the situation, she finds success, preserving the family, fulfilling Nicia's greatest desire (on terms that suit her), and taking Callimaco as her "contracted" husband.[56]

Far from being manipulated by Friar Timoteo, Lucrezia takes control by ordering Nicia to pay the friar well for "churching" her, which is the point of the ceremony organized by the priest on the morning after, a

symbolic wedding of Lucrezia and Callimaco. In most contemporary interpretations, the scene in church is just another "deception," one that
Machiavelli cannot really mean for us to take seriously. But that view fails
to take account of the importance of appearances in Florentine culture, a
judgment that is reflected in Machiavelli's advice to the prince to pretend
to be virtuous, even when he is not.

Ferroni finds the supposedly naive Lucrezia the true "sage" of the play;
Callimaco and Ligurio simply provide the "external 'occasion' [opportu-
nity] that Fortune offers." While Callimaco suffers the "madness" of love,
the "wise" Lucrezia keeps her eye on the ball. Pointing out that Machiavelli has little patience for "sterile and unproductive emotional hesita-
tions," Ferroni quotes Callimaco's advice to himself: "Turn your face to
luck, flee mischance, or, not being able to flee from it, bear it like a
man"—which describes exactly how Lucrezia responds to the opportunity
the ruse of the mandragola affords her.[57]

In Ferroni's view, Ligurio is not the hero, although he is in charge of
the action in the beginning when he sets the scenes and moves the prin-
cipals on and off the stage. But once Lucrezia is made aware of the plot,
she becomes the center of the play, "autonomously" deciding how to
respond to *Fortuna*,[58] and deserving the accolade by which Ligurio first
describes her: "a beautiful woman, well-behaved, and capable of ruling a
kingdom."[59]

Machiavelli's "Il Femminino"

Machiavelli's ability to imagine women as princes—and to admire the
bold Caterina Sforza—does not make him an admirer of "womanly" virtues, however.[60] On the contrary, the word "effeminate" is one of the
harshest in his vocabulary, and he repeatedly dismisses the "feminine"
qualities of weakness and indecisiveness as unworthy, lauding the "opposing" qualities of *animo*, or spiritedness, and *virtù*. More than mere courage, *virtù* is a moral quality, the "major bulwark" against "luxury, idleness,
softness and the pusillanimity that lie in wait to rob the *animo* of its fiber
and manhood and turn it into an *animo effeminato*."[61]

Machiavelli associates feminine qualities with political failure. "Christian indolence" and moral weakness are the qualities that, he believes,
bear the greatest responsibility for the sorry plight of the Italian states.[62]

Softness in leaders invites challenge. Machiavelli's patron and employer Piero Soderini was elected "*Gonfaloniere* for Life." But he was overthrown, Machiavelli writes, because his "patience and gentleness" made him too good to hold onto power, bringing disaster to Florence—and, as Pitkin reminds us, to Machiavelli himself.[63]

Not only is an "effeminate" Christian concept of virtue of no use in a corrupt world, but corruption inevitably takes hold if *virtù* is not regularly put to the test. Machiavelli rejects the Greek ideal of equilibrium, and would certainly find the contemporary feminist position—that peace would emerge naturally if it were not for militarized *eros* and the masculine state—both unconvincing and undesirable.

Nonetheless, I believe his attack on "the feminine" is not an attack on women. Machiavelli includes women in his writings in a variety of roles and with a range of personal qualities. As real individuals and in his imagination, women are capable of exhibiting the highest *virtù*. Machiavelli "knows well that history is full of examples of women who did much better than men in political affairs," Maurizio Viroli contends, in response to Pitkin's charge that Machiavelli is "anxious and defensive" about his manhood and determined to maintain his autonomy. Machiavelli values love as much as political action, with which it shares elements of risk and vulnerability, Viroli argues. Repeatedly falling in love, Machiavelli repeatedly risked the autonomy that Pitkin insists he is so determined to preserve.[64]

Machiavelli often "speaks of women as friends and equals." In *The Golden Ass* he portrays the hero talking with Circe's damsel "as one friend speaks to another" about many things, including politics.[65] In his own life, it is evident that Machiavelli cared for his wife and his children. In a cultural context where men took lovers as a matter of course, some of his lovers were also his friends. For Machiavelli, Viroli concludes, "love of women, of family, and of friends, as well as the pleasures and pains of ordinary life, are important."[66]

Finally, if "the feminine" is cowardly and soft, how can Machiavelli imagine *Fortuna* as such a strong and active force? Bonnie Honig offers a paradoxical answer. Machiavelli's men are not as masculine as they are often portrayed. The relation between *virtù* and *Fortuna* is "less adversarial . . . than indebted and mimetic," as the "highest overall excellence of Machiavelli's man of *virtù* is his ability to be like [*Fortuna*], to be as capricious, unpredictable, and wily as she."[67] Honig provides another perspective on why fraud may be a superior form of power. It is more flexible than force, enabling the prince to change his position rapidly while still maintaining the appearance of a leader who is decisive and capable of cruelty, which is essential to deter those who would attack him.[68]

One way to reconcile Machiavelli's rejection of the effeminate with his portrayal of *Fortuna* and his admiration for women who lead is to put his work in the context of Renaissance understandings of sex and gender. The modern position is that biological sex determines cultural gender, that anatomy is destiny. But, if Thomas Laqueur is correct, the Renaissance view was just the opposite. According to Galenist biology, gender determined sex. Female sexual organs were not differentiated from those of males, but were understood as *inverted* versions. "In this world the vagina is imagined as an interior penis, the labia as foreskin, the uterus as scrotum, and the ovaries as testicles." Women were not men's *opposites:* they were *lesser men*. In Galen's view (but not Aristotle's, who gave men the credit for the only active role in procreation), both men and women produced sperm. If both sperm were "strong," the child would be a boy, and if "weak," a girl. Both men and women could produce either strong or weak seed.[69]

Gender differences were rationalized by teleology: "just as mankind is the most perfect of all animals, so within mankind the man is more perfect than the woman, and the reason for his perfection, is his excess of heat."[70] The view that women are not radically different from men did not inhibit the enforcement of patriarchal ideology, however. For Galen as for Aristotle, "man is the measure of all things."[71] The differences in male and female roles, in the "obligations" of women and the "rights" of men, were taken as givens. Machiavelli's plays are subversive in that women are portrayed as both powerful and moral, against the gender stereotypes of his time.

Two features of Galenism help explain aspects of Machiavelli's portrayal of Lucrezia that Pitkin and O'Brien find offensive. In the Galenist view, women actively seek sexual pleasure, and they must experience orgasm in order to become pregnant. This makes it harder to see Machiavelli's portrayal of Lucrezia as intending to deny her virtue. And all individuals, men and women, are a mix of male and female characteristics, of "hot" and "cold," "wet" and "dry." There were "feminine men," and "masculine women."[72] As Renaissance historian Ian Maclean writes, "there was no necessary connection between 'manliness' and 'maleness,' 'effeminacy' and 'femaleness.'"[73] Machiavelli could thus imagine women who showed male *virtù*, yet were incontestably biologically female. And he could excoriate "the feminine" without dismissing women as a class.

Although he finds most women too eager for luxury and thus a source of "license,"[74] Machiavelli usually refrains from generalizing about "women's nature." In the famous chapter of *The Discourses* where he cites Aristotle's claim that women are "a danger to the state," Machiavelli discusses women's *roles* in society (as men's intimates or as the objects of disruptive male passion), not their *natures*. In this he differed from many of his contemporaries, including the influential Spanish jurist Juan Luis Vives, who argued that women should "not meddle with matters of realms or cities" because they know "neither measure nor order."[75]

Fortune Is a Woman . . .

I have left *Fortuna* (nearly) to the last. The provocative language of the penultimate chapter of *The Prince* colors everything else we read by Machiavelli. I reverse this process, and suggest that his metaphor be viewed in light of the arguments made thus far. My argument depends on a point at issue: whether Machiavelli understood *Fortuna* as a causal force in human history or only as a useful metaphor that reflected his deep ambivalence toward women. Anthony Parel has argued that, like many of his contemporaries, Machiavelli believed in astrology. Parel's thesis ties together several aspects of Machiavelli's thinking that otherwise seem anomalous to modern readers: his references to signs and omens, his cyclical characterization of history, and the role of *Fortuna* herself.[76]

In Parel's interpretation, Machiavelli believed that "the heavens are the general cause of all particular motions—human, elemental, and natural—occurring in the sublunar world." The "motions of history as well as of states are subject to the motions of the heavens," but they do not fully determine man's fate. *Fortuna* represents "the chance events which occur in a universe so determined."[77] Christians had seen history as determined by God but, by emphasizing *Fortuna*, Machiavelli expands the possibilities for human initiative.

Parel points out how Machiavelli differentiates *Fortuna*'s role in *general matters* as compared to *particular cases*, a distinction that is important to understanding why Machiavelli suggests the prince must act boldly. In

Renaissance astrology, the reference to *Fortuna* "in general" refers to *states*, but in "particular cases" refers to *individuals*. The distinction figures prominently in the introduction to Machiavelli's famous metaphor, which occurs in chapter 25 of *The Prince*. The chapter begins:

> It is not unknown to me how many have been and are of the opinion that worldly events are so governed by fortune and by God, that men cannot by their prudence change them. . . . [F]or this they may judge it to be useless to toil much about them, but let things be ruled by chance. . . . Nonetheless, that our freedom may not be altogether extinguished, I think it may be true that fortune is the ruler of half our actions, but that she allows the other half or thereabouts to be governed by us. I would compare her to an impetuous river that, when turbulent, inundates the plains, casts down trees and buildings . . . still, when it is quiet, men can make provision by dikes and banks. . . . This must suffice as regards opposition to Fortune in general.

Contrasting the role of *Fortuna* in general to her role in particular cases, he argues that *Fortuna* makes it hard to predict the consequences of human efforts and therefore flexibility, rather than habit or principled rigidity, is the path to success:

> I would point out how one sees a certain prince today fortunate and tomorrow ruined, without seeing that he has changed in character or otherwise. . . . [This is] because the prince who bases himself entirely on Fortune is ruined when fortune changes. . . . For one sees that men . . . proceed in various ways; one with circumspection, another with impetuosity, one by violence, another by cunning, one with patience, another with the reverse, and each by these diverse ways may arrive at his aim.

Given that there is no rule of reason that can be consistently applied,[78] what strategy should be followed by a leader who wants to have an impact on history? It is at this dramatic juncture that Machiavelli writes,

> I conclude then that Fortune varying and men remaining fixed in their ways, they are successful as long as these ways conform to circumstances, but when they are opposed then they are unsuc-

cessful. I certainly think that it is better to be impetuous than cautious, for Fortune is a woman, and it is necessary, if you wish to master her, to conquer her by force; and it can be seen that she lets herself be overcome by the bold, rather than those who proceed coldly. And therefore, like a woman, she is always a friend to the young, because they are less cautious, fiercer, and master her with audacity.[79]

It has always been hard to explain why Machiavelli the political scientist would place *Fortuna* at the center of his theory of causality and place such credence in omens and signs. It is good feminist methodology to take anomalies as a signal of internal stress in a theorist's work. To some, this is an invitation to put the theorist on the couch and try a psychoanalytical approach. Both Pitkin and O'Brien take that path. To Pitkin, Machiavelli's treatment of *Fortuna* reveals the underlying fear and resentment Machiavelli feels toward women; to O'Brien, the conflict between *virtù* and *Fortuna* is a story of the victory of male power over female innocence, a metaphor for the domination of nature by science.

Pitkin points out that the most commonly used translation, in which Machiavelli calls on the youthful prince to "take" *Fortuna* "by force," is in fact incorrect. She suggests a translation of "cuff and maul her"; Parel and Zuckert use the more literal "to hold her down, to beat her and strike her down."[80] Unlike "take her by force," these translations suggest that, although Machiavelli is suggesting an aggressive approach, he is not prescribing rape.[81]

When he is describing *Fortuna*, Machiavelli usually follows the classical sources, borrowing many of the metaphors many modern readers assume are original with Machiavelli. But, Pitkin observes, although *Fortuna* was "powerful and sometimes capricious," the classical role "of *virtus* with regard to [*Fortuna*] seems always to have been limited and respectful."[82] By contrast, Machiavelli is counseling the prince to boldness in terms that are unmistakably gendered.

Pitkin then makes an analytical leap. Citing Machiavelli's contemporary, Pico della Mirandola, who comments that references to *Fortuna* "attribut[e] to the heavens powers that reside within ourselves," Pitkin rejects the interpretation that Machiavelli took astrology seriously. Instead, Pitkin asserts, Machiavelli is projecting his own fears and hopes onto this richly metaphorical image.[83]

There is no doubt that Machiavelli was engaging in an aggressive call to action. But to say, as Leo Strauss contended and Pitkin quotes to feminist effect, that Machiavelli thinks *Fortuna* "can be vanquished by the right kind of man" goes too far.[84]

Parel and Pocock do take Machiavelli seriously when he talks of *Fortuna* as a causal force. But where Parel sees *Fortuna* as chance in a mechanical universe governed by movements of the stars and planets, Pocock describes uncertainty in broader, humanist terms. In both cases, however, *Fortuna* is a bridge to the present—to the modern notion that humans can shape history.

Pocock argues that *Fortuna* as human innovation affects Machiavelli's views of power and autonomy. Hereditary princes can rely on the balance between *virtù* and *Fortuna* that arises out of custom and acceptance; kings enjoy legitimate and stable political authority. But, he declares, *The Prince* is not a handbook for kings, and Machiavelli's new prince "lack[s] legitimacy altogether," and must use force and fraud to establish his rule. *The Prince* is organized to illustrate the various kinds of relations that can exist "between princes and contingency." Pitkin sees Machiavelli's fear of dependency as a male fear of dependency on women. Pocock offers a broader interpretation: The more a prince depends on the wills of others, the more he is "exposed" to *Fortuna*. The sooner he can "transfer to himself the habitual legitimacy enjoyed by his predecessor . . . the less urgent his need of *virtù*."[85]

Thus, Pocock concludes, the relation between *virtù* and *Fortuna* "is not simply antithetical." By *virtù* we innovate, and "let loose sequences of contingency beyond our prediction or control," which makes us "prey to *Fortuna*". By *virtù* we "resist *Fortuna*" but, because innovation is "formally self-destructive," there is an "incompatibility between action . . . and moral order."[86]

To turn his power into authority, the new prince must move quickly to provide laws and cultivate *virtù*. But without good arms there are no good laws. Machiavelli seems to suggest that in the end all states are based on coercion. Jane Mansbridge makes a similar point, against the feminist grain, in the context of recent debates about democracy and power. She argues that, without coercion, democracies could never act. Some people will always disagree about change or its direction. What democracies do is guarantee that this dissent will be heard, but not that it will always prevail. Legitimacy rests not in consensus, but in the way decisions will be made.[87] Thus, to act as a group is to accept the necessity of "power over" as well as "power to."

A "Masculine Birth of Time"?

Pocock argues that *virtù* imposes order on uncertainty and moral order on a corrupt polity. It is a short step from there to the feminist gloss that *virtù* is male order imposed on an unruly (female) nature. O'Brien reads *La Mandragola* as the story of male science conquering natural innocence. The chaste Lucrezia is like nature in that men want to control her; *virtù* is the violence required to tame her. The notion that Lucrezia gives up so completely is the expression of a male fantasy. "Women/nature/nurture challenges man/polity/violence in a primordial way," O'Brien asserts, and the male version of the story—i.e., Lucrezia's seduction—"denies even the possibility of complementarity." Taking up Pitkin's focus on Machiavelli's preoccupation with masculine autonomy, O'Brien argues that "manliness" is the "crucial individual quality demanded by the tension between biological and civil society." "The struggle for an autonomous and scientific politics is the struggle in which political man, by whatever means he can devise, breaks free from the chains that bind him to biological and affective life."[88]

Machiavelli can be directly linked to some of the intellectual shifts that led to the development of modern, empirical science.[89] The gendered rhetoric Evelyn Fox Keller finds in Sir Francis Bacon's work reflects Machiavelli's rhetorical style and even borrows some of his metaphors, most drawn, as Pitkin has shown, from classical sources. Like Machiavelli, Bacon uses aphorisms to categorize and discipline his unwieldy material; similarly, his empiricism is a form of practical reason rather than systematic science. Bacon's call for a "masculine birth of time," taken by Keller as an indication of the gendered foundation of science,[90] is in keeping with the masculine *animo* so admired by Machiavelli, whose work Bacon knew.

Neither Machiavelli nor Bacon saw *Fortuna* or nature as passive or innocent. *Fortuna* might have been "unruly," but she was too powerful to be coerced. Machiavelli never ridicules or discounts her power. As Robert Orr writes, he "sees her as an active sharer in the making of events."[91] A prince may succeed without *Fortuna*, but he can never prevail against her.

There are also important differences between Machiavelli's and Bacon's understanding of nature. Machiavelli would have been horrified at the world imagined by Bacon, where prudent management promised to bring a world of plenty. Machiavelli thought the best states were formed where the land was less productive, because a life that was too easy would sap a nation's *virtù*. Nor would he have accepted the radical break between biology and politics that O'Brien attributes to him. For Machiavelli, men are first and last part of nature; they are subject to desires, embedded in families, embodied. Christian doctrine may suggest that nature can be transcended, but Machiavelli does not.

Citizens and Soldiers

I have argued that many of the generalizations commonly made about Machiavelli, and used by feminists to denounce him, are flawed. Machiavelli does not see all individuals as "evil" and therefore argue that they require a coercive state to govern them. He does not separate the private from the public, justify the excessive use of force, or support domination as a form of power. I have tried to show that his depiction of the relation of *virtù* to *Fortuna* is neither a sign of men's hostility to women nor a call for male control over nature. Machiavelli does not exclude women from politics or distinguish between men and women on the basis of intelligence or moral character, sex differences that have been conventionally used to bar women from public life.

This reading of Machiavelli does more than repel the charge of misogyny. It opens the way to a more balanced assessment, one that recognizes the many ways in which Machiavelli has contributed vital elements to a modern concept of participatory citizenship that is fully shared by feminists.

His first contribution is to construct an image of the political world that is dynamic rather than static, open and eclectic rather than closed and exclusionary. Pitkin puts it very well: "For Machiavelli, at his best, the real point is not some unified harmony at which politics theoretically aims, but the activity of struggling toward agreement with and against each other, in which citizens take active charge of the historical processes that would otherwise direct their lives. And that activity is not mere courtly dialogue, but a genuine conflict, in which needs and important interests are at stake." But political conflict must not degenerate into civil war. The struggle must be kept "open and public"; it must involve a "genuine appeal to principle"; and citizens must "be kept aware of their interdependence, their shared stake in fair rules and right principles, the civil limits (*i termini civili*) that forbid wiping out their opponents."[92]

Pocock adds to this understanding in a way that is significant for feminist analysis. He points out that Machiavelli's politics were directed *against* "the politics of grace"—not *toward* a rational end. Challenging the view that Machiavelli thinks like a natural scientist, Pocock argues that he conceives of citizens as people who "are not engaged in knowing (and so creating) the universe and themselves so much as in managing the relationships between one another's minds, wills and purposes."[93] In politics as in moral philosophy, Machiavelli accepts the possibility of irreconcilable values, and therefore of pluralism. Conflict, if it does not degenerate into violence, contributes to the development of good laws and good citizens.[94]

In my view, Machiavelli's view of individuals as "natural" beings is a corrective both to the view that humans should be self-denying and solely focused on salvation and to the extreme forms of individualism that treats people as "rational actors" pitted against one another for power. He recognizes, even celebrates, passion; at the same time he knows that the passions must be harnessed to *virtù* and an ideal of civic life, and not be allowed to degenerate into a privatized politics of license. Sebastian de Grazia has written that the key problem for Machiavelli is that men are created by nature but their politics are not. We cannot leave it to nature to create harmony, or live in a world without politics or power. But we can build dikes and channels, and establish the rule of law. Machiavelli teaches that political order does not emerge without human innovation, which he sees as a prerequisite to all forms of sustained human cooperation.

Some problems remain. Machiavelli's Enlightenment successors— liberal, radical, and conservative—all value a citizenship of action and focus on whether the political, economic, and social conditions in which people live are conducive to truly autonomous choice. Yet many feminists today would counter that we should focus less on the politics of rights and more on the politics of care. Dependency, not autonomy, is the basic human condition; it must be recognized and incorporated into citizenship, not ignored or denied.[95]

Here it is significant that Machiavelli's construction of a republican politics based on an ideal of *virtù* rejected privatized self-interest and justified power as a means to a common end, not as the dominance of some over others. As Pitkin herself argues, Machiavelli developed an idea of autonomy that is "highly political," assuming "neither the solidarity postulated by organic theorists nor the atomistic, unrelated individuals postulated by social contract theorists." Instead, "he focuse[d] on the way in which citizens in political interaction continually recreate community out of multiplicity."[96] This is far from the idea of mutual care, but not as narrow as the "Hobbesian" construction of man, which some have characterized, too simplistically, I believe, as based on Machiavelli's prince.

A more intractable issue is Machiavelli's preoccupation with the citizen-soldier. Machiavelli defends citizen militias and opposes mercenaries, famously argues that good laws depend on good arms, and instructs the prince above all to study war. Have we skirted the Scylla of Hobbes only to founder on the Charybdis of the Homeric warrior ideal?

However troubling, Machiavelli's vision of the soldier-citizen does not suggest the destructive male *eros* that Nancy Hartsock traces from Greek theory to the present, or the kind of hostility toward women (and toward their own desires) she ascribes to them.[97] The discipline of the soldier, "persistent courage and no braggadocio," is Machiavelli's ideal, Martin Fleisher argues, "not stoic self-control."[98] And, although Machiavelli firmly excludes women from military affairs, his *Art of War* is curiously distanced from the blood and bonding of battle. Pitkin finds it a "pastoral of military life."[99]

R. Claire Snyder attempts a defense of the citizen-soldier that is consistent with feminist values. She sees Machiavelli's ideal as "the centerpiece of a *citizenship of civic practices*"[100] and finds the citizen-soldier a more satisfactory basis for citizenship than geographical accident (*jus solis*) or family or ethnic ties (*jus sanguinis*). Drawing on Pocock, Snyder agrees that "when citizen-soldiers fight to defend their republic and their ability to govern themselves through the formation of man-made laws, they fight for a secular political order."[101] The army "constructs" citizens, and makes them public-spirited and committed to a common good. Citizen soldiers help bridge the gap between the "new" prince and the institutionalized republic and, as citizens as well as soldiers, they have a dual view of the world, ensuring that the army does not become alienated from the wider public.

However, this ideal excludes women and "the feminine," which is especially troubling when military service creates a privileged form of citizenship. A more serious flaw is that military *virtù* requires having enemies to fight. Machiavelli felt that the conflict and turmoil of popular republicanism required an expansive state to keep internal oppositions in balance.[102] *Virtù* defined as war-making inevitably constructs an ideal of masculinity that emphasizes violence and denigrates women, even when women are recruited as soldiers.[103] But, Snyder counters, once citizenship is conceived of as constructed rather than natural, it should be possible to redefine both citizens and soldiers on grounds more congenial to feminism.[104]

In conclusion, the Machiavelli who emerges from this analysis is both smaller and larger than the Machiavelli of legend. Smaller because he is more down to earth and human than we usually think of him, and larger because he is morally engaged, neither a cynic, a misogynist, nor a defender of tyranny. Reading his political theory in the light of his plays and letters, it is hard to picture Machiavelli as "the author of an austere priesthood of single-minded politicians," as O'Brien describes him.[105] Maurizio Viroli's characterization seems more apt: Machiavelli's work is "pervaded by irony and self-irony," he writes, "tolerant [of] the variety of the human world and human frailty."[106]

With regard to citizenship, we owe important debts to Machiavelli, not the least for his contributions to a secular, republican, and pluralist ideal of political community. The modern view of the citizen as an active, skeptical, public-spirited individual, a member of a class, a family, and a nation, interdependent yet autonomous, has a Machiavellian core that we continue to value deeply, although we rarely acknowledge him as its source.

Notes

1. Sheldon Wolin emphasizes that Machiavelli's view that "all men are wicked" is a Christian, not a classical, view, which is ironic given Machiavelli's rejection of the relevance of Christian values to politics. See Wolin, *Politics and Vision* (Boston: Little, Brown, 1960), 237. Part of my larger intent is to question Wolin's interpretation that Machiavelli creates mass men who are vulnerable to political manipulation and mass politics because men are all the same and driven by interests rather than higher values. The part of the case presented (briefly) in this chapter emphasizes that Machiavelli has a complex view of human beings as political actors. I underline, agreeing with Harvey Mansfield as well as John Pocock and Hannah Pitkin as discussed in more detail below, the importance of the fact that Machiavelli portrays history as guided by human choice, not divine intervention. See Harvey C. Mansfield, *Machiavelli's Virtue* (Chicago: University of Chicago Press, 1996), 57.

2. Quoted in Maurizio Viroli, *Machiavelli* (Oxford: Oxford University Press, 1998), 93–94. The phrase "beyond good and evil" is Nietzsche's; its use to describe Machiavelli is Benedetto Croce's:

"It is known that Machiavelli discovers the necessity and autonomy of politics which is beyond or, rather, below, moral good and evil, which has its own laws against which it is useless to rebel; politics that cannot be exorcised or driven from the world with holy water." Benedetto Croce, *Politics and Morals*, trans. Salvatore J. Castiglione (New York: Philosophical Library, 1945), 59.

3. Leo Strauss debates whether Machiavelli or Hobbes is the first modern; see the discussion by Anthony J. Parel in *The Machiavellian Cosmos* (New Haven: Yale University Press, 1992). For a negative assessment of Machiavelli's "scientific" approach to politics, see Sheldon Wolin, "Political Theory as a Vocation," in *Machiavelli and the Nature of Political Thought*, ed. Martin Fleisher (New York: Athenaeum, 1972).

4. Jean Bethke Elshtain, *Public Man, Private Woman: Women in Social and Political Thought* (Princeton: Princeton University Press, 1981), 99.

5. See Mary O'Brien, "The Root of the Mandrake," in *Reproducing the World: Essays in Feminist Theory* (Boulder, Colo.: Westview Press, 1989).

6. I am arguing that Machiavelli does not divide public from private, separating the political world of "realpolitik" from the "private realm," as Elshtain suggests (*Public Man*, 99).

7. See Jane S. Jaquette, "Power as Ideology," in *Women's Views of the Political World of Men*, ed. Judith H. Stiehm (Dobbs Ferry, N.Y.: Transnational Publishers, 1984).

8. Hannah Fenichel Pitkin, *Fortune Is a Woman: Gender and Politics in the Thought of Niccolò Machiavelli* (Berkeley and Los Angeles: University of California Press, 1984).

9. Susan Bordo, *The Flight to Objectivity: Essays on Cartesianism and Culture* (New York: SUNY Press, 1987).

10. Women's alleged weaker intellectual and moral capacities have been used by many theorists to exclude them from citizenship. See, for example, Genevieve Lloyd, *The Man of Reason: "Male" and "Female" in Western Philosophy* (London: Methuen, 1984) and Karen Green, *The Woman of Reason: Feminism, Humanism, and Political Thought* (New York: Continuum, 1995).

11. Isaiah Berlin, "The Originality of Machiavelli," in *Against the Current: Essays in the History of Ideas* (Harmondsworth: Penguin Books, 1979), 25–79. The lack of a "systemic" theory is what commends Machiavelli to postmodern defenders like R. B. J. Walker. See "The Prince and 'The Pauper': Tradition, Modernity, and Practice in the Theory of International Relations," in *International/Intertextual Relations: Postmodern Readings of World Politics*, ed. James Der Derian and Michael J. Shapiro (Lexington, Mass.: Lexington Books, 1989), 25–48.

12. See Neal Wood, "The Value of Asocial Sociability," in Fleisher, *Machiavelli*, 282–91.

13. Niccolò Machiavelli, *The Prince*, in *The Prince and The Discourses*, ed. Max Lerner (New York: The Modern Library, 1940), chap. 17, 61; chap. 18, 65.

14. *The Prince*, chap. 17, 61.

15. Machiavelli advises that the prince must be a both a lion and a fox—that is, use both force and deception—when men act like beasts themselves and cannot be ruled by laws. This implies that, under some conditions, men *are* capable of being ruled by laws, when they are not corrupted and living under established authority (*The Prince*, chap. 18, 64). Parel writes that Machiavelli finds "[t]he directing of ambition for private glory, for making others the means of one's own ends, is the essence of tyranny, of which Caesar was also guilty." Parel, "Commentary," in Fleisher, *Machiavelli*, 149–50.

16. Niccolò Machiavelli, *The Discourses*, in *The Prince and The Discourses*, ed. Max Lerner (New York: The Modern Library, 1940), introduction, 104.

17. Machiavelli writes that "all human things are kept in perpetual motion," a thesis of restlessness that anticipates Hobbes, and calls the idea of a perfect equilibrium an "impossibility": "Seeing then the impossibility of establishing . . . a perfect equilibrium, and that a precise middle course cannot be maintained [both references to classical ideals], it is proper in the organization of a republic to select the most honorable course" *Discourses* 1.6, 129.

18. *The Prince*, chap. 3, 6. In conditions of uncertainty, Machiavelli advises that founders should

"start with the assumption that all men are bad and ever ready to display their vicious natures" (*Discourses*, 1.3, 117).

19. Pocock, *The Machiavellian Moment* (Princeton: Princeton University Press, 1975), 77.

20. Elshtain states that "Machiavelli's politics can be seen in large measure as a defense against the softer, 'womanly' Christian virtues" (*Public Man, Private Woman*, 95).

21. For a discussion of the relation between "time" and "free will," see Cary J. Nederman and Kate Langon Forhan, "Introduction," in *Medieval Political Theory—A Reader: The Quest for the Body Politic, 1100–1400* (London: Routledge, 1993), 6–7.

22. Pocock, *Machiavellian Moment*, 49.

23. O'Brien, *Reproducing the World*, 104.

24. This aspect of Machiavelli's definition of "license" will become a part of Hobbes's definition of anarchy—that everyone acts according to his or her own private will. I disagree with Catherine H. Zuckert (whose interpretations of Machiavelli's plays I find generally insightful) when she argues that "[i]n order to attach human beings more firmly to the goods of this world, he seeks to downplay, to privatize, if not entirely to suppress human eroticism." Machiavelli strongly opposed privatization and believed that *virtù* arose out of adversity. Nor is his eroticism repressed; indeed, contemporary readers seemed to have found him too earthy for their tastes. Catherine H. Zuckert, "Fortune Is a Woman—But So Is Prudence: Machiavelli's *Clizia*," in *Finding a New Feminism: Rethinking the Woman Question for Liberal Democracy*, ed. Pamela Grande Jensen (Lanham, Md.: Rowman & Littlefield, 1996), 25. On Machiavelli's concept of license, see Markus Fischer, *Well-Ordered License* (New York: Lexington Books, 2000).

25. "The Tale of Balfagor," in *The Literary Works of Machiavelli*, ed. J. R. Hale (London: Oxford University Press, 1961), 195–96.

26. Arlene Saxonhouse, *Women in the History of Political Theory: Ancient Greece to Machiavelli* (New York: Praeger, 1985), 19.

27. Women, who are men's moral inferiors in the Artistotelian/Christian worldview, become men's moral anchors by the nineteenth century, in their roles as mothers and wives.

28. This is well illustrated in Harvey C. Mansfield Jr.'s essay, "Party and Sect in Machiavelli's *Florentine Histories*," in Fleisher, *Machiavelli*, especially 251–60.

29. *Discourses*, 3.3, 417; 3.3, 422 and passim.

30. *The Prince*, chap. 8.

31. *Discourses*, 3.46, 534.

32. Mary O'Brien criticizes Machiavelli for finding kinship "a very destructive basis for politics" and for rejecting "hereditary ties as the 'most fallacious means of identifying the best men to rule'" (*Reproducing the World*, 107). Perhaps she is suggesting that heredity rather than merit or skill should determine leadership? Harvey Mansfield Jr. maintains that Machiavelli's contempt for Christian values was illustrated by the fact that they allowed one family, for example the Medici, to dominate: "Florentine partisanship feeds on the Christian spirit, as Machiavelli sees it, of absolute revenge" ("Party and Sect," in Fleisher, *Machiavelli*, 255).

33. *Discourses*, 3.26, 489; 3.6, 412: "As to attacking men's honor, that of their wives is what they feel most, and after than their being themselves treated with indignity." Of course, men's defense of their wives' honor is part of a larger cultural package that is unquestionably patriarchal.

34. Quentin Skinner has emphasized the importance of Machiavelli's use of the rhetorical technique of "paradiastole," which can be defined "as a method of excusing the vices by redescribing them as virtues." *Reason and Rhetoric in the Philosophy of Hobbes* (Cambridge: Cambridge University Press, 1996), 163–71.

35. Pitkin, *Fortune Is a Woman*, 6.

36. For the political and social themes raised, see, for example, J. R. Hale's discussion in his introduction to *The Literary Works of Machiavelli*, xi–xxvi; and Giulio Ferroni, "'Transformation' and 'Adaptation' in Machiavelli's *Mandragola*," in *Machiavelli and the Discourse of Literature*, ed. Albert

Russell Ascoli and Victoria Kahn (Ithaca: Cornell University Press, 1993), 81–116. On bourgeois life in Florence, see Hale, "Introduction," *Literary Works*.

37. *Clizia*, in Hale, *Literary Works*, 84–85. Pitkin discusses this passage to show that Machiavelli is ambivalent about fatherhood, drawing on his comment in *The Florentine Histories* that "[c]aring for children and political greatness are 'an almost impossible combination'" (*Fortune Is a Woman*, 252). This could also be taken as evidence of Machiavelli's recognition that childcare is demanding work.

38. *Clizia*, 84–85. This is very close to his description of political decay in *Discourses*, 1.2, 114: "Each individual only consulted his own passions, and a thousand acts of injustice were daily committed."

39. The "public" space of social control can work for or against women, but it is largely controlled by women, and has never been adequately theorized. For accounts that parallel Sophronia's actions, see Sandra Cavallo and Simona Cerutti, "Female Honor and Social Control of Reproduction in Piedmont between 1600 and 1800," in *Sex and Gender in Historical Perspective*, ed. Edward Muir and Guido Ruggiero (Baltimore: Johns Hopkins University Press, 1990), 73–109.

40. Zuckert notes that *sofronia* meant "suffering" in the Italian of Machiavelli's time, but that its classical root is *sophrosynē*, or practical reason ("Fortune," 30).

41. Hale, "Introduction," xxiv. Zuckert calls the play "original with Machiavelli." Although this is rarely commented upon by scholars, the plot of *Mandragola* is virtually identical to a Spanish play, *The Celestina* by Fernando de Rojas, written in Spain and published in 1499; Rojas paints a much grimmer picture of human failings, reducing the possibilities for human action to existential choices.

42. I have used Hale's English spelling for the heroine of *La Mandragola*, but spell the name of the historical Lucretia (wife of Lucius Tarquinius Collatinus, whose rape provoked the overthrow of the Tarquin kings and the emergence of the Roman republic) with a *t* instead of a *z*, to distinguish between them. Hale, "Introduction," xxv.

Ligurio represents someone "on the make," a sign of changes in the old social order. In fact, in both plays, the characters often change clothes and pretend they're someone else. The lack of correspondence between appearance and reality is a Machiavellian trope, perhaps a sign of the social discomfort that accompanied the disintegration of the feudal order and the rise of new opportunities for social mobility.

43. Ronald L. Martinez opens his "Benefit of Absence: Machiavellian Valediction in *Clizia*" with the statement that audiences identified Machiavelli with Nicomaco: "Students of *Clizia* have recognized that the play's plot . . . fictionalizes the self-reprobation of Machiavelli's passion, late in life, for the singer Barbara Saluti." Quoted in Ascoli and Kahn, *Machiavelli and the Discourse of Literature*, 117. Barbara Saluti's role in a performance of *La Mandragola* is referred to in Machiavelli's letter to Guicciardini, October 16–20, 1525 (letter 299), in *Machiavelli and his Friends: Their Personal Correspondence*, ed. and trans. James B. Atkinson and David Sices (DeKalb: Northern Illinois University Press, 1996), 367–68.

44. As many other Machiavelli scholars have argued, including G. Gilbert and Theodore Sumberg. See also Pitkin, *Fortune Is a Woman*, 30 n. 22.

45. Pitkin, *Fortune Is a Woman*, 30, 31, 32.

46. Ibid., 33, 39.

47. Ibid., 47, 111–12.

48. This follows a tradition that sees Machiavelli as weak and resentful because he himself cannot rule and because he must always be a "courtier."

49. O'Brien, *Reproducing the World*, 115, 120.

50. Zuckert compares Plautus's play *Casina* unfavorably with the moral tone and treatment of women in *Clizia*, concluding that "[s]o much for the superior morality—or 'virtue'—of the Romans" ("Fortune," 30). Gisela Bock argues that Machiavelli finds superiority in some Florentine political

institutions and values; see her "Civil Discord in Machiavelli's *Istiorie Fioretine*," in *Machiavelli and Republicanism*, ed. Gisela Bock, Quentin Skinner, and Maurizio Viroli (Cambridge: Cambridge University Press, 1990), 188–94.

51. After showing that *La Mandragola* has "never lacked admirers," J. R. Hale speculates that its neglect has been due "not to its quality, but to fashion," including "a preference, as far as bawdy was concerned, for the suggested rather than the stated" (*Literary Works*, xxiv). Ferroni cites one source that connects "Machaivellian anthropology" with "the 'carnivalesque' strain of European culture as reconstructed by Mikhail Bakhtin" ("Transformation/Adaptation," 92 n. 21).

52. See Thomas Laqueur, *Making Sex: Body and Gender from the Greeks to Freud* (Cambridge, Mass.: Harvard University Press, 1990), 2–3. According to Laqueur, "[t]he commonplace of much contemporary psychology—that men want sex while women want relationships—is the precise inversion of pre-Enlightenment notions that, extending back to antiquity, equated friendship with men and fleshliness with women" (3–4). But, as Roger Boesche points out, Machiavelli took sexual license—especially of older men—as a sign of corruption: "the young are lazy, the old licentious, and both sexes of every age abound in vile habits" (*History of Florence*, quoted in Boesche, *Theories of Tyranny from Plato to Arendt* [University Park: Pennsylvania State University Press, 1996], 141).

53. Ronald L. Martinez strongly contrasts the two plays, describing *La Mandragola* as "audacious" and *Clizia* as a "valedictory" return to classical values, closer to the "revisionist" *Florentine Histories* and "more meditative regarding collective institutions and the historical cycles that transcend individuals" ("Benefit of Absence: Machiavellian Valediction in Clizia," in Ascoli and Kahn, *Machiavelli and the Discourse of Literature*, 117–22).

54. *The Prince*, chap. 25, 93. See also his letter to Piero Soderini of January, 1513, and his poem *On Fortune*, discussed in Parel, *The Machiavellian Cosmos*, 74–75.

55. I developed the argument that Lucrezia was Machiavelli's prince before reading Ferroni's essay, but Ferroni takes the idea further by speculating that adapting to Fortune is one of the most important lessons Machiavelli is trying to teach the prince.

56. This explains why Lucrezia takes Callimaco for her "lord, master and guide, father, defender and the sole source of all my happiness," language that makes no sense except in the way it binds both Callimaco and Lucrezia to a relation that is stipulated in the language of church vows, not only by Callimaco's vow, but more importantly Lucrezia's vow to him. This is formalized in the church scene, where Nicia asks Callimaco to take his wife's hand, as though giving her in marriage.

57. Ferroni, "Transformation/Adaptation," 96, 111. "Turn your face to luck" is "precisely" the term Machiavelli uses to signify the individual's adaptation to the unforeseeable variations of *Fortuna* (90).

58. In the more robust translation that appears in Ferroni, Lucrezia makes the following speech to Callimaco, "Now that your cleverness, the idiocy of my husband, the stupidity of my mother and the wickedness of my confessor have led me to do what I should never have done on my own account, I want [*voglio*] to judge that this comes to pass because of a heavenly decree that has so willed it, and I am not sufficient to refuse what heaven bids me to accept" (113).

59. From translation in Ferroni; in Hale's edition, the same phrase is rendered in more "feminine" terms as "beautiful, amiable, discreet and fit to be a queen" (*La Mandragola*, 14).

60. Captured along with her six children, Caterina Sforza persuades her captors to let her enter the fortress to tell the castellan to surrender, leaving her children as hostages. But once inside, she refuses to surrender and, going to the top of the castle wall, "bares her 'genital members' to her enemies," telling them to "do their worst," for she can always make more children (Pitkin, *Fortune Is a Woman*, 49).

61. Fleisher, "A Passion for Politics," in Fleisher, *Machiavelli*, 123.

62. See Bonnie Honig, *Political Theory and the Displacement of Politics* (Ithaca: Cornell University Press, 1993), 68–69; Pocock, *Machiavellian Moment*, 31–35.

63. Pitkin, *Fortune Is a Woman*, 252. Machiavelli finds Soderini "a single and most remarkable

example . . . who believed that he would be able by patience and gentleness to overcome the determination of the new sons of Brutus to return to another form of government; in which, however, he greatly deceived himself" (*Discourses*, 3.3, 405).

64. Viroli, *Machiavelli*, 29, 30. In his letter to Francesco Vettori of August 3, 1514, Machiavelli writes: "So, if you want to write about your lady, do so, and discuss other things with those who value them more and understand them better, for they have brought me nothing but loss, while in love I have always found pleasure and profit" (*The Literary Works*, 152). These protestations are taken by Pitkin as sour grapes: as I cannot do politics I will waste my time with women instead. Machiavelli does write about love in terms of a military campaign and, as with Fortune, he is often defeated. Still, as he says to Vettori in a letter of February 25, 1514, quoting Boccaccio: "better to act and repent than to do nothing and repent" (*The Literary Works*, 149). De Grazia's interpretation is that Machiavelli argues that there is an analogy in men's love of women and the love they bear their country. Sebastian de Grazia, *Machaivelli in Hell* (Princeton: Princeton University Press, 1989), 145–62.

65. Viroli, *Machiavelli*, 30–31. Pitkin finds "Circe's damsel" a strong character, but "anti-political" (see discussion in *Fortune Is a Woman*, 122–30), to which Viroli responds that her interpretation "ignores the fact that the hero's political reflections are prompted by the woman's considerations on the variations of earthly things and on the best way to face them" (31).

66. Viroli, *Machiavelli*, 35. This is also de Grazia's view; see *Machiavelli in Hell*, 132–36, 266.

67. Honig, *Political Theory*, 16.

68. Ruth W. Grant offers an extended defense of hypocrisy as "inextricably connected to politics. Political relations, ordinarily understood as power relations, can just as readily be conceived as relations of dependence . . . among people who require another's voluntary cooperation, but whose interests are in conflict. Trust is required but highly problematic, and the pressures toward hypocrisy are immense." In these circumstances, "doing the right thing" may call for "deception, ethical posturing, or both" (Grant, *Hypocrisy and Integrity: Machiavelli, Rousseau, and the Ethics of Politics* [Chicago: University of Chicago Press, 1997], 2–3).

69. Laqueur, *Making Sex*, 4, 39–40. If mixed, it would depend on the relative quantities of each.

70. Laqueur, quoting Galen, *Making Sex*, 28.

71. Laqueur, *Making Sex*, 62.

72. *Webster's New Universal Unabridged Dictionary* gives the first definition of "virago" as "woman of strength and courage," but *Roget's Thesaurus* puts "virago" under "irascibility," along with "shrew," "termagant," and "spit-fire."

73. Ian Maclean, *Renaissance Notion of Woman* (Cambridge: Cambridge University Press, 1980), 53.

74. See Fischer, *Well-Ordered License*.

75. In *Instruction of a Christian Woman* (1523), written "at the request of Catherine of Aragon for guidance in the education of Mary" (quoted in Constance Jordan, *Renaissance Feminism: Literary Texts and Political Models* [Ithaca: Cornell University Press, 1990], 119).

76. Parel makes this argument in considerable detail in *The Machiavellian Cosmos*.

77. Parel, *The Machiavellian Cosmos*, 7–8.

78. Here Parel is arguing against Eugene Garver's thesis that that Machiavelli is developing a particular form of reason, *phronesis* or prudence, which is neither "heuristic" nor "algorithmic." See Garver's introduction to *Machiavelli and the History of Prudence* (Madison: University of Wisconsin Press, 1987); and the discussion in Parel, *Machiavelli's Cosmos*, 78–81. Zuckert also refers to Machiavelli's practical reason, noting that "Sophronia" and "*phronesis*" share the same root. *Clizia*, as Ronald Martinez has observed, is the more cautious play. See "Benefit of Absence: Machiavellian Valediction in Clizia," 122 n. 65.

79. *The Prince*, chap. 25, 92–94.

80. Zuckert, "Fortune," 24.

81. This is not to argue that Machiavelli thought it was appropriate for men to beat women: Nicomaco's attempt to assert his right to use force to get his way is treated with contempt by his wife and laughed at by the audience, although the play and historical accounts both indicate that wife-beating was widely accepted at the time.

82. Pitkin, *Fortune Is a Woman*, 141.

83. Ibid., 143. Pico della Mirandola may have been referring to the Catholic response to the threat of astrological alternatives, which maintained that the soul had free choice and was not governed by the stars.

84. Strauss, *Thoughts*, 216, quoted in Parel, *Machiavellian Cosmos*, 83. Pitkin writes: "The image of Fortune as a woman, then, challenges men in terms of their masculine identity: she is there for the taking—if you're man enough" (*Fortune Is a Woman*, 293). Machiavelli is contrasting "masculine" action to "Christian" *ozio*.

85. Pocock, *Machiavellian Moment*, 161, 162.

86. Ibid., 167.

87. Jane Mansbridge, "Using Power/Fighting Power: The Polity," in *Democracy and Difference: Contesting the Boundaries of the Political*, ed. Seyla Benhabib (Princeton: Princeton University Press, 1996), 139–52.

88. O'Brien, *Reproducing the World*, 110, 122–23.

89. Note the contrast between the colorful rhetoric used by Machiavelli and Bacon, and the "plain language" of Hobbes and modern science. Carolyn Merchant's argument on science and the "death of nature" is focused on the way materialist and mechanistic views replaced hermetic and neoplatonic concepts of nature; see Merchant, *The Death of Nature* (San Francisco: Harper and Row, 1980). Parel's argument suggests that detachment and manipulation is not limited to the materialist forefathers of modern science but is shared by the hermetics. Pocock finds hermeticism incompatible with republicanism. Neoplatonists may be substituting "knowledge" for the loss of the polis, but "hermetics are no substitute for politics if they cannot set up a scheme of relationships between men as equal individuals" because "magic, the manipulation of objects through knowledge of their natures, is an activity supremely unsuited to a relation between political equals" (Pocock, *Machiavellian Moment*, 98, 99).

90. Evelyn Fox Keller, *Reflections on Gender and Science* (New Haven: Yale University Press, 1985), 38–40.

91. Robert Orr, "The Time Motif in Machiavelli," in Fleisher, *Machiavelli*, 199.

92. Pitkin, *Fortune Is a Woman*, 301; and see the discussion of this paragraph in Garver, *History of Prudence*, 145.

93. Pocock, *Machiavellian Moment*, 99.

94. See Bock et al., *Machiavellian Republicanism*, for a range of views on this issue.

95. See Joan C. Tronto, *Moral Boundaries: A Political Argument for an Ethic of Care* (New York: Routledge, 1995); Eva Feder Kittay, *Love's Labor: Essays on Women, Equality, and Dependency* (London: Routledge, 1999); and Grace Clement, *Care, Autonomy, and Justice; Feminism and the Ethic of Care* (Boulder, Colo.: Westview Press, 1998). The rights/care distinction is, of course, from Carol Gilligan's *In a Different Voice* (Cambridge, Mass.: Harvard University Press, 1982).

96. Pitkin, *Fortune Is a Woman*, 286.

97. Nancy C. Hartsock, *Money, Sex, and Power* (New York: Longman, 1983), chaps. 7 and 8. Zuckert tries to argue this for Machiavelli, although I do not think she succeeds: see "Fortune," 25.

98. Fleisher, "A Passion for Politics," in Fleisher, *Machiavelli*, 123.

99. Pitkin, *Fortune Is a Woman*, 70.

100. R. Claire Snyder, *Citizen-Soldiers and Manly Warriors; Military Service and Gender in the Civic Republican Tradition* (London: Rowman & Littlefield, 1999), 15, italics in original.

101. Snyder, *Citizen Soldiers*, 22.

102. Machiavelli writes, "if Heaven favors [a state] so as never to be involved in war, the contin-

ued tranquility would enervate her, or provoke internal dissensions, which together, or either of them separately, would be apt to prove her ruin" (*Discourses*, chap. 6, 129). Note the difference between a perpetual state of potential war caused by the expansion of republics seeking to maintain *virtù* and Hobbes's understanding of war as a result of anarchy. Machiavelli may have used the example of Rome's empire to justify the attempt by Florence to control nearby cities in order to defend against the growing power of consolidating nation states like France and Spain. See Michael Mallet, "The Theory and Practice of Warfare in Machiavelli's Republic," in Bock et al., *Machiavelli and Republicanism*, 173–80.

103. As Cynthia Enloe argues in *Maneuvers: The International Militarization of Women's Lives* (Berkeley and Los Angeles: University of California Press, 2000).

104. See especially Snyder, *Citizen Soldiers*, chap. 2.

105. O'Brien, *Reproducing the World*, 105.

106. Viroli, *Machiavelli*, 11.

13

Machiavelli and Feminist Ethics

Andrea Nicki

In contemplating the future of feminist ethics, Alison Jaggar identifies two assumptions that all feminist approaches to ethics must share: "that the subordination of women is morally wrong" and "that the moral experience of women should be treated as respectfully as the moral experience of men." The claim advanced in the second assumption is not that there is some universal moral experience that women have but that women's experiences as informed by sexual oppression may make them uniquely qualified for identifying male bias in ethics. Jaggar claims that these assumptions ground a practical agenda for feminist ethics: "first, to articulate moral critiques of actions and practices that perpetuate women's subordination; second, to prescribe morally justifiable ways of resisting such actions and practices; and third, to envision morally desirable alternatives that will promote women's emancipation."[1] With these considerations in mind, in this chapter I will argue that while some current feminist approaches to ethics challenge traditional conceptions of female virtues that promote subservient roles for women, their attempt to transcend traditional moral frameworks requires more force. The insight of these particular approaches that deviant behavior can have moral value needs to be pushed further in keeping with feminist ethics' practical agenda of empowering women and other oppressed groups. I will show that feminist ethics can benefit from Machiavelli's thought, and provide a sketch of a feminist Machiavellian account of morality, drawing particularly on Sarah Hoagland's *Lesbian Ethics* and Antonio Gramsci's discussion of *The Prince*.

Feminist Ethics

Sheila Mullett argues that feminist theory stresses the moral relevance of the great amount of human destructiveness in the world, in particular male destructiveness toward women.[2] Referring to the radical alteration of consciousness that feminist ethical theory demands, she writes:

> Feminist moral consciousness begins with an anguished awareness of violence, victimization and pain. The highly developed capacity of human beings to avoid painful experience, to ignore, suppress, deny, and forget the agonies of life, is shifted aside and they fill our consciousness. We lose our moral callousness and see the violence around us: "It is astonishing to note the profound silence in ethics regarding violence against women—rape, battering, child sexual abuse and incest. . . . This silence must be broken."[3]

According to Marilyn Frye, feminist theory is about identifying and explaining the forces sustaining "the subordination of women to men" and justifying the need for women to separate "from men and from institutions, relationships, roles and activities which are male-defined, male-dominated or operating for the benefit of males and the maintenance of male-privilege."[4] According to her view, the feminist moral agent challenges patriarchal laws, principles, and taboos and pursues alternate values. Feminist theory involves fundamentally both a turn inward, a discovery of resources and affirmation of female powers, and a turn outward to other women with whom one can engage in meaning-making, finding commonalities in experiences.

For Sandra Bartky, "[f]eminist consciousness is consciousness of *victimization*. To apprehend oneself as victim is to be aware of an alien and hostile force outside of oneself which is responsible for the blatantly unjust treatment of women and which enforces a stifling and oppressive system of sex-role differentiation. For some feminists, this hostile power is 'society' or 'the system'; for others, it is simply men."[5] Essentially, Bartky presents the female moral agent as confronting and battling patriarchy and maleness, and thus identifies a force or forces external to women as the cause or causes of women's oppression. In understanding women's oppression, she emphasizes women's victimization. Bartky acknowledges that feminist consciousness may also involve a consciousness of privilege, such as skin-color privilege for a white woman, and thus of one's implication in the victimization of others. But for her, consciousness of victimization is the hallmark of feminist consciousness: "In sum, feminist consciousness is the consciousness of a being . . . who sees herself as victim and whose victimization determines her being-in-the-world as resistance, wariness and suspicion." According to Bartky's view, feminist consciousness is somewhat paranoid: one is continually on the defensive, wary both of sexist attack or disparagement and of oneself, about the possibility of anger from sexist injury being vented in "imprudent" or "dangerous" aggressive behavior.[6]

Bartky's account of feminism may be seen as subscribing to what might be called a "reactive model of empowerment." Her emphasis on women's victimization under patriarchy, rather than on their survival, presents women, however unwittingly, as passive objects on which oppressive forces act rather than as already existing forces with which these operate. For Bartky, feminist consciousness is consciousness of the possibility of "the release of energy long suppressed,"[7] not that of mobilizing energy already manifest.

Sarah Hoagland's *Lesbian Ethics*

While Hoagland claims that breaking away from men and patriarchal institutions is necessary for constructing an alternative ethics, she does not emphasize women's victimization. In *Lesbian Ethics* she argues that portraying women as victims ignores their choices under oppressive conditions and thus denies their moral agency. Though they are coerced in such circumstances, women must nonetheless act, making good or bad choices on the basis of their needs and resources. Some women pursue femininity and completely align their interests with those of men, believing that they can only find value and meaning in their existence as subordinate persons with limited options. Others embrace femininity, simmering on the back burner of men's wants and projects, gently warming male egos in the pursuit of feminist goals. Both of these types of choices, she emphasizes, no less than the choice to focus completely on women and women's projects, are "survival choices."[8]

Frye advances a similar point in her discussion of female sexual slavery, arguing that a woman may act in a self-sacrificing way out of survival if "she is in a situation where she cannot, or reasonably believes she cannot, survive without the other's provision and protection, and where the experience has made it credible to her that the other may kill her or abandon her if and when she displeases him."[9]

Unlike feminists such as Bartky, who highlight women's victimization, Hoagland does not assume a dualism between freedom and oppression, where moral agency is a matter of exercising power over forces such as men and patriarchy that are judged to be alien. In her view, moral agency does not involve an ability to choose under conditions that do not limit this ability, but rather an ability to choose in limited situations. In contrast to traditional, impartialist ethics, Hoagland maintains that one need not and should not strive to transcend the boundaries of particular situations in order to exert moral agency. Such limits are actually deeply relevant for moral agency in that they help us to "create value through what we choose, and to conceive of ourselves as ones who are able to make choices"; "contexts, in other words . . . help us give form to and create depth of meaning."[10] Specific situations may be seen as providing opportunities for the discovery of new sorts of moral possibilities, of values that will undermine women's oppression, such as the value of separating from men and male-defined institutions.

Hoagland writes: "It is through understanding the boundaries and limits of our paths, that we can, by means of our choices, and interactions, seek to transform our selves in certain respects and hence to change certain boundaries and limits." According to this view, although moral agency is consistent with an acknowledgment of personal constraints, and is actually informed by them, we do not have to relate to each other antagonistically as we come to better understand these boundaries. Rather we can perceive ourselves as acting in cooperative relations with others. Acknowledging our boundaries involves, in part, acknowledging our separateness and distinctness from others but also appreciating a need for others to help us expand our boundaries: "By perceiving our selves as one among many, . . . we can perceive our possibilities as enhanced by our engagement with others, engagements which create possibilities that did not exist before."[11] In seeing each other as one oppressed woman among many, women can unite in solidarity to challenge oppressive structures in protests, support networks, crisis centers, and battered women refuges, challenges that could not emerge in isolation. In understanding their boundaries and limits as women, the ways in which their paths are constricted, and seeking to expand these, women can discover new possibilities of moral value and thus achieve greater resistance under oppression.

Although when faced with others that have power over oneself, one has little choice but to adhere to their values, this does not necessarily mean that one's personal boundaries are defeated or lose all force. As Hoagland claims, developing a sense of our boundaries involves becoming better aware of when others are "trespassing" over these "and, if they have power over us, of ways to retain our moral sense of self despite the trespass."[12]

Preserving our ability to make choices as moral agents can be very difficult, Hoagland argues, when people are so manipulated under oppression to internalize the values of dominance and subordination that they act in a way that destroys their own systems of values. She gives the example of the hero of the film *Sophie's Choice* who, while in a concentration camp, is told that she must choose which of her two children will be killed; otherwise both children will die. She chooses that her daughter be killed and as a result her son is spared. Another example Hoagland presents involves Lucy Andrews, who petitioned the South Carolina government to let her become a slave and was eventually granted her wish. She was only sixteen years old, with two children, without employment, and without permanent address. It is true that in certain cases like the ones Hoagland describes the agents are so constrained, the options are so bad, that there is no possibility for the discovery of any new sort of moral insights, aside from the realization that the situation one is in is so demoralizing that there are no acceptable choices. But while it is potentially dangerous to assume a cooperative attitude when this attitude is not reciprocated, accepting the dominant/subordinate framework need not always involve demoralization. Separating from this framework is one way of avoiding demoralization, as when a woman leaves an abusive partner. But sometimes separation is not enough, as Hoagland recognizes: "I am not saying that we can successfully separate ourselves and resist demoralization in all oppressive circumstances."[13] Sometimes, in order to challenge oppression a woman must resort to "the master's tools,"[14] finding new values within the dominant/subordinate framework. Sometimes, by *not* separating from the dominant belief system, we can challenge oppression.

Machiavelli

The position I am defending is in a significant sense Machiavellian. As Arlene Saxonhouse argues, in both his political writings and his plays Machiavelli challenges traditional understandings of good and evil, of virtue and vice, addressing particularly the different virtues and vices associated with men and women.[15] This reassessment proceeds from a rejection of classic utopian thought, which derives ethical principles from a vision of a perfect society. For Machiavelli, praiseworthy behavior is not based on knowledge of the Forms, in particular of the Good, which affords clear insight into moral rightness and wrongness, but instead on unadorned truths of human social behavior. As a hard realist, he fully acknowledges the presence of selfishness, dishonesty, and cruelty in the world and sees these traits as absolutely necessary to take into account when one is considering how to act: "how we live is so far removed from how we ought to live, that he who abandons what is done for what ought to be done, will rather learn to bring about his own ruin than his preservation," since "a man who wants to make a profession of good in all regards must come to ruin among so many who are not good." People are not, as a matter of fact, most often motivated by benevolent intentions. And to strive to remain pure when contending with so much impurity is foolhardy and irrational: "If one considers well, it will be found that some things which seem virtues would, if followed, lead to one's ruin, and some others which appear vices result in one's greater security and well being."[16]

For Machiavelli, what appears to be condemnable and vicious when examined in isolation sometimes seems praiseworthy and beneficial when seen in a specific context. Like Hoagland, he emphasizes the creation of values in contexts. He constructs a bridge connecting virtue and vice, between which he travels procuring ingredients for the stability and happiness both of the prince and of the people. As Harvey Mansfield argues, his account of virtue sharply contrasts with that of Aristotle, which presents virtues as separate and distinct from vices, as the mean between two extremes.[17] Whereas for Aristotle virtue is its own reward, for Machiavelli virtue has a definite practical function: virtue is not the end of human life but a means for bettering it. "The really good things are those that do good for the greatest number, and in which the greatest number find satisfaction." According to Aristotle's view, the virtuous character consistently realizes the moral mean. Machiavelli, on the other hand, recommends a more mobile character, able to move freely between extremes: "Thus it is well to seem merciful, faithful, humane, sincere, religious, and also to be so; but you must have the mind so disposed that when it is needful to be otherwise you may be able to change to the opposite qualities." Thus he stresses that a prince must learn how to alternate between two natures: the man and the beast, the latter of which is divided between the fox and the lion in order to advise on cunning and ferocity. Unlike Plato, Machiavelli does not presume some hierarchy in human nature according to which a rational, human part rules over an emotional, bestial part. Calm reason does not govern the passions and allow them to be expressed in moderation: both parts must be equally strong and able to overcome the other's demands. He writes that "the prince must know how to use both natures and . . . the one without the other is not durable."[18]

Throughout *The Prince* Machiavelli stresses a distinction between cruelty used for good ends and cruelty used for bad ends, maintaining that the former kind is strategically wise whereas the latter is foolhardy. A prince must, above all, strive not to be hated by the people; one who indulges in cruelty, who performs cruel acts when these are not necessary for conserving a state, will inevitably come to a brutal end. In the nineteenth chapter of *The Prince* Machiavelli gives several examples of princes overthrown because of excessive ferocity and cruelty. Antoninus, he states, was "a man of great ability" and possessed admirable traits that made him popular with both the people and the soldiers. But his rapacity was so great, having "caused a large part of the population of Rome and all that of Alexandria to be killed, that he became hated by all the world and . . . was finally killed by a centurion in the midst of his army."[19] Further, in admonishing princes against excessive pride, in *The Discourses* Machiavelli explicitly states: "To bring hatred on himself without any return is in every way rash and imprudent."[20] In the cases of outrageously cruel leaders, these leaders pursue ends—sadism for the sake of sadistic pleasure—that Machiavelli rejects as beyond the realm of the political. Clearly, Machiavelli has specific ends in mind when he states that "in the actions of men, and especially of princes, . . . the end justifies the means. Let a prince therefore aim at conquering and maintaining the state, and the means will always be judged honourable and praised by every one, for the vulgar is always taken by appearances and the issue of the event."[21]

Machiavelli makes a clear distinction between well-used and ill-used cruelty in his discussion on Agathocles:

> It cannot be called virtue to kill one's fellow-citizens, betray one's friends, be without faith, without pity, without religion; by these methods one may indeed gain power, but not glory. For if the virtues of Agathocles in braving and overcoming perils, and his greatness of soul in supporting and surmounting obstacles be considered, one sees no reason for holding him inferior to any of the most renowned captains. Nonetheless, his savage cruelty and inhumanity, with his infinite crimes, prevent him from being considered among men of great excellence.[22]

The ability to use cruel techniques does not alone make for a great prince. Despite his bravery and greatness of soul, having lost sight of the true role of the prince—to be harsh or cruel only when constrained—Agathocles could not be considered a truly great prince.

Further, in *The Discourses* Machiavelli considers whether sternness or kindness is better in a prince, and discusses a general embodying each trait: Manlius Torquatus, who was very harsh toward his soldiers, never allowing them any break in their work, and Valerius Corvinus, who maintained his soldiers' obedience through affability and kindness. He concludes, rather tentatively, that harshness as a method for preserving the state is better than kindness: "[Manlius's] way is wholly for the benefit of the state and does not in any respect regard private ambition, since by his way a leader cannot gain partisans, for he shows himself always harsh to everybody and loves solely the common good." But, he emphasizes, when it comes to judging who is the better prince, Valerius is, without hesitation, to be preferred, "for a prince ought to seek in his soldiers and in his subjects obedience and love. . . . For a prince to be in high favour as an individual and to have the army as his partisan harmonizes with all the other demands of his position." Just as too much hardness in a prince can cause his ruin, as in the case of Antoninus, too much kindness can also cause a prince's downfall. The magistrate Piero Soderini believed that through persistent goodness and patience he could put an end to evil factions. But because he refused to be Brutus-like he could no longer keep the state safe and lost his position and reputation.[23] Machiavelli writes: "He should never have allowed an evil to continue for the sake of a good, when that evil could easily crush that good."[24] In contrast, when Scipio's soldiers and friends rebelled against him out of restlessness and fearlessness, Scipio wisely restored order by becoming fearsome and turning to cruel methods that he had previously avoided.[25]

The crux for Machiavelli is toward what aim 'evil' is being expressed. Nietzsche makes a similar point in criticizing Christianity: "Ultimately the point is to what *end* a lie is told. That 'holy' ends are lacking in Christianity is *my* objection to its means. Only *bad* ends: the poisoning, slandering, denying of life, contempt for the body, the denigration and self-violation of [humanity] through the concept of sin—*consequently* its means too are bad."[26] In maintaining the state, a prince is not justified in using any means *whatsoever*. When the prince does not have as his end maintaining the state but more precisely the destruction of a people, or to quote Nietzsche "the denigration and self-violation of [humanity]," the means must also be bad.

Sartre also amplifies the kind of point Machiavelli is making in *Notebooks for an Ethics*. He claims that to choose to attain an end by any means whatsoever is not to choose "the universe of violence" if means other than violence (e.g., honesty, cooperation, deception, theft) are sufficient to realize the end. He states that in deciding to steal food to relieve his hunger it is not a matter of determining to use any means whatsoever to realize this end. Certain means, Sartre states, such as murder and forced entry, are not considered. These are excluded, it seems, because he knows that theft will be sufficient to realize his end: "So I go out, determined to steal something from a grocery that I know quite well and where I have noticed one can steal something without being seen."[27]

Sartre illustrates two different meanings of the formula "the end justifies the means," arguing that the formula's meaning depends on the context in which it is applied. He claims that if he is dying of thirst and comes upon a bottle that he cannot open, the violence of breaking its neck does not change the end of satisfying his urgent thirst. Breaking the bottle's neck has no effect on relieving extreme thirst since it is required for that end to be achieved. If, however, he claims, he is invited for a drink with friends, breaking the bottle in this context does change the end of social drinking, based on an adherence to certain rules, in particular those demanding the respectful use of objects.[28] The goal changes from social drinking to *orgy*, so that violence is both the means and a part of the end: violence is used for the sake of violence. The first case, and not the second, captures the meaning of Machiavelli's recommendation of using 'evil' to realize morally good ends.

Just as in the first case, as Sartre claims that violence "is justified in that it is no longer really violence,"[29] for Machiavelli 'evil' that is required to realize good ends is justified since by virtue of its necessity it loses its status as (absolute) evil. The crude interpretation of the maxim "the end justifies the means," according to which it is thought that any means *whatsoever* (e.g., unnecessary violence) is justified by an end is un-Machiavellian and is expressed in Sartre's second case.

Machiavelli's belief that so-called evil means are sometimes required to realize morally praiseworthy ends also appears in his plays. As Saxon-house argues, in La Mandragola and Clizia, Machiavelli challenges and inverts traditional meanings of virtue and vice by depicting human beings as needing to let loose 'the beast' when human harmonies are disrupted. The plot of La Mandragola (for a summary, see Appendix A) presents the view that the value of faithfulness is subverted and replaced by that of adultery, proving itself, in this instance, to have far-reaching beneficial effects: Lucrezia has a virile lover; Callimaco has Lucrezia; Nicia will have the children he so longs for; Sostrata can be a proud grandmother; and Friar Timoteo will profit financially through his association with the rich Nicia and Callimaco.[30] Just as when the end is acquiring and maintaining the state the means should be judged "honourable and praised by everyone,"[31] so also, when the aim is achieving and preserving a harmonious household, should the means be similarly regarded. Through Lucrezia's acceptance of Callimaco—through her agency—universal happiness is secured. As Saxonhouse states, "in the kingdom of her home she is not only fit to rule, she does rule."[32]

Hanna Fenichel Pitkin presents a very different account of the world of Machiavelli, maintaining that therein, traditional female virtues are left unchallenged and remain intact. She claims that in Machiavelli's plays young women are almost always presented as mere sex objects with no independent wills of their own. In discussing Lucrezia, however, she does concede that she is not wholly passive or without personality. But she asserts that her characteristics are "inconsistent and puzzling," failing to produce a compelling portrait of Lucrezia as "a real person, a person in her own right." Pitkin writes, "[t]his paragon of virtue not only turns out to be so malleable in the hands of her foolish husband, wicked mother, and corrupt priest that she agrees to commit an obvious sin (which may still be within the bounds of credibility) but is transformed after one night with her lover into a resolute and competent adulteress who, with-out pangs of conscience, knows just how to arrange things so that she and her lover may continue to cuckold her husband as long as he lives."[33] First, it certainly is the case that the Judeo-Christian tradition considers adultery a sin, that within the framework from which the concept of sin derives its meaning it is sinful. But it is not clear how in this particular case adultery is sinful in the sense of being morally wrong if one assumes that moral standards are not synonymous with previously established Judeo-Christian laws, or that these laws are the only morally viable ones. In his emphasis on basing one's behavior on how people act rather than on how they ought to act, Machiavelli rejects the view that moral action instantiates a vision of a perfect society.[34] It is with tongue in cheek that Machiavelli has Lucrezia say "I can only believe that some divine influ-ence has willed this, and, as it is not for me to resist what heaven decrees, I surrender."[35] Lucrezia progresses morally, knowing "how to arrange things," not so that she can continue to indulge in sin, but so that she can enjoy several goods that her revaluation of adultery, her new moral insight, has served to secure. In a world in which many are corrupt, it is self-destructive to pursue values that can only result in one's ruin.[36] The "Song" appearing before the prologue of the play may be seen as articu-lating Lucrezia's wise progression of mind (see Appendix A).

Pitkin assumes that the only alternative to conventional morality is corruption, which she sees Sostrata as embodying in advising Lucrezia to choose the best among bad choices.[37] In contrast, Clizia's Sofronia, Pitkin argues, is "an agent of virtue, of good and order,"[38] who advises that "one ought to do good at all times, and it counts all the more when others are doing wrong."[39] Her next words, however, are these: "But it seems to me that when we do do good, it only works against us,"[40] leaving some doubt about whether she really believes that doing 'good' is always good. As Pitkin acknowledges, Sofronia later on participates in 'evil' herself: "Although she is an agent of morality, however, her methods are those of manipulation and deceit. . . . [She] controls the outcome through her 'beautiful cleverness.' "[41]

While *Clizia*, like *La Mandragola*, also involves the theme of romantic love and men's pursuit of a young female beauty, this theme merely serves as a backdrop for the display of female autonomy and power (for a summary, see Appendix B). Just as in *La Mandragola* the 'virtue' of faithfulness is supplanted by the 'vice' of adultery, with fecund, beneficial effects, so also in *Clizia* the 'virtues' of love, honesty, kindness, gentleness, and forgiveness are surpassed by the 'vices' of pride, anger, deceit, and cruelty, lending a superhuman aura to the play's characters. In the world of Machiavelli there is no natural order that determines that men must rule over women, that Sofronia should, as the foolish Nicomaco claims, "act according to [his] rule"[42]—that virtue must balk at vice, and human beings must refrain from committing 'evil.'[43] Thus human beings must become like gods and decide what is good and right, casting off all superstitious legacies.

Machiavelli and Feminism

In Antonio Gramsci's discussion of Machiavelli's politics he makes an important distinction between the "diplomat" and the "politician." Drawing on the work of Hegel and Marx, he refers to the notion of "effective reality," meaning the objective, given situation—"what is." Gramsci writes: "The diplomat can only move within an effective reality, since his specific activity is not that of looking for new equilibriums, but of conserving an existing equilibrium within a certain judicial framework." The diplomat seeks to maintain the existing order, and the laws and rules by which it operates, not looking beyond that order and considering the possibility of a different order. The politician, by contrast, "wants to create new relations of forces and because of this cannot help concerning himself with 'what should be,' though not in the moralistic sense."[44] He is a creator or initiator, who seeks not to maintain the existing order but to establish a new order.

Gramsci identifies Machiavelli as more truly a politician than a diplo-

mat, challenging the impartiality of existing laws and rules while rejecting impartiality itself. But as "a partisan with mighty passions," the
politician does not act simply on the basis of subjective whims. "He bases
himself," Gramsci emphasizes, "on effective reality." The difference between the diplomat and the politician is that whereas for the former
effective reality is "something static and immobile," for the latter "it is a
relationship of forces in continuous movement and change of equilibrium." For instance, for the diplomat, socialist revolution is something
abstract, external to the capitalistic order, in no intrinsic relation with
it. In contrast, for the politician, who wants to change the existing order,
socialist revolution is a project that emerges within capitalism, from
forces that can be made to struggle against it. Gramsci writes: "To apply
the will to the creation of a new balance of the really existing and operating forces, basing oneself on that particular force which one considers
progressive, giving it the means to triumph, is still to move within the
sphere of effective reality, but in order to dominate and overcome it (or
contribute to this)." For example, the marxist politician perceives capitalism, in its institutions, as preventing the free development of people
and productive powers. Judging the working class as the force that pushes
forward, he seeks to mobilize that force against capitalism in the project
of transforming the present. Thus, Gramsci concludes, " '[w]hat should
be' is therefore concrete."[45]

In claiming that Machiavelli, as a politician, concerns himself with
'what should be,' Gramsci does not mean to imply that he is interested
in moral ideals; however, his distinction between the diplomat and the
politician is helpful for identifying Machiavelli's contribution to ethics,
in particular feminist ethics. Machiavelli's account of good and evil, of
virtue and vice, may be seen as political in attributing a political function
to virtue, depicting the individual as an instrument of social change.
In contrast, traditional, impartialist moral theories may be perceived as
diplomatic. The moral agent they depict is bent on preserving the existing equilibrium, on ending conflicts through the application of impartial
principles of justice.

According to a feminist Machiavellian account of morality, the moral
agent is an active politician seeking to overcome the patriarchal order.
Acutely aware of the continuous movement and change in equilibrium of
existent forces, she strives for a new balance of these forces, basing herself
"on that particular force which [she] considers progressive, giving it the
means to triumph."[46]

As the existing dynamics of relations are subject to change, her disposition will be flexible so that when a situation calls for harm-producing action, for rage, cruelty, or deceit—when challenging oppressive structures requires 'evil'—the feminist Machiavellian moral agent will act accordingly: "[The prince] needs to have a spirit disposed to change as the winds of fortune and variations of things command him, and . . . not depart from good, when possible, but know how to enter into evil, when forced by necessity."[47] Instead of *reacting* to patriarchy as if to a force external to herself, the feminist, much like the judoist, mobilizes certain features of patriarchy to realize her own ends. Feminist consciousness is as offensively oriented as it is defensive. In struggling against women's oppression, feminists make use of certain aspects of female experience, products of that oppression. For example, women can mobilize the feminine trait of nurturing, directed under patriarchy toward sustaining patriarchal institutions like the male-headed family, in the interest of emancipatory female bonding.

In *La Mandragola*, Lucrezia, by using the female virtue of subservience, by being complicit in subverting her husband's authority and playing the obedient and innocent wife, ultimately determines the outcome of events.[48] In *Clizia*, Sofronia mobilizes the vices that Machiavelli depicts as female—pride, deceit, hardness, cruelty, disdain, jealousy, and spite—to overthrow her husband's authority. The moral goodness that results in both plays does not simply consist in the large amount of happiness achieved but in the defeat of oppressive, patriarchal authority, which accords women only instrumental value. The actions of Lucrezia and Sofronia are not morally good simply because of the kinds of consequences that they produce but because they are expressions of self-respect. Lucrezia comes to realize that those who refuse to engage in so-called evil for the sake of happiness are naive. Her actions express her discovery of her right to self-determination, to determine the nature of her existence, an existence guided by enlightened choice. Further, in humiliating her husband, Sofronia also asserts her right to self-determination, to not have her household's good name besmirched by her husband's foolish, no longer exemplary behavior. In a speech of soaring feminist righteousness, she says: "I never wanted to make a fool out of you [Nicomaco] . . . The only way to bring you to your senses was to . . . shame you before witnesses."[49]

Similarly, consider Flora, the hero of the British Broadcast Company (BBC) production *The Politician's Wife*. In this Machiavellian film, Flora's husband, the leader of a national political party, is publicly revealed to have been having an affair that was unbeknownst to her but known to some of her friends all along. The dynamics of the couple's relationship change; the equilibrium is disrupted. Taking advantage of others' perception of her as a pure and innocent, dutiful wife, Flora engages in deceit, cunning, and manipulation and turns her husband's supporters against him by feigning acceptance of her husband's betrayal; enhances her femininity by giving herself a make-over; and indicates utmost devotion to her husband by lying to a powerful friend that though he had cheated on her in the past, she had forgiven him. As a result, she succeeds in getting her husband removed from office and winning his position for herself.

Again, deceit, cunning, and manipulation are not in this instance morally good simply because of the results they produce, but because in playing "the fox," in seeking revenge, Flora recovers that aspect of herself that her husband's betrayal had devastated, namely, her self-worth. Flora comes to realize that not only is her husband's monogamous commitment to her void; so are his commitments to his children and political party, commitments that she shares and values greatly. In a poignant scene her son asks her to define the soul. She considers the question very seriously and tells him to say a prayer for her, uncertain of the morality of her behavior but feeling she has no other choice. From Flora's perspective and what circumstances make necessary to preserve her self-respect, causing her husband's downfall is morally required. Flora's enhancement of her femininity is not simply morally good because of the worthy ends she seeks to achieve by virtue of it—the downfall of her politically irresponsible husband, the integrity of the political party she supports, her own rise as the party's leader—but because (given the positive meaning she attaches to it) it is an assertion of self-worth, as if she were proclaiming her sexual desirability, which her husband's affair had challenged. Similarly, deceit and cunning are morally right in her situation, in part because they too express self-respect. It is as if she were saying, "You think I am naive, child-like, and obedient, needing male protection; think again. I am not a mere puppet you can so easily make to accept my husband's betrayal. I am a full-grown, intelligent adult, with needs and feelings of my own that should be respected, not depreciated, not neglected." The deceitful practices Flora engages in would still have been morally right even if they had not produced the results she desired.

Through understanding the boundaries of her situation Flora creates value through what she chooses, discovering new moral possibilities. The greater richness of Flora's ideals causes her to refuse to be subordinate and self-sacrificing but also to recognize that whatever act is necessary to affirm her self-worth is morally right. By pushing out the limits of her situation with an enlarged ethical self, Flora succeeds in resisting demoralization and resignation under oppression. But it cannot be denied that Flora avoids being demoralized precisely by moving within the dominant/subordinate framework and waging war on her husband. The more powerful, more independent self that she forges is one that recognizes the moral significance of 'evil' for the sake of good.

Conclusion

While in the examples discussed above I depict the moral agent as mobilizing aspects of female experience and products of women's oppression in the struggle against that oppression, the feminist moral agent is not limited to protecting and advancing women's interests alone. In fact, it is not clear what precisely that endeavor would mean, since women's systematic subordination intersects with other forms of oppression such as those based, for example, on class and race. Thus a feminist Machiavellian account of morality presents a moral agent who mobilizes aspects of female/black/working-class experience in struggling against oppressive structures. Moving within the existing order, she judges the oppressed as that force which pushes forward and acts in a way that furthers liberation.

Admittedly, it is often very difficult to know what action will challenge oppressive structures, or challenge them the most, or whether a particular harm-producing action is actually necessary to preserve one's self-worth and thus morally good. In other words, we will not always know if a so-called evil action is necessary because of the constraints of apprehending the full context, or whether one that does less or no harm is sufficient. But this is not a problem peculiar to the kind of moral perspective being propounded here. For instance, in utilitarianism we may have difficulty deciding what action will produce the most happiness or how many people it will benefit. Similarly, in care ethics we often do not know what action is the most caring one, expressing kindness or compassion rather than self-interest.

To be sure, I am not embracing a moral agent who charges recklessly ahead to achieve her goals, knocking others down without a moment's pause. The end of maintaining self-worth is not justified by any means *whatsoever*. For instance, a woman applying for a job might justify sabotaging another women's chances at it by claiming that her destructive action is required so that the other, more qualified woman will not get the job. However, the goal of securing a job is based on a notion of fair play where one job candidate respects another candidate's right to seek the same job without interference. In sabotaging another woman's efforts to obtain the job by, for instance, destroying her research files, a woman changes the goal of securing the job to vanquishing one's opponent as in war, where 'all is fair.' She uses 'evil' means to instantiate a vision in which others are either obstacles or instruments for one's use; she uses 'evil' for a morally repugnant end.

According to Jaggar, feminist ethics is "transitional, a temporary adaptation" to a world overflowing in violence, cruelty, callousness—a tool for coping with and overcoming this world geared toward the creation of a world in which explicit feminist commitments no longer have a function.[50] Feminist approaches to ethics "must recognize the often unnoticed ways in which women and other members of the underclass have refused cooperation and opposed domination while acknowledging the inevitability of collusion and the impossibility of *totally clean hands*."[51] I hope to have shown, with the examples of the characters Lucrezia, Sofronia, and Flora, that a feminist Machiavellian moral account does precisely this.

Notes

1. Alison Jaggar, "Feminist Ethics: Projects, Problems, Prospects," in *Feminist Ethics*, ed. Claudia Card (Lawrence: University Press of Kansas, 1991), 89.

2. Sheila Mullett, "Shifting Perspective: A New Approach to Ethics," in *Feminist Perspectives*, ed. Lorraine Code, Sheila Mullett, and Christine Overall (Toronto: University of Toronto Press, 1987), 109–26, especially 114.

3. Ibid., 114.

4. Marilyn Frye, *The Politics of Reality: Essays in Feminist Theory* (Freedom, Calif.: Crossing Press, 1983), xi, 96.

5. Sandra Bartky, *Femininity and Domination: Studies in the Phenomenology of Oppression* (New York: Routledge, 1990), 15, emphasis in original.

6. Ibid., 16, 19, 21.

7. Ibid., 16.

8. Sarah Hoagland, *Lesbian Ethics: Toward New Value* (Palo Alto: Institute of Lesbian Studies, 1988), 50, 51, 53.

9. Frye, *The Politics of Reality*, 73.

10. Hoagland, *Lesbian Ethics*, 232.

Feminist Interpretations of Niccolò Machiavelli

11. Ibid., 232, 238, 241.

12. Ibid., 240.

13. Ibid., 209, 215.

14. Audre Lorde, "The Master's Tools Will Never Dismantle the Master's House," in *Sister Outsider: Essays and Speeches* (Freedom, Calif.: Crossing Press, 1984), 112.

15. Arlene W. Saxonhouse, *Women in the History of Political Thought: Ancient Greece to Machiavelli* (New York: Praeger, 1985), 152.

16. Niccolò Machiavelli, *The Prince*, trans. Luigi Ricci (New York: Nal Penguin, 1980), 84, 85.

17. Harvey C. Mansfield, *Machiavelli's Virtue* (Chicago: University of Chicago Press, 1996), 18.

18. Machiavelli, *The Prince* (1980), 31, 92, 93.

19. Ibid., 101.

20. Niccolò Machiavelli, *Discourses on the First Decade of Titus Livius*, in *The Chief Works and Others*, ed. and trans. Allan Gilbert (Durham: Duke University Press, 1965), 3.24, 485.

21. Machiavelli, *The Prince* (1980), 94. Some commentators claim that the phrase "the end justifies the means" is a misleading translation of Machiavelli. James B. Atkinson favors the following, more literal translation: "When there is no court of appeal, people judge all men's actions, and particularly those of a prince, by the final outcome" (Niccolò Machiavelli, *The Prince*, trans. James B. Atkinson [Indianopolis: Bobbs-Merrill, 1976], 285). George Bull presents a similar translation: "In the actions of all men, especially of princes, where there is no court of appeal, one judges by the result" (Niccolò Machiavelli, *The Prince*, trans. George Bull [Baltimore: Penguin Books, 1961], 101). In an annotation, Atkinson claims that the translation "the end justifies the means" has led to the crude interpretation that Machiavelli is advocating that one do anything to achieve one's goals (284). However, as he asserts, and as I will argue, for Machiavelli the end justifies the means only when the end is truly praiseworthy (284). Machiavelli is simply making the psychological observation that people tend to evaluate results irrespective of the means used to achieve them; therefore a prince will not lose public respect if in obtaining good ends he has to resort to means that would be judged reprehensible in themselves.

22. Machiavelli, *The Prince* (1980), 60.

23. Machiavelli, *The Discourses*, 3.3, 425; 3.22, 379; 3.22, 483.

24. Ibid., 3.3, 425; my emphasis.

25. Ibid., 3.21, 478.

26. Friedrich Nietzsche, "Twilight of the Idols," in *The Portable Nietzsche*, ed. and trans. Walter Kaufman (Middlesex: Penguin Books, 1984), section 56, p. 642; emphasis in original.

27. Jean-Paul Sartre, *Notebooks for an Ethics*, trans. David Pellauer (Chicago: University of Chicago Press, 1992), 244.

28. Ibid., 172.

29. Ibid.

30. Saxonhouse, *Women in the History of Political Thought*, 162–75, especially 168.

31. Machiavelli, *The Prince* (1980), 94.

32. Saxonhouse, *Women in the History of Political Thought*, 168, 169.

33. Hanna Fenichel Pitkin, *Fortune Is a Woman: Gender and Politics in the Thought of Niccolò Machiavelli* (Berkeley and Los Angeles: University of California Press, 1984), 110–11, 112.

34. Saxonhouse, *Women in the History of Political Thought*, 152.

35. Machiavelli, *La Mandragola*, act 5, in *The Literary Works of Machiavelli*, ed. and trans. J. R. Hale (London: Oxford University Press, 1961).

36. Machiavelli, *The Prince* (1980), 85.

37. Pitkin, *Fortune Is a Woman*, 119; Machiavelli, *La Mandragola*, act 3.

38. Pitkin, *Fortune Is a Woman*, 119.

39. Machiavelli, *Clizia*, act 2, in *The Literary Works of Machiavelli*.

40. Ibid., act 2, p. 81.

41. Pitkin, *Fortune Is a Woman*, 119.

42. Machiavelli, *Clizia*, act 3, p. 91.

43. Saxonhouse, *Women in the History of Political Thought*, 171.

44. Antonio Gramsci, "The Modern Prince: Essays on the Science of Politics in the Modern Age," in *The Modern Prince and Other Writings*, trans. Louis Marks (New York: International Publishers, 1975), 163.

45. Ibid.

46. Ibid.

47. Machiavelli, *The Prince* (1980), 70.

48. Saxonhouse, *Women in the History of Political Thought*, 169.

49. Machiavelli, *Clizia*, act 5.

50. Jaggar, "Feminist Ethics," 95, 97.

51. Ibid., 98, emphasis in original.

References

Bartky, Sandra. *Femininity and Domination: Studies in the Phenomenology of Oppression*. New York: Routledge, 1990.

Frye, Marilyn. *The Politics of Reality: Essays in Feminist Theory*. Freedom, Calif.: Crossing Press, 1983.

Gramsci, Antonio. "The Modern Prince: Essays on the Science of Politics in the Modern Age." In *The Modern Prince and Other Writings*, trans. Louis Marks, 135–88. New York: International Publishers, 1975.

Hoagland, Sarah. *Lesbian Ethics: Toward New Value*. Palo Alto, CA: Institute of Lesbian Studies, 1988.

Jaggar, Alison. "Feminist Ethics: Projects, Problems, Prospects." In *Feminist Ethics*, ed. Claudia Card, 78–104. Lawrence: University Press of Kansas, 1991.

Lorde, Audre. "The Master's Tools Will Never Dismantle the Master's House." In *Sister Outsider: Essays and Speeches*, 110–13. Freedom, Calif.: Crossing Press, 1984.

Machiavelli, Niccolò. "Clizia." In *The Literary Works of Machiavelli*, ed. and trans. J. R. Hale, 63–120. London: Oxford University Press, 1961.

———. "Discourses on The First Decade of Titus Livius." In *Machiavelli: The Chief Works and Others*, ed. and trans. Allan Gilbert, 175–529. Durham: Duke University Press, 1965.

———. "La Mandragola." In *The Literary Works of Machiavelli*, 1–61.

———. *The Prince*. Trans. George Bull. Baltimore: Penguin Books, 1961.

———. *The Prince*. Trans. James B. Atkinson. Indianapolis: Bobbs-Merrill, 1976.

———. *The Prince*. Trans. Luigi Ricci. New York: Nal Penguin, 1980.

Mansfield, Harvey C. *Machiavelli's Virtue*. Chicago: University of Chicago Press, 1996.

Mullett, Sheila. "Shifting Perspective: A New Approach to Ethics." In *Feminist Perspectives*, ed. Lorraine Code, Sheila Mullett, and Christine Overall, 109–26. Toronto: University of Toronto Press, 1987.

Nietzsche, Frederick. "Twilight of The Idols." In *The Portable Nietzsche*, ed. and trans. Walter Kaufman, 565–656. Middlesex: Penguin Books, 1984.

Pitkin, Hanna Fenichel. *Fortune Is a Woman: Gender and Politics in the Thought of Niccolò Machiavelli*. Berkeley and Los Angeles: University of California Press, 1984.

Sartre, Jean-Paul. *Notebooks for an Ethics*. Trans. David Pellauer. Chicago: University of Chicago Press, 1992.

Saxonhouse, Arlene W. *Women in the History of Political Thought: Ancient Greece to Machiavelli*. Ed. Rita Mae Kelly and Ruth B. Mandel. New York: Praeger, 1985.

Appendix A

Summary of *La Mandragola*

Niccolò Machiavelli

Canzone
... Because life is short and many are the pains
That every man bears who lives and stints himself,
Let us go on spending and wasting the years as we will,
For he who deprives himself of pleasure
Only to live with labor and toil
Does not understand the world's deceits,
And what ills and what strange events
Crush almost all mortals. ...

Prolog

"Callimaco Guadagni, a young man just arrived from Paris . . . greatly loved a prudent young woman and tricked her, as you will learn, and I

Niccolò Machiavelli, *Chief Works and Others*, ed. and trans. Allan Gilbert (Durham: Duke University Press, 1989), 2:776–821. Occasionally I have restored some of the better-known spellings or terms to the translation, e.g., Lucrezia instead of Lucretia (Latin), so as to give it a more authentic texture. I have also kept intact those speeches that clearly illustrate Machiavelli's "ethical" views as well as his supposed views on women in general. [Ed] hope you'll be tricked as she was. . . . The writer is not very famous, yet [if he fails to make you laugh][1] he will be ready to pay for your wine. . . . And if this material . . . does not befit a man who likes to seem wise and dignified, make this excuse for him, that he is striving with these trifling thoughts to make his wretched life more pleasant, for otherwise he does not know where to turn his face, since he has been cut off from showing other powers with other deeds, there being no pay for his labors."

Act 1

Callimaco lived in Paris for twenty years, determining never to return to Italy after King Charles had "ruined this country." But he met Cammillo Calfucci from Florence, who praised a relative of his, Lucrezia, the wife of an old jurisdoctor, Nicia Calfucci, for such "beauty and manners that we were all spellbound . . . and letting every other plan go . . . I set out for this place" in order to seduce Lucrezia. However, on arriving he discovers that "the nature of the woman fights against me, because she's very chaste and a complete stranger to love dealings. Her husband is very rich and lets her rule him entirely. . . . No tradespeople get into her house; she has no maid or servant who's not afraid of her; so there's no chance for bribery."

Nevertheless, there are two factors favoring their meeting: one, Nicia is "the stupidest and silliest man in Florence," and two, he and Lucrezia both long to have children. Callimaco remarks that Lucrezia's mother, Sostrata, "has been a lovely dame, but she's rich so I don't know how to handle her."

Callimaco's friend Ligurio, a former marriage broker and an "amusing man" able to "beg suppers and dinners" from his friends, is very intimate with Nicia and "bamboozles him," promising to help Callimaco "with all his might" to set up a tryst with Lucrezia. In return Callimaco promises "if he succeeds, to give him a lot of money; if he doesn't succeed, he'll get a luncheon and a supper out of it."

Ligurio first tries to induce Nicia to take his wife to the baths to "cure" her infertility so that Callimaco might meet her there, but Nicia does not want to get out of sight of the "cupola" [Duomo]. Callimaco is so frustrated he fears "I shall certainly die." Ligurio tells Callimaco that Lucrezia is virtuous, courteous, and "fit to rule a kingdom" and that he should keep up his hopes. He suggests that Callimaco pretend to have studied medicine and practiced in Paris, because "Nicia is so foolish . . . you can say something to him in Latin" and he will be easily bamboozled. By arranging a meeting immediately Ligurio believes Nicia will not have time to investigate Callimaco's background.

Act 2

Ligurio assures Nicia that Callimaco has not practiced medicine in Florence because "he's rich . . . and at any moment he's likely to return to Paris." Nicia greets Callimaco in minimal Latin and asks if he can cure his wife's sterility. Callimaco gives several possible causes for Lucrezia's and/or Nicia's infertility, all in Latin, implying that if Nicia is impotent there might be no cure. Nicia is so impressed by his response that he declares his trust in Callimaco, who then agrees to make up a potion for Lucrezia after first examining a specimen of her urine.

Nicia returns with the specimen, complaining of the difficulty he had in obtaining it. Siro, Callimaco's servant, tells him: "Be patient; with gentle words you can usually get a woman where you want her to go." Callimaco looks at the urine and declares "this specimen shows weakness of the kidneys" and utters a few more phrases in Latin, thereby impressing Nicia even more. When Callimaco ventures a guess that Lucrezia is "poorly covered at night," Nicia replies, "She always has a good blanket over her. But she does keep kneeling four hours to string off paternosters before she gets into bed, and acts like a fool about getting chilly."

Callimaco promises that he will make up a potion and "if a year from today, your wife doesn't have her own son in her arms, I bind myself to pay you two thousand ducats." Nicia declares he is "ready to believe you in everything and to trust you more than my confessor." Callimaco tells him that the potion will be made from the root of the mandrake, which he has personally tested on the Queen of France, but that the first man who lies with her after she consumes it will die in eight days. If Nicia can find someone to "draw to himself all the poison of the mandrake" he will be able to lie with her afterward, begetting a child, without any danger.

At first Nicia protests that he will not turn his wife into a whore and himself into a cuckold, so Callimaco asks if it is possible that Nicia hesitates to do "what the King of France has done, and all the lords in that country?" Nicia wonders "Whom do you suppose I could find to do such a crazy thing? If I tell him, he won't do it. If I don't tell him, I victimize him, and that's a matter for the Eight [Criminal Court]." Callimaco responds that after giving Lucrezia the potion and putting her to bed, they will all disguise themselves and go hunting in the marketplaces and as soon as they find "an idle young fellow, we'll pull a sack over his head, and to the music of blows . . . we'll put him in the bed and tell him what he's got to do, and there'll be no difficulty at all."

Nicia agrees because "kings and princes and lords have used this method . . . but don't let it be known because of the Eight." However, his wife must also give her consent. Ligurio suggests they ask her confessor, Fra Timoteo, to help and together "you, I, money, our rascality, theirs" will convince her to do it. To ensure their success they will have Lucrezia's mother take her to her confessor.

Act 3

Sostrata agrees, saying, "I've always heard that it's the part of a prudent man to take the best among bad choices. If for having children you don't know any other way, then you'll have to accept this one, if it doesn't burden the conscience."

Nicia remarks to Ligurio that the reason "we have to tell so many stories to get my wife to consent" is that "She used to be the sweetest person in the world and the most accommodating, but a neighbor of ours told her she'd become pregnant if she vowed to hear the first mass at the Servi [Santissima Annunziata] for forty mornings, and she . . . went there for twenty or so . . . [when] one of those nasty friars began to hang around her, so she didn't want to go back there any more. It certainly is a bad thing, though, that those who ought to set us good examples should be of that sort. . . . From that time on she's had ears like a rabbit, and when almost nothing is said to her, she finds a thousand difficulties in it."

Ligurio asks for twenty-five ducats to give Fra Timoteo and tells Nicia to pretend he is deaf and to say nothing. They see the Friar speaking to a woman who is requesting masses to be said for her dead husband and is asking if he might be in purgatory for what he did to her [implying sodomy] and expressing the fear of impaling if the Turks should invade Italy that year.

Much to the surprise of Nicia, Ligurio tests Fra Timoteo by telling him that Nicia and another man will donate several hundred ducats to charity and have selected Timoteo to distribute it if he will help them with a matter of much urgency. The daughter of Nicia's nephew, Cammillo Calfucci, Ligurio says, was left in a nunnery while he went to France, and is now four months pregnant. Since the entire family as well as the nunnery will be disgraced, they want him to convince the abbess to give the girl a medicine which will make her miscarry. Ligurio remarks "I believe good is what does good to the largest number, and with which the largest number are pleased."

Fra Timoteo agrees: "So be it, in God's name. . . . Let it be done for God and for charity," and takes the money. Ligurio returns a little while later with the news that the girl has miscarried on her own and then asks for help with their plan for getting Lucrezia pregnant—a matter for which there would be "less blame." The Friar says he understands what he must do and asks them to bring the women to the church.

After Ligurio and Nicia leave Fra Timoteo proclaims: "I don't know which of us has bamboozled the other. This rascally Ligurio came to me with that first story to test me . . . but all this bamboozling brings me profit. . . . This affair is certain to be kept secret, because the telling of it is as serious for them as for me. However things go, I don't repent of it. . . . [T]here'll be difficulty, because Madam Lucrezia is cautious and good; but I'll bamboozle her by using her goodness. For all women lack brains, so when one of them knows enough to say two words, it makes her famous, because in a city of the blind, a man with one eye is Duke."

Sostrata meets with her daughter and asks her to consult with the Friar because "if Fra Timoteo tells you it isn't a thing to burden your conscience, you should do it without even thinking about it." Lucrezia laments, "I've always been afraid that Messer Nicia's wish to have children would make us commit some sin, and for this reason, whenever he's spoken to me of anything, I've always been suspicious and afraid, especially after . . . [the incident at the Servi]. But of all the things that have been tried, this seems to me the strangest, to have to submit my body to this shame, to be the cause that a man should die as the result of shaming me. . . . I'm sweating with anxiety."

Fra Timoteo tells Lucrezia: "In truth I've been at my books for more than two hours, studying this case, and in my researches I've found many things that support us." Lucrezia asks: "Are you speaking seriously or are you joking?" He replies: "There are many things that at a distance seem terrible, unbearable, strange, yet when you get close to them they seem mild, bearable, normal. . . . You must, as to conscience, accept this rule: where a good is certain and an evil uncertain, you ought never to give up the good for fear of the evil. Here you have a certain good, that you will become pregnant, gain a soul for the Lord. The uncertain evil is that the man who lies with you after you take the medicine may die, yet there are also those who don't die. But because the matter is uncertain, it's not a good thing for Messer Nicia to run this risk. As to the action, the notion that it's a sin is a fairy story, because the will is what sins, not the body, and what would make it a sin would be your husband's displeasure, but you will be pleasing him; or if you should take pleasure in it, but you will get displeasure from it. Besides this, one's purpose must be considered in everything; your purpose is to fill a seat in paradise, to please your husband. The Bible says [regarding Lot's daughters, that] because their intention was good, they did not sin."

Sostrata urges Lucrezia to be persuaded by these words: "Don't you see that a woman who doesn't have any children doesn't have any home? When her husband dies, she is left wretched, deserted by everybody. . . . What are you afraid of . . . there are fifty women in this city who would lift their hands to heaven for it." Lucrezia consents but adds, "I don't believe I shall be alive at all tomorrow morning. . . . God and Our Lady help me and keep me from shame!"

Canzone

Pleasant indeed is the trick
Carried on to the dear conclusion that has been dreamed of,
That takes one out of distress
And makes sweet every bitter thing that has been tasted.
Oh restorative splendid and rare,
You show the straight path to wandering souls; . . .

Act 4

Callimaco, waiting to hear of the outcome of Ligurio's activities, ruminates: "It's true that Fortune and Nature keep their account balanced; the first never does you a good turn that on the other side something bad doesn't come up. . . . Nicia's folly makes me hope; Lucrezia's caution and firmness make me fear. . . . When you get her, what'll it amount to? . . . Don't you know how little good a man finds in the things he has longed for, compared to what he expected to find? On the other hand, the worst you can get from it is that you'll die and go to Hell. But how many others have died! And in Hell how many worthy men there are! Are you ashamed to go there? Face your fortune . . . bear it like a man . . . don't be a coward like a woman."

When Ligurio tells Callimaco the news he is ecstatic, declaring "I'm ready to die for happiness." Ligurio comments: "What a man this is! Now for happiness, now for sorrow—this fellow wants to die no matter what." He then asks what kind of medicine he will send Nicia. Callimaco replies, "A glass of hypocrats, that is good to settle the stomach, cheers the brain," then realizes that if he goes with them to catch the victim, he cannot go to Lucrezia without being recognized.

Ligurio says he will get Fra Timoteo to disguise himself as Callimaco, imitating his voice and dress, while Callimaco will wear a short jacket, carry a lute, twist up his face, show his teeth, close one eye and wear a false nose. Ligurio also instructs him that "You must win her over in the course of this night, and before you leave, let her know who you are, confess the trick to her, show her your love for her, tell her of the happiness you wish for her, show her that without disgrace she can be your friend, and with great disgrace, your enemy. It's impossible she'll not come to an understanding with you, and that she'll want this night to stand alone."

Siro delivers the medicine to Nicia's house with the instructions that it be given to Lucrezia after supper and that she be immediately put to bed. Ligurio, disguised as a hunchback, arrives at the meeting place with Fra Timoteo and while the others go off to disguise themselves, the Friar declares: "They tell the truth who say that bad company brings men to the gallows; and many times one comes to harm by being too accommodating and too good, as well as by being bad. God knows I wasn't thinking of harming anybody . . . all at once this devil of a Ligurio . . . made me put my finger in a sin, then I have put in my arm and my whole body, and I don't know yet where I'm going to end. Yet I comfort myself that when an affair's important to many, many have to be careful about it."

Ligurio and Siro return, followed by Nicia, who is "wearing a little jacket that doesn't cover his ass," with "one of those furs the canons wear" on his head, and a "little sword at his belt." Nicia complements "the doctor" (Fra Timoteo) on his excellent disguise, and Ligurio tells him that he's "had [Timoteo] put two nuts in his mouth so he won't be recognized by his voice." When Nicia approves of that tactic Ligurio gives him two aloes to disguise his, which Nicia immediately spits out. The four men then head for the marketplace in search of their victim, with the battle-cry, "Saint Cuckoo!" [cuckold], the saint most honored in France, Ligurio assures Nicia. Ligurio describes this battle formation as "Callimaco" (Fra Timoteo in disguise) on the right horn, himself on the left, Nicia in the center, and Siro in the rear.

Siro is then sent out to scout the marketplace and he soon returns with the real Callimaco, "the prettiest chap you ever saw" in a "short jacket playing a lute." They cover his head, muffle him up, and spin him around, then take him to Nicia's house.

Act 5

The next morning, Nicia, Ligurio, and Siro bring out "the prisoner." They once again spin him around while Ligurio tells him to be off: "If I hear of your talking, I'll cut your throat."

Nicia tells Ligurio and Siro, who had stayed in the cellar to drink, that the night before he took the victim to a store room and told him to undress. "His face is ugly. He had a great big nose, a twisted mouth; but you never saw finer skin . . . and don't ask about the other things. . . . I wanted to see if he was healthy; if he had had syphilis. . . . I took him into the bedroom; I put him in the bed, and before I would go away I wanted to touch with my hands how the thing was going." Ligurio complements him on how sensibly he was "managing this affair." Then Nicia tells them that he stayed up all night talking to Sostrata, imagining the baby that would soon be "in my arms." At seven he went back to the bedroom but "couldn't make the big rascal get up. . . . He'd liked his rich diet." When Nicia tells Ligurio that he is "troubled" by "[t]hat poor boy, who's got to die so soon and whom this night is going to cost so dear," Ligurio tells him not to worry about it: "Let him take care of it."

Later Callimaco tells Ligurio, "I was anxious until three o'clock, and though I was having a very good time, it didn't seem to me right. But then I made myself known to her and made her understand my love for her, and how easily, because her husband is so stupid, we could live in happiness without any scandal, and promised her that when God removed him, I'd take her as my wife. Besides my sound reasons, too, she felt what a difference there is between the way I lie with her and the way Nicia does, and between the kisses of a young lover and those of an old husband."

Lucrezia had replied: "Your cleverness, my husband's stupidity, my mother's folly, and my confessor's rascality have brought me to do what I would never have done of myself. So I'm forced to judge that it comes from Heaven's wish that has ordered it so, and I'm not strong enough to refuse what Heaven wills me to accept. I take you then for lord, master, guide; you are my father, you are my defender; I want you as my chief good; and what my husband has asked for one night, I intend him to have always. You'll make yourself his best friend; you'll go to the church this morning, and from there you'll come to have dinner with us; after that your comings and stayings'll be as you like, and we can be together at any time without suspicion."

Meanwhile, Nicia proposes to Lucrezia that he take her to the church for "the churching," because "this morning it's exactly as though you were born a second time." They all meet Fra Timoteo outside the church. Nicia "introduces" Lucrezia to "Doctor" Callimaco as "the man who'll cause us to have a staff to support our old age," for which she thanks him and tells him she wants him to be "our closest friend." Nicia invites Callimaco and Ligurio to dine with them and gives them "the key of the room on the ground floor in the loggia, so they can come there when it's convenient, because they don't have women at home and live like animals." When he assures the Friar that the money for charity has already been sent, Lucrezia tells him to add ten grossi for the churching. Sostrata comments, "Who wouldn't be happy?" and everyone goes into the church satisfied.

Note

1. Niccolò Machiavelli, *Chief Works and Others*, ed. and trans. Allan Gilbert (Durham: Duke University Press, 1989), 2:777 n. 3.

Appendix B

Summary of *Clizia*

Niccolò Machiavelli

Prolog

"If into the world the same men should come back, just as the same events come back, never would a hundred years go by in which we should not find here a second time the very same things done as now. . . . This story is called *Clizia*, because that is the name of the girl . . . these gentle-

Niccolò Machiavelli, *Chief Works and Others*, ed. and trans. Allan Gilbert (Durham: Duke University Press, 1989), 2:822–64. I have changed certain names—e.g., Palamede instead of Palamed, Eustachio instead of Eustace, Raimondo instead of Raymond—and have left intact some important speeches. [Ed]

men [Nicomaco, an old man, his son Cleander, and two servants, Pirro and Eustachio], are going to fight over. Do not expect to see her, because Sofronia [Nicomaco's wife], who has brought her up, does not, for modesty's sake, want her to come on the stage. . . . The author of this comedy is a man of great refinement, and he would take it badly if you should think, as you see it acted, that there is anything immodest in it . . . [but] if in this play anything immodest is said, it will be said in such a way that the ladies here can listen to it without blushing."

Act 1

Cleander, son of Nicomaco, tells his friend Palamede that in 1494 when the French King invaded Italy, a French officer was quartered in the house of Nicomaco, with whom he formed a close friendship. When French troops were forced out of Naples by an alliance between the Papacy, the Emperor, Milan, and Venice, this officer left a Neopolitan girl of five, part of the "spoils of war," with Nicomaco for safekeeping, telling him no more of her background than her name, Clizia. Soon after, the officer disappeared and was presumed dead in battle, so Nicomaco and his wife, Sofronia, raised the pretty child as though she were their own daughter. In the twelve years that followed Cleander fell madly in love with her, but because no one knew whether Clizia was of high birth or low, rich or poor, Nicomaco would not allow him to marry her since she had no dowry. Cleander insisted he "would take her as wife, mistress, or in any way I could."

Unfortunately, Nicomaco had also fallen in love with Clizia and therefore decided to marry her off to his servant, Pirro, who would be willing to share her with him, "because to try to get her before she was married seemed to him something wicked and repulsive." Sofronia, "who for sometime had realized he was in love, discovered this trick and, driven by jealousy and anger, is working as hard as she can to spoil it." But all she can do is put another suitor in the field, the foreman of their farm, Eustachio, and Nicomaco determines, despite all opposition, to have the wedding that very day. He has rented a little house next door, belonging to Damon, a neighbor, and he intends to buy it for Pirro, "furnish it with household goods, open a shop for him, and make him rich."

When Palamede asks Cleander if it matters to him which servant gets the girl, Cleander replies, "This Pirro's the worst rascal in Florence [and] besides having made this bargain about her with my father, he's . . . always hated me, so I should prefer to have the Devil from Hell get her." He then sends for Eustachio and hopes to make the same deal with him that his father made with Pirro.

When alone, Cleander observes, "Certainly the man who said that the lover and the soldier are alike told the truth. The general wants his soldiers to be young; women don't want their lovers to be old. It's a repulsive thing to see an old man a soldier; it's most repulsive to see him in love. . . . Equally in war and in love, secrecy is needed, and fidelity and courage. The dangers are alike, and most of the time the results are alike. The soldier dies in a ditch and the lover dies in despair." Eustachio arrives, bringing his musings to a close, and Cleander tells him to clean up and wait in the church.

Act 2

As Nicomaco tells Pirro he is determined that the wedding take place this day, Sofronia is commenting that she has just shut Clizia and Doria, Sofronia's servant, in their room. "I have to protect that poor girl from my son, my husband, my servants; all of them have laid siege to her." She then tells Nicomaco that "since we have in our house a girl who's very good and pretty, whom we've brought up with a lot of trouble, we should take care that we don't throw her away now, so that even though earlier everybody praised us, now everybody will blame us, since we'll be giving her to a guzzler, with no brains, who doesn't know how to do anything except a little shaving, that a fly couldn't live on."

Nicomaco replies that Pirro has the three good points in a husband: "youth, beauty, and love," and that "I'm thinking of buying for him that house I've taken on a lease from Damon our neighbor, and furnishing it with household goods; and then, even though it may cost me four hundred florins to put him . . . in a shop . . . I'm not going to consider the expense." Sofronia responds: "Are you really intending to take from your son, with this wild plan, more than is right, and give to this fellow more than he deserves? . . . I suspect there's something else underneath. . . . With this dowry or a smaller one, couldn't we marry her better?"

Nicomaco argues that they could, but that he's moved by love of them both since he raised them both and he's glad to help them both at once. Sofronia replies that they also brought up Eustachio, who "knows how to do something . . . who's in the habit of trading, of doing business, of being thrifty, of managing other people's affairs and his own . . . a man who could live on water, [who has] laid up a nice property, [while] Pirro . . . is never anywhere except in the taverns or gambling." As for the money Nicomaco would give Pirro, she says, "You've spent money in bringing her up, and I've put labor into caring for her, and so, since I've a share in these things, I intend to see for myself how they'll turn out—or I'll say so many bad things and stir up so much scandal that you'll think you're in a bad way . . . I'll turn not merely our house but Florence upside down."

Nicomaco then suggests they consult their friends and Fra Timoteo, their confessor, who's already worked the miracle, through his prayers, of getting Madam Lucrezia Calfucci pregnant. Sofronia replies: "A fine miracle, a monk to make a woman pregnant! It would be a miracle if a nun should make her pregnant!"

On her way to mass, Sofronia laments to herself: "Anybody who knew Nicomaco a year ago and who has dealings with him now would have a right to be shocked on seeing the great change in him. For he was always serious, steadfast, cautious. He spent his time as a good man should. He got up early in the morning, heard mass, bought the provisions for the day. Then if he had business in the public square, in the market, with the magistrates, he attended to it; if he didn't, he either joined with some citizen in serious conversation, or he went to his office at home, where he wrote up his ledger and straightened out his accounts. Then he dined pleasantly with his family, and after he had dined, he talked with his son, advised him, taught him to understand men, and by means of various examples, ancient and modern, showed him how to live. Then he went out. He spent the whole day either in business or in dignified or in honorable pastimes. When it was evening, the Ave Maria always found him at home; he sat a little while with us by the fire, if it was winter, then went to his office to go over his affairs. At nine o'clock he had a cheerful supper. . . . But since this infatuation for that girl has got into his head, his affairs are neglected, his farms are going to ruin, his business ventures fail; he's always scolding and doesn't know why; he comes into the house and goes out a thousand times a day without knowing what he's doing; he never comes back at such an hour that he can have dinner and supper on time; if you speak to him, he doesn't answer or doesn't answer to the point. The servants, seeing this, make a game of him, and his son has given up respecting him . . . I'm afraid, if God doesn't furnish us a cure, that this poor house will be ruined."

Meanwhile, Pirro and Eustachio almost come to blows when they see each other, and declare their eagerness to see which one "Fortune favors."

Act 3

When Nicomaco is unable to get Cleander to agree to the marriage of Clizia to Pirro, he accuses Cleander of taking sides with Sofronia and warns him that "I'll throw you and [Eustachio] into the Stinche [prison]; and I'll give her dowry back to Sofronia and send her away; for I intend to be master of my own house. . . . I'm going to have this wedding come off this evening. Or . . . I'll set this house afire."

When alone, Cleander bewails his bad luck in having his father as his rival: "Though my mother aids me, she does not do it to aid me but to hinder her husband's affair. And for this reason I can't show myself boldly in this business, because she would at once believe I had made with Eustachio the very bargain my father has made with Pirro . . . and I should be entirely done for."

Cleander tells Sofronia of Nicomaco's threats. When Sofronia asks him what he says about this affair, he replies, "I say what you do, for I love Clizia as a sister, and it would cut me to the heart if she fell into Pirro's hands." Sofronia says, "I don't know how you love her. But . . . if I believed I was taking her from Nicomaco's hands to put her in yours, I wouldn't trouble myself about it. But I think Eustachio'll want her for himself, and you'll forget your love because of your wife (for we're soon going to give you one)." Cleander agrees but says that it might be better to leave things as they are if possible, because "Heaven may let us find her parents, and if they should be noble, they'd not thank you for having married her to a servant or a peasant."

Nicomaco arrives and tries to get Sofronia to "make a fool of herself" by pretending to flirt with her. But Sofronia says he is drunk and smells of perfume, complaining that he is always going to a whorehouse or tavern, gambling and spending money recklessly. Nicomaco and Cleander then promise to try to dissuade each other's candidate from pursuing this contest and "the one who persuades his man wins."

Nicomaco tells Eustachio, who is thirty-eight, that he's too old for marriage and that after a few months with him Clizia would look for a younger man, he'd be wretched and lose his job, and she would go begging. Eustachio replies, "In this city a man with a pretty wife can't be poor because the more you give the more is left for you." Nicomaco tells him to get his accounts ready to hand over and leave the farm. Eustachio responds, "This doesn't worry me if I get Clizia."

After Sofronia similarly speaks with Pirro, Pirro tells Nicomaco he's afraid if he marries Clizia he will make enemies of Sofronia, Cleander, and all the others in his household, so that if Nicomaco dies, "the saints'd give me pretty bad treatment." Nicomaco promises him that he'll "make such provision for you that the saints won't be able to give you much trouble; and if they try it, the magistrates and the laws'll protect you, if only through your help I get a chance to sleep with Clizia."

When Pirro still protests, Nicomaco decides to convince Sofronia to have the two servants draw lots to see "who shall have Clizia," and trusts in God that the lot won't go against him. Pirro then says to himself, "Oh crazy old man! He thinks God will lend a hand to this wickedness of his." And to Nicomaco he says, "I believe that if God should worry about such things, Sofronia too might trust in God."

Seeing Sofronia with Eustachio, Nicomaco proposes that the matter be turned over to Fortune by putting both names in one bag and in another bag putting Clizia's name and a blank slip, so that "first the name of one of them'll be drawn, and the one to whom Clizia's name goes shall have her." Sofronia agrees and tells Eustachio to make up the slips and put them into the bags. Pirro wins the draw and Nicomaco immediately orders the wedding to be prepared. Sofronia asks why they can't wait until the next day: "Are we going to carry on the affair like heathens? Isn't there going to be a wedding mass?" Nicomaco replies: "The bean mass! [referring to the fava bean, a male sexual symbol] She can hear it some other day." Sofronia departs determined to disrupt Nicomaco's plans.

Canzone[1]

He who once angers a woman,
Rightly or wrongly, is a fool if he believes
To find in her, through prayers or laments,
Any mercy.
    When she enters upon this mortal life,

Along with her soul she brings pride, anger,
And disregard of pardon.
   Deceit and cruelty escort her
And give to her such aid that in every
Undertaking she gains her wish;
   And if anger harsh and wicked moves her,
Or jealousy, she labors and watches; and her strength
Mortal strength surpasses.

Act 4

Cleander ponders the outcome of the lottery: "How can my mother have been so little on the watch as to turn herself over to chance in this way, about a thing on which the honor of our house entirely depends? . . . How unlucky I am! . . . O Fortune! Because you're a woman, you've always had the habit of befriending young men; but this time you've befriended the old men. . . . You couldn't have done me a greater injury, since with this blow you've taken from me at once my sweetheart and my money." Cleander sees Nicomaco and Pirro coming, so he hides and listens in.

Nicomaco is delighted with the outcome and tells Pirro, "This obligation I have to you, I'm going to pay you double for." He tells him to take Clizia to Damon's house after the wedding, which Damon's wife, Sostrata, will arrange. Sostrata will put Clizia into bed and Pirro is to pretend to undress; Nicomaco will then slip into bed beside Clizia. Before daylight Nicomaco will leave and Pirro will then take his place in bed.

Pirro warns him that he should fortify himself "in such a way that you'll seem young, because I'm afraid your old age will be found out in the dark." Nicomaco replies that he will take an aphrodisiac, which he'll follow with a "salad of cooked onions, then a mixture of beans and spices . . . because they are hot and windy, [and] would make a Genoese carrack make sail. . . . I'll have a big pigeon roasted, so underdone it'll bleed a little . . . [and] though I haven't many teeth, my gums are as strong as steel." At that Pirro remarks he doubts he'll even touch Clizia afterwards, because he has "a vision of that poor girl broken to pieces."

Nicomaco then tells Damon to have his wife Sostrata come to help Clizia get ready for the wedding as soon as she's called by Sophronia, and to have her servant with her. Sophronia, who's been told of Nicomaco's plot by Cleander, is determined to make both Damon and Nicomaco ashamed of themselves. When Damon asks her if she wants his wife to come help Clizia, she replies: "Let her be; I don't wish to trouble her. I'll call her when the time comes."

When Nicomaco asks where Sostrata is, Sofronia then tells him Sostrata didn't want to come. Nicomaco then berates Damon, who replies, "The offer was made to your wife. She didn't want her to come, and so you get me mocked and then you complain of me." He nevertheless agrees to do what Nicomaco wants.

Suddenly a noise erupts from the house and Doria, Sofronia's servant, comes running out, yelling "I've been killed! I've been killed! Run, run, get that knife out of her hand." Doria tells Nicomaco that Pirro had given Clizia the ring and had gone to see the notary. Clizia then seized a dagger, and "with her hair flying loose, completely crazy, shrieked: 'Where's Nicomaco? Where's Pirro? I'm going to kill 'em . . . no matter what.' . . . Pirro's run into the kitchen and hidden behind the basket of capons. I'm sent here to warn you not to come into the house."

Nicomaco then promises Doria "a pair of slippers and a kerchief" if she can get Clizia to put down the dagger. To herself, Doria comments: "In how many ways we make game of this old man! . . . [T]hey have undressed Siro, our servant, and put his clothes on Clizia, and put Clizia's clothes on Siro, and they're going to have Siro act as bride in place of Clizia." When Nicomaco asks Doria if Clizia has quieted down she tells him yes, and that Clizia has promised Sofronia to do as he wants, but that "Sofronia thinks it'd be well for you and Pirro not to come into her sight, so her anger won't blaze up again. Later, when she is put to bed, if Pirro can't tame her, it'll be his fault."

Sofronia and Sostrata take the weeping "Clizia" up to bed and Nicomaco remarks to Damon that Clizia "acts very melancholy . . . did you see how tall she is? She must have helped herself out with high heels." Damon assures him that he is very lucky but warns him that if he doesn't handle himself well "it won't be easy for you to come back again."

Canzone
Pleasant indeed is the trick carried on
To the dear conclusion that has been dreamed of,
That takes one out of distress. . . .
    You conquer, with your sacred counsels alone,
Rocks, enchantments, and poisons.

Act 5

The next morning Doria relates the story of the wedding night: "I've never laughed so much before and I'm certain I'll never laugh as much again." Everyone has been laughing all night, even Pirro. She listens as Nicomaco comes out of the house and talks to Damon. "I'm disgraced forever," he tells Damon. Weeping, he describes how he got into bed with Clizia but when he tried to touch her she wouldn't let him, and pushed his face away when he tried to kiss her. "I tried to put myself on top of her, and she punched me with her knee in such a way that she's broken a rib." Though he turned to "soft words" when force wouldn't work, she still refused to speak to him or "grant him" anything else.

He then began to threaten her until "she all at once drew up her legs and gave me a couple of such kicks" that he almost bounced into the middle of the room. Being bewildered and tired from all the exertion, he drowsed a bit until he found himself "stabbed in the side, and here under the rump five or six cursed hard strokes given me. . . . I hurriedly put my hand there and found something hard and sharp; I was so scared that I jumped out of bed, remembering the dagger." He told Pirro to get a light and when he returned, "instead of Clizia we saw Siro, my servant, raised up on the bed all naked, and in contempt . . . he was making faces at me . . . and finally the *manichetto* [an obscene gesture]."

Damon laughs also and advises him that "you'll have to give yourself into the hands of your Sofronia, and tell her that from now on she can do as she likes about Clizia and about yourself. She too'll have to think about your honor, because, since you are her husband, you can't be disgraced without her sharing in it." He promises to go to the marketplace and if he hears any rumors about this affair he'll try to cover it up.

When Nicomaco sees Sofronia he begs her not to make a joke of him. She replies that he was the one who wanted to make a joke of everyone, including himself. "Did you think you were dealing with blind people, or with those who couldn't upset these shameful plans of yours? . . . [I]f I was to make you come to your senses, there was no other way than to get so many witnesses to your actions that you'd be ashamed . . . [I]f you wish to come back to your duty and be that Nicomaco you were a year ago and before, we'll all return to you, and the matter'll not be known." Nicomaco replies, "My Sofronia, do what you like; I'm prepared not to go beyond the limits you set, if only the thing doesn't get known."

She then tells Nicomaco that she'd sent Clizia off to a nunnery the night before dressed in Siro's clothes, and that Cleander is happy that the marriage is broken off, but "he's very sad because he doesn't see how he can have Clizia." Nicomaco then gives Sofronia "all responsibility for Cleander's affairs" as well. But since they don't know who Clizia really is they both agree it wouldn't be right to give her to Cleander. Meanwhile, Sofronia says, the marriage to Pirro must be annulled.

She later tells Cleander and Eustachio what's been decided and that neither Eustachio nor Pirro nor Cleander is to have Clizia, and that Clizia will return to the house or not, "just as I decide." Suddenly Damon returns from the marketplace full of good news. Clizia's father, a very rich Neapolitan gentleman named Raimondo, has just come to the city looking for his daughter. The entire family gathers to hear the news and to greet the gentleman. Damon explains that he has persuaded Raimondo to allow Clizia to marry Cleander, if Nicomaco and Sofronia agree. Sofronia then tells the audience to go home, because now "we can arrange for the new wedding, which will be female, and not male, like Nicomaco's."

Note

1. Although a "canzone" precedes each act of this play and the previous one, I have only included those to which the authors in this volume make a specific reference, or that are especially reflective of Machiavelli's unique viewpoint. [Ed]

Selected Bibliography

Behuniak-Long, Susan. "The Significance of Lucrezia in Machiavelli's *La Mandragola*." *Review of Politics* (Spring 1989): 264–80.

Breisach, Ernst. *Caterina Sforza: A Renaissance Virago*. Chicago: University of Chicago Press, 1967.

Brown, Wendy. *Manhood and Politics: A Feminist Reading in Political Theory*. Totowa, N.J.: Rowman & Littlefield, 1988.

Coltheart, Lenore. "The Virago and Machiavelli." In *Stereotypes of Women in Power*, ed. Barbara Garlick et al., 141–55. Westport, Conn.: Greenwood Press, 1992.

D'Amico, Jack. "The *Virtù* of Women: Machiavelli's *Mandragola* and *Clizia*." *Interpretation: A Journal of Philosophy* 12 (May 1984): 261–73.

Elshtain, Jean Bethke. *Public Man, Private Woman*. Princeton: Princeton University Press, 1981.

———. "Reflections on War and Political Discourse Realism: Just War and Feminism in a Nuclear Age." *Political Theory* 13 (February 1985): 39–57.

———. *Meditations on Modern Political Thought: Masculine/Feminine Themes from Luther to Arendt*. University Park: Pennsylvania State University Press, 1986.

Flaumenhaft, Mera J. "The Comic Remedy: Machiavelli's *Mandragola*." *Interpretation: A Journal of Philosophy* 7 (May 1978): 33–74.

Freccero, John. "Medusa and the Madonna of Forlì: Political Sexuality in Machiavelli." In *Machiavelli and the Discourse of Literature*, ed. Albert Russell Ascoli and Victoria Kahn, 161–78. Ithaca: Cornell University Press, 1993.

Garlick, Barbara, Suzanne Dixon, and Pauline Allen. *Stereotypes of Women in Power: Historical Perspectives and Revisionist Views*. New York: Greenwood Press, 1992.

Grant, Ruth W. *Hypocrisy and Integrity: Machiavelli, Rousseau, and the Ethics of Politics*. Chicago: University of Chicago Press, 1997.

Hairston, Julia L. "Skirting the Issue: Machiavelli's Caterina Sforza." *Renaissance Quarterly* 53 (Autumn 2000): 687–712.

Honig, Bonnie. *Political Theory and the Displacement of Politics*. Ithaca: Cornell University Press, 1993.

Kahn, Victoria. *Machiavellian Rhetoric: From the Counter-Reformation to Milton*. Princeton: Princeton University Press, 1994.

Matthes, Melissa M. *The Rape of Lucretia and the Founding of Republics*. University Park: Pennsylvania State University Press, 2000.

McIntosh, Donald. "The Modernity of Machiavelli." *Political Theory* (May 1984): 184–203.

O'Brien, Mary. "The Root of the Mandrake: Machiavelli and Manliness." In *Reproducing the World: Essays on Feminist Theory*, 103–32. Boulder, Colo.: Westview Press, 1989.

Pitkin, Hanna Fenichel. *Fortune Is a Woman: Gender and Politics in the Thought of Niccolò Machiavelli*. Berkeley and Los Angeles: University of California Press, 1984. Reprint, Chicago: University of Chicago Press, 1999.

Saxonhouse, Arlene W. *Women in the History of Political Thought: Ancient Greece to Machiavelli*. New York: Praeger, 1985.

Shin, John Juncholl. *The Functional Sex*. Ph.D. diss., University of California, Berkeley, 2001.

Snyder, R. Claire. *Citizen-Soldiers and Manly Warriors: Military Service and Gender in the Civic Republican Tradition*. London: Rowman & Littlefield, 1999.

Struever, Nancy S. *Theory as Practice: Ethical Inquiry in the Renaissance*. Chicago: University of Chicago Press, 1992.

Sullivan, Vicki B. *Machiavelli's Three Romes: Religion, Human Liberty, and Politics Reformed*. DeKalb: Northern Illinois University Press, 1996.

———, ed. *The Comedy and Tragedy of Machiavelli: Essays on the Literary Works*. New Haven: Yale University Press, 2000.

Tylus, Jane. "Theatre and its Social Uses: Machiavelli's *Mandragola* and the Spectacle of Infamy." *Renaissance Quarterly* 53 (Autumn 2000): 656–86.

Vesna, Marcina. *Re-Thinking Republicanism: A Feminist Perspective on the Political Thought of Machiavelli and Arendt*. Ph.D. diss., University of California, Santa Barbara, 2001.

Zerilli, Linda M. G. "Machiavelli's Sisters: Women and 'the Conversation' of Political Theory." *Political Theory* 19 (May 1991): 252–76.

Zuckert, Catherine H. "Fortune is a Woman—But so is Prudence: Machiavelli's *Clizia*." In *Finding a New Feminism: Rethinking the Woman Question For Liberal Democracy*, ed. Pamela Grande Jensen, 23–37. Lanham, Md.: Rowman & Littlefield, 1996.

List of Contributors

WENDY BROWN is Professor of Political Science at the University of California, Berkeley, and the author of *Manhood and Politics* (Rowman & Littlefield, 1988). Her most recent book is *Politics out of History* (Princeton University Press, 2001).

MARIA J. FALCO is Professor Emerita of Political Science at DePauw University, the former Academic Vice President of DePauw, and former Dean of the College of Arts and Sciences of Loyola University in New Orleans. She has authored or edited five previous books and several articles in political science, including *Feminist Interpretations of Mary Wollstonecraft* (Pennsylvania State University Press, 1996).

JANE S. JAQUETTE is Bertha Harton Orr Professor of Liberal Arts and Professor of Political Science at Occidental College. She has written extensively on women and politics, women and development, and international feminism. Her most recent book, co-edited with Susan L. Wolchik, is *Women and Democracy: Latin America and Central and Eastern Europe* (Johns Hopkins University Press, 1998).

DONALD McINTOSH is a private scholar and author of *The Foundations of Human Society* (University of Chicago Press, 1969) and many articles on Freud and Weber. His most recent book is *Self, Person, World: The Interplay of Conscious and Unconscious in Human Life* (Northwestern University Press, 1995).

MELISSA M. MATTHES is an independent scholar and Visiting Lecturer at Wesleyan University. She is the author of *The Rape of Lucretia and the Founding of Republics* (Pennsylvania State University Press, 2000).

VESNA MARCINA teaches political science at Citrus College in Glendora, California. She recently completed her dissertation, titled *Rethinking Republicanism: A Feminist Perspective on the Political Thought of Machiavelli and Arendt*. Her research interests continue to focus on women and democratic theory.

MARTIN MORRIS teaches political science at York University in Toronto. He is the author of *Beyond the Communicative Turn: Adorno, Habermas, and the Problem of Communicative Freedom* (SUNY Press, 2001), as well as numerous articles on topics related to political theory and political communication.

CARY J. NEDERMAN is Professor of Political Science at Texas A&M University, where he directs the graduate program. The author or editor of numerous books and articles on the history of Western political thought, his latest book is *Worlds of Difference: European Discourses of Toleration, c. 1100–c. 1550* (Pennsylvania State University Press, 2000).

ANDREA NICKI is currently a Research Associate with the Simone de Beauvoir Center at Concordia University in Montreal and, until recently, was a post-doctoral fellow at the Center for Bioethics at the University of Minnesota. She has published articles on feminist virtue ethics and trauma. She was the special guest editor of the Spring 2002 issue of the APA Newsletter on feminist virtue theory and ethics, and is working on a book tentatively titled *Marginalized Moral Voices: Feminist Virtue Ethics and Psychiatric Suffering*.

MARY O'BRIEN, a native of Walmer, Kent, England, was originally a nurse midwife who became active in the Scottish Labour Party before moving to Canada. She completed her Ph.D. at York University in Toronto, publishing her thesis as her first book, *The Politics of Reproduction* (Routledge and Kegan Paul, 1981). Her second was a series of essays on feminist political theory, *Reproducing the World: Essays on Feminist Theory* (Westview Press, 1989). She taught graduate studies at the Ontario Institute for Studies in Education and at the University of Toronto, was active in Women against Violence against Women, and was a founding member of the Feminist Party of Canada before her death in 1998.

HANNA FENICHEL PITKIN is Professor Emerita of Political Science at the University of California, Berkeley, and is the author of numerous articles and books including *Fortune is a Woman: Gender and Politics in the Thought of Niccolò Machiavelli* (University of California Press, 1984; 2d ed. with "Afterthoughts," University of Chicago Press 1999), *Representation* (Atherton, 1969), and *The Attack of the Blob: Hannah Arendt's Concept of the Social* (University of Chicago Press, 1998).

ARLENE W. SAXONHOUSE is Professor of Political Science at the University of Michigan and the author of *Women in the History of Political Thought: Ancient Greece through Machiavelli* (Praeger, 1985). She is also the author of *The Fear of Diversity* (University of Chicago Press, 1992) and *Athenian Democracy* (University of Notre Dame Press, 1996).

JOHN JUNCHOLL SHIN holds a doctorate in political science from the University of California, Berkeley, and has taught in the Sociology Department of the University of Oregon. He is currently an independent scholar and homemaker in Eugene, Oregon, and is writing a book on the history of masculinity as reflected in political theory and popular culture.

R. CLAIRE SNYDER is Assistant Professor of Government and Politics in the Department of Public and International Affairs at George Mason University, where she teaches and writes in the fields of democratic and feminist theory. She is an Associate of the Kettering Foundation and the author of *Citizen Soldiers and Manly Warriors* (Rowman & Littlefield, 1999).

CATHERINE H. ZUCKERT is Professor of Political Science at Carleton College and the author of several books on political philosophy, including *Natural Right and the American Imagination* (Rowman & Littlefield 1990) and *Postmodern Platos* (University of Chicago Press, 1996).

Index

ability, republicanism threatened by, 237
action: autonomy and, 51; conflict as, 64; Habermas' theory of speech and, 281–84; judgment and, 71–73; Machiavelli's concept of, 57–63, 94–95, 341; Machiavelli's Founder in context of, 60–63; politics as, 52–53; sexual power and, 97; timeliness of, for Machiavelli, 131–32, 167 n. 51; *virtù* and, 132–35
Adriani, Marcello Virgilio, 4, 30 nn. 11, 20
Aeneid, 315–16
aesthetic theory: in *La Mandragola*, 189–90, 195 n. 50; political theory and, 173–76
aggression, Machiavellian political theory and, 83–87
Alammanni, Lodovico, 315
Alberti, Leon Battista, 170 n. 154
Albrecht-Carrie, Rene, 30 n. 15
Alexander VI (Pope), 5
Alghieri, Dante, 125, 170 n. 154, 173
Alvarez, de, Leo Paul S., 30 n. 18, 31 nn. 28–29
ambition: Machiavellian political theory and role of, 83–87, 124–30; *virtù* and, 131–35, 143–46, 167 n. 49
amor fati (Nietzsche), 61–62
Andrews, Lucy, 371–72
animality: in *La Mandragola*, 187–88; Machiavelli's discussion of, 119–24
animo feminato concept, 348–51
Apulieus, Lucius, 165 n. 8, 166 n. 9
Aquinas, Thomas, 50, 95–96, 170 n. 154
Arendt, Hannah, 68, 87, 147, 162; defense of Machiavelli by, 197–98; public versus private life and, 174; on Roman authority, 257
arete, *virtù* and, 130–31, 143–46, 198

Aretino, Pietro, 183
Ariosto, 314–15
Aristotle: medieval philosophy and, 95–97; poetics of, 7, 90 n. 17, 91 n. 18, 92 n. 49, 183–84, 194 nn. 36–37; political theory of, 17–18, 50–51, 117–18, 147, 151–53, 209–10, 222; on reproduction, 135–36, 350; on virtue, 373; on women, 170 nn. 140, 154, 343, 350–51, 361 n. 27
Armstrong, Karen, 31 n. 34, 34 n. 88
Art of War, The, 9, 30 n. 13, 169 n. 131, 193 n. 18, 194 n. 20; citizen soldier as ideal in, 228, 244 n. 31, 245 n. 60, 307 n. 2, 358
atheism, in Machiavelli's writing, 31 n. 34
Atkinson, James B., 29 n. 9, 30 nn. 14, 17, 19, 32 n. 47, 33 n. 62, 211 nn. 8, 10–11, 16–17, 264 n. 9, 362 n. 43, 384 n. 21
Augustine (Saint), 94
Austin, J. L., 280
autarky, Machiavellian concept of, 151–65
authority: Machiavelli's Founder in context of, 60–63; *virtù* and, 354
autonomy: citizenship and, 79–80; *Fortuna* and, 354; Machiavelli's political theory and, 50, 60–63; sovereignty and, 87–90
avarice, Machiavellian political theory and, 83–87, 124

Bacon, Francis (Sir), 24, 355–56, 365 n. 89
Bales, Robert F., 44
"Balfagor: The Devil Who Married," 137–38
Baron, Hans, 29 n. 6, 34 n. 78, 219–20, 243 nn. 1, 6–7, 12, 244 n. 25
Bartky, Sandra, 24, 369–70, 383 nn. 5–7

Baudrillard, Jean, 258, 266 nn. 30–31
Beauvoir, Simone de, 48 n. 18, 90 n. 10, 211 n. 5
Becchi, Ricciardo, 29 n. 9
Beckett, Samuel, 175, 193 n. 4
Behuniak-Long, Susan, 266 n. 46
Belfagor, The Devil Who Married, 10, 22, 137, 167 n. 68, 168 n. 75, 171 n. 179, 289; feminist critique of, 342, 361 n. 25; prince's role in, 296–300
Benjamin, Jessica, 291–92
Benson, Pamela, 314, 327–28
Berlin, Isaiah, 1, 29 n. 1, 48 n. 6, 331, 335 n. 43, 339, 360 n. 11
biological continuity: gender in Renaissance culture and, 350–51; Machiavellian political theory and, 181–82; polity and, 190–93
Bocaccio, 314–15, 364 n. 64
Bock, Gisela, 362 n. 50
body imagery: domination and, 139–40; Machiavellian political theory and, 118, 154–65
Boethius, 115 n. 11
Book of the City of Ladies, 313–15
Bordo, Susan, 338
Borgia, Cesare, 5, 155, 307 n. 3
Borgia family, 8
Botero, Giovanni, 7, 31 n. 21
Brecht, Berthold, 72, 91 n. 21, 174
Brown, N. O., 123, 147, 149, 169 n. 112
Brown, Wendy, 15–17, 19, 33 n. 73, 117–65, 227, 231, 242, 245 nn. 55, 57, 246 nn. 76–78, 107, 296, 311–12, 334 nn. 10–11
Burckhardt, Jacob, 167 n. 69, 175–76, 193 nn. 6–7, 194 n. 23
Burke, Edmund, 78, 91 n. 35
Butler, Judith, 277

Caesar, Augustus, 30 n. 18
Caesar, Julius, 30 n. 18, 320
Casina, 111–12, 200–210, 362 n. 50
Cassirer, Ernst, 31 n. 27, 243 nn. 6–9, 245 n. 37, 246 n. 104, 335 n. 45
Castiglione, 314
Castruccio Castrocani, The Life of, 10, 158, 170 n. 156
Catholic Church: astrology and, 365 n. 83; bridal metaphor in, 96–97, 115 n. 8; *Dio* concept and, 301–3; Machiavelli's criticism of, 8–9, 253; republican citizenship and, 331
Celestina, The, 362 n. 41

centaur, in Machiavelli's work, 119–21
Chabod, Federico, 29 n. 4, 31 n. 22, 33 n. 62, 133, 167 n. 59, 193 n. 5
Charles V (Emperor), 10–11
Chodorow, Nancy, 291
Christianity: effeminate male and, 100–104, 349–51; *Fortuna* in context of, 56–58; history and time in, 341; Machiavelli's rejection of, 7–8, 337–38, 348–49, 359 n. 1, 361 n. 32; medieval philosophy and, 95–97; Nietzsche's discussion of, 375; republicanism and, 222, 245 n. 37; virtue in context of, 99–100. *See also* Catholic Church; religion
Cicero, Marcus Tullus, 7, 94, 228, 269–73, 278–80, 282–84
Cincinnatus, Machiavelli's discussion of, 324
Ciompi Rebellion, 73–77
Citizen Machiavelli, 216
citizenship: autonomy and, 79–80; of blood, 232–34; civic virtue and, 321–26; civil practices of, 213–42, 358–59; diversity of individuals and, 234–37; feminist interpretations of Machiavelli and, 18–19, 22–24, 311–12, 331–33, 333 n. 9, 337–59; functionality and, 290; gender and, 232–34; Machiavelli's republicanism and, 9, 215–18; membership and, 64–71; power and, 152–65; private morality and, 252–57; public speech and, 272–74; public versus private in, 341–43, 361 n. 24; republican women and, 326–31
citizen-soldier: feminist interpretations of, 18–19, 311–12, 338–39, 356–59, 360 n. 10; images of masculinity and, 292–96; legislation and role of, 219–22; Machiavelli's concept of, 9–11, 132, 167 n. 52, 193 n. 18, 213–42; republican citizenship and, 330–31; republican theory and, 217–18; war and importance of, 238–42, 254–57, 265 n. 19
Citizen-Soldiers and Manly Warriors: Military Service and Gender in the Civic Republican Tradition, 18–20
civic practices: citizen-soldier ideal and, 213–42; individual diversity and, 234–37
civic virtue: in *Discourses*, 311–13; of women, 318–26
civil life: *Fortuna* as enemy of, 274–77; human drives and needs and, 83–87; judgment and, 79–80; Machiavelli's concept of, 25–26, 56–58; membership and, 64–71; necessity

and *virtù* in, 142–46; private life versus, 174–76

Clausewitz, Karl von, 162

Clement VII (Pope), 9–11. *See also* Medici, Giuliano dei (Cardinal)

Cleugh, James, 33 n. 59

Clizia, 10; *Casina* compared with, 362 n. 50; cultural legacy of, 363 n. 53; ethics discussed in, 376–78, 380–83; feminist interpretations of, 14–15, 18, 24–25; political theory in, 204–10, 211 n. 12; portrayal of women in, 110–14, 137, 199–210, 343–48, 362 n. 34; public versus private life in, 344–48; summary of, 397–406

cogito concept, 292–96

Coleridge, Samuel Taylor, 173–74

Colish, Marcia L., 29 n. 9

Colonna, Prospero, 11, 32 n. 52

Coltheart, Lenore, 17–18

comedies of Machiavelli, political theory in, 182–93, 247–64

common good: citizenship in context of, 234–37; civic virtue and, 322–26; private morality and, 252–57

community: ambition's impact on, 125–28; republicanism and role of, 272–74; self-identity in, 82–83

conflict: in Machiavellian political theory, 180–82, 194 n. 22, 259–64; membership and, 65–71

conquest: Machiavelli's theories in context of, 215, 260–64; republican ideal and, 238–42

conspiracy: in *La Mandragola*, 184–93; Machiavelli's discussion of, 107–9, 211 n. 12, 316–17, 342–43

Cornazzano, 314

corruption: civic virtue and, 318–26; *Fortuna* and, 181–82; judgment and politics and, 71–73; Machiavelli's discussion of, 62–63, 88–90; *virtù* and, 132–35, 167 n. 53

Credi, Lorenzo de, 30 n. 12

Croce, Benedetto, 1, 12, 34 n. 78, 193 n. 5, 243 n. 10, 359 n. 2

Cromwell, Oliver, 178–79, 194 n. 19

cruelty, Machiavelli's discussion of, 373–78

cynicism, in Machiavelli's work, 74–77

dagger imagery, in *La Mandragola*, 252–53, 265 n. 12

D'Amico, Jack, 14, 33 n. 67

deception, in *La Mandragora*, 346–48

democratic theory: Italian republics and, 4–5; Machiavelli's doctrines and, 1–2, 6–9, 29 n. 2

Demosthenes, 146

dependence, civic virtue and, 324–26, 357–58

De Profundis, Machiavelli's use of, 8

Derrida, Jacques, 265 n. 16

Descartes, Rene: feminist critique of, 291–96, 338; Machiavelli and, 22, 289

Detmold, Christian E., 30 n. 13

di Lando, Michele, 75–77

Dinnerstein, Dorothy, 66–67, 90 nn. 11–15

Dio, Machiavellian concept of, 295–96, 300–303

Di Scala, Spencer M., 30 n. 15

discipline, Machiavelli's discussion of, 104

Discourse on Method, 292–93

Discourses on the First Ten Books of Titus Livius, 8–9; ambition discussed in, 124–25, 128–30; animality in, 120–21; citizen-soldier ideal in, 219–22, 228–34; civic virtue in, 311–13, 318–26; conspiracy discussed in, 184, 316–17; ethics discussed in, 374–78; family structure discussed in, 178; feminist interpretations of, 12–13, 310–13; fortresses discussed in, 102–4; founding stories in, 254–55; geography and climate in, 140–41; historical cyclicality in, 156, 340–41; laws and armies discussed in, 219–22; power discussed in, 200–201; pride discussed in, 374; rape discussed in, 250–57; republicanism in, 215, 243 n. 12, 328–31; role of community in, 272–74; theatrical paradox in, 261–64; transformation of values in, 93–95; *virtù* discussed in, 131–35; women discussed in, 104–9, 198–201, 210 n. 3, 316–17, 351

diversity, citizenship and role of, 234–37

domination, form-matter paradigm and, 155–65

Donne, John, 175

drama, in political theory, 146–50, 169 n. 120

dualism: in feminist ethics, 370–72; in *La Mandragola*, 189–93; in Machiavellian political theory, 179–82

duty, Machiavelli's discussion of, 77–80

Early History of Rome, 250–57

economics, Machiavellian discussion of, 189, 195 n. 51

"economy of violence," in Machiavelli, 21

economy of violence, feminist interpretation of, 268–84
education, Machiavelli's concept of, 73–77, 178
effective reality, Machiavelli and, 378–83
"effectual truth," Machiavelli's concept of, 94–95
effeminacy: *animo feminato* concept, 348–51; biological necessity and, 190–91; Christianity and, 100–104, 292–96; definitions of, 307 n. 2; *Fortuna* and concept of, 138–39, 168 n. 76, 179–82, 194 n. 20; in *La Mandragola*, 185–93; *virtù* as antidote to, 224–25, 289–90, 311–13
Eisenstein, Zillah R., 48 n. 10
Elshtain, Jean Bethke, 13, 16, 19, 23, 33 n. 64, 233; citizen-soldier ideal critiqued by, 311–12; *virtù* concept analyzed by, 267–68; on women and Christianity, 341, 361 n. 20
"ends justify the means" concept, 374, 384 n. 21
Engels, Friedrich, 48 n. 17
Enlightenment, Machiavelli in context of, 26–27, 357–58
Epigram, 10
equality: citizenship and diversity in context of, 234–37; Machiavelli's discussion of, 74–77
equilibrium, Machiavelli's rejection of, 349
Erasmus, 31 n. 27
ethics: feminist critique of Machiavelli's work on, 24–25, 367–83; Machiavelli's political theory and, 17–18, 117–18, 372–83; modern versus premodern interpretations, 39–40; public versus private, 343
Eve, Machiavelli's transformation of values and, 95–97
evil, Machiavelli's theories concerning, 7–8, 197–98, 215, 337–39, 359 n. 1, 374–78, 384 n. 21
"Exhortation to Penitence, An," 8
expressivity: modern concepts of, 44–47; in *virtù*, 48 n. 1

Fabius, Machiavelli's discussion of, 324
Fabius Maximus, 109
family structure: in *Clizia*, 344–48, 362 n. 37; in *La Mandragola*, 174–76, 347–48; membership and, 65–71; polity and, 176–82, 342–43, 361 n. 27; in premodern society, 44; republican citizenship and, 328–31
fantasia, Machiavellian concept of, 144–46
Farrell, Warren, 306–7

femininity: cultural concepts of, 291–96; definitions of, 307 n. 2; of fortune, 56–58, 98–100; Machiavellian political theory and role of, 40–43, 97, 115 n. 10, 317–31, 348–51; medieval philosophy and, 95–97; membership and, 66–71; republicanism threatened by, 226–34; resentment and, 62–63; transformation of values in Machiavelli and, 93–95
Feminism and Psychoanalytic Theory, 291
feminist theory: citizenship and, 18–19, 22–24, 311–12, 331–33, 333 n. 9, 337–59; citizen-soldier ideal and, 338–39, 356–59, 360 n. 10; critique of Machiavelli, 2–3, 12–25, 310–13, 331–33, 338–59, 378–83; economy of violence and, 268–84; ethics in Machiavelli, 367–83; Habermas critiqued by, 280–84, 284 n. 2; masculinity critiqued by, 291–96; political theory and, 174–76; public versus private in Machiavelli critiqued in, 341–43; republican citizenship and, 326–31
Ferrara, House of, 194 n. 20
Ferroni, Giulo, 347–48, 363 nn. 51, 55–59
Fichte, 215
"Five Curators of the Walls," 11–12, 32 n. 57
Flanagan, Thomas, 31 n. 26, 170 n. 154
Flaumenhaft, Mera J., 13, 33 n. 63, 116 n. 32
Flax, Jane, 291–93
Fleisher, Martin, 116 nn. 32, 36; 194 n. 22, 358, 360 nn. 3, 15, 361 nn.28, 32, 363 n. 61, 365 n. 98
Florentine Histories: family structure in, 362 n. 37; historical cyclicality in, 156, 161, 169 n. 120, 171 nn. 167, 172; political theory in, 10, 21, 75–77, 287–90, 363 n. 53; women in, 304–7, 315–16
Florentine Republic: collapse of, 6, 10–11, 244 n. 13; family structure in, 177–82; Machiavelli's analysis of, 75–77, 161–65, 171 n. 172, 253–57, 304–7; Machiavelli's career during, 8–9; military threat to, 219–22; political culture in, 3–5, 29 n. 6; role of appearances in, 346–48
Fonte, Moderata, 314, 334 n. 19
force: feminist critique of Machiavelli's philosophy, 338–39; *Fortuna* and use of, 353–54, 364 n. 81; gender and rhetoric and, 277–79; Machiavelli on use of, 133, 254–57, 265 n. 18, 341; public versus private forms of, 342–43; social formation and, 271–72; theatrical dimensions of, 149–50

form-matter paradigm: historical cyclicality and, 157–65; political theory and, 135–39, 152–65

Fortuna (fortune): ambition and, 127–30; in Clizia, 112–14, 344–48; Dio concept and, 295–96, 300–303; as feminine attribute, 55–58, 98–100, 179–82, 349–54; feminist interpretation of, 13–16, 20–21, 24–25, 310–13; form-matter paradigm and, 136–39, 168 nn. 70, 73; gender amibiguity concerning, 316; Habermas' theory of speech and, 283–84; instrumentalism and, 39–40, 46–47; in La Mandragola, 174–76, 185–93, 348, 363 nn. 55–57; Machiavellian concept of, 7, 10, 170 n. 154, 266 n. 47; necessity and, 144–46; political theory and, 56–58, 118–19, 158–65, 170 n. 154; power of, 355–56; in The Prince, 198–99; republicanism and, 224–34; rhetorical tradition concerning, 268; seduction of, 259–64; violence and, 268, 274–79; virtù and, 134–35, 190–93, 275–78, 312–13, 334 n. 15; women as republican citizens and, 327–31

"Fortune," 251–52

Fortune Is a Woman: Gender and Politics in the Thought of Niccolò Machiavelli, 14, 33 nn. 69, 71, 115 n. 10, 194 n. 38, 198–99

Foucault, Michel, 277

founders and founding stories: civic virtue and, 321–26, 334 n. 32; Machiavelli's use of, 58–63, 253–57; role of innovation in, 339–40, 360 n. 18

fox imagery, in Machiavelli, 14, 33 nn. 69, 71, 115 n. 10, 194 n. 38, 198–99, 297–98, 360 n. 15; in La Mandragora, 345–46

Fraser, Antonia, 194 n. 19

fraud: Machiavelli on use of, 133; political effectiveness of, 252–57; theatrical dimensions of, 149–50, 169 n. 120

freedom, virtù and, 138–39, 168 nn. 79, 82

free will: Machiavellian concept of, 7, 14, 342–43, 361 n. 24; time and, 361 n. 23

Freud, Sigmund: action in context of, 62–63; Fortuna and virtù in context of, 40–43, 91 nn. 39–40, 277–79, 363 n. 62; Machiavelli in context of, 13–14, 26, 48 nn. 3–4, 11–13, 80–83; oppression and, 135; sexuality and, 45–46

Frye, Marilyn, 368–70, 383 nn. 4, 9

Frye, Northrop, 186, 195n46

functionality: in Machiavelli, 22–23; in The Prince and Belfagor, 296–98; virtù and, 289–90

Galen, 24, 350–51, 364 n. 70

Garlick, Barbara, 34 n. 79

Garver, Eugene, 31 n. 29, 364 n. 78

gender: civic practices and, 224–34; civic virtue and, 309–33; force and, 277–79; form-matter paradigm and, 136–39, 153–65, 168 n. 71; heroic ethic and, 343–48; in Machiavelli's comedies, 109–14; Machiavelli's discussion of, 199–200; in Machiavelli's work, 93–115, 310, 312–13; male functionality and, 306–7; in medieval philosophy, 95–97; membership and, 65–71; modern versus premodern concepts of, 44–47; political theory and role of, 13–15, 86–87, 118–19, 134–35, 163–65, 171 n. 180; in Renaissance culture, 314–15, 350–51; terminology concerning, 307 n. 2; violence and, in Machiavelli, 267–84; virtù and fortuna in context of, 40–43, 57–58, 98–100

geography, in Machiavelli's work, 140–41

Gilbert, Alan, 30 n. 13, 32 n. 50, 90 n. 4, 115 n. 1, 165 n. 1, 193 n. 1, 194 n. 40, 243 nn. 1, 12, 264 nn. 1, 4–6, 307 n. 2, 333 n. 4, 334 n. 24, 384 n. 20, 387, 397

Gilbert, Felix, 33 n. 59, 134, 167 nn. 58, 60, 181, 194 n. 25, 195 n. 51

Gilligan, Carol, 365 n. 95

Giovanna, Queen of Naples, 288–90, 303–7

glory, Machiavellian discussion of, 131–35, 167 n. 50, 216–18, 244 n. 18

Godman, Peter, 29 n. 6, 30 nn. 11, 20, 31 n. 34, 32 n. 40, 33 n. 59

Golden Ass, The, 10; ambition and power in, 129–30; human nature and animality in, 121–24, 165 n. 8, 166 n. 9; women in, 349, 364 n. 65

Goldoni, Carlo, 183, 194 n. 32

Gomez, Tatiana V., 274

Gonfalonieri (Chief Executives), Machiavelli family members as, 3–5, 29 n. 7

goodness: appearance of, Machiavellian concept of, 7–8, 31 n. 34, 349–51, 364 n. 68; citizen-soldier ideal and, 222–34; Machiavelli's public/common good concept, 150–51; Machiavelli's rejection of, 94–95; in The Prince, 373–78

Gramsci, Antonio, 25, 368, 378–82, 385 nn. 44–46

grandi structure, 177, 193 n. 10

Grant, Ruth W., 364 n. 68

gratitude, Machiavelli on role of, 170 n. 147

Grazia, Sebastian de, 29 nn. 4, 8, 30 n. 17, 31 nn. 25, 30, 32, 32 n. 48, 33 n. 62, 34 n. 78, 230–31, 236, 239–40, 243 n. 11, 244 nn. 13, 22, 245 n. 41, 246 nn. 75, 88, 307 n. 3, 357, 364 n. 64

greed, Machiavellian political theory and, 83–87

Greek culture, politics and family in, 342–43, 361 n. 27

Guelf-Ghibelline conflict, 304

Guicciardini, Francesco, 10–12, 30 n. 14, 33 n. 59, 48 n. 5, 167 nn. 58, 60, 194 n. 29, 315, 362 n. 43

Habermas, Jürgen, 21, 268, 279–84, 284 n. 1

Hairston, Julia L., 30 n. 12

Hale, John R., 29 n. 4, 32 nn. 54–55, 33 n. 60, 48 n. 7, 194 nn. 29, 31, 211 nn. 8, 10–11, 13–14, 16, 361 nn. 25, 36, 362 nn. 37, 41–42, 363 nn. 51, 59

Hamlet, 182, 194 n. 29

Hannibal, 198, 322

Harding, Sandra, 293

Hartsock, Nancy, 358, 365 n. 97

Hegel, Georg W. F., 52, 90 n. 2, 174, 215, 243 n. 5, 378

Heidegger, Martin, 61

heredity: Machiavelli's discussion of, 176–82, 194 n. 20, 343, 361 n. 32; *virtù* and *Fortuna* and, 354

heroic ethic: in *Belfagor*, 302–3; family life as threat to, 181–82; *Fortuna* in context of, 100, 116 n. 13; gender and, 343–48; Machiavelli's republicanism and, 89–90, 216–18; war and, 239–42, 246 n. 102

Hexter, J. H., 288–89

Highet, Gilbert, 182–83, 194 nn. 30, 34

history: cyclicality of, 156–65, 340–41; *Fortuna* and role of, 351–54; in Machiavelli's *Discourses*, 104–9; Renaissance reevaluation of, 222

History of Florence. See Florentine Histories

Hoagland, Sarah, 24, 34 n. 87, 368–73, 383 nn. 8, 10, 384 nn. 11–13

Hobbes, Thomas: anarchy defined by, 361 n. 24;

on human nature, 53, 125, 358; Machiavelli's influence on, 18; on natural law, 142; reason and theory of, 133; science and philosophy of, 360 n. 3, 365 n. 89; state of nature theories of, 291, 360 n. 17

Homer, 198

Honig, Bonnie, 226, 237–39, 245 nn. 51–53, 246 nn. 93, 96, 310, 312, 333 n. 3, 334 n. 12, 349–50, 363 n. 62, 364 n. 67

Hulliung, Mark, 19, 31 n. 34, 34 n. 78, 216–17, 225–26, 239–40, 243 nn. 1, 3, 244 nn. 15–18, 245 n. 50, 246 nn. 100–102, 272

human nature: ambition and, 128–30; flux as natural state for, 340–41, 360 n. 17; in *The Golden Ass*, 121–24; in *La Mandragola*, 185, 195 n. 44; Machiavellian political theory and role of, 51–55, 118–65, 249–50, 264 nn. 6–7, 373–78; masculinity and, 339–40; political action and, 359 n. 1

hypocrisy, Machiavellian political theory and, 349–50, 364 n. 68

ideals and practice, in Machiavelli's work, 71–77, 91 n. 20

imitation, Machiavelli's doctrine of, 59–63

imperialism, Machiavelli's theories interpreted as, 215

indecisiveness, *virtù* and, 133–35

individuality: ambition and, 125–28; citizenship and, 234–37; Machiavellian concept of, 357–59; Machiavelli's membership and, 63–71

innovation, Machiavellian political theory and role of, 340–41

instrumentalism, Machiavellian ethics and, 39–40, 43–47

irony, in *La Mandragola*, 186–93, 195 n. 46

Istorie. See Florentine Histories

Italy, political divisions in, 4–5

Jacobson, Norman, 146–47, 149, 169 nn. 105–6, 108

Jaggar, Alison, 24, 367–68, 383, 383 n. 1, 385 nn. 50–51

Jaquette, Jane S., 23–24, 337–59, 360 n. 7

Jefferson, Thomas, 8

Joan of Arc, 330

judgment: ambition and, 126–28; autonomy versus, 51; civil life and role of, 79–80; Freudian theory and, 80–83; human needs and, 86–87; Machiavelli's discussion of, 71–73; politics as, 52–53

Kahn, Victoria, 31 n. 21, 34 n. 78, 268, 362 nn. 36, 43
Kant, Immanuel, 65, 79, 91 n. 38, 307 n. 2
Kateb, George, 48 n. 1
Keller, Evelyn Fox, 355
kinship, Machiavellian political theory and, 343, 361 n. 32
Kissinger, Henry, 29 n. 4

La Mandragola, 10, 32 n. 49; childbirth in, 258–59, 265 nn. 28–29; Clizia compared with, 201–2; critical analysis of, 182–83, 194 n. 32; cultural legacy of, 347, 363 nn. 51, 53; ethics discussed in, 376–78, 380–83; feminist interpretations of, 13–17, 20, 24–25; instrumentalism in, 45; as male science, 355; mandrake imagery in, 257–58; plot outline of, 184–85, 194 n. 40; political theory in, 174–76, 182–93, 261–64; public versus private life in, 344–48; rape metaphor in, 250–57, 299–300, 308 n. 5; serious and comedic in, 248–50; sex and politics in, 48 n. 7; Spanish version of, 362 n. 41; summary of, 387–95; women's power in, 110–11, 136–38, 155–56, 168 n. 75, 202, 317, 345–48, 363 n. 56
Laqueur, Thomas, 350
laws: citizens' maintenance of, 249–50, 264 n. 6; citizen-soldier ideal and role of, 219–22, 228–34; diversity in interpretation of, 235–37; Machiavelli on role of, 141–42
laziness, Machiavelli's discussion of, 159–60
Leacock, Eleanor, 48 n. 17
Ledeen, Michael A., 29 n. 4
Leo X (Pope), 6, 8–9, 307 n. 3
Lesbian Ethics, 368–72
Letters of Machiavelli, 303
Lévi-Strauss, Claude, 195 n. 44
lewdness, in Renaissance comedy, 183, 194 n. 35
liberal feminism, Machiavelli's impact on, 199–200
license, Machiavellian concept of, 351, 361 n. 24
Life of Castruccio Castrocani, The, 10
linguistics: Habermas' theory of, 280–84; social organization and, 269–72

lion imagery, in Machiavelli, 14, 33 nn. 69, 71, 115 n. 10, 194 n. 38, 198–99, 360 n. 15
literati, Machiavelli's participation in, 9, 32 n. 46
Livy (Titus Livius), 3, 8–9, 20, 136, 143, 200–201; in Belfagor, 299–300, 308 n. 5; civic virtue in works of, 324–26, 346; in Machiavelli's Discourses, 104–10, 247, 250–64, 264 n. 7, 265 n. 24
Locke, John, 142; Machiavelli's influence on, 18; state of nature theories of, 291
Lorenzo, Duke of Urbino, 6, 30 n. 20
Lorenzo "The Magnificent." See Medici, Lorenzo (the Magnificent)
loyalty, Machiavelli on role of, 155–56, 170 n. 147
Lukács, George, 189, 195 n. 50
Luther, Martin, 91 n. 20

Macaulay, Thomas Babington (Lord), 182–83, 194 nn. 32–33
Machiavelli, Bernardo, 3
Machiavelli, Niccolò: critical condemnations of, 214–18; death of, 12; deposition and exile of, 6, 181–82, 194 n. 28; differing interpretations of, 1–2; diplomatic missions of, 4–6, 378; early life of, 3–4; epitaph of, 12, 33 n. 62; imprisonment and torture, 6, 30 n. 17; influence on political theory of, 2–3, 29 n. 4; literary creations of, 9–10, 182–83; observations on Savonarola, 4, 29 n. 9; political career of, 4–5
machismo: in Machiavelli's work, 40–43, 277–79; membership and, 69–71
Maclean, Ian, 350–51
Mailer, Norman, 174
Manhood and Politics, 15–16, 231
Manlius Capitolinus, 323–24, 374–75
Mansbridge, Jane, 354, 365 n. 87
Mansfield, Harvey C., Jr., 116 n. 20, 215, 245 nn. 37, 39, 45, 359 n. 1, 361 n. 32, 373
Marcina, Vesna, 22–23, 309–33
market economy, women as commodity in, 47
marriage, Machiavellian discussion of, 178
martial practices, virility of, 224–34
Martines, Lauro, 29 n. 8
Martinez, Ronald, 264 n. 8, 265 n. 27, 362 n. 43, 363 n. 53, 364 n. 78
Marx, Karl, 67–68, 378; aesthetic theory of, 189, 195 n. 50; poetry of, 174
Mary (Virgin), Machiavelli's transformation of values and, 95–97

masculinity: Christianity and effeminate male
and, 100–104; citizen-soldier ideal and, 218,
222–34; cultural concepts of, 291–92; definitions of, 307 n. 2; feminist theory and concept of, 291–96; Machiavellian attributes of,
15–17, 19–24, 51, 289–307, 339–40; power
and, 135–39, 168 n. 75; in *The Prince and
Belfagor*, 296–98; time as attribute of,
355–56; in *virtù* concept, 40–43, 56–58,
138–39, 168 n. 76, 179–82, 194 n. 20; *virtù*
in women and, 303–7; war as element of,
239–42; in women, 315–17
Matthes, Melissa M., 20–21, 34 n. 86, 247–64,
266 n. 42
McCormick, John P., 29 n. 2
McIntosh, Donald, 13–14, 29 n. 3, 33 n. 66, 39–
47, 278
Medici, Cosimo d', 3, 9, 193 n. 10
Medici, Giovanni delle Bande, 5–6
Medici, Giuliano dei (Cardinal), 3–4, 6, 8–10,
307 n. 3. *See also* Clement VII (Pope)
Medici, Lorenzo (Duke of Urbino), 6, 30 n. 30,
131, 297, 303, 306
Medici, Lorenzo (the Magnificent), 3–4, 9, 132,
192; Catholic Church and, 301–3; as *Prince*
protagonist, 297–98, 307 n. 3
Medici family, 3–4, 108–9; Catholic Church
and, 301–3; Machiavelli and, 6, 8–9, 31 n.
35, 32 n. 40, 307 n. 3, 361 n. 32; overthrow
of, 11; political theory in relation to, 176
medieval philosophy, Machiavelli's transformation of values and, 95–97
Meinecke, Friedrich, 21, 39, 167 n. 49, 215,
240–41, 243 n. 6, 244 nn. 12–13, 246 nn.
103, 106
membership: autonomy versus, 51; Machiavelli's
concept of, 63–71; politics as, 52–53
mercenary troops: Machiavelli's criticism of, 5,
9, 11, 132, 185, 193 n. 18, 195 n. 45; as
threat to republicanism, 220–22, 245 n. 32
Merleau-Ponty, Maurice, 78–79, 91 n. 37, 147–
50, 169 n. 107, 243 n. 10, 260, 266 nn. 35,
40–41
Michelangelo, 32 n. 57
military power: feminist critique of Machiavelli
concerning, 338–39; as male prerogative,
46–47; republican citizenship and, 330–31;
republicanism and threat of, 219–22
Milton, John, 173
Minogue, K. R., 144, 147, 149, 169 nn. 96, 110,
121

"mirror of princes" pamphlets, 94–95
misogyny, of Machiavelli, 21–22, 254–57; membership and, 67–71; *virtù* in women and,
304–7
mixed government, Machiavellian concept of,
319–26, 334 n. 33
modernism, Machiavelli's influence on, 7,
39–47
monarchism, Machiavelli's republicanism and,
215–18, 244 n. 13
morality: feminist ethics and, 368–72; in Machiavelli, 373–83; politics as separate from, 215
Morris, Martin, 21, 267–84
mother-matter paradigm, political theory and,
135–39
Mullet, Sheila, 24, 368, 383 nn. 2–3
Musa, Mark, 31 n. 28
mutuality, membership and, 65–71

Najemy, John M., 31 nn. 28, 32, 32 n. 47
nationalism, Machiavelli's influence on, 215,
240–42
nation-states: in *Belfagor* and *The Prince*, 302–3;
Machiavelli's discussion of, 6
natural world: ambition in context of, 125–28;
human nature in, 121–24; Machiavelli's
concept of, 247–48, 275–78, 355–56
necessity: *Fortuna* and role of, 183–84; Machiavellian political theory and, 118–19, 160–
65, 171 n. 169; polity and, 191–93;
republican citizenship and, 328–31; *virtù*
and, 142–46
Nederman, Cary J., 21, 31 nn. 23, 34, 33 n. 76,
267–85
needs, Machiavellian political theory and,
83–87
Nicki, Andrea, 24–25, 34 n. 87, 367–86
Nietzsche, Friedrich: *amor fati* concept of,
61–63; evil discussed by, 337, 359 n. 2, 375,
384 n. 26; Machiavelli and, 25; philosophy
and political theory of, 173, 211 n. 5
Notebooks for an Ethics, 375–76

object-relations theory: Machiavelli and, 22;
masculinity and, 291–96
O'Brien, Mary, 16–17, 20, 23, 33 n. 77, 173–95,
195 n. 52, 346, 350, 353, 355–56, 359, 360
n. 5, 361 nn. 23, 31–32, 362 n. 49, 365 n.
88, 366 n. 105
Odyssey, The, 198

Okin, Susan Moller, 355 n. 39
Olds, James, 44
Olschki, Leonardo, 168 n. 70
oppression: in feminist ethics, 370–72; power of, 135–39
Orco, Ramirro de, 5, 30 n. 16, 155
order: Machiavellian concept of, 151–65; power and, 155–56; statehood and, 157–65
"Ordinances of Justice," 177
"Originality of Machiavelli, The,"
Orlando Furioso, 315
Orr, Robert, 138, 355
Ortega y Gasset, Jose, 171 n. 182
Orti Oricellarii, 9, 32 n. 46
other, membership and relation to, 65–71
otium, 272, 279; Machiavellian concept of, 8
ozio (indolence), Machiavellian concept of, 102–4, 116 n. 20, 194 n. 20, 340–41

papal nepotism, Machiavelli's discussion of, 176–82, 193 n. 9
"paradiastole" device, 361 n. 34
paradox: in La Mandragola, 186–93; of theater, in Renaissance culture, 262–64
Parel, Anthony J., 31 nn. 24, 26, 29, 34, 34 n. 78, 167 n. 49, 168 n. 70, 351–54, 360 nn. 3, 15, 363 n. 54, 364 nn. 76–78, 365 nn. 84, 89
parents, Machiavelli's discussion of, 60–63
Parsons, Talcott, 44, 48 n. 9
partisanship, republicanism and, 229–34
passion: feminist assessment of Machiavelli's work on, 338–39, 360 n. 10; virtù and, 130–35, 167 n. 46
Patch, Howard R., 274
patriarchy: in Clizia, 344–48, 362 n. 37; feminist ethics and, 369–70; in La Mandragola, 251–57; Machiavellian political theory and, 180–82, 190–93; in Machiavelli's work, 14–17; modern civilization and, 46–47; as myth, 306–7; sexual honor and, 343, 361 n. 33
patriotism, Machiavelli's republicanism and, 241–42
Paul (Saint), 96
Pazzi conspiracy, 3–4, 29 n. 8
Pazzi family, 4
philosophy, political theory and, 53–55
Phyllis (mistress of Alexander), 95–97
Piaget, Jean, 90 n. 5

Pico della Mirandola, Giovanni, 27, 31 n. 27, 34 n. 89, 180–81, 191, 353, 365 n. 83
Pitkin, Hanna Fenichel: on citizen-soldier, 358; on civic virtue and dependence, 324–26; Clizia discussed by, 362 n. 37; critique of Machiavelli's virtù, 14, 18–19, 23, 33 nn. 69, 71, 198, 211 n. 9, 290, 357–58; ethics in Machiavelli discussed by, 343, 376–78; on Fortuna, 2–3, 21, 49–90, 115 n. 10, 194 n. 38, 198–200, 268, 353–54, 365 n. 84; fox/lion imagery discussed by, 308 n. 4; on gender in Machiavelli, 291–96, 311–13; history in Machiavelli and, 359 n. 1; La Mandragola discussed by, 345–46, 350; Machiavelli's citizen-soldier and, 217–18, 224–27, 231; on Machiavelli's political theory, 339, 356–57; masculinity in Machiavelli discussed by, 309, 349, 355; women and Machiavelli discussed by, 364 nn. 64–65
Pizan, Christine de, 313–15, 334 n. 18
Plamenatz, John, 167 n. 49, 168 n. 80, 179–80, 194 n. 21
Plato, 94, 114, 162, 169 n. 126, 173, 209, 338, 363 n. 52, 373
Plautus, 111–12, 182, 200, 204–10, 248, 344, 361 n. 50
Pocock, John G. A., 19, 42; citizen-soldier ideal and, 224; on cyclical history, 340–41; on evil in Machiavelli, 197–98; on Fortuna, 354; Machiavellian political theory and, 222, 357; on Machiavellian state, 240–42, 245 n. 37, 359 n. 1; science and Machiavelli and, 365 n. 89; on virtù, 355
Poggio, 176
polis, Machiavelli's philosophy and concept of, 50–51
political theory: aesthetics and, 173–76; ambition and, 83–87, 124–30; autonomy in context of, 50–51; of Cicero, 269–72; citizen-soldier tradition and, 214–18; in Clizia, 200, 204–10; cyclical history and innovation in, 340–41; "effectual truth" in, 94–95; family structure and, 176–82; feminist critique of Machiavelli's work in, 15–16; Fortuna (fortune) and, 351–54; Gramsi's analysis of Machiavellian politics, 378–83; Habermas' perspective on, 283–84; human autonomy and, 51–55; human drives and needs and, 83–87; judgment and, 71–73; law and, 141–42; Machiavelli's influence on, 2–3,

political theory (*continued*)
  6–7, 26–29, 29 n. 4; masculinity and,
  135–39; membership and, 63–71; necessity
  and, 160–65, 171 n. 169; philosophy and,
  53–55; power in context of, 151–65; in *The
  Prince*, 5–7; republicanism and, 215–18, 243
  n. 12, 244 n. 13; separation of ethics from,
  17–18, 117–18; sexuality and, 42–43, 48 n.
  7; theatrical dimension in Machiavelli of,
  146–50; *virtù* and, 130–35
Politician's Wife, The, 380–82
polity: biological necessity and, 190–91; as social structure, 191–93
Polybius, 156, 244 n. 13, 334 n. 31, 340
"post-masculinist politics," Brown's concept of,
  16
power: ambition and, 129–30; effeminacy as
  threat to, 348–51, 363 n. 63; feminist critique of Machiavelli concerning, 338–39;
  feminist ethics and, 370–72; force and,
  135–39; *Fortuna* and, 354; geography and,
  140–41; in Greek philosophy, 150, 209–10;
  human nature and, 339–40, 360 n. 15; in *La
  Mandragora*, 346; Machiavelli's discussion
  of, 74–77; necessity and, 145–46; political
  theory and role of, 151–65; Renaissance
  family structure and, 176–82; speech and social order in relation to, 279–84; support of
  people and, 254–57; theatrical dimensions
  of, 148–50; *virtù* and, 132–35; of women,
  109–14, 136–39, 163–65, 168 nn. 73, 75,
  171 nn. 180–82. *See also* authority; autonomy
pragmatism, in Machiavellian political theory,
  175–76
premodern society: ethics in, 39–40; family
  structure in, 44
Prince, The: ambition discussed in, 129–30; animality in, 119–21; autocratic theory in, 215;
  Christianity and effeminate male and,
  101–4; citizen-soldier ideal in, 219–22, 228;
  Clizia compared with, 206–10; conspiracies
  in, 342–43; *Dio* concept in, 300–303; ethics
  discussed in, 368, 373–78, 384 n. 21; feminist critique of, 310–13; form-matter paradigm in, 136–39; *Fortuna* (fortune) in,
  40–41, 98–100, 111, 158–59, 275–78,
  352–54; founding stories in, 254–57; fox/
  lion imagery in, 14, 198–99, 298–300; functionality in, 22; hereditary monarchies in,

  194 n. 20; *La Mandragola* compared with,
  188–89; laws and armies discussed in,
  219–22; masculine functionality in, 296–98,
  305–7; nationalism influenced by, 215; political theory in, 5–7, 200–201; republicanism in, 215–18, 243 n. 12; transformation of
  values in, 93–95; *virtù* in, 226–34, 288–90;
  women discussed in, 105, 198–99, 316–17,
  345; writing and dedication of, 6–7, 30 n. 18
"principle of communion" (Merleau-Ponty),
  78–79
private life: comedy as, 182–93; in *La Mandragola*, 174–76, 184–93; versus public citizenship, 338–39, 341–43, 360 n. 6, 361 n. 24
Pro Sestio, 271
protofascism, Machiavelli's theories in context
  of, 215
prudence, Machiavelli's theories concerning, 7,
  31 n. 29
Public Man, Private Woman, 13
public opinion, republicanism and, 272–74
public versus private citizenship: control of
  women and, 345–48, 362 n. 38; feminist critique of, 338–39, 341–43, 360 n. 6, 361 n.
  24; republicanism and, 229–34

querelle des femmes, 313–15

Ranke, 215
rape: in *Clizia*, 201, 203–4; in *Discourses*,
  105–9, 201–2; *Fortuna* and, 353–54, 364 n.
  81; in *La Mandragora*, 20–21, 110–11, 250–
  64, 265 n. 26, 346–48; power and, 165, 171
  n. 182, 180–82; republican citizenship and,
  329–31, 335 n. 41. *See also* seduction metaphor
*Rape of Lucretia and the Founding of Republics,
  The*, 20–21
rationality: fortune and violence and, 274–77;
  in Machiavelli's work, 7, 31 n. 24, 43–44;
  virtù and, 132–35
realism, in Machiavelli's work, 41–43
reason: *Fortuna* (fortune) and, 352–54; polity
  and, 191–93; *virtù* and, 133–35, 167 n. 58
Rebhorn, Wayne A., 268
rebirth, in *La Mandragora*, 110–11
religion: bridal imagery in, 96–97, 115 n. 8;
  Christianity and effeminate male and,
  101–4; in *Clizia*, 207–10, 211 n. 15; *cogito*
  concept and, 292–96; *Dio* concept and,
  300–303; Machiavelli's discussion of, 7–8,

31 n. 34, 253, 265 n. 13; as political tool, 331; republicanism and, 222, 245 n. 37; theatrical dimensions of, 148–50

Renaissance culture: Machiavellian political theory and, 4–5, 167 n. 50, 331–33; Machiavelli's comedies in context of, 183–84; sex and gender in, 347, 350–51, 363 nn. 51–52; sexual equality in, 167 n. 69; women in, 261–64, 314–15, 327–31

repression, judgment and, 80–83

Reproducing the World, 16, 346

reproduction, Machiavellian aesthetics and role of, 190–93, 258, 265 n. 28

republicanism: citizen-soldier ideal and, 213–18, 224–34, 243 n. 12, 244 n. 13; corruption and, 319–26; family structure and, 176–82, 193 nn. 9–10; feminist critique of Machiavelli's theory, 18–20, 23–24, 339; Habermas' theory of, 284 n. 1; laws and armies in context of, 219–22; Machiavelli's political theory and, 3–4, 6–9, 33 n. 78; militaristic conquest and, 238–42; in Renaissance Italy, 4; rhetoric and, 272–74; women citizens and, 326–31

resentment, as feminine trait, 62–63

ressentiment, Nietzsche's concept of, 61–63

"return to beginnings": judgment in context of, 82–83; Machiavelli's doctrine of, 59–63, 75–77

reverence, Machiavelli's Founder in context of, 60–63

rhetorical tradition: economy of violence and, 268–84; force in context of, 277–79; Habermas' theory of, 280–84, 284 n. 1; Machiavellian "paradiastole," 361 n. 34; power and social bond and, 279–84; republicanism and, 272–74

Riarii (Rovere) family, 3–4, 193 n. 9

Ridolfi, Roberto, 29 nn. 4, 7, 9, 32 nn. 44, 46, 48–49, 53, 58, 265 n. 20

Rojas, Fernando de, 362 n. 41

role differentiation, in premodern society, 44

Roman culture: in *Belfagor*, 299–300, 308 n. 5; citizenship in, 234–37, 272–74; civic virtue and, 320–26; in *Discourses*, 263–64; family structure in, 178; historical cyclicality in, 156–57; influence on Machiavelli's comedies of, 182, 204–10; *La Mandragora* influenced by, 346–48; Machiavellian political theory and, 102–4, 143–46, 253–57, 366 n.

102; role of women in, 107–9; sacking of (1527), 11; Senate in, 30 n. 18; *virtù* concept influenced by, 198

Romeo and Juliet, 176

Rosamund (Queen), 304–5

Rousseau, Jean-Jacques, 23, 153, 173, 334 n. 38, 338

Rucellai family, 9

Ryan, Mary P., 43 n. 10

Sabadino, 314

sadism, *Fortuna* and *virtù* in context of, 41

Sallust, 189, 195 n. 51

Saluti, Barbara, 362 n. 43

Sartre, Jean-Paul, 25, 375–76, 384 nn. 27–29

Savonarola, Fra Girolamo, 3–4, 11, 29 n. 9, 30 n. 10, 32 n. 38, 33 n. 61

Saxonhouse, Arlene, 14–18, 22–25, 33 n. 72, 93–115, 211 n. 7, 309–13, 319–26, 329, 334 nn. 13–14, 16–17, 335 nn. 40, 42, 361 n. 26, 372, 376, 384 nn. 15, 30, 34, 385 nn. 43, 48

"scholastic-customary" historical theory, 222

science, Machiavelli and, 338, 355–56, 360 n. 3, 365 n. 89

Scipio, 322–26

Searle, John, 280

secular state, Machiavelli's concept of, 7, 33 n. 78

seduction metaphor, in *La Mandragora*, 258–64, 266 n. 32

self-interest: in *Clizia*, 207–10; feminist ethics and, 370–72; judgment and, 81–83; membership and, 66–71; politics and role of, 357–59

self-rule, versus autocracy, 235–37

self-sacrifice, republicanism and, 224–34

sexuality: ambiguity of, in Machiavelli's work, 93–115; cultural concepts of, 291–96; in *La Mandragola*, 183–93; in Machiavelli's comedies, 109–14; in Machiavelli's works, 13–15, 86–87, 199–200; in medieval philosophy, 95–97; membership and, 65–71; modern versus premodern concepts of, 44–47; in Renaissance culture, 347, 350–51, 363 nn. 51–52; self-restraint concerning, 343, 361 n. 33; *virtù* and *fortuna* in context of, 40–43, 57–58, 98–100

Sforza, Caterina (Countess of Forli), 5, 15, 30 n. 12, 70, 101, 107, 114, 193 n. 9, 195 n. 48, 210 n. 3, 315–17, 326, 330, 334 n. 26, 348–51, 363 n. 60

Sforza family, 176, 193 n. 9, 316
Shakespeare, William, 176, 183, 194 n. 29
Shaw, George Bernard, 174
Shin, John Juncholl, 21–23, 287–307
Siegel, Jerrold, 133, 167 n. 57, 168 n. 93
Signoria, Machiavelli family members in, 3–5, 29 n. 7
Sismondi, J. C. L. de, 30 n. 10
Sixtus IV (Pope), 193 n. 9
Sixtus VI (Pope), 3–4
Skinner, Quentin, 29 n. 4, 42, 48 n. 6, 116 n. 12, 223–24, 243 n. 11, 245 nn. 40, 42, 296, 358, 361 n. 34, 363 n. 50
Slate, Philip E., 44
Snyder, R. Claire, 18–20, 22–24, 34 n. 83, 213–46, 311–12, 333 n. 9, 358–59, 365 n. 101, 366 n. 104
social organization: in *La Mandragola*, 345, 362 n. 42; linguistics and, 269–72; speech and power and, 279–84
Soderini, Piero, 4–6, 10, 32 n. 52, 127–28, 159, 251, 264 n. 5, 349, 363 nn. 54, 63, 375
Song (Donne), 175
Song of Songs (Old Testament), 115 n. 8
Sophie's Choice, 371–72
sovereignty, autonomy and, 87–90
"species being" (Marx's concept of), 67–68
spectacle, political theory and role of, 261–64
speech. *See* rhetorical tradition
state: corruption in, 318–26; flux as natural order of, 340–41, 360 n. 17; in *La Mandragola*, 347–48; Machiavelli's concept of, 7, 9, 32 n. 45, 240–42; religion as tool of, 7–8; women's role in, 106
stato. *See* state
Strauss, Leo, 31 n. 34, 211 nn. 4, 18, 215, 243 n. 2, 335 n. 44, 338 n. 3, 354, 360 n. 3, 365 n. 84
Strozzi, 314
Studio (University of Florence), 4, 30 n. 11
sublimation, judgment and, 80–83
Sullivan, Vickie B., 31 n. 34
surrealism, in Machiavelli's work, 42

teleology, gender and, 350
"Tercets on Ambition," 129–30
"Tercets on *Fortuna*", 158–60, 275–78, 316
Tertullian, 95, 98
theatricality, in Machiavelli's political theory, 146–50, 169 n. 120, 261–64

Thucydides, 150, 169 n. 127
time, Machiavellian discussion of, 355–56
transformation of values: Machiavelli's *Fortuna* and, 98–100; in Machiavelli's work, 93–95, 373–78; medieval philosophy and, 95–97
tyranny: citizen-soldier as defense against, 221–22; rape as, 250–57

utopianism, Machiavelli's rejection of, 94–95

validity, Habermas' theory of speech and, 280–84
Valla, Lorenzo, 31 n. 27
Vatter, Miguel E., 274
Vespasiano, 314
Vettori, Francesco, 10, 12, 30 n. 17, 31 n. 28, 33 nn. 59, 62, 247–48, 247–50, 249, 264 nn. 1, 4, 307 n. 3, 315, 325–26, 364 n. 64
victimization, feminist ethics and, 369–70
Villari, Pasquale, 29 n. 4, 30 n. 10, 33 n. 61
violence: form-matter paradigm and, 155–65; *Fortuna* and, 268, 274–77; gender in Machiavelli and, 267–68; Machiavellian political theory and, 254–57; public versus private forms of, 342–43; rhetorical tradition and, 269–72; Sartre's discussion of, 375–76; social formation and, 271–72
"Virago and Machiavelli, The," 17–18, 34 n. 79
Viroli, Maurizio, 29 n. 4, 30 n. 21, 31 n. 34, 32 nn. 37, 44–46, 52, 55, 241–42, 246 n. 105, 268, 325–26, 334 n. 36, 349, 359, 359 n. 2, 363 n. 50, 364 nn. 64–65, 364 nn. 64–66, 366 n. 106
virtù, Machiavellian concept of, 7–9; ambition and, 131–35, 167 n. 49; citizen-soldier tradition and, 214, 218, 222–34, 245 n. 39, 358–59, 365 n. 102; civic virtue and, 322–26; in *Clizia*, 207–10; expressivity of, 40, 48 n. 1; family structure and protection of, 344–48, 362 n. 37; feminist interpretation of, 13–16, 18, 22–25, 33 n. 74, 198–210, 310–13, 338–39; form-matter paradigm and, 153–65; *Fortuna* (fortune) and, 134–35, 190–93, 275–78, 312–13, 334 n. 15, 354; functionality and, 289–90; human drives and needs and, 83–87; instrumentalism and, 39–40, 46–47; interdependence and, 88–90; in *La Mandragola*, 111, 174–76; as masculine attribute, 57–58, 99–100, 179–82, 198, 292–96; necessity and, 142–46; origin of terminol-

ogy, 136–39; political theory and, 130–35, 163–65, 167 n. 46; public-private dimensions of, 99–100, 116 n. 12; republicanism and, 215, 244 n. 13; women in context of, 267–68, 287–90, 303–7

Visconti family, 3, 176

vivere civile. See civil life

Vives, Juan Luis, 351

Waiting for Godot, 175

war: Cicero's discussion of, 269–72; in Machiavellian political theory, 161–65, 171 n. 172, 254–57, 265 n. 18, 358–59, 365 n. 102; republican citizenship and, 238–42, 330–31

wealth, Machiavelli's discussion of, 86–87

Weber, Max, 43, 48 n. 8, 277–79, 291

will to power, Machiavellian ambition and, 126–28

Wolin, Sheldon, 340, 359 n. 1, 360 n. 3

Woman as Image, 115 n. 11

woman(en): Aristotle on, 170 n. 140; Christianity and effeminate male and, 101–5; citizen-soldier ideal and exclusion of, 358–59; in *Clizia*, 110–14, 137, 199–210, 343–48, 362 n. 34, 362 n. 40; in *Discourses*, 104–9; feminine qualities of, 317–26; as *Fortuna*, 55–58, 98–100, 179–82, 349–54; in *La Mandragola*, 110–11, 136–38, 155–56, 168 n. 75, 202, 317, 345–48, 363 n. 56; Machiavelli's discussion of, 10, 14–24, 109–14, 116 n. 32, 198–210, 210 n. 3, 334 n. 25; masculine qualities of, 315–17; moral role of, 342–43, 361 n. 27; political role of, 163–65, 171 n. 180, 175–76, 232–34, 343, 348–51, 364 n. 64; power of, 136–39, 168 nn. 70–71, 73, 75; in Renaissance culture, 167 n. 69, 261–64, 314–15, 327–31; as republican citizens, 326–31; shepherdess in the *Golden Ass*, 121–24, 166 n. 11; as threat to republicanism, 226–34; transformation of values and, 93–95; *virtù* concept and, 267–68, 287–90, 303–7

Women in the History of Political Thought, 13–14

Wood, Neal, 160–62, 168 nn. 79, 82, 171 n. 166, 173–75, 193 n. 18, 194 nn. 20, 22, 272, 360 n. 12

Xenophon, 209

Zedlich, Morris, 44

Zeitlin, Froma, 262, 266 n. 45

Zuckert, Catherine H., 18, 31 n. 29, 34 n. 82, 197–210, 345, 353, 361 n. 24, 362 nn. 40–41, 50, 364 nn. 78, 80, 365 n. 97